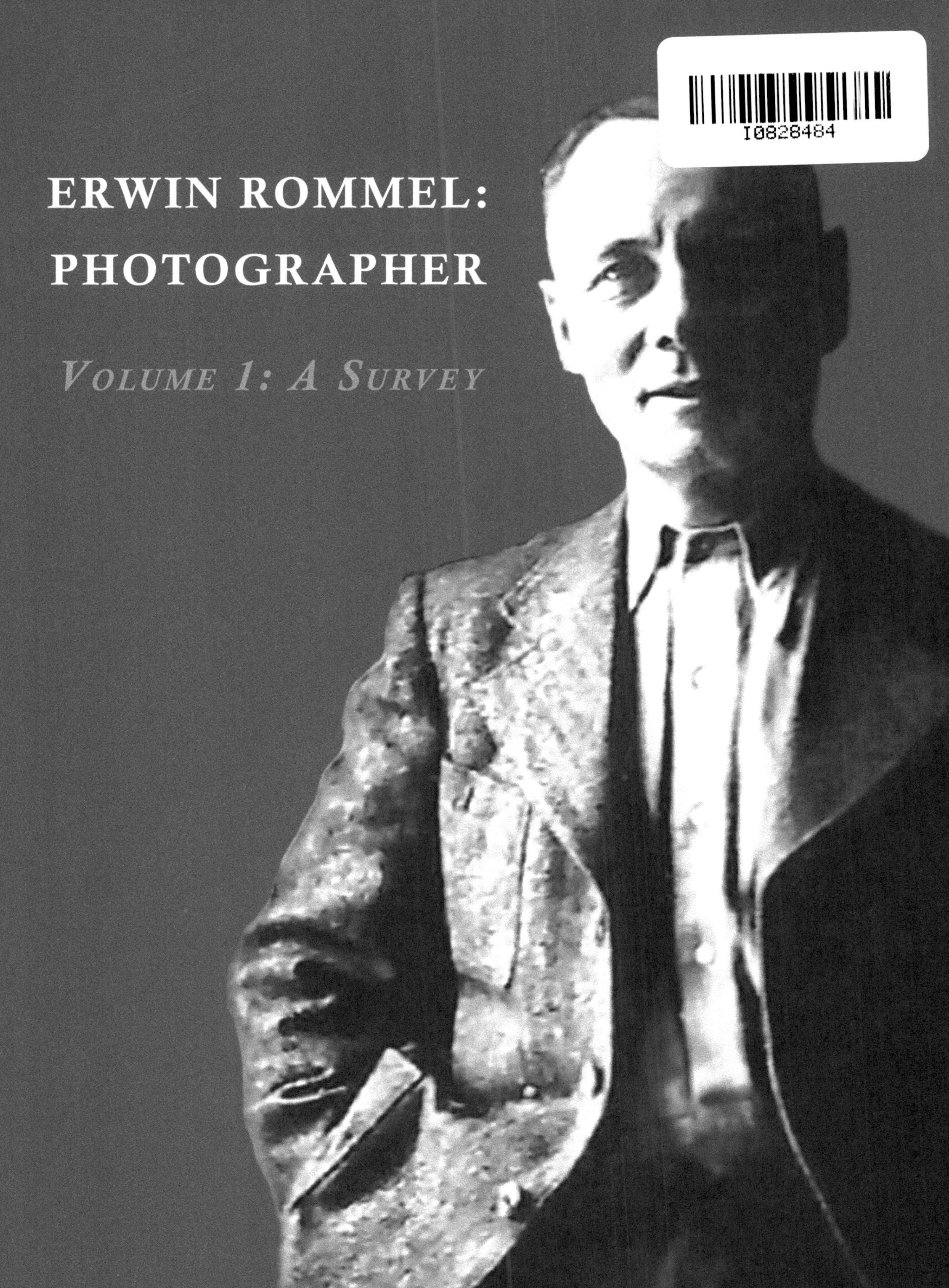
ERWIN ROMMEL:
PHOTOGRAPHER
VOLUME 1: A SURVEY

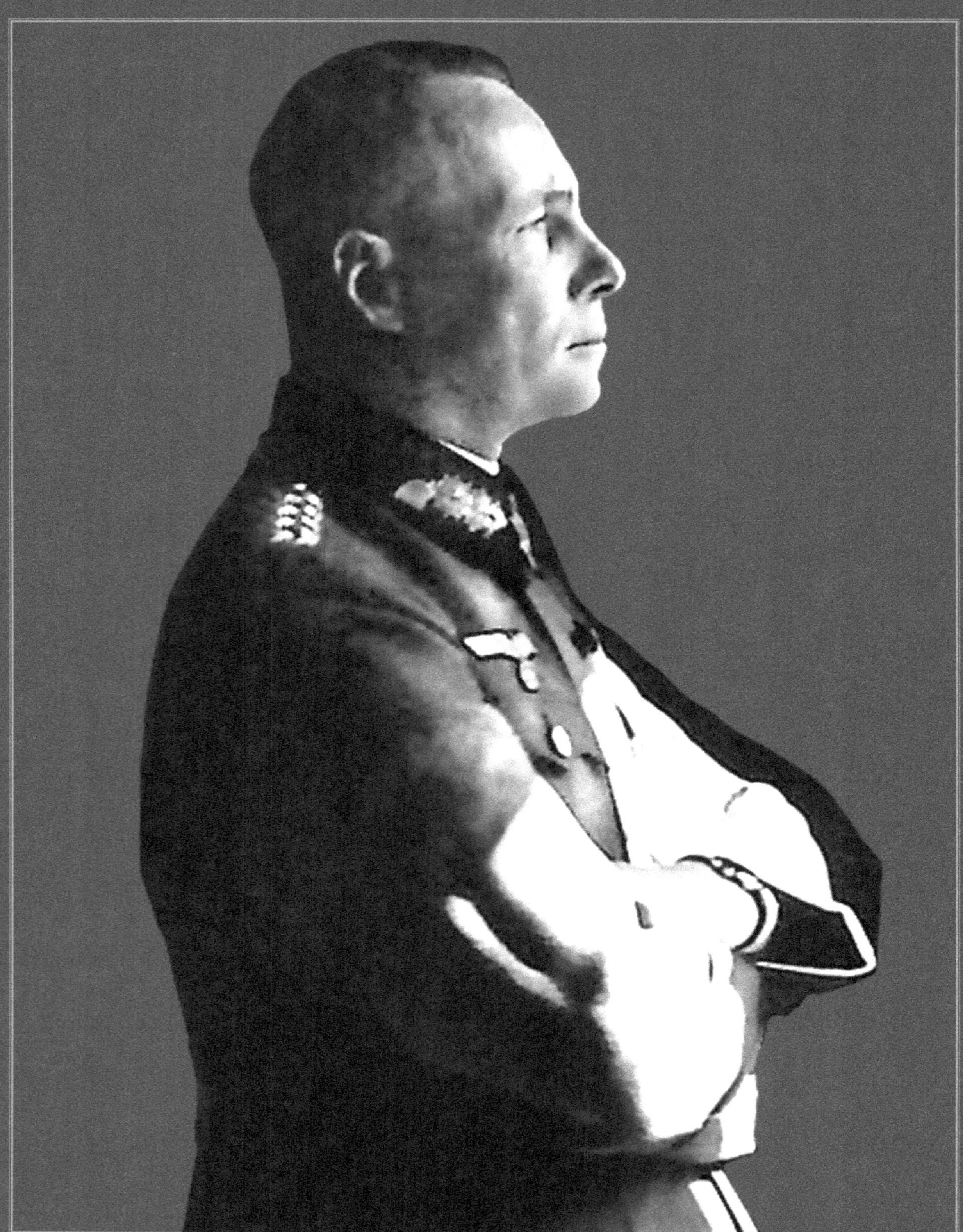

ERWIN ROMMEL: PHOTOGRAPHER

Volume 1: A Survey

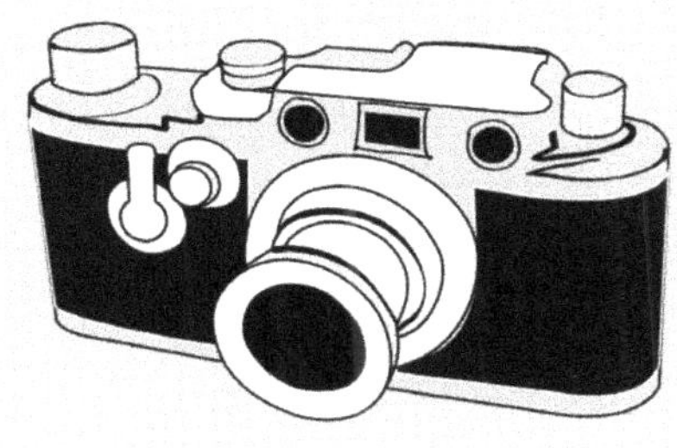

by Erwin Rommel & Zita Steele

FLETCHER & CO. PUBLISHERS
www.fletcherpublishers.com

NOTE: The photographs in this collection belonged to the private collection of Erwin Rommel before they were seized from his widow by U.S. military forces during the final stages of World War II. Rommel, an avid photographer, intended to author another book on military strategy if he survived the war. Some of these photos he took to illustrate his strategy and maneuvers, while others were intended for his personal interest. To the best of my knowledge, all photos were taken by Rommel unless he is shown in a picture taken by someone else, either an unidentified German war photographer or close personal associate.

DISCLAIMER: This book does not in any way promote Nazi ideology. In addition, Rommel was never a member of the Nazi party, nor was he responsible for any war crimes or genocide.

Erwin Rommel: Photographer—*Volume 1: A Survey*

By Erwin Rommel & Zita Steele
Fletcher & Co. Publishers

Cataloging-in-Publication data for this book is available from the Library of Congress.
Library of Congress Catalog Number 2015942027

Photography: Erwin Rommel
Author, Editor & Illustrator: Zita Steele
Interior design: Noël Fletcher
Photos of Zita Steele by Noël Fletcher
First Edition
Published in the United States of America

Cataloging information
ISBN-10 1941184057
ISBN-13 978-1-941184-05-9

Dedication

For Mama —

Thank you for encouraging me to discover and explore my German heritage. Thank you for standing behind me and my work when I faced opposition. Thank you for helping me develop my talents and pursue my dreams, and for always supporting me and cheering me on.

Acknowledgements

I would like to especially thank the following:

- ▣ John Taylor— for introducing me to the Rommel photo collection in the first place. Taylor joined the National Archives and Records Administration in Washington, D.C. at the end of World War II and worked there for 63 years. The National Archives named its intelligence and espionage books in his honor as the John E. Taylor Collection. A specialist in military history, he helped me locate the Rommel photo collection before his death in 2008.
- ▣ The late Manfred Rommel and his wife, Liselotte—for their kindness and willingness to help. I am very grateful to the Rommels, who, despite geographical distance, took time to correspond with a U.S. college student.
- ▣ The University of South Florida Honors College—for the opportunity to begin this project, which had its academic origins as my undergraduate Senior Honors Thesis.
- ▣ The Camera Heritage Museum in Staunton, VA—for the use of an image of a World War II-era Leica camera.

Contents

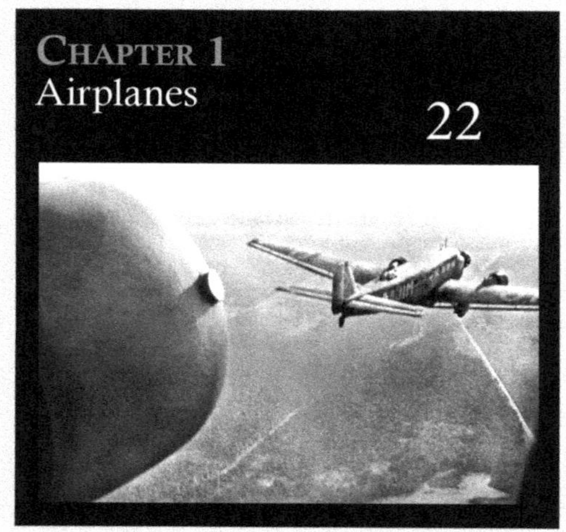

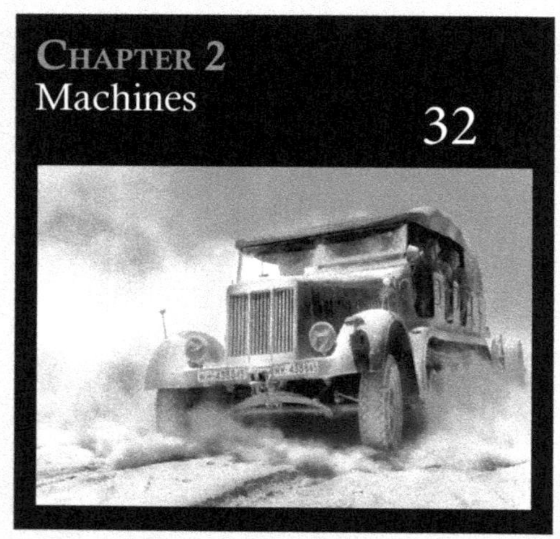

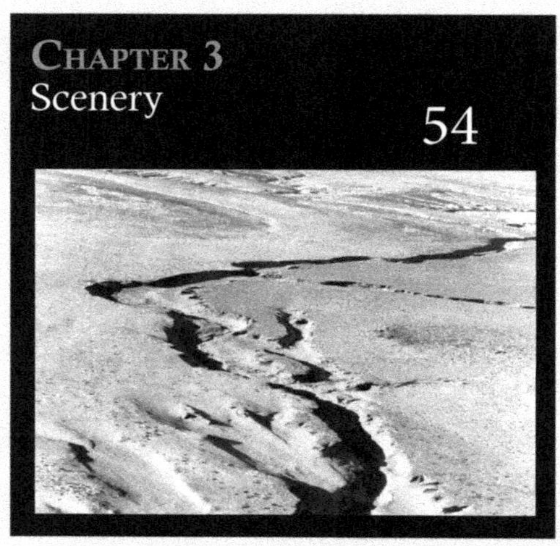

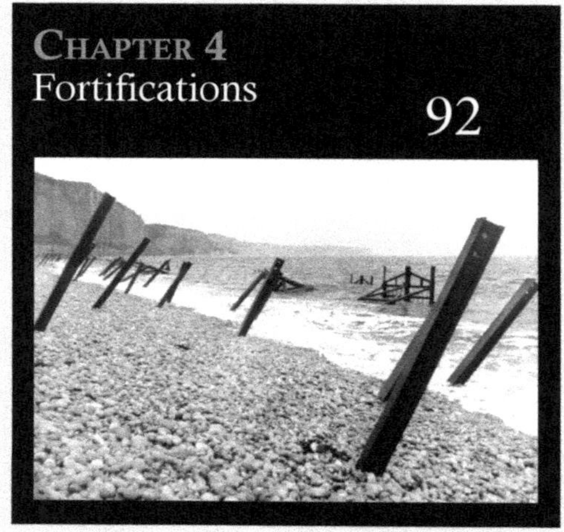

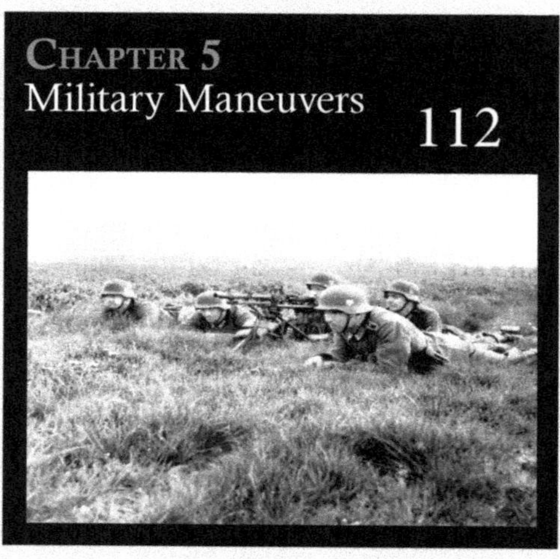

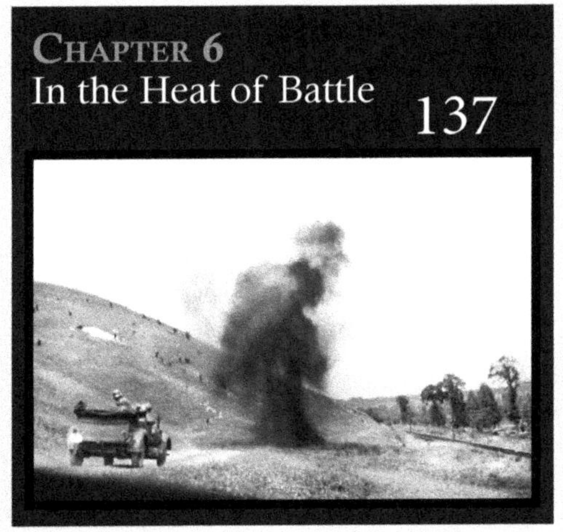

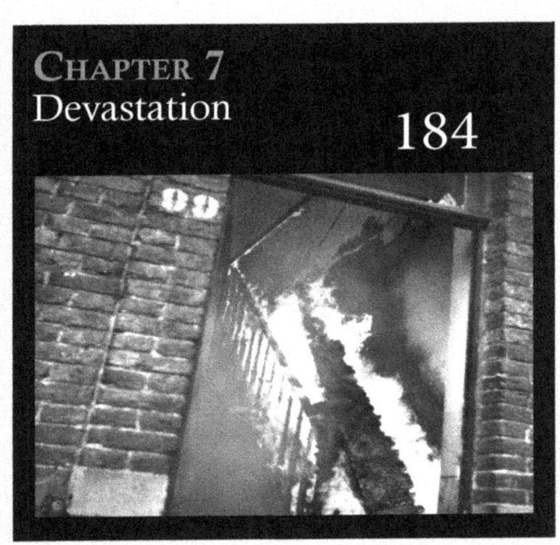

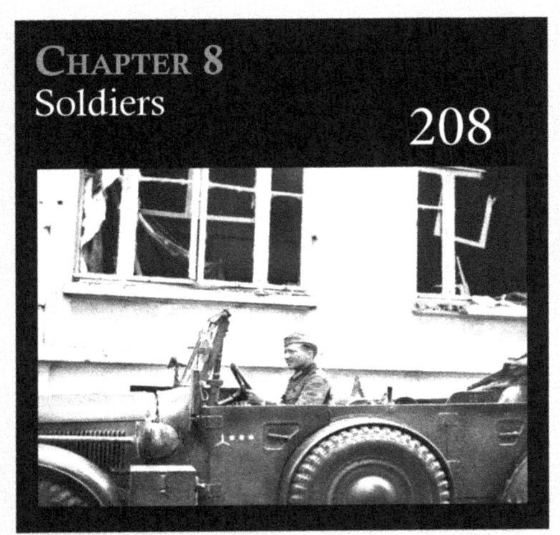

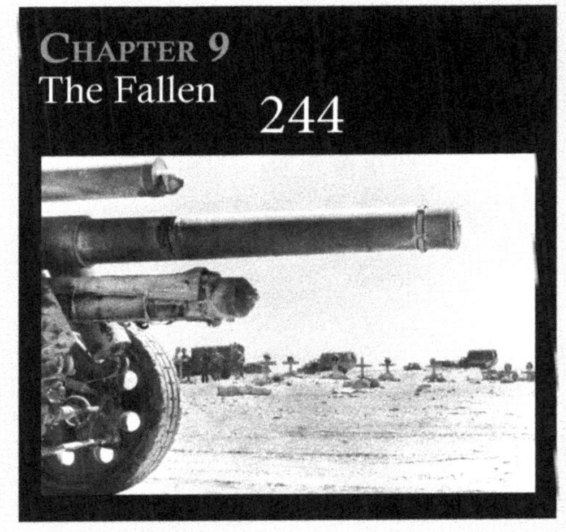

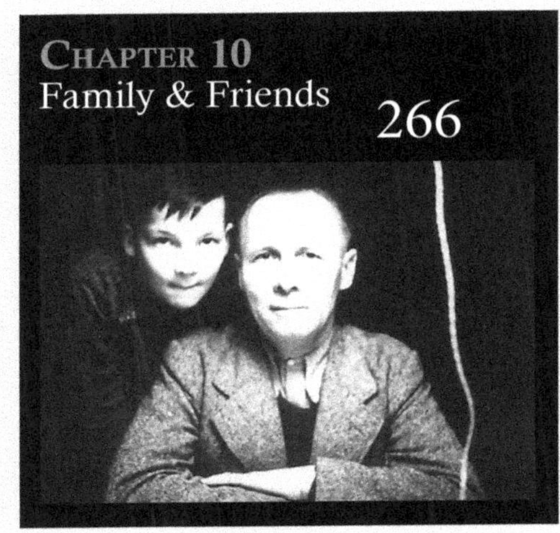

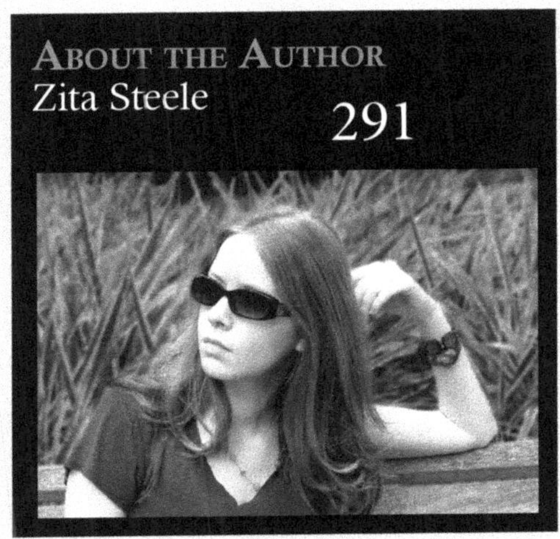

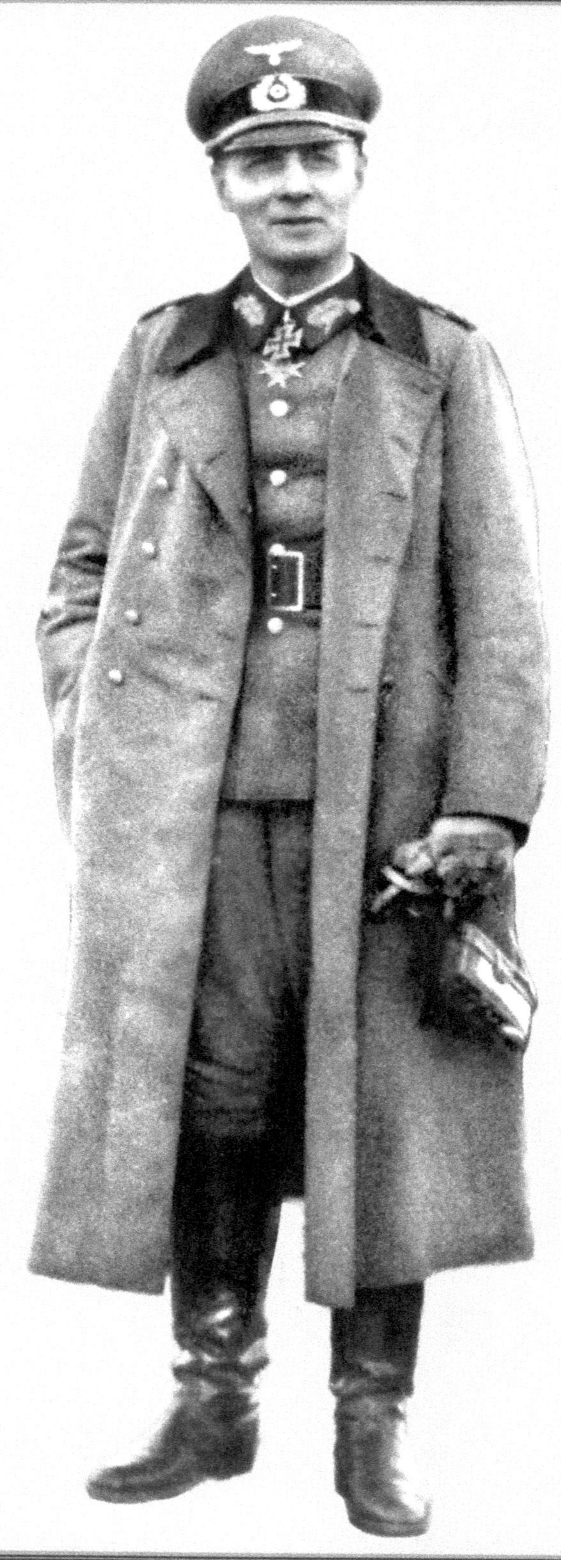

About this Collection

Photography was one of Field Marshal Erwin Rommel's favorite pastimes. Between 1940 and 1942, he took thousands of photos. These images cover a wide variety of subjects reflecting both Rommel's military and personal interests.

Rommel was meticulous in labeling his photos. He also penned several diaries detailing his activities, some of which are the subjects of his photos. Also, he frequently scrawled captions on the photos during his time away from the battlefield. He intended many of these pictures to be illustrations in a manual on military tactics that he planned to write after World War II. His untimely death prevented him from doing so.

Although historians have noted Rommel's photography hobby, no one has ever published a collection of his photography before this book.

THIS SERIES

My goal is to create a series of photography books that provides readers with the opportunity to gain insights into Rommel through both the photos he took and those he collected. The photos are presented to provoke thought and allow people to make their own interpretations. This series offers a unique perspective on Rommel, while providing a glimpse of what he experienced and saw in the war.

You will witness what Rommel saw through his lens—as if accompanying him on the battlefield and during private family moments. You will see what scenes captured his attention and imagination in France and North Africa. From high-angle viewpoints, Rommel took many pictures while flying in airplanes or riding atop tanks.

Rommel also collected pictures of himself taken by German war photographers and others. Rommel evidently saved the images to document or remember important events in his life. These photos are interspersed throughout each book in this series.

VOLUME I: A SURVEY

This first book contains a broad overview of Rommel's photographic work. It analyzes overarching themes, artistic composition of his images, and frequent subjects found within his images. The other books in the *"Erwin Rommel: Photographer"* series will explore individual themes in greater detail.

THE MAN BEHIND THE CAMERA

Erwin Rommel was born in 1891 in the Kingdom of Württemberg, a German state ruled by Emperor Wilhelm II. Rommel's hometown was Heidenheim near the Brenz river, an offshoot of the Danube. This rural southwestern region of Germany is called Swabia. The area has a landscape of rolling green hills, forests, and vineyards. Swabian people are known for being thrifty and hardworking. They speak a distinct dialect of German called "Schwäbisch."

Young Rommel was described as a quiet, but energetic boy who considered becoming an engineer. Ultimately, he decided to be a soldier. Fighting on the frontlines in World War I, he demonstrated exceptional leadership qualities and a remarkable sense of strategy. Wounded several times, he won the Pour le Mérite, Germany's highest award for heroism.

After WWI, Germany was required to reduce its military forces under conditions of the Treaty of Versailles. Rommel, noted for his promising abilities, kept his position in the army. He became a military instructor and taught at academies in Germany and Austria.

Following a civil war and an era of political turmoil in Germany, the Nazi Party took control of the country and established the Third Reich in 1933.

In 1937, Rommel published a military textbook based on his experiences in WWI. The book, called *"Infantry Attacks,"* showed Rommel's extraordinary sense of battlefield tactics and was noticed by Hitler. When World War II eventually broke out, Hitler placed Rommel in command of a tank division.

During WWII, Rommel led campaigns in France and North Africa. He became famously known as the "Desert Fox" and was given the rank of Field Marshal, the role for which he is most well known. At age 49, he was the youngest Field Marshal in German history.

During the course of WWII, Rommel became an opponent of Hitler and the Nazi regime. In 1944, Rommel met with various other political dissidents and made plans to conclude a separate peace with the Allies. After a failed assassination attempt on Hitler, the Nazi Party conducted a crackdown, and Hitler discovered Rommel's connection with his political challengers. Convalescing from an injury, Rommel was trapped at his home in Germany and surrounded by Gestapo and Schutzstaffel (SS) forces. Representatives of Hitler threatened Rommel's family and forced him to commit suicide. Rommel died in October 1944 before WWII ended.

Erwin Rommel is a controversial figure, about whom people have many different opinions. He is an undisputed strategic genius, who is recognized for his humane conduct on the battlefield.

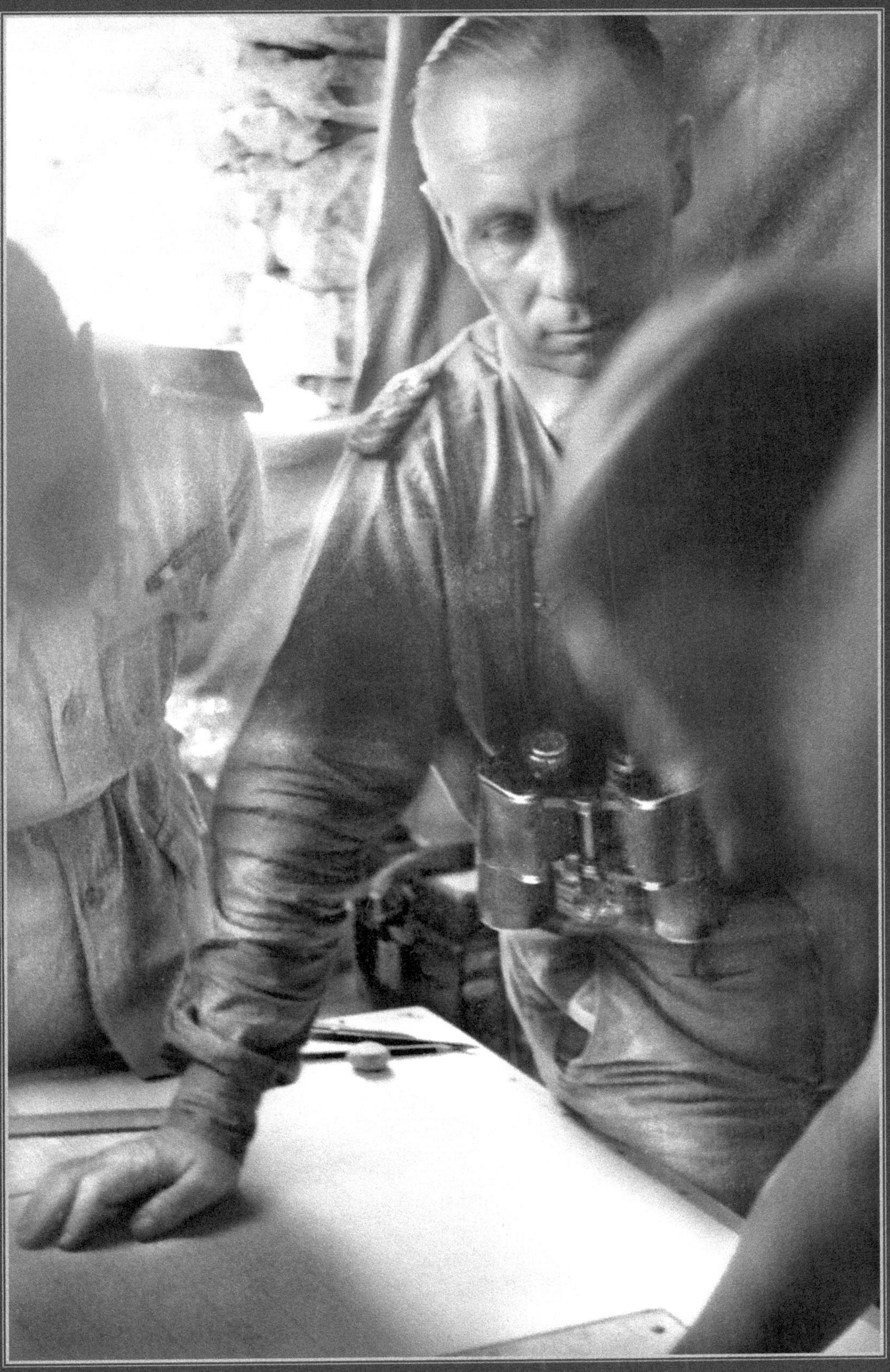

Background: The Origin of This Series

I've always had an interest in diverse cultures and people. I'm a descendant of Spanish settlers who emigrated to New Mexico in the 1600s. I was raised in a multicultural environment. I'm also of German heritage. My German ancestors were farmers from Württemberg who came to America in the 1800s and settled in the Midwest. As Swabians, they were of the same ethnicity as Rommel.

As a teenager, I decided to write a historical fiction novel set in North Africa during WWII. While in Washington, D.C., I went to the National Archives. I made research inquiries and discovered the Rommel photo collection.

I found Rommel's photos very interesting. They demonstrated excellent composition, and many seemed as if they could have been taken by a photojournalist. Numerous images were very striking. I also was impressed by the fact that someone commanding an army could find the time and energy to take so many pictures.

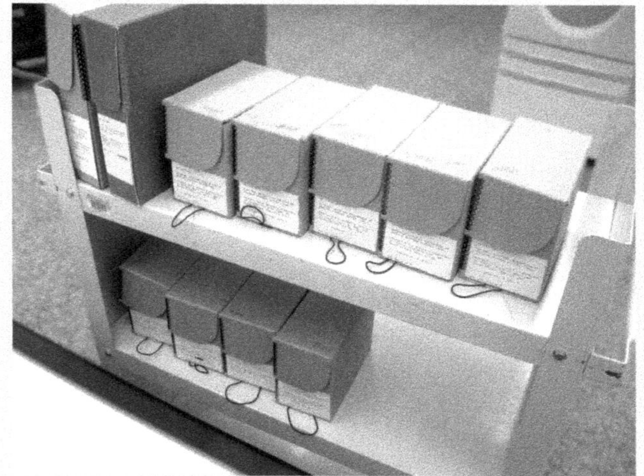

To create this book, I delved through hundreds of photos, slides, negatives, and photographic contact prints in these boxes at the National Archives, where Rommel's personal photos are stored after having been seized by American forces during World War II.

The photo collection motivated me to do more research about Rommel and WWII in North Africa. I planned to write a book using the photos as illustrations. As years passed, I continued to research this subject.

While attending the Honors College at the University of South Florida, I was required to complete a thesis as a senior undergraduate capstone project. I decided to create a thesis project involving the Rommel photos. This allowed me to demonstrate my capabilities in analysis, creative thinking, writing, and independent research. I also made use of my German language skills to learn more about the photographs.

My thesis provided the groundwork for this book and others that will follow in this series. It is my hope that this work will make a contribution to modern history.

Opposition to This Work

As I worked on this project, I was confronted by opposition from many people. This primarily stemmed from antagonism against Germany due to prejudices related to Hitler, Nazis, the SS, and the Holocaust. People treated me badly for even speaking the German language. This hostility came from fellow students, professors, university staff, personal acquaintances, and even members of my own family.

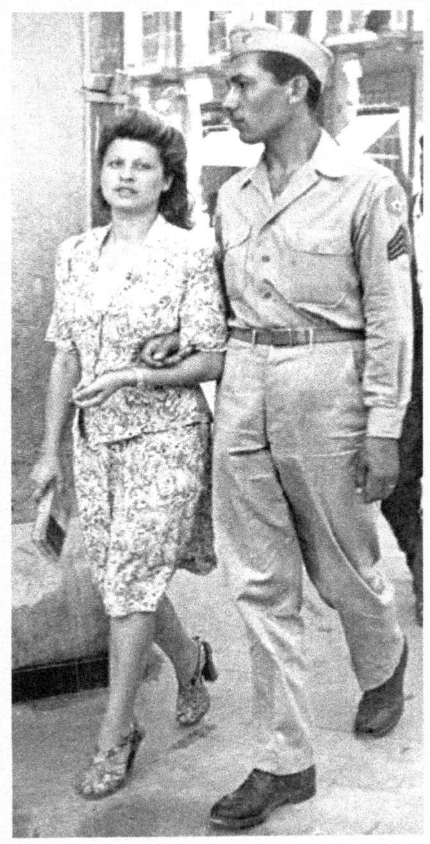

Pedro Perea, my great-grandmother's brother, who fought against Rommel in WWII.

I found these reactions to be narrow-minded and intolerant. I don't believe in prejudice. My goal is to understand other people as human beings, not to make judgments about them based on history or politics.

While writing this book, I also encountered strong misperceptions about Rommel—namely that he was a member of the Nazi Party or an SS officer, neither of which were true. I also found that most authors who have written about Rommel primarily have been concerned about determining what Rommel's political views were and what his association was with Hitler. While doing research with the Rommel photos, I found a few wartime photos of Rommel with Hitler—and I chose deliberately not to include them. This book is not about Hitler or Nazism.

During World War II, my maternal grandfather served the U.S. Army in a medical role, treating men wounded in the Pacific Theater. One of my other relatives, Pedro "Uncle Pete" Perea, fought in North Africa against Rommel's Afrika Korps. I never knew him since he died a year before I was born. My mother visited him 2 weeks before he died, and he spoke about his time in North Africa even then. I grew up hearing stories about how he was wounded in the leg by a German antitank gun and had acted as an Italian interpreter.

War is a terrible thing which incurs suffering for everyone involved in it. This book is not about taking sides. It is not about passing moral verdicts.

Whatever your personal views may be, it's unquestionable that Erwin Rommel was an important historical figure. This photo collection is significant because it sheds new light on his personality, allows us to view him from a creative standpoint, and adds a groundbreaking dimension to the history of World War II.

My Approach to These Photos

As a graphic artist and writer, I am well aware of the power and intrinsic ability of images to convey information using visual elements that are stronger than printed words. Images, however, can be distorted through various means, such as cropping and design manipulations. In this manner, photographs, especially in this digital age, can be taken out of context, altered from the original image, or slanted to show a different viewpoint contrary to the intent of the photographer.

One of the most important goals of my restoration was to preserve the photographer's original work. The contents within the images have not been distorted in any way.

All photos taken by Rommel are shown in full frame, as they actually appeared when he captured the shot. For some photos, I have extracted close-up sections and placed them next to Rommel's full-frame images so readers can see interesting details I observed in certain areas within the pictures.

The only photos which have been cropped are those taken by others of Rommel himself. This was done to make it easier for viewers to see Rommel clearly, particularly in pictures of him surrounded by other people. In some cases, I have extracted close-ups of Rommel, cropped them to provide greater visibility of him, and placed them next to the original photos of himself that he collected.

Rommel used a Leica camera for much of his photography. While the exact model is unknown, the Leica III D camera (below) was popular during World War II. Rommel's camera and accessories were stolen after his death from his home in Germany by American soldiers, who even took his uniforms.

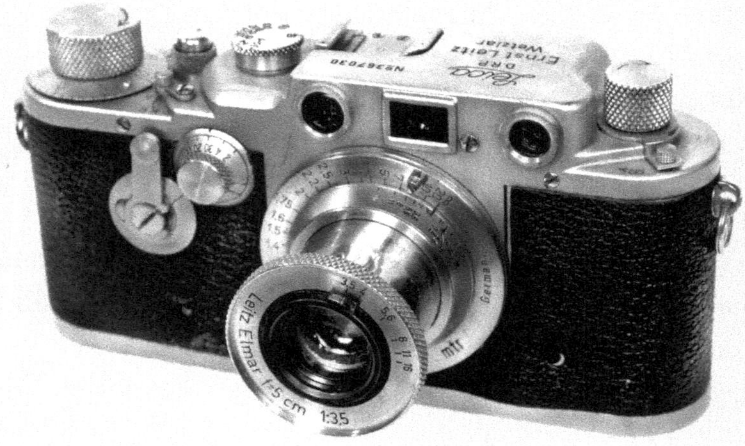

Photo courtesy of Camera Heritage Museum at www.cameraheritagemuseum.com.

Rommel's Images & My Photo Restoration

The Counterintelligence Corps of the U.S. military seized Rommel's private photo collection in 1945 from his widow in Germany. They confiscated his Leica equipment and 3,000 photos that he had taken.

The images, which fill about a dozen boxes in the National Archives, are in various conditions. Many are jammed together in stacks so tightly that some images are stuck to others. Some are slides encased in plastic sleeves. Others are large contact prints that contain several series of images from film negatives. Most, however, are still photos printed on different types of paper and in a variety of sizes.

The majority of the photographs in Rommel's collection are badly damaged. In some cases, the photos are stained, yellowed, or darkened by age. Many are creased and slightly torn. Other photos contain significant amounts of scratching, dust, and blotches due to the conditions in which they were taken and developed.

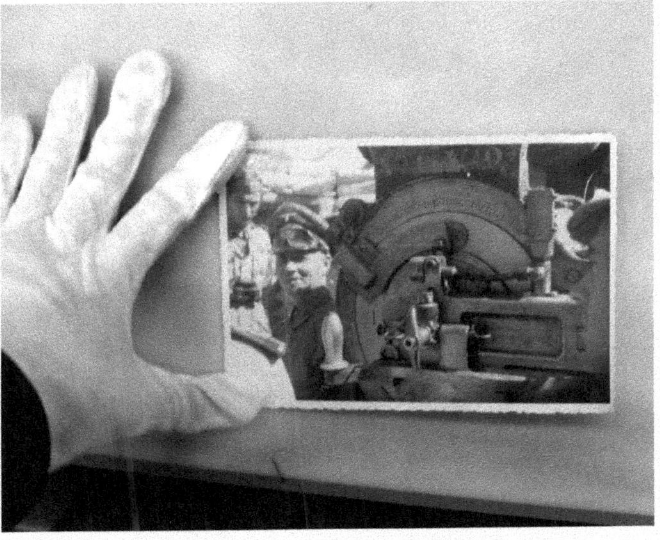

While examining the photos at the National Archives, I placed a picture on the table while wearing cloth gloves.

I am responsible for the restoration of all photos in this book. My graphic design and multimedia skills are central to my work as an author and artist. All the photos in this book have undergone a painstaking, digital-restoration process.

I used a three-phased approach to the restoration; I worked on each photo at least three times to address various components of the images. The process is described below.

- *Repaired and Lightened*—Because the photos were all very dark, they had to be lightened in order to be visible. Scratches, dust particles, rips, stains, and other forms of damage were repaired.
- *Balanced*—Due to poor lighting conditions that occurred when many of the photos were taken, not all key elements within the photos were equally apparent. Therefore, I balanced the toning and lighting as needed.
- *Revived*—I made a special effort to bring out all the details in each image. I wanted to bring the images to life by making each aspect of the subjects as clear as possible.

Three examples of my restoration work in the various phases are shown below.

REPAIRED & LIGHTENED

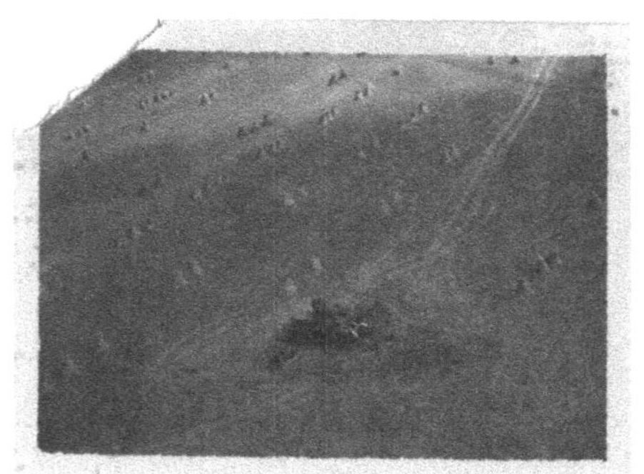
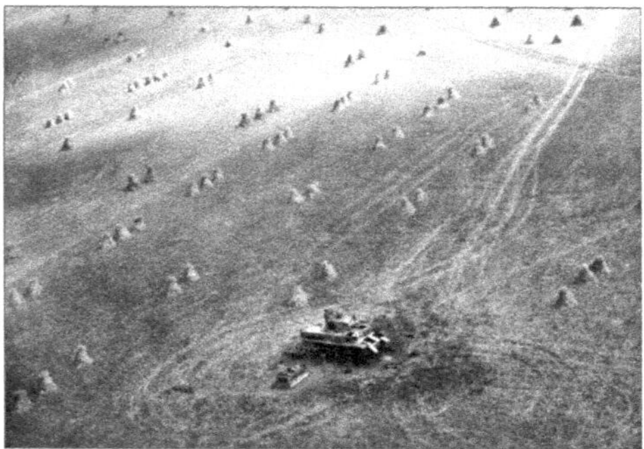

Rommel's original photo (left). The same photo after my restoration (right).

BALANCED

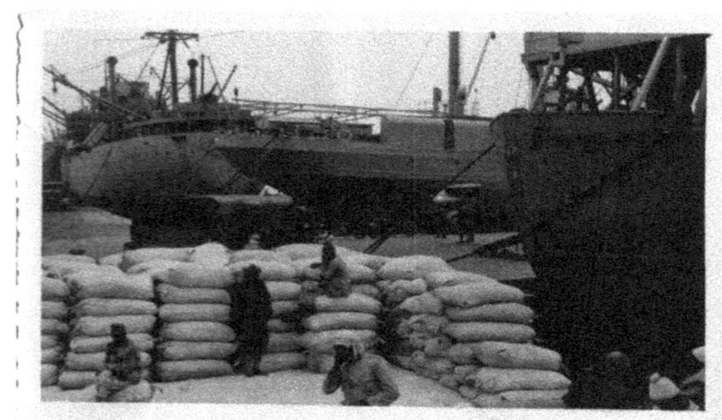
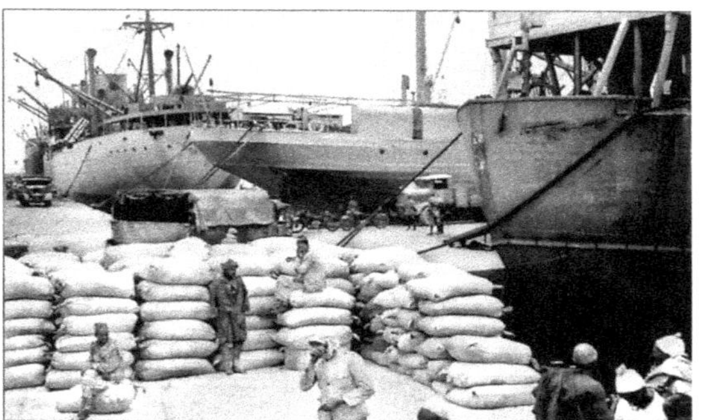

Rommel's original photo (left). The same photo after my restoration (right).

REVIVED

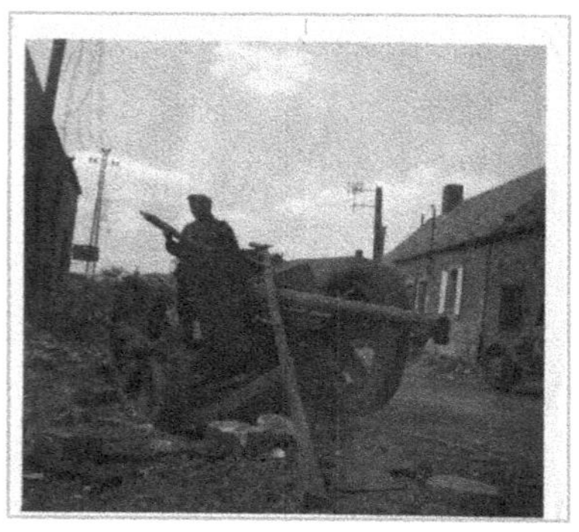
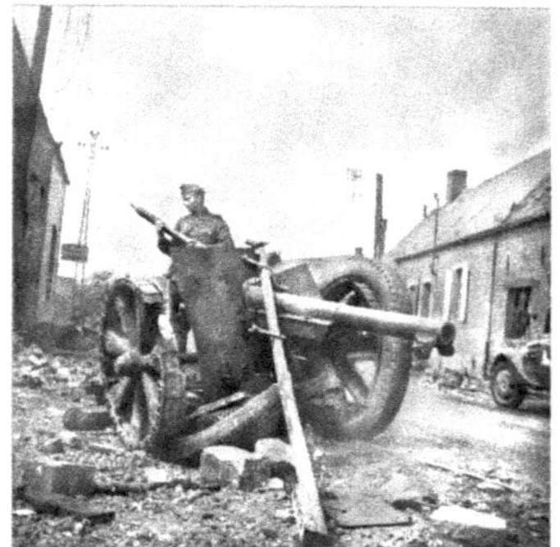

Rommel's original photo (left). The same photo after my restoration (right).

Rommel's Handwriting

All of Rommel's handwriting in this book is authentic. The handwritten words shown on chapter title pages were chosen for artistic effect. Their meaning in German is relevant to the chapters in which they appear. All of these were taken from Rommel's own captions, which he had written on photos in his collection.

Some of Rommel's captions are shown throughout the chapters. They usually appear next to the photos on which they were originally written.

Rommel's signature shown at the beginning of the book is from an item in my private collection.

A sample of one of Rommel's handwritten captions on his photos.

Themes in Rommel's Photos

While studying Rommel's collection, I identified particular themes which Rommel appeared to have been interested in photographing: nature, machinery, his men, battlefield action, and other subjects. (The themes are categorized in the chapters of this book.) Rommel also demonstrated distinct characteristics as a photographer. These idiosyncrasies recur throughout his entire collection.

All of Rommel's photos, including action snapshots, demonstrate methodical precision. His photography was controlled and deliberate. Subjects are nearly always centered within the frame—or, if they are not centered, they are carefully aligned in relation to other objects. (This is noteworthy, given that many of these photos were taken quickly in the middle of battle.) His photos demonstrate strong composition, often with a large centered focal point.

Most of the photos also reveal what appears to be his mathematical interest. Rommel paid unique attention to geometric shapes, patterns, and curves. In the majority of his photos, a curving diagonal line of some type appears in the middle of the image. In many instances, the backgrounds are planar surfaces with layers of intersecting lines. Additionally, Rommel was attentive to shadows. In many pictures, shadows and lights dramatize the subject matter.

Rommel had a tendency to capture contradictions and possible ironies. For example, a photo may show order amid disorder, machines that are broken or dysfunctional, or an intact object among wreckage.

Many of Rommel's photos feature lone figures set against overpowering backdrops: a single man is often shown amid a vast landscape, or tiny human figures are framed against overwhelming action or chaos.

It is also significant that Rommel paused during the heat of battle to snap action photos, while simultaneously avoiding enemy fire and directing military actions.

His photos appear to indicate a respect for people. There are no photographs of corpses on either side, nor are there any photos of people in degrading or inhumane situations. In terms of human subjects, Rommel focused on frontline soldiers—both German and Allied—as well as ordinary people he encountered.

Rommel took many photos of graves. Despite having fought in two world wars, he was apparently not so battle-hardened as to prevent him from feeling the loss of those around him who sacrificed their lives. Rommel did not expect this photo collection to be publicized in its entirety. It is likely that the grave photos were for private memories and personal reflections. Not all of the men whose graves Rommel photographed are documented in his writings. When possible, I have included the documentation. I have also included Rommel's documentation of military comrades who died whose graves are not pictured here.

This book concludes with Rommel's family photos that were seized along with his military images. They include pictures of Rommel interacting with his wife, Lucie, and son, Manfred.

The majority of photos that depict Rommel and his troops in Europe were taken in France, 1940. Rommel returned to France in 1944, during which time he photographed Atlantic Wall fortifications. By this time, he was too disillusioned with Hitler and the war to photograph other subjects. The majority of photos from North Africa were taken in 1941. Some appear to have been taken in the early part of 1942. The family photos were probably taken during Rommel's leaves throughout the war.

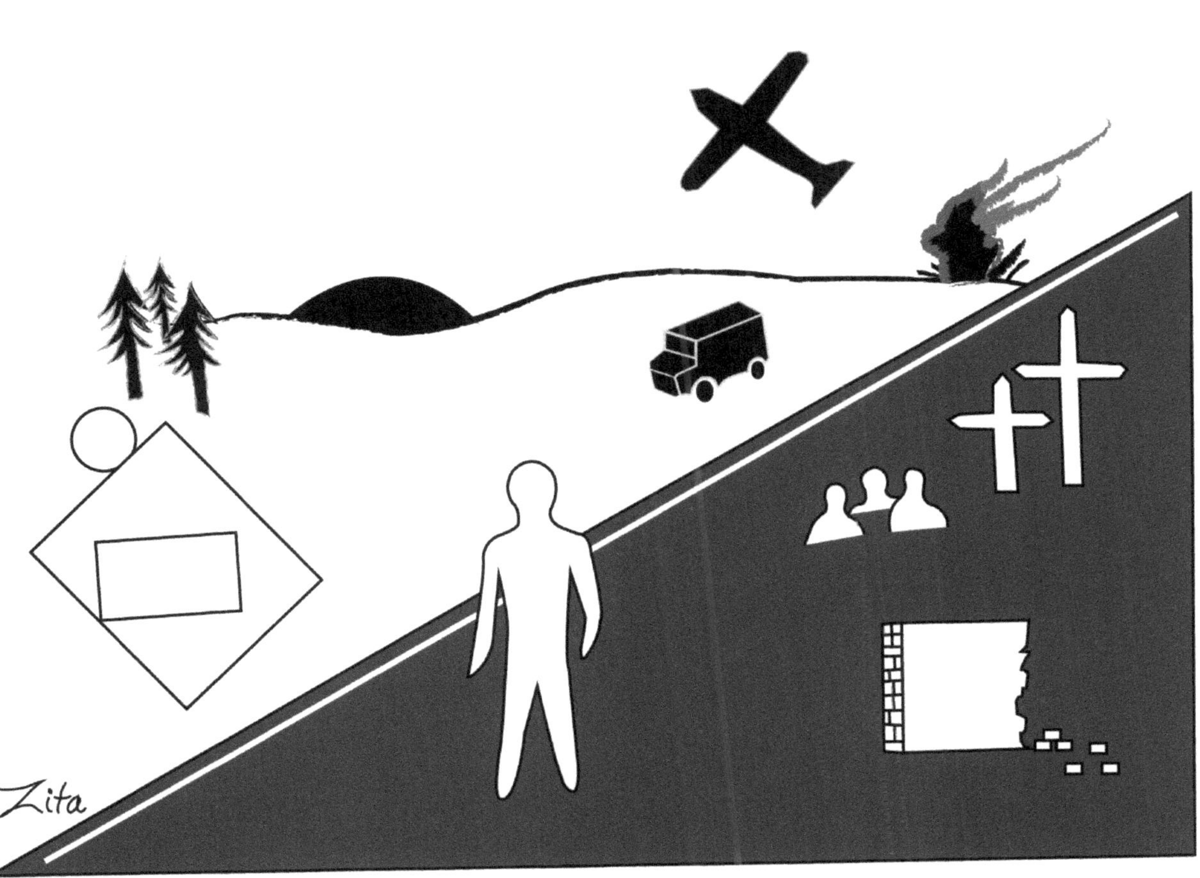

1

Airplanes

Am frühen Morgen

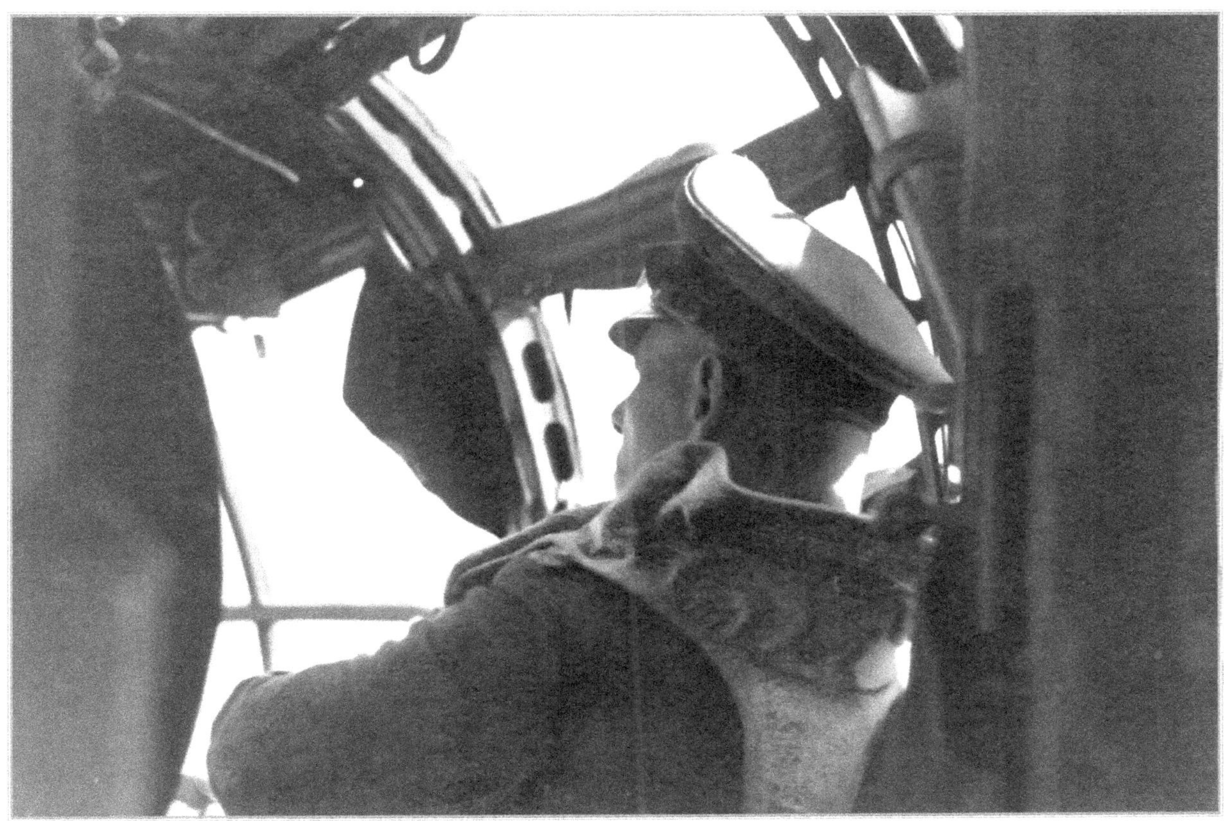

Rommel is seated in the cockpit of a plane (date and location unknown).

Flying was one of Rommel's hobbies as a youth; at age 14 he attempted to build and fly a glider. He incorporated his interest in flying into his military activities. Although he had no formal training, he often flew his own plane in North Africa while monitoring troop movements or conducting reconnaissance. Rommel's preferred reconnaissance aircraft was called a Fieseler Storch.

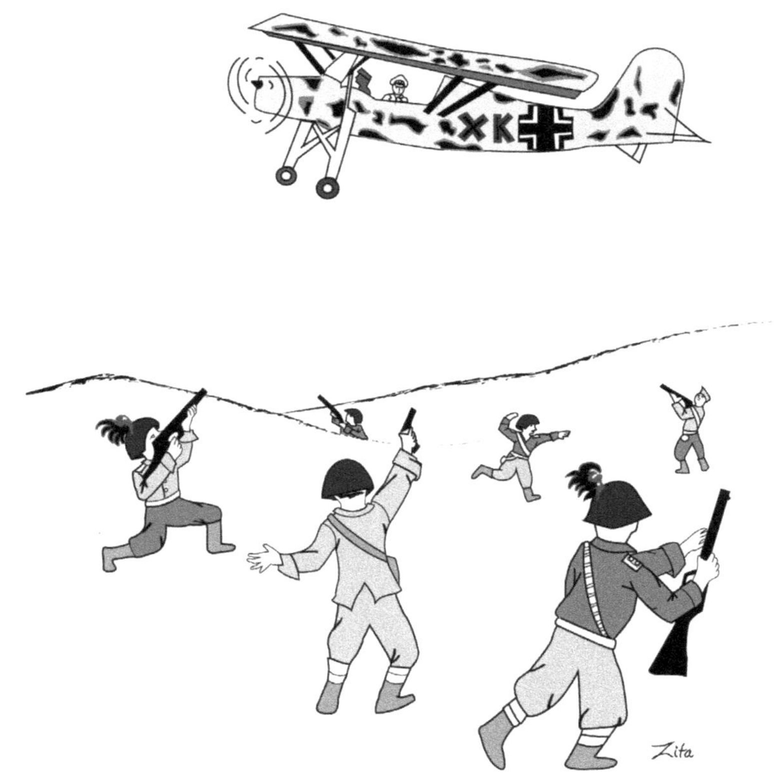

Sometimes Rommel had dangerous experiences when flying his aircraft in North Africa. On one such occasion, Rommel's plane, flying at about 150 feet, was mistakenly targeted by his own Italian troops in the North African desert.

> "The Italians had apparently never seen a Storch before and were so completely bewildered by our sudden appearance over their heads that they fired on us from all directions. At the range of 50 to 100 yards, it was a miracle that we were not shot down, and it did not speak well for Italian marksmanship...Having no wish to be shot down by my own Italians I had the aircraft climb to 3,000 feet, from where we observed the situation in safety."

— Rommel

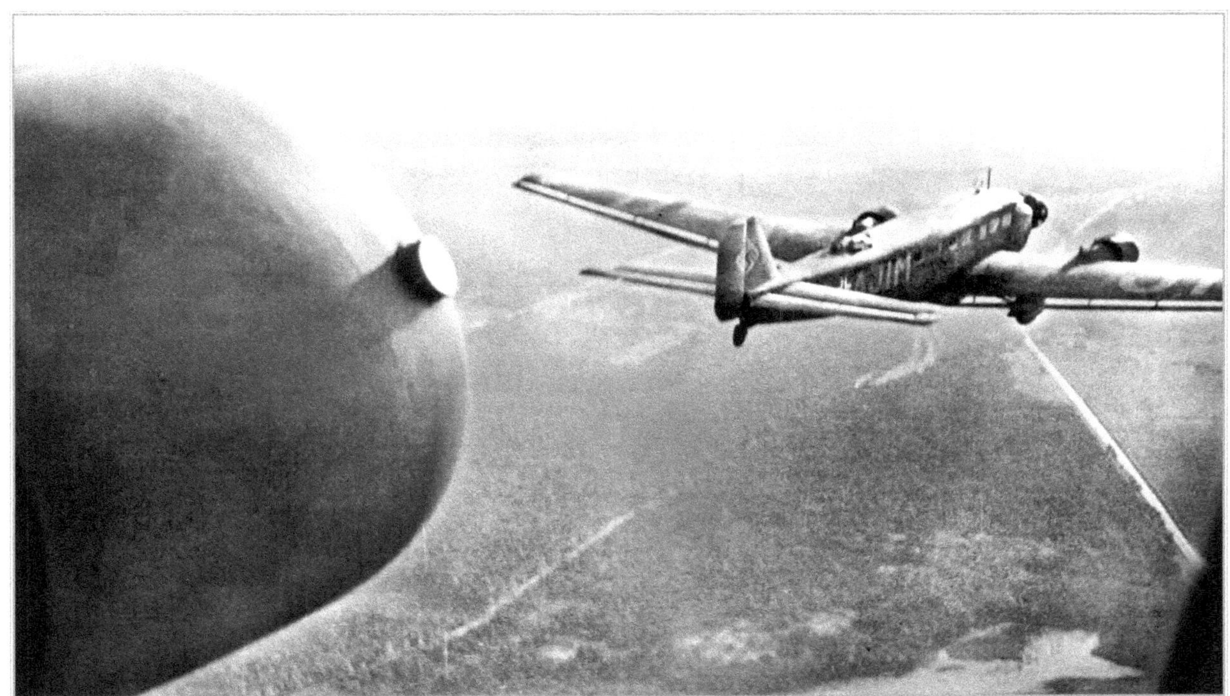

Another aerial shot of Rommel's plane flying under German escort over France.

Rommel captured many striking images from the window of his airplane while conducting aerial reconnaissance. His photos often show bold compositions (as in this image), which contain central focal points with horizontal straight or curving lines around them.

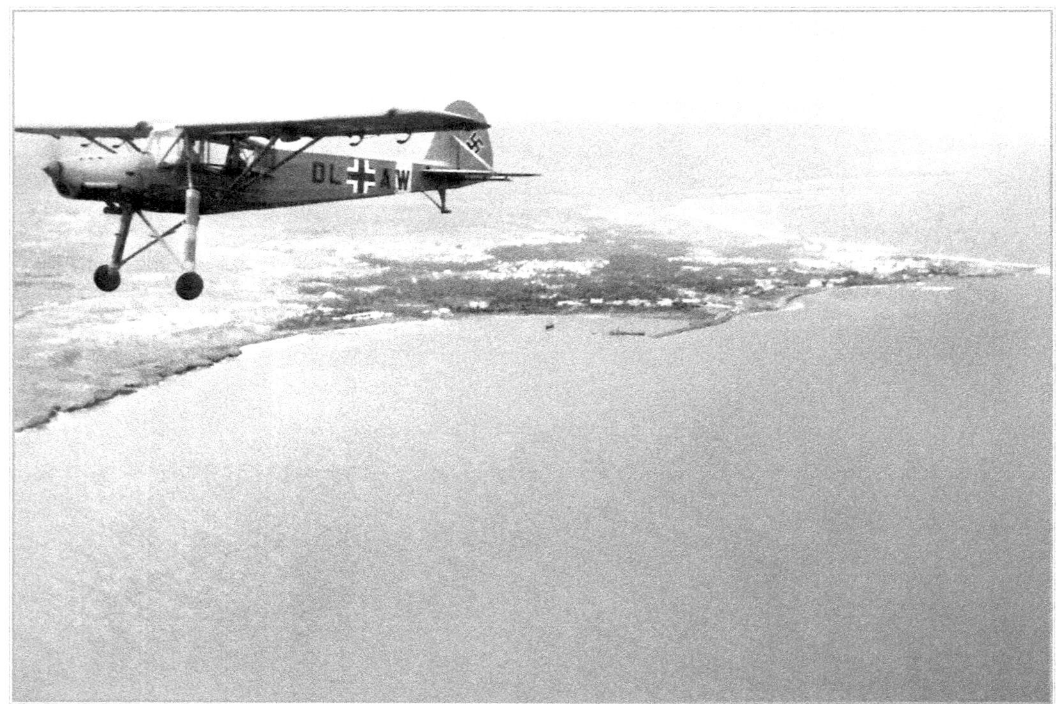

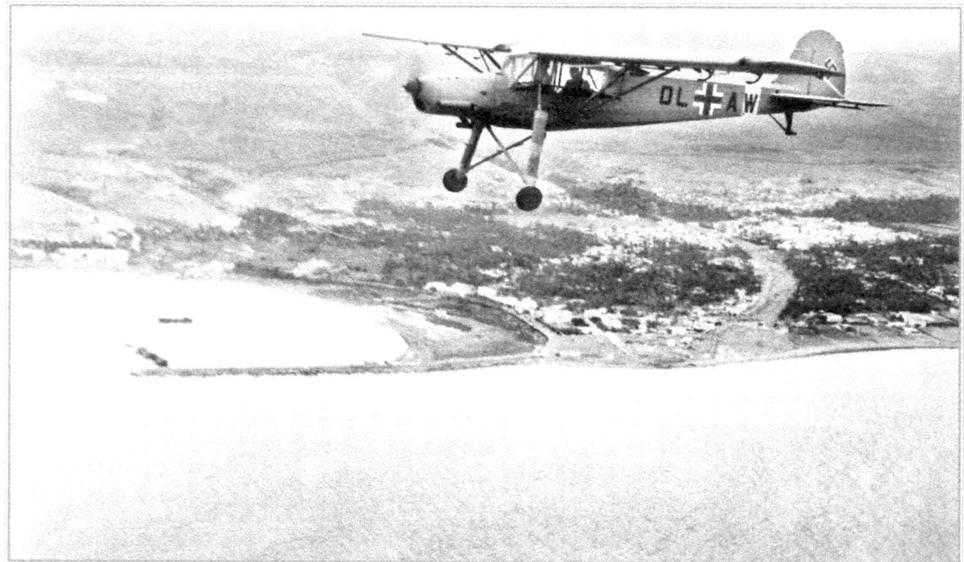

While riding in a plane, Rommel photographed two pictures of a companion German aircraft (a Fieseler Storch) gliding over the sea.

It appears that Rommel took these photos out of personal rather than military interest. They demonstrate his characteristic tendency to contrast a strong dramatic focal point against a simple, unassuming backdrop.

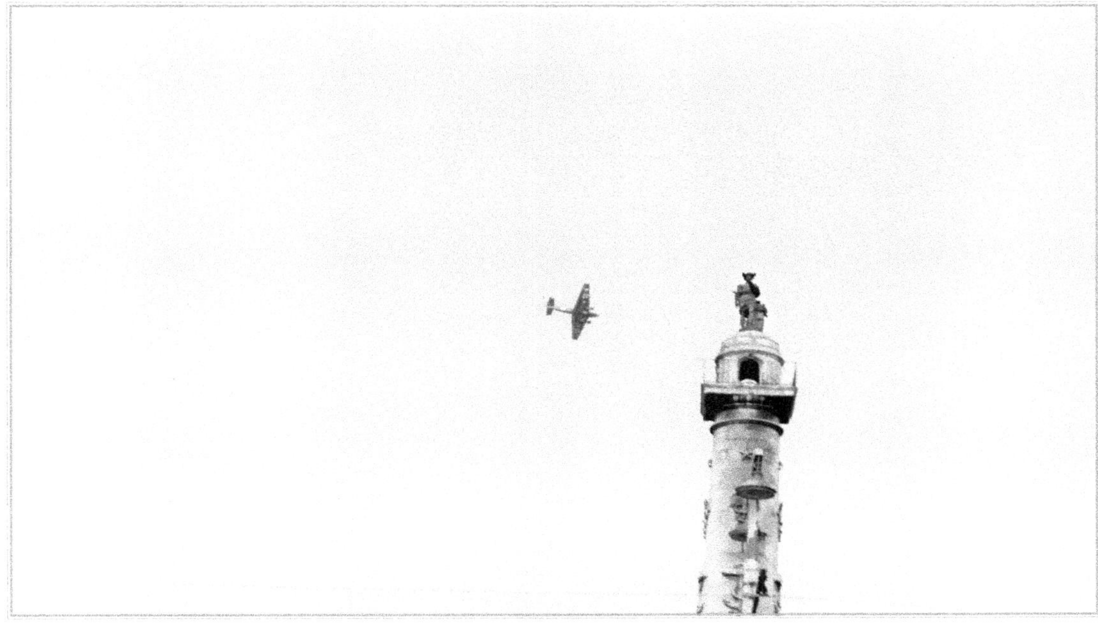

A German plane swoops by a statue on a pinnacle in France.

This image is unique among Rommel's pictures because of its empty background.

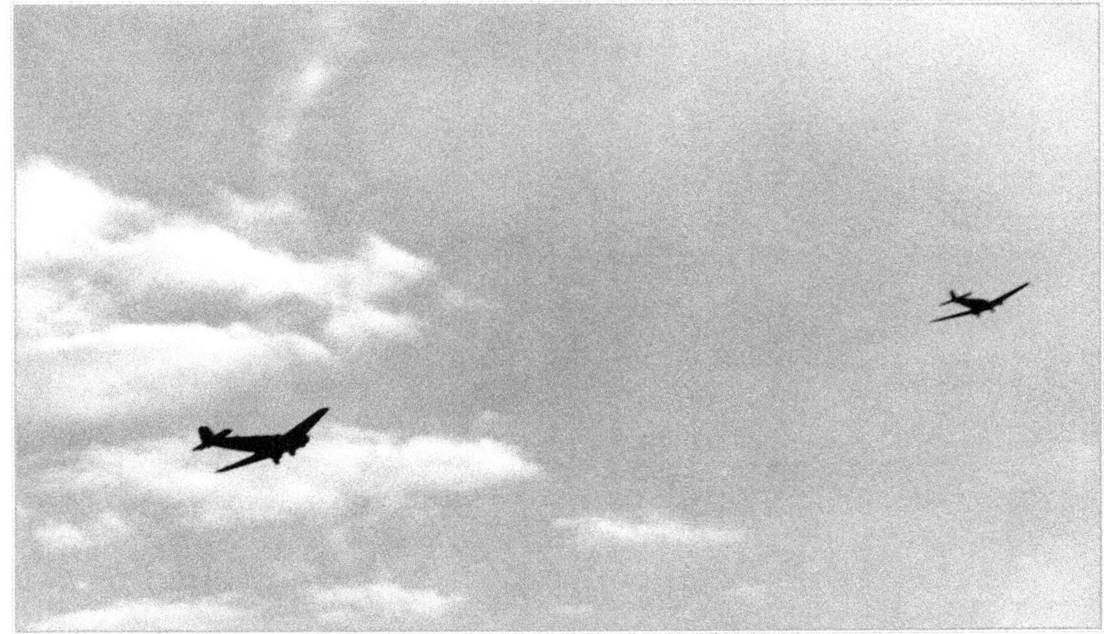

Silhouettes of German airplanes fly through the sky (date and location unknown).

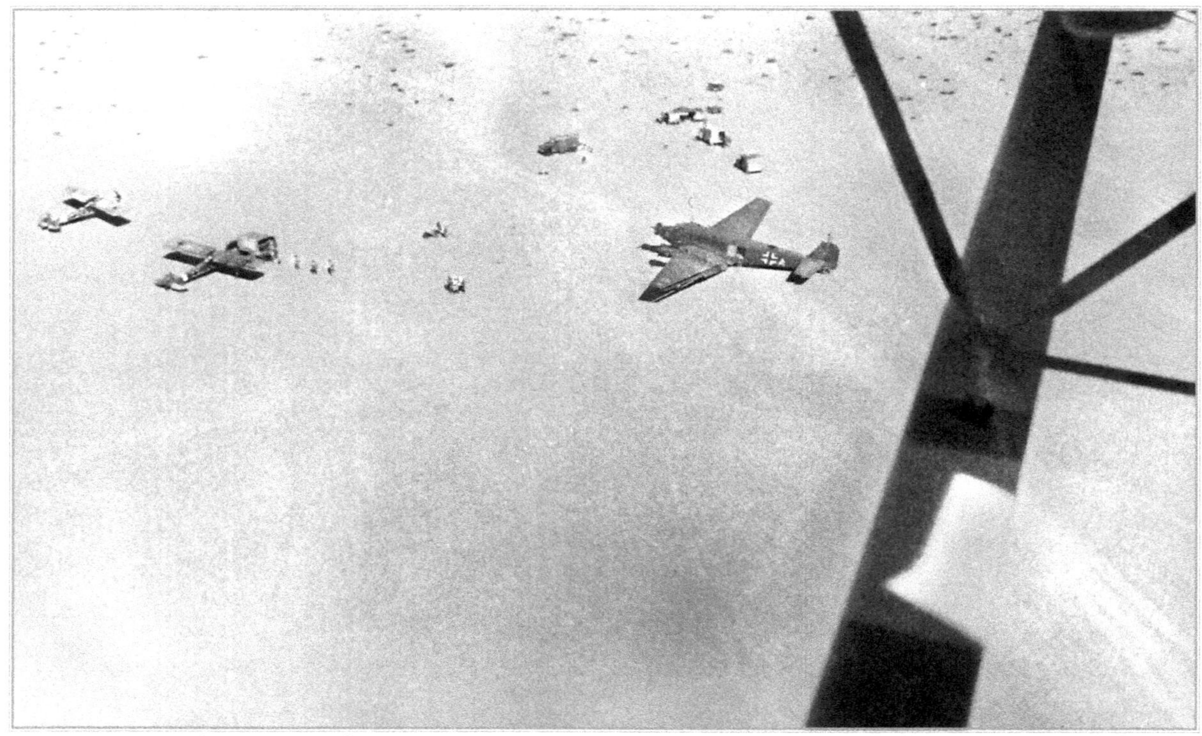

Rommel's airplane flies over a makeshift airfield in the desolate sand of the North African desert.

The large dark plane on the right appears to be a cargo plane. Groups of men stand in the center of this airfield. A truck is parked in front of one airplane (left) as a row of men walk behind the vehicle.

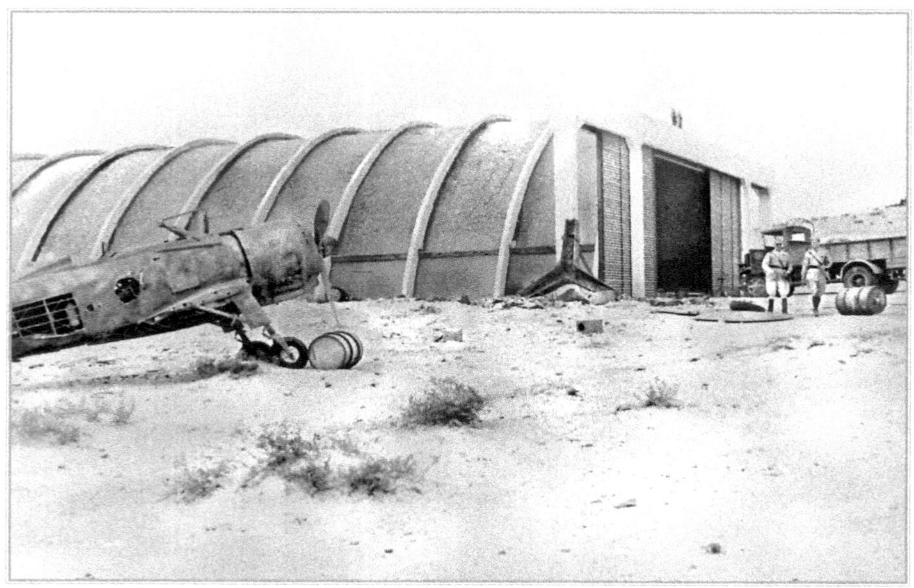

A disabled airplane (left) near a hangar in the desert.

Two Italian officers walk past a metal barrel. They appear to be approaching Rommel as he takes this photograph.

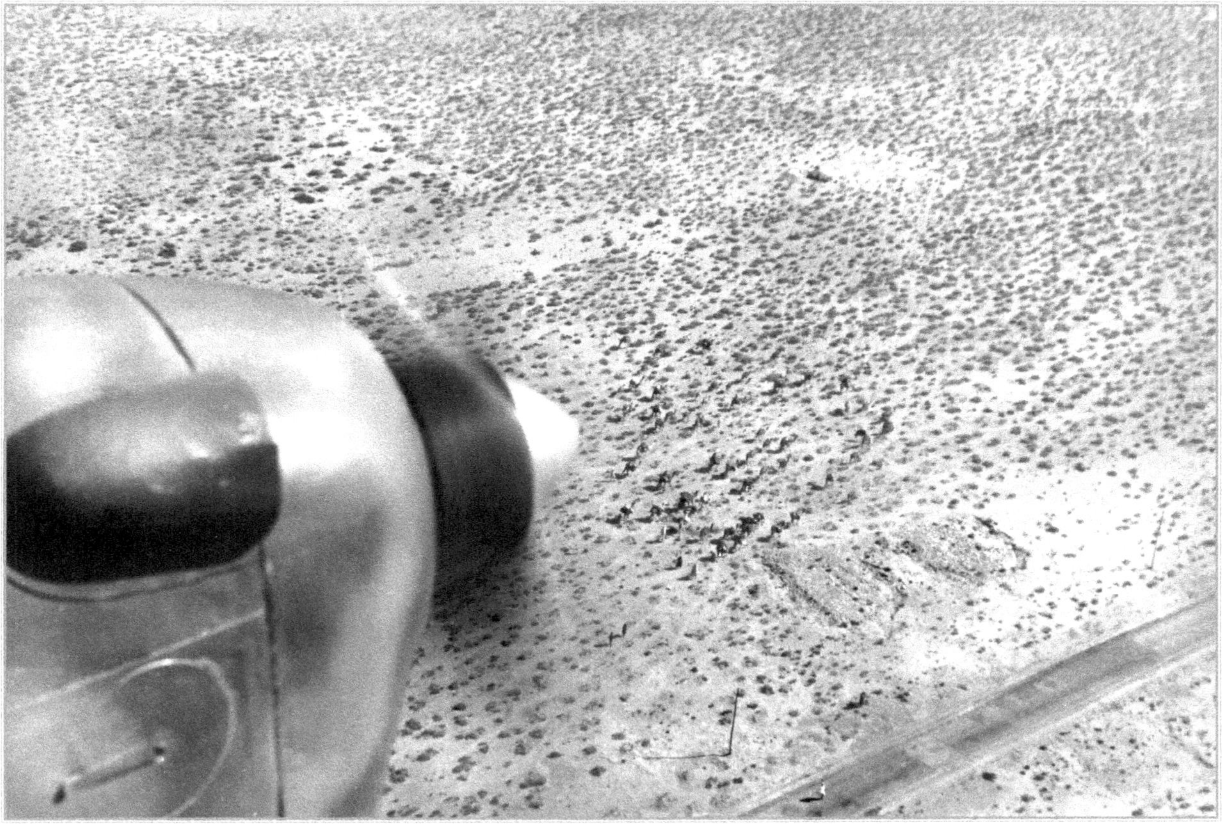

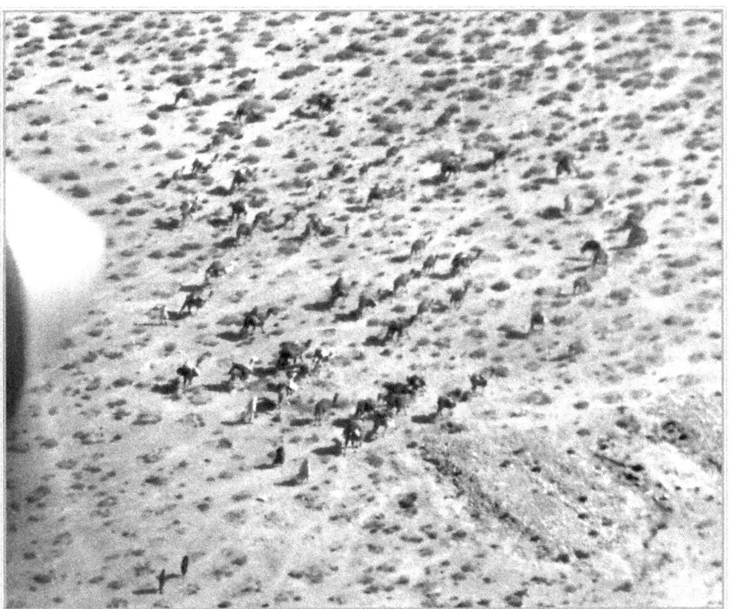

A herd of camels travel across the desert in North Africa. The road (lower right) creates a diagonal element in the image, which is a feature in many of Rommel's photos.

The close-up (left) was cropped from Rommel's photo and enlarged to provide a more detailed view of the camels that Rommel saw from the seat of his airplane.

An airplane propeller points to herd of camels (above) in North Africa.

Rommel had another risky aerial experience when he used his Storch airplane to search for lost German troops in the desert.

Flying at 2,000 feet, he sighted what he believed to be the missing Germans and began to land his airplane. He then had a surprising close call, which he recorded in his memoirs.

> "Several men laid out a landing cross between the vehicles. At the last moment I suddenly spotted the flat helmets of British troops. We immediately banked and made off, followed by machine-gun fire from the British troops. We were lucky to get away practically unscathed, with only one hit in the tail."
>
> — *Rommel*

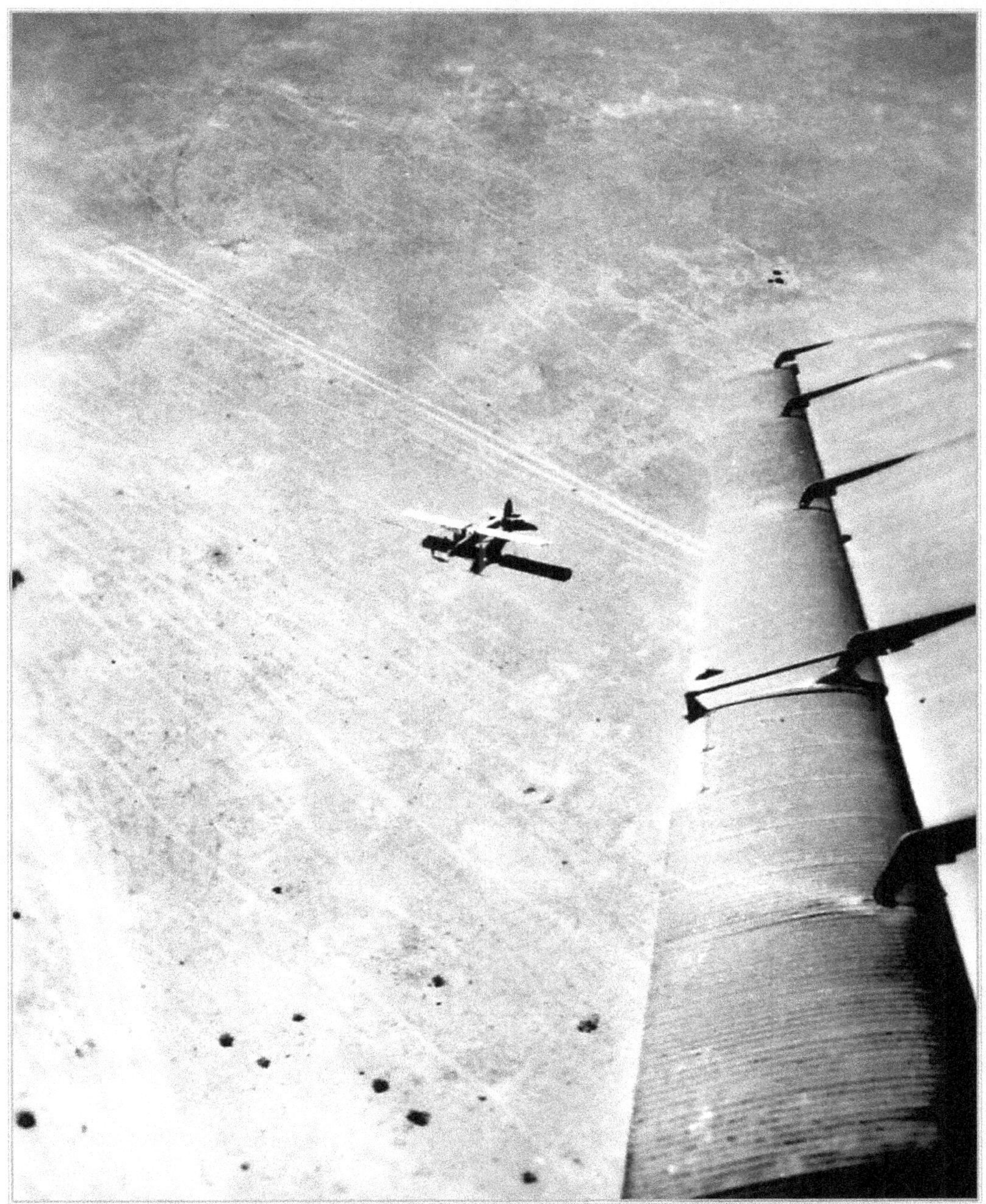

Looking over the wing of his aircraft, Rommel captured this bold image of what appears to be a makeshift airfield in Libya (April 5, 1941).

An airplane has landed in a dirt clearing. Multiple tire tracks indicate this area was in heavy use. This photo contains many diagonal lines, characteristic of Rommel's photographs.

2

Machines

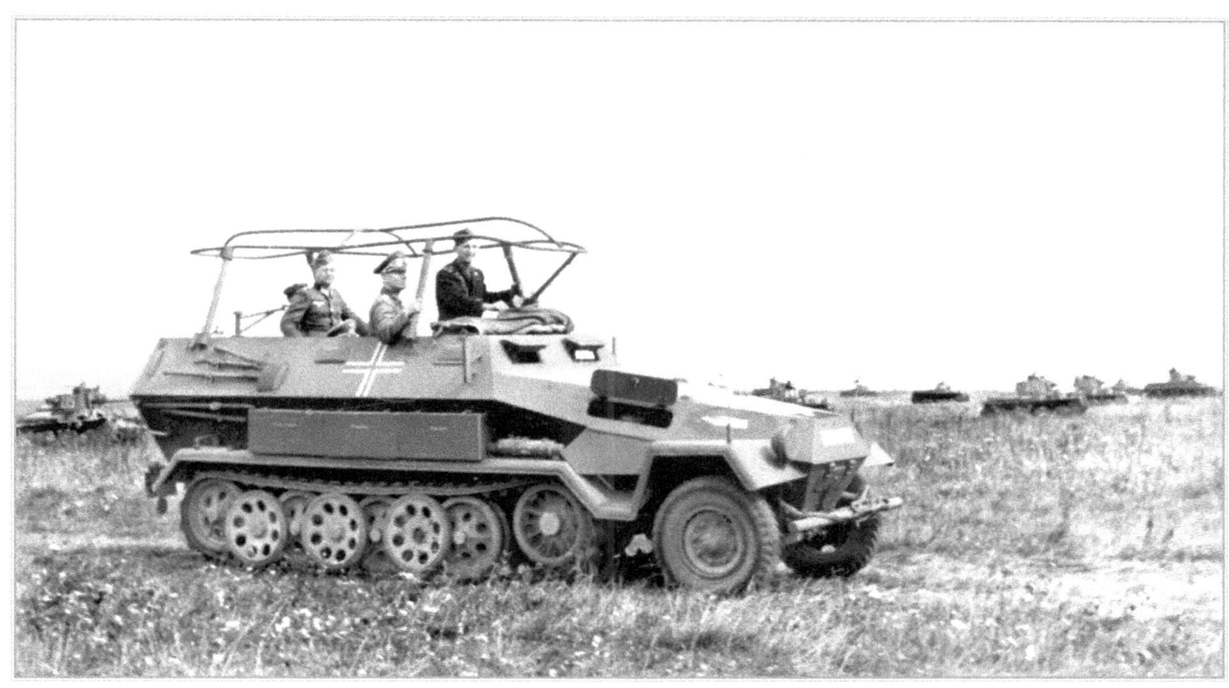

Rommel rides in a German half-track Sonderkraftfahrzeug (Sd.Kfz.) military vehicle while accompanying a Panzer formation across a field in France.

Nearly a dozen tanks can be seen accompanying Rommel in his command vehicle into the countryside through France.

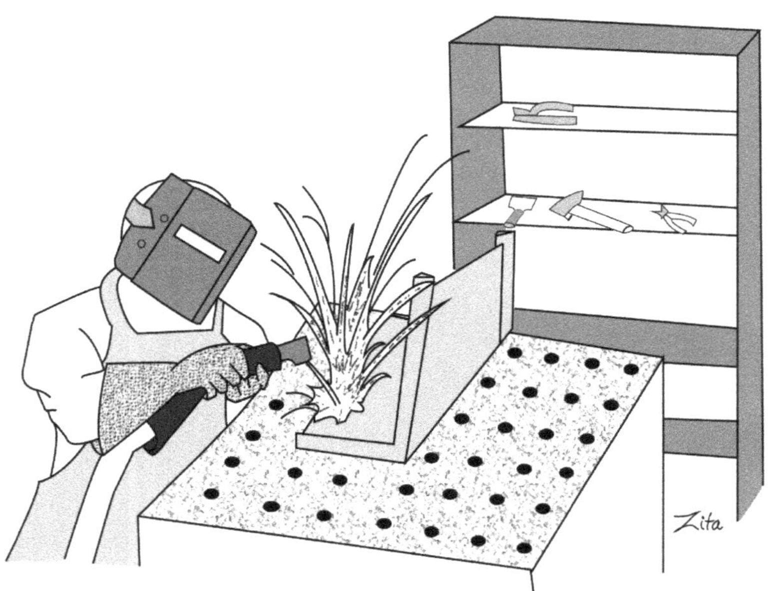

Rommel had a lifelong passion for mechanics and engineering. He demonstrated an interest in technical things from an early age. As a young man, he considered becoming an engineer.

According to those who knew him, Rommel could build or fix anything, and he enjoyed making things. He completely took apart and rebuilt both his car and his motorcycle in order to understand how the vehicles worked and how to fix them. In his writings, he analyzed and critiqued different types of military machinery. His photos reveal that he was interested in cars, engines, equipment, boats, and other types of motorized vehicles and construction.

Rommel's interest in technology is typical of people from the Swabian region of Germany.

Swabia always has been one of the most scientifically and technologically advanced areas of Germany. Rommel's home state of Württemberg (now known as Baden-Württemberg) is today considered Germany's industrial and engineering powerhouse. In Rommel's era, the area was known for its metal craftsmanship and high-quality machinery. Home to some of the most famous German inventors, it also is the birthplace of the motorcycle, the electric drill, the diesel engine, the mechanical calculator, and Zeppelin airship.

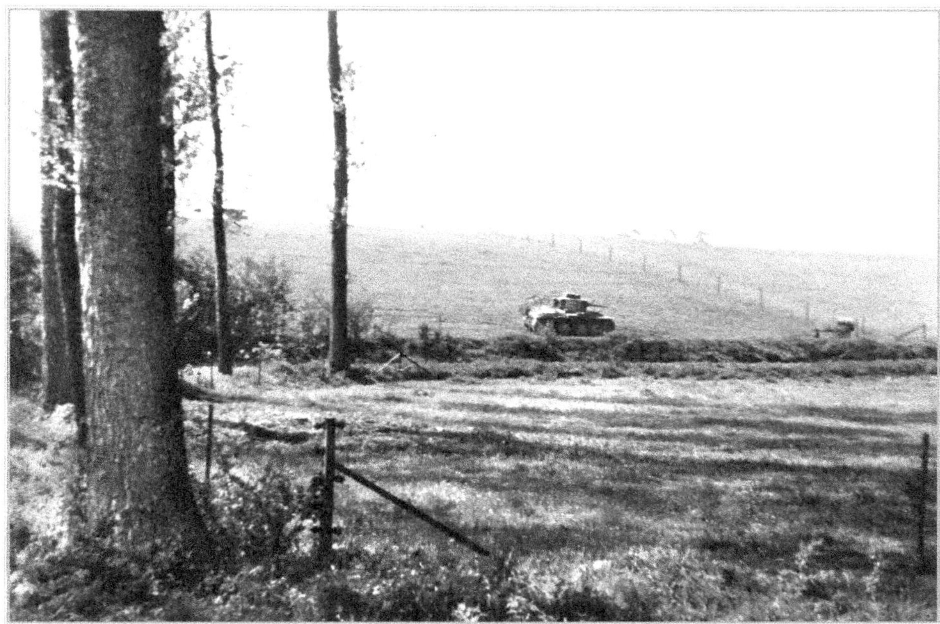

A disabled tank sits alone in a field in France.

A closer view reveals that the tank skidded wildly as it came to a stop, leaving marks in the ground. The tank appears to have a large hole in the turret.

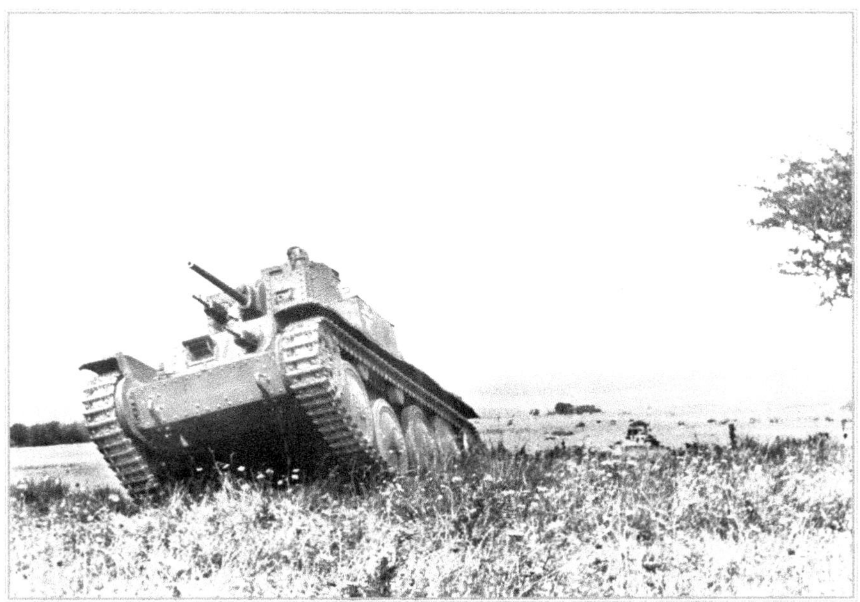

A Panzer ascends a hill in France.

With gun barrels ready, this tank leads another Panzer (right) over a ridge. This photo shows Rommel's interest in photographing tanks from a low angle, giving them a monumental presence and emphasizing their mechanical aspects.

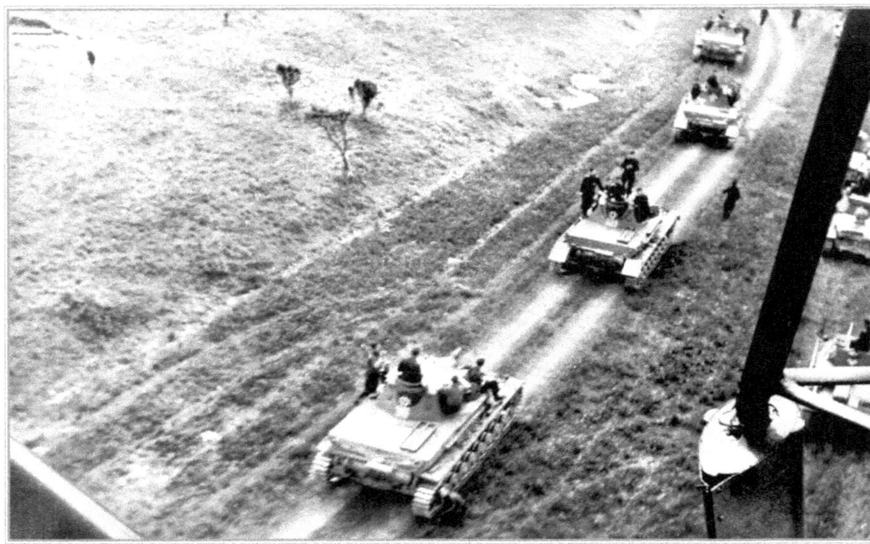

Panzer tanks of Rommel's so-called "Ghost Division" advance deeper into France.

Rommel took this photo from a plane that appears to be flying at a dangerously low altitude. The Panzer crews sit on the tanks, which are driving forward. Some German soldiers walk beside the tanks.

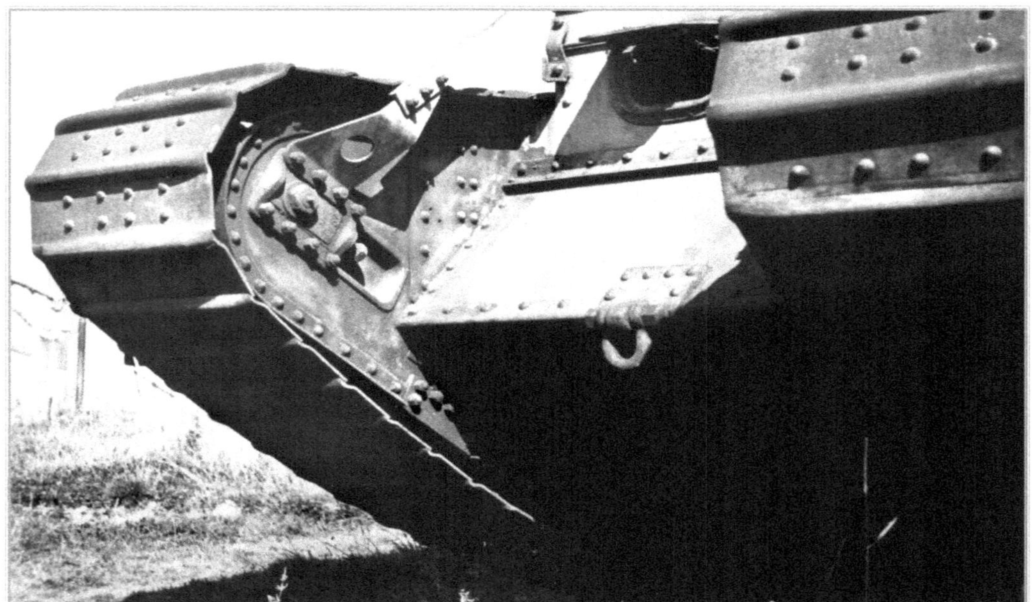

This dark, moody image depicts a tank in France.

Rommel evidently crouched low on the ground to achieve this shot. The tank appears ominous and overpowering. The picture is also very mechanical; the bolts and tread of the tank dominate the composition. The round bolts contrast the rigid angles of the metal plates.

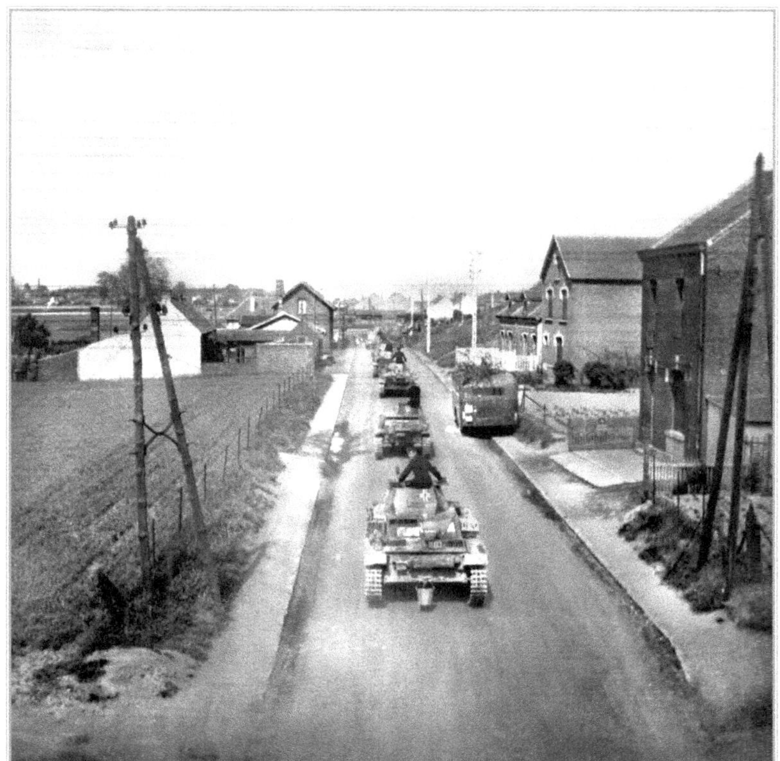

Panzers travel in formation on a street, likely in France.

The soldier on the Panzer in the foreground (right) turns around as this photo is taken. Rommel was standing at a high level to capture this image. The roadway is nearly centered within the photo. A vehicle parked on the shoulder of the road has branches as camouflage on its roof.

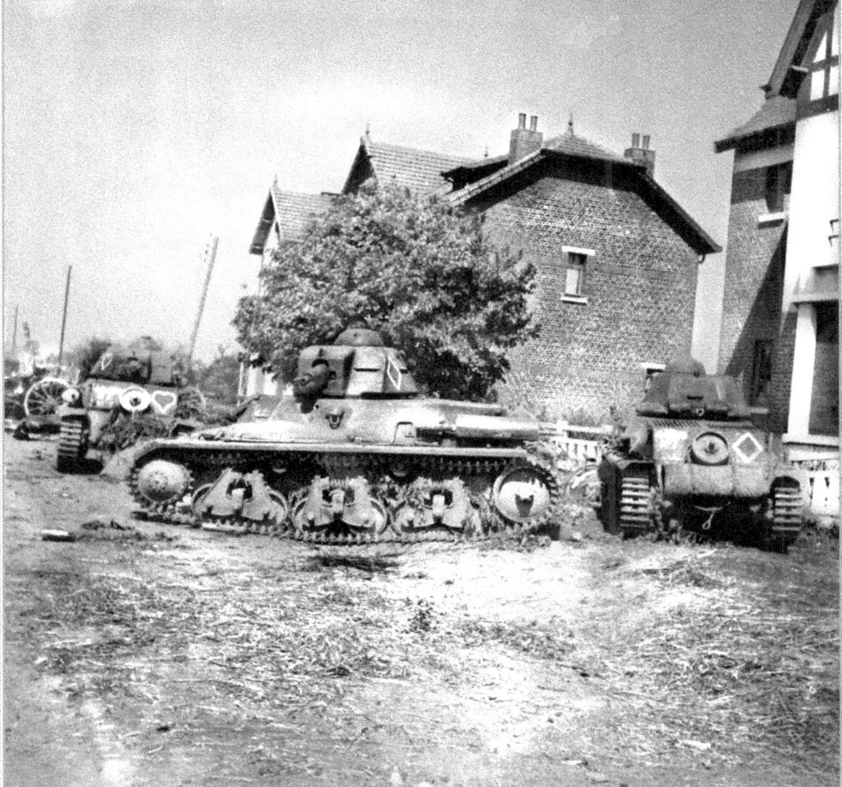

Three tanks surround brick buildings, possibly in France.

A gun from a turret (center) points towards Rommel in this photo. Diamond symbols are marked on the tanks in the center and right. Heart shapes are drawn on the tank to the left.

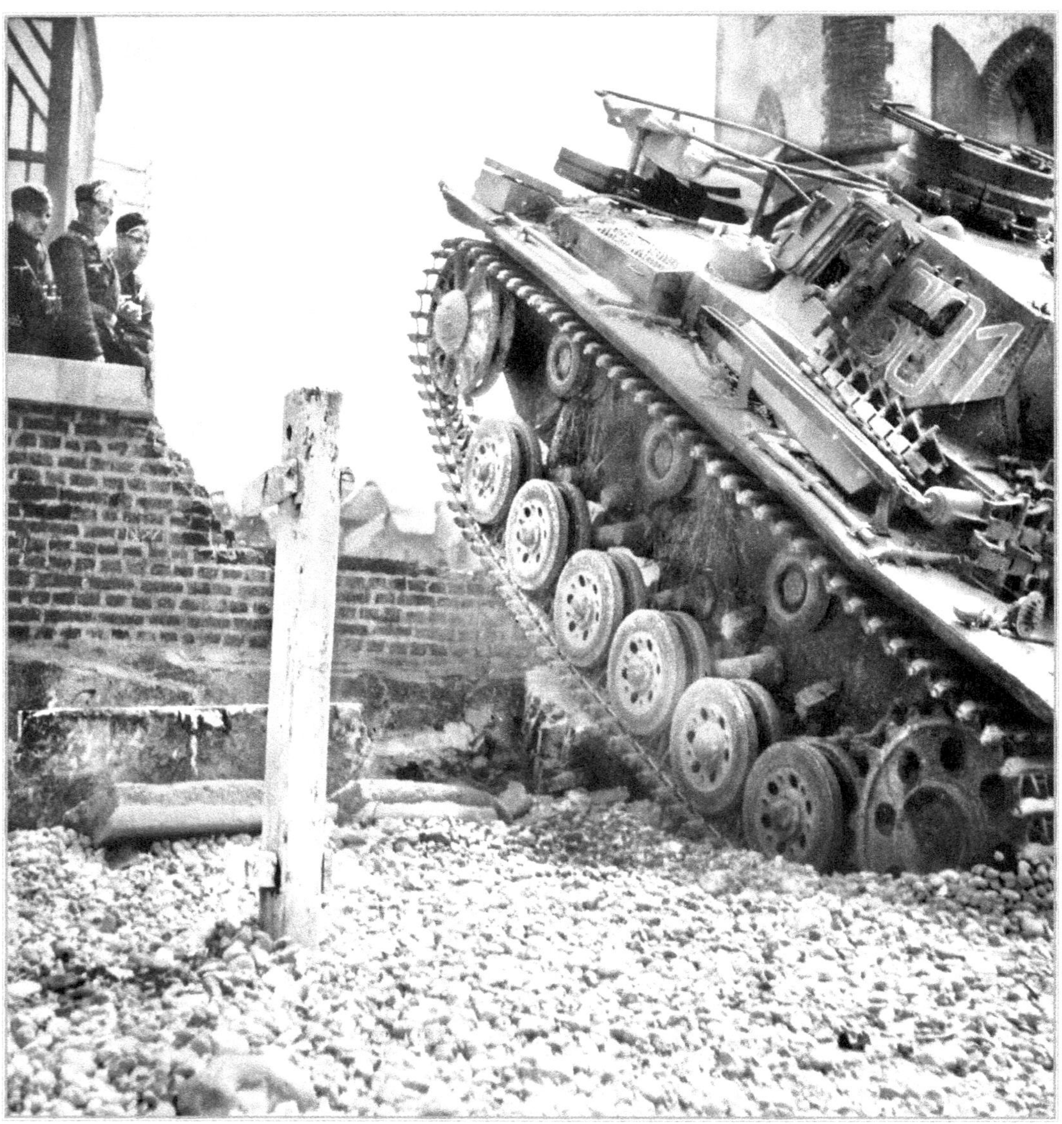

German soldiers watch a tank arrive on Les Petites-Dalles beach on France's Normandy coast (June 10, 1940).

Visible near the numbers on the tank, a crewman (right) prepares to exit from the command tank of Colonel Karl Rothenburg, which has just crashed through a wall in descent to France's northern coastline. The German soldiers were excited to arrive on the beach. This picture is one of many Rommel took to commemorate the occasion. Rothenburg died in Russia in 1941.

10. 6. 40.
Petite Dalles.
B01 will wieder zurück.

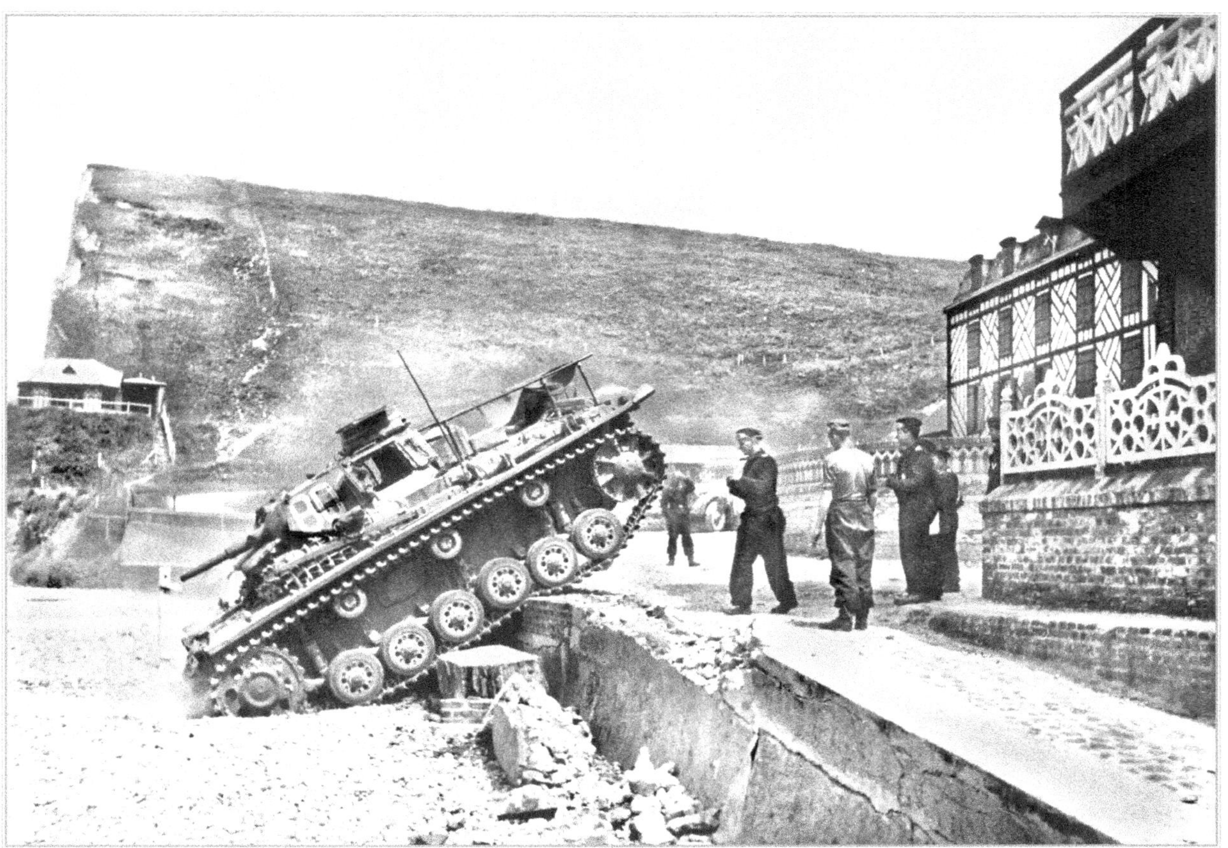

Colonel Rothenburg's command tank returns over a crumbled wall along the Normandy coast in France.

The tank is heading right, with its turret facing to the left side. The crumbling wall forms a linear diagonal element moving from the right to the center of the frame.

This tank (right) was one among many that was engaged in battle against Lieutenant Paul Lauterbach, a German officer in the 25th Panzer Regiment.

The Germans were constructing a bridge crossing when suddenly they were faced by an onslaught of advancing French and British tanks, approaching them from the other side of the river canal.

The Germans were not, at that time, sufficiently equipped to defend themselves. The Allied tanks were in a position to overrun the bridge crossing and decimate the German soldiers.

Rommel, who described the situation as "extremely critical," sent a Panzer III across the makeshift bridge to defend the troops from the approaching tanks.

Lauterbach managed to cross the bridge in his Panzer III, after nearly slipping into the water, and engaged the Allied tanks in battle. He was one of a few German officers who single-handedly repelled the tank attack and, therefore, preserved the lives of his fellow soldiers, including Rommel, who stood vulnerable on the other side of the canal. Lauterbach was killed during this fight.

Rommel memorialized Lauterbach in three photo captions and took two pictures of his grave. (See pages 245–246.)

Although Rommel photographed the graves of many fallen soldiers, he did not photograph any grave twice except for Lauterbach's.

Lauterbach is also the only soldier who Rommel recalled three times in written captions. Clearly Rommel must have been moved by this man's sacrifice.

21.5.40.

Angriff auf Haute Avesnes.
Engl. Pz., der den Lt. Lautenbach abschoss, dann auch Geschütze in Deckung brachte, aber schließlich von uns abgeschossen wurde.

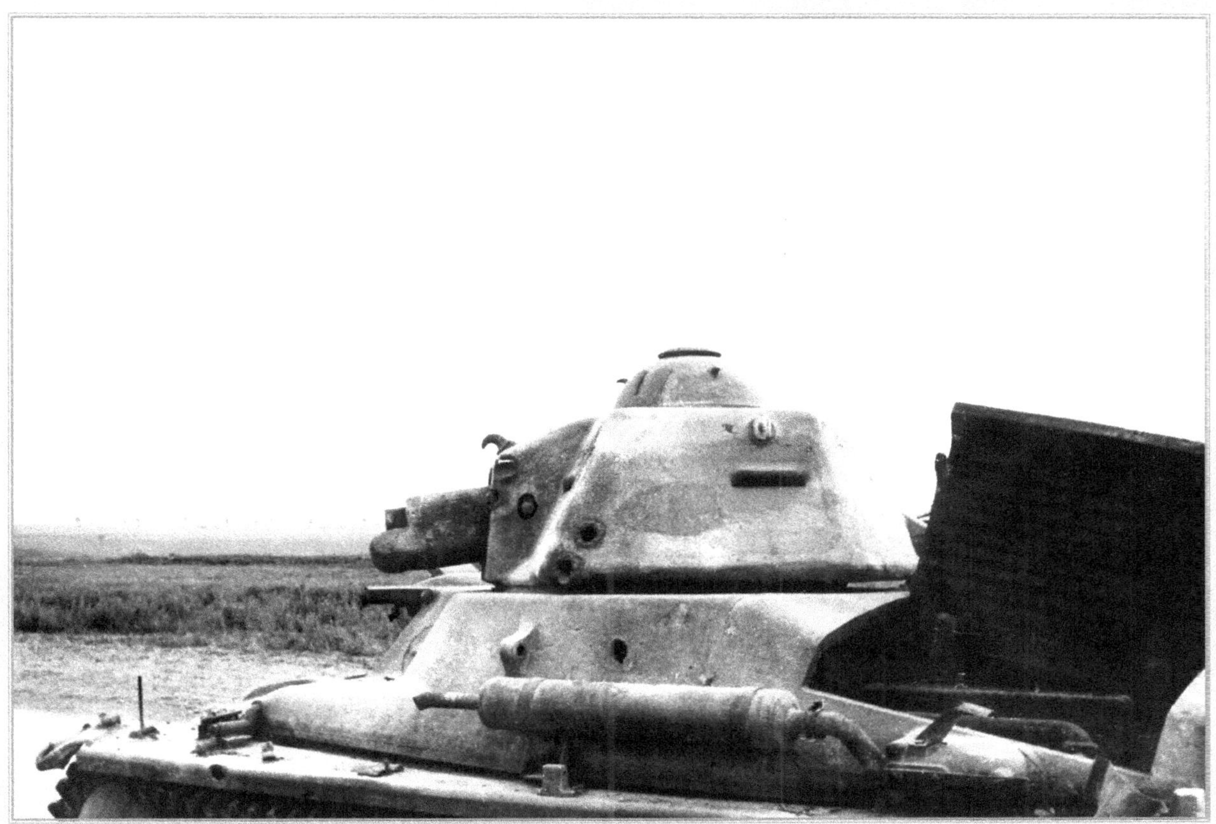

A disabled Allied tank sits near the edge of a field in France.

Several large shell holes are visible in and around the turret. The tank dominates this photo, with the turret in the center.

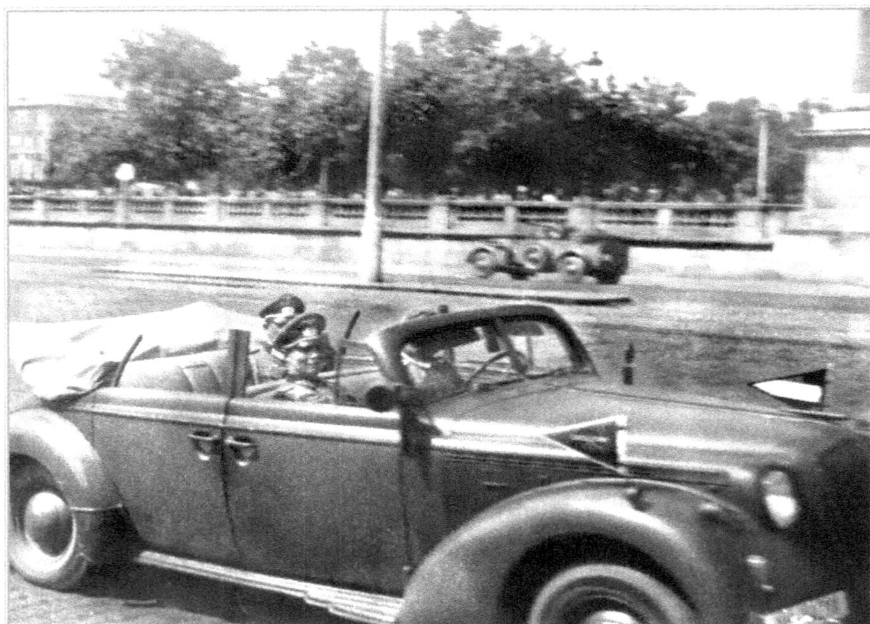

Rommel rides in a convertible in France.

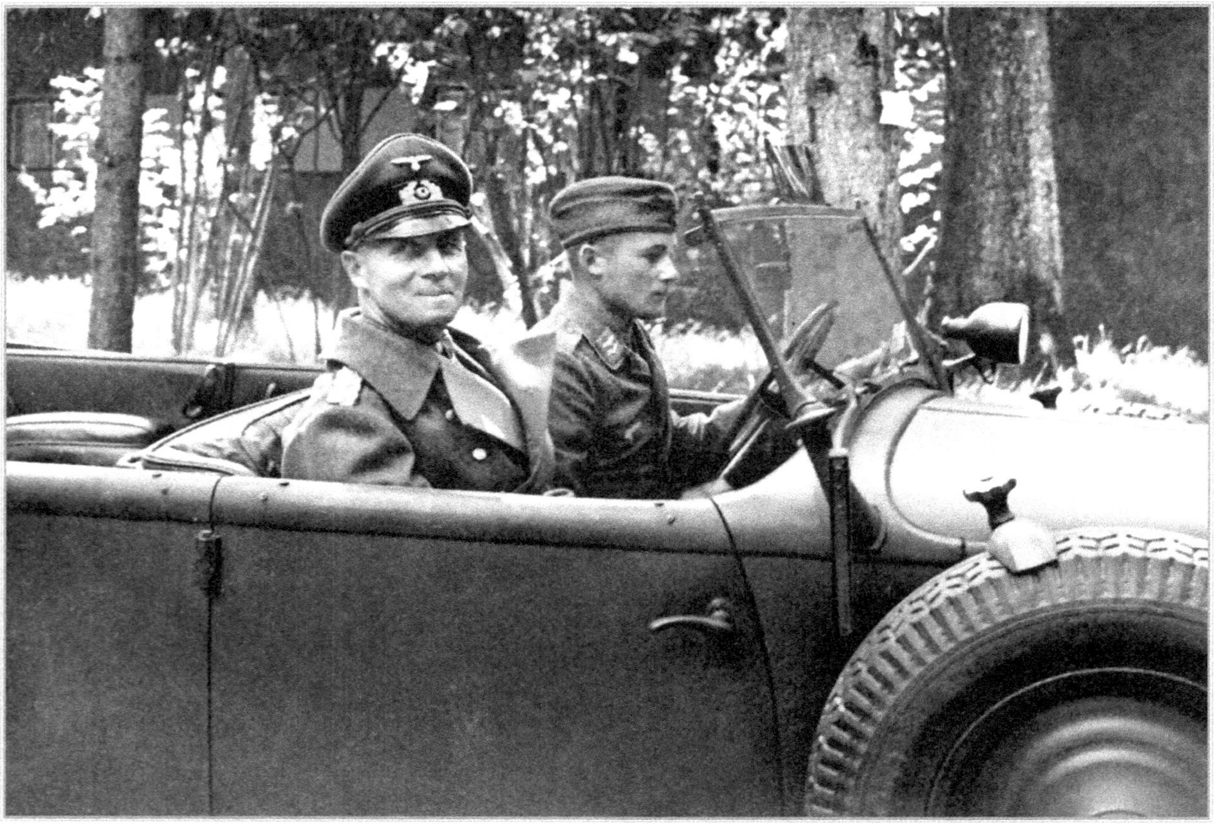

Rommel looks past the photographer taking his picture as he sits beside a military driver in Europe (date unknown).

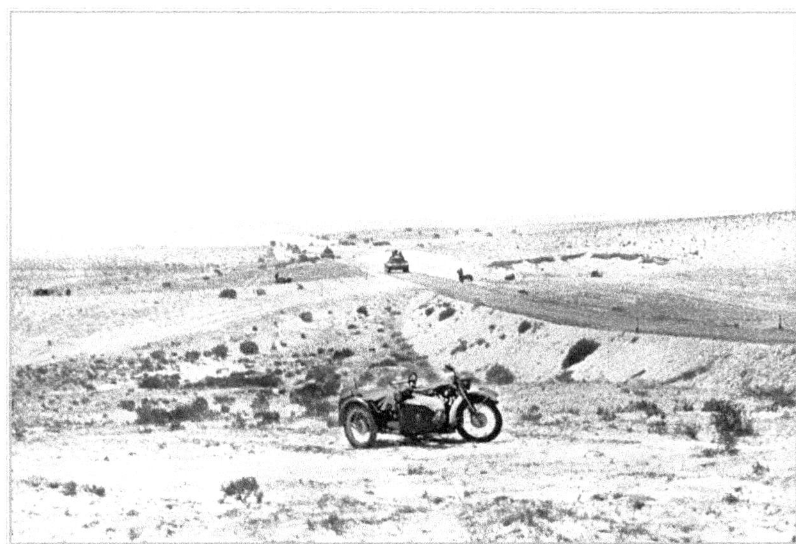

A lone motorcycle stands by a roadside in North Africa.

Rommel shows characteristic attention to lines and patterns. He aligned the intersecting roads and the motorcycle in the center of the frame. This alignment adds more dimension to the photo. This is a good example of Rommel's mathematical precision, which he employed both in his photography and on the battlefield.

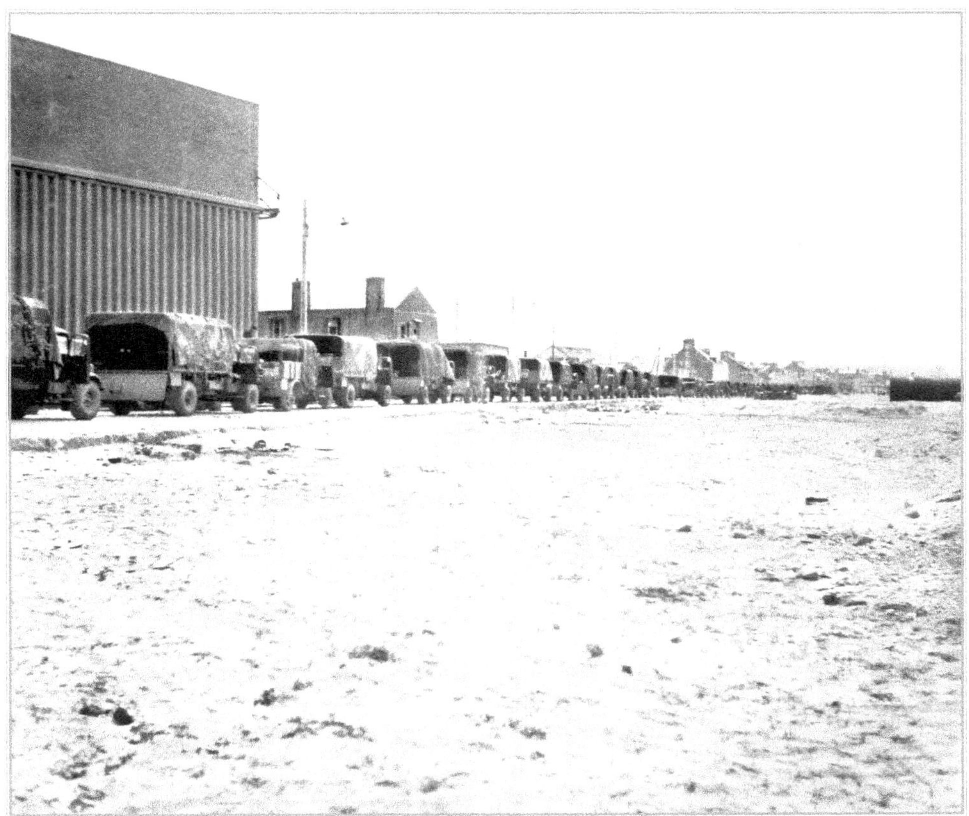

A line of trucks at a standstill (date and location unknown, possibly France, 1940).

Rommel depicts the trucks gradually decreasing from larger to smaller as they cross the middle of the image. This creates an optical effect of infinity. Rommel used this technique in many of his photographs.

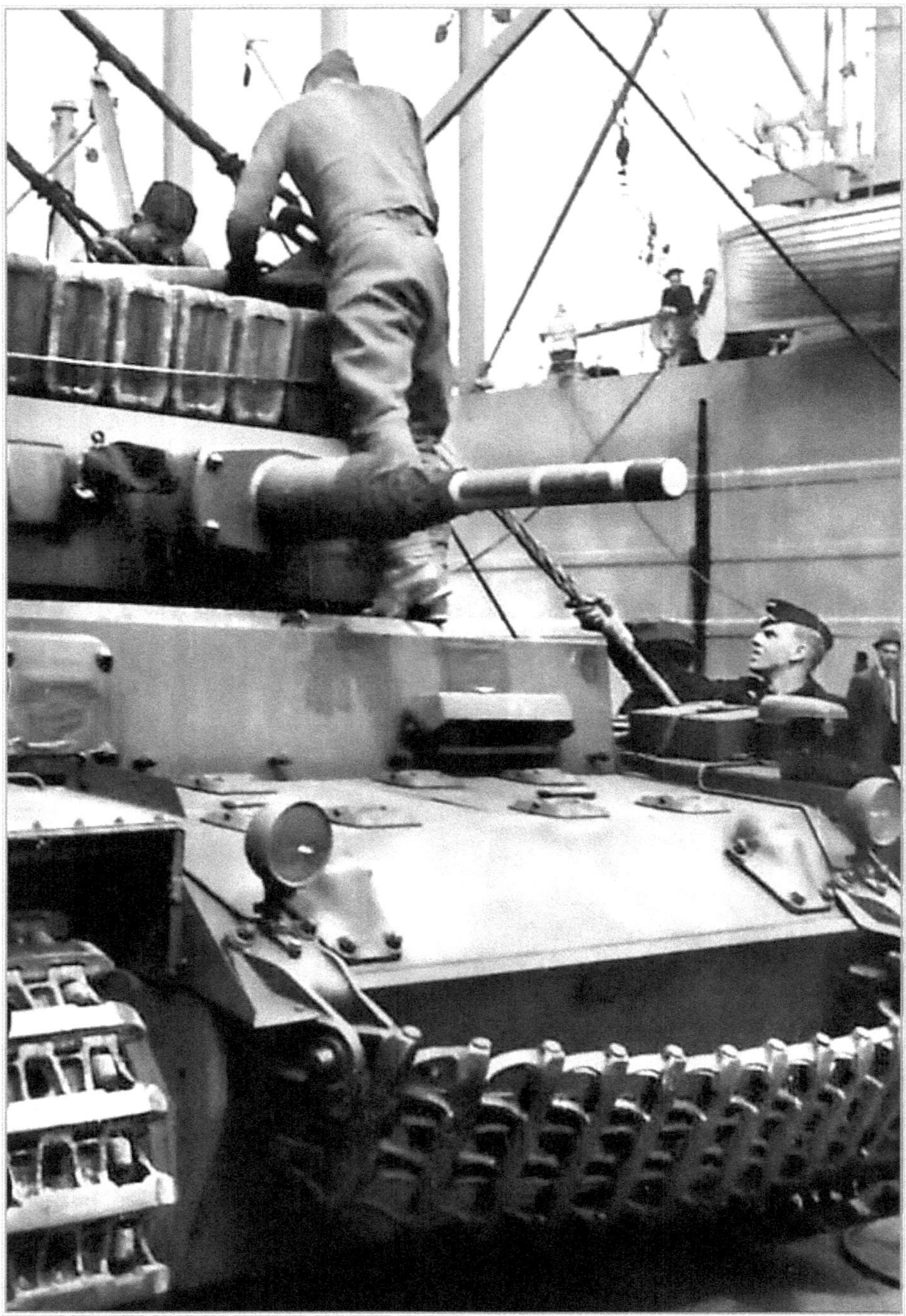

German soldiers prepare a tank for use after it is unloaded at the shipyard in North Africa.

This is a very busy and chaotic image. Actions are taking place on multiple levels. The picture also shows Rommel's interest in mechanics and shapes. The tank's track is depicted prominently. The upper half of the image is filled with the angles of the tank's structure and the intersecting ropes surrounding it.

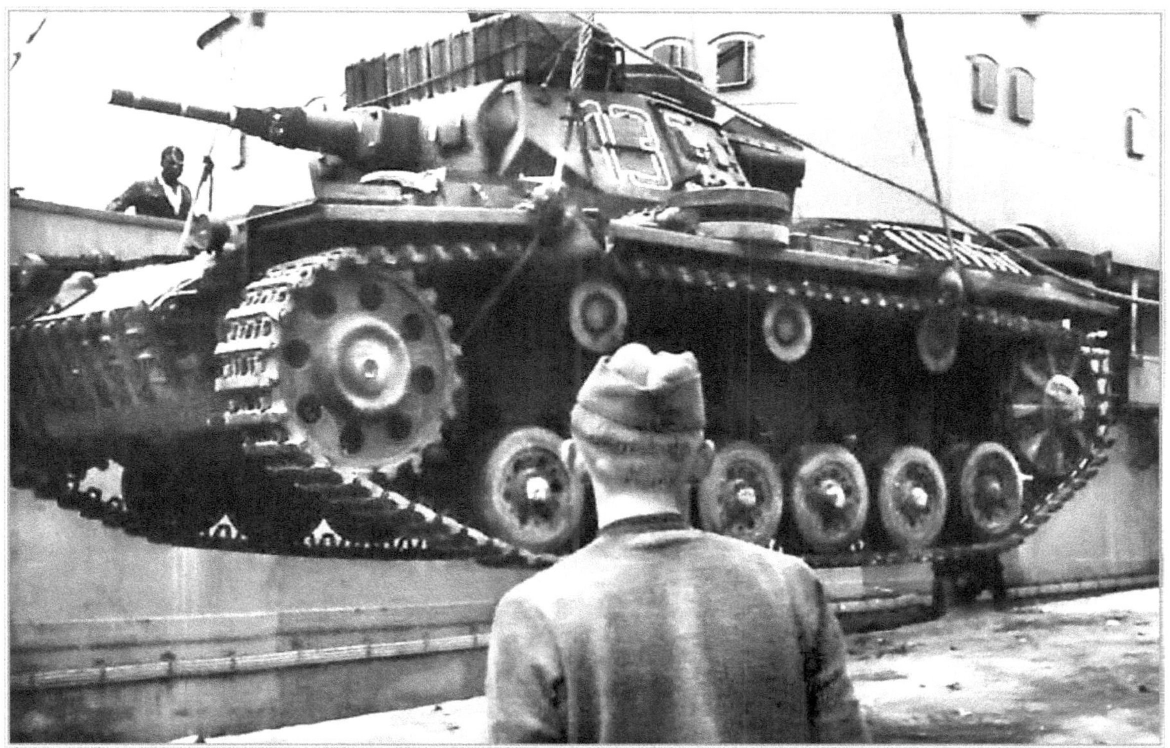

A tank is unloaded from a cargo ship in North Africa.

This is another balanced photo from Rommel showing a German soldier's point-of-view looking at the tank as it is lowered to street level.

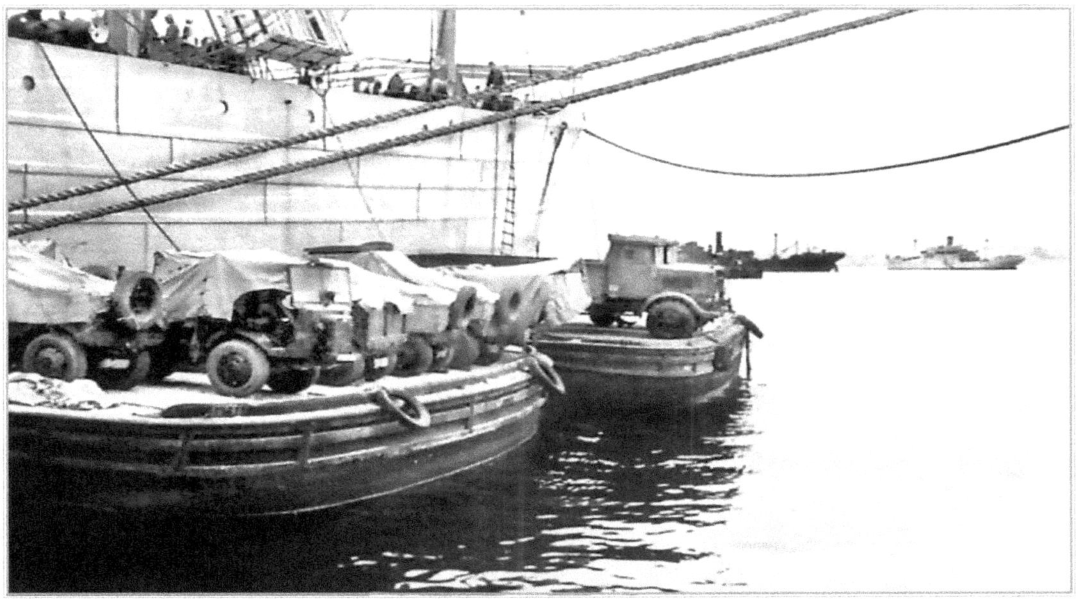

Military vehicles en route from a cargo ship to the battlefield in North Africa.

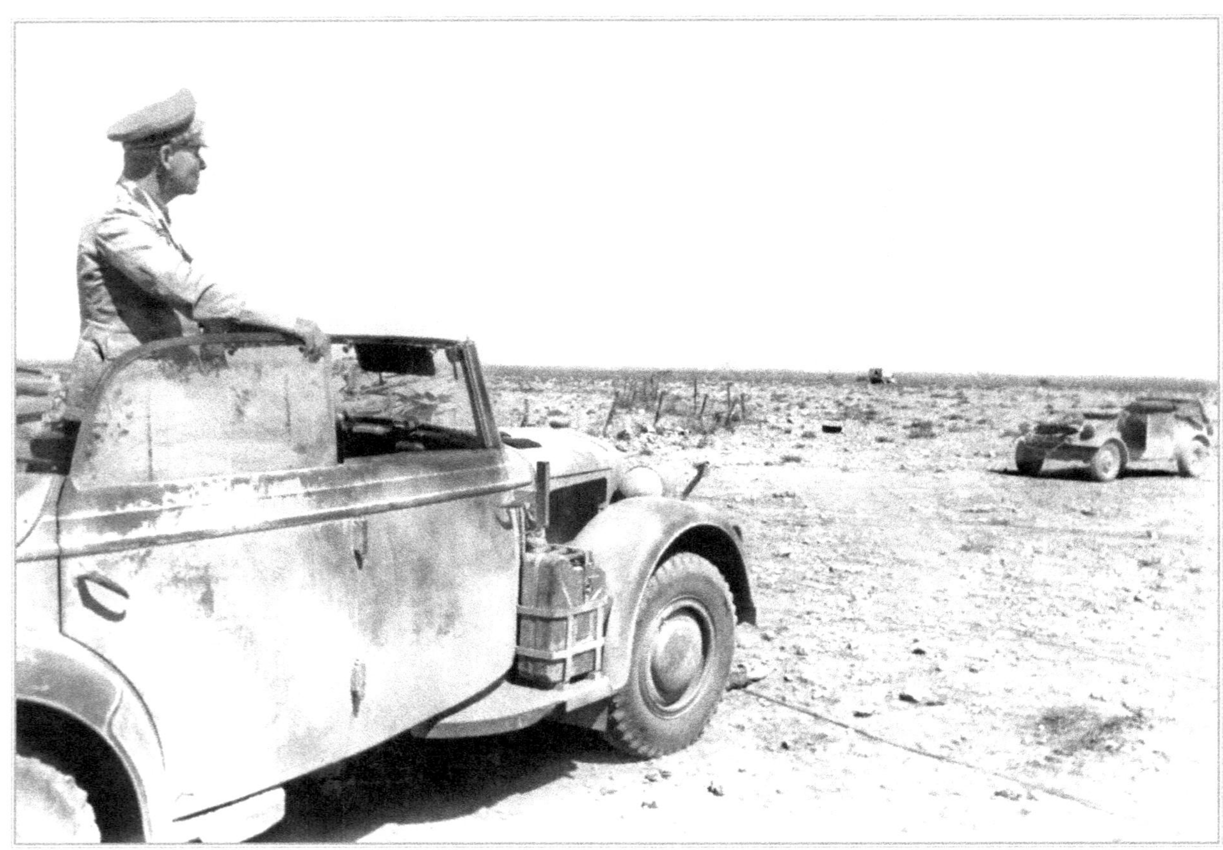

Rommel stands in his car in North Africa.

Rommel took a hands-on approach to strategy and was known to travel by car to different areas of the battlefield. This often made him difficult to find. At times, Rommel also found himself behind enemy lines. He had several close encounters with British forces—once he walked in and out of a New Zealand hospital which was occupied by British troops. On other occasions, he drove across British airstrips in his car. He was often chased, but always managed to escape.

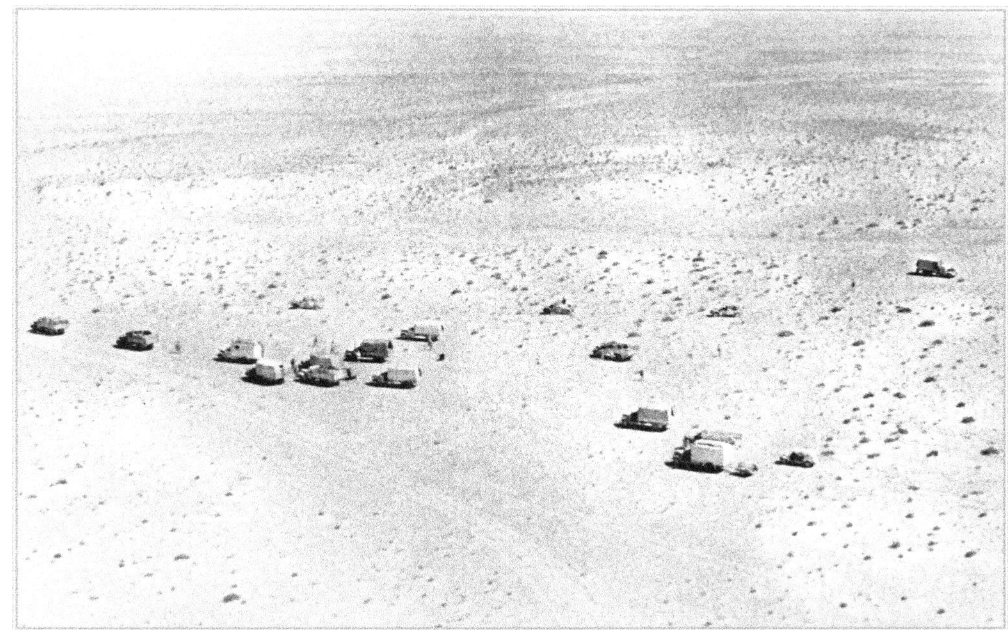

A variety of different types of German trucks dot the barren landscape in North Africa.

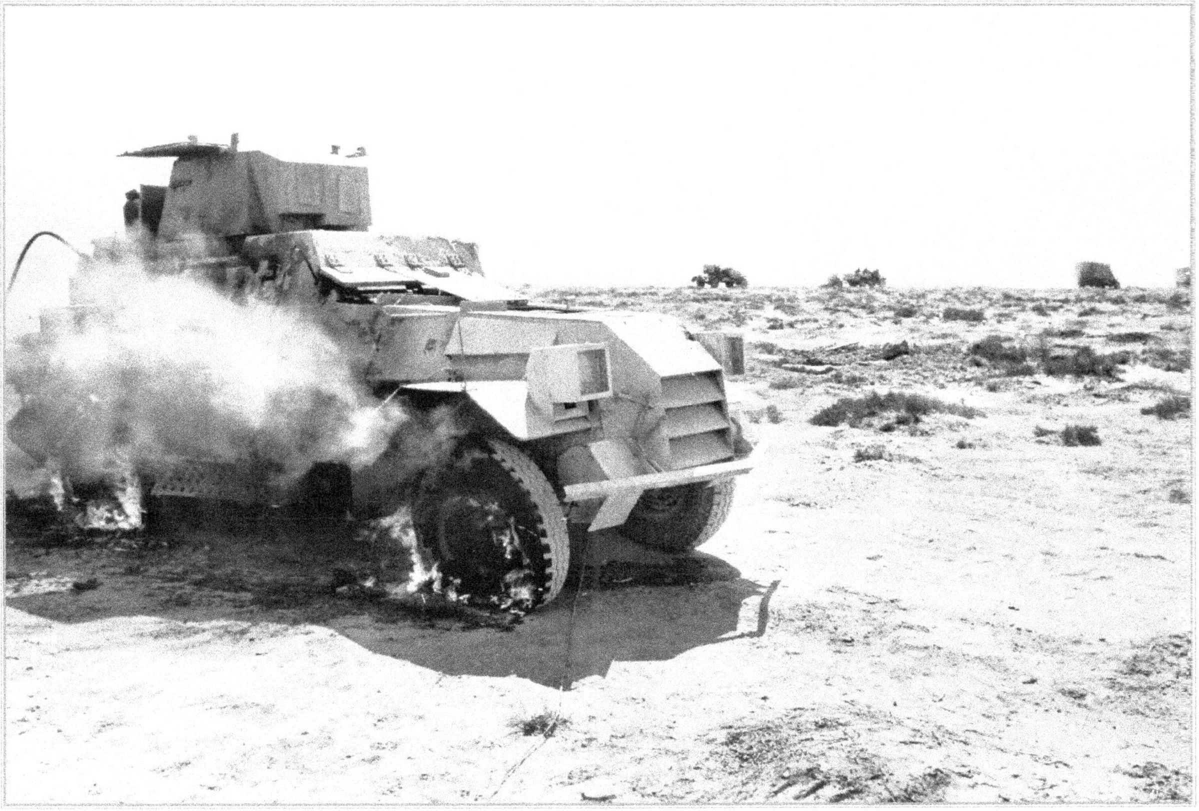

A vehicle burns in North Africa, with flames shooting out from the bottom.

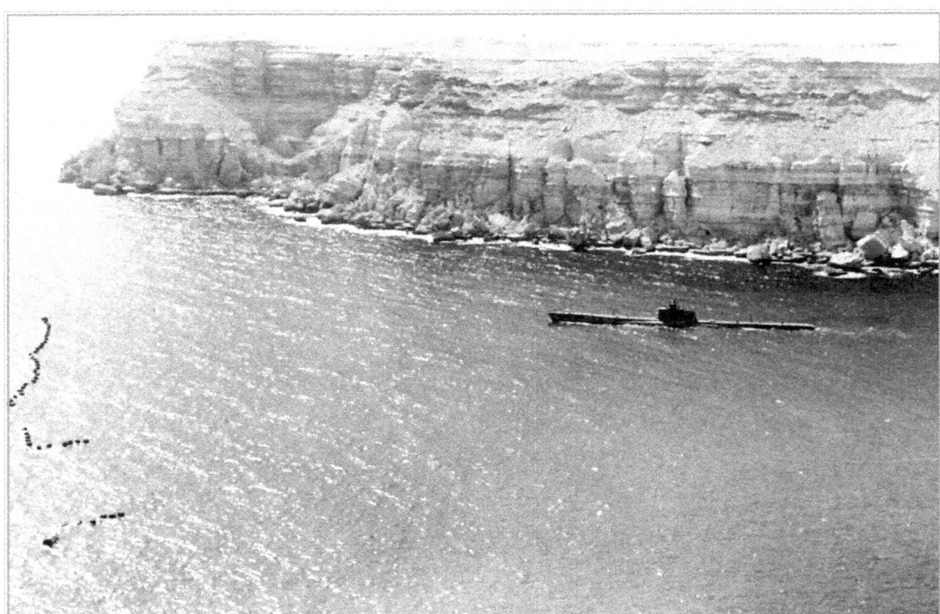

A submarine heads out to sea from the North African coast.

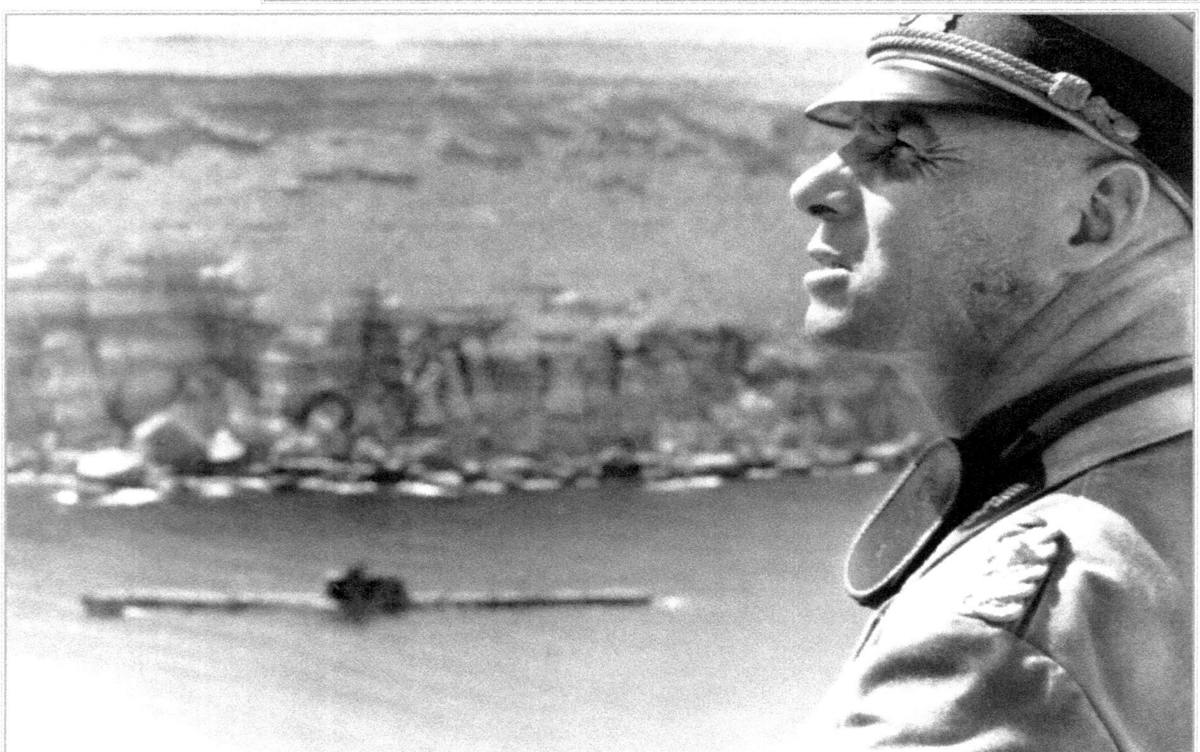

Rommel watches the coastline as the submarine departs.

A binocular strap and a camera strap are visible around his neck, which indicates this image of Rommel was taken when he was photographing the submarine. Rommel's physical appearance is notably different; he shows signs of ill health. He became very sick in North Africa.

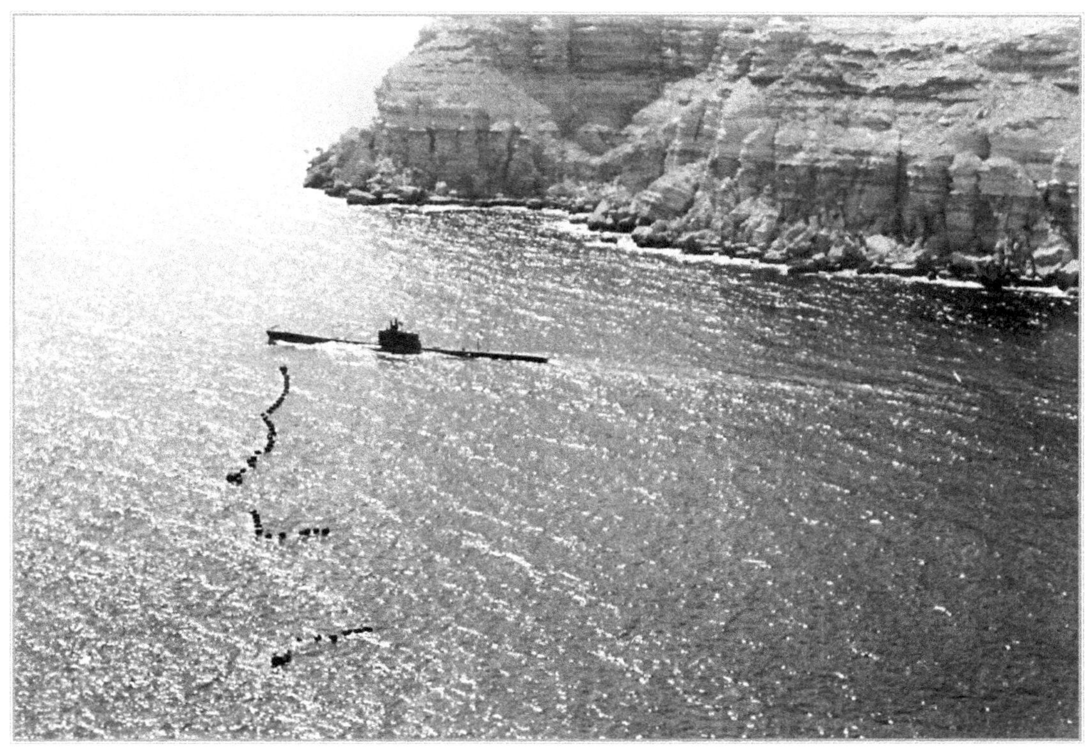

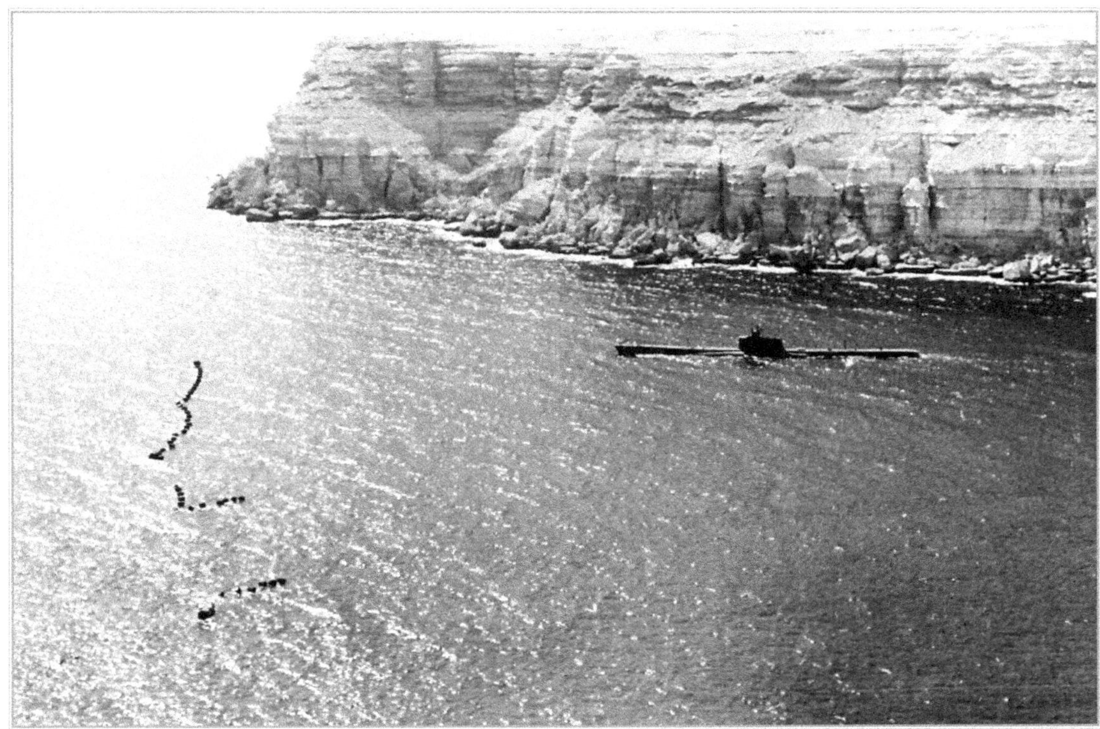

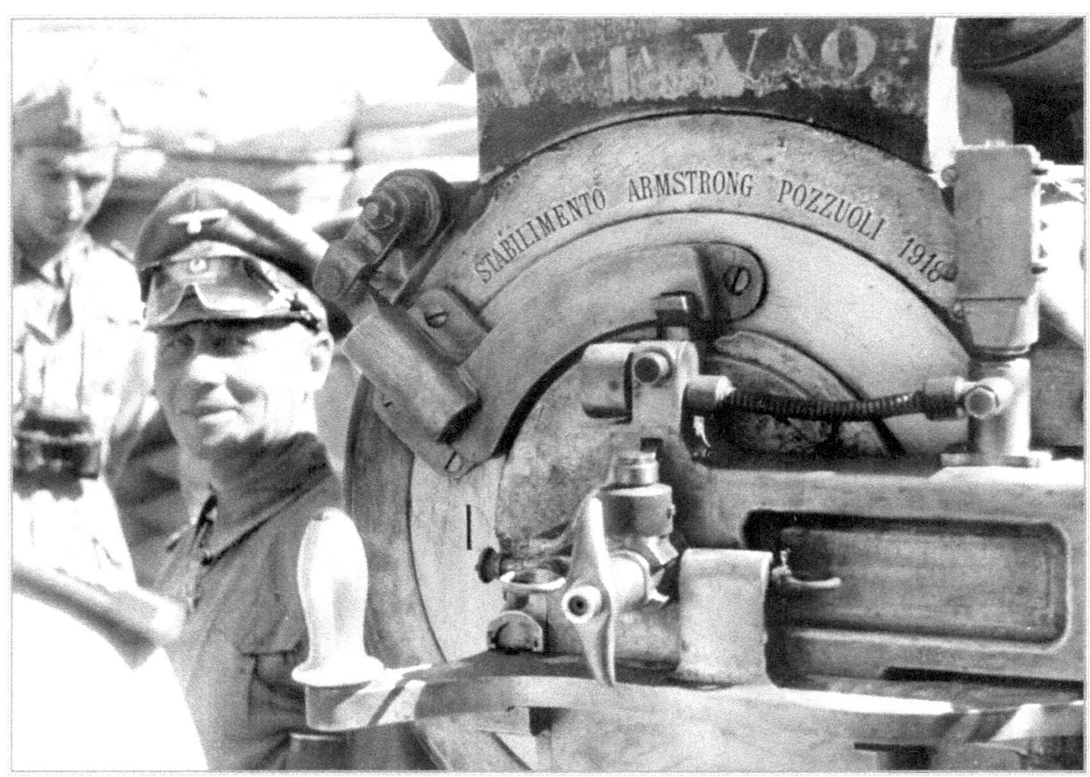

Rommel, in North Africa, stands flanked by a piece of outdated Italian machinery made in 1916.

Most Italian equipment in North Africa was antiquated and had been made during the First World War. Italian tanks were frequently put out of action—most of the time due to mechanical malfunction or engine failure. Moreover these tanks had no radios, and signals had to be given using flags. Rommel was exasperated by the state of Italian armor and referred to it as "antediluvian." His writings on the subject often reveal both frustration and ironic humor.

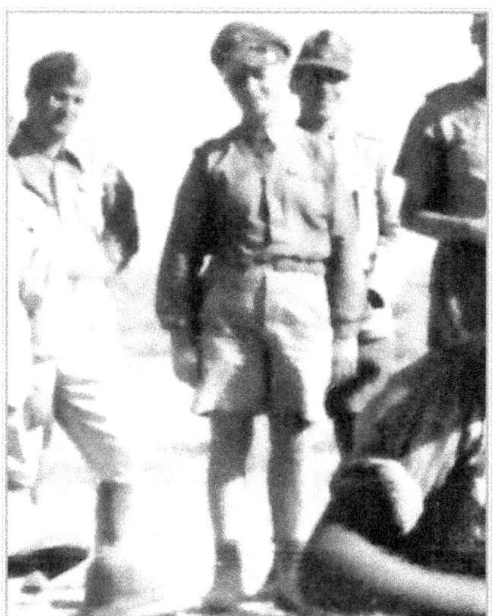

The photo on the right is a close-up of Rommel that was enlarged from the image below to provide a better view of Rommel as he stood among the troops.

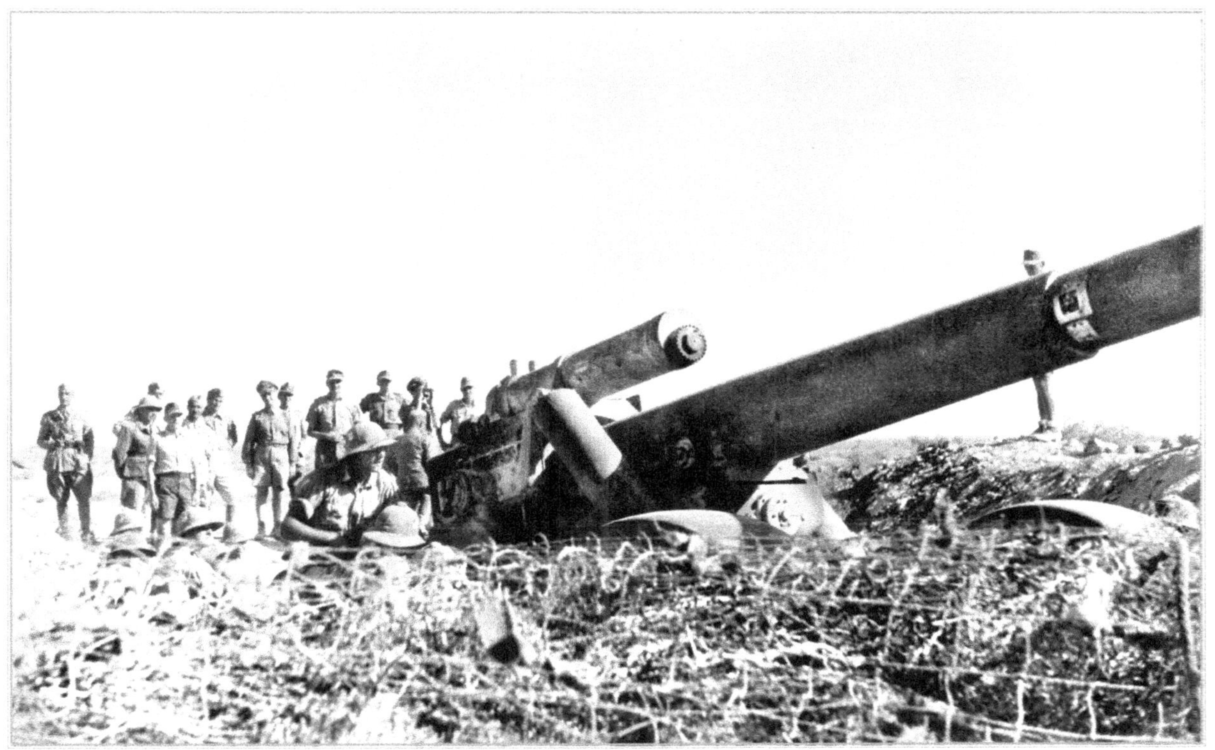

Rommel stands among a group of men next to a powerful long-range gun in North Africa.

Rommel was known for the revolutionary tactic of using long-range, anti-aircraft guns against tanks. He joins other soldiers in posing alongside an anti-aircraft gun. The pith helmets of some of his troops are visible above the netting in the foreground.

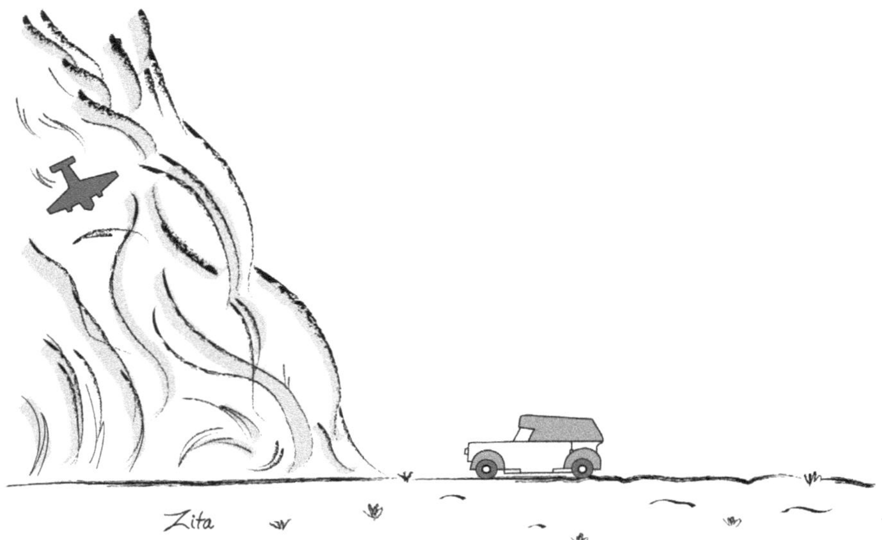

Sandstorms were a formidable element of the North African landscape. These harsh walls of flying sand were driven by winds, which often reached speeds of over 100 mph. The storms were blinding and caused men to become lost during maneuvers. Some German soldiers, who left their tents during sandstorms, disappeared and never returned. At other times, the storms provided a strategic advantage, allowing German troops to carry out particular plans while the enemy was unable to see.

Rommel first experienced a North African sandstorm while being flown to his new military headquarters in 1941. At the first sight of the storm, the pilot turned the plane around and headed back, in spite of Rommel's indignation and arguments to continue the flight. After returning to the airfield, Rommel, determined to reach his destination, attempted to drive. He described his experience in his writings:

> "Now we realized what little idea we had of the tremendous force of such a storm. Immense clouds of reddish dust obscured all visibility and forced the car's speed down to a crawl. Often the wind was so strong that it was impossible to drive...Sand streamed down the windscreen like water. We gasped in breath painfully through handkerchiefs held over our faces and sweat poured off our bodies in the unbearable heat...Silently I breathed my apologies to the pilot. A Luftwaffe officer crashed in a sandstorm that day."
>
> — *Rommel*

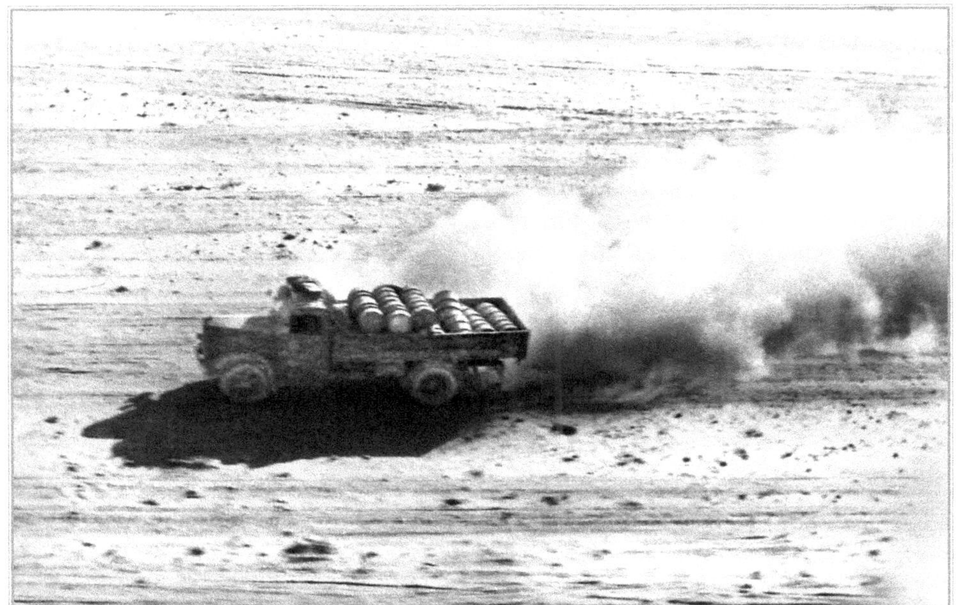

A German supply truck races through the desert in North Africa and leaves clouds of dust in its wake.

The truck, the focal point, is framed by the dust and the shadow.

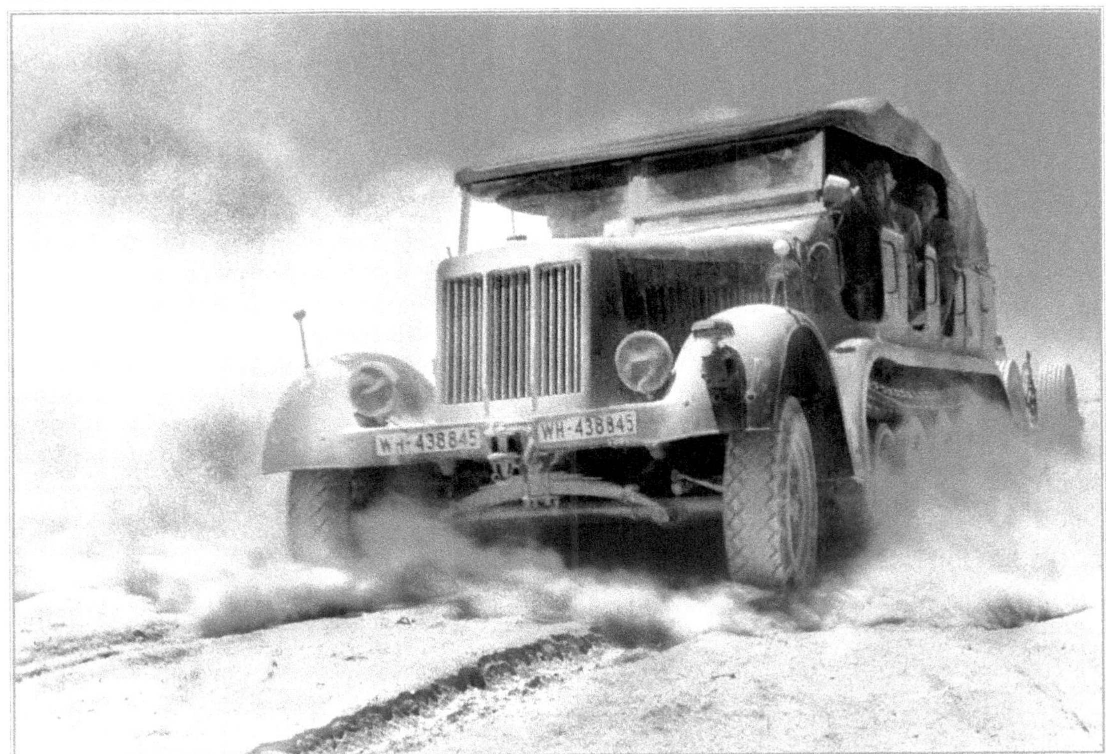

Windblown sand blasts a vehicle carrying German soldiers across the desert in North Africa.

This photo appears to have been taken from a low angle, as if Rommel crouched to capture the image. The soldiers in the vehicle are looking at the camera.

3

Scenery

Petrike Dulles.

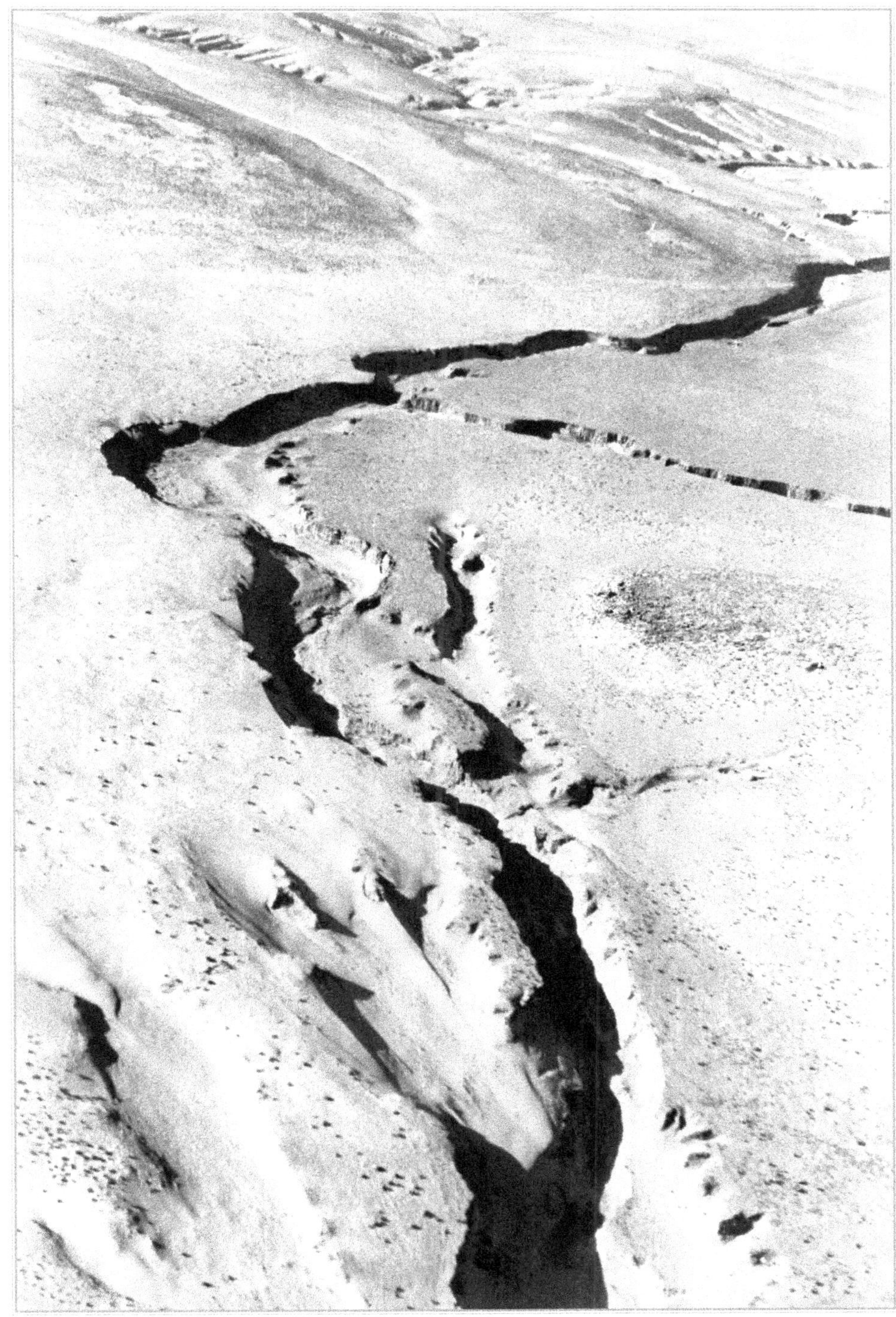

An aerial view of a deep crevice in the desert in North Africa.

Rommel shows a frequent interest in patterns within nature scenes.

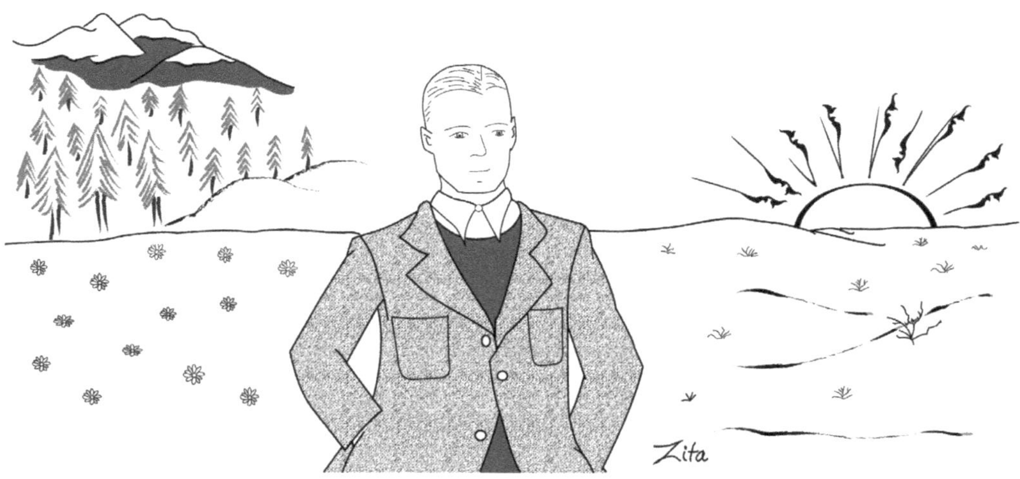

Rommel was evidently interested in landscapes. In addition to desert terrains, his photos contain a heavy emphasis on wooded areas and trees.

Germans, in general, have a special appreciation for nature, particularly forests. Approximately 1/3 of Germany is forested. Rommel's native Württemberg (Baden-Württemberg), is one of the most verdant regions of Germany, with 3/4 of the region consisting of meadows, forests, vineyards, hills, and fields.

Significantly, there are also many photos of the rugged North African wilderness. The fact that Rommel took so many pictures of desert landscapes indicates his appreciation for the stark and barren scenery of North Africa, which was so very different from the greenery of his native Germany.

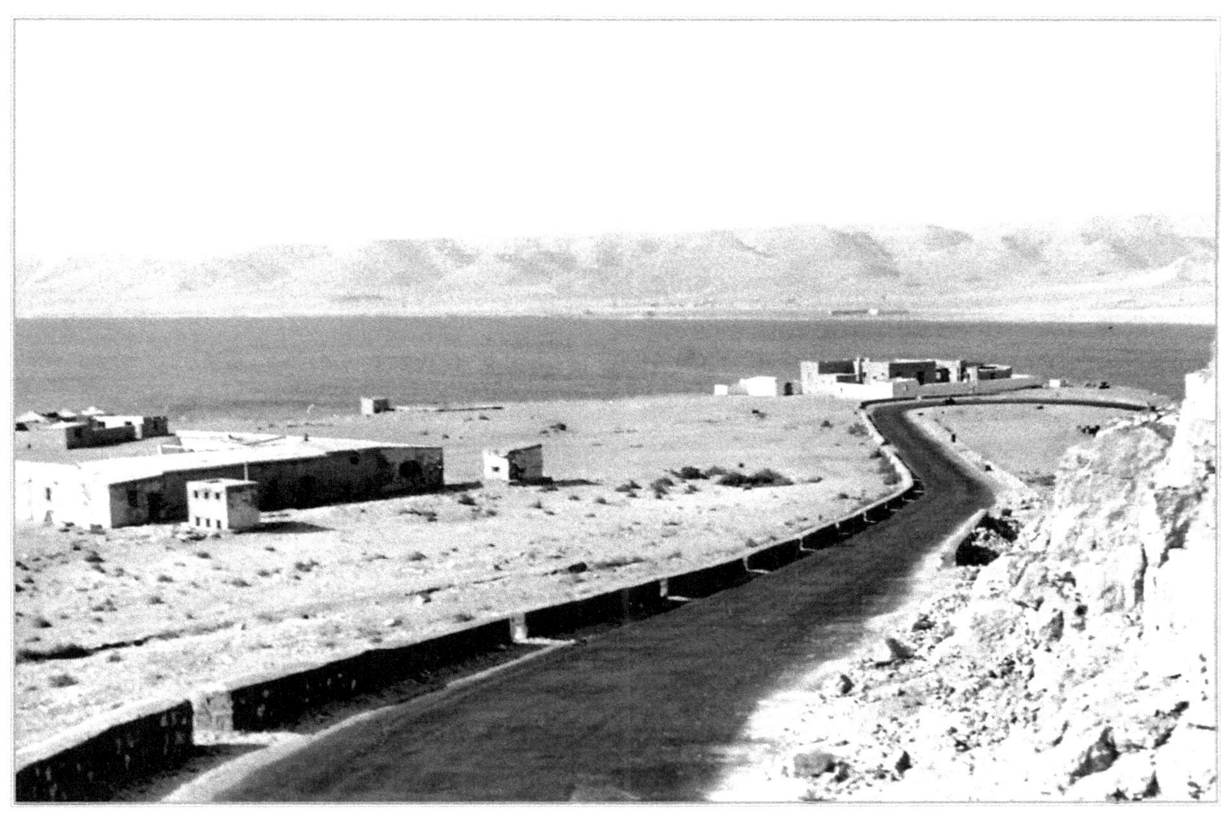

A desert road snakes through the arid landscape of North Africa.

Rommel clearly noticed and appreciated curving and intersecting lines on planar surfaces. This is likely due to the fact that Rommel was a skilled mathematician.

Rommel composed this off-center view of camels that form a diagonal pattern. He evidently was intrigued by camels, judging by the numerous camel photos in his collection. Rommel liked animals, especially horses and dogs. Rommel kept pets in North Africa. He and another officer shared two pet chickens. Rommel also had an interest in wildlife. In a letter to his son, Rommel described different wild animals in North Africa, including cheetahs and bustards. During World War I, a young Rommel even posed for a photo in his tent with a fox.

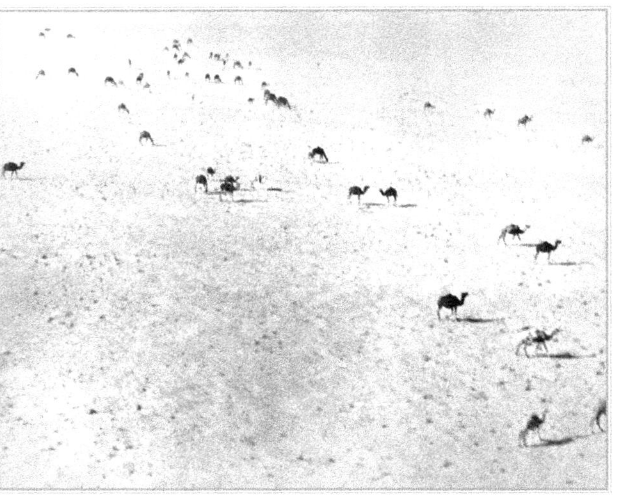

Aerial view of camels taken from Rommel's airplane.

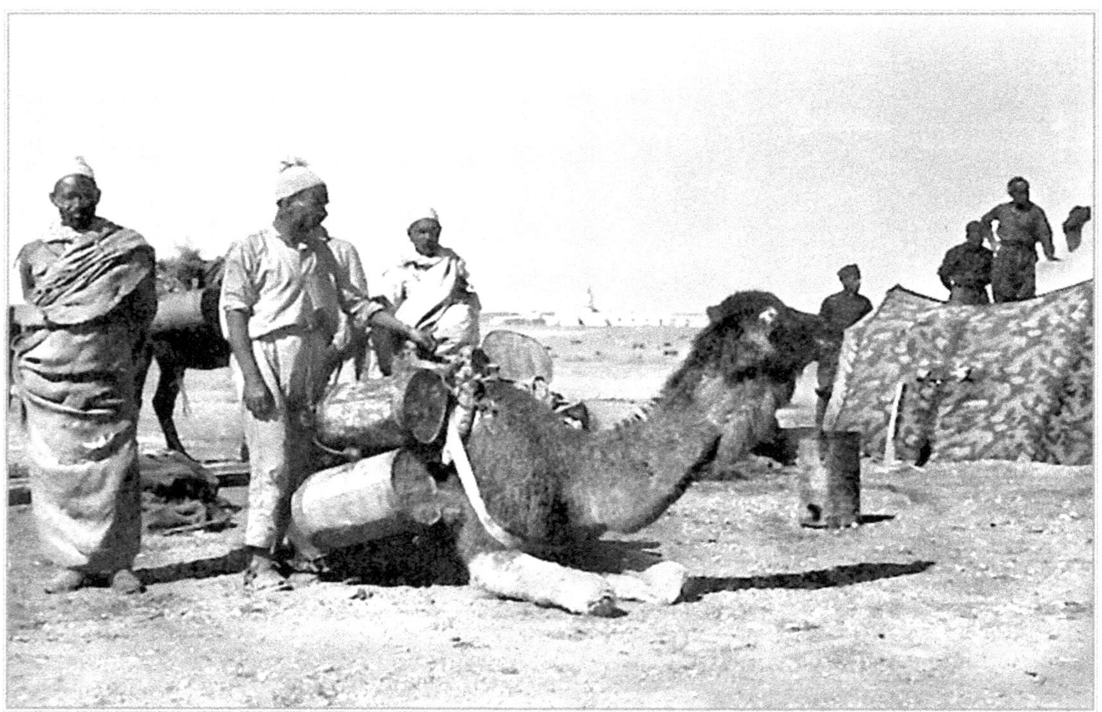

A group of Arabs stand around a camel laden with drums at a camp in North Africa.

The camels are carrying canisters that appear to be military supplies. Soldiers are nearby next to a camouflage tent.

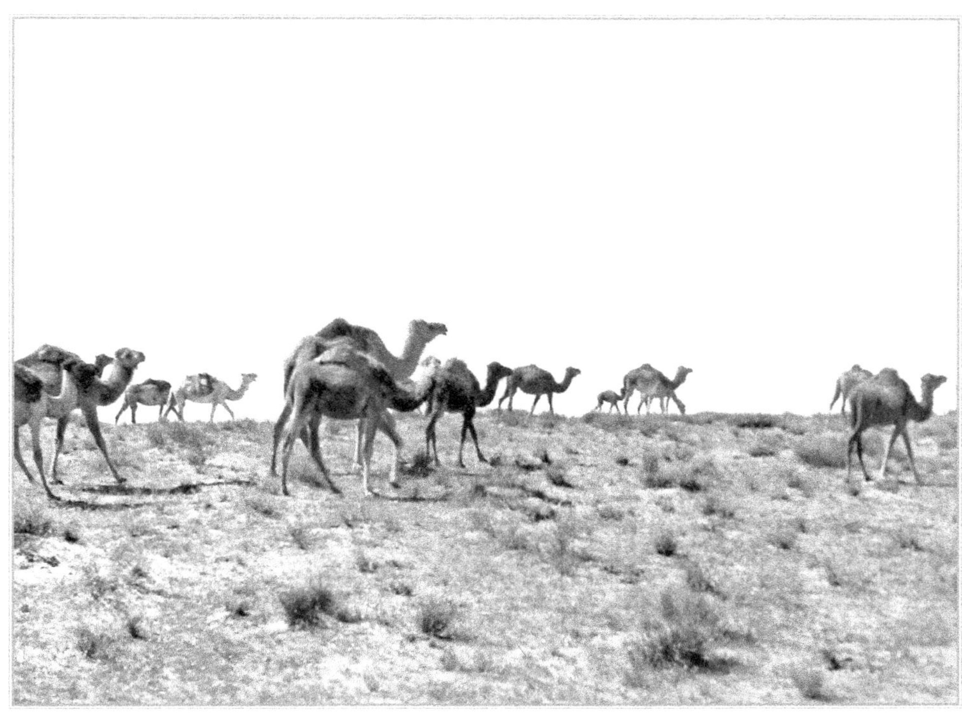

Rommel apparently was walking among the camel herd when he took these photos.

Camels move across the desert (above and below) in North Africa.

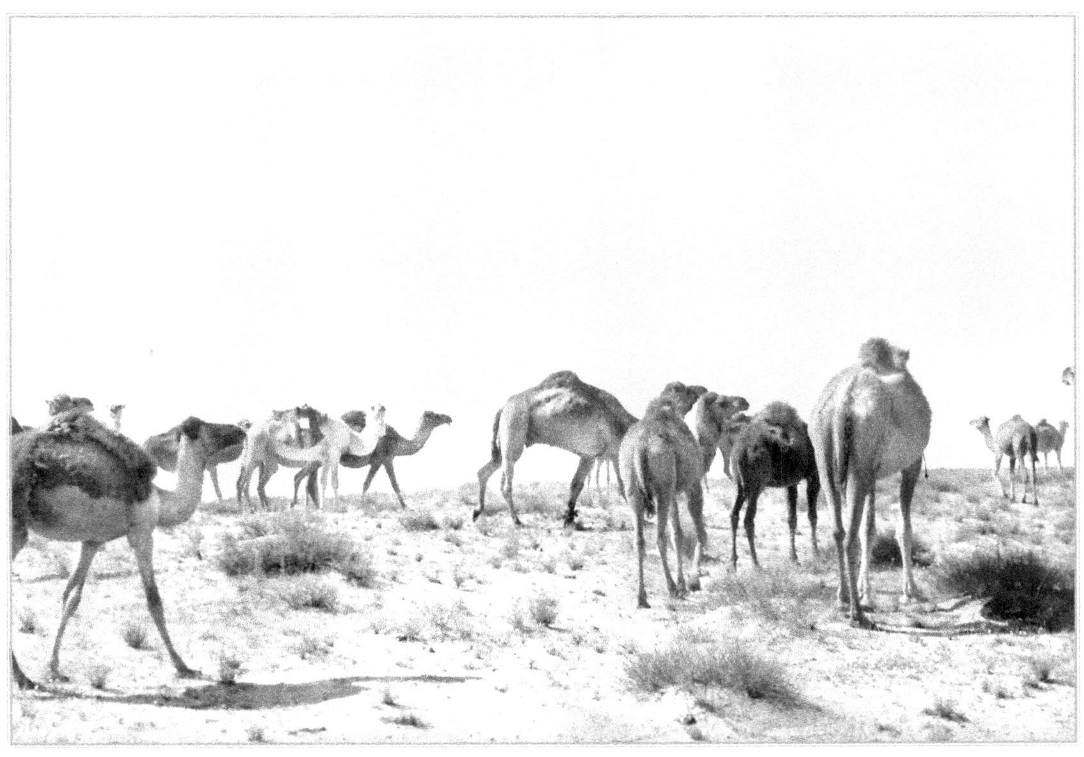

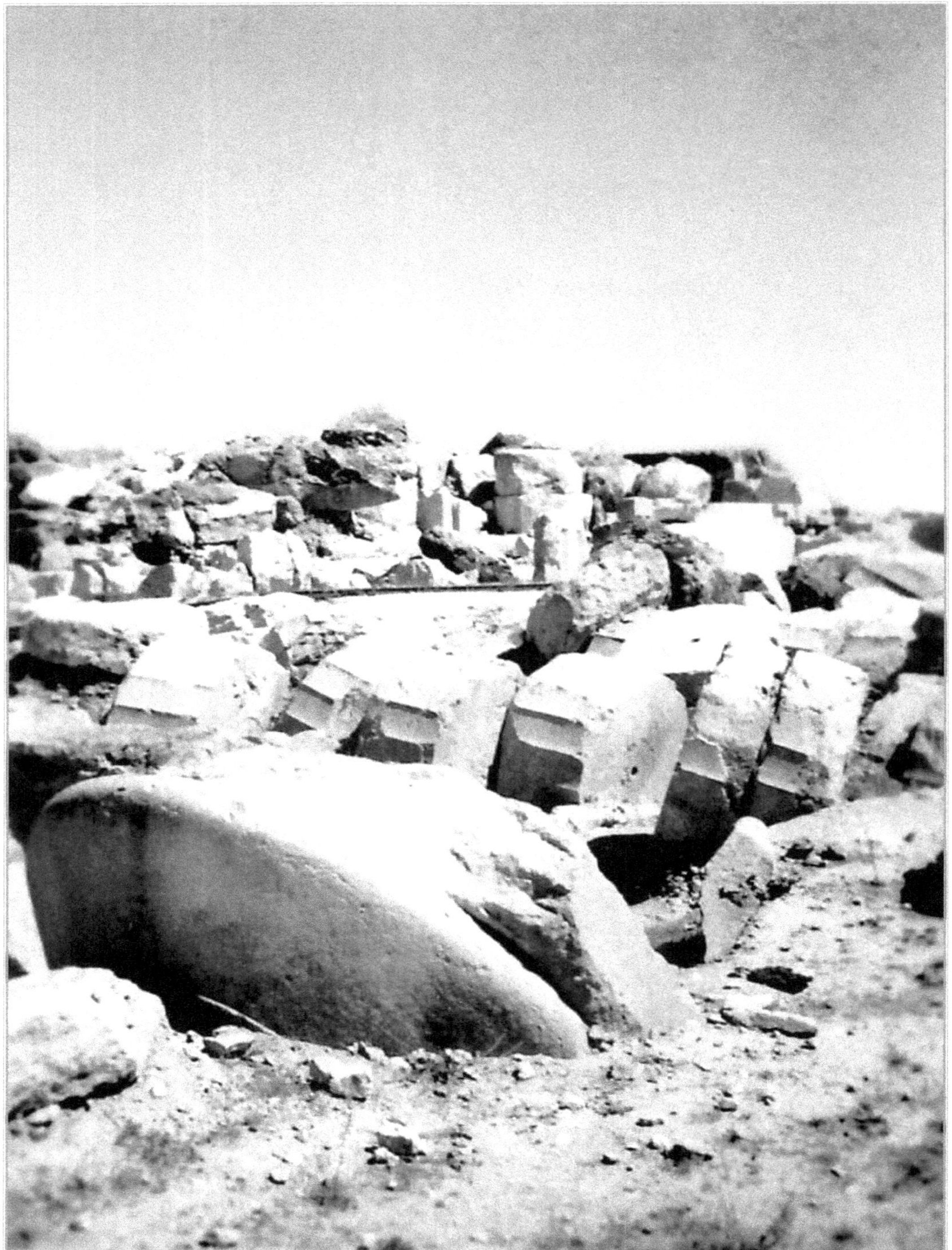

The ruins of ancient pillars in North Africa.

Rommel visited several Roman ruins in North Africa during WWII. This photo shows his continuing attention to geometric shapes.

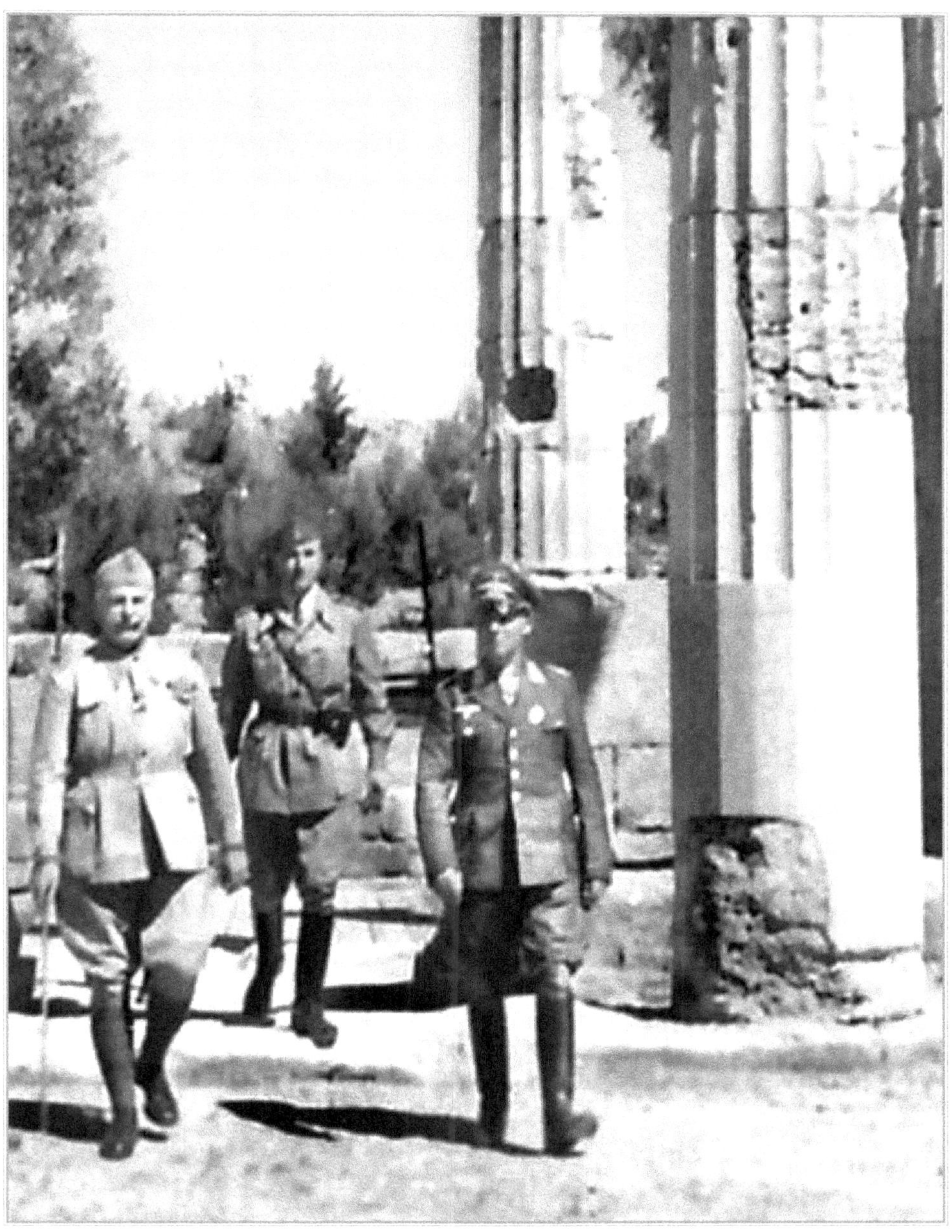

Italian commanding officer Italo Gariboldi accompanies Rommel through the ancient ruins of Cyrene, Libya (circa 1941).

After Italy joined the Allies in 1943, Gariboldi became a German prisoner of war (POW) until he was freed by the Allies a year later. He died in 1970.

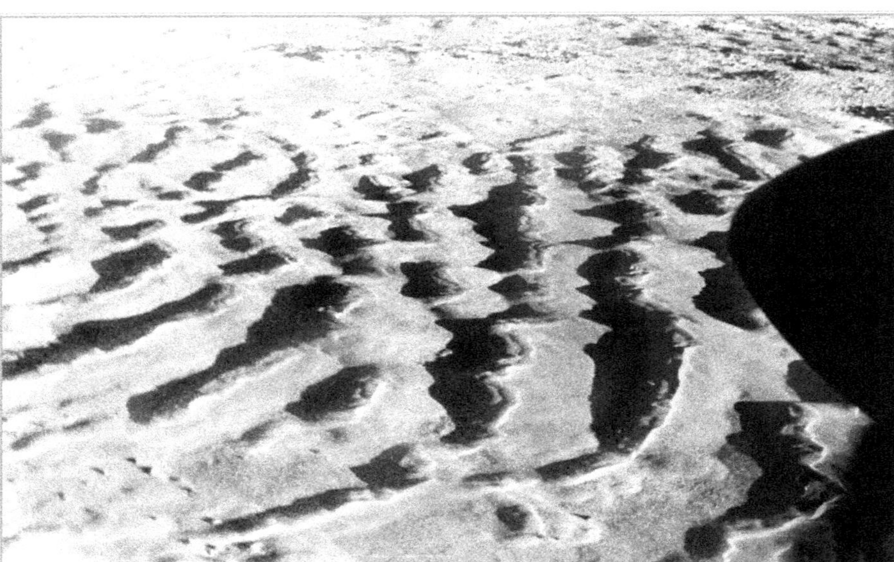

Another aerial view of sand dunes in North Africa.

Part of the plane is visible on the right side of the frame. This sight apparently caught Rommel's fancy while he was conducting reconnaissance.

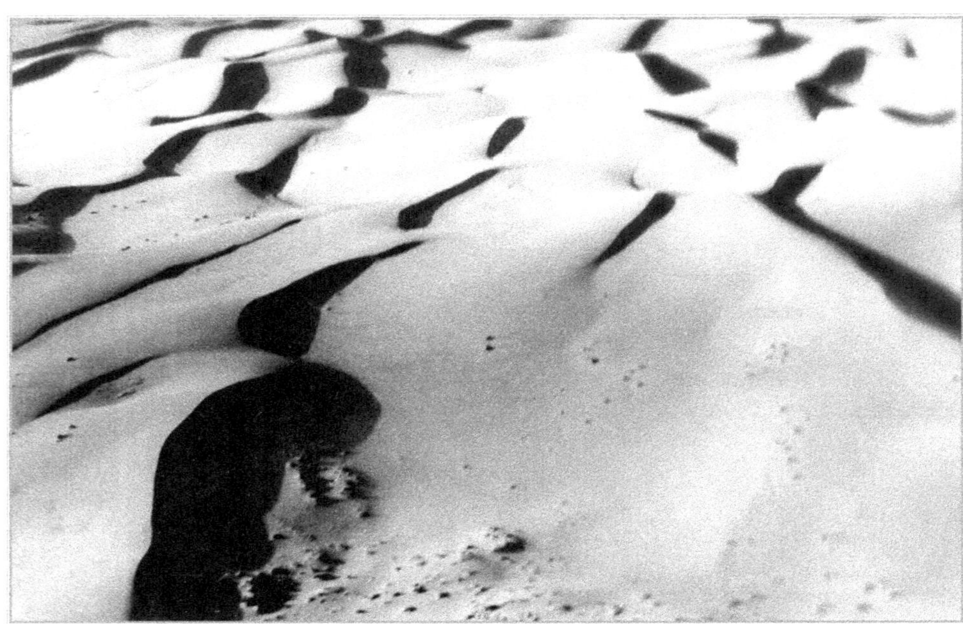

Shadows and sand dunes form a ripple pattern in the North African desert.

Rommel often made comments in his letters and writings about the impressive landscapes he saw in North Africa. He described the Qattara Depression, a wide expanse of salt marshes and sand dunes in Libya, as a "fantastic sight." He also praised the beauty of dawn in the desert and referred to a particular region as a "real moon landscape." His letters also contain descriptions of flowers, greenery, and wildlife. Although life in the desert was difficult, Rommel wrote to his wife that he was better suited to the simplicity of rugged North Africa than the "fleshpots of France."

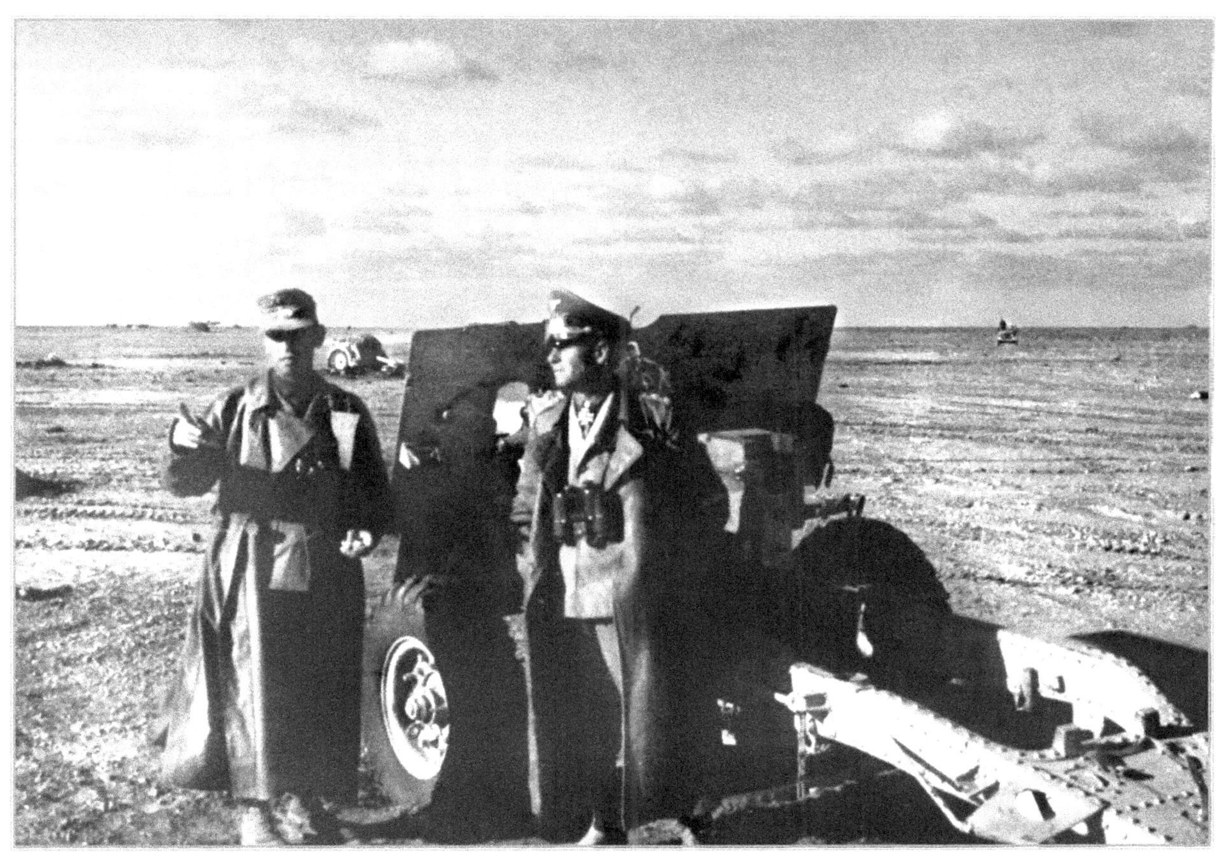

Rommel stands next to an unidentified German soldier in front of an antitank gun.

In this picture, his binoculars are clearly visible. During the World War II, Rommel spent much time looking through binoculars across great distances.

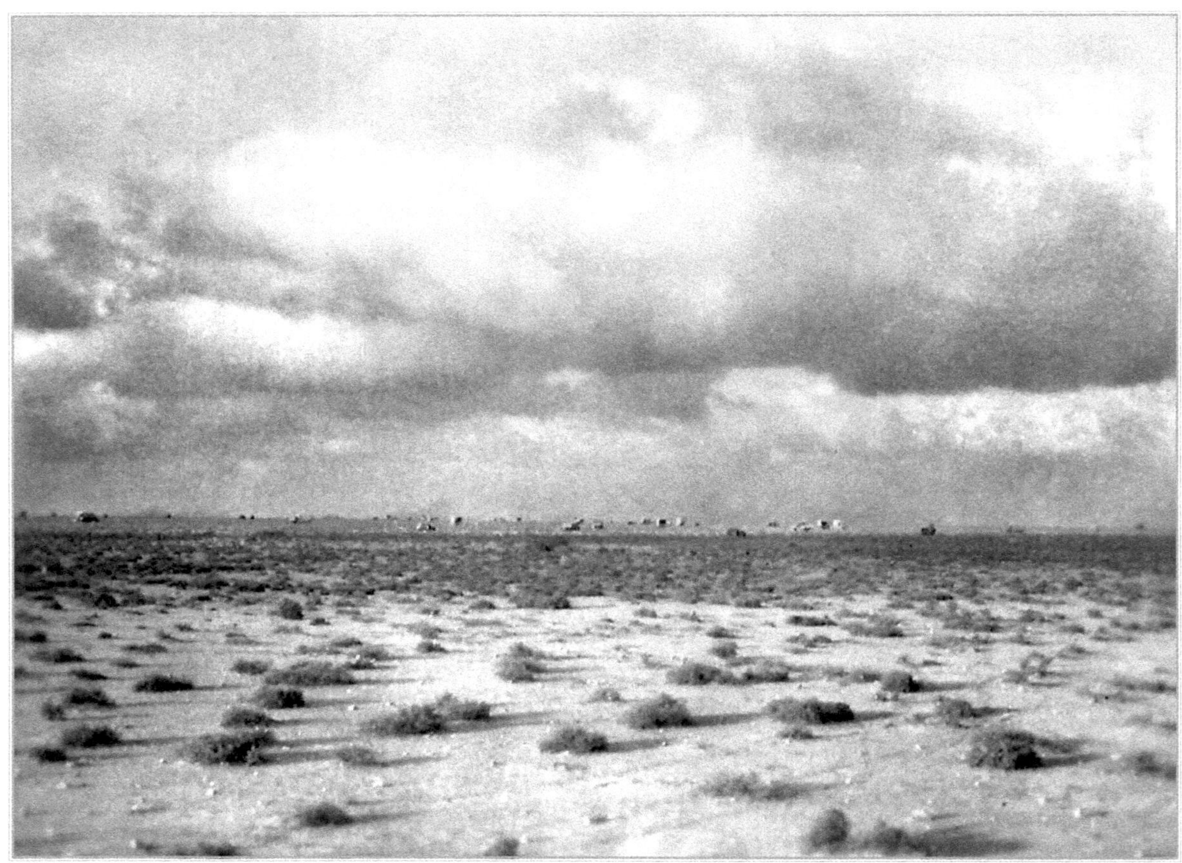

German vehicles dot the horizon in North Africa.

The vehicles are carefully balanced in the frame between the clouds and the sandy desert brush. Although it is possible that life in the desert offered little variation in subject matter for photography, Rommel made use of the desolate landscape to create many images of varying types.

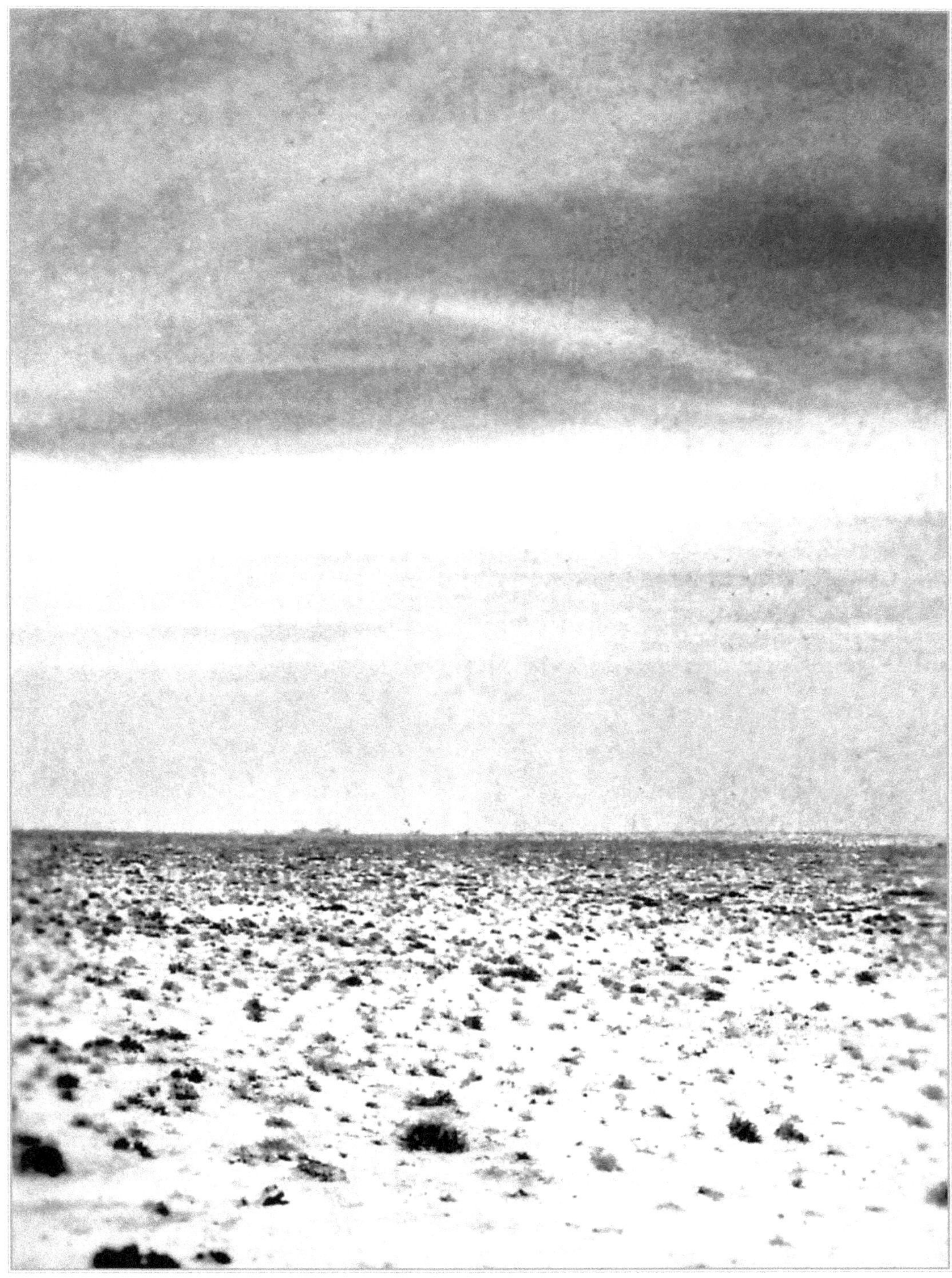

Another view of a desert horizon in North Africa.

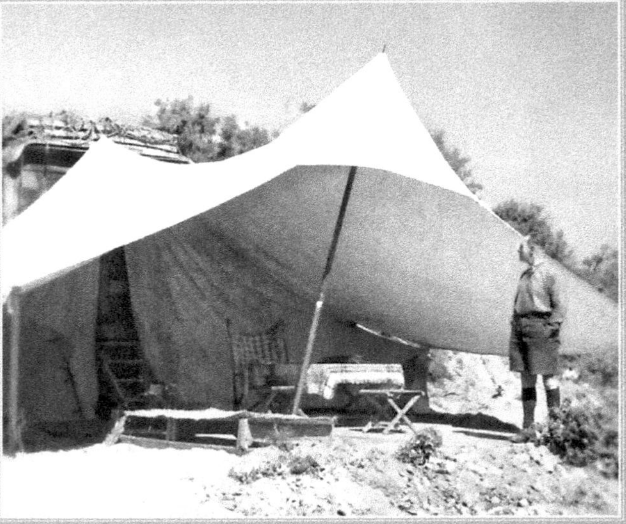

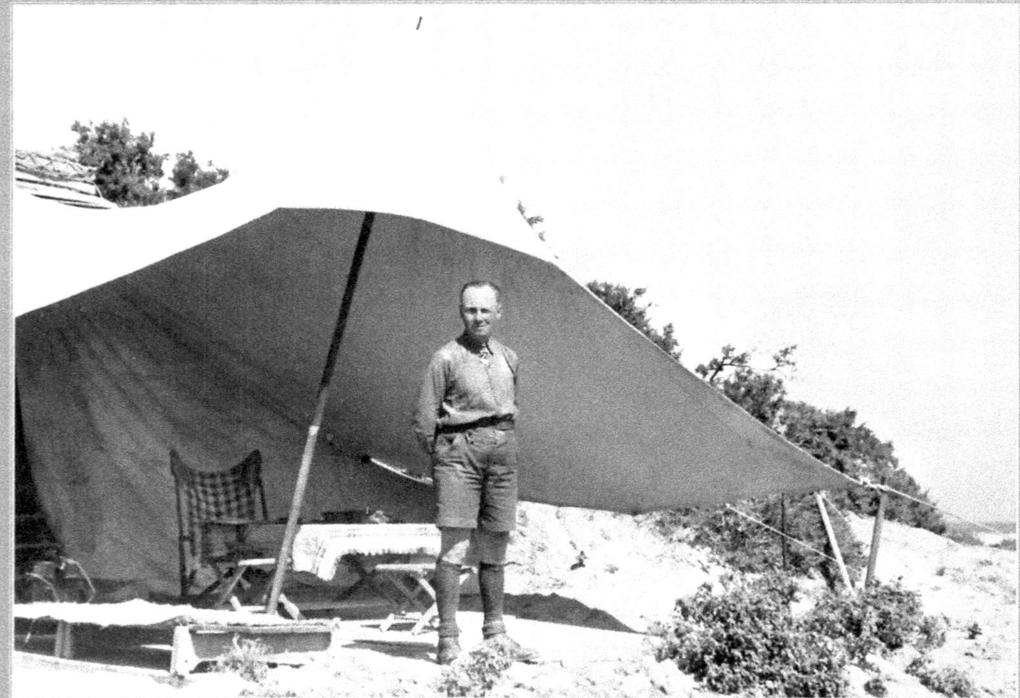

Rommel poses outside his van on the beach near Tobruk in North Africa.

This van (covered by a tent on the outside) was a gift to Rommel from the Italians. According to his writings, Rommel very much appreciated the van. It allowed him to have shelter and much-needed sleep after hours spent formulating strategies and touring the battlefield. During a military campaign, particularly in a harsh environment such as North Africa, it was important for a commander to be rested and in good health in order to fulfill his responsibilities as a tactician and lead his troops efficiently.

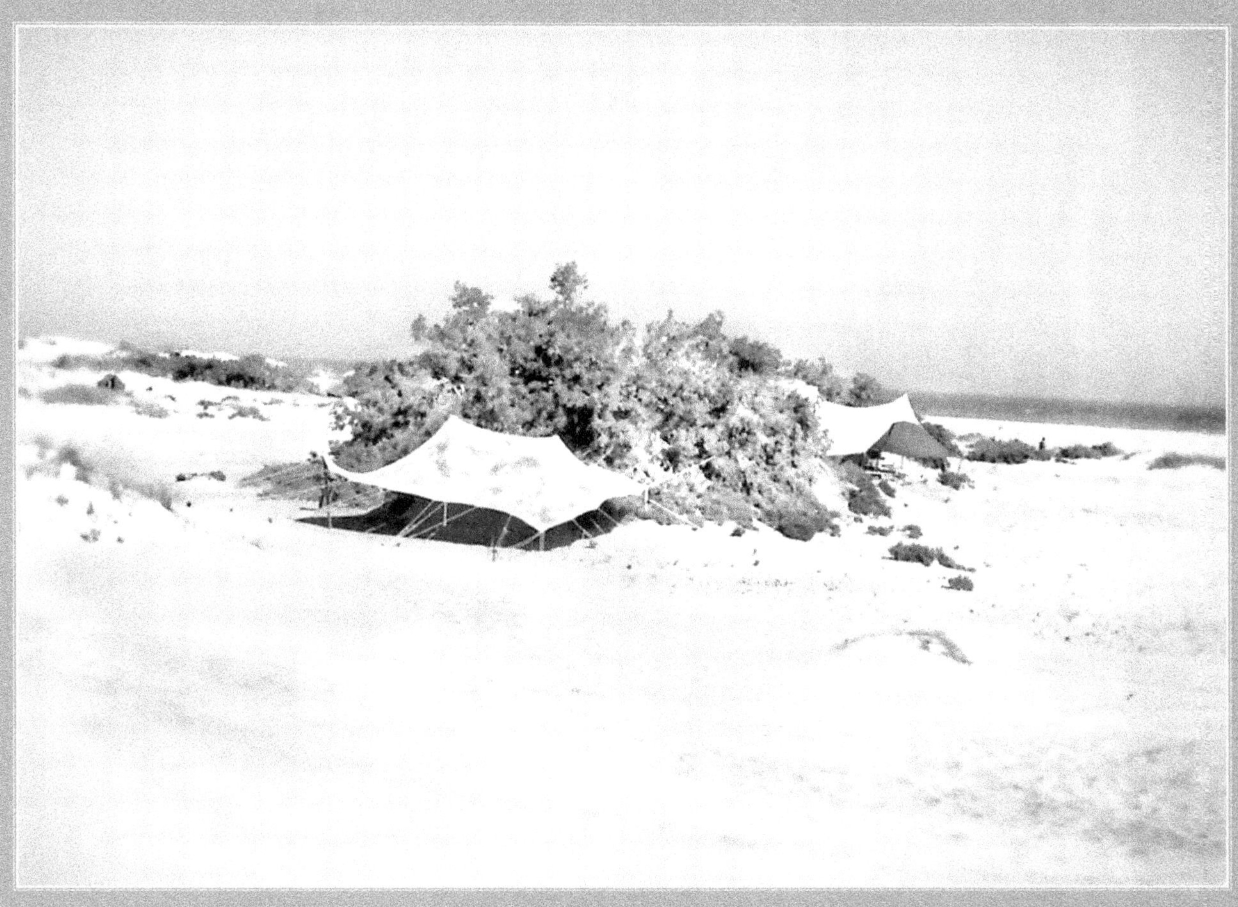

Rommel's headquarters located on the beach near Tobruk, Libya (April 1941).

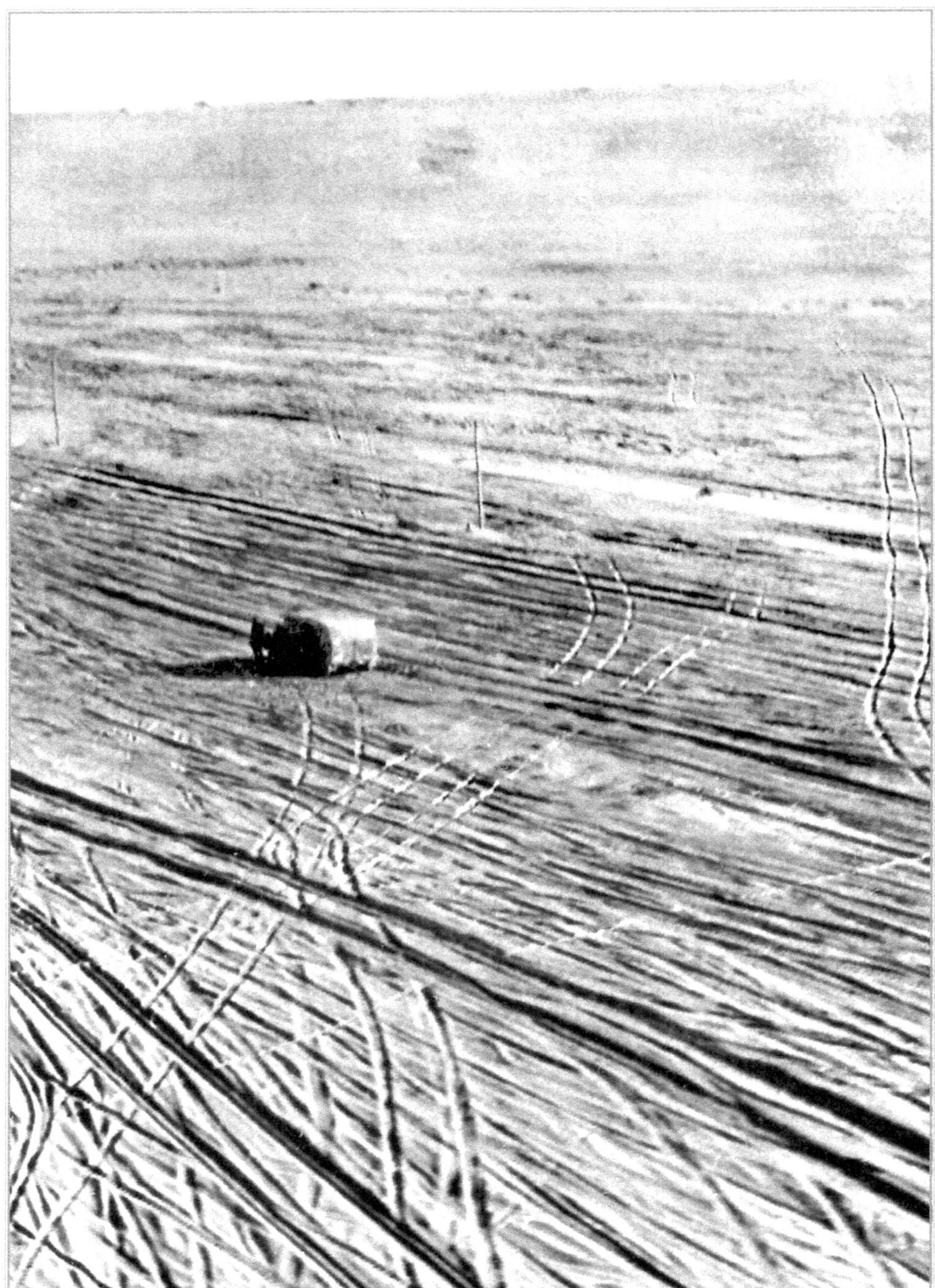

A truck is parked among a maze of tire tracks in North Africa.

Rommel appears to have taken this photo from an aircraft. The picture has no military relevance. It is likely Rommel was intrigued by the chaotic scene of the tire tracks across the desert sand. The layers of diagonal track lines are predominant in this photo.

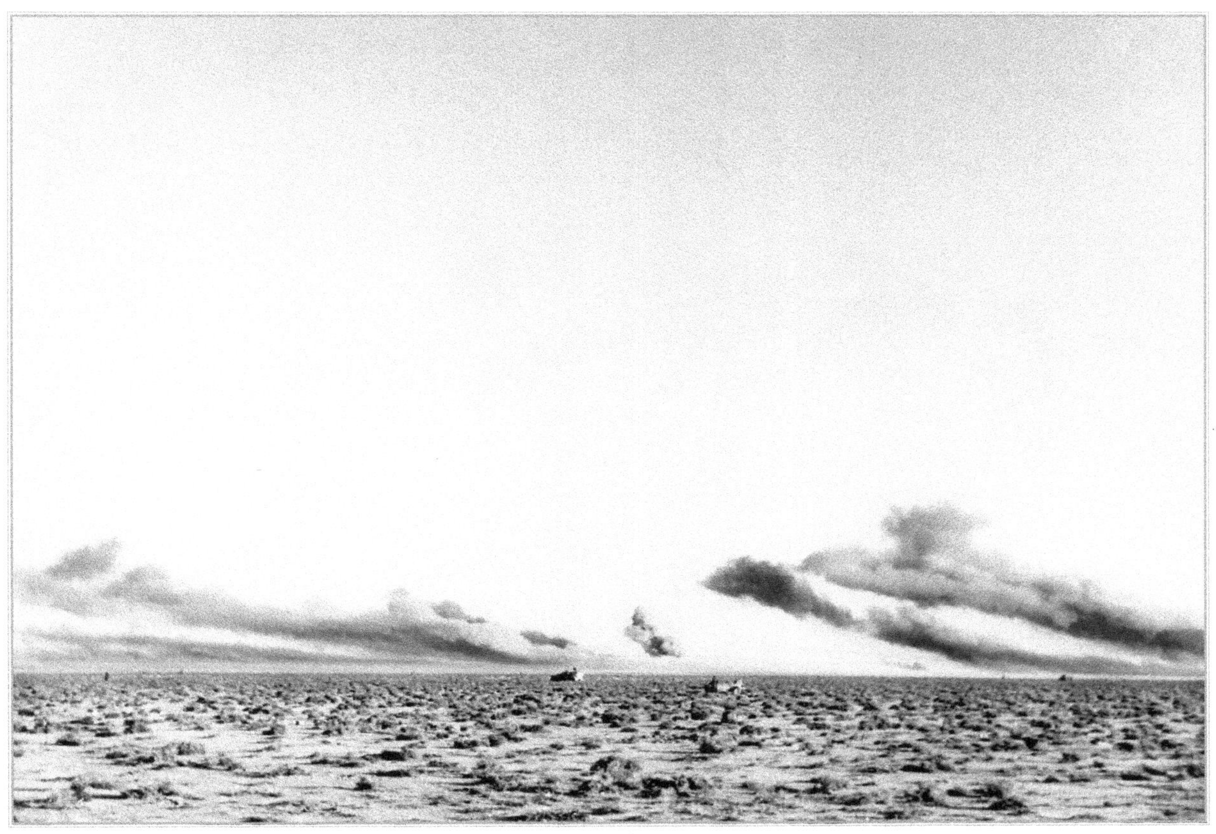

Smoke plumes drift diagonally across a clear desert sky in North Africa.

"It was a typical picture of a desert battle. Black smoke clouds rolled up to the sky, giving the landscape a curious sinister beauty."

— *Rommel*

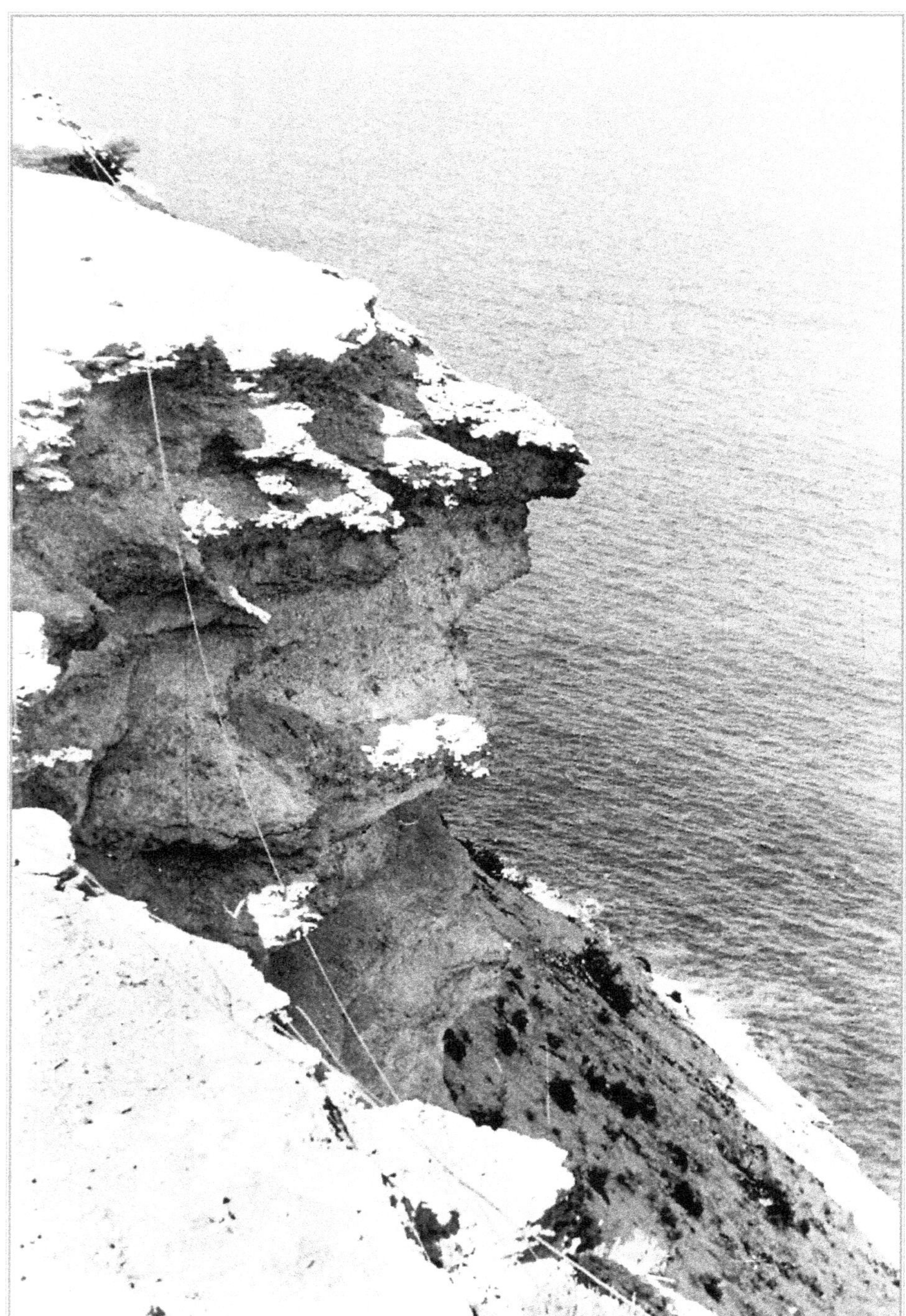

A craggy cliff juts out towards the sea in North Africa.

The rim of this cliff forms a jagged diagonal pattern, which divides the image in half between the land and sea. It is likely Rommel took this picture in North Africa while encamped near the Mediterranean.

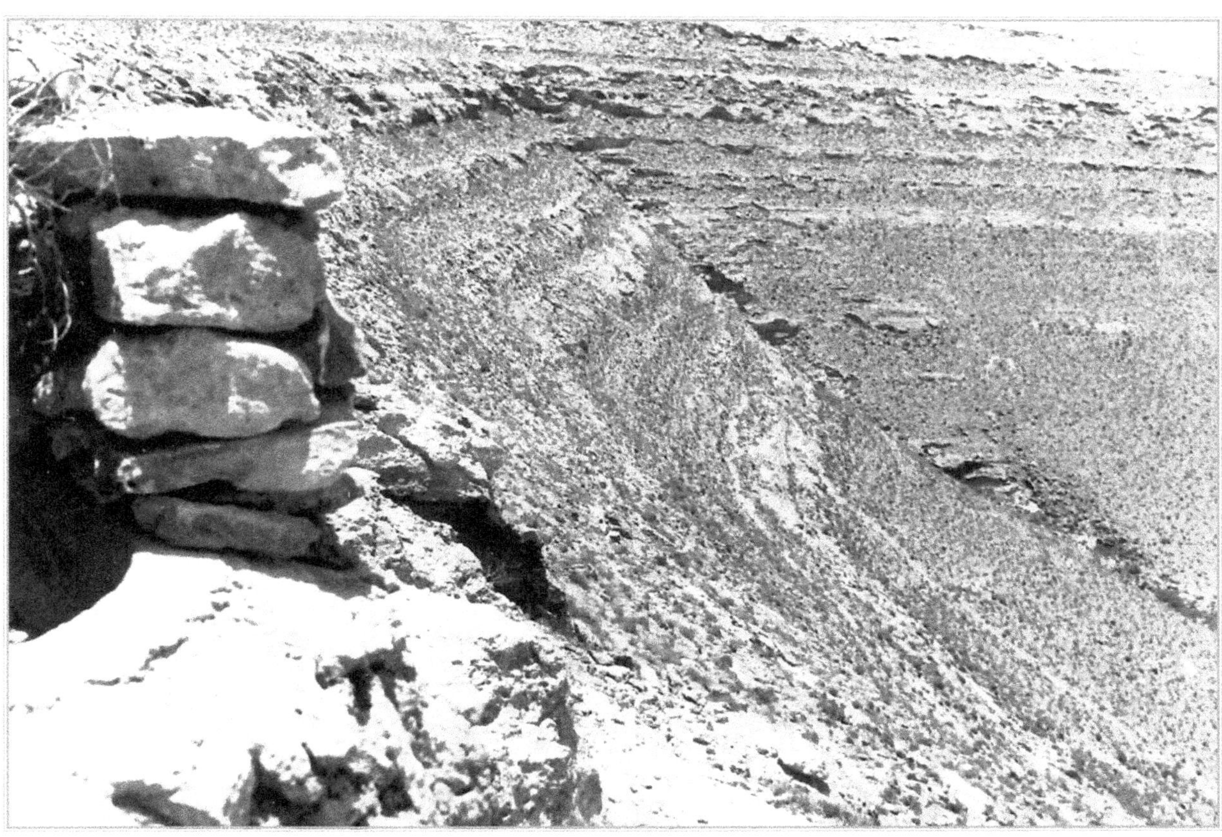

A rugged slope forms a steep precipice in North Africa.

When composing this photo, Rommel contrasted the rocks in the foreground against the patterns formed by sedimentary rock stratum in the distance. A split in the earth on the right side of the photo forms a curving diagonal line, a characteristic feature of Rommel's photography.

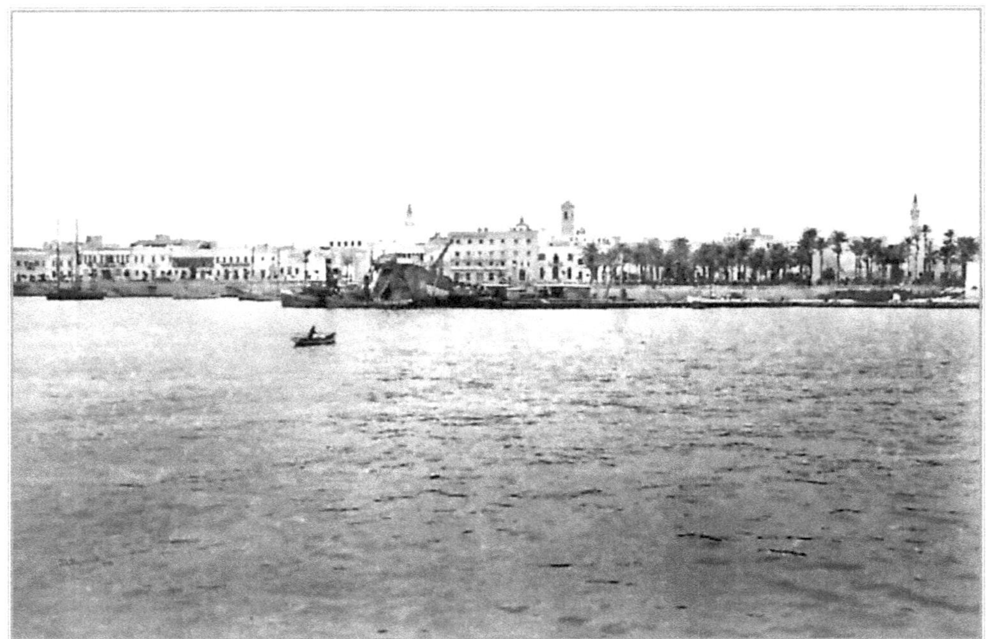

A lone figure rows a boat in a North African harbor.

A lone figure or object against a vast backdrop is a typical subject in Rommel's photos.

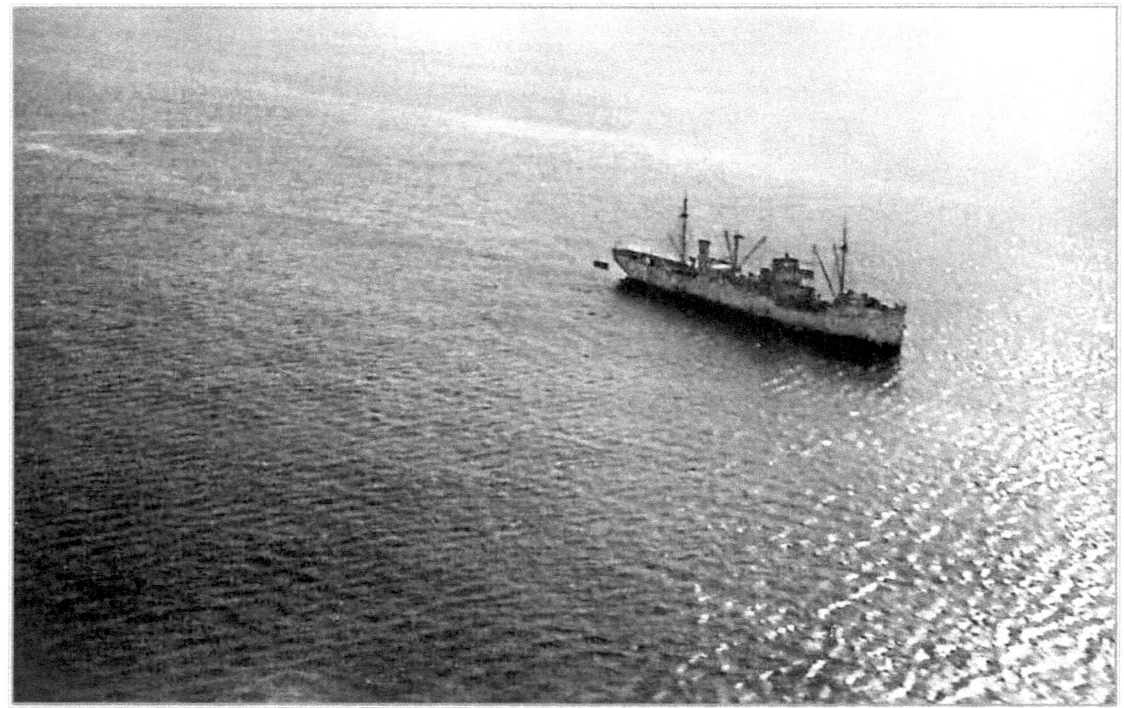

A battleship glides through tranquil waters (date and location unknown).

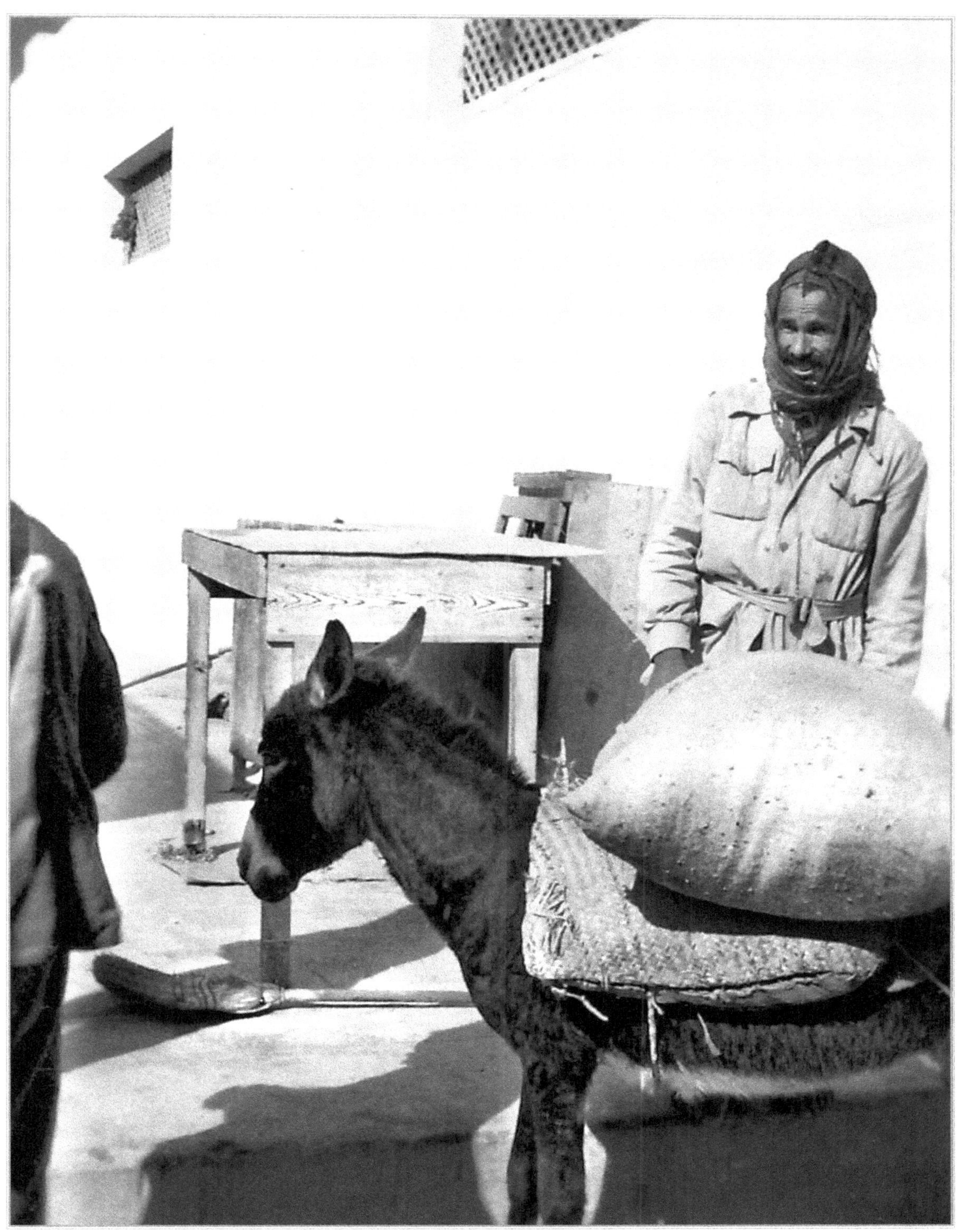

An Arab man and his donkey stand in a street in North Africa.

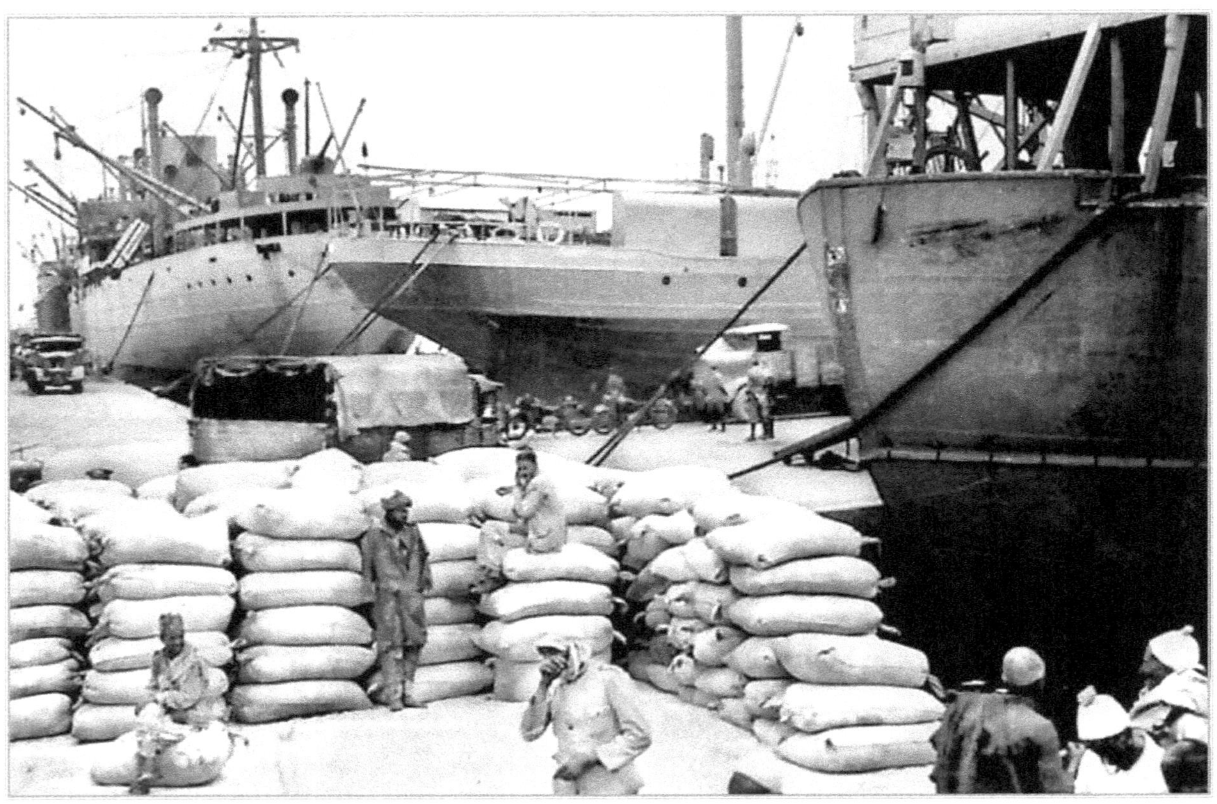

Dockyard workers take a rest in a port in Tripoli, Libya (1941).

Rommel took this photo at a high angle. Judging from the comparative differences in height between the ships, docks, and the truck parked behind the sandbags, it would seem Rommel captured this image by standing atop a vehicle. The dockworkers, gathering next to an L-shaped wall of sacks, are the central object of this photo.

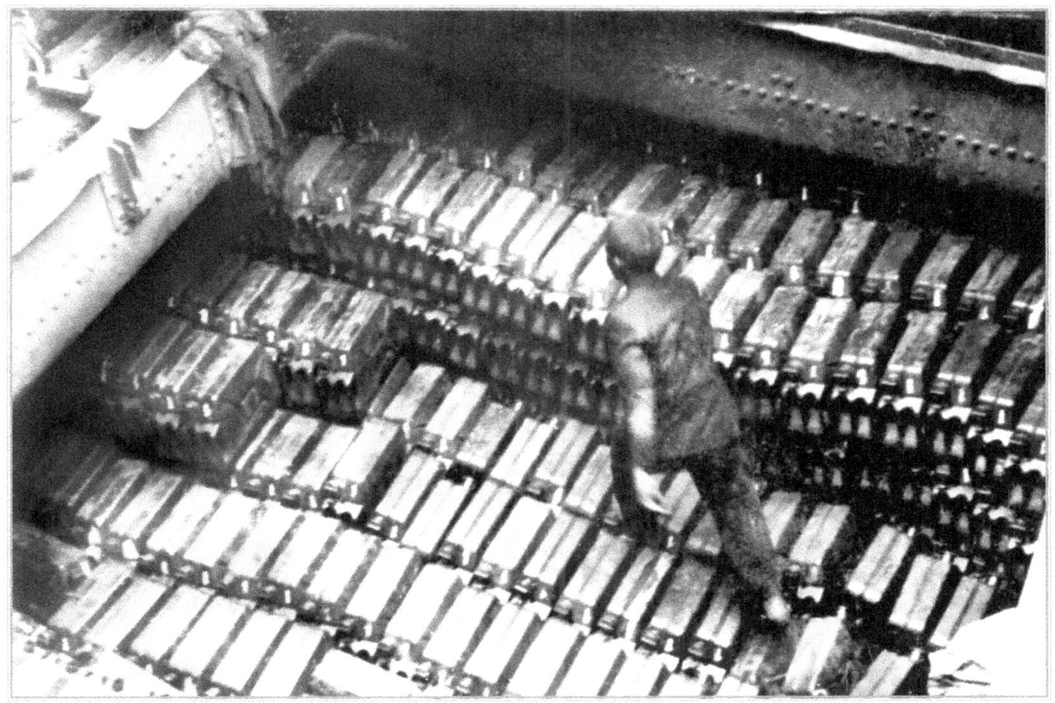

A dock worker sprints across military cargo in a ship in Libya (1941).

The man is a single focal point set against a patterned diagonal backdrop.

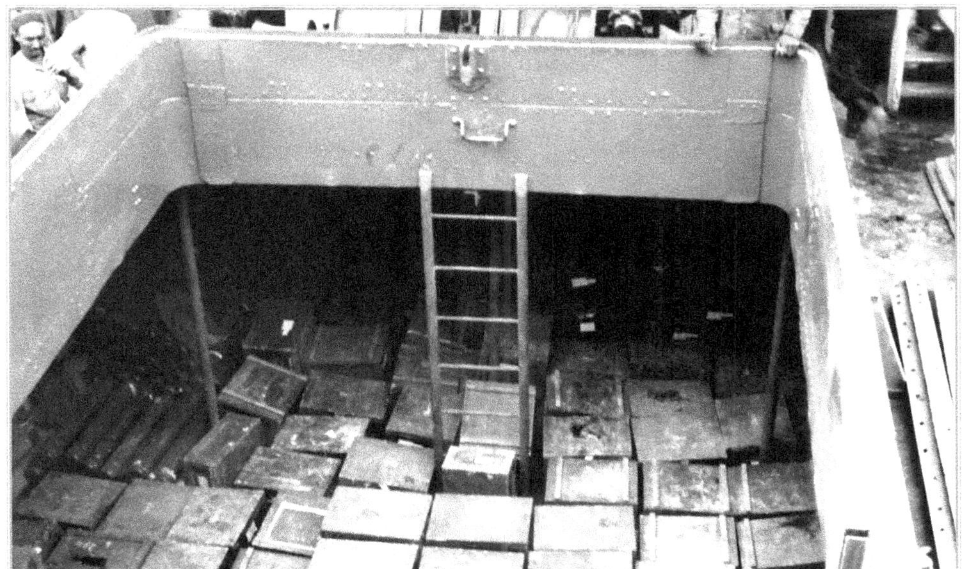

Cargo is ready to be unloaded from a ship in Libya (1941).

The ladder in the center balances the composition of this image. The rectangle shapes within the ladder's openings are similar to the square shapes of the boxes and deck opening.

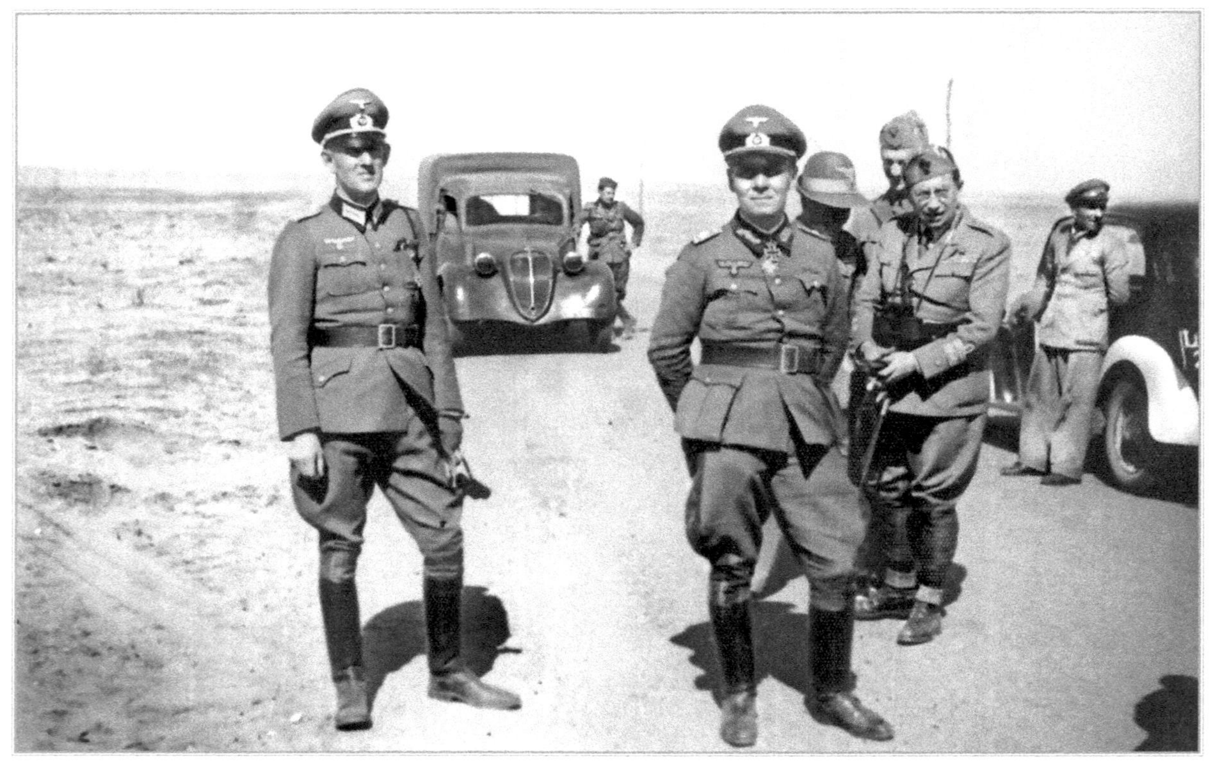

Rommel poses for a photo in the middle of the barren desert of North Africa, surrounded by German and Italian officers.

It is interesting to note that the German and Italian drivers in the background appear lost in thought as they stand ready near their vehicles. The shadow of the photographer appears in the lower right corner of the frame.

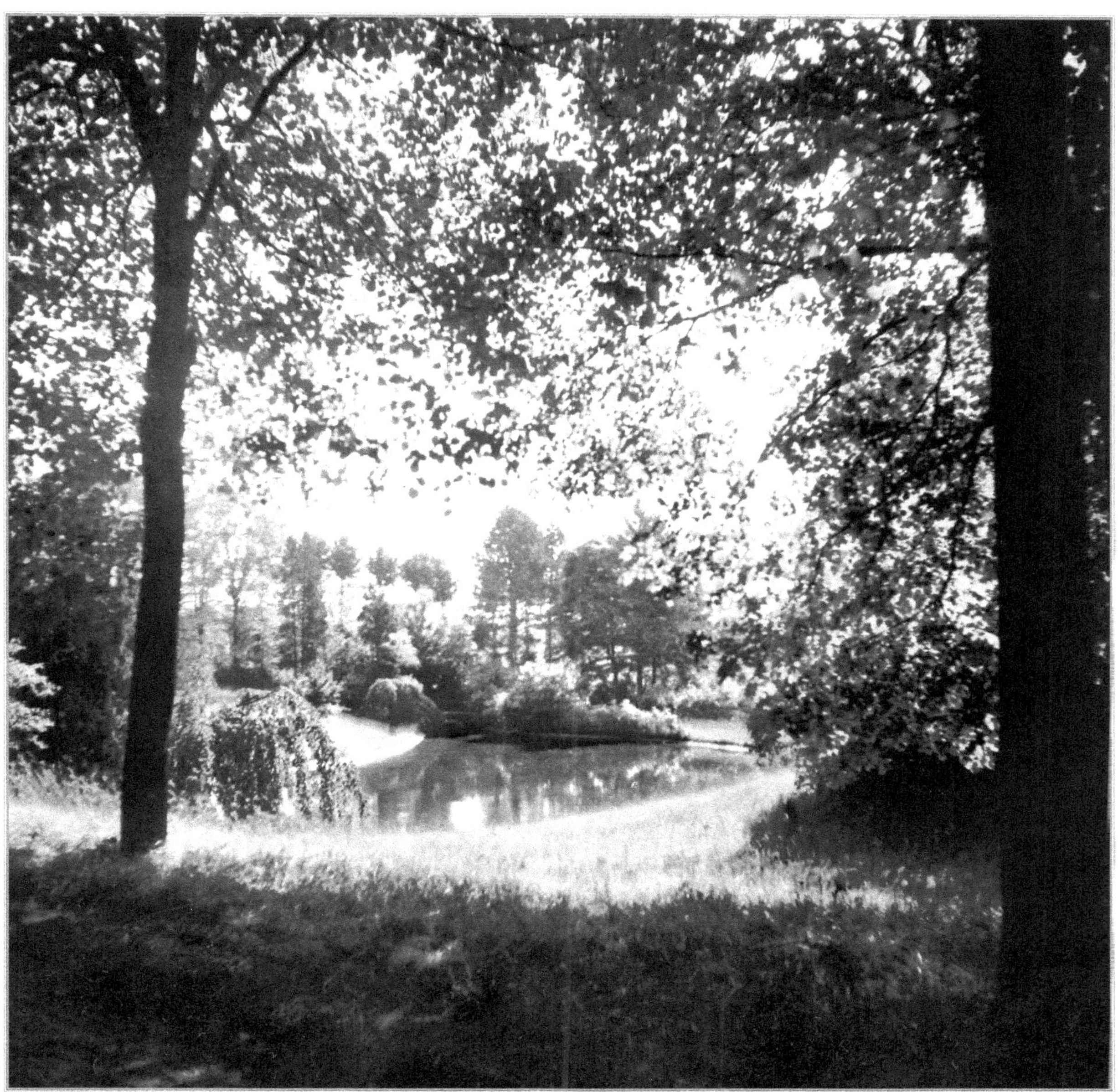

A forest in Europe (circa 1940).

This photo contains a frame within a frame. The trees on both the right and left form a border around the water and trees in the distance. As in many of his pictures, Rommel also contrasts nearness and farness.

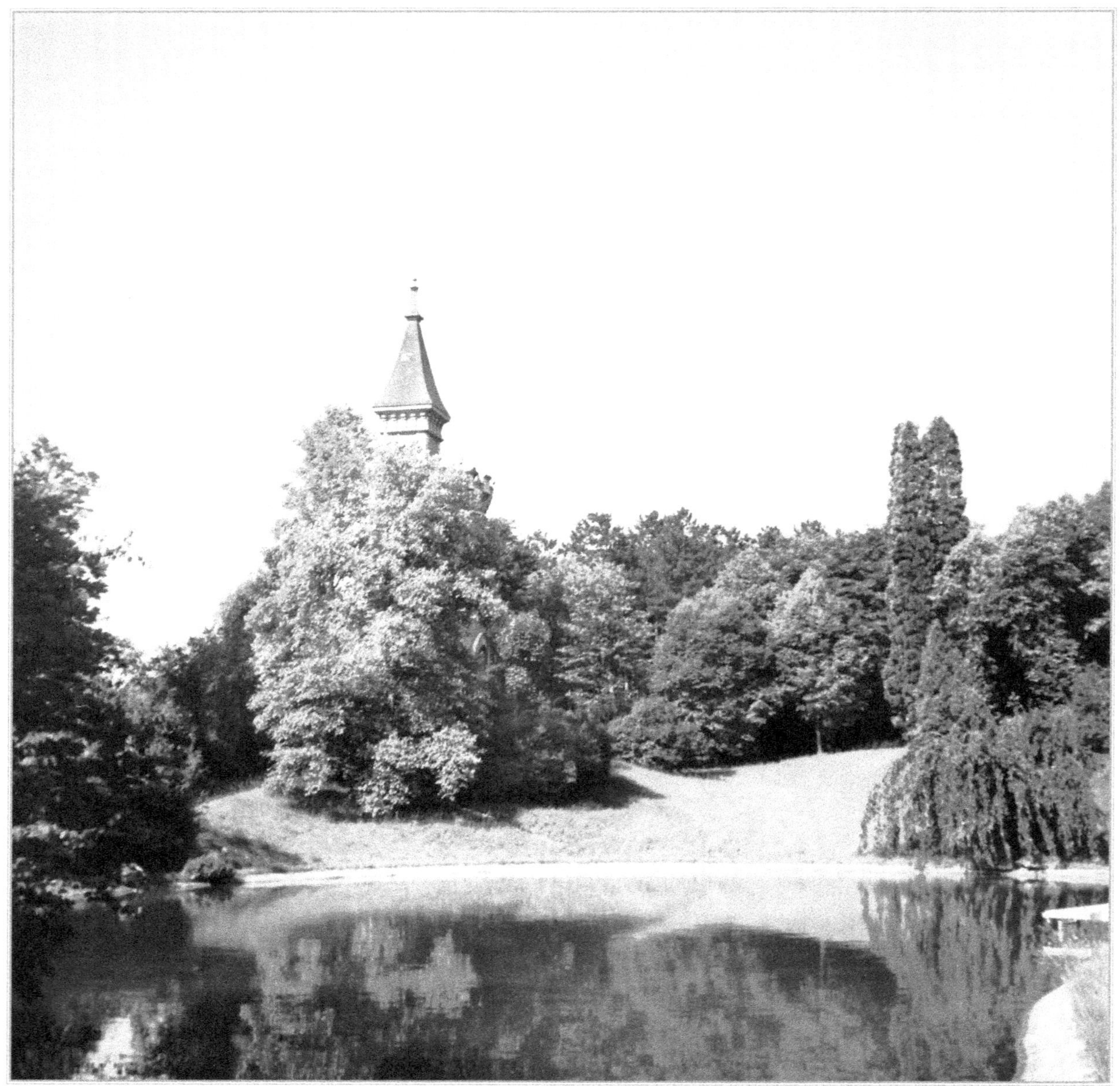

Another scene from Europe.

This photo conveys Rommel's recurring attention to natural beauty. A shoreline in the middle ground curves across the frame. The trees on both the right and left sides of the image balance the composition.

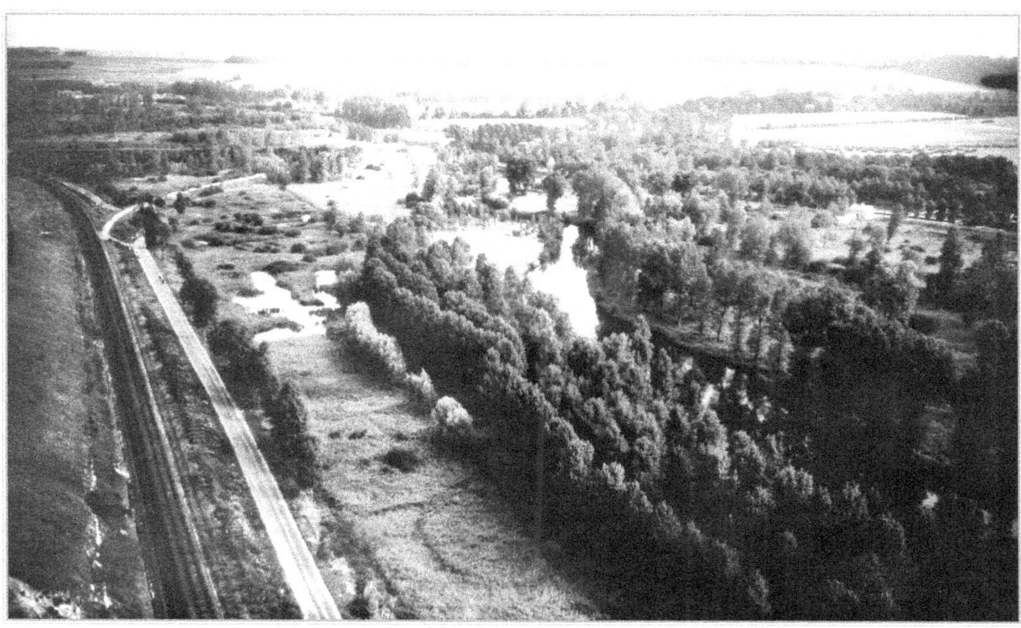

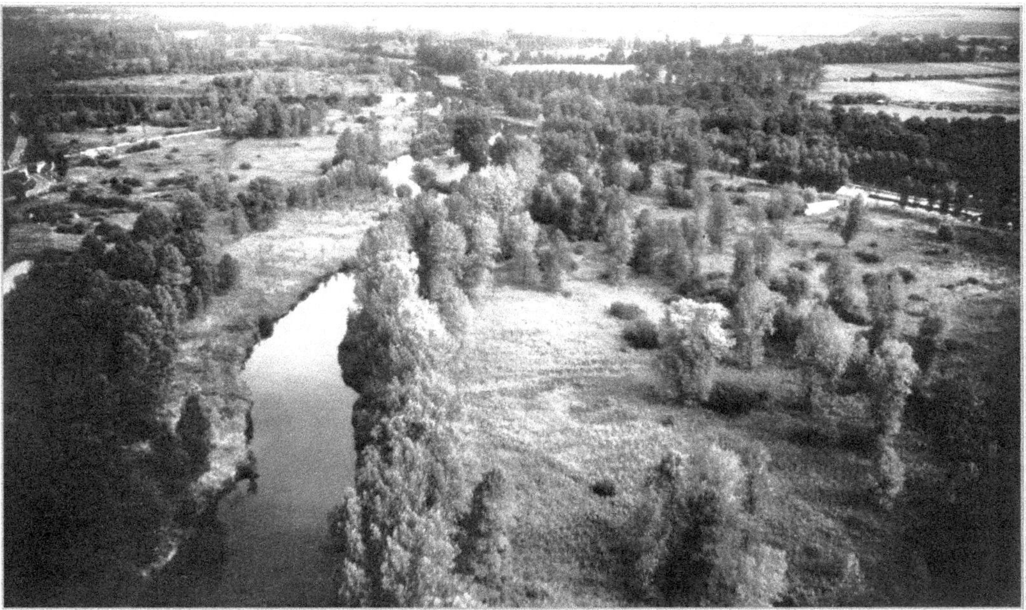

Aerial view of the countryside in France.

These photos were taken by Rommel as he accompanied the advancing German military. In both photos, Rommel fills 1/3 of the frame with a linear shape (a river and a railway track).

A horse munches grass next to a tank as a soldier walks past (date and location unknown).

The motion of the German soldier walking into the frame indicates Rommel was photographing the horse and tank when the soldier suddenly appeared.

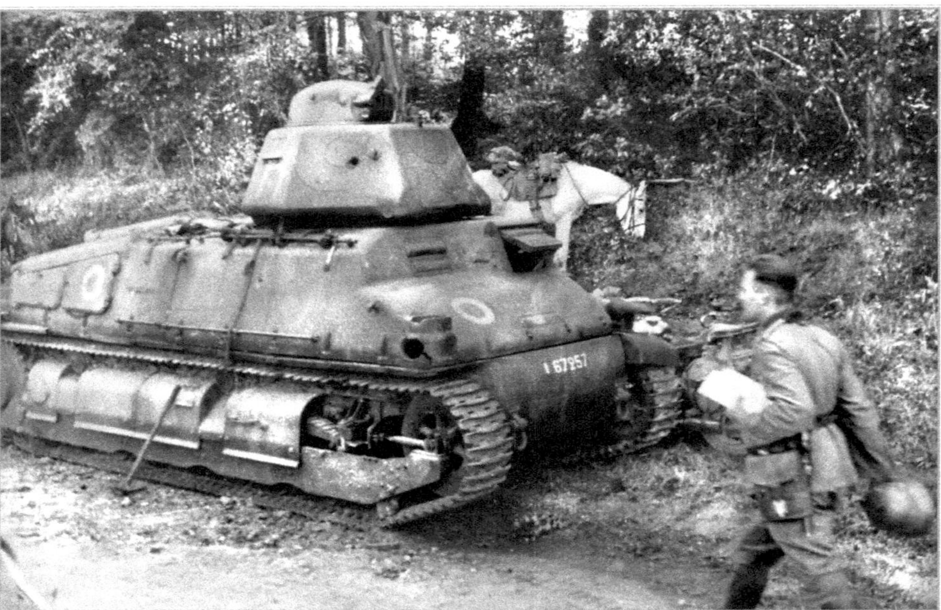

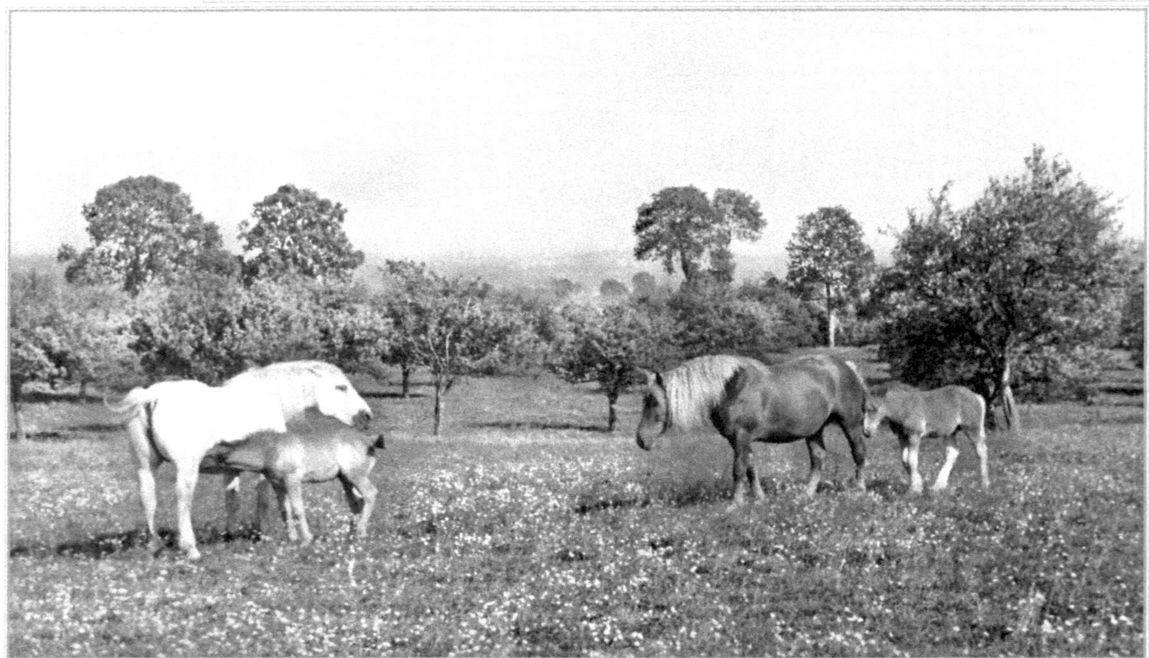

Horses and foals approach each other in a pasture (location and date unknown).

Rommel loved horses. He first encountered horses at age 22, when he became part of a horse-drawn artillery regiment in Ulm. His enthusiasm for horses and riding became a lifelong passion. He went on riding excursions with his wife, Lucie. Rommel was even pictured in riding gear, standing beside his toddler son, who was seated on the back of a horse. Rommel also kept riding saddles at his home. After his death, these saddles were stolen from his widow by American G.I.s.

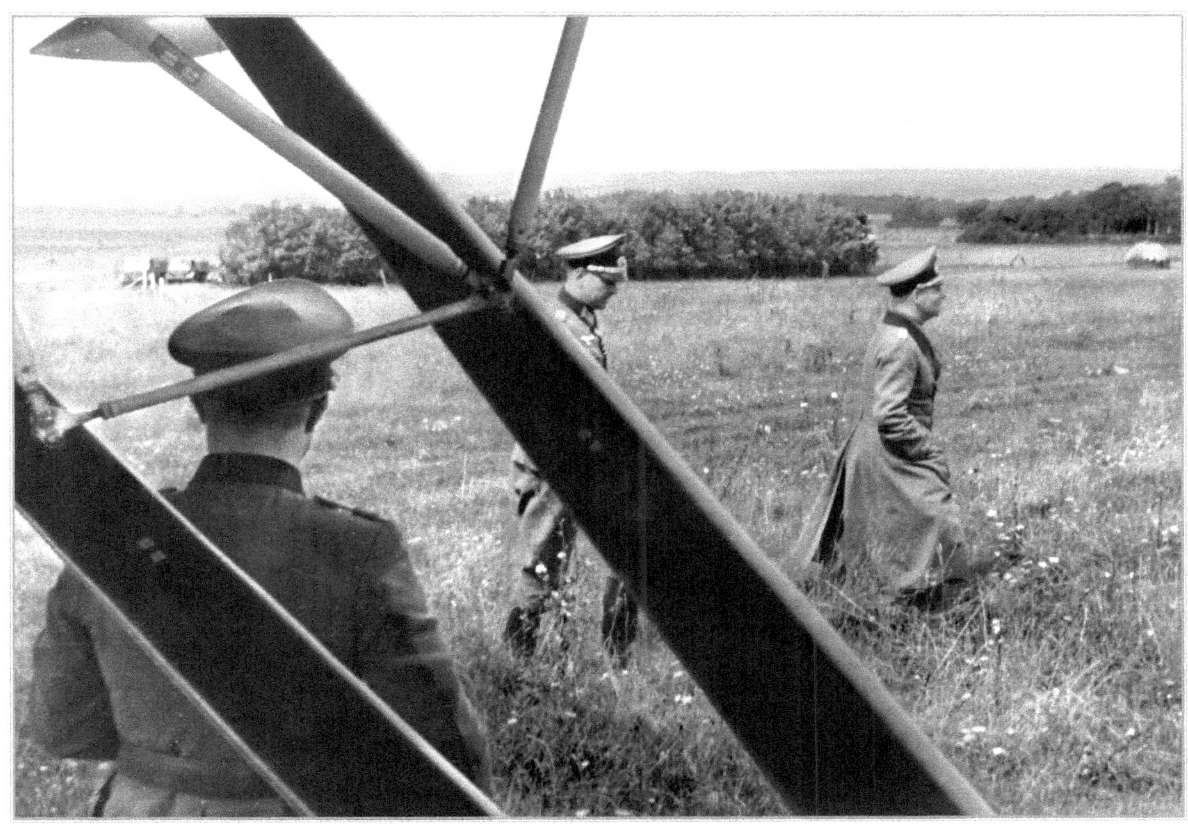

Rommel walks past an airplane in a flowery field in Europe (1939–40).

This airplane in the photo could have been one that Rommel was traveling in while conducting aerial surveillance of military operations.

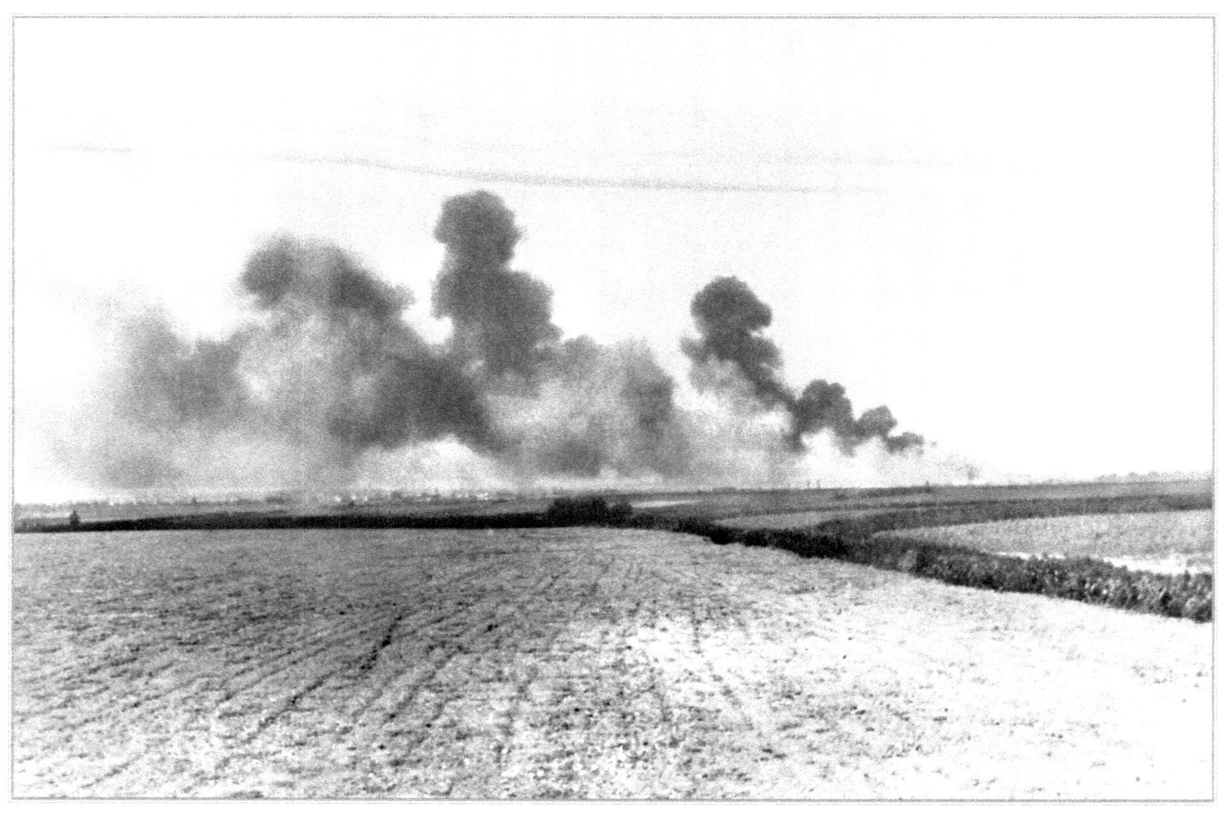

Smoke rises from a distant battle in France.

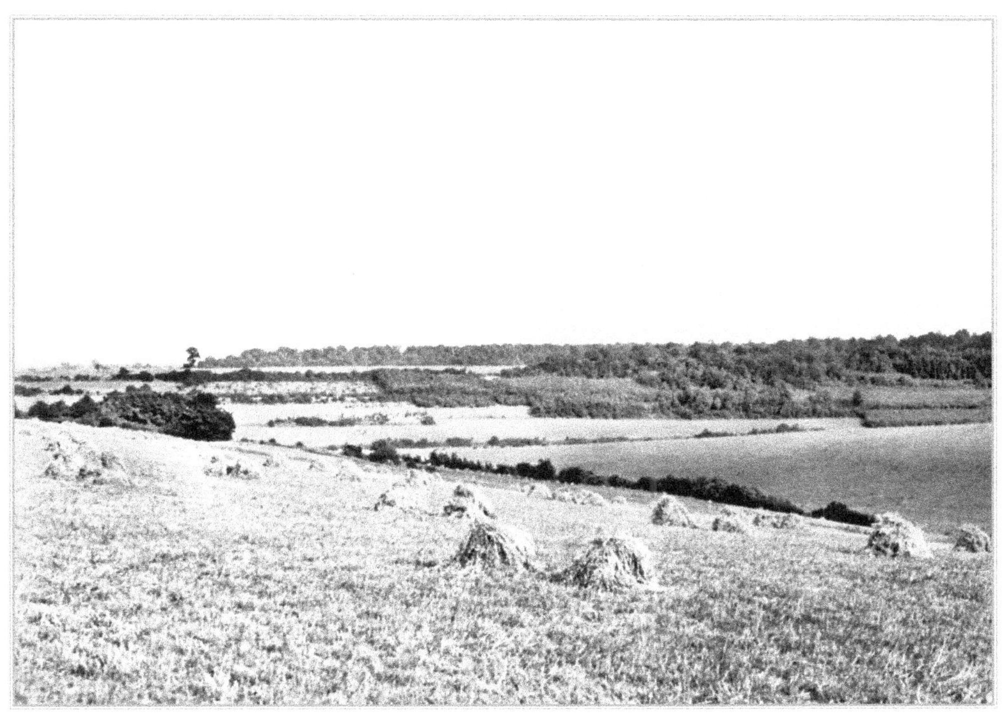

Haystacks dot a sloping hill in France.

The incline of the hill and the fields beyond form many free-flowing horizontal lines.

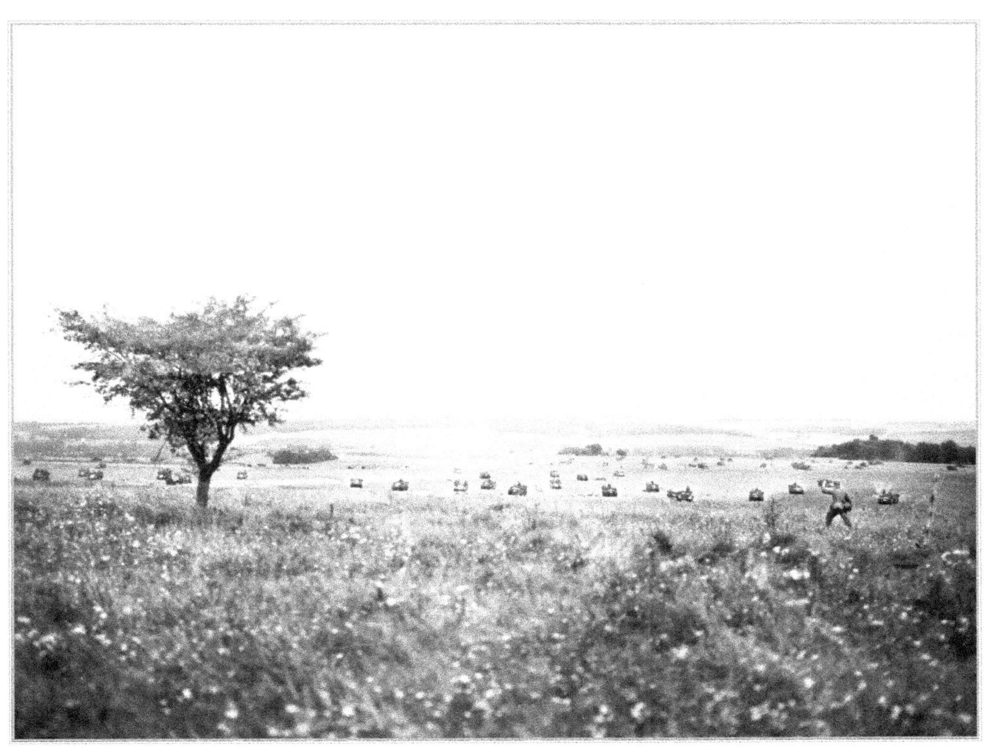

A formation of Panzers approaches a lone German soldier, who waves to them in a flowery field in France.

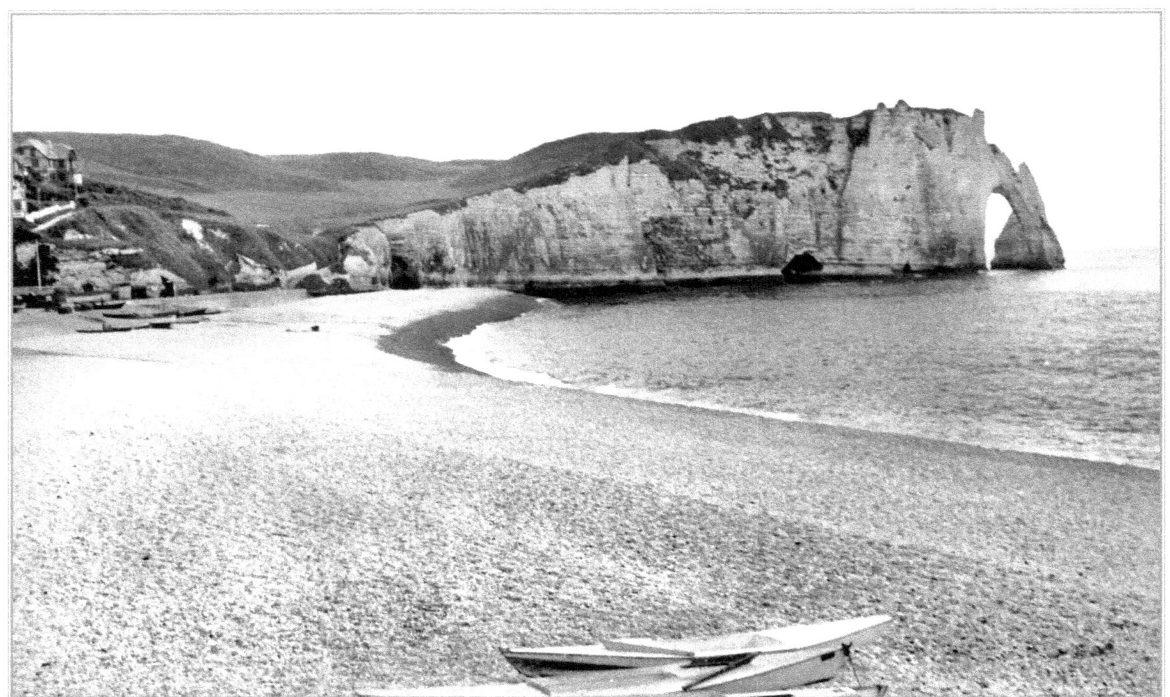

Monumental cliffs rise above the ocean on the Normandy coast of France.

The shoreline of the beach curves dramatically in this composition. The curving line is similar to the rugged circular rim of the cliffs overlooking the water.

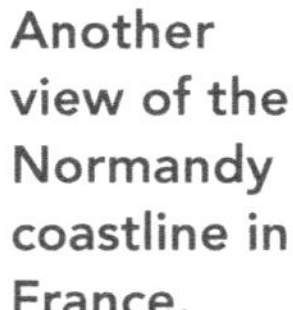

Another view of the Normandy coastline in France.

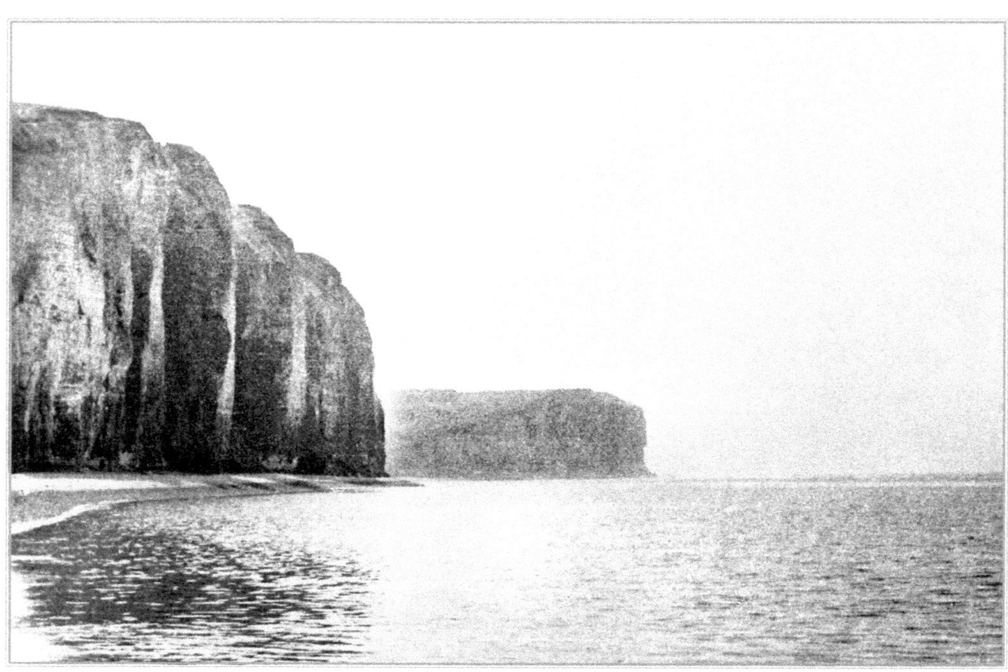

The edge of the beach seems to blend into water in the distant horizon.

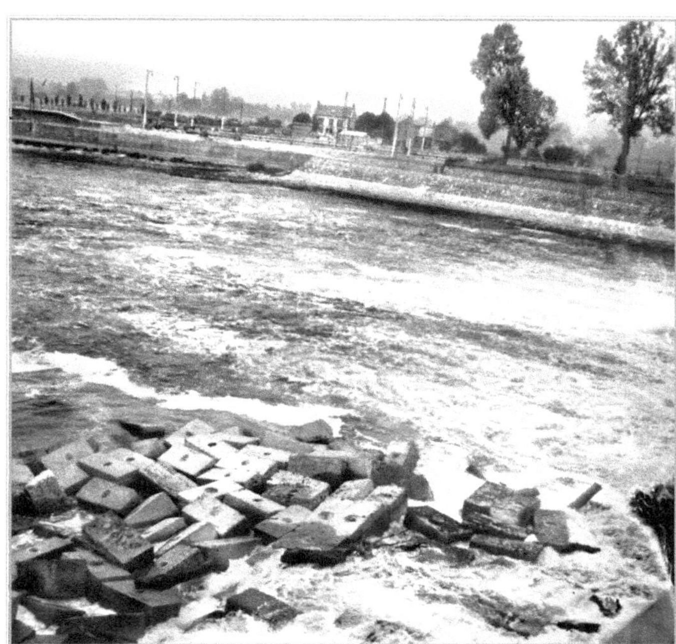

Turbulent water flows alongside rural houses in Europe (date and location unknown).

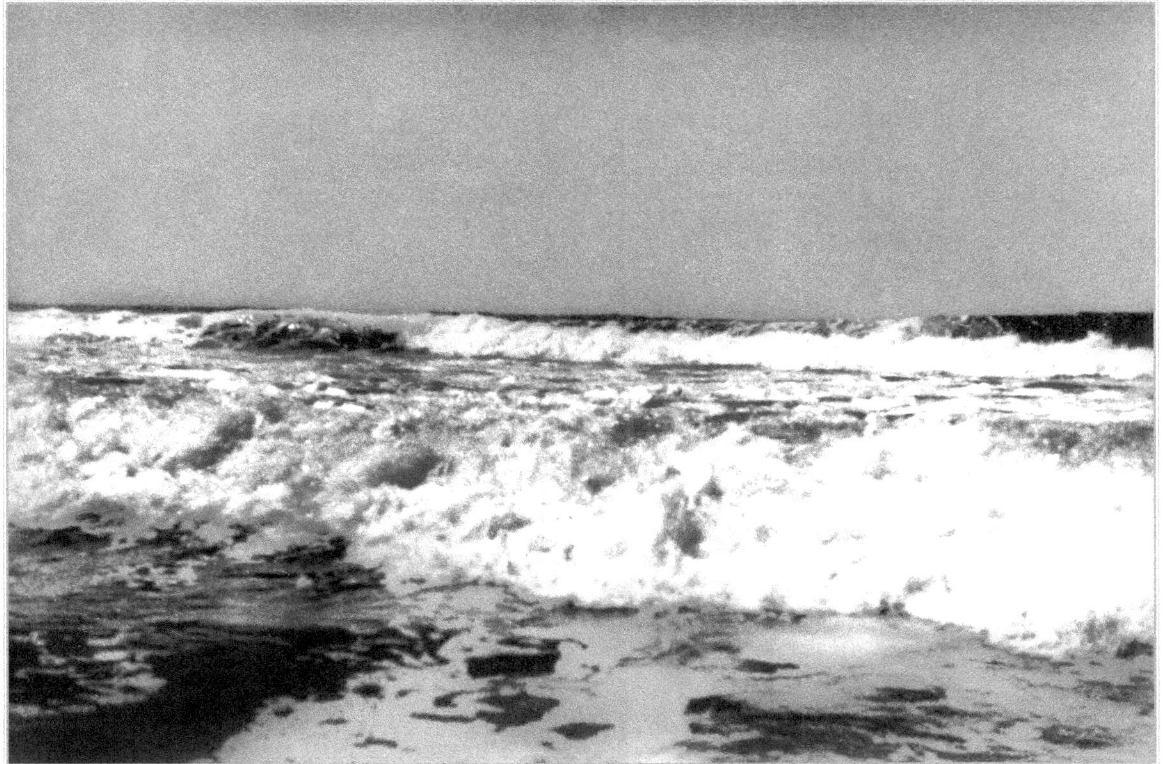

Waves crash onto the beach of the northern coast of France.

This photo contrasts a calm sky with raging waters. It is divided evenly in thirds by the sky, water, and wet sand.

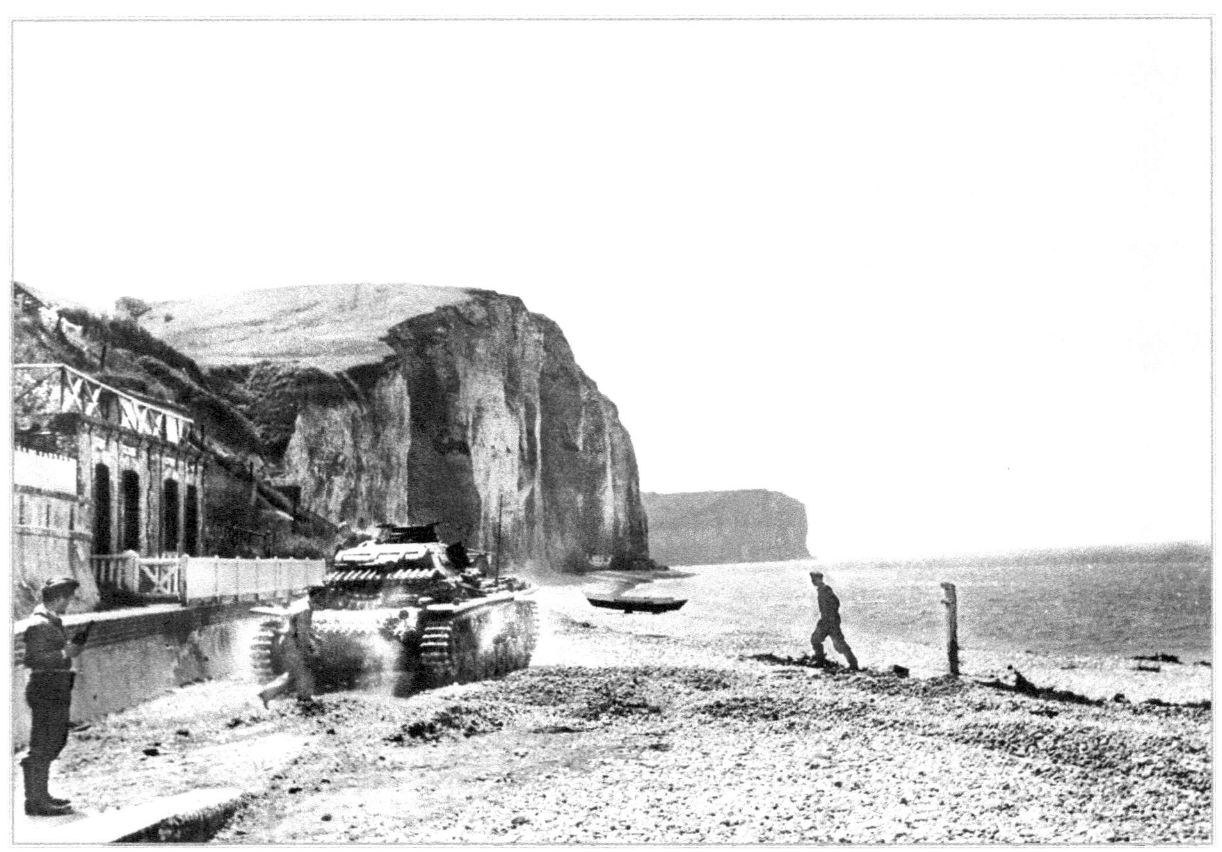

German troops arrive on Les Petites-Dalles beach of France's Normandy coast (June 10, 1940).

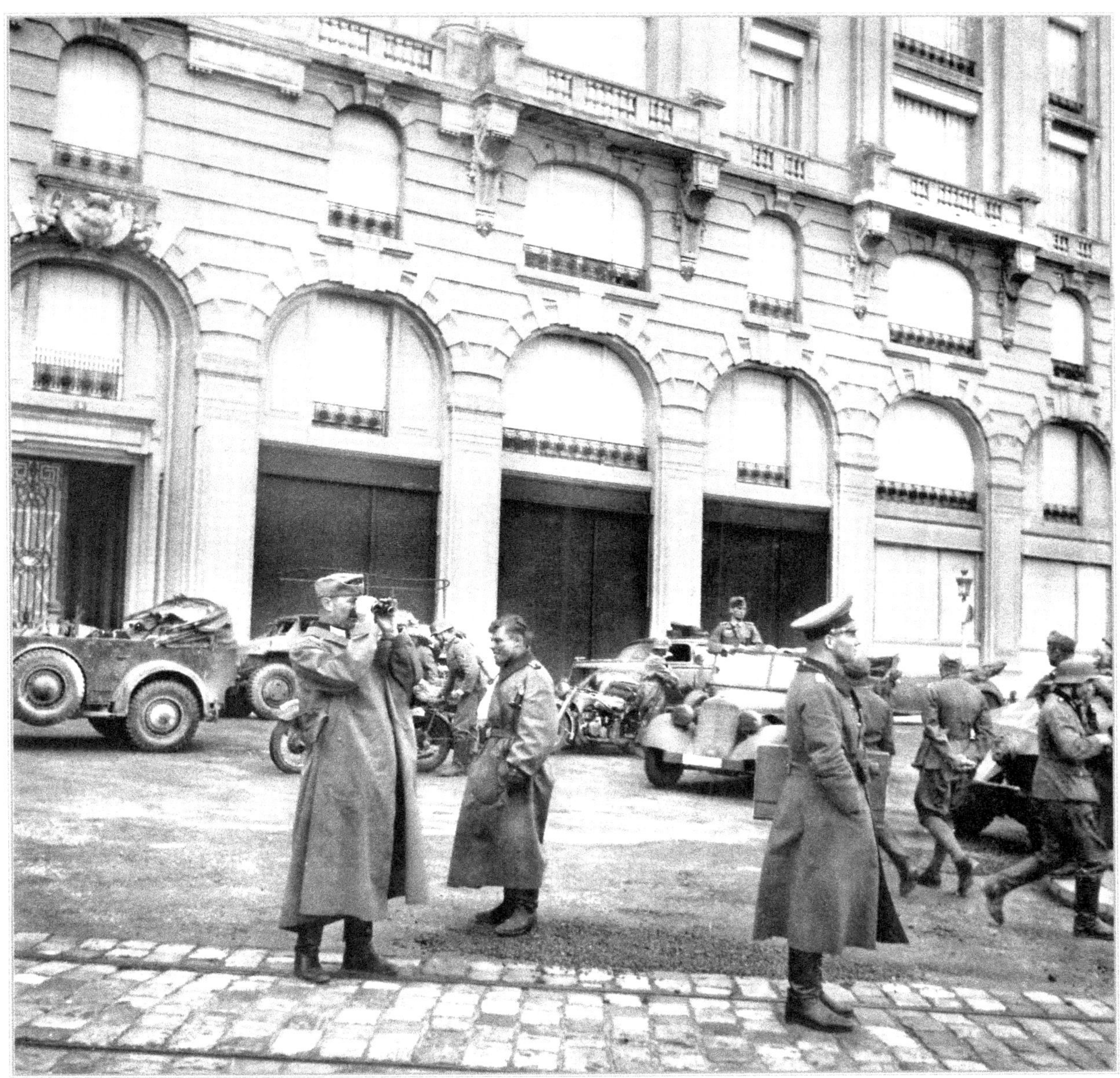

Rommel, unaware that he is being photographed, stands among other German soldiers in a street in France.

It is unknown why Rommel included this image among his private photo collection. He may have been struck by the irony of the picture. Rommel looks intently at something out of view, as a German soldier behind him peers through binoculars. At the same time, a photographer is watching them both through a camera lens.

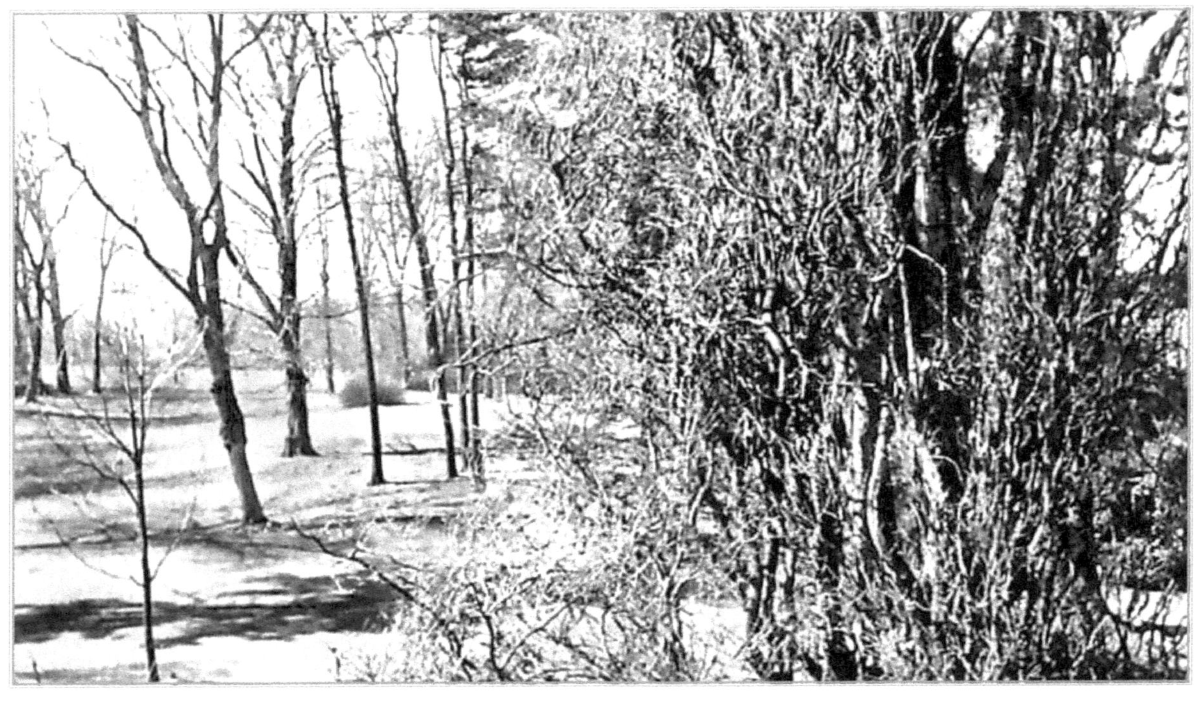

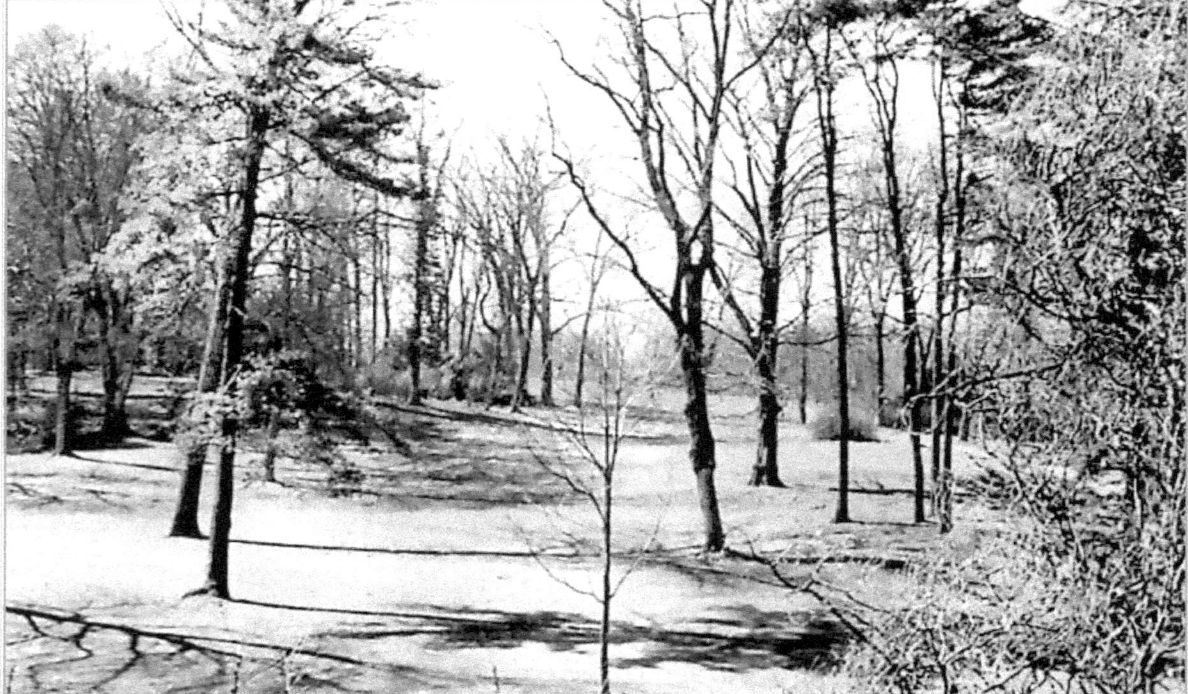

Barren trees create a bleak and gloomy atmosphere in these two photos of a wooded area in Europe (circa 1940).

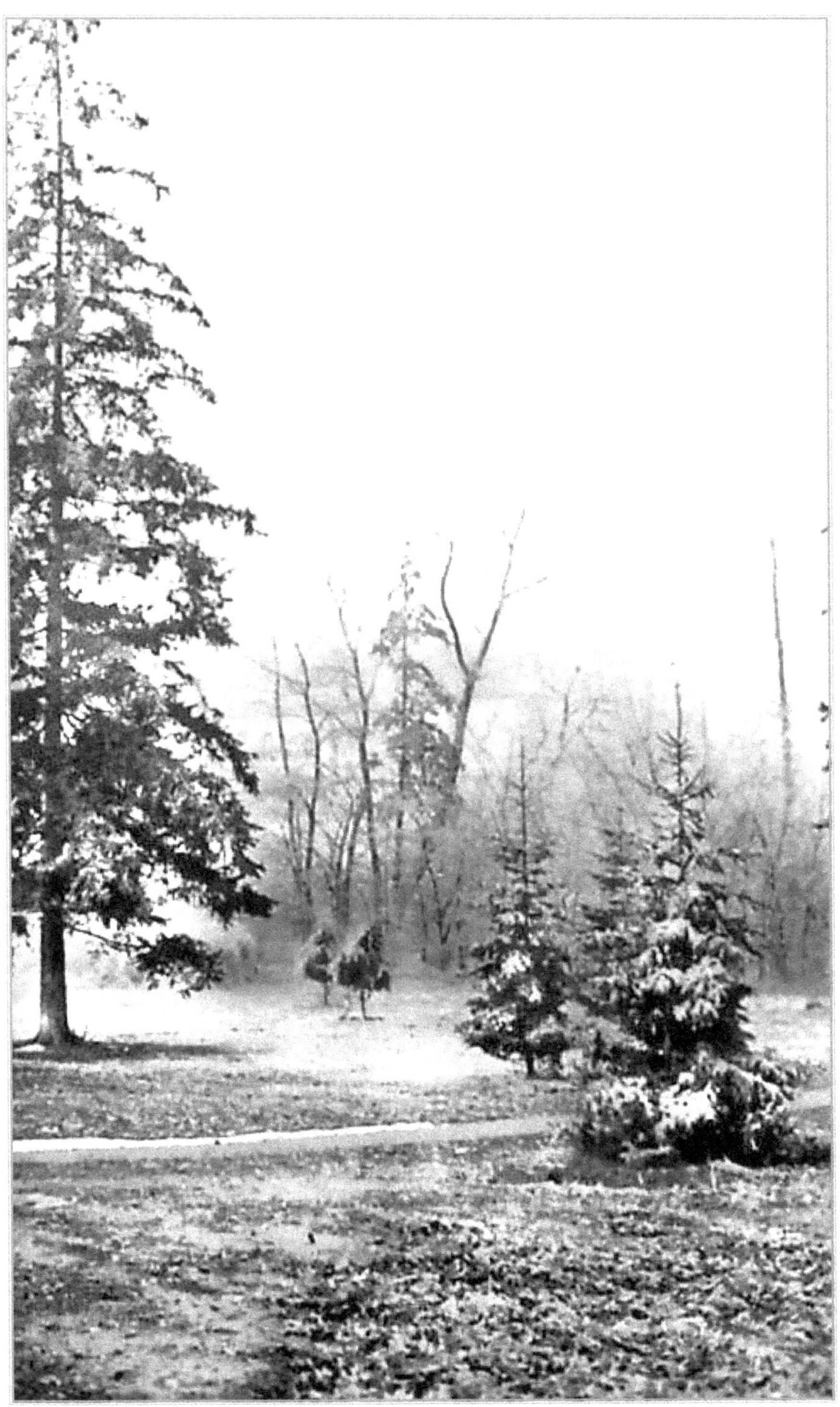

An autumn scene in a forested area (date unknown).

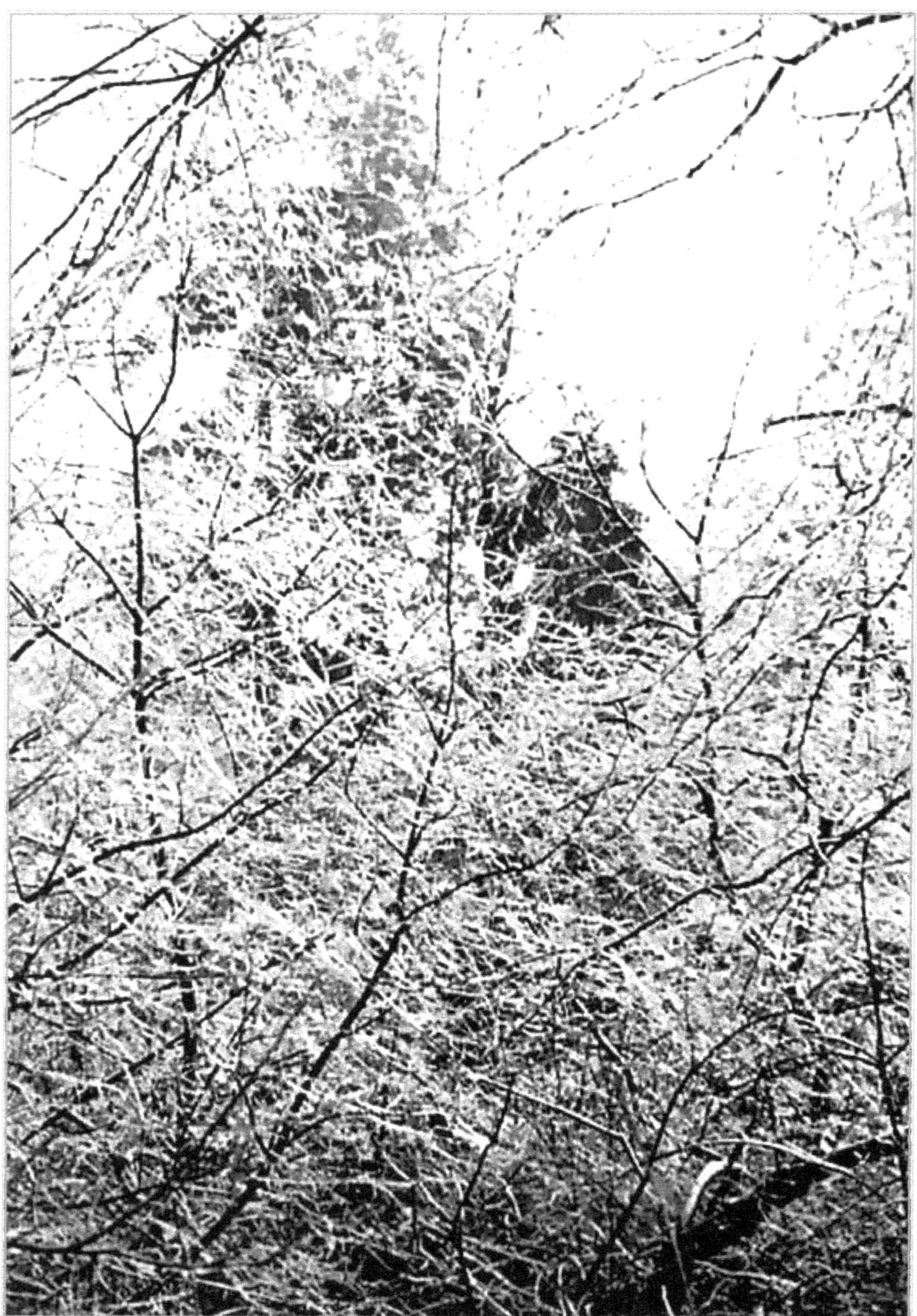

Jagged tree branches show a coarse distinction between light and darkness in this photo (date and location unknown).

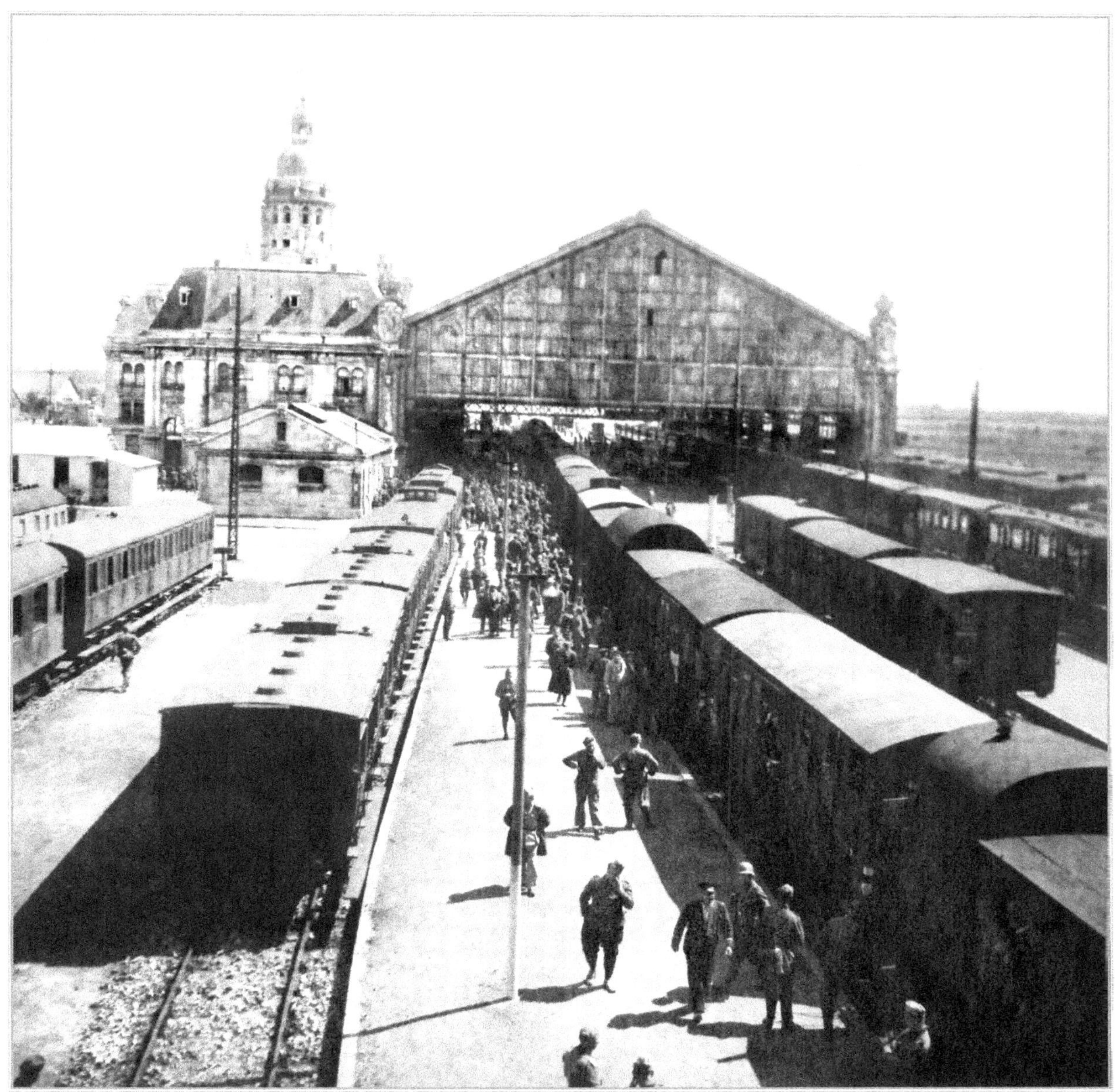

German soldiers mingle with civilians at a train station in Europe (date unknown).

Rommel took this photo from a high angle. The shadows and lines in the image create an almost painterly effect. Instead of focusing on a lone individual, this time Rommel captures various interplays of curving lines: trains, people, and tracks all intersect in the center of the photograph.

4

Fortifications

GETARNT ZU WERDEN.

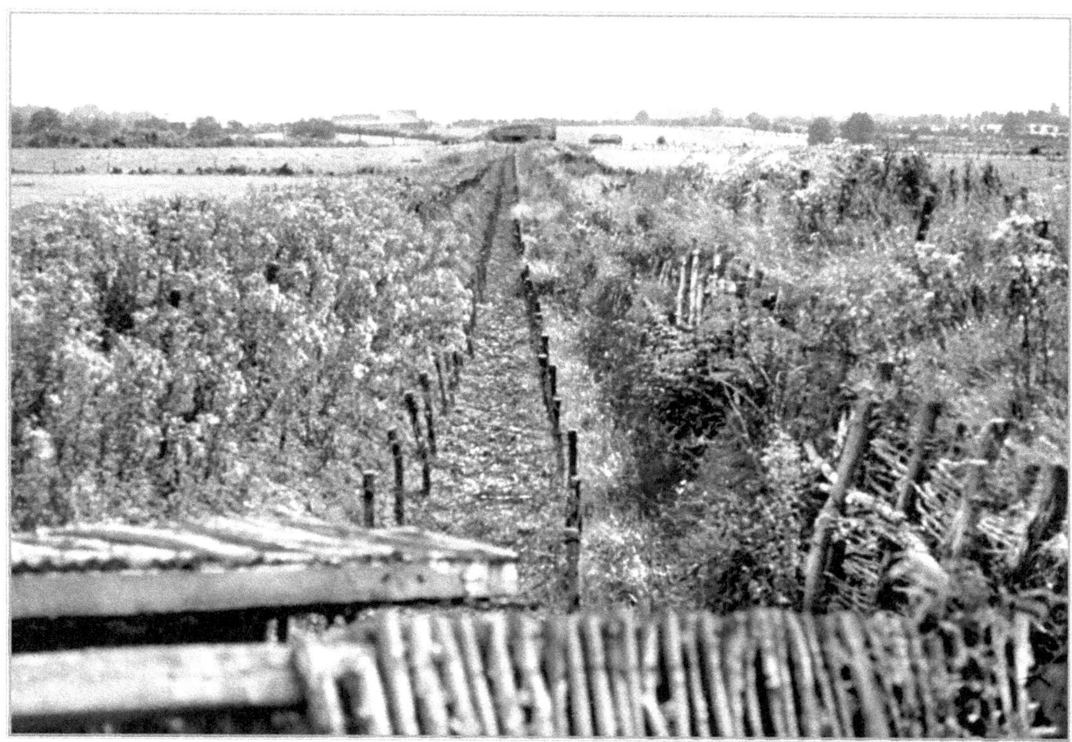

A fortified barrier marks the Maginot Line in France.

Rommel fought as an infantryman in the trenches during WWI. He was wounded three times in combat, including a shot through the leg that nearly shattered his thigh. Because of his experiences, he had strong feelings about casualties in war. In his book, Rommel wrote several emotional tributes to his fellow German soldiers killed in action between 1914 and 1918. Crossing the Maginot Line in France 1940 was clearly a meaningful moment for Rommel. He took many pictures of the Maginot Line as the German troops traveled over it. He wrote the following passage in his memoirs:

> "We were through the Maginot Line! It was hardly conceivable. Twenty-two years before we had stood for four and a half long years before this self-same enemy and had won victory after victory and yet finally lost the war. And now we had broken through the renowned Maginot Line and were driving deep into enemy territory. It was not just a beautiful dream. It was reality."
>
> — *Rommel*

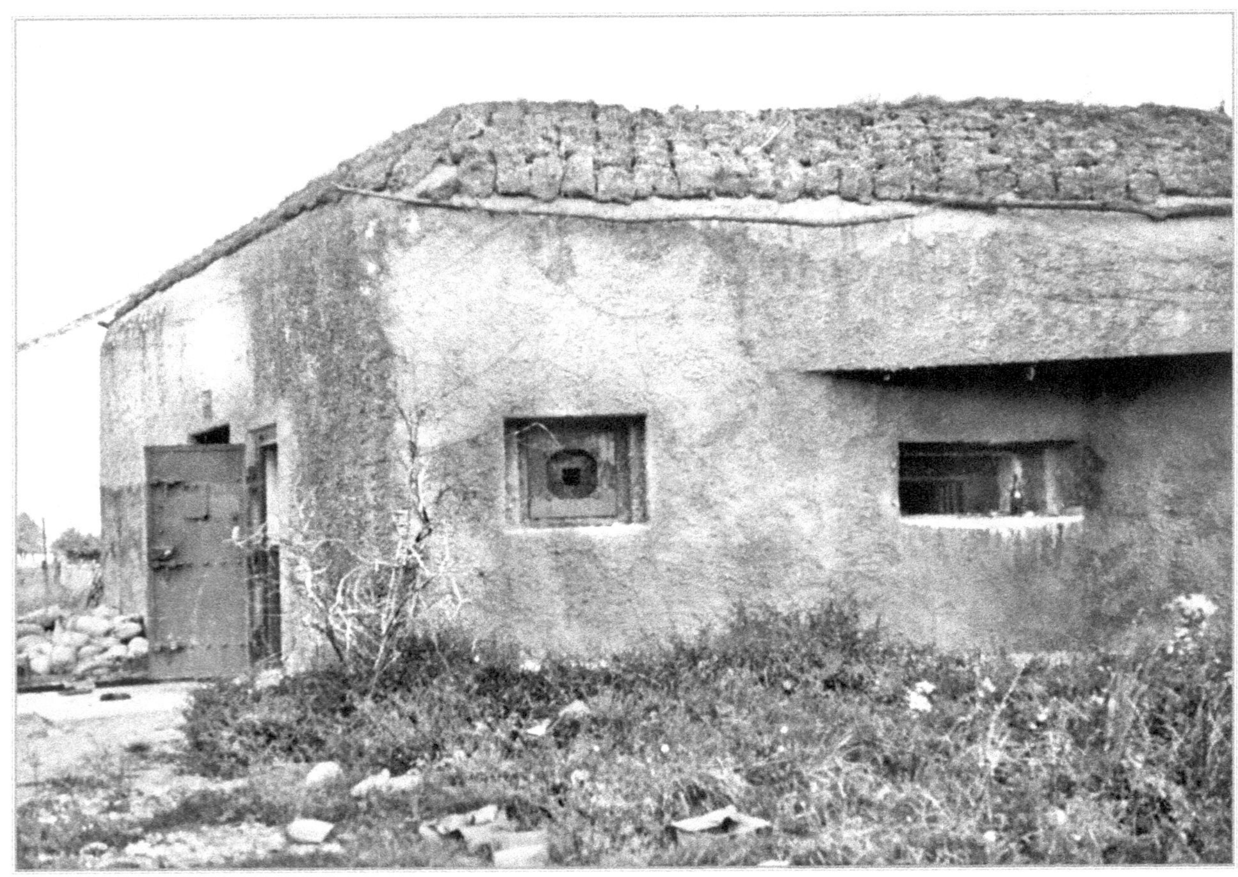

A bunker stands on France's Maginot Line (1940).

This photo contains multiple square and rectangle shapes, such as the roof, door and windows. The windows of the bunker are centered within the frame. A lone bottle stands in the window on the far right. It appears Rommel took this photo for personal interests rather than for military use.

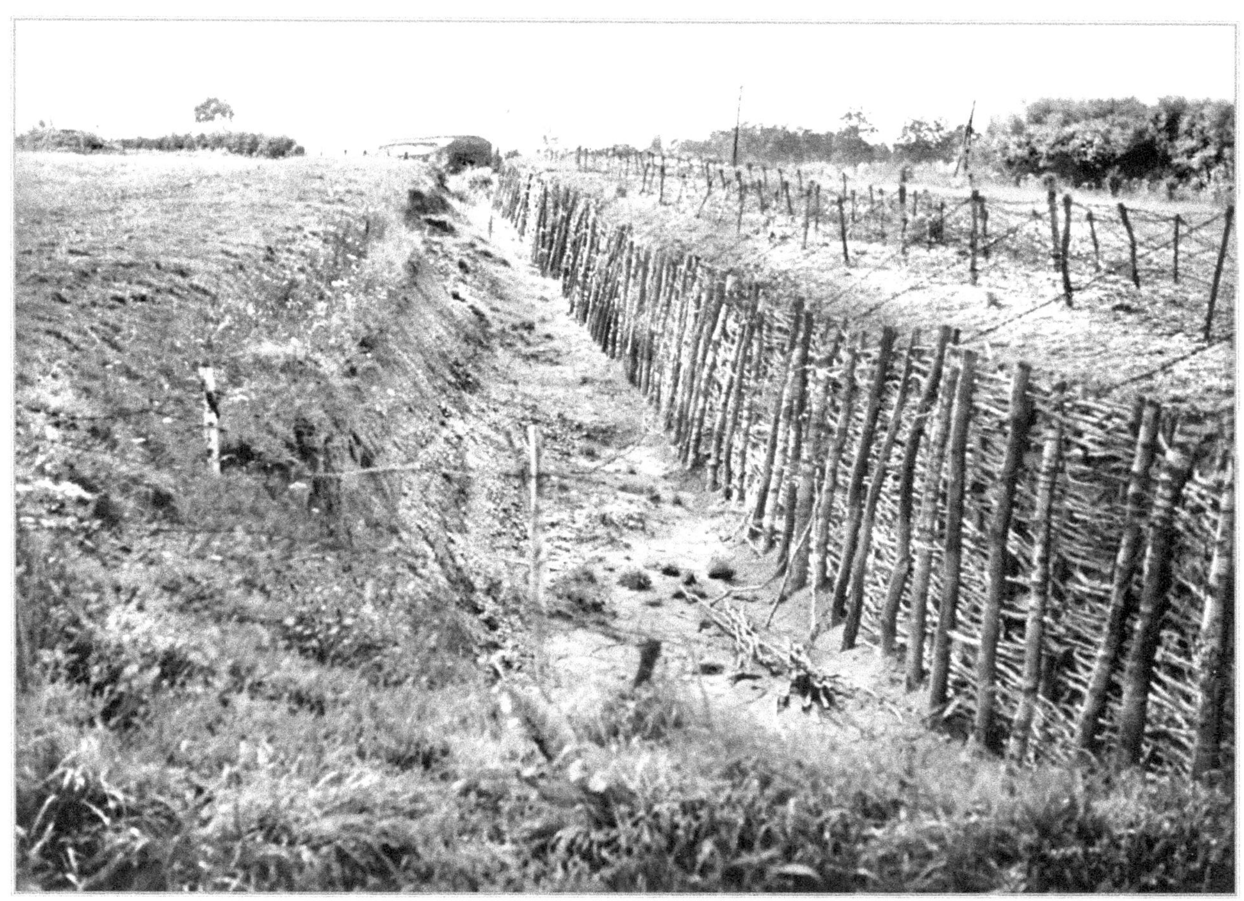

A fortified trench, with barbed wire, leads to a bunker on the Maginot Line (France, 1940).

Rommel appears to have composed this photo while standing on the grass above the trench. The trench provides a central focal point as it disappears into the horizon. Rather than taking a close-up photo of the fortifications on the right, he positioned his lens so that the surrounding areas appear equally on both sides. It is likely he took this image to illustrate the military manual he wanted to write after WWII.

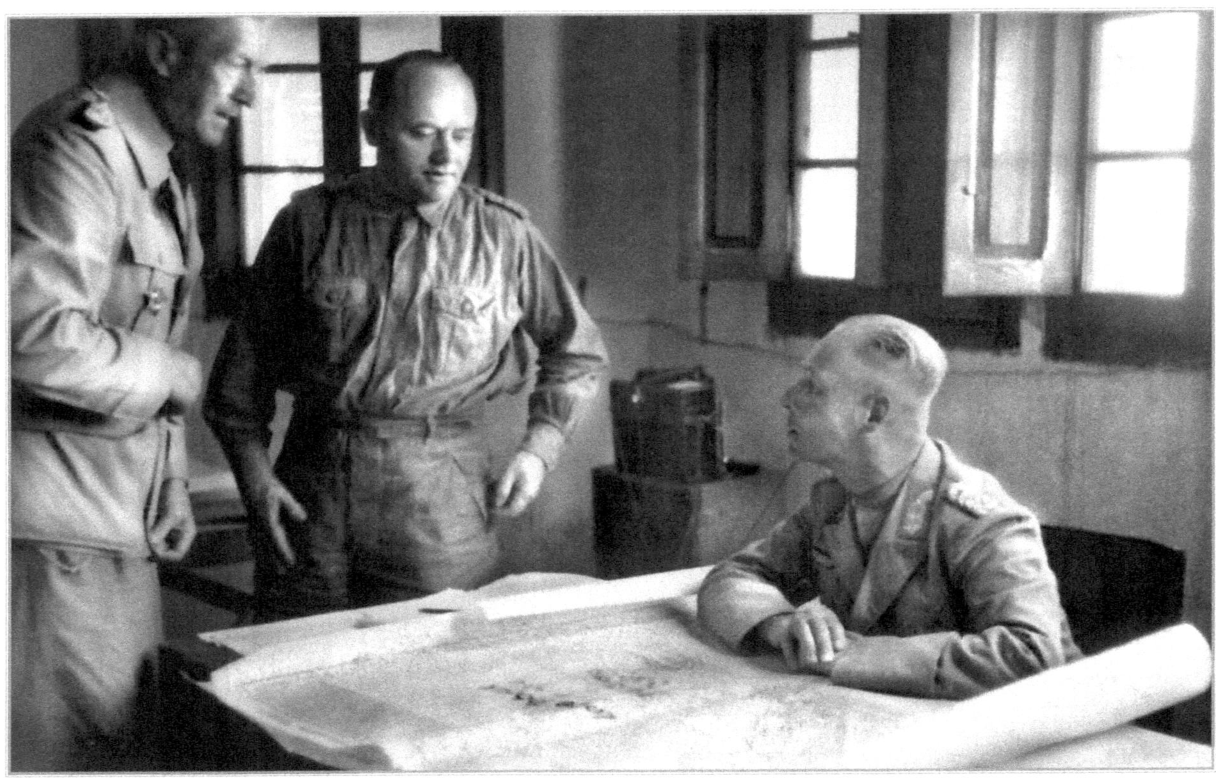

Rommel discusses military strategy with two officers in North Africa.

The spontaneous motions of the officers on the left and Rommel appearing to be in the middle of speaking would indicate this was an impromptu photo rather than a propaganda image.

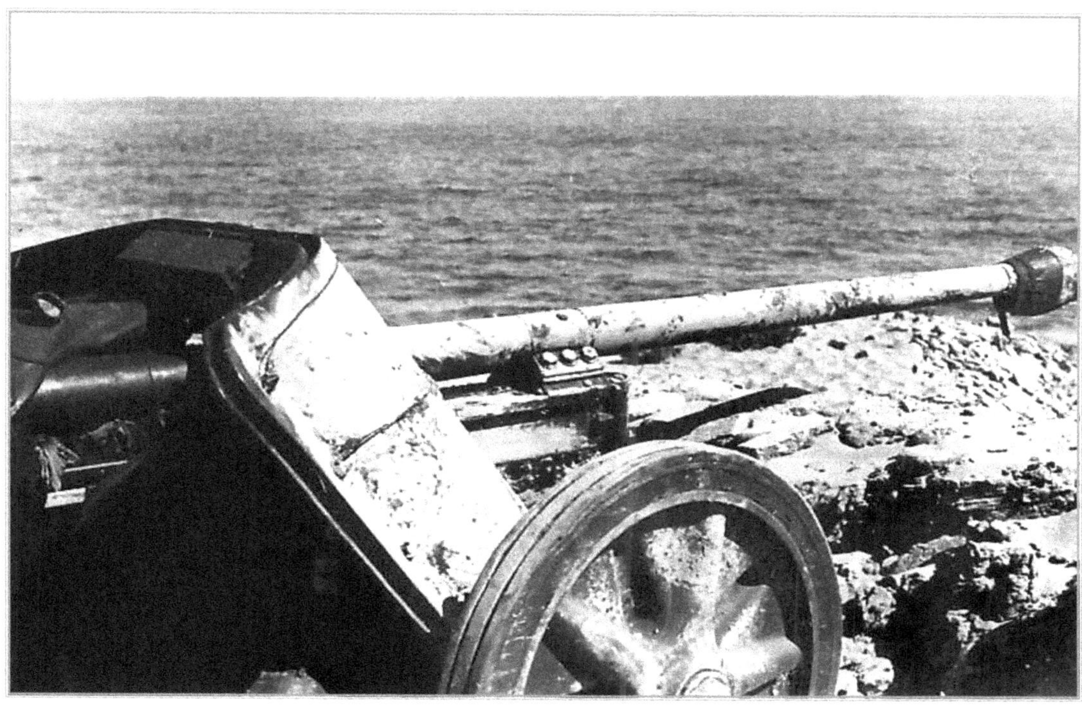

A German antitank gun sits positioned near the coast in North Africa.

This is a very striking composition. The hard mechanical surfaces of the gun contrast the softer patterns of the sand and sea.

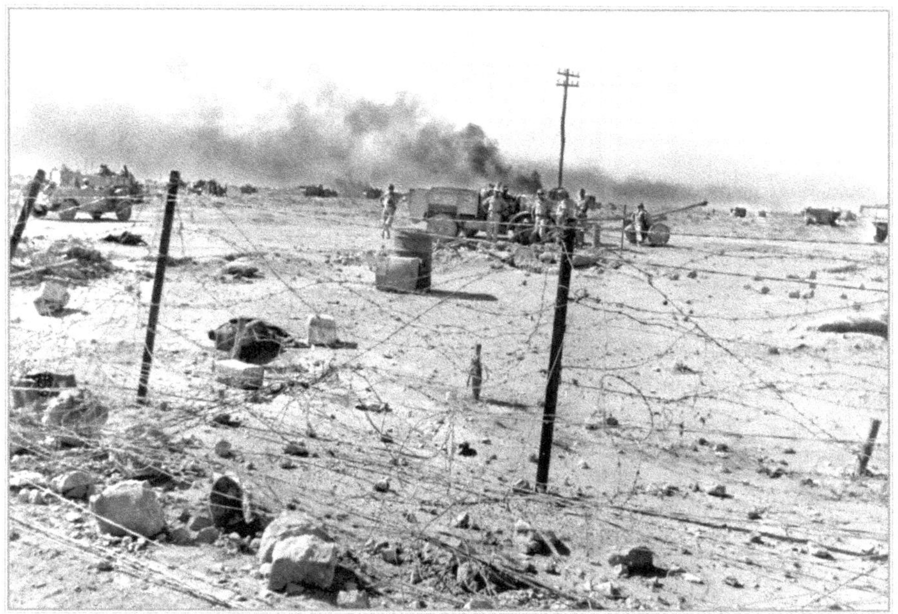

Soldiers stand beside their vehicles as black smoke billows above barbed wire in North Africa.

The soldiers in the center of the image are looking at Rommel as he takes their photo. Other vehicles congregate in the background.

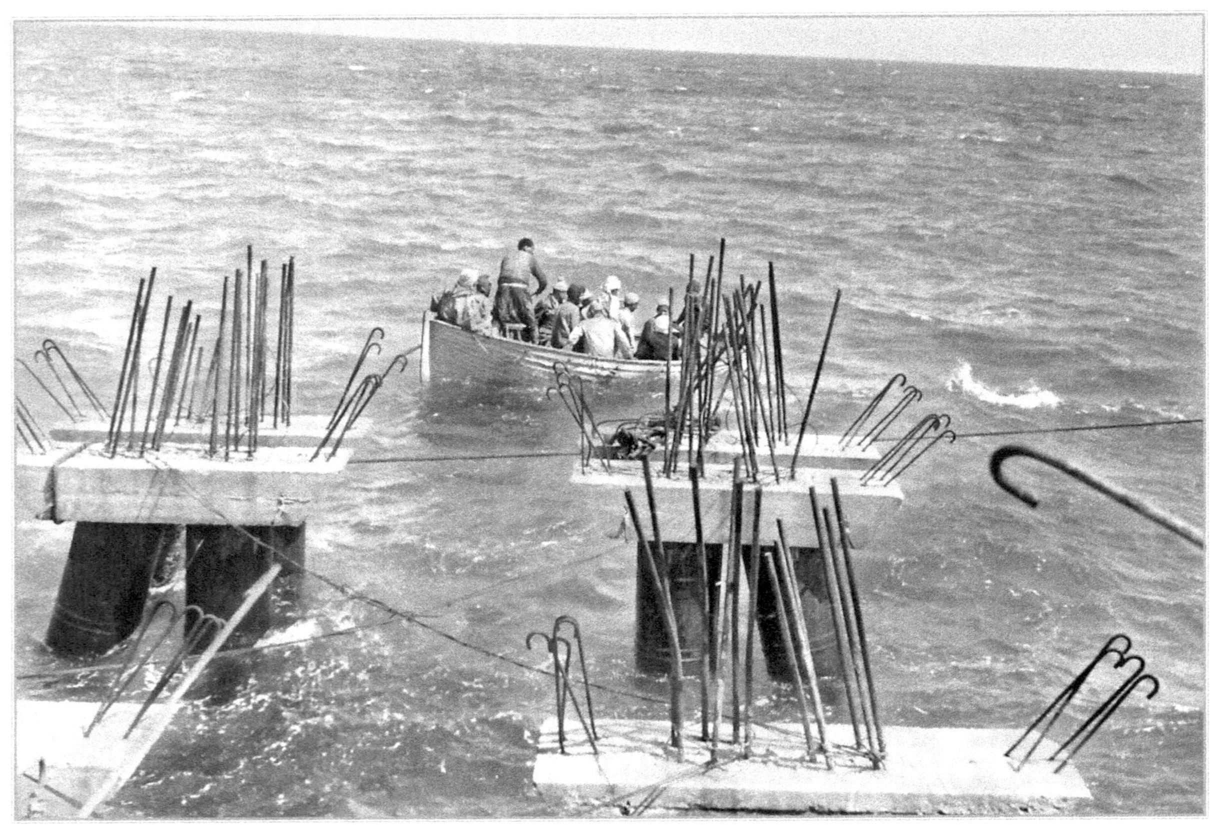

Arab men in a boat sail away from ongoing construction in the sea in North Africa.

This photo is unusual for Rommel because of its jumbled foreground. Rebar juts from concrete-topped piles. Although the boat is almost perfectly centered in the middle of the photo, it is partially obstructed from view, which is also uncharacteristic of Rommel's compositions.

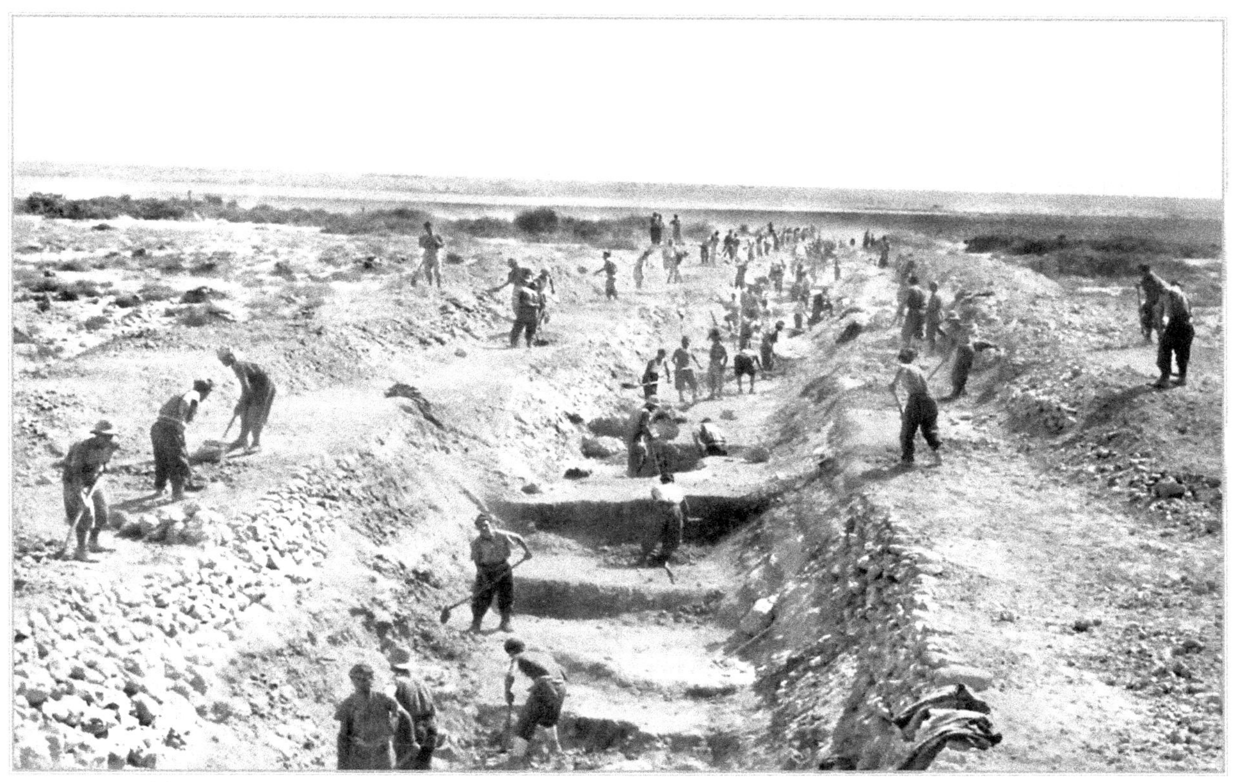

Soldiers wearing pith helmets and caps dig a trench and create concealing earthworks alongside it in North Africa.

The digging men are Germans and Italians. The trench is the main focal point as it curves and becomes smaller in the distance, where it meets vegetation on the horizon. The image is layered with many types of curving lines, such as those formed by the men, the trench, and the ridges of the earthworks.

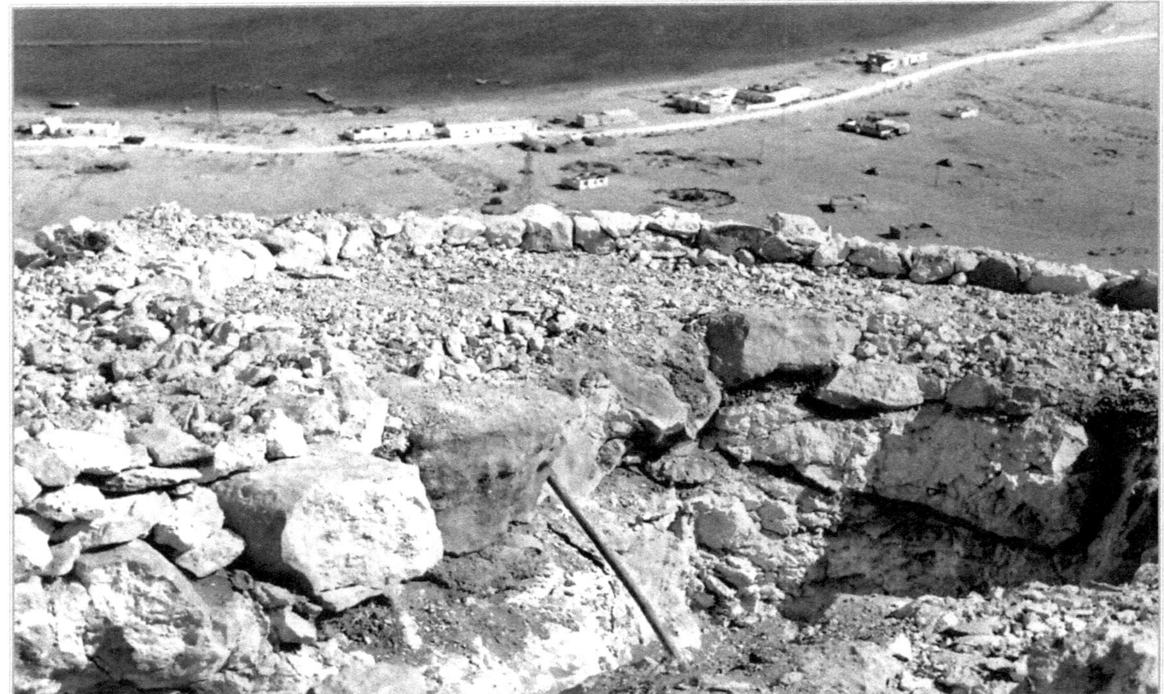

The wooden handle of a tool lays diagonally against a rocky barrier on a hill overlooking the coastline in North Africa.

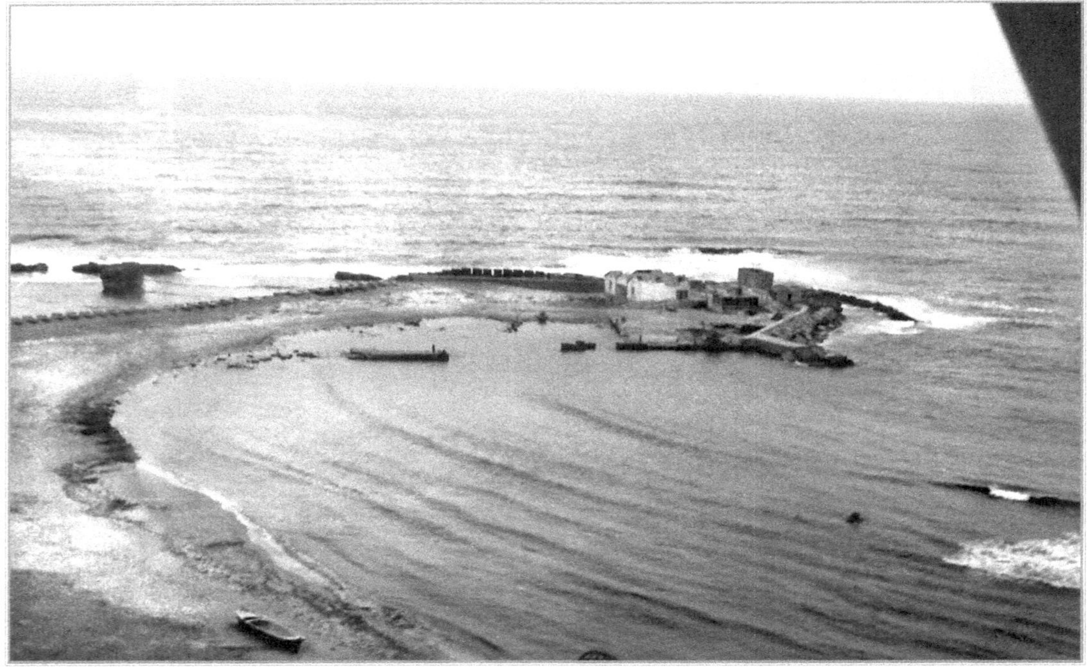

A boat sails away from a group of buildings in North Africa.

Both photos feature curving lines that dominate the compositions.

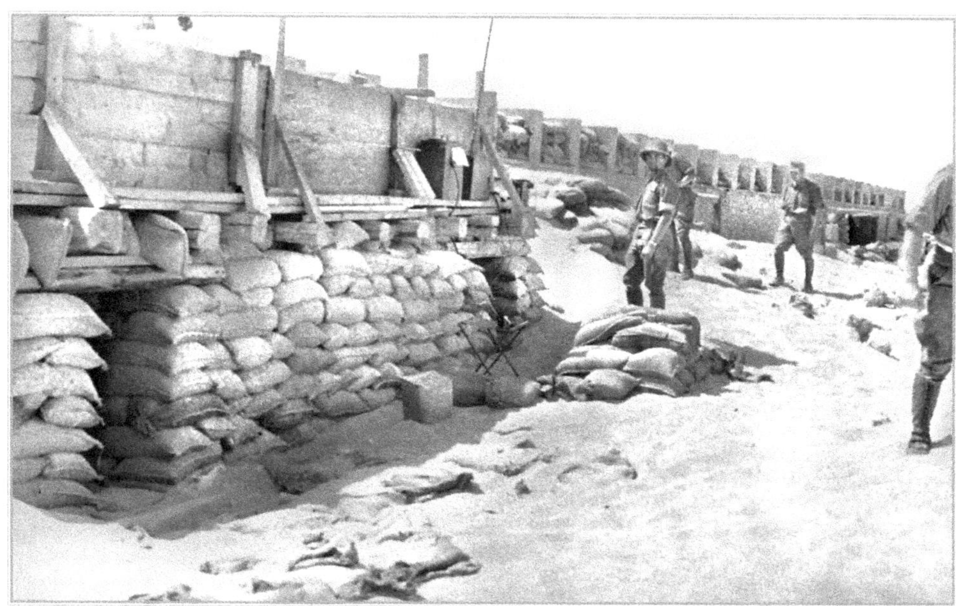

A soldier pauses near a barricade to watch his picture being taken in North Africa.

Both soldiers and barricades are visible. In the center of the frame is a folding stool with sandbags on both sides of it.

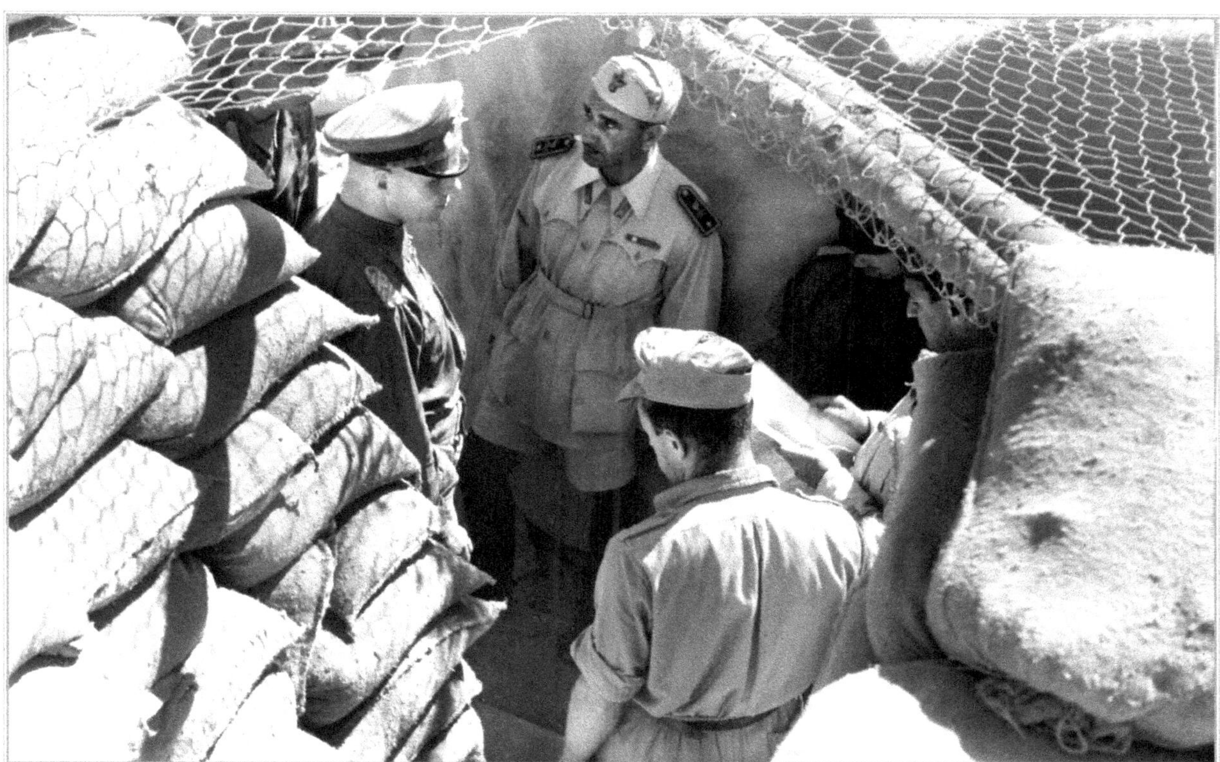

Rommel speaks with German and Italian officers in a fortified structure in North Africa.

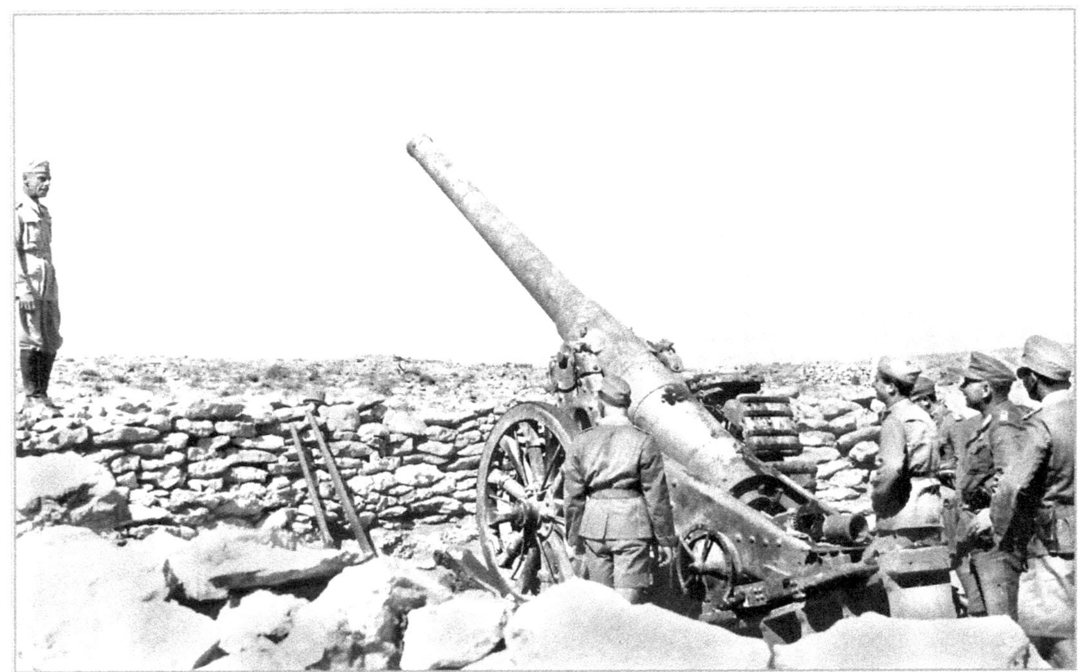

Soldiers next to an artillery gun look at an Italian officer standing on a wall in North Africa.

The rocks in the foreground indicate that Rommel stood near a wall when he took this photo.

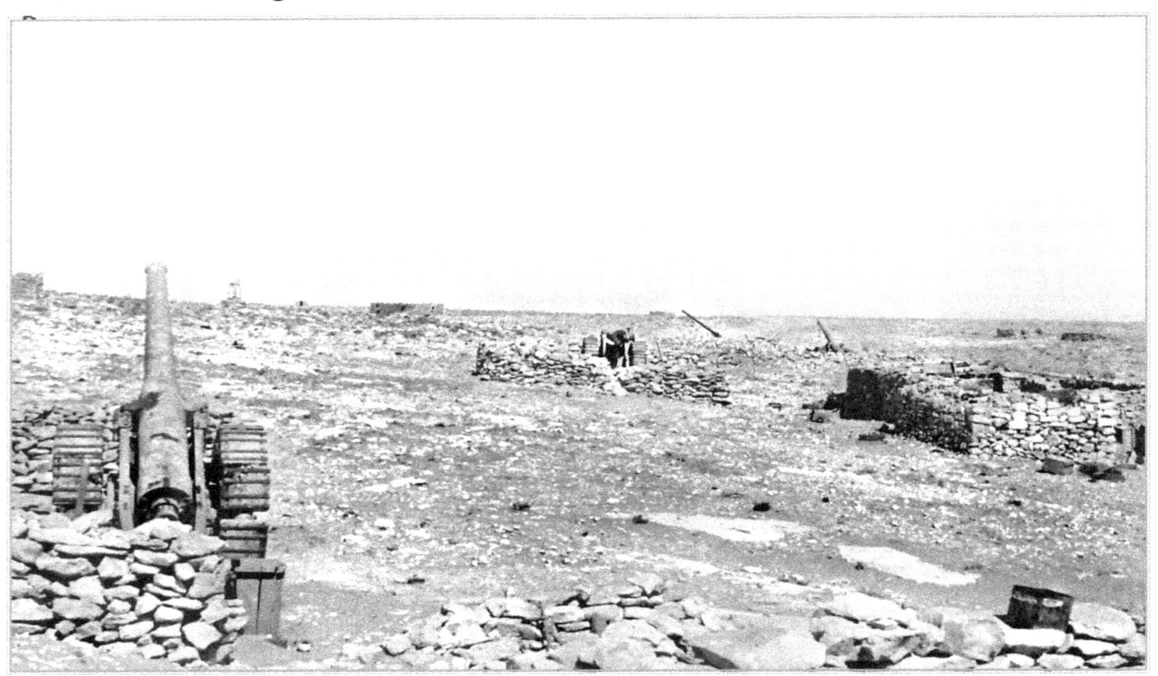

The barrels of several antitank guns point in different directions in North Africa.

This photo would appear to be unbalanced if not for the gun located perfectly in the center of the frame.

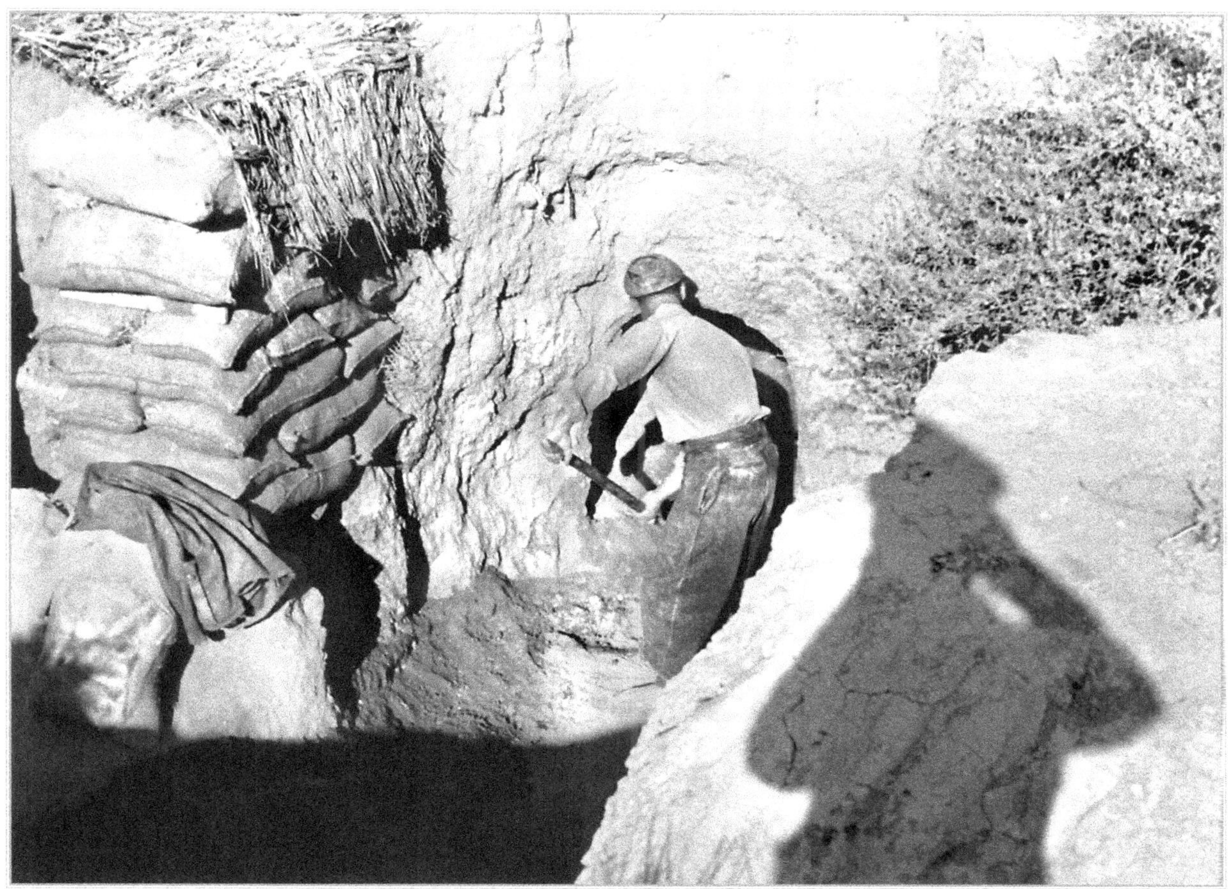

A soldier digs a hole in North Africa.

Standing on the ground above, Rommel photographs the soldier in the exact center of the composition. Rommel's shadow appears on the right. Judging from the height of the ground surface, it is clear that the hole was being dug deep. On the left side of the image, the sandbags are stacked high and covered by woven thatching. Digging in the desert was intensive labor. The soldier's shirt appears soaked with perspiration. His jacket has been removed and placed on a ledge near the sandbags.

Rommel carefully composed this photo. The top of the gun almost perfectly divides the frame between the horizon and the ground.

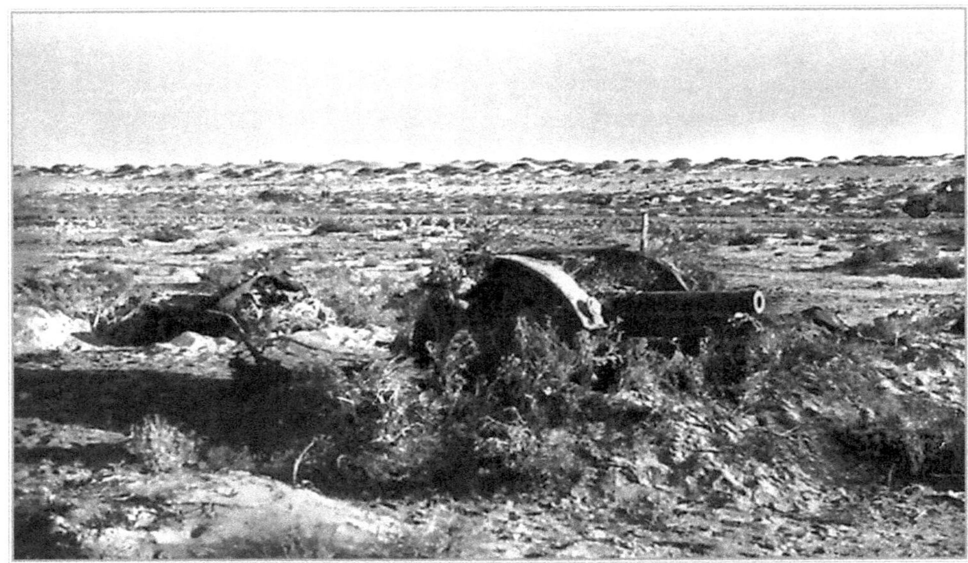

An antitank gun is obscured by camouflage in North Africa.

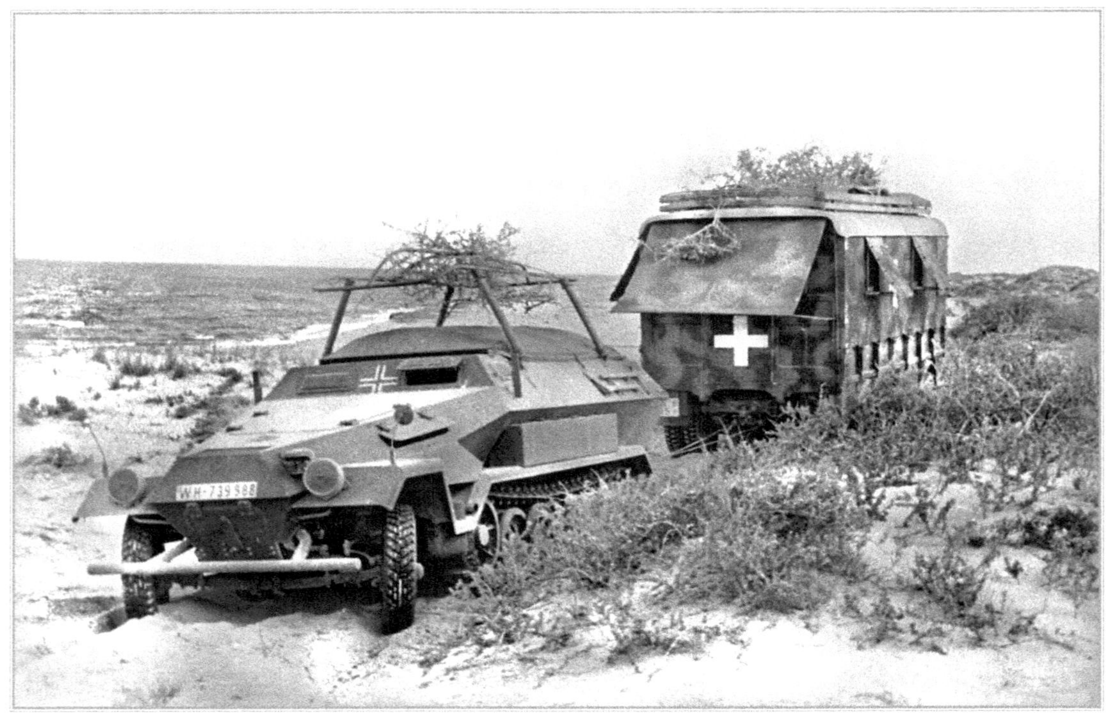

Rommel's favorite Mammoth vehicle (far right) hauls a half-track vehicle through the dense sand in North Africa.

The rugged terrain of the North African desert created problems for cars and drivers. Tires often became stuck in sand. German supply trucks also were impeded by potholes, which formed in dirt roads.

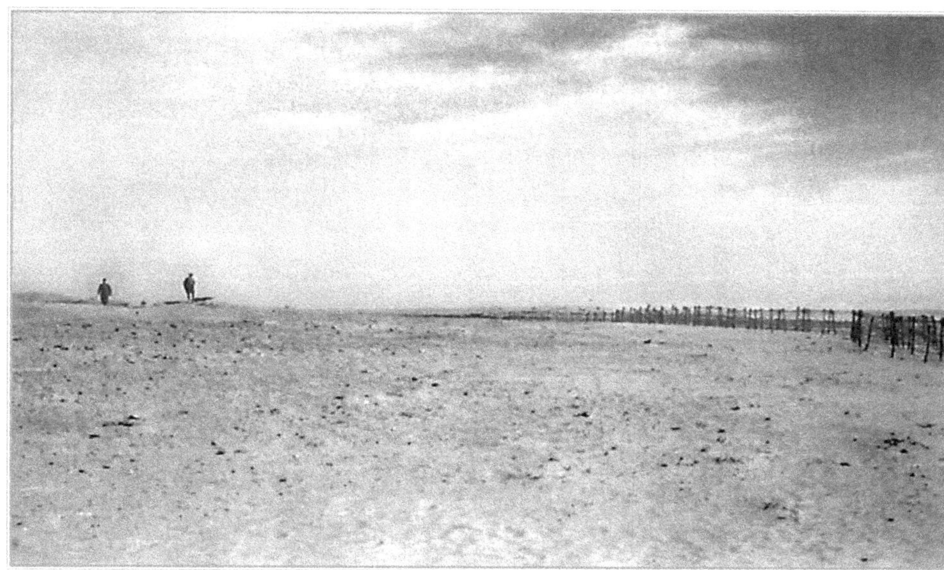

This moody photo is balanced by two men on the left and a curving barrier on the right. The barrier appears to stretch into infinity in the center of the horizon.

Two soldiers stand opposite a fortification in North Africa.

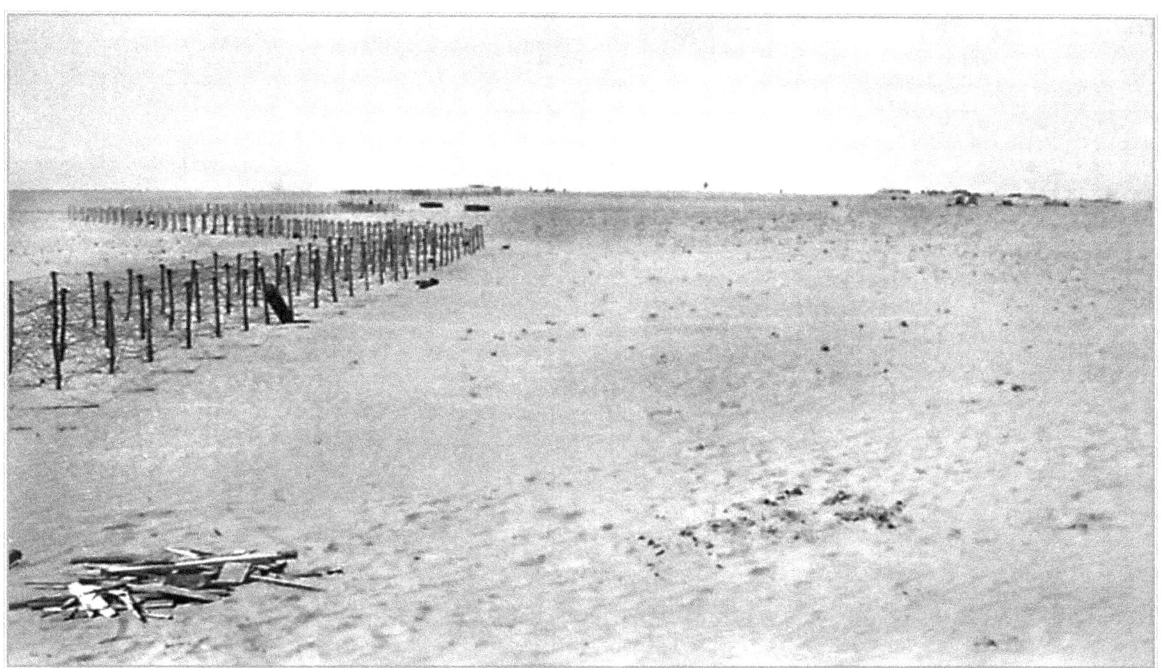

A double row of barbed wire fences (left) provide a defensive fortification for the vehicles and campsite (right) in North Africa.

In this second photo from the same film strip, Rommel uses a curving line on the left to balance the negative space of the sand.

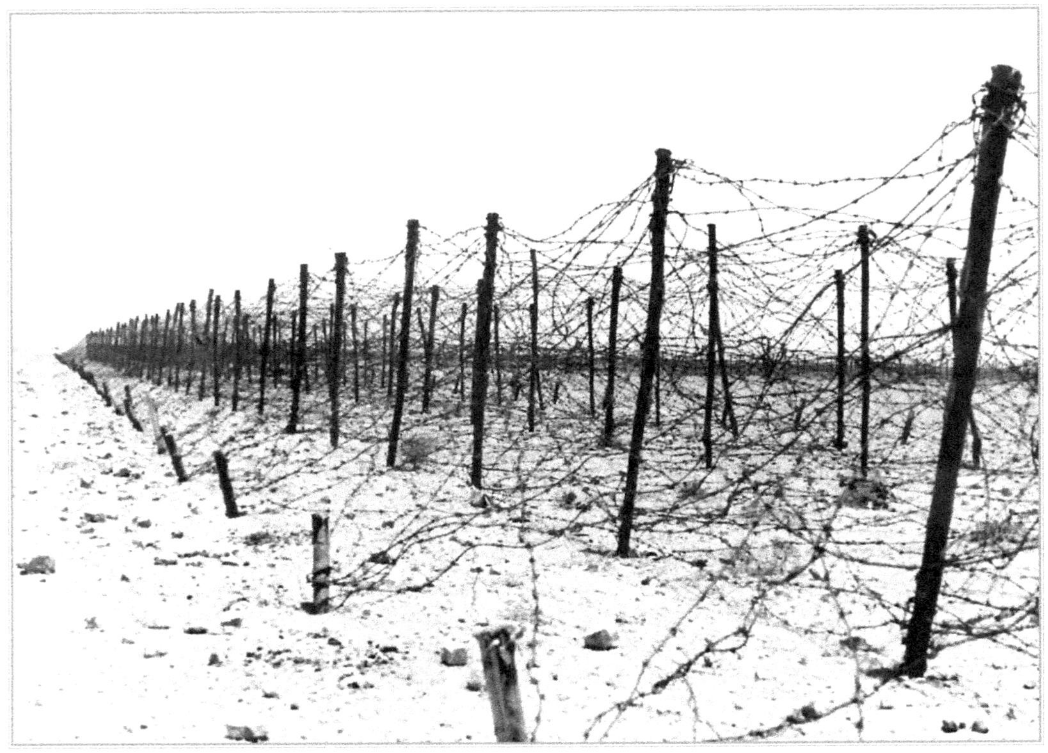

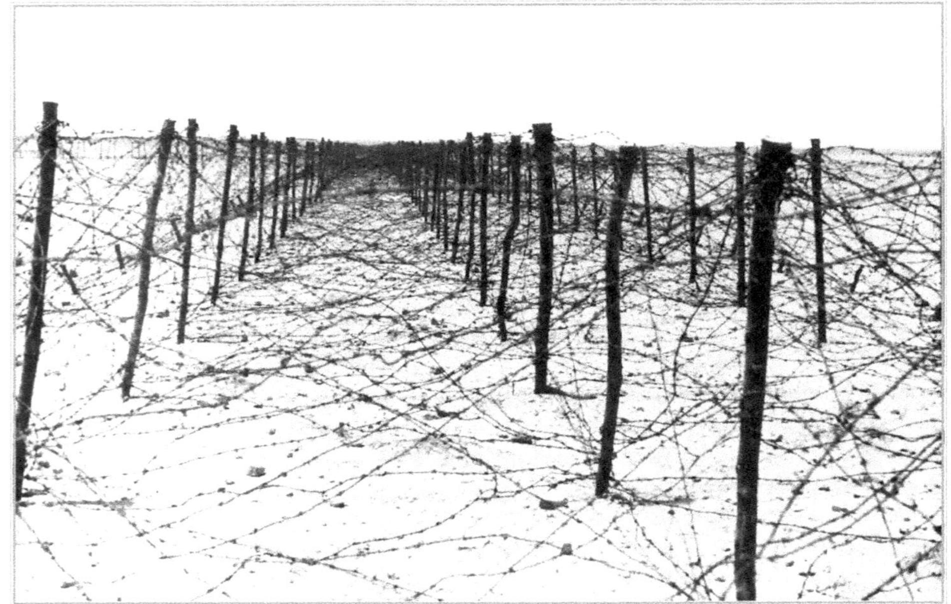

Barbed wire fortifications jut from the sand in North Africa.

The photos on both pages create an optical illusion of infinite fences. One (top) has a diagonal view, while the other (lower) features a centered view.

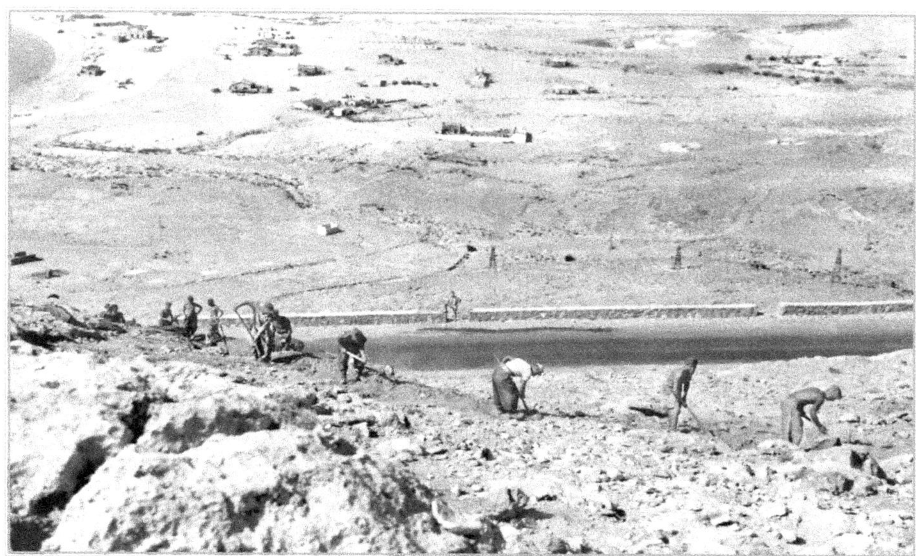

Beneath a blazing sun, soldiers dig a road in North Africa.

The men, paved road, and stone wall form intersecting lines. In the center, a lone man stands with one leg propped on the wall. Most soldiers are shirtless and tanned, indicating their frequent exposure to the hot sun.

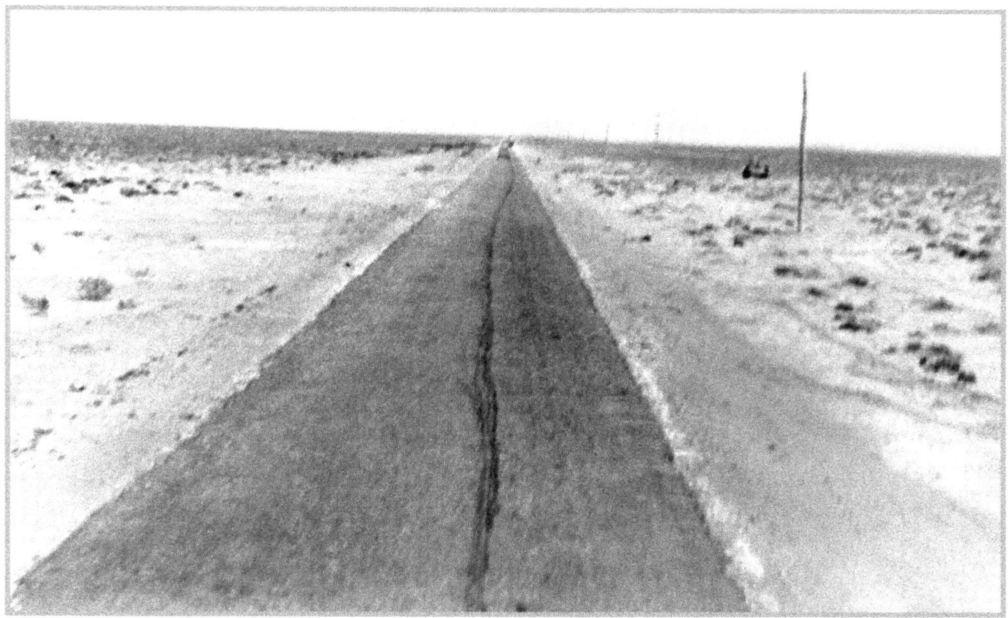

Vehicles disappear into the horizon on the Via Balbia, a road in North Africa that Rommel and his men used to transport fortifications.

Rommel took this photo from a high angle when driving ahead of other vehicles. It displays a sense of infinity. The road in the center disappears into a horizontal plane.

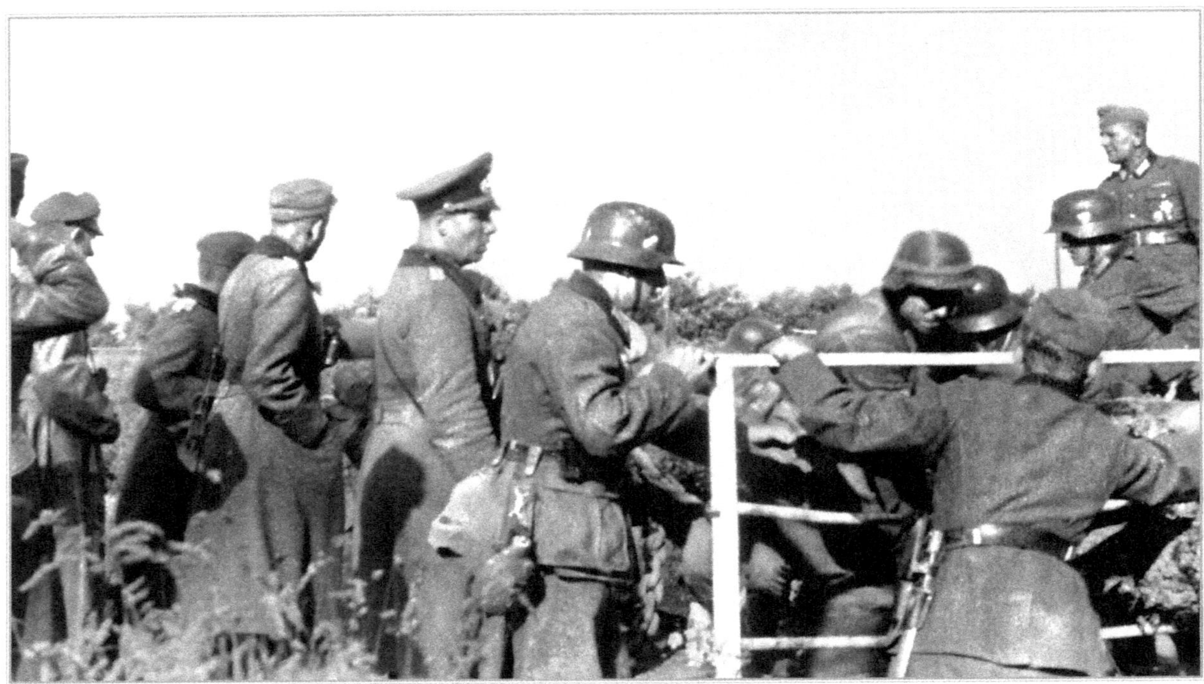

Rommel oversees the movement of a metal frame in France.

In this photo, Rommel looks toward the right, the direction where the German soldiers are moving the metal frame. The other soldiers behind him watch something else beyond the view of the camera. The officer on the far upper right is standing at a higher level than the others. His head and that of the solider in the helmet beneath him are turned in the opposition direction from Rommel's gaze. This photo in Rommel's collection was likely taken by an amateur photographer rather than a propaganda professional, particularly since Rommel's mouth is parted, giving him a less polished appearance.

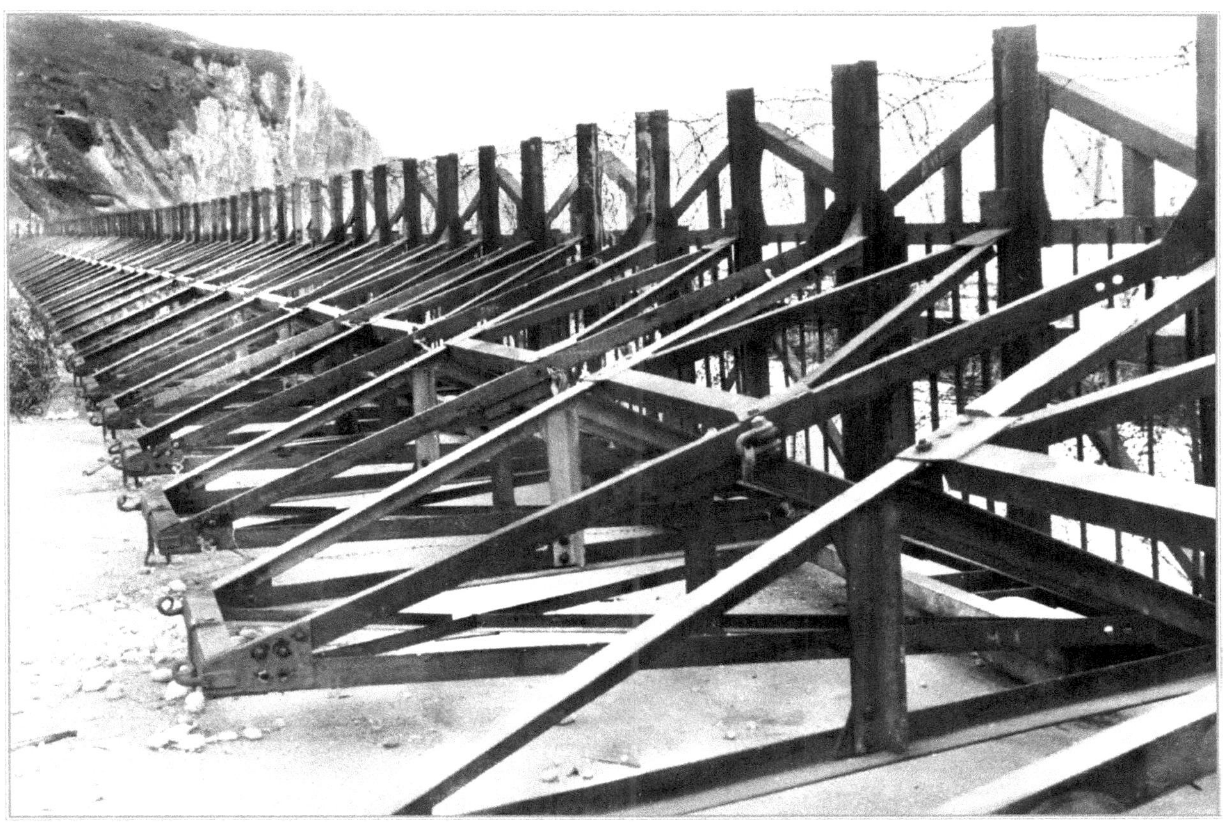

A view of Rommel's fortifications along the Normandy coast before the Allied Invasion of Europe in 1944.

This photo of beach fortifications is more technical than aesthetic in nature. Rommel could have intended it for use in the military manual that he planned to write. Instead of taking the photo from behind the barrier facing toward the coast, Rommel captured a close-up of the fortifications at a diagonal angle. The tops of the barrier fill the frame on the right, but disappear into infinity as it diminishes in size to the left.

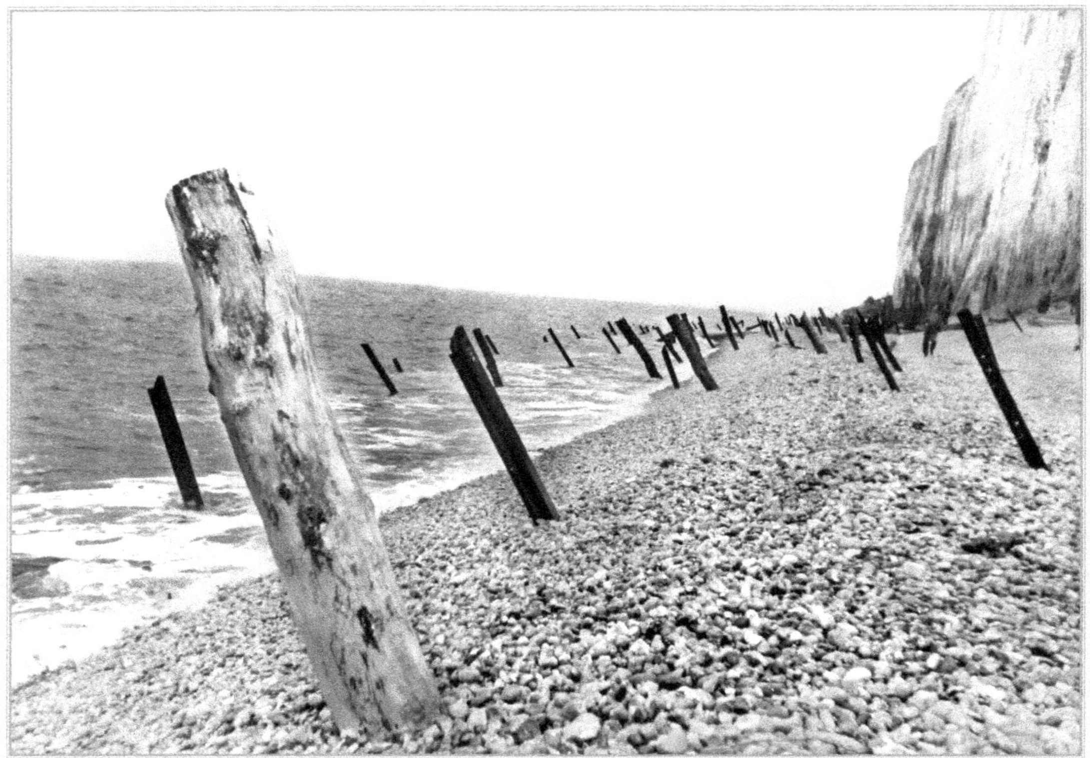

Rommel's fortifications stand on the northern beaches of France preceding the Allied invasion in 1944.

At the time these pictures were taken, Rommel had reached a major turning point in his life. A series of difficult events had changed him—he was no longer the optimistic Panzer General who had led a lightning charge of tanks across France in 1940.

Rommel had recently recovered from a serious illness. While in North Africa, he caught diphtheria which, left untreated, caused him severe intestinal problems. Unable to rest due to his constant activity on the frontlines, Rommel's physical fatigue and mental stress worsened his condition. His symptoms became severe and resulted in dangerously low blood pressure, weakening Rommel to the point of exhaustion and causing him to have blackouts on the battlefield.

While struggling with his health, Rommel suffered a bitter defeat in North Africa. Following a series of military crises, Hitler removed Rommel from command of the Afrika Korps. Rommel found himself stranded in Europe while his entire army, including his former staff officers and military comrades, surrendered to the Allies and were sent to POW camps in the United States and Canada. Rommel was embittered by this ultimate separation from his troops, a sentiment he expressed frequently in his personal letters and writings.

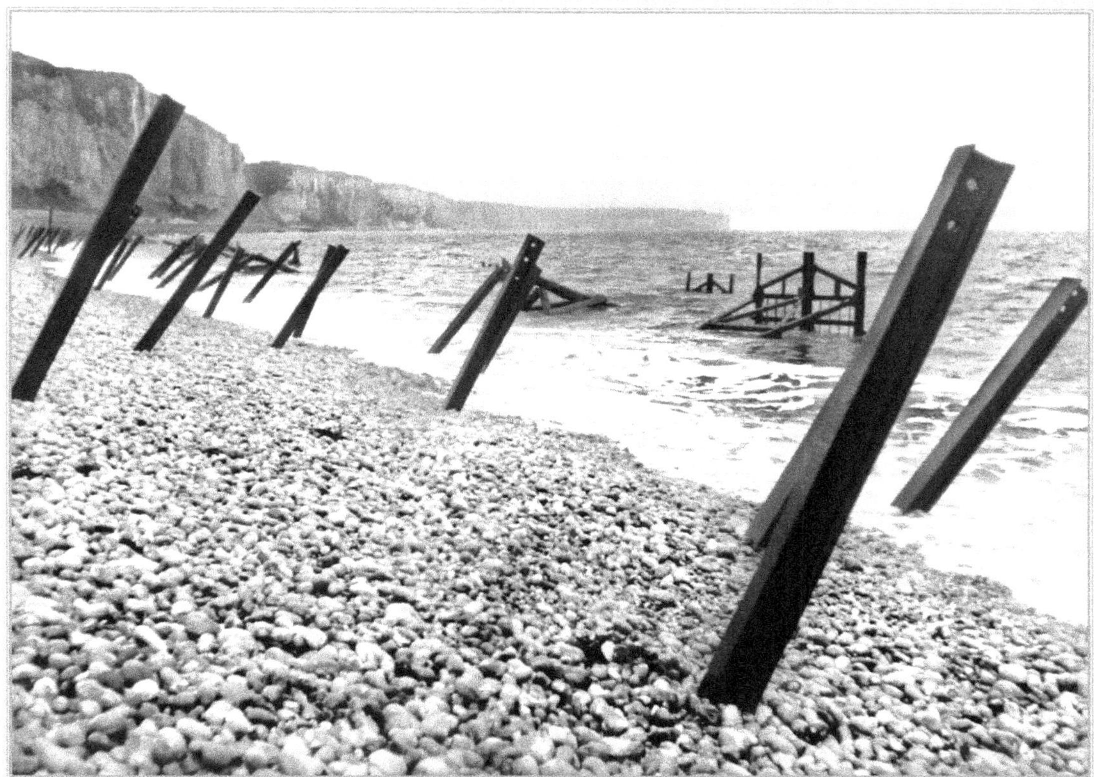

Both of these photos of beach fortifications reflect a somber tone.

Rommel came into constant conflict with Nazi Party members, military officers of the High Command, and also with Hitler himself. These disillusionments and disputes occurred during Rommel's time in North Africa and intensified in 1943 during Axis operations in Italy.

By 1944, Rommel had become thoroughly opposed to Hitler. Given his principles as a professional soldier, Rommel hesitated to take a direct role in overthrowing his country's government. However, his sense of patriotism forced him to take action.

At the time these photos were taken in 1944, Rommel, who was in charge of strengthening and defending the Atlantic Wall, was making plans to conclude a separate peace with the Allies. While opposed to the idea of assassinating Hitler, he also was in contact with conspirators who intended to remove the Nazis from power. Rommel's decision to act against the Nazi regime and its leader cost him his life later this same year.

5

Military Maneuvers

Tobruks

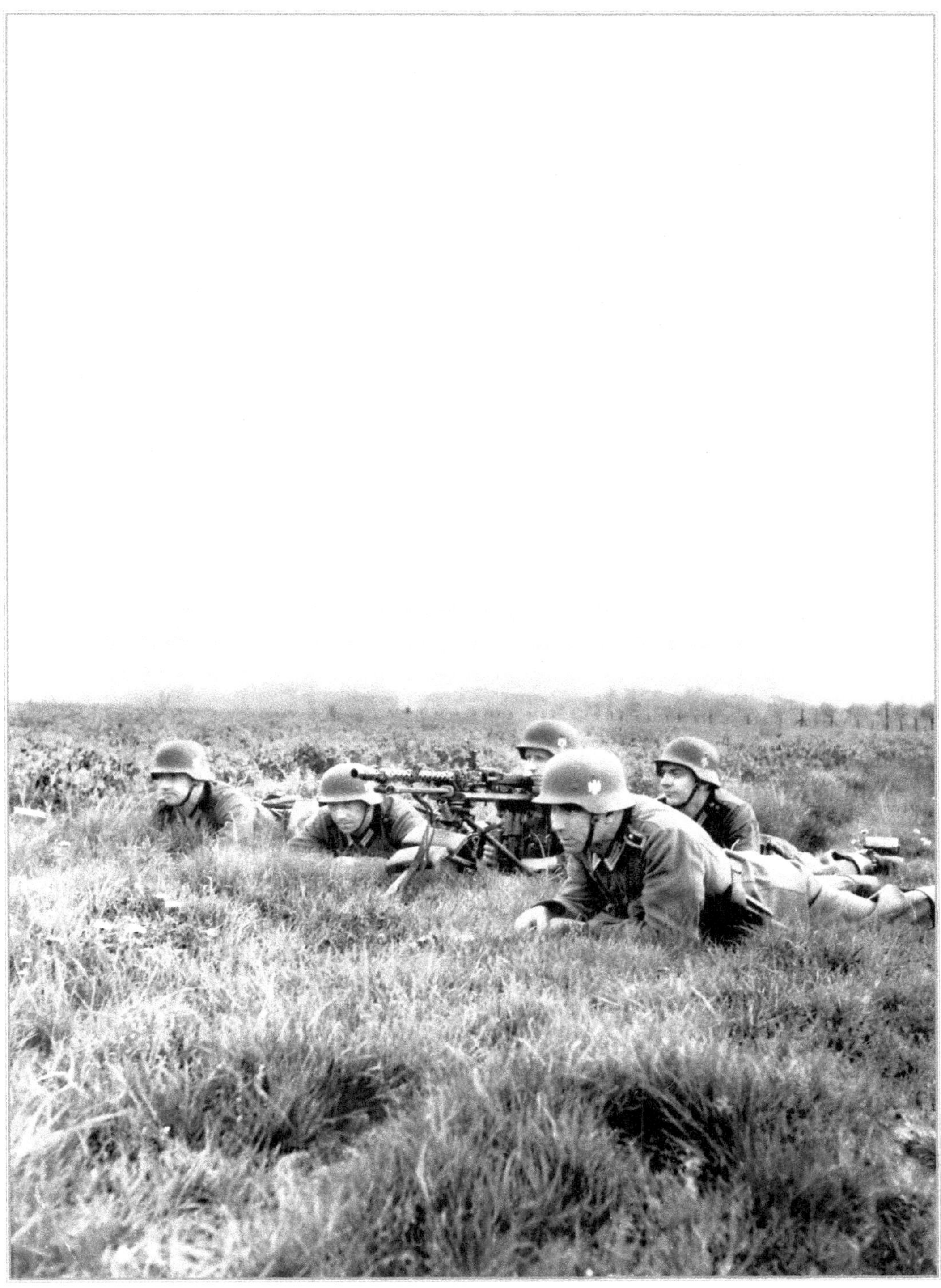

German soldiers lie in position beside a machine gun in a field in France.

Rommel's focal point is the gun barrel with soldiers on each side.

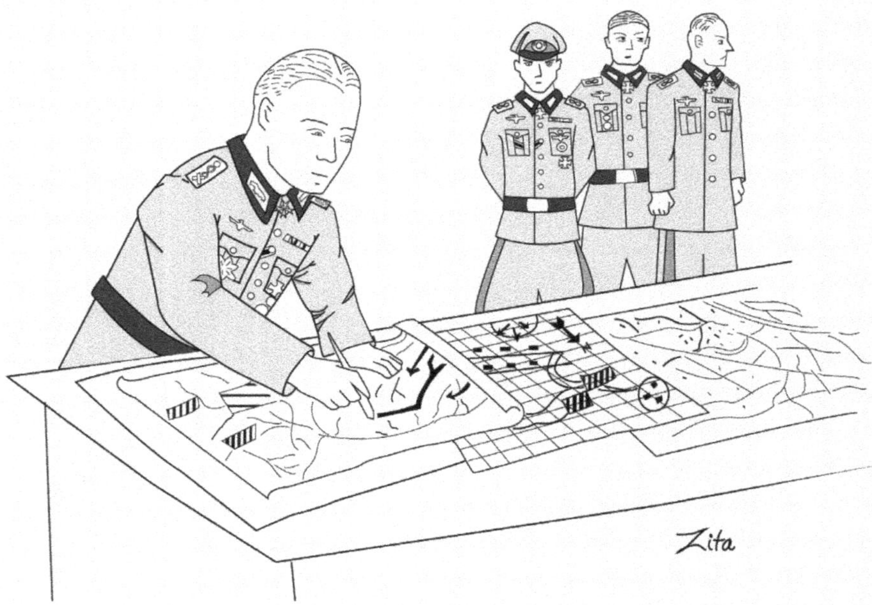

Rommel is known as a strategic and tactical genius. During his lifetime, he displayed daring and cleverness on the battlefield, which earned him a formidable reputation. His methods are still studied in military schools today.

As a commander, Rommel often adopted unconventional approaches to situations. He believed strongly in being a hands-on leader and wished to have complete freedom of movement. He devised many new techniques to make actions flexible, fast, and adaptive—both on the battlefield and behind the lines. He often was criticized by military administration for not following standard rules. However, Rommel's ideas usually had winning results and earned him great fame, irritating his critics and resulting in jealousy among his peers.

Many of Rommel's military superiors belonged to an elite, close-knit group of officers from aristocratic families. Many were landowners with titles who came from the German Kingdom of Prussia; collectively they are sometimes known as *Junker*, or members of the Officer Corps. Members of the Junker class looked down on Rommel because of his Swabian origin and lack of pedigree, and dismissed him as an interloper. They also disapproved of his creative military ideas.

Yet, Rommel was a typical Swabian. People of Swabia are recognized in Germany for their ingenuity and ability to create and improve things. Swabians have made numerous contributions to the sciences and technology. They are known for using their imagination to develop innovative solutions to problems and invent items with practical applications.

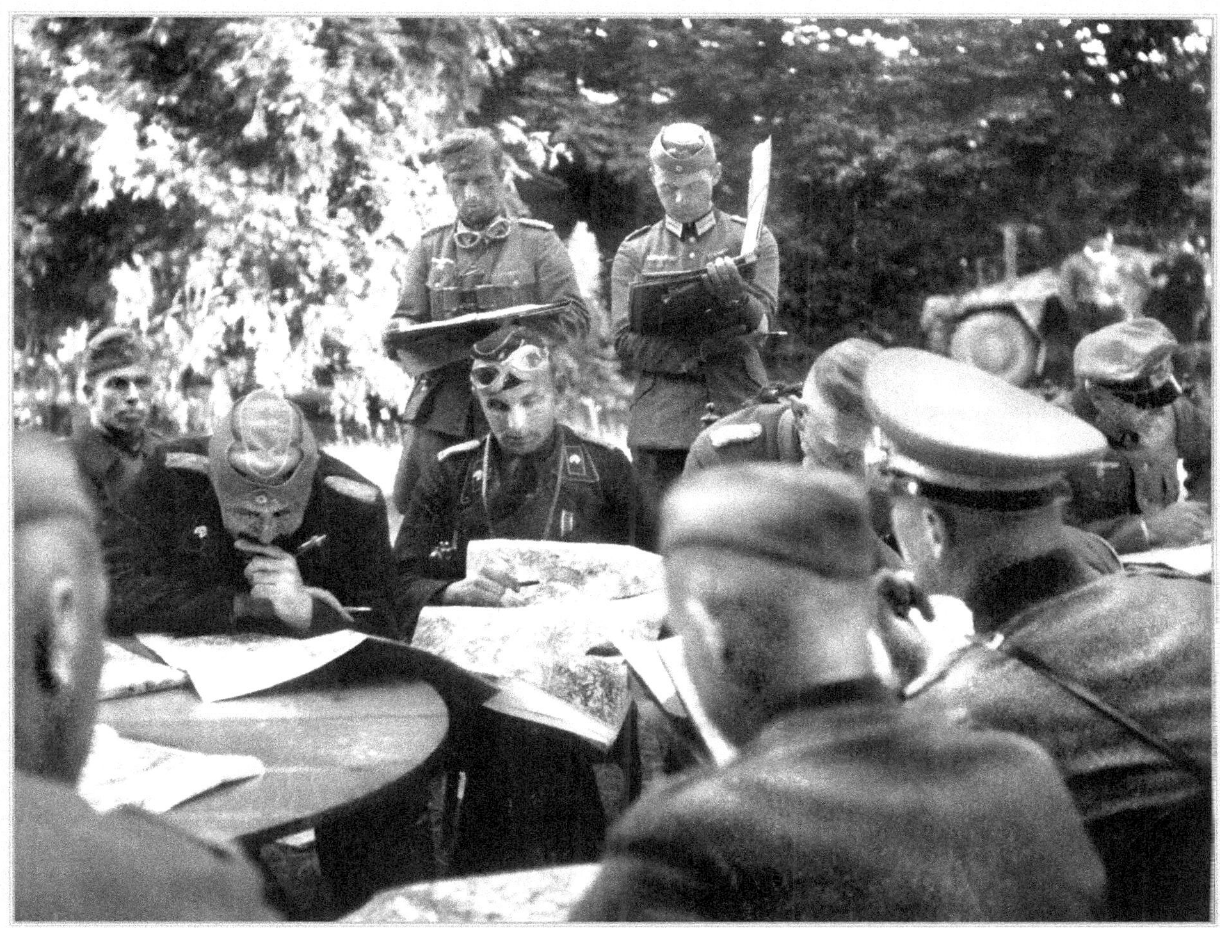

Rommel (wearing a hat on the far right) participates in a military briefing in France.

The strap of Rommel's camera is slung around the back of his uniform as he sits among officers during the briefing. The fact that he wore his camera in this way shows he had it constantly with him and in easy reach for taking photographs at a moment's notice. This depiction of Rommel with his camera is but one example of how photography was an integral part of his life.

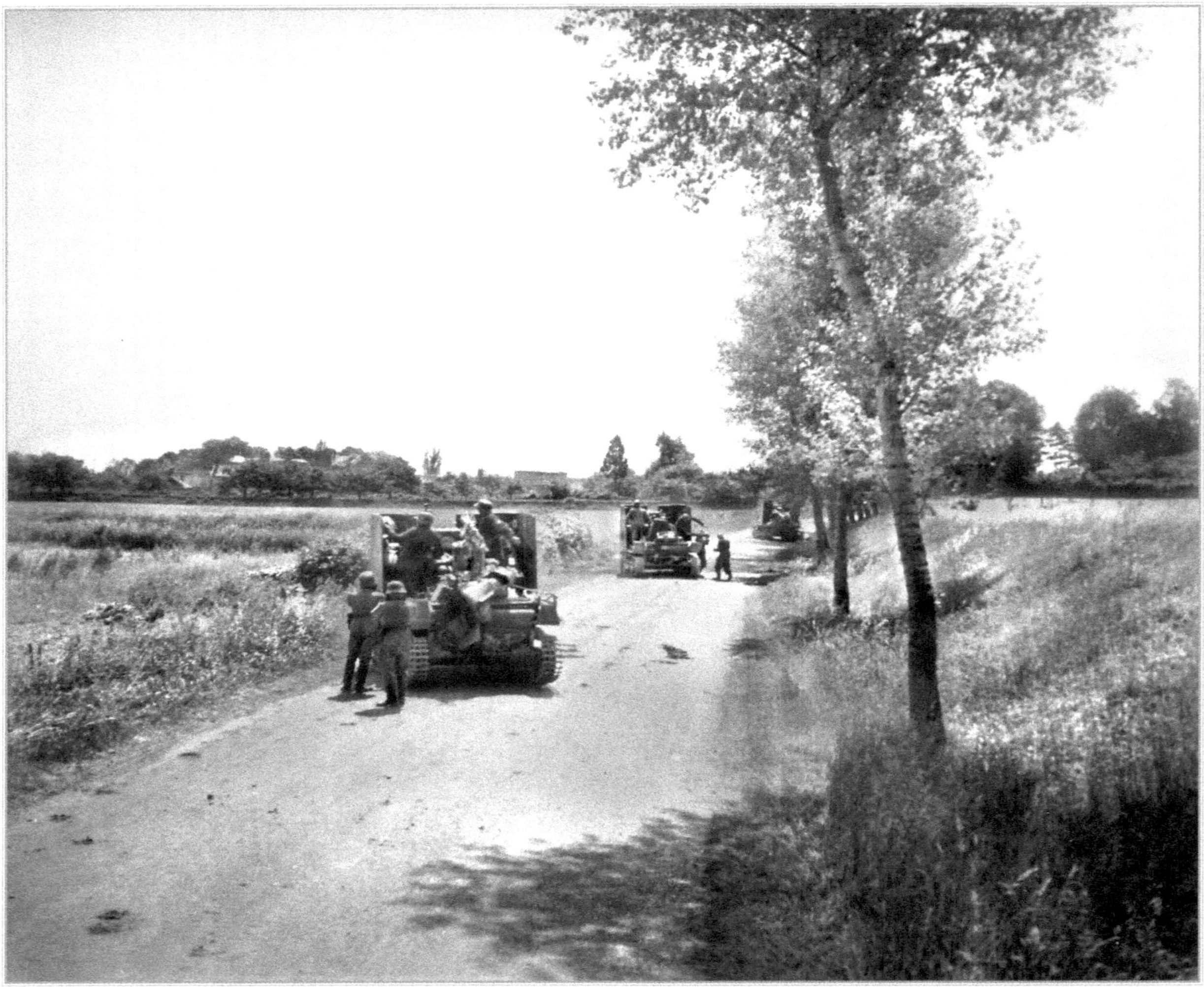

German soldiers in three howitzers stop in a road and engage in a firefight in France (extracted close-up below).

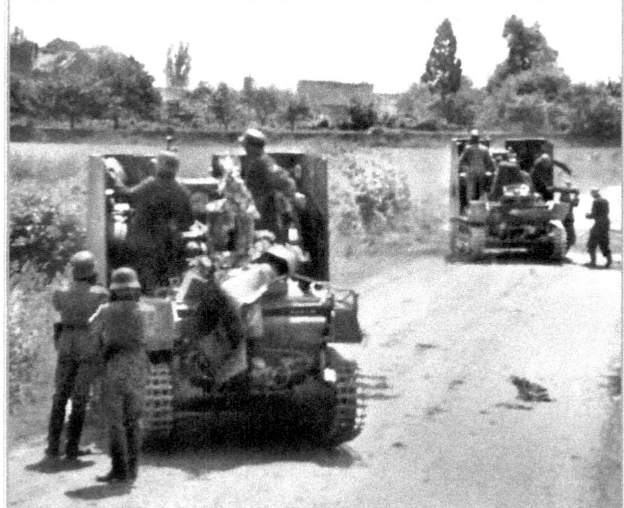

The perspective of this photo suggests Rommel snapped it while riding on top of an armored vehicle. The angle of the camera appears to be higher than street level and pointed down slightly at the men on the road. The men look anxiously out towards the field to the left. Two helmeted soldiers, standing near the foremost howitzer, cover their ears—indicating that the gun has just been fired. Down the road, soldiers hurry to load ammunition into the second howitzer.

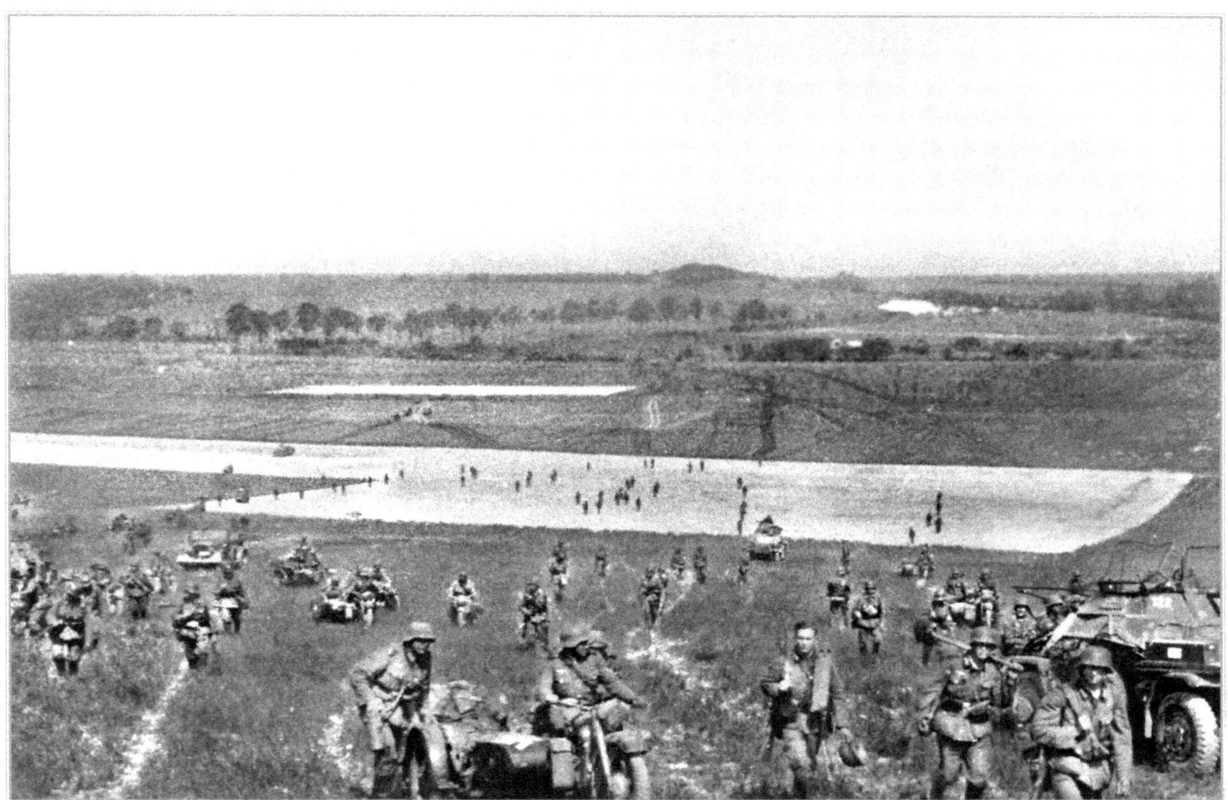

German soldiers march up a hill in France.

Rommel seems to have been standing at the top of the hill looking down at the men when he took this photo. Although some of the German soldiers are traveling in motorcycles with sidecars, they don't appear to be in a hurry. The soldiers marching alongside the Panzer (right) seem to be keeping a steady pace.

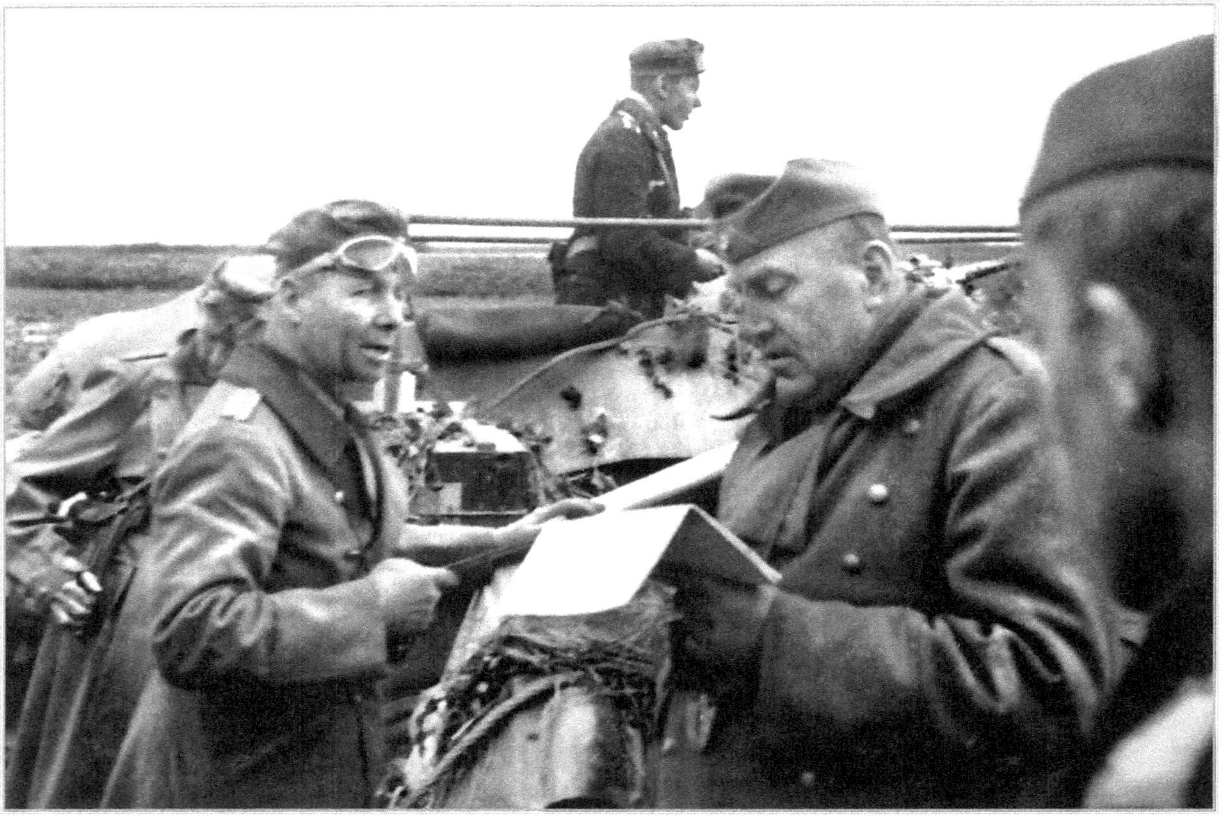

Rommel, wearing goggles, converses with an officer in France.

This candid photo shows a disheveled-looking Rommel speaking to another officer beside an armored vehicle. Rommel is wearing a cloth cap and goggles. His face appears dusty, with white stripe marks around his nose and eyes where his goggles previously were. The German officers in this image were likely his aides.

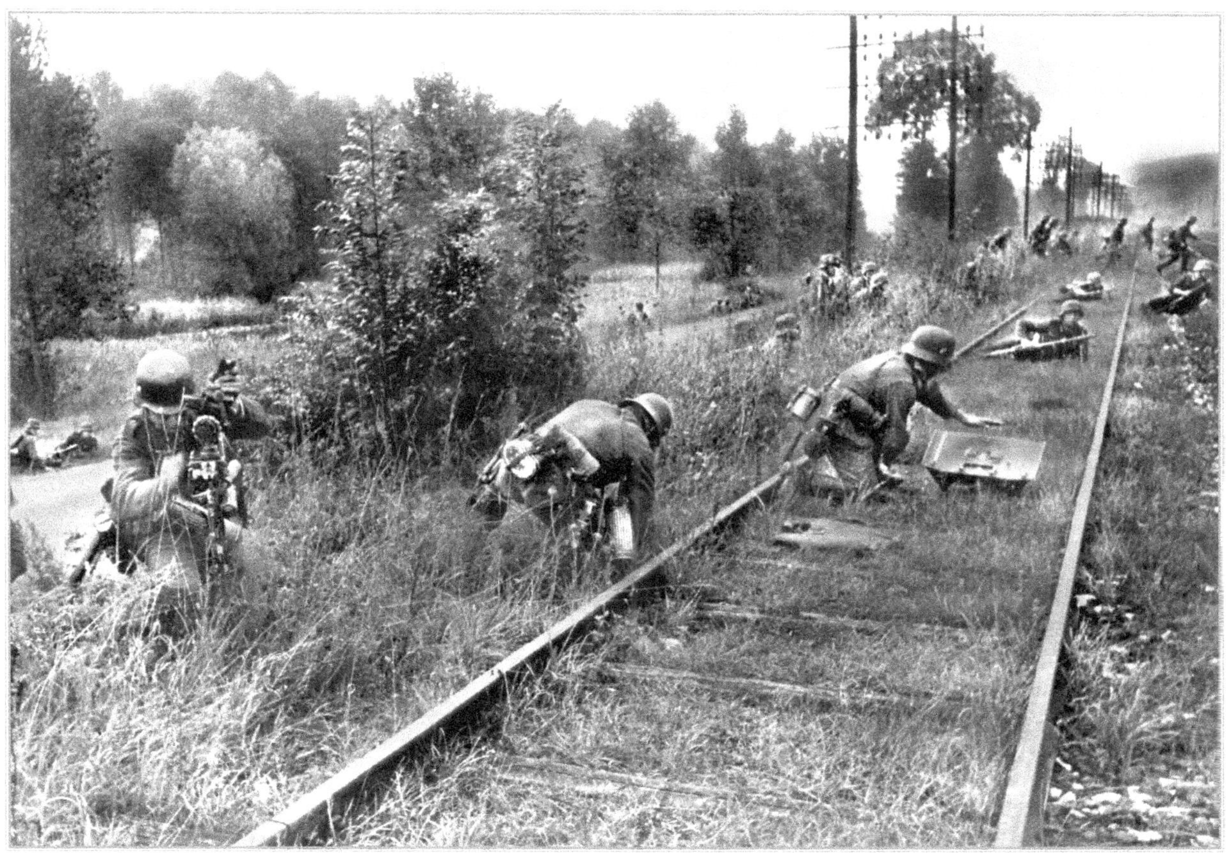

German soldiers rush over train tracks in France.

The soldiers fill the composition. They appear in the foreground, middle ground, and background. The soldiers are visible as they climb over a road (far left), cross the tracks in the foreground, and make their way towards a hill (right). This action photo has a strong diagonal element—the train tracks that dominate the front of the image form a diagonal line which decreases into the background on the upper right.

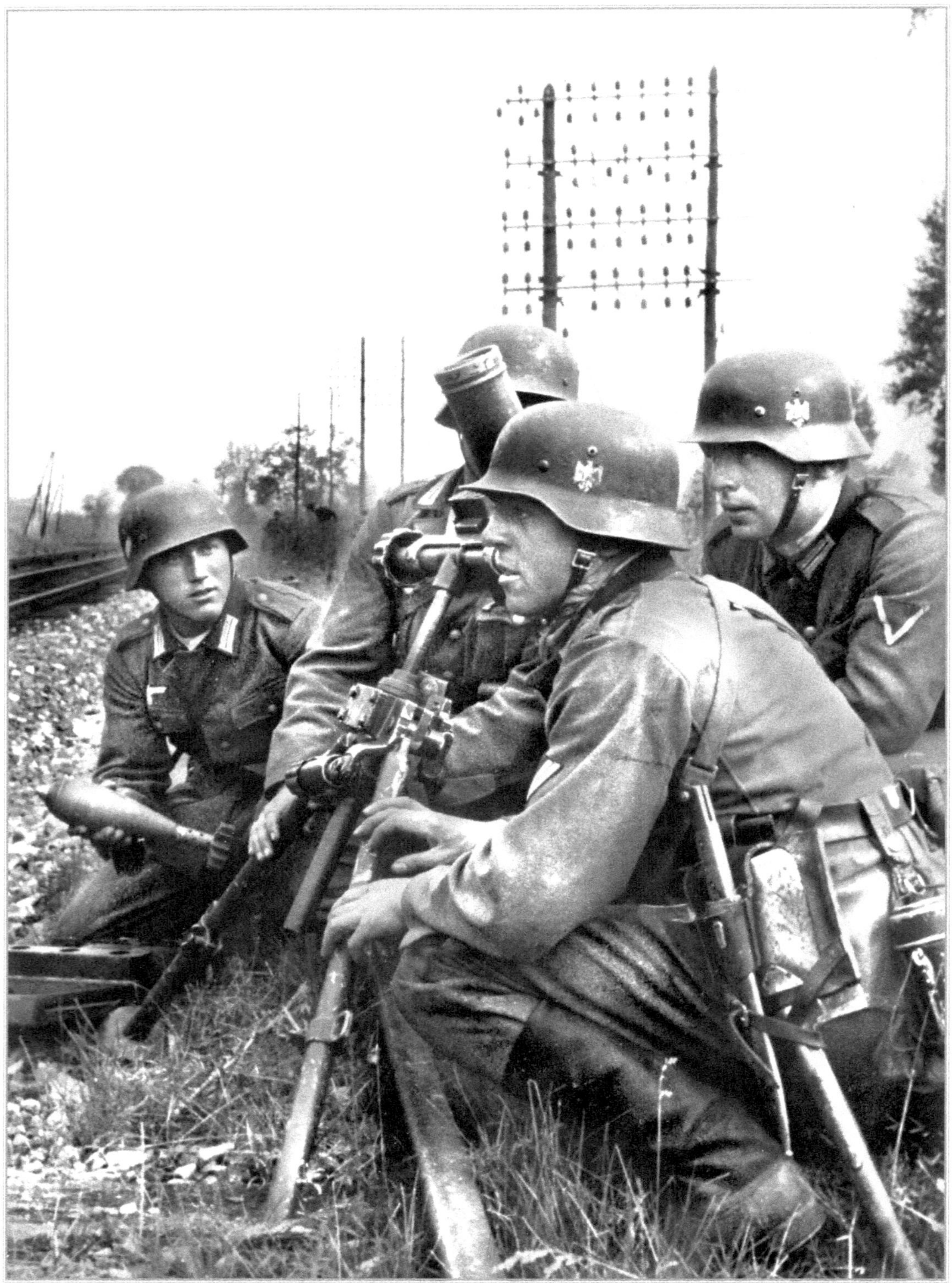

German soldiers prepare to launch offensive maneuvers (above and left) in France.

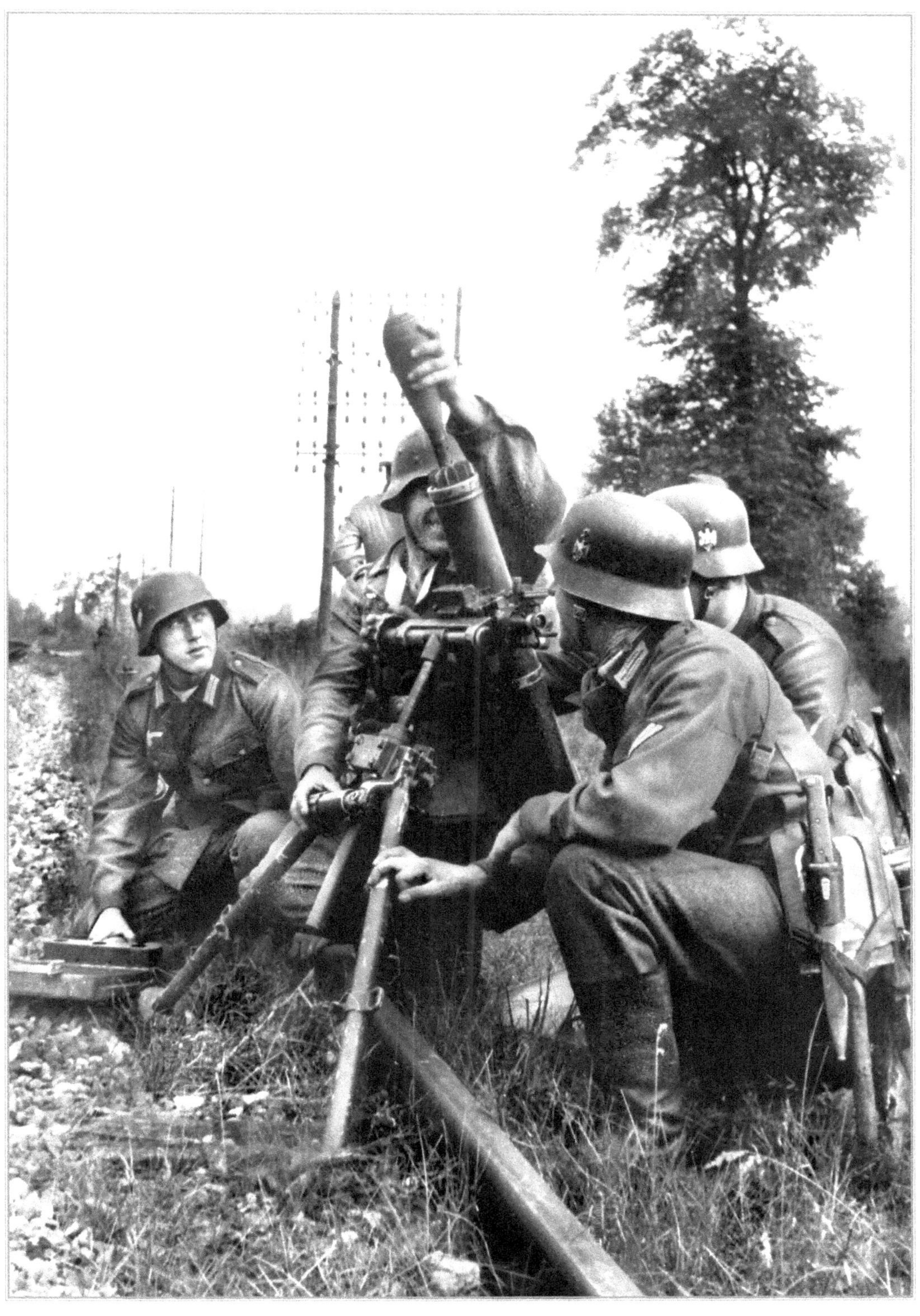

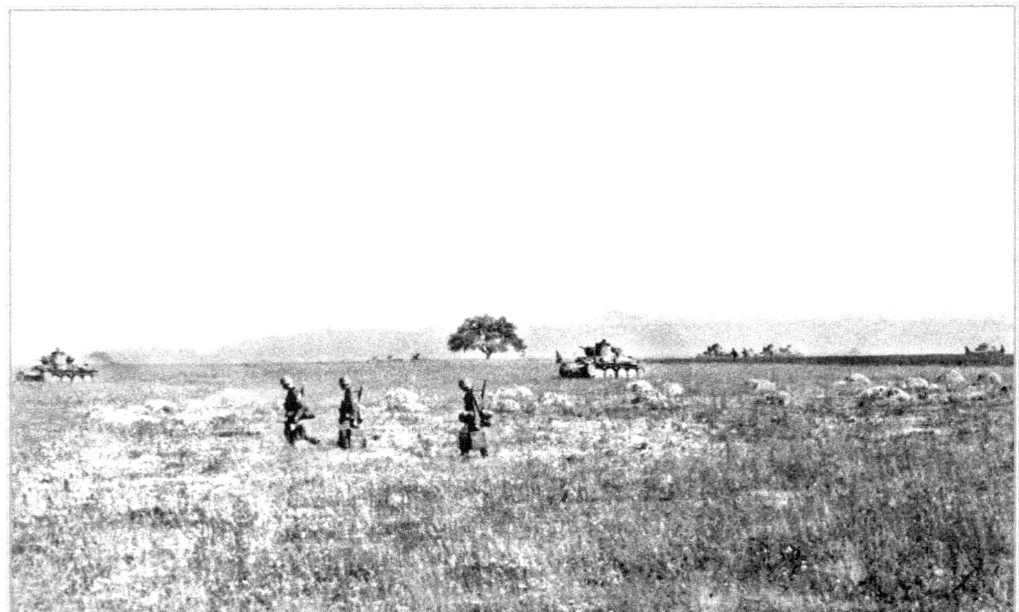

A trio of German soldiers plod through an open field in France as Panzers travel in the same direction.

Tanks dot the horizon. A solitary tree is perfectly centered in the frame.

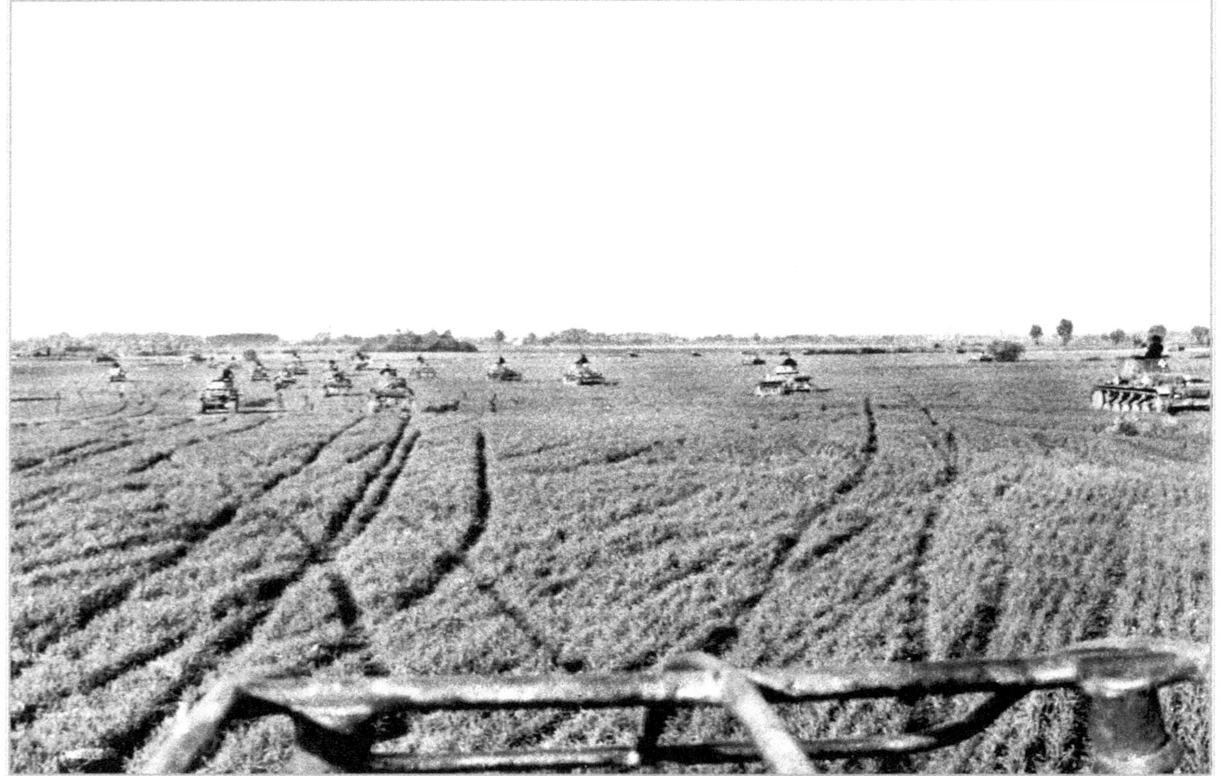

German tanks cut jagged tracks through farmlands in France.

It is apparent that Rommel took this photo while riding atop a command vehicle, visible in the lower part of this image.

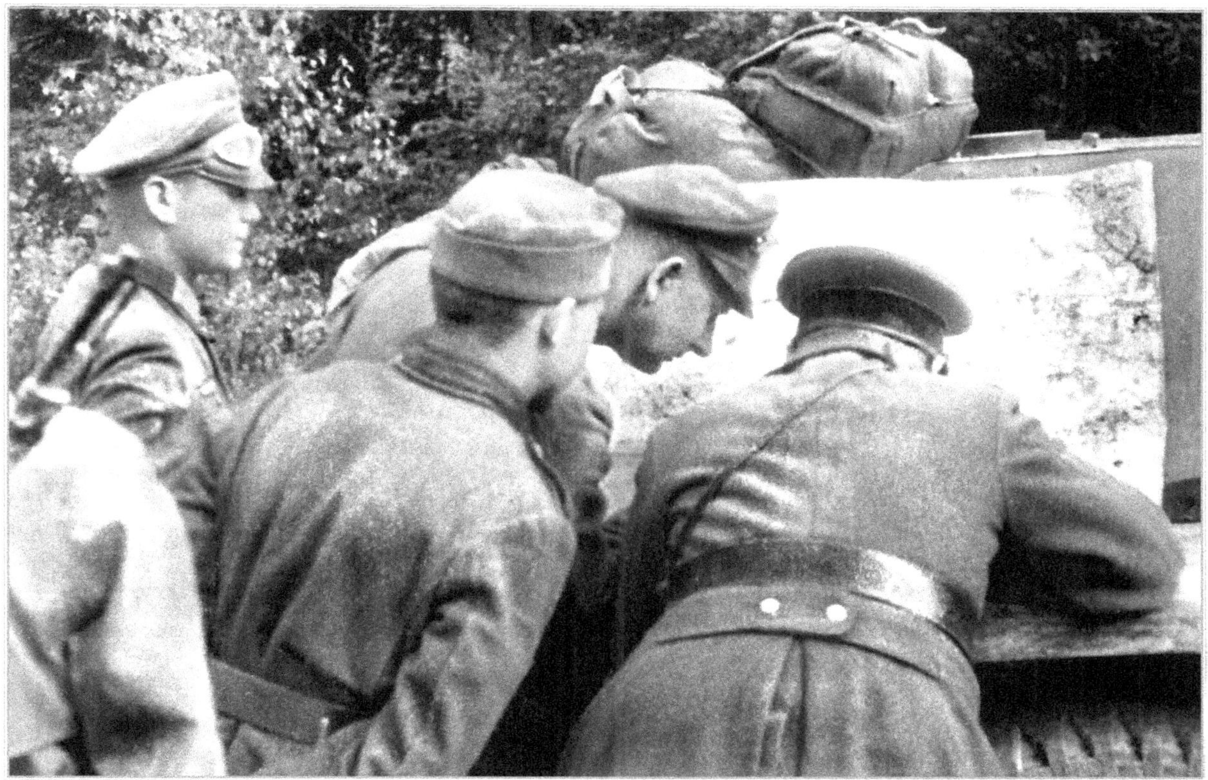

Surrounded by German officers peering over his shoulder, Rommel (right) looks intently at a map in France.

Rommel's camera strap is visible, slung over his shoulder as he bends down to study the map. This image appears to be another impromptu photo in Rommel's personal collection—part of a soldier and his gun barrel (left) appear awkwardly in the frame. Like other photos which Rommel saved of himself, this looks more amateurish than stylized propaganda photography. It may have been taken by one of Rommel's associates.

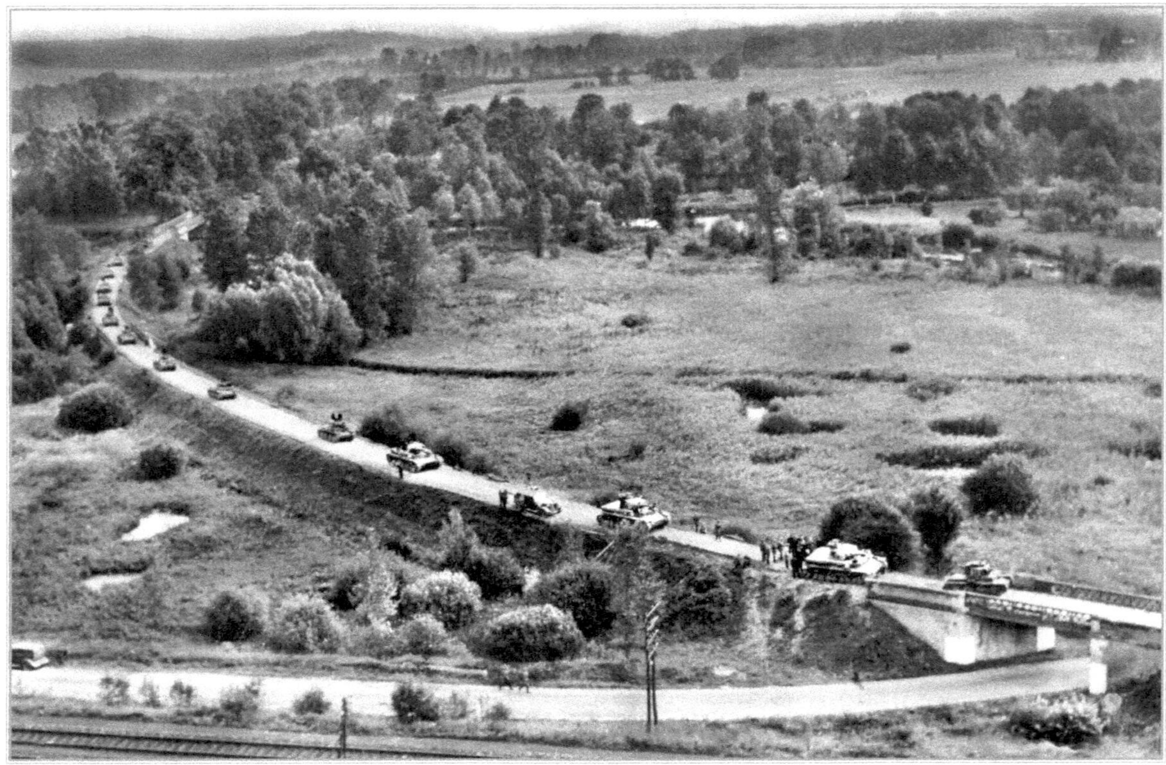

German tanks advance through France.

This aerial photo demonstrates Rommel's characteristic attention to curving lines that divide landscapes.

Rommel took a series of aerial photos of Panzers as they advanced. He may have intended these photos for the military textbook he planned to write.

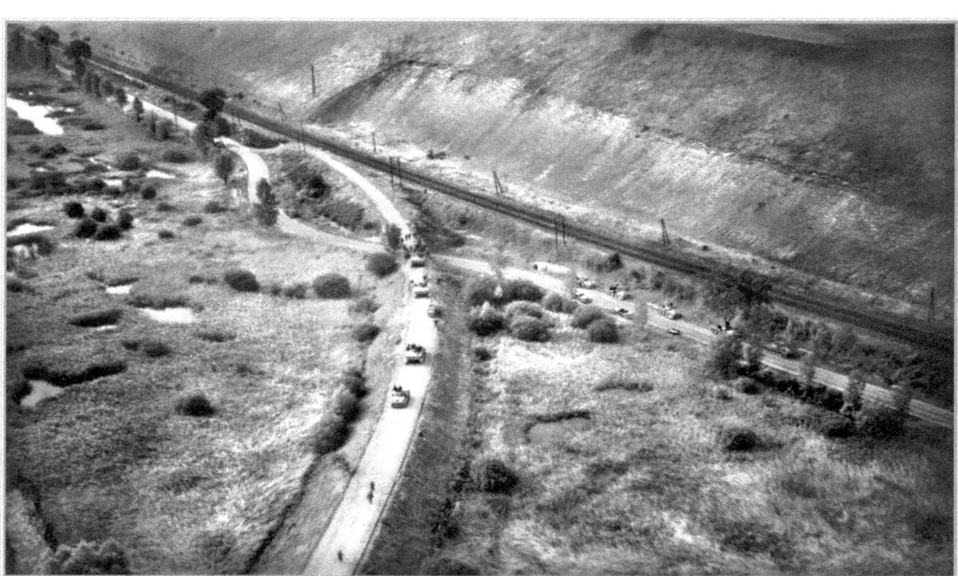

Another aerial view of German tanks in France.

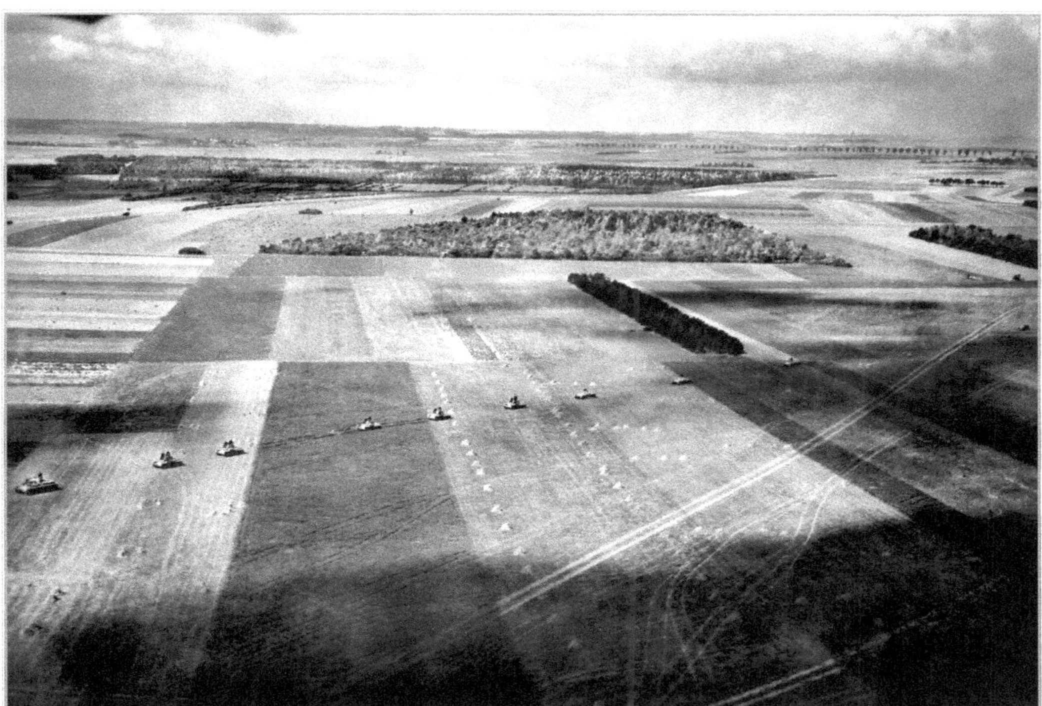

German tanks travel diagonally across country fields in France.

There are many geometric shapes within this image. A curving line of tanks intersects with the rectangular patterns of the field.

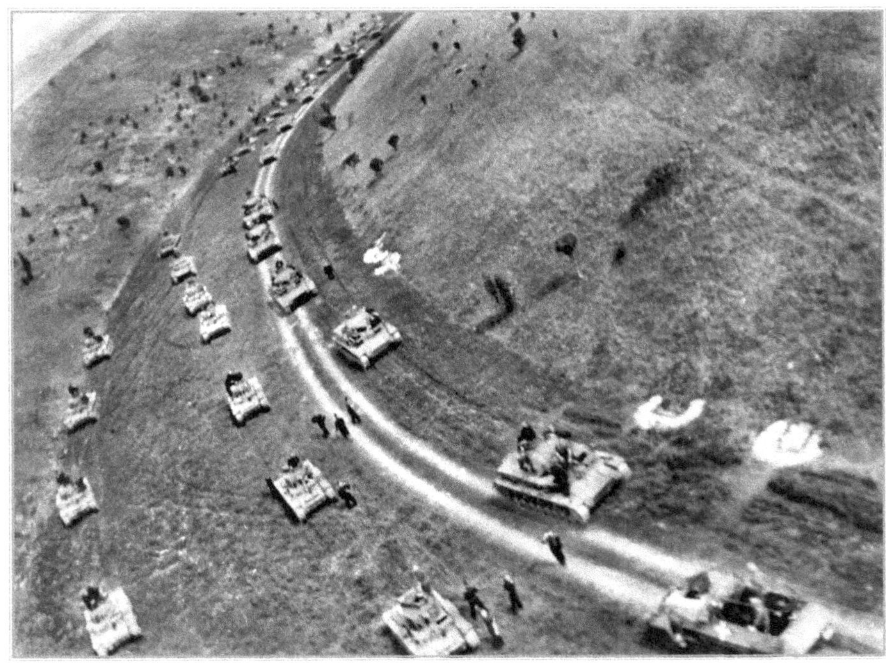

German tank crews prepare to drive their Panzers onward into France.

In these aerial photographs (above and left), Rommel portrays a multitude of parallel curving lines: the tank formations, vehicles tracks in the fields, and various parts of the roadway.

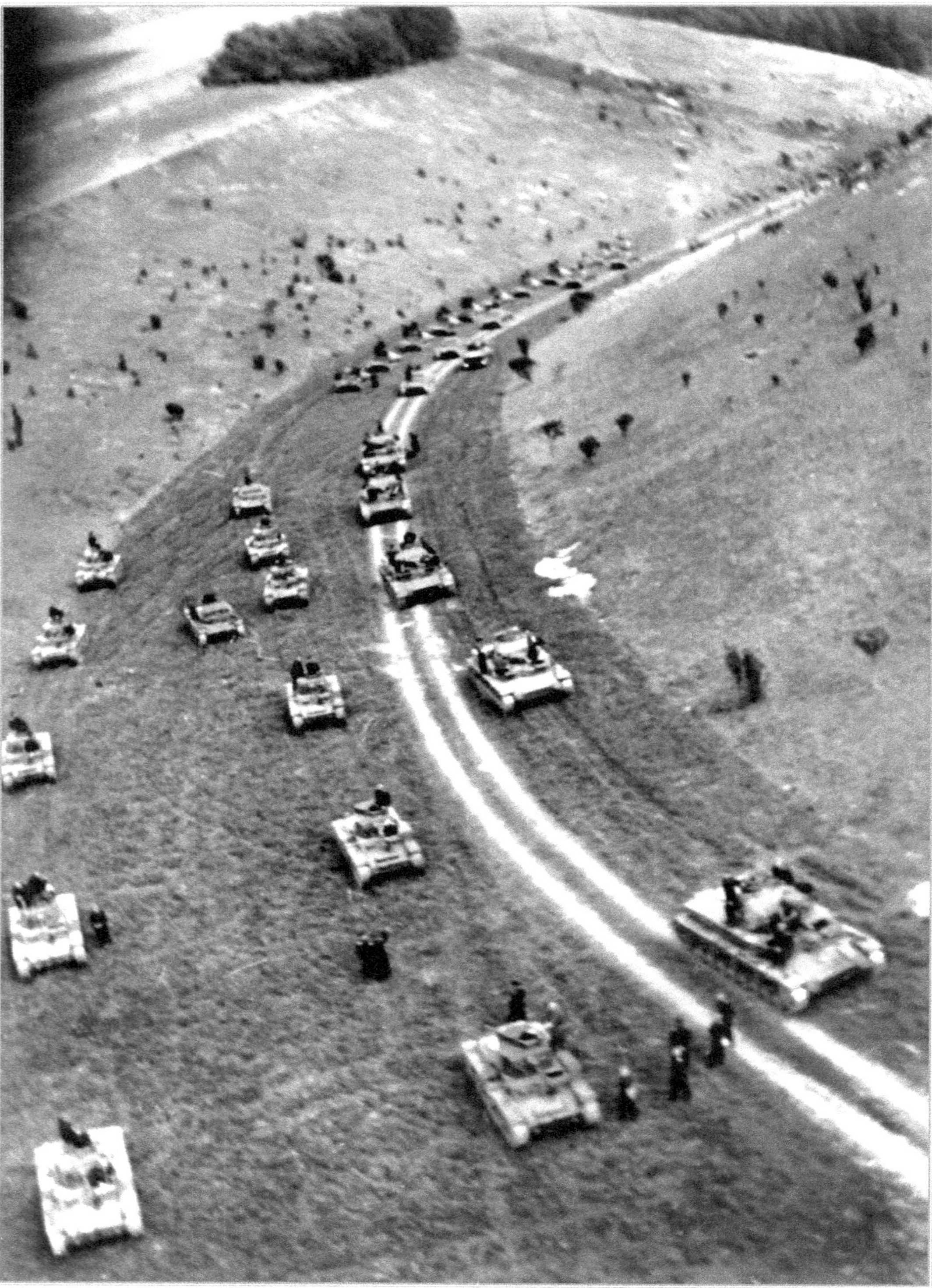

A low-altitude aerial view of Panzer crews standing and sitting on their tanks in France.

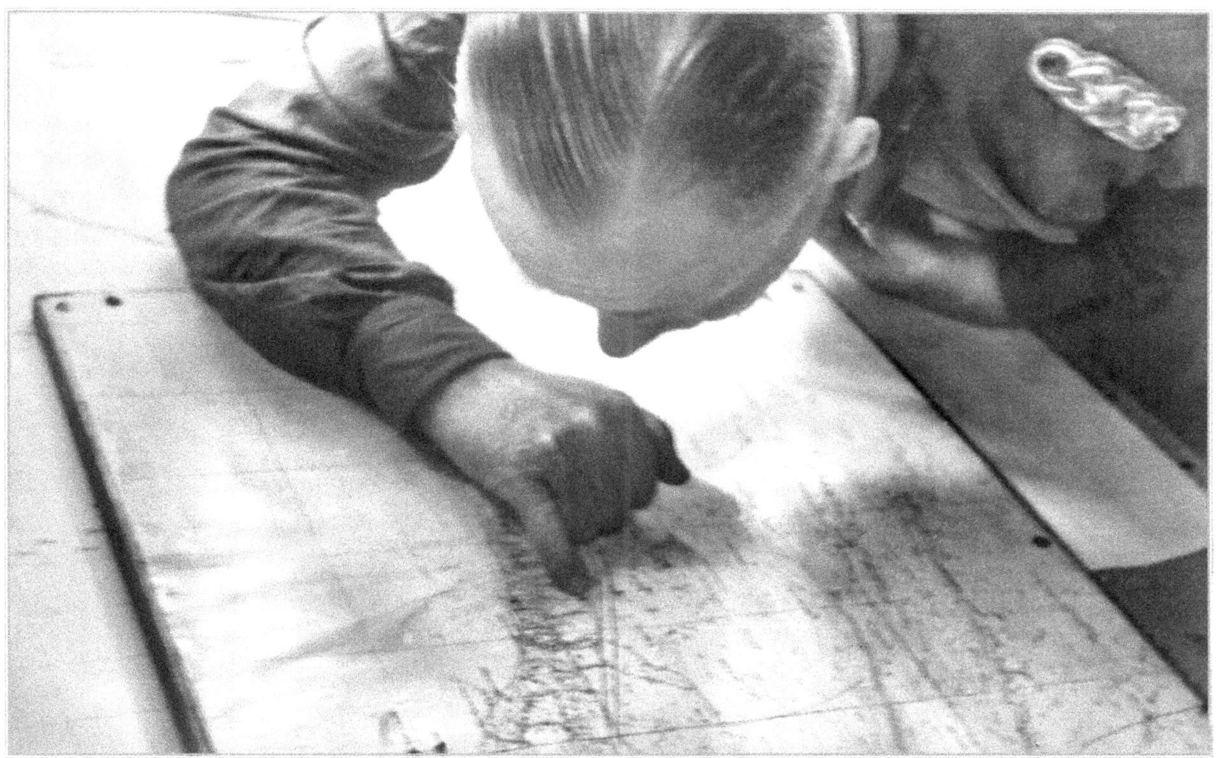

Rommel analyzes a map in North Africa.

Rommel first arrived in North Africa when he was 49 years old. In this photo, he is pictured without a hat and part of his receding hairline is visible. Despite his age at the time, Rommel was tougher physically than many German soldiers who were much younger. He had a reputation among his officers for being very physically strong and resilient.

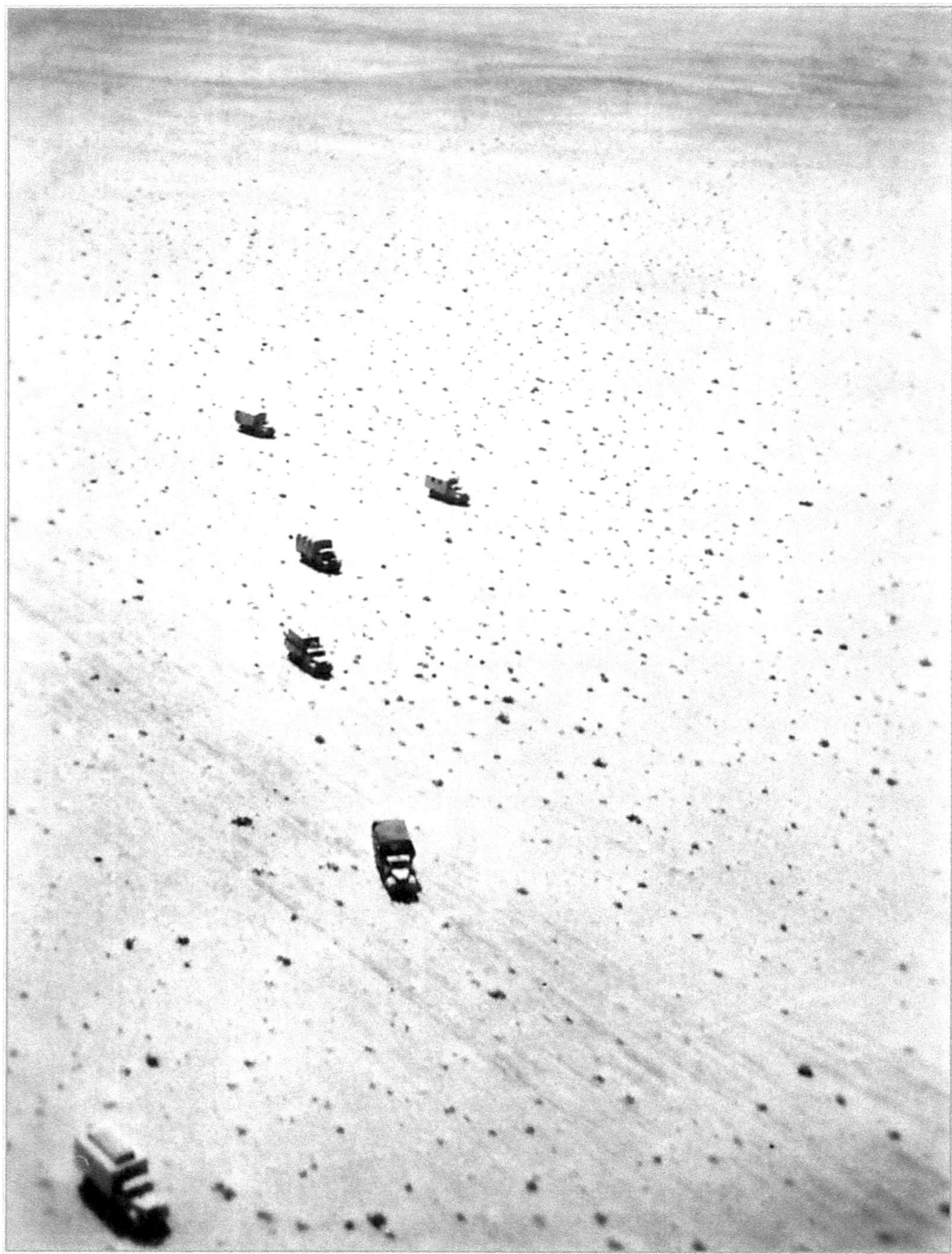

German trucks wend their way across a bleached expanse of sand and shrubs in Libya (April 5, 1941).

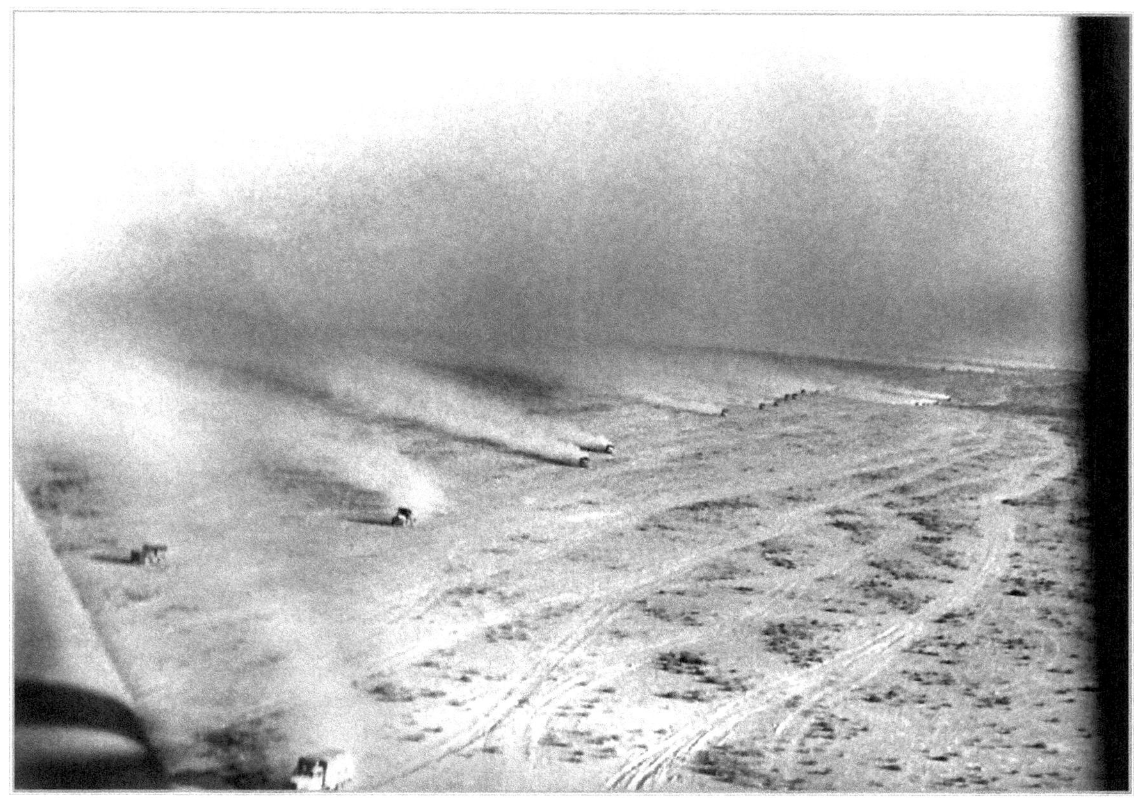

Military vehicles speed through the North African desert, leaving huge trails of sand clouds in the air.

Part of Rommel's airplane is visible within the frame of this photo. The wing comes into view on the left, and part of the window in the cockpit is visible on the right. The prominence of the convoy truck (lower left) in the foreground shows that Rommel's airplane was flying at a low altitude while this event was unfolding. Multiple rows of tire tracks on the right side of this image create curving diagonal lines. Rommel could have easily turned his camera on the vehicles alone without framing this image with the tire tracks. However, curving lines and patterns are characteristic of Rommel's photo compositions. Also, he showed a tendency to align his camera with subjects that appear larger in the foreground and become smaller until they merge into the horizon. Rommel also achieves this illusion of infinity with the trucks in this image.

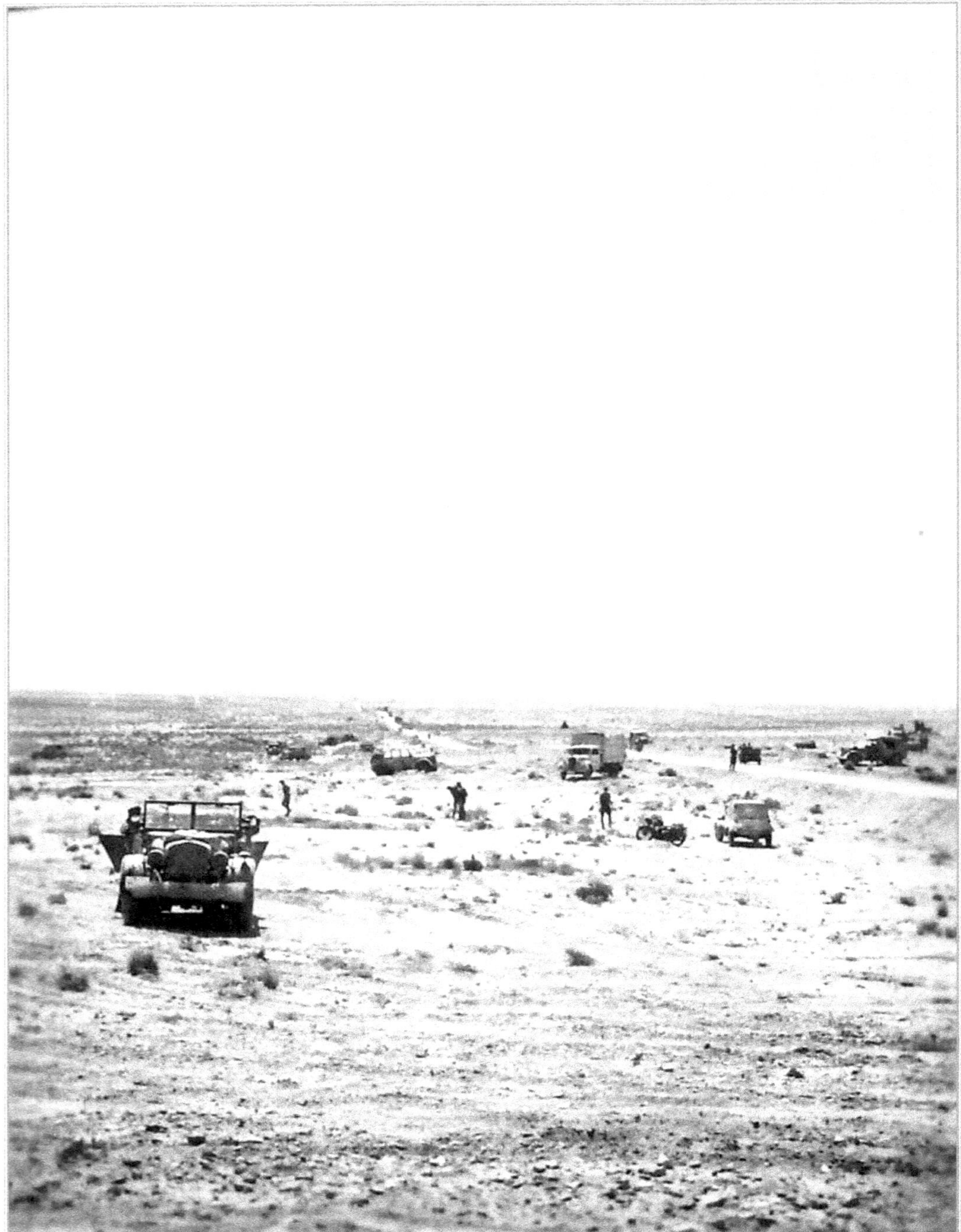

Soldiers, including POWs, congregate beside a dirt road in North Africa.

In the middle ground, three figures appear to stand at equal distances apart. This image contains British soldiers who seem to have just been taken captive.

Close-up of Rommel standing on the roof of his Mammoth command vehicle.

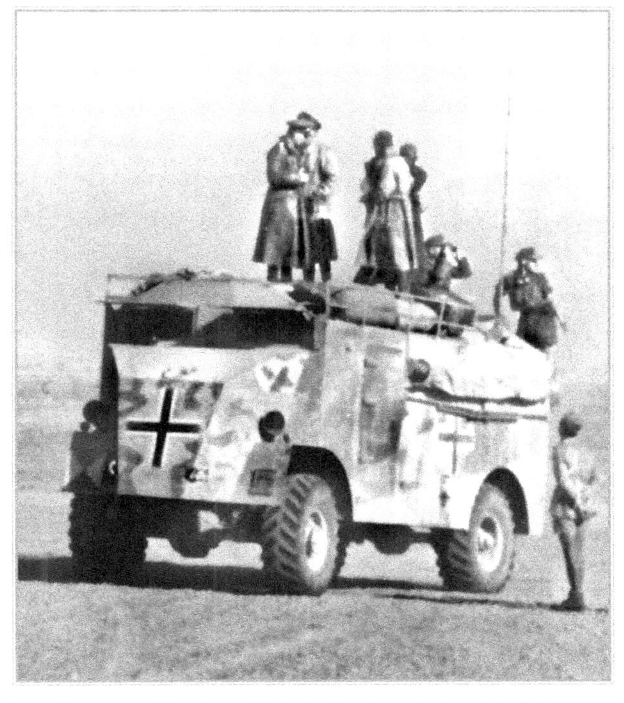

This close-up of Rommel has been cropped and enlarged for greater visibility. Rommel (left) appears to be looking downward as if listening to the German officer next to him. Two soldiers on the right side of the roof are looking at something in the distance. One is peering through binoculars.

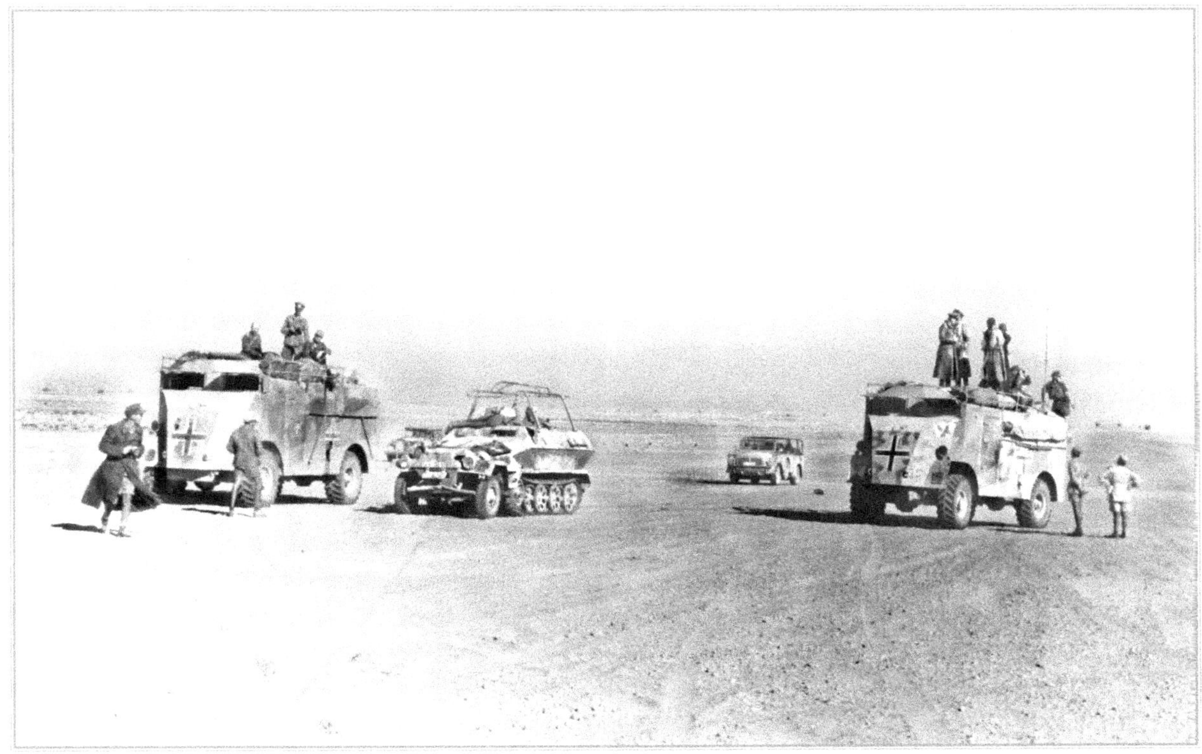

Rommel stands on top of his Mammoth command vehicle (far right) surrounded by his men in North Africa.

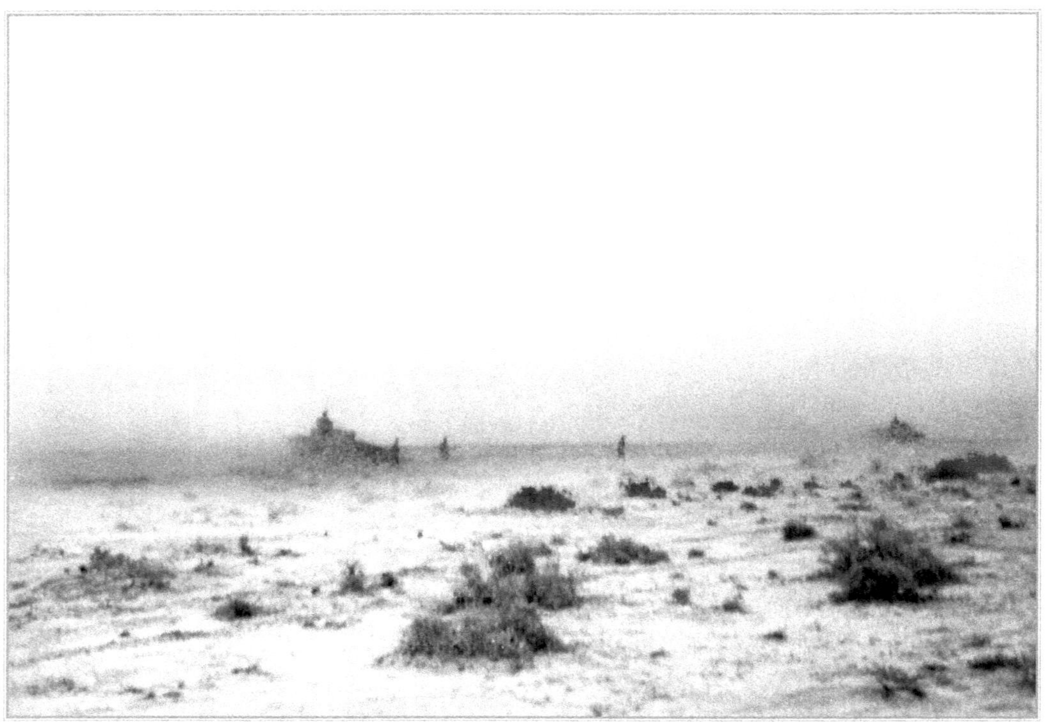

This slightly blurred image depicts German soldiers advancing through a sandstorm in North Africa.

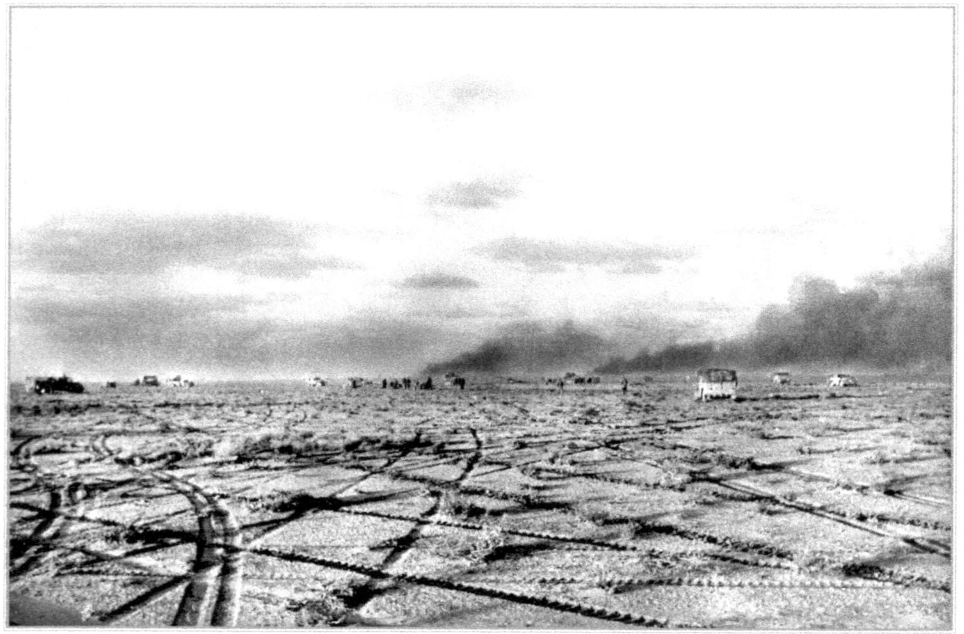

Smoke rises from a distant battleground in North Africa.

This photo seems to have no military value. The patterns of intersecting lines in the sand must have interested Rommel. This image was taken at a high vantage point above the ground.

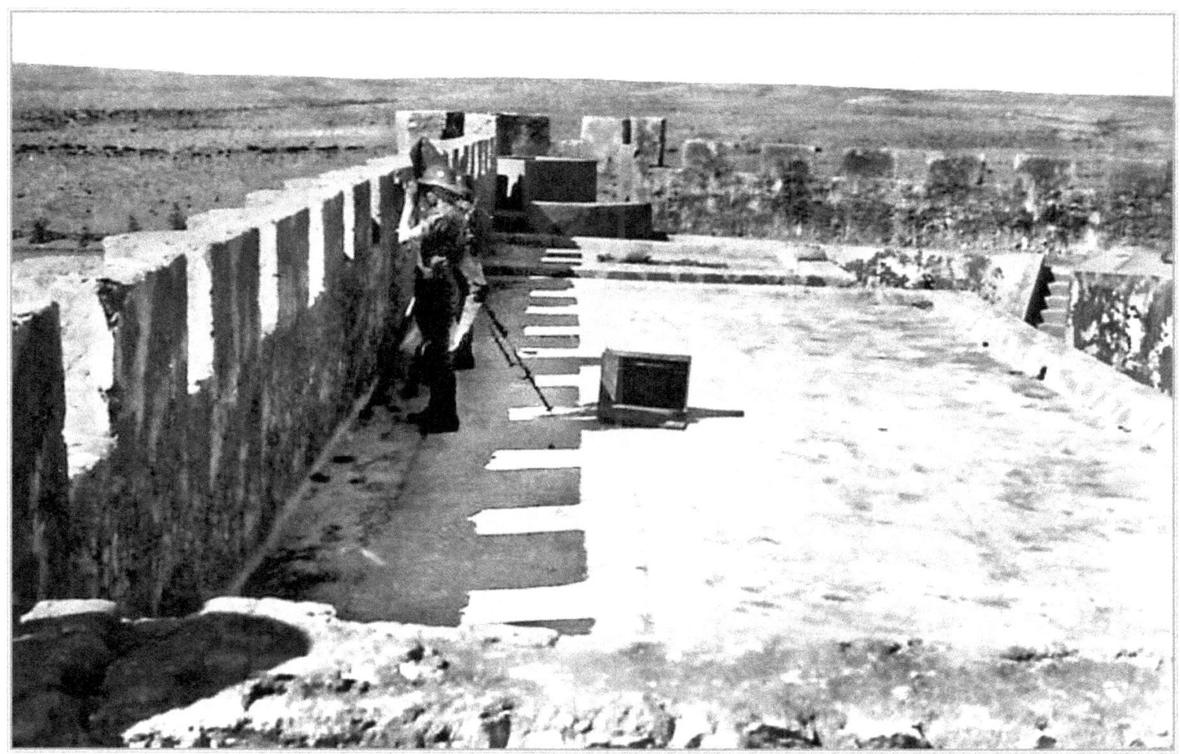

German soldiers wearing pith helmets gaze through binoculars from the stone wall of a fort in North Africa.

Rommel composed this photo with great precision. There are many rectangular shapes which overlap, including the wall and the shadows on the left. The soldiers in the pith helmets stand within a rectangular shadow on the fort's rooftop. Behind them, in the center of the frame, is a rectangular object that appears to be a box. Since the soldiers are located on the side of the image, it appears Rommel was interested in photographing the men in the context of their surroundings rather than merely focusing on them as the centerpiece of the photo.

Close-up of Rommel in another command vehicle.

This photo has been cropped and enlarged from the one below to provide a close-up of Rommel (right) inside the command vehicle as he monitors the activity of his troops.

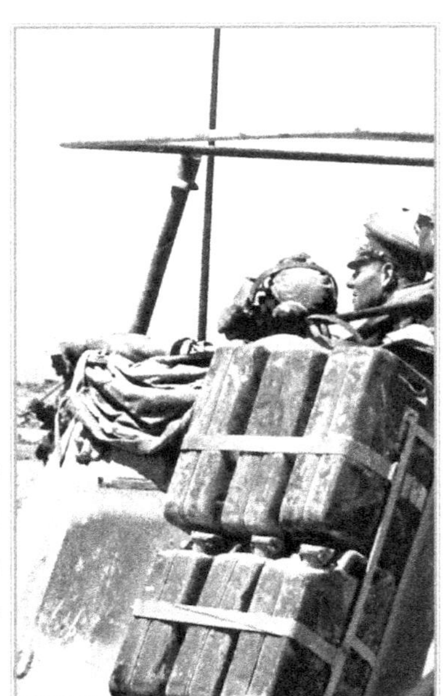

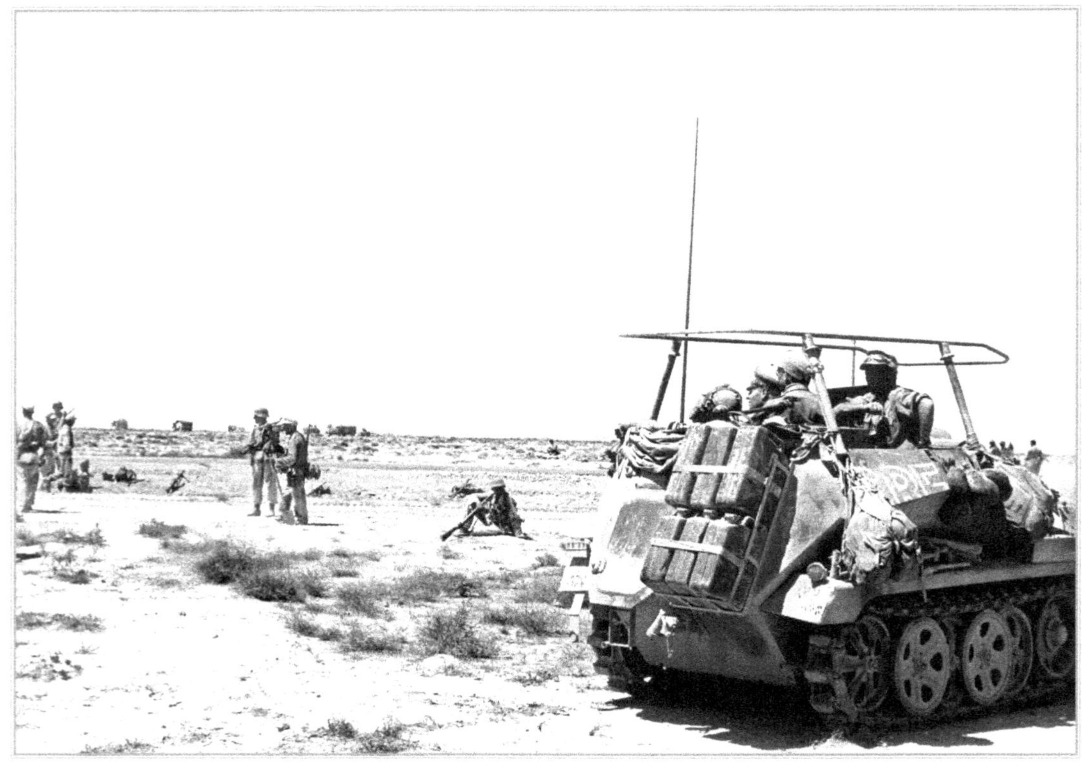

Rommel, seated in his "GREIF" command vehicle, looks intently at his troops in North Africa.

Inside the vehicle, Rommel and the officers nearby look intently into the distance. However, the soldiers in the dirt appear to be relaxing. One soldier even sits on the ground to rest. In the distance, military vehicles line the road.

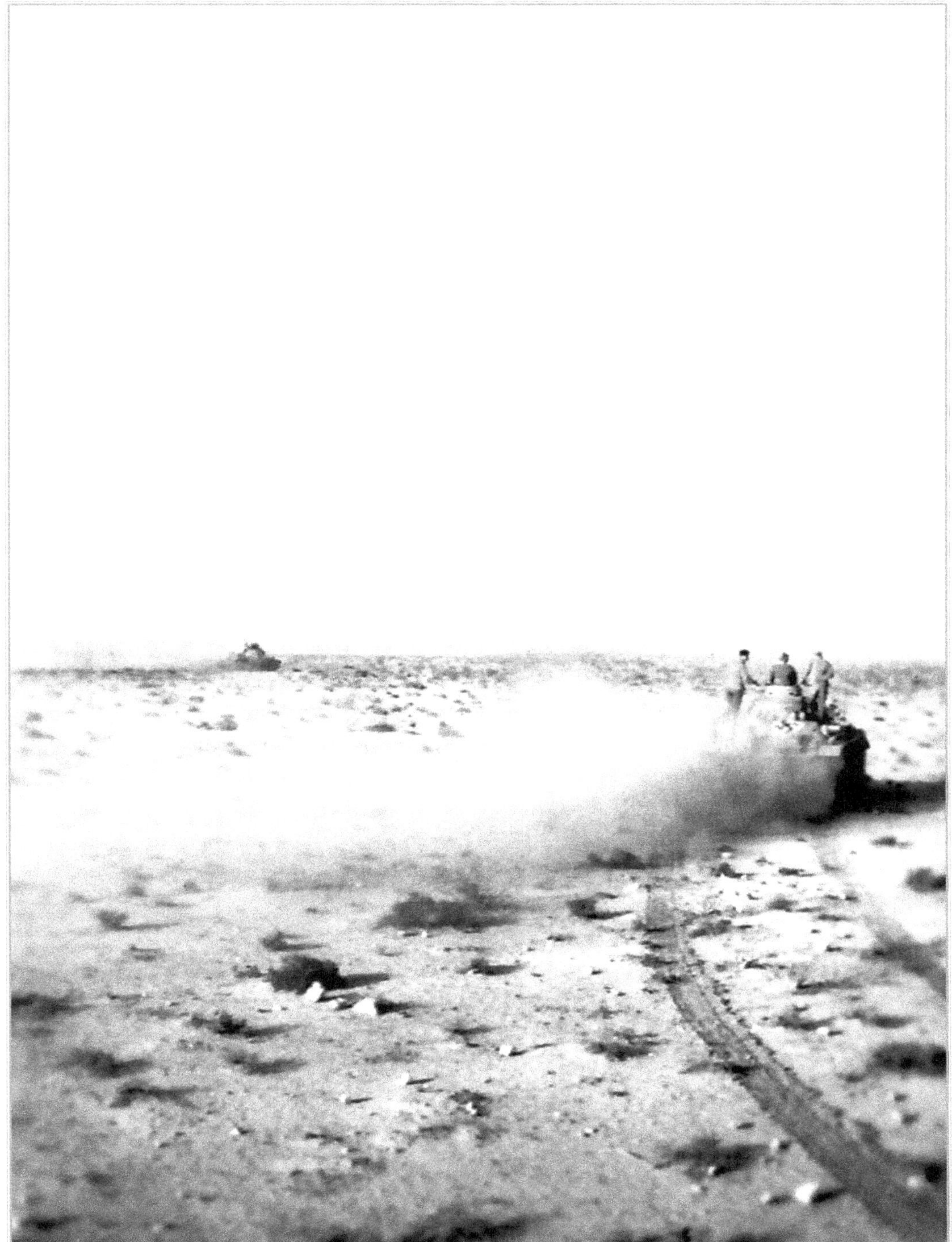

Panzers ride off into the North African desert while creating clouds of dust.

It is likely Rommel took this picture while following behind the tank. The tracks make deep ruts in the sandy ground. Plumes of dust form horizontal clouds across this image.

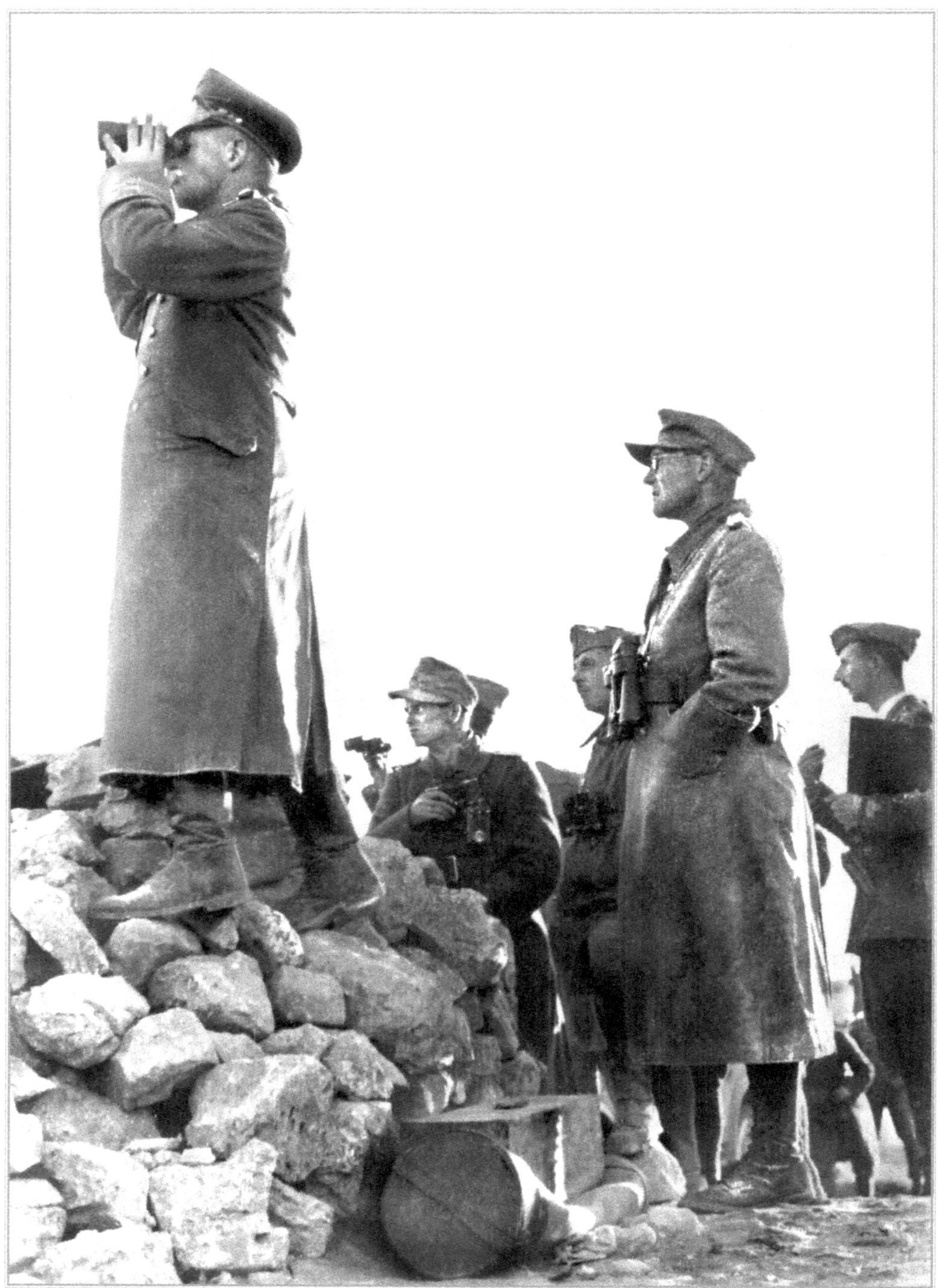

Rommel perches on a pile of rocks to peer from binoculars in North Africa.

Behind Rommel stands Lieutenant General Karl Böttcher (right), with his hand in his pocket. Böttcher, in charge of Rommel's artillery, was captured by the Allies. He survived the war and died in 1973.

6

In the Heat of Battle

Angriff

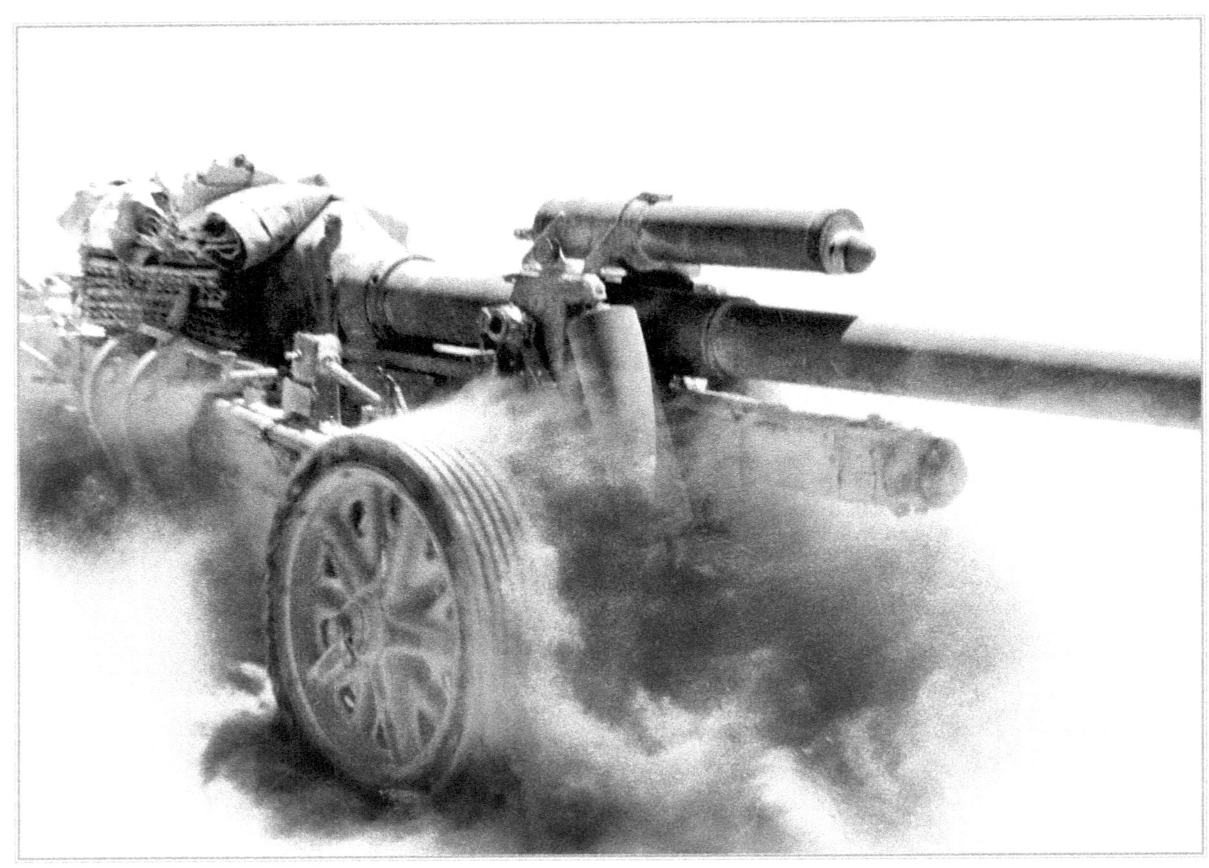

A German antitank gun caught firing in motion.

Rommel took this image at close range as it was firing. The convergence of the smoke and dust add movement as well as drama to this photo.

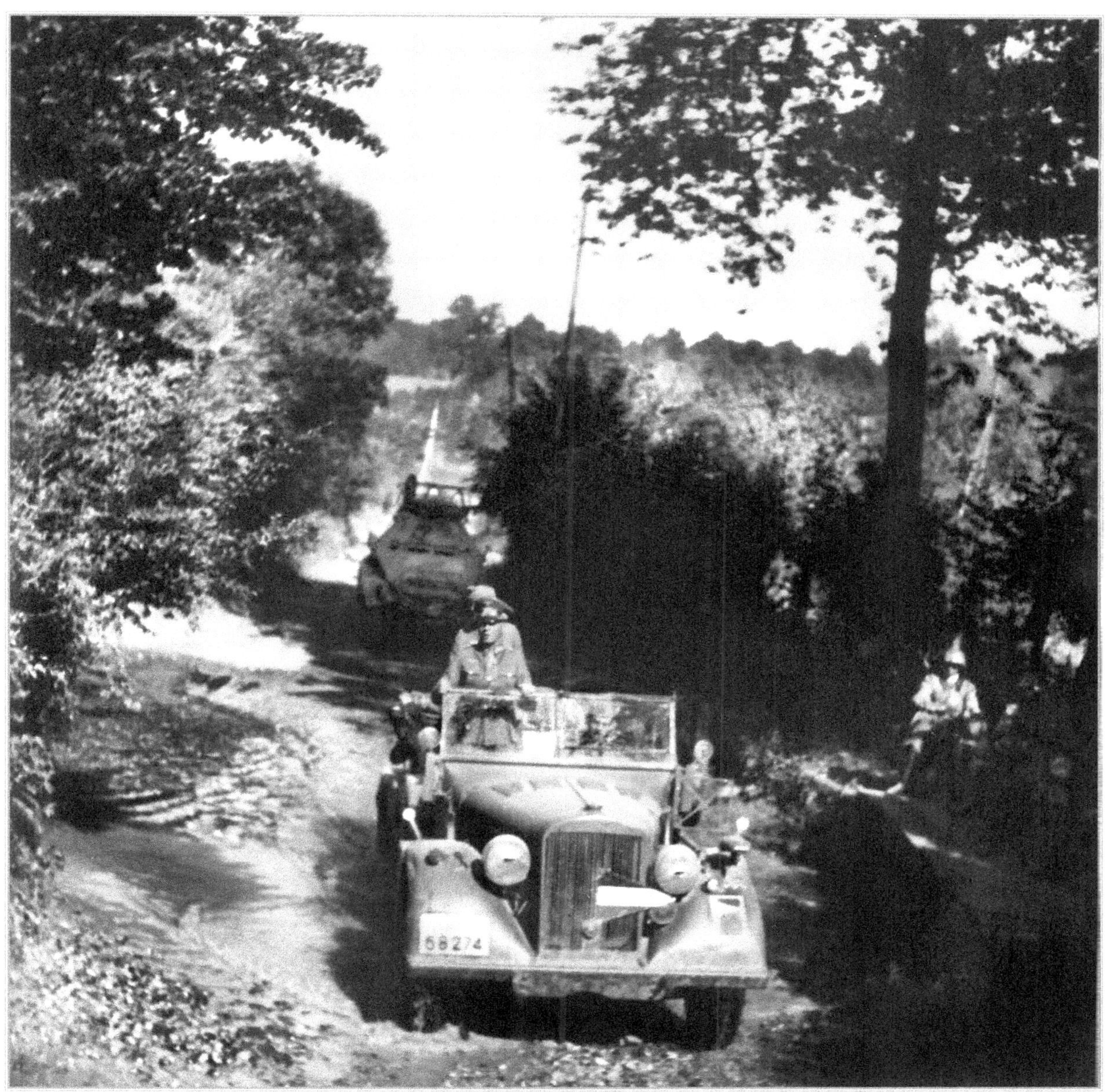

Rommel stands upright in his jeep as it travels through a stream in France (date unknown).

Rommel precedes an armored vehicle and is flanked by German soldiers on motorcycles (right). The face of Rommel's driver is visible through windshield.

In wartime, Rommel liked to be in the thick of the fighting action. Unlike other commanders, he preferred to lead his troops from the frontlines—a characteristic which made him popular among his men, but resulted in criticism from military superiors and administrative officers.

Rommel's "hands-on" method of command often placed him in perilous situations. In the following passage, Rommel, riding in a Panzer III, describes a narrow escape during a tank battle in France 1940.

> "Shells landed all around us and my tank received two hits one after the other, the first on the upper edge of the turret and the second in the periscope. The driver promptly opened the throttle wide and drove straight into the nearest bushes. He had only gone a few yards, however, when the tank slid down a steep slope on the western edge of the forest and finally stopped, canted over on its side, in such a position that the enemy, whose guns were in position about 500 yards away on the edge of the next forest, could not fail to see it.
>
> "I had been wounded in the right cheek by a small splinter from the shell which had landed in the periscope. It was not serious though it bled a great deal. I tried to swing the turret around so as to bring our 37-mm. gun to bear on the enemy in the opposite forest, but with the heavy slant of the tank it was immovable. The French battery now opened rapid fire on our forest and at any moment we could expect their fire to be aimed at our tank, which was in full view.
>
> "I therefore decided to abandon it as fast I could, taking the crew with me. At that moment the subaltern in command of the tanks escorting the infantry reported himself seriously wounded, with the words: 'Herr General, my left arm has been shot off.' We clambered up through the sandy pit, shells crashing and splintering all around."
>
> — *Rommel*

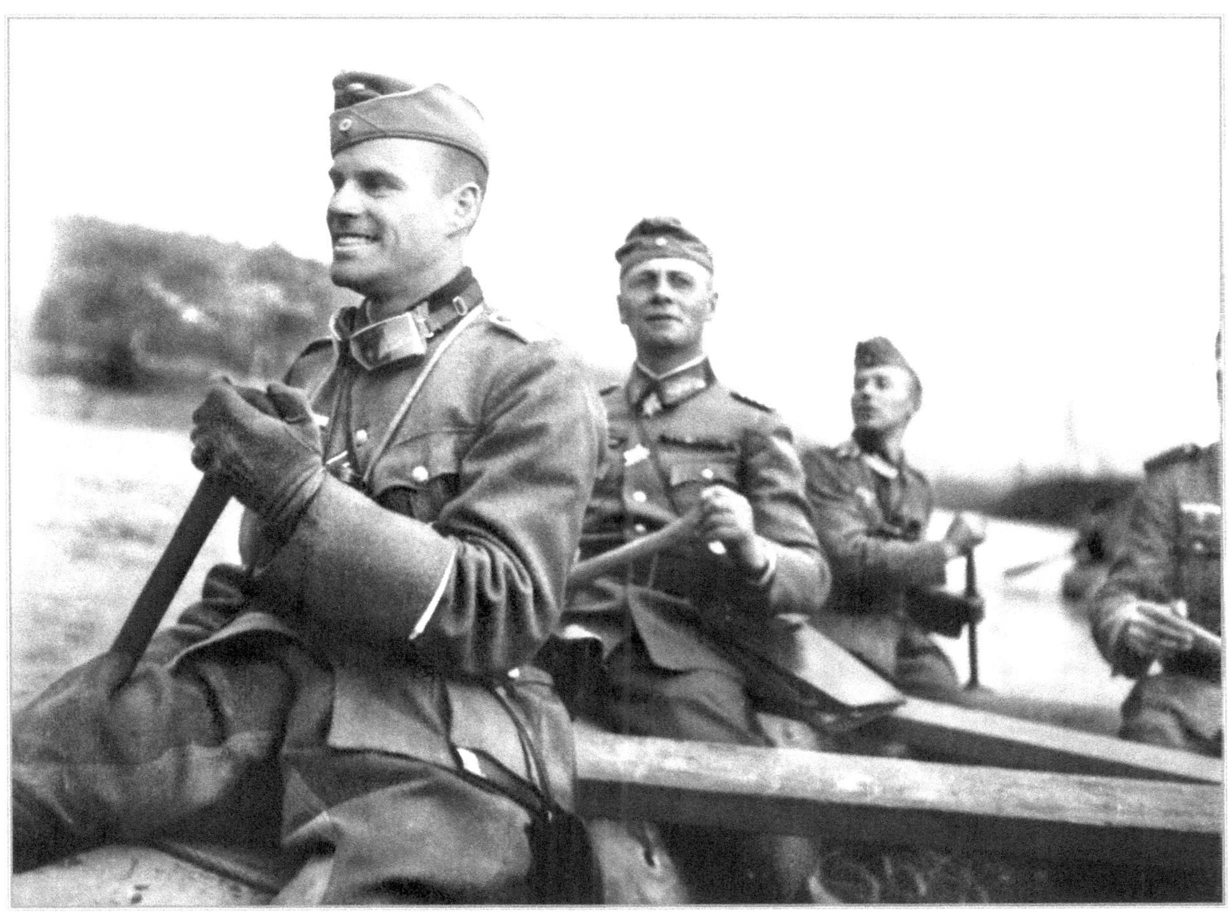

Rommel crosses a river in France accompanied by his aides.

According to his war diary, Rommel was among the first German soldiers to cross the Meuse River into French territory during the invasion.

Snipers located across the river frequently shot the Germans as they attempted to cross the water in rubber boats, making the crossing very dangerous and difficult.

Accompanying Rommel in the boat was Lieutenant Most, who stayed constantly at Rommel's side and shared many harrowing experiences with him during battle. Most later was killed in action.

Rommel was deeply saddened by the death of Most and photographed his gravesite in France to memorialize him. (See pages 254–255.)

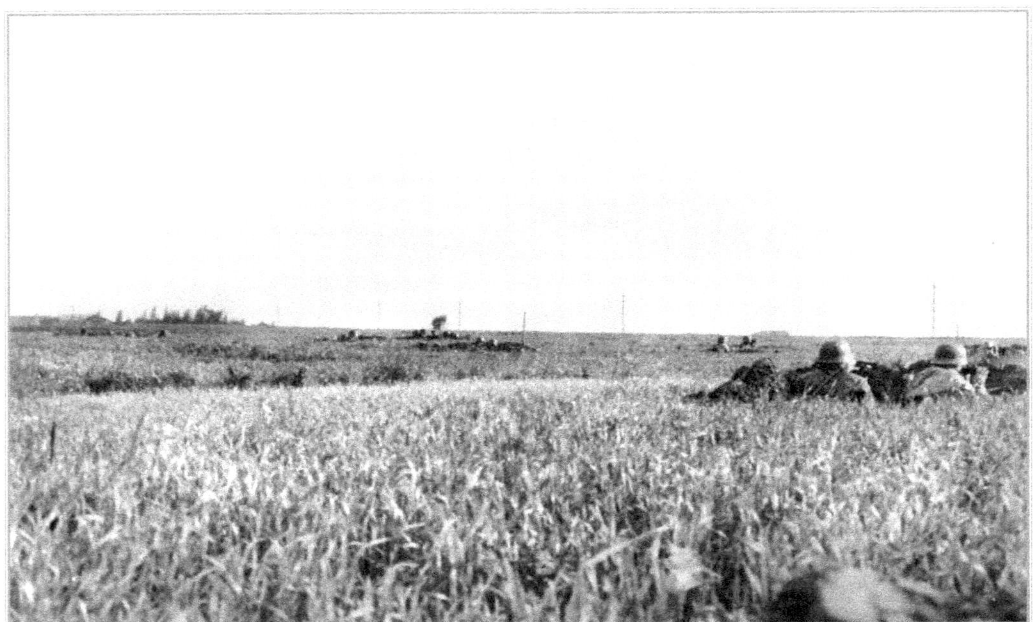

Clusters of German soldiers crouch in machine gun nests in an open field in France.

Rommel took this photo from the same level as the men on the right side, indicating that he also was crouching low in the grass like the others. Rommel's composition is atypically off-centered. The gunners on the right side loom largely in the foreground, while distant gun nests appear simultaneously in the middle ground and background.

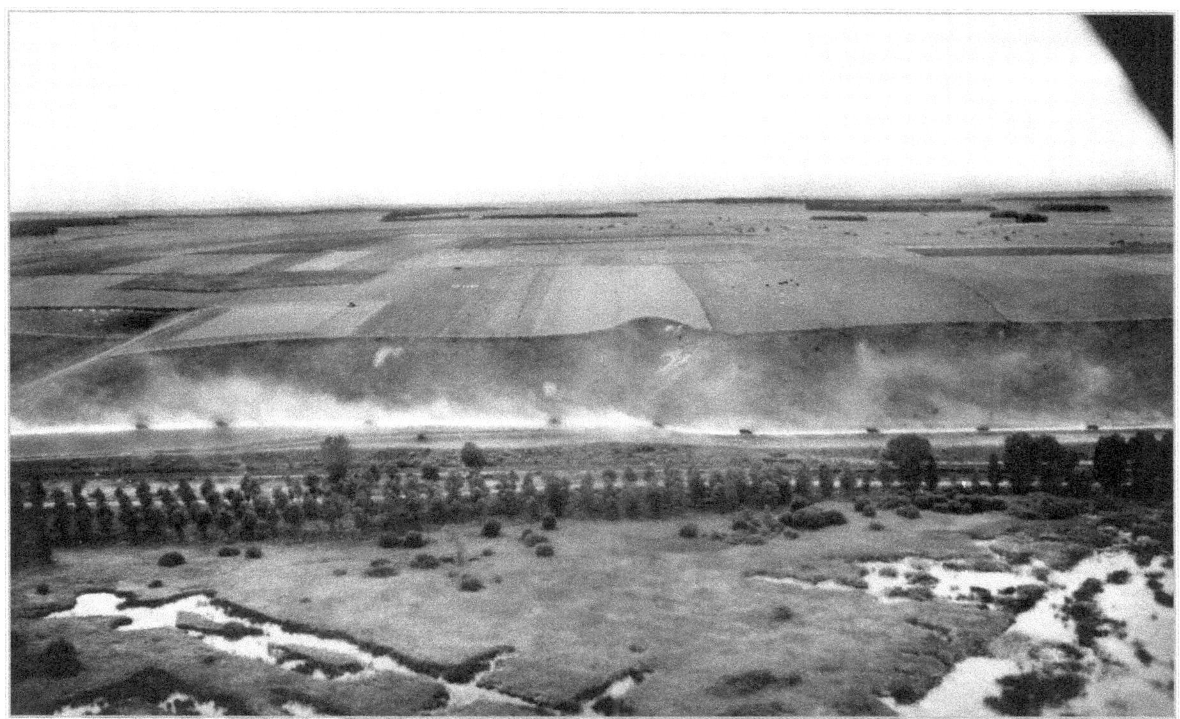

German vehicles race along a flat roadway in France.

This aerial view consists of layers of horizontal lines: the horizon, the top of the hillside, the column of vehicles, the roadway, and the treetops.

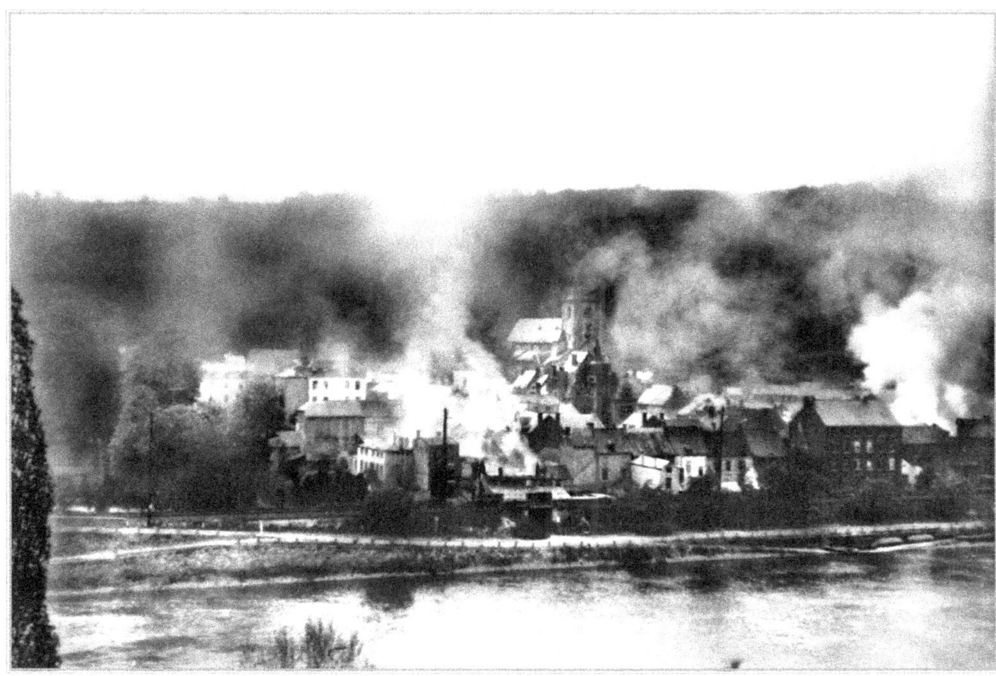

An aerial view of a town under attack in France.

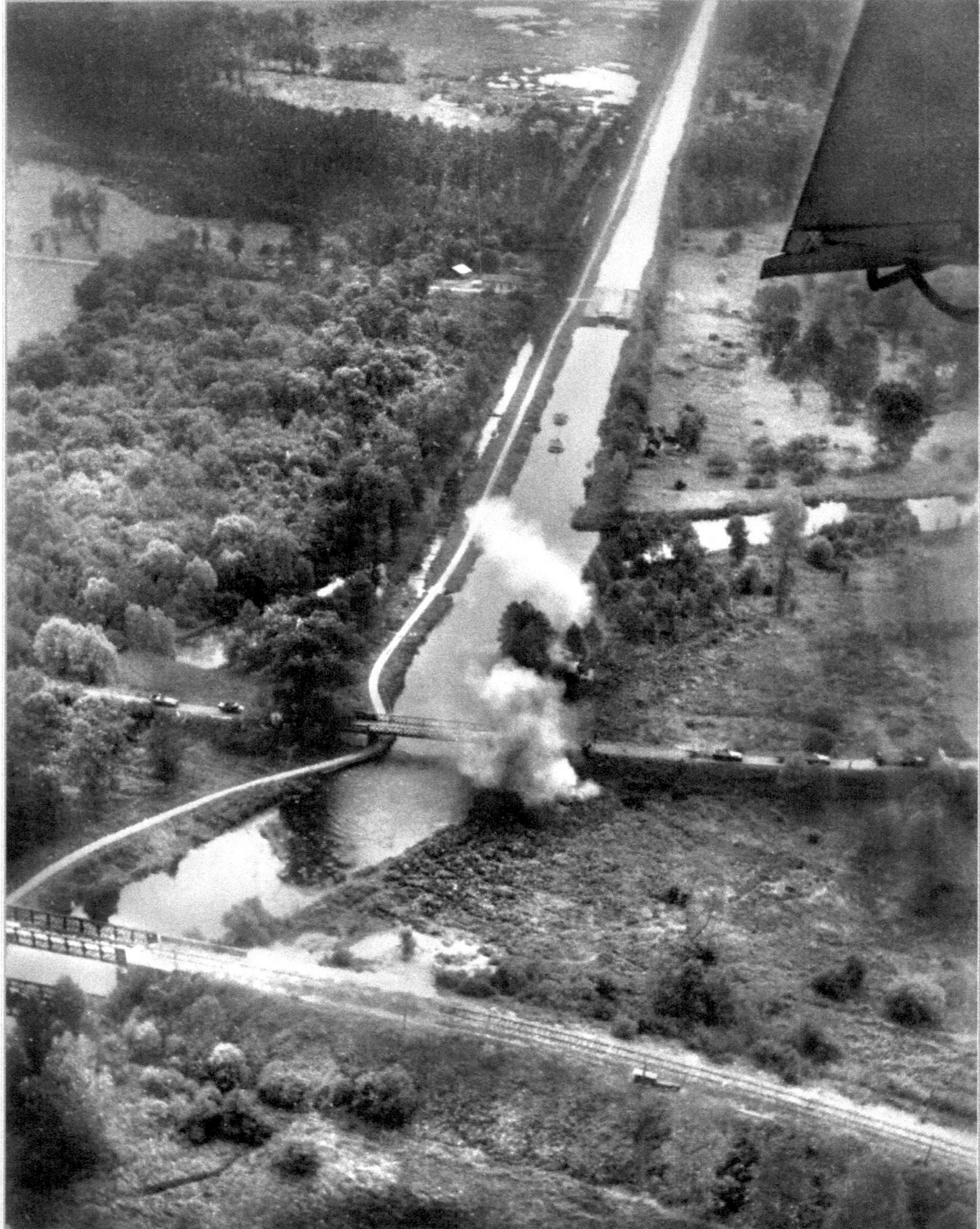

Shells fall beside German vehicles crossing the Somme river (France, 1940).

The tip of Rommel's airplane appears in both photos. Both images feature perfectly arranged lines in the center. This photo (above) was the first taken as Rommel, accompanying the advancing tanks, passed by the bridge in his plane.

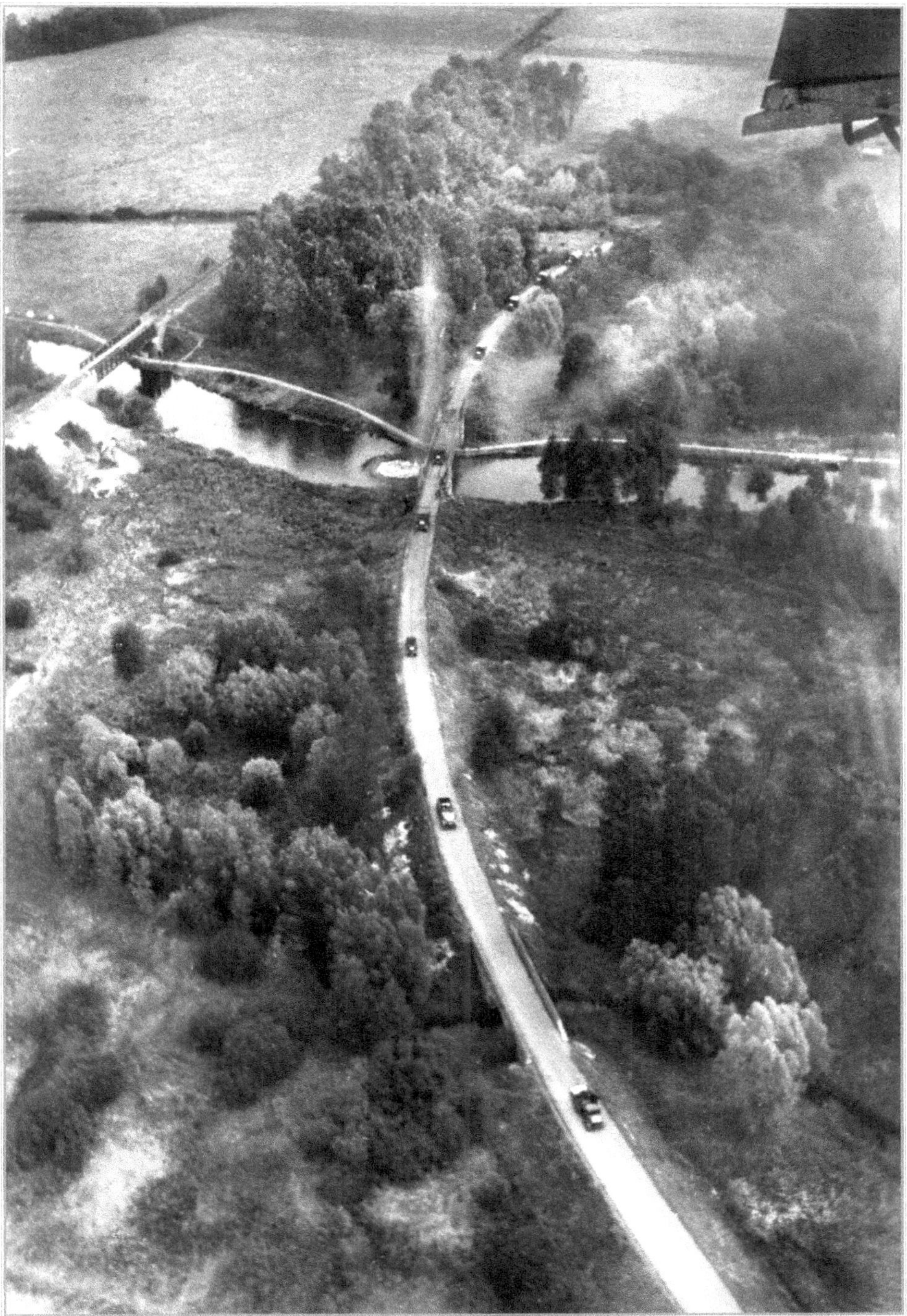

A plume of water from the river shoots up into the air from a shell falling near the vehicles.

Rommel's airplane has circled around from the bridge (upper left) to meet the oncoming German vehicles. The plane is now flying at a lower altitude, allowing Rommel a closer view of the action. The bombshell makes a deep splash in the water.

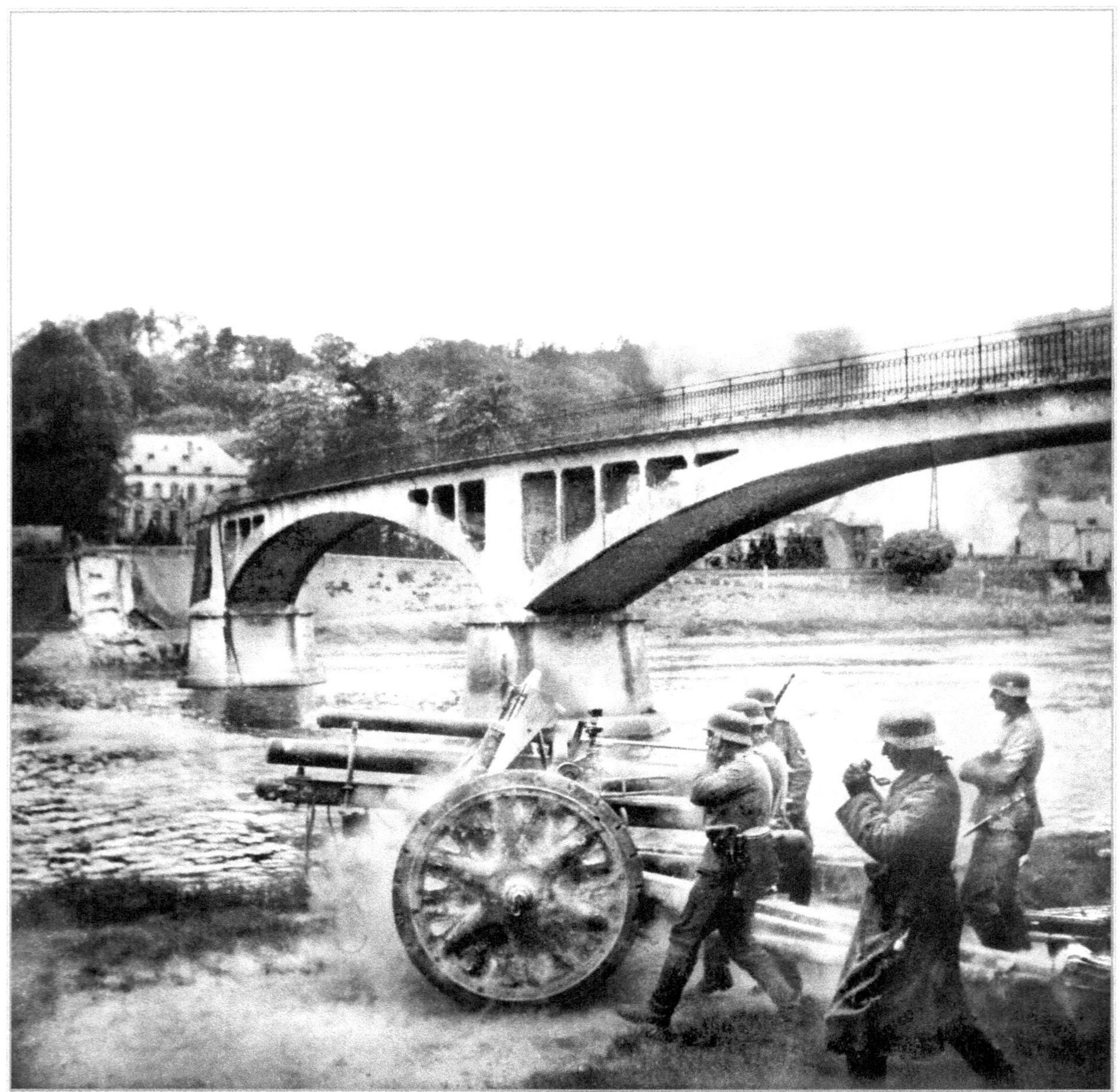

German soldiers fire artillery in the thick of a battle near a bridge in France.

Rommel's focal point is the weapon in action amid the swirling dust and smoke on both photos. This photo (above) appears to have been taken before the other in this series (left). One German soldier covers his ears, while another behind him lifts a pair of binoculars.

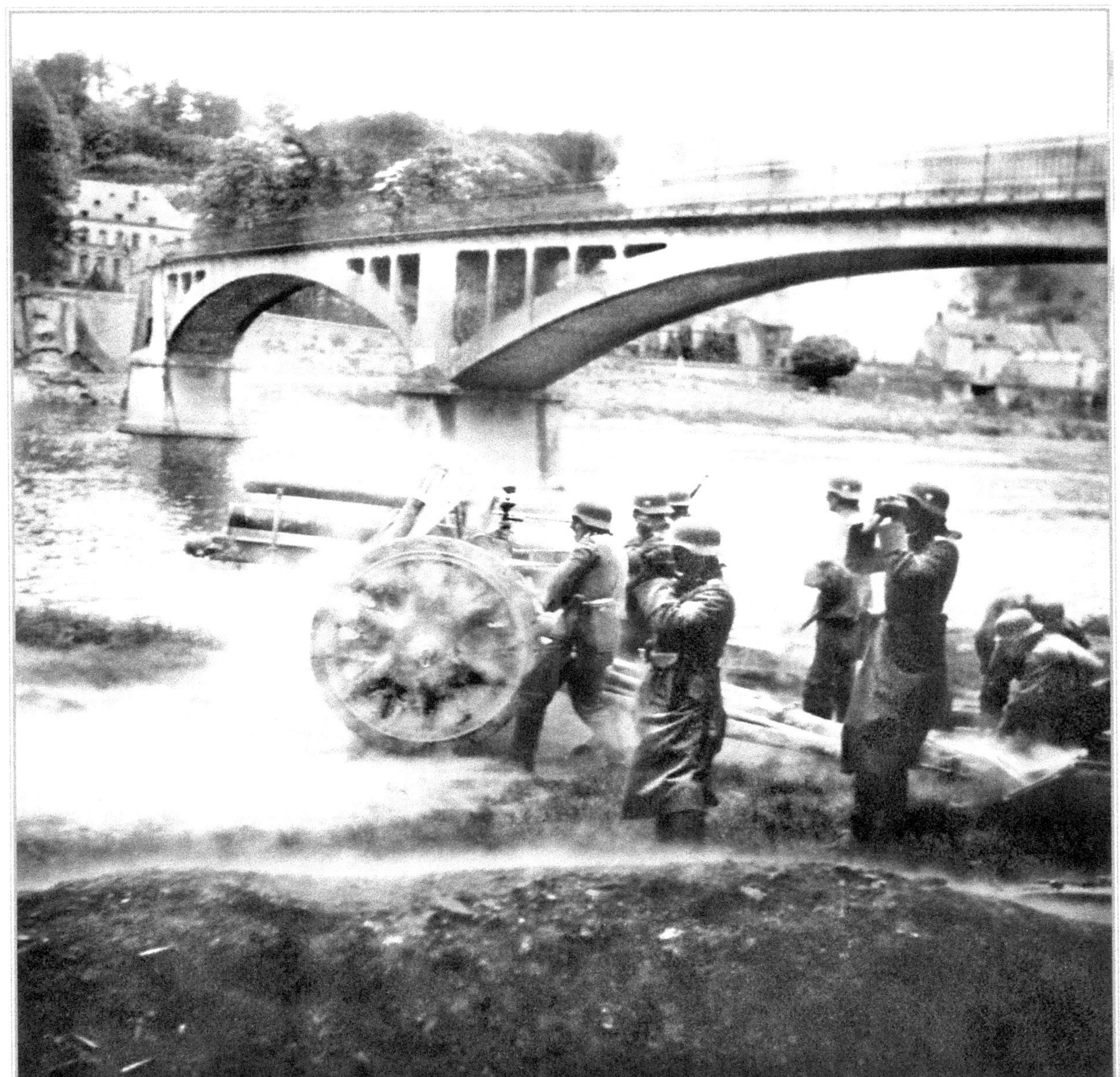

Dirt swirls around the crew of soldiers after an artillery blast.

The soldier on the right looks through the binoculars in the direction where the shot was fired. Rommel was standing very close to the firing gun while taking these pictures. More of the gunner crew is visible in this photo.

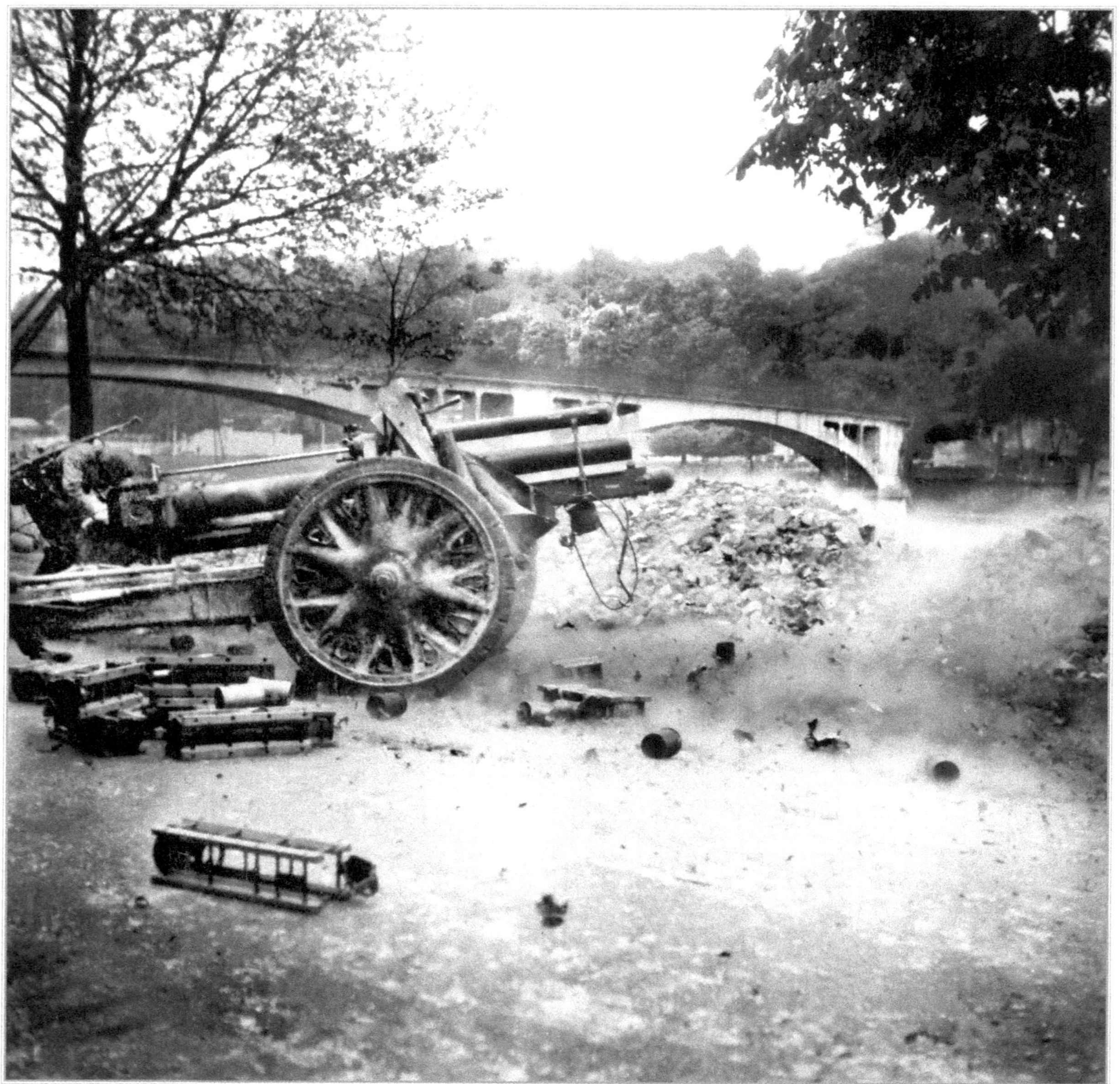

Another German soldier fires from an alternate position along the river in France.

A close-up view of this photo reveals that the gun has just been fired. A cloud of dust is shaken up from the earth, and pieces of debris appear blurred, indicating movement.

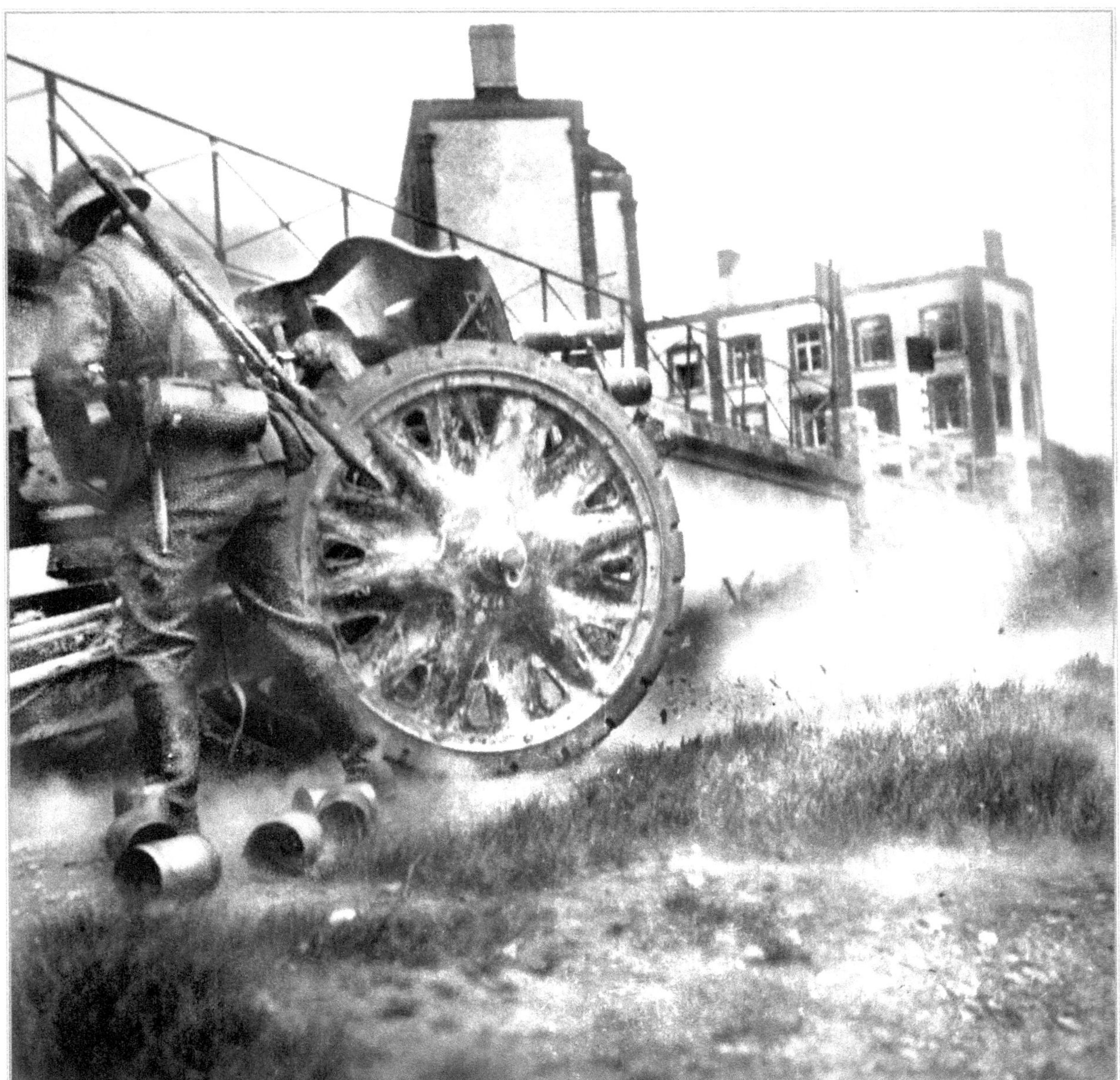

A German soldier reloads another artillery round in France.

Rommel seemingly crouched low to the ground to capture this side view of firing artillery. In his composition, the gun fills most of the frame, with the gunner appearing on the left side. The side of the wall is concealing the position of the gun from enemy view.

17.5.40.

Pommereuil

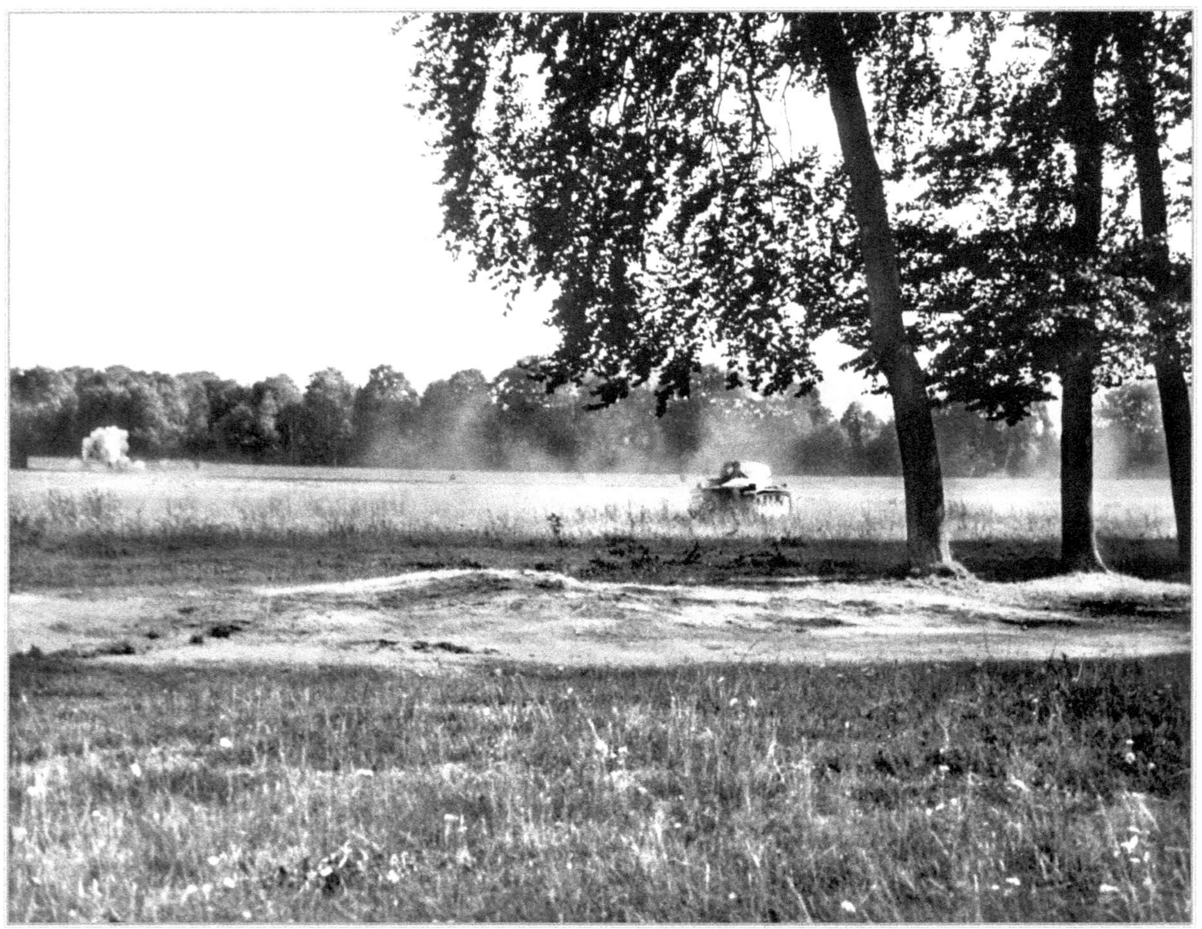

German tanks come under heavy fire from the woods as they advance near Pommereuil in northern France (May 17,1940).

At first, this photo appears asymmetrical. However, the central tank is balanced by three trees (right) and large plumes of smoke (left). Near the edge of the field, small puffs of smoke reveal a formation of tanks engaged in battle in the distance. Judging from the high vantage point, Rommel appears to have taken this photo series while approaching in a tank. In the following two photos, the tree branches shown above are visible hanging directly in front of Rommel's lens.

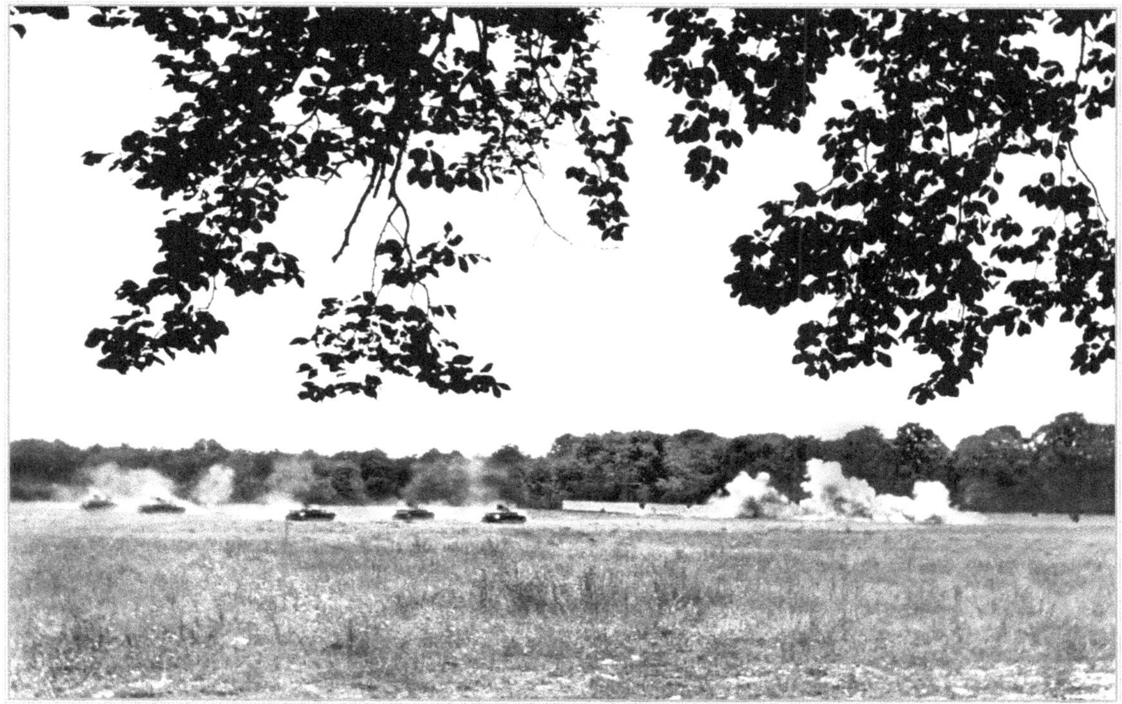

A formation of five Panzers race across a field in France.

The Panzers are traveling from left to right, apparently firing on a target. Clouds of smoke ensue from tank shell bursts.

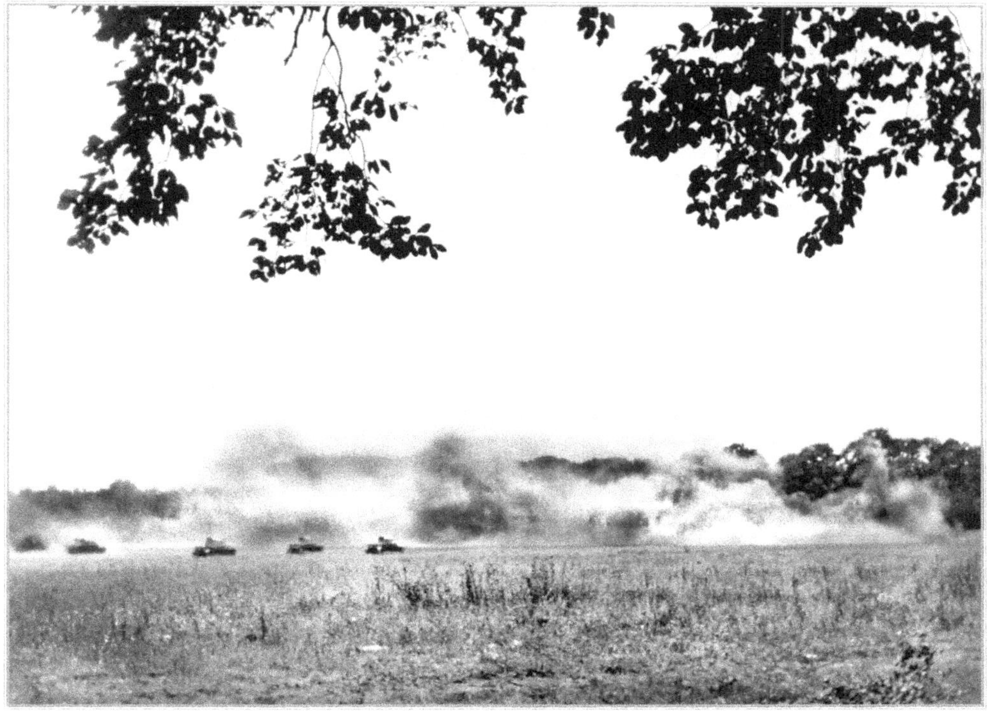

Another view of the tanks as they progress further across the field.

Rommel was monitoring the battle from a nearby grove of trees. The leaves and grass in the photo above appear closer than the lower image (left).

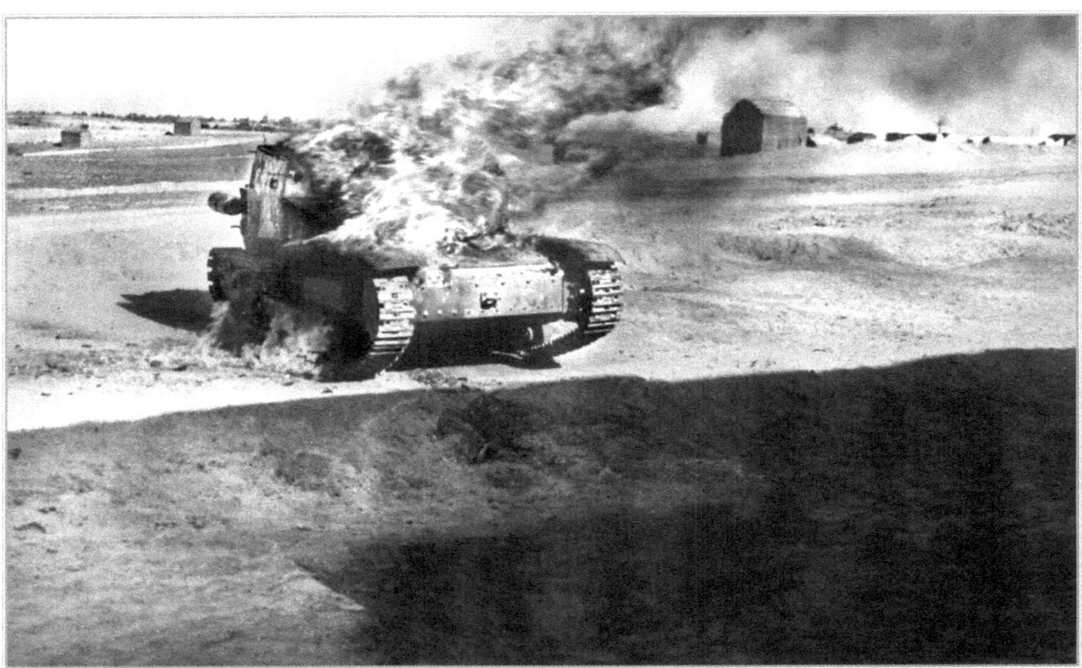

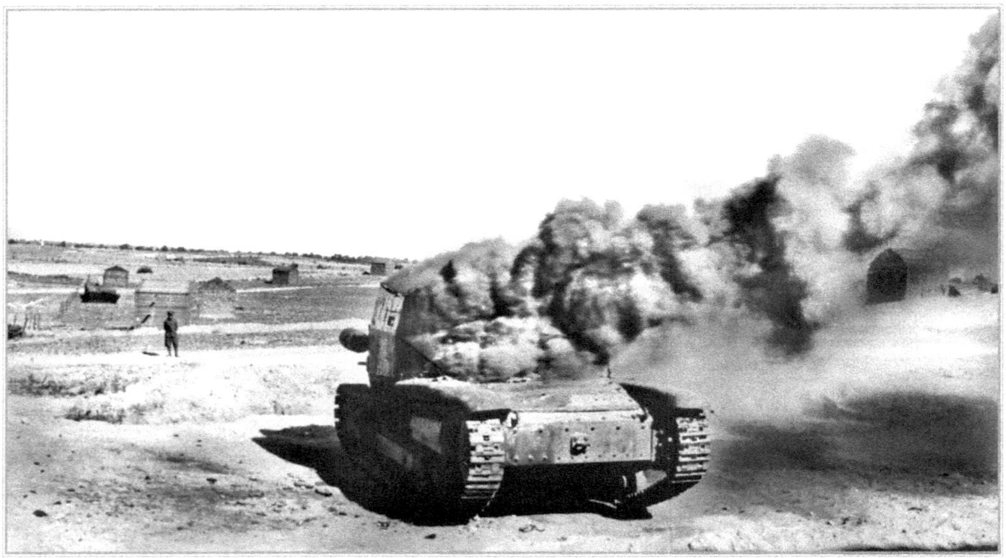

A tank is engulfed in flames in France.

Flames consume the tank (top) in the countryside. The large dark shadow that appears on the ground may have ensued from a nearby building.

In the second photo (above), Rommel has stepped closer to the tank. Only a sliver remains of the shadow compared to the first photo. The fire in the tank has changed into thick smoke. A man in a uniform stands by while watching both the tank and the photographer.

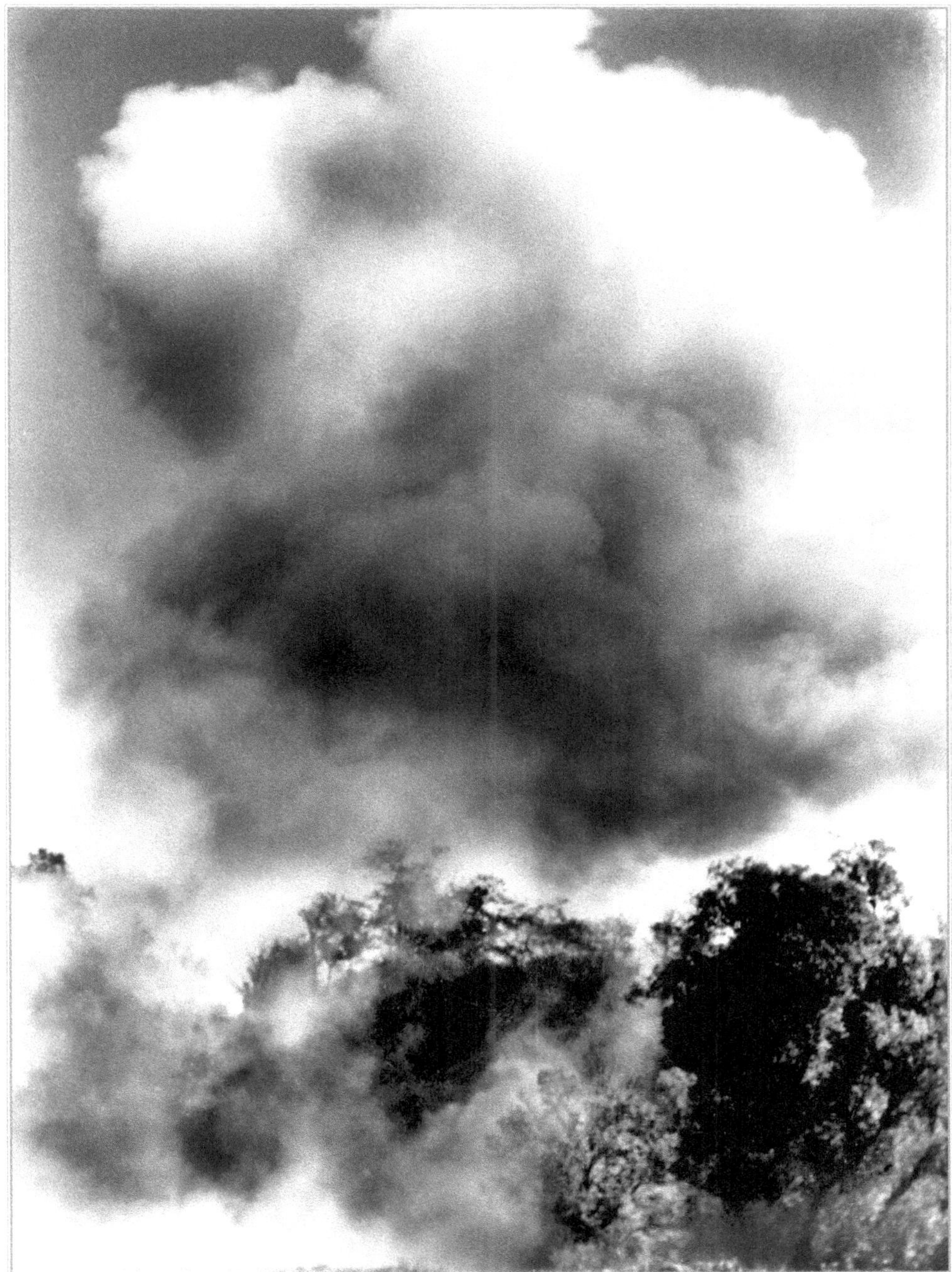

A cloud of smoke from a bomb blast billows above trees in France.

This image does not seem to have military value. The formation of billowing smoke is similar to the round shapes of the treetops.

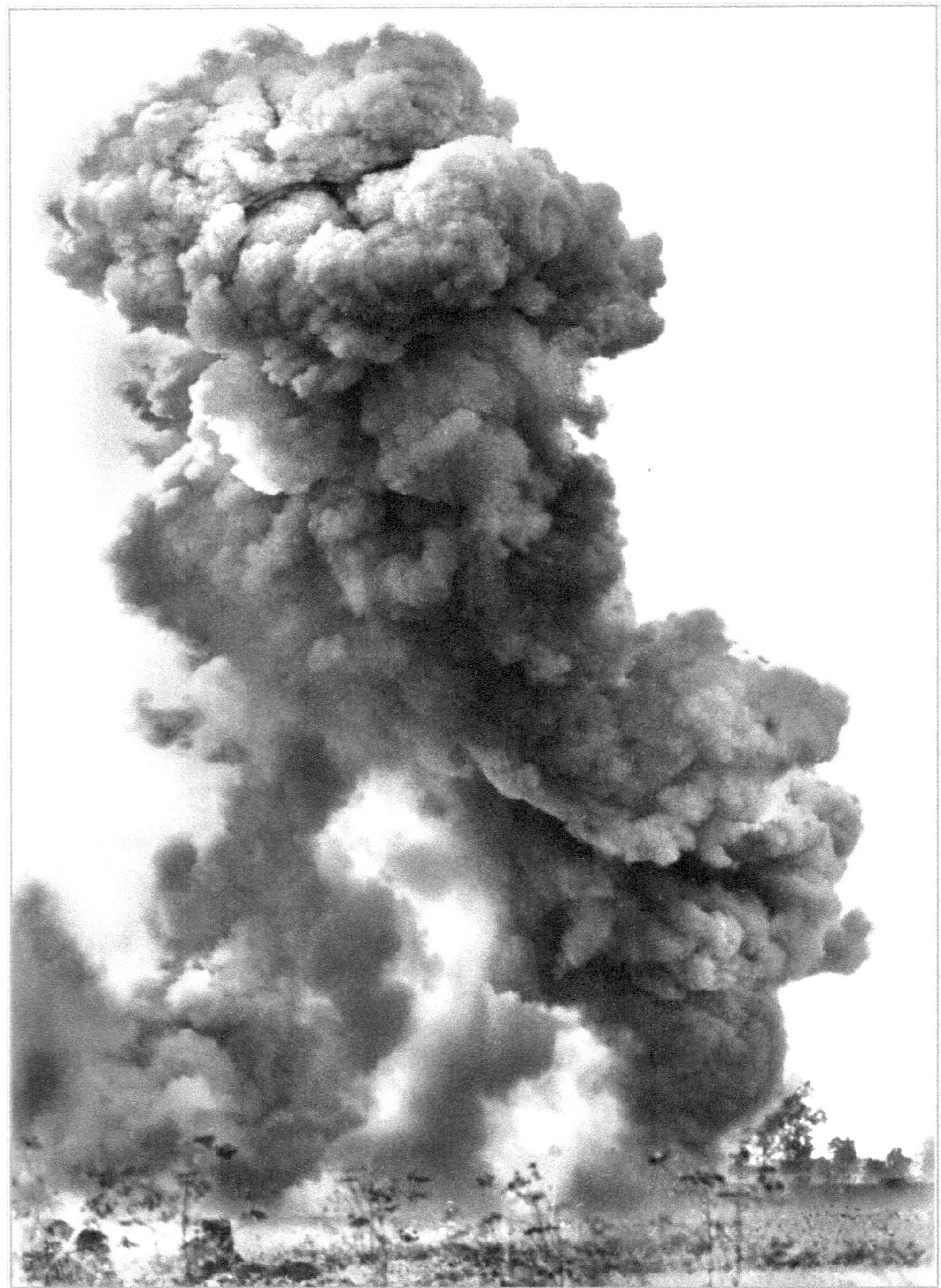

An enormous explosion sends a pillar of smoke flying into the sky in France.

Rommel was obviously very close to the explosion when he took this photo. He must have felt the immediate effects of the blast, such as ash and the strong smell of smoke.

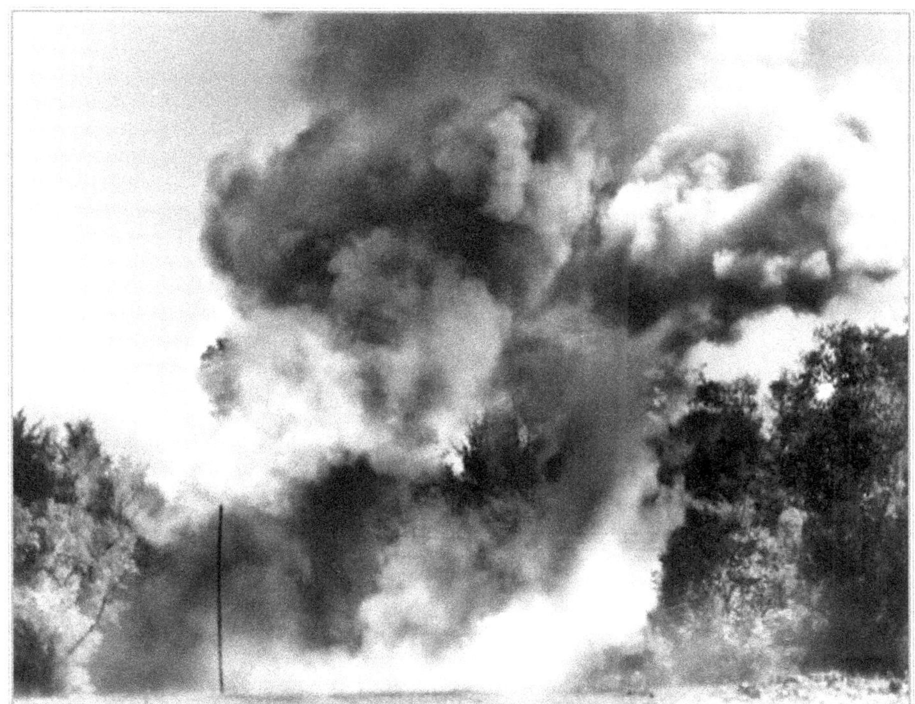

Smoke soars from a blast in a grove of trees in France.

A lone pole stands in the foreground (left), which suggests the trees were next to a road. The high level at which this image was photographed indicates Rommel was atop a command vehicle as he took this picture.

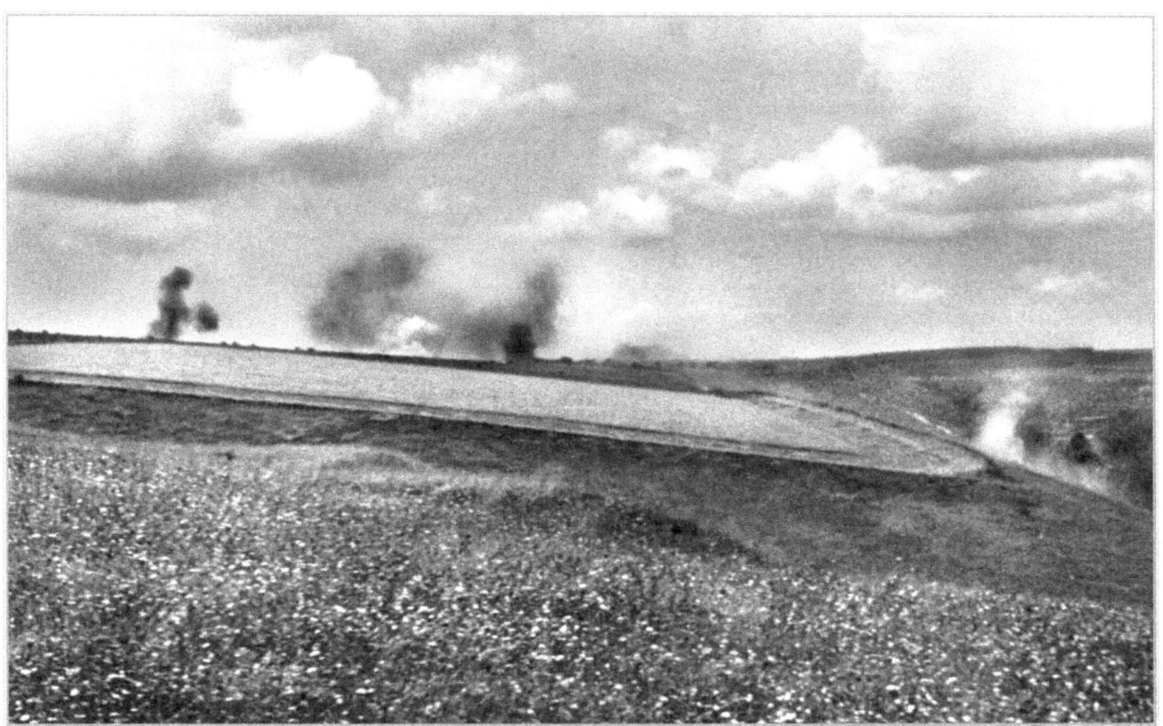

Smoke plumes rise from a series of blasts around the perimeter of a clearing in France.

Blick auf das brennende St. Valery nach der Einnahme von der Höhe westl. d. Stadt.

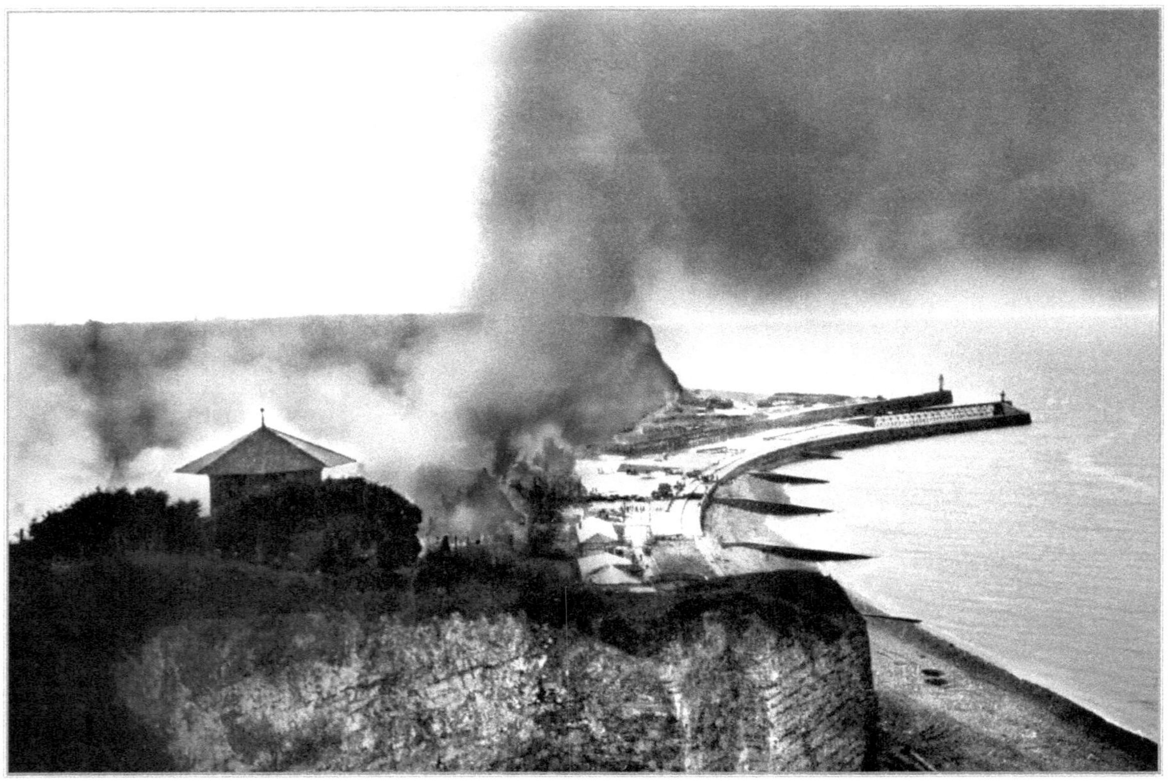

Smoke fills the sky following the German siege of Saint-Valery-en-Caux in France.

Rommel likely took this photo while standing on a height overlooking the town. He captures the smoke plume precisely in the center of the frame.

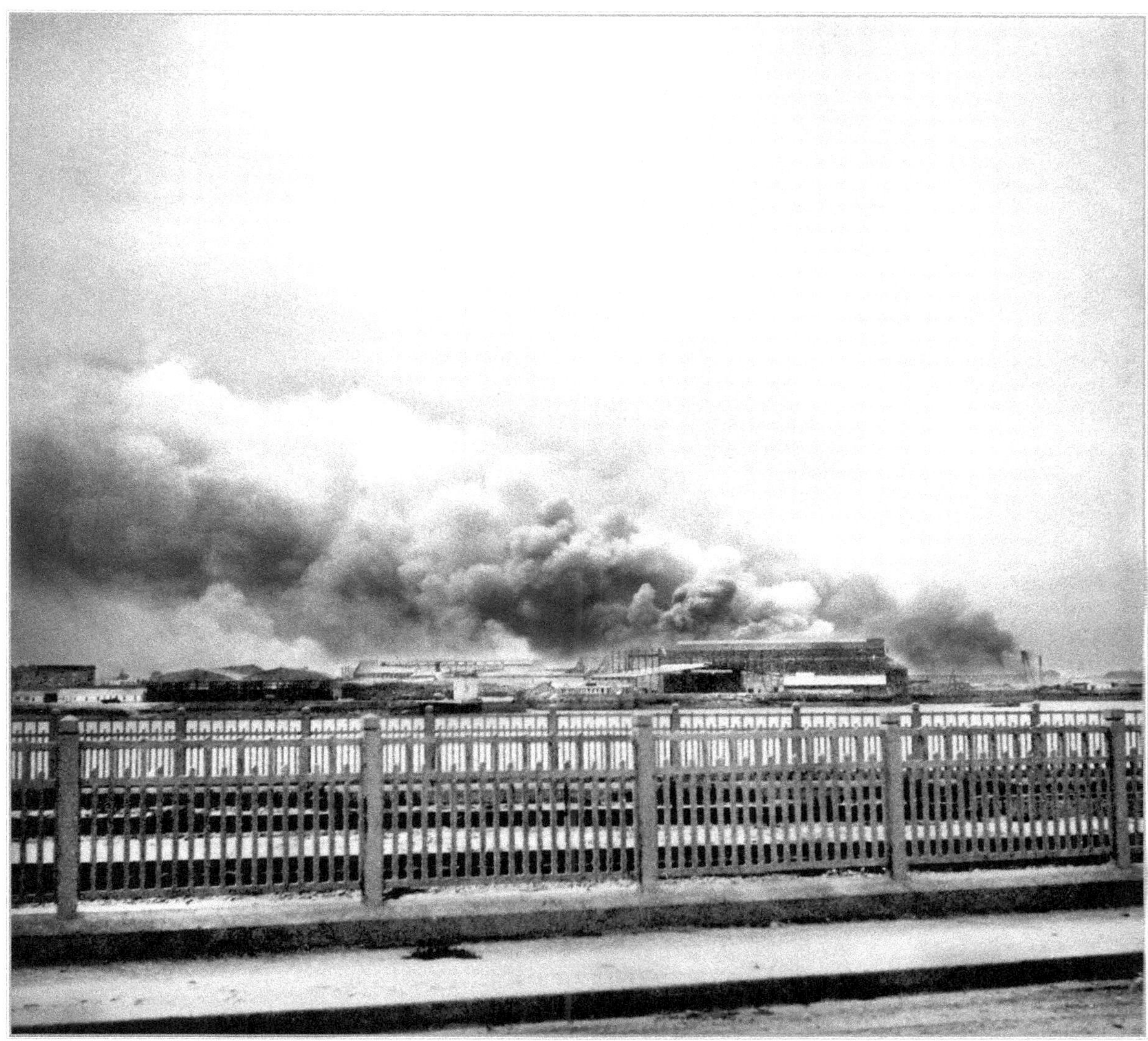

A roadside view of another German bombing in France.

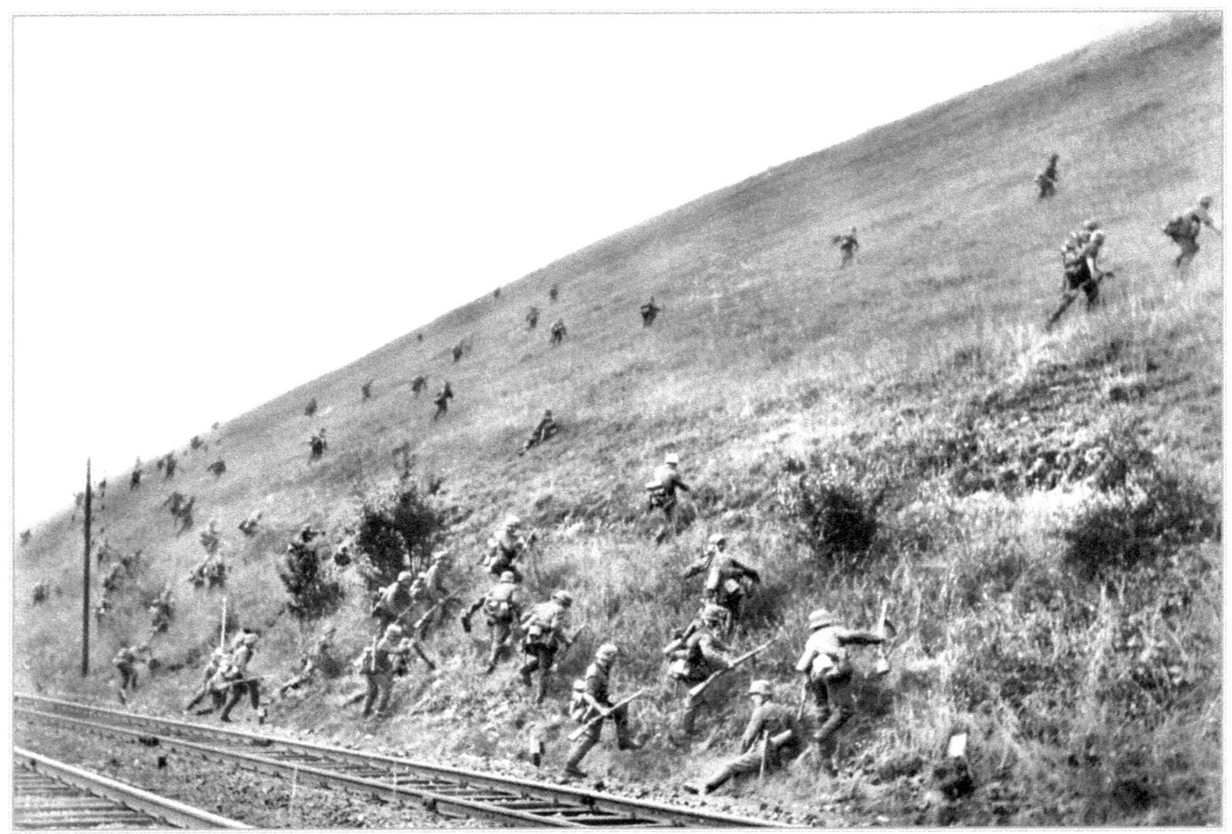

German soldiers charge up a hill in France.

Rommel photographed various angles of this scene (above and right) as the event unfolded. While watching and overseeing the action, he documented the activities in this photo series. He may have wanted to use these photos in the military manual he wished to write.

He shows characteristic patterns in this photo. Two train tracks form a diagonal element, and, as in many of his other photos, the subjects decrease in size from one side of the frame to the other. One of the soldiers (lower right) appears to have slipped down the hill beside the railroad tracks. The others nearby balance themselves using rifles in their right hands as they ascend the steep hillside.

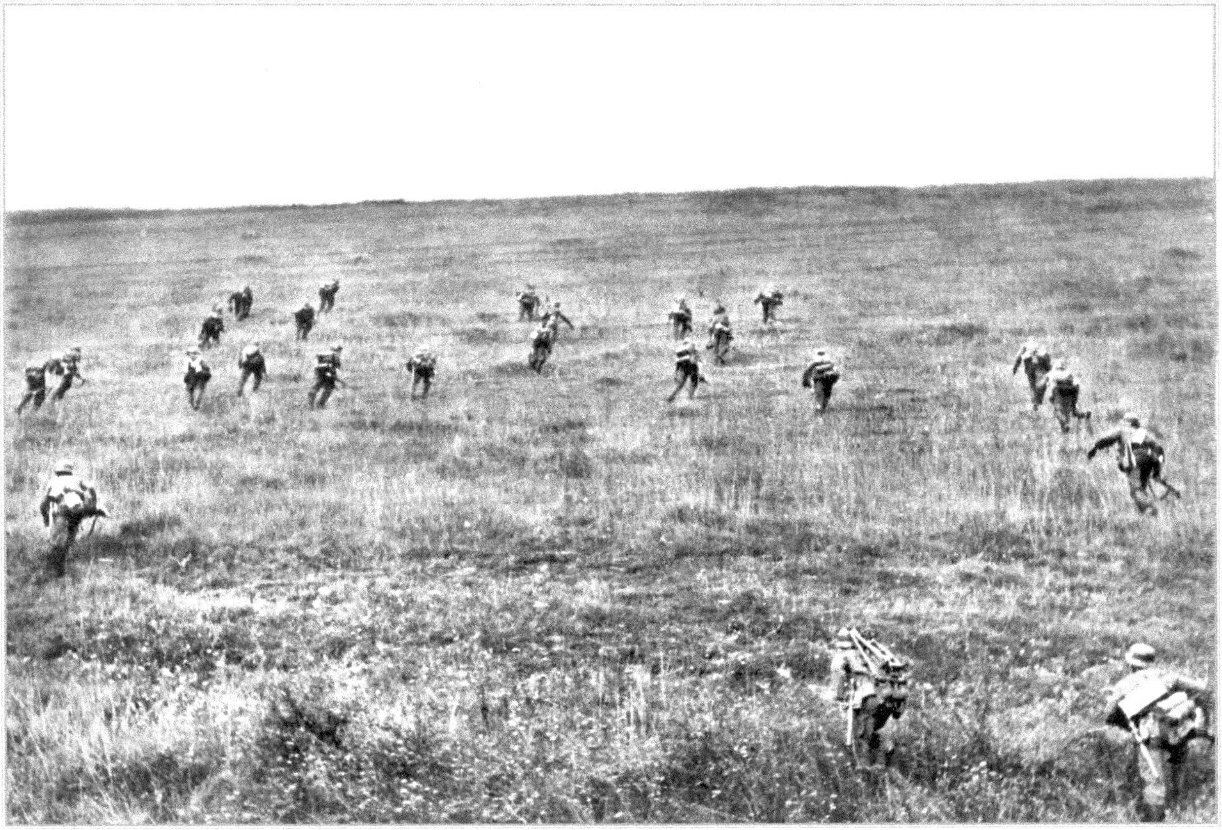

German infantry (above and below) ascend a hill in France.

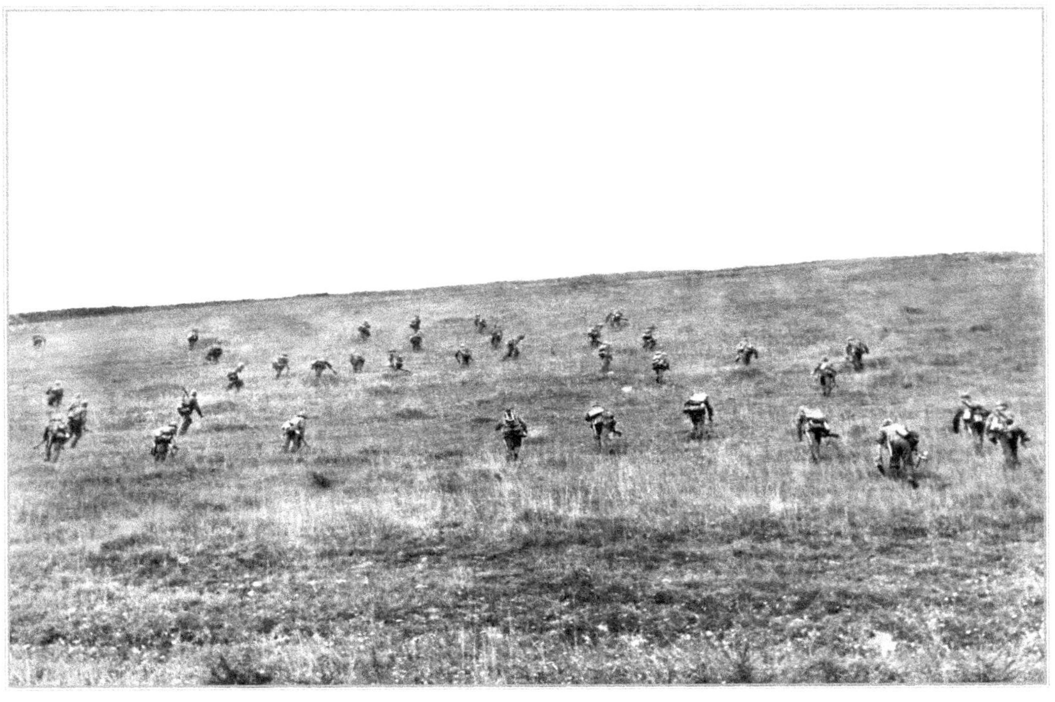

Different types of equipment can be seen on the soldiers' backs, which are bent under their heavy loads.

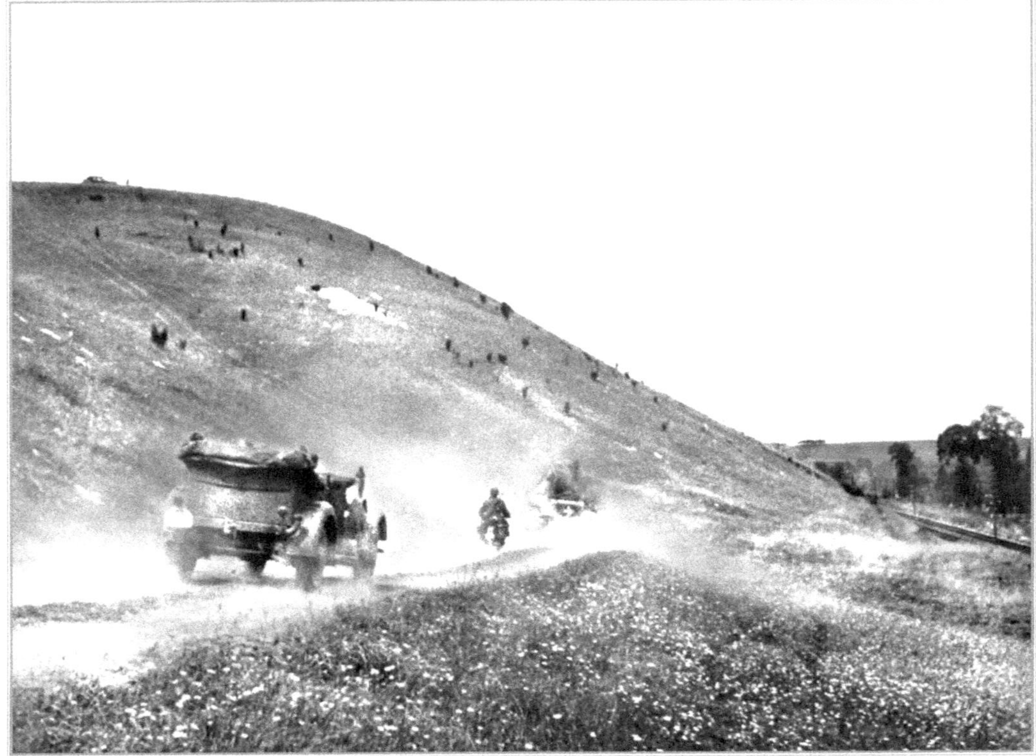

An armored car leads the column. Railway tracks can be seen on the right. Two men's helmets are apparent in the back of one car. In the center, a motorcyclist is visible in the dust.

German vehicles (above and below) press onward into France.

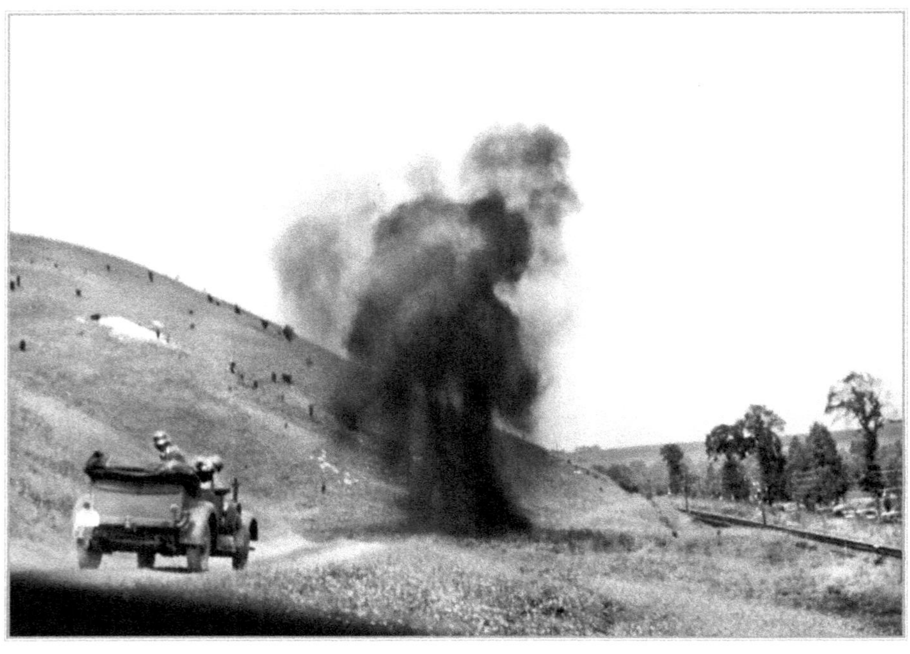

A shell hits the ground as the Germans advance further down the road. The motorcyclist is no longer visible. One soldier in the vehicle stands and recoils from the blast. This photo is slightly out-of-focus, indicating Rommel moved during this shot as the blast hit. Part of Rommel's vehicle appears in the left corner of the frame.

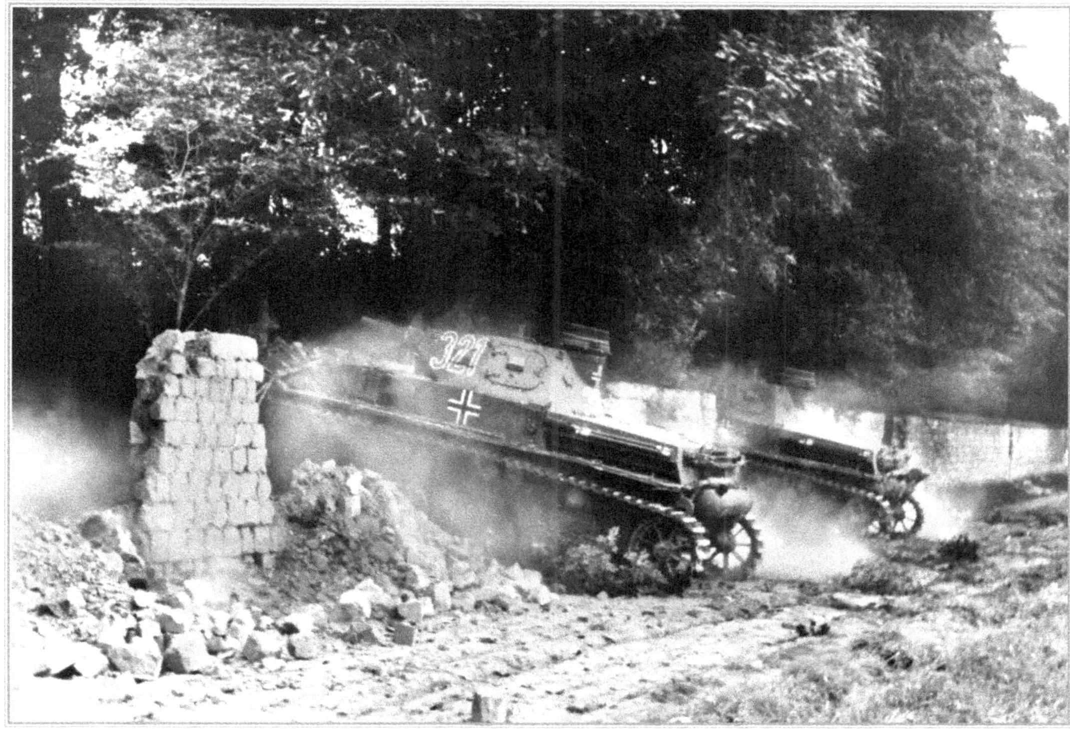

German tanks crash through a brick wall during their advance through France.

This photo was taken at very close range. The destruction of the wall is magnified by the flying dust and the motion of the pair of tanks. The precise composition shows Rommel's ability to capture rapidly moving objects with methodical accuracy.

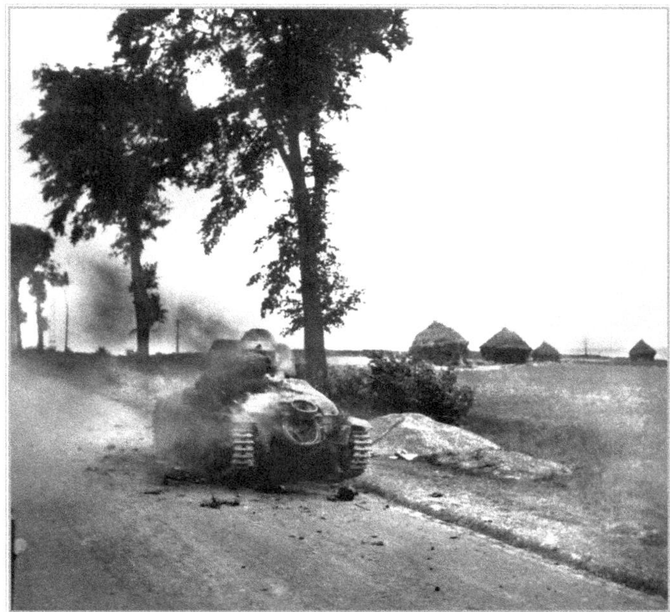

Debris surrounds a smoldering tank in France.

The tank took a direct hit in the front below the turret. The impact caused debris to scatter several feet away from the tank.

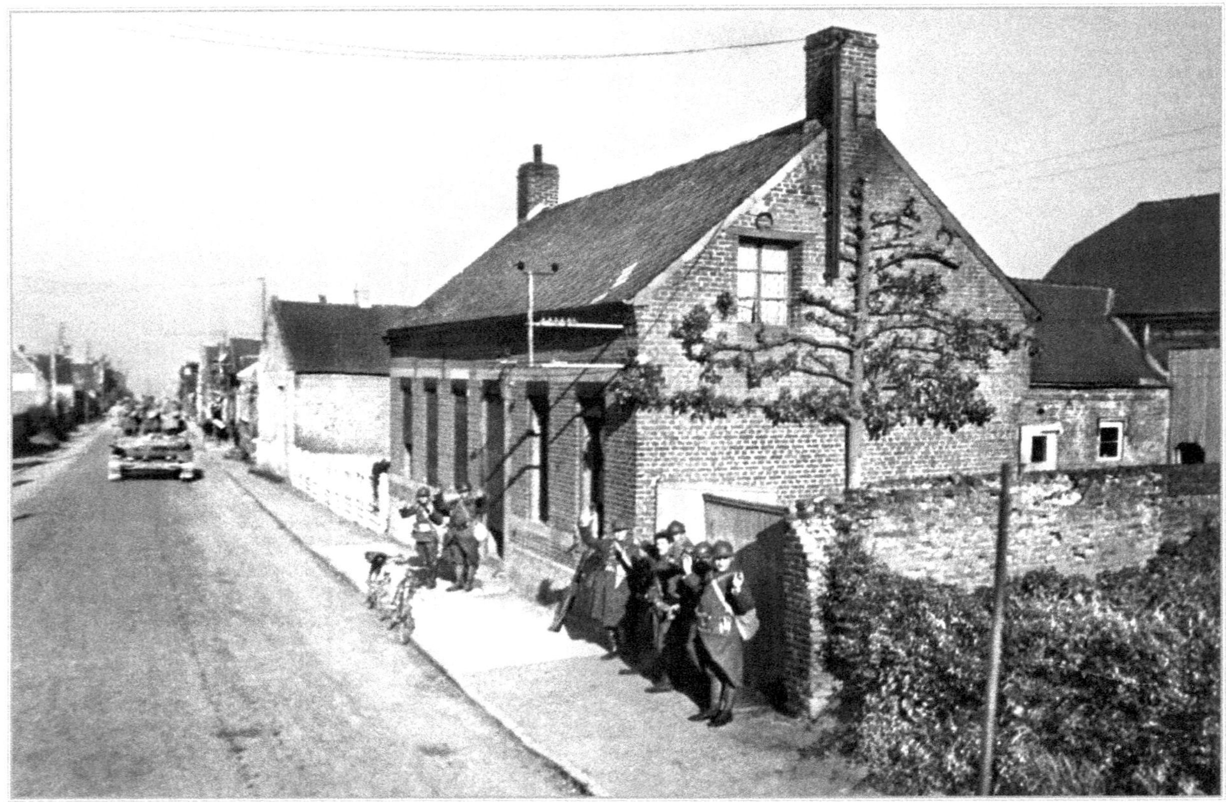

French soldiers raise their hands in surrender to German troops.

A Panzer unit has just passed the French soldiers, who stand aside on the sidewalk as Rommel approaches. Judging from Rommel's vantage point, he seems to have been riding on a tank. Two French soldiers look directly up at Rommel. The others stare at something on the roadway beyond—probably at the column of tanks following Rommel's.

In Rommel's war diary, he stated that many French soldiers surrendered to the Germans with minimal or no resistance during the invasion. This was partially due to the sudden and swift appearance of Rommel's "Ghost Division," which took many French troops by surprise. There also was confusion among French officers as to whether an armistice with Germany had been agreed on, making some of them unwilling to fight. The combination of these factors resulted in disorganization and chaos among the French ranks.

Many French soldiers fled immediately at the sight of German tanks. Some were taken as POWs, while others ran away into wooded areas shortly after surrendering. There were so many French soldiers surrendering at once that the Germans could not manage to take all of them as POWs and allowed many simply to desert.

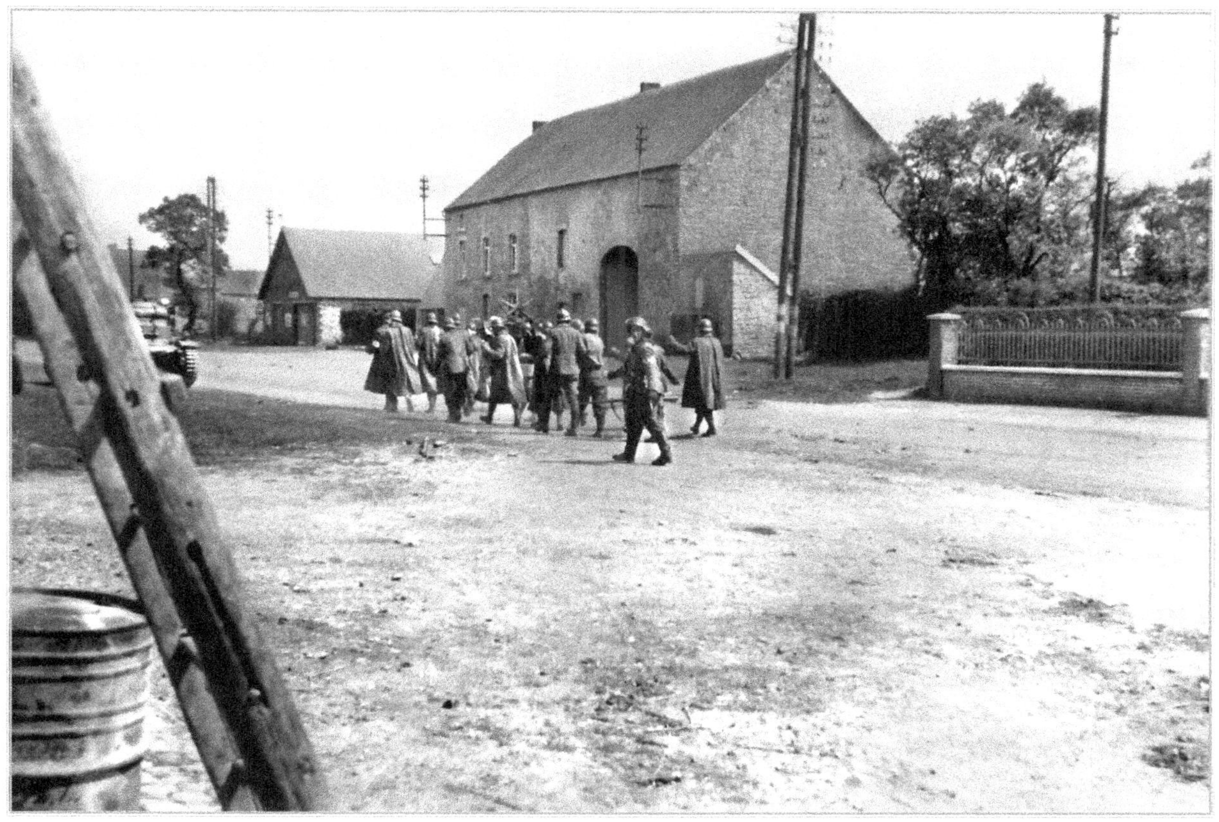

A German soldier escorts more than a dozen captured French soldiers.

The German soldier, who carries a rifle in this right hand, turns away from the group to face Rommel as this photo is taken. A Panzer is visible beyond the ladder on the left.

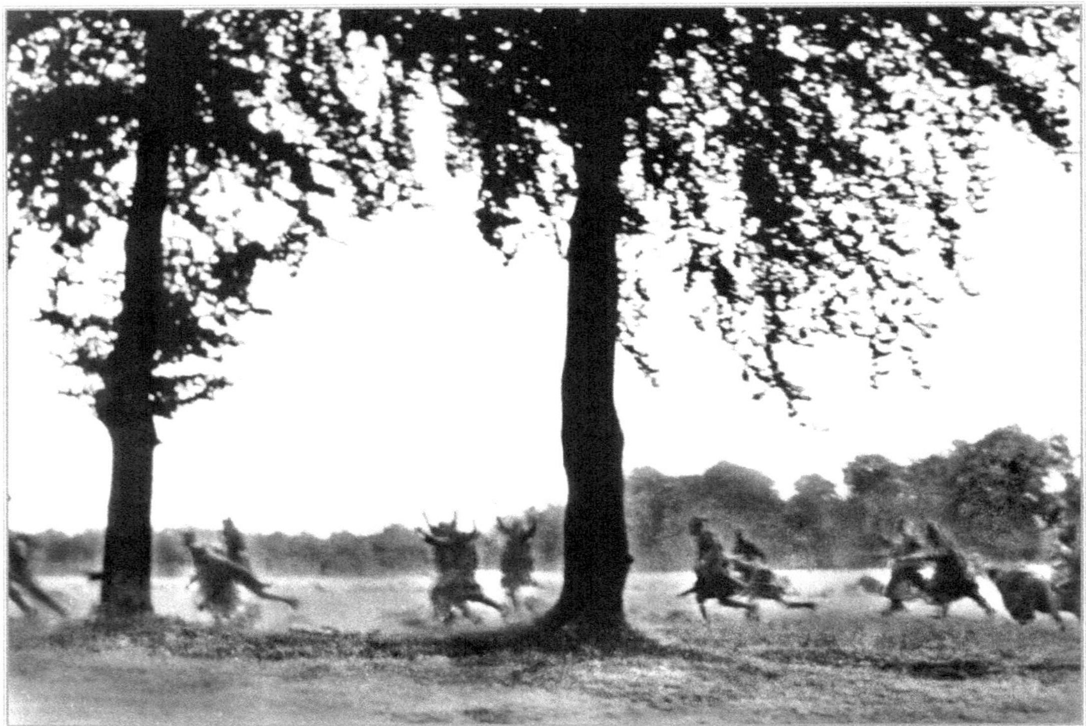

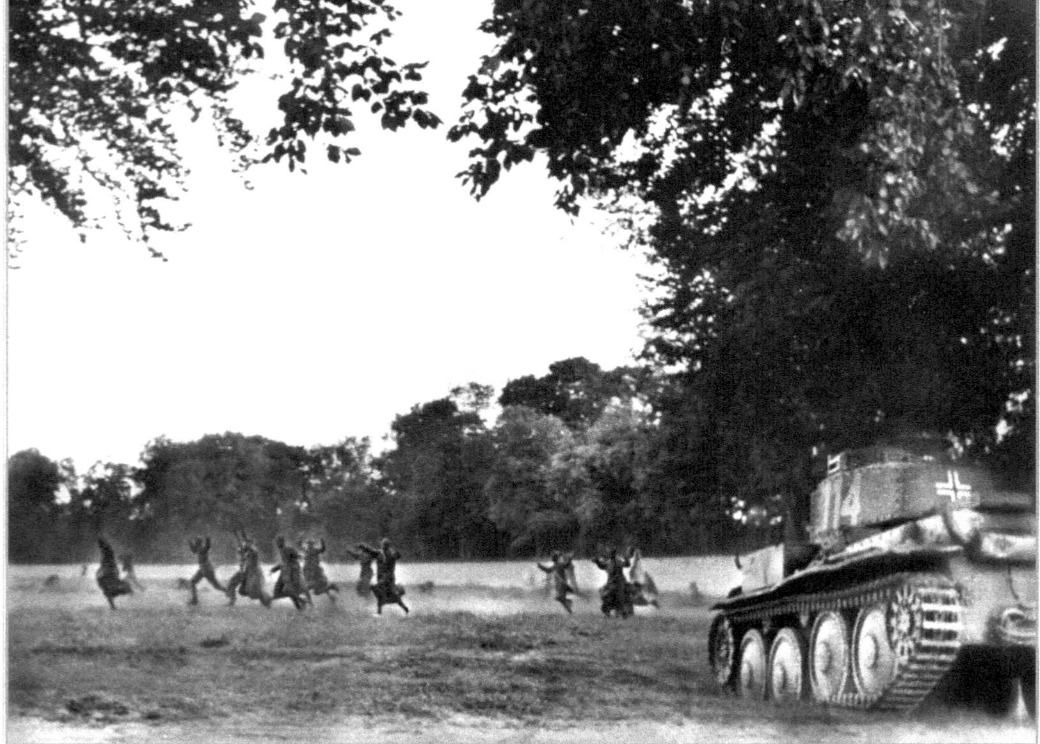

French soldiers surrender and flee (above and below) from the Germans in France.

Die „[illegible] zeigt Erfolg.
„A bas les armes!"

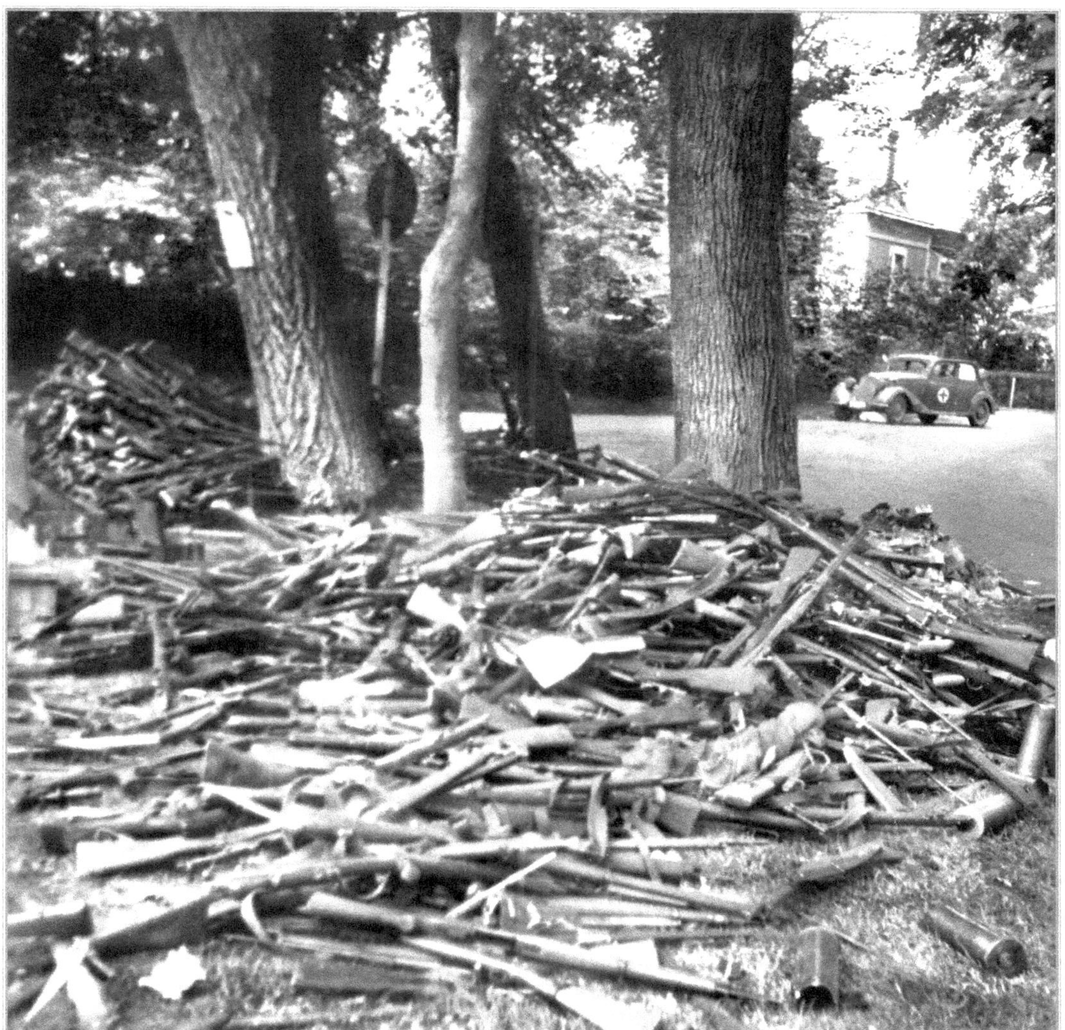

French rifles are thrown in a heap after being discarded by deserting and surrendering French soldiers.

As the Germans advanced, they shouted to the French to lay down their arms. Many French soldiers cast aside or turned in their weapons. The Germans arranged the discarded rifles in piles by the roadside.

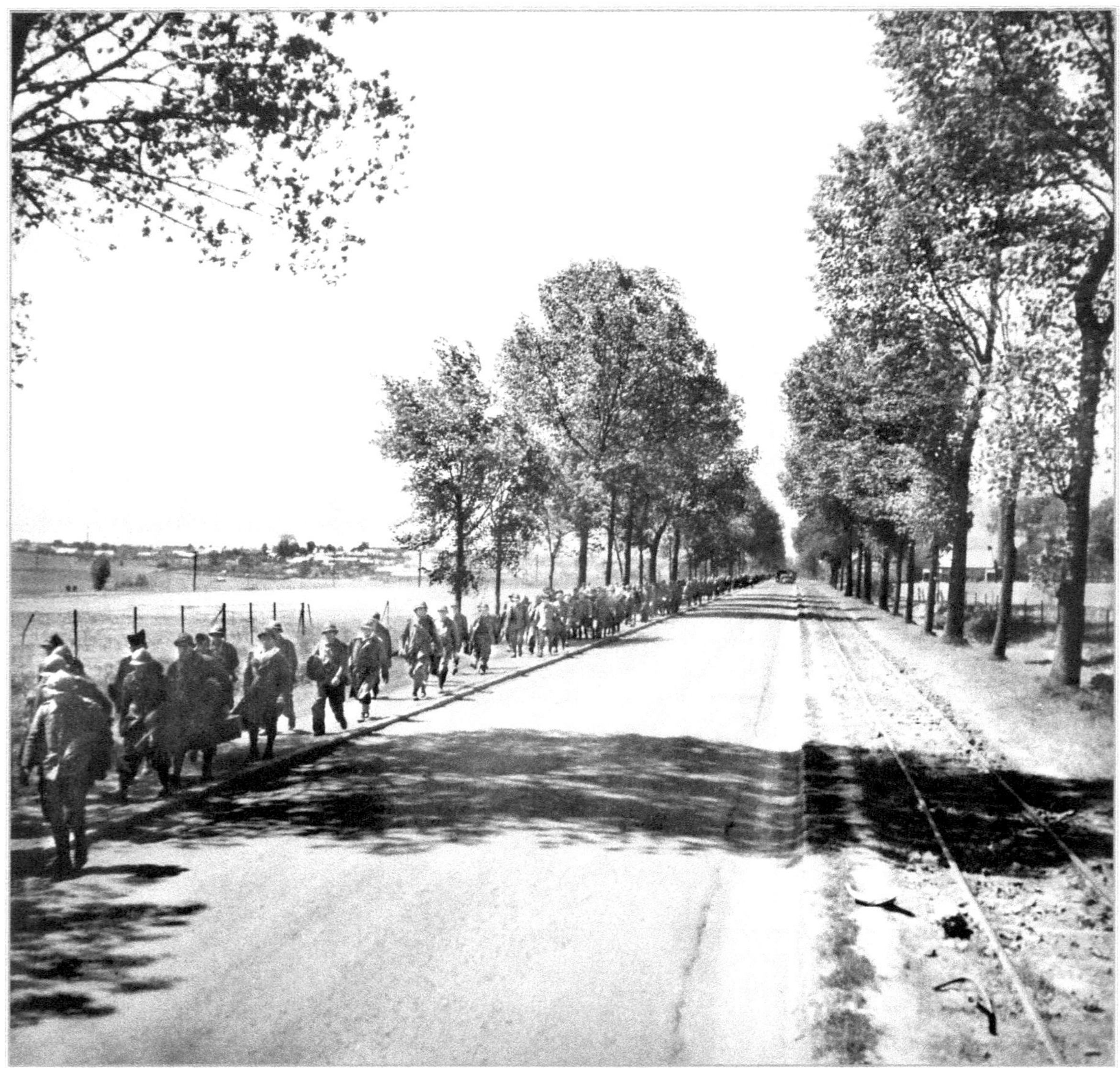

French soldiers trudge along a roadside after having surrendered to the advancing Germans.

In Rommel's memoirs, he notes that the roads in France were typically crowded with French deserters, surrendering soldiers, and civilians fleeing en masse from towns and cities. In this photo, only French soldiers walk down the street on the left. French POWs frequently marched alongside German columns. In the center of the road, a German vehicle approaches the camera. It appears that Rommel turned around while inside a car to take this photo. The straight lines on each side of the road converge in the center of the image, creating Rommel's characteristic optical illusion of infinity.

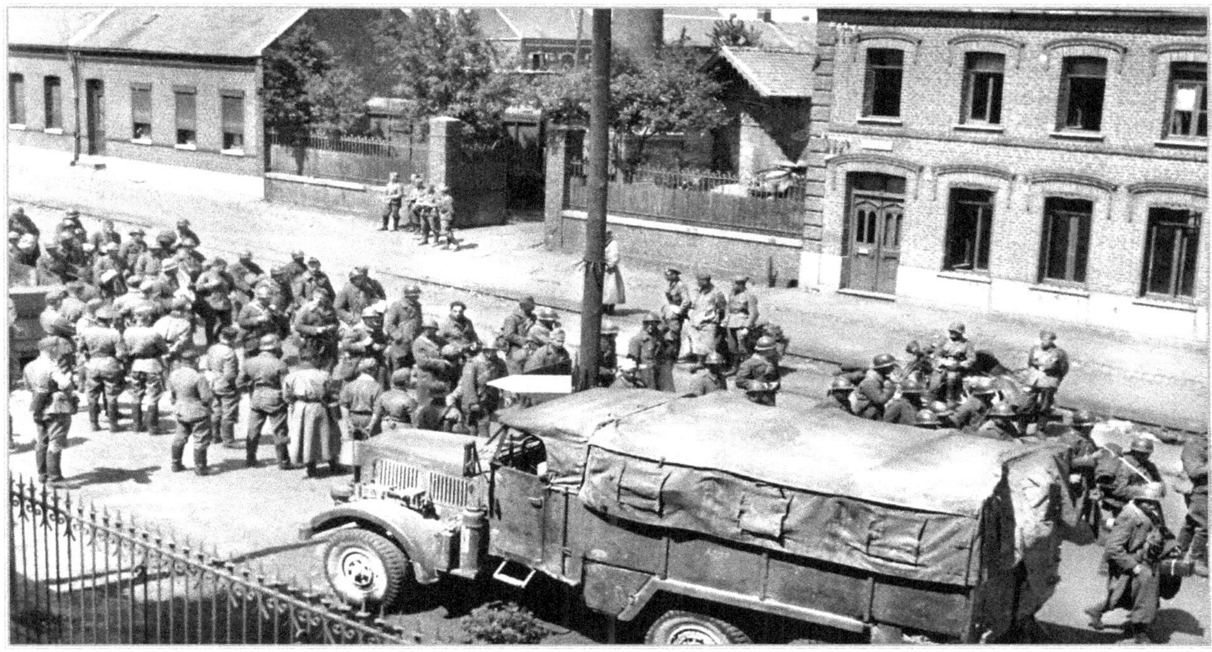

Captive French soldiers march past a truck in France.

German troops stand on each side of the street facing the French soldiers, who are marching to the right of the frame. Most of the POWs are carrying their equipment and belongings. Rommel seems to have taken this photo from a building facing the street.

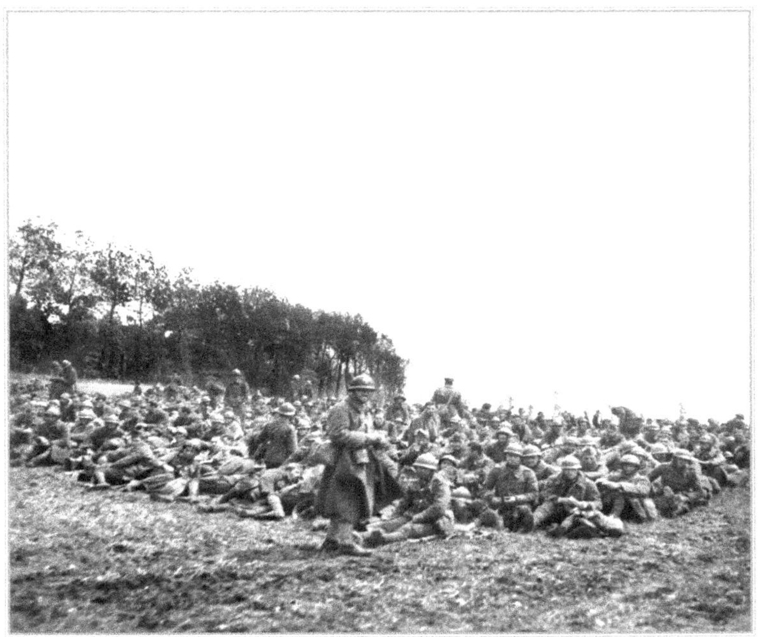

A large group of French soldiers gathers in a field in France.

One French soldier (center) is flanked by others who look at the camera as Rommel takes this photo.

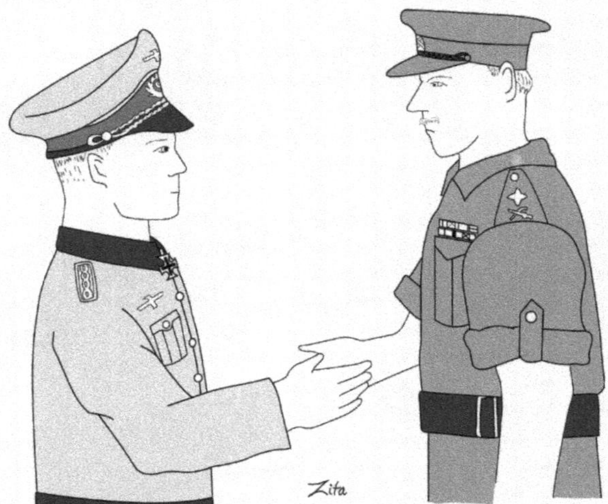

During the invasion of France in 1940, Rommel won two major victories by capturing the fortified cities of St. Valery-en-Caux and Cherbourg along the Normandy coast.

In St. Valery, Rommel's actions led to the surrender and capture of 12,000 Allied soldiers, including 12 generals. Among the high-ranking POWs were four divisional commanders, including General Marcel Ihler of the French 9th Corps and General Victor Fortune of Britain's 51st Highland Division.

Afterwards, Rommel successfully negotiated the surrender of the heavily armed fortress of Cherbourg following a brief bombardment of the city's military targets, including the forts and the naval dockyard. It was one of the last decisive German victories in France 1940.

In both places, Rommel agreed on conditions of surrender with Allied commanding officers, which were communicated to all captured soldiers. Rommel ordered surrendering troops to carry prominent white flags so that the German forces stationed at a distance could see that hostilities had ended, thus preventing unnecessary fire. Formal ceremonies of surrender were arranged at set times.

Rommel's personal letters and writings from those days indicated he was proud of these accomplishments. Pictures of these events, taken by war photographers, were saved among his photo collection.

It is said that Rommel greatly respected British General Fortune, captured at St. Valery. Rommel apparently spoke to his family about Fortune with soldierly admiration.

After his repatriation to Britain in 1945, Fortune also reportedly sent a message of condolence to Rommel's widow in Germany. General Fortune suffered a stroke while he was a POW and died in 1949. General Ihler, a POW until 1945, died in 1975.

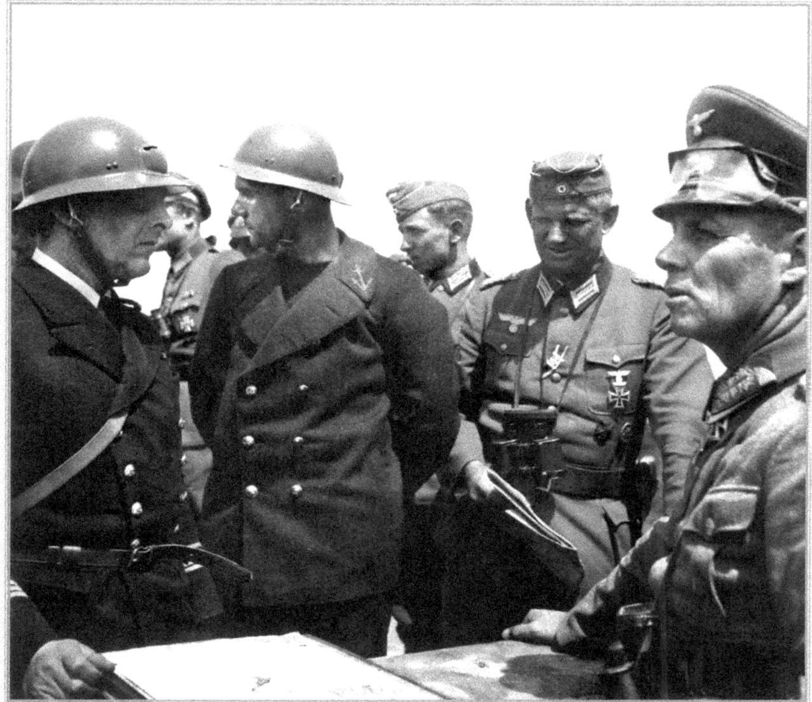

French naval officers write Rommel's terms of surrender outside of Cherbourg, France. Col. Karl Rothenburg is present.

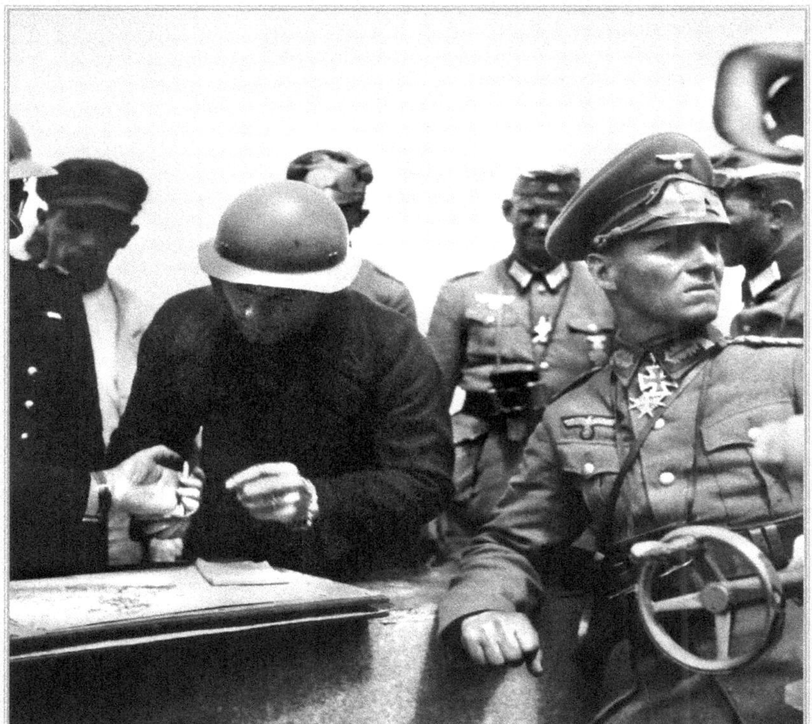

Rommel's camera hangs out of view on his right side (above).

"After a quick exchange of salutes with my officers, I addressed the senior French officer, through the interpreter, in roughly the following terms:
'As Commander of the German troops at Cherbourg, I take note of the fact that the fortress has surrendered and wish to express my pleasure that the surrender has taken place without bloodshed among the civilian population.'

The French Chief of Staff then had me informed, on behalf of the officers, that the fortress would not have surrendered if sufficient ammunition had been available."

— *Rommel*

POWs are walking in small groups at the base of the cliffs towards the camera. Others walk across the beach to an unknown location. Rommel's characteristic curving lines and infinity effect appear in this image.

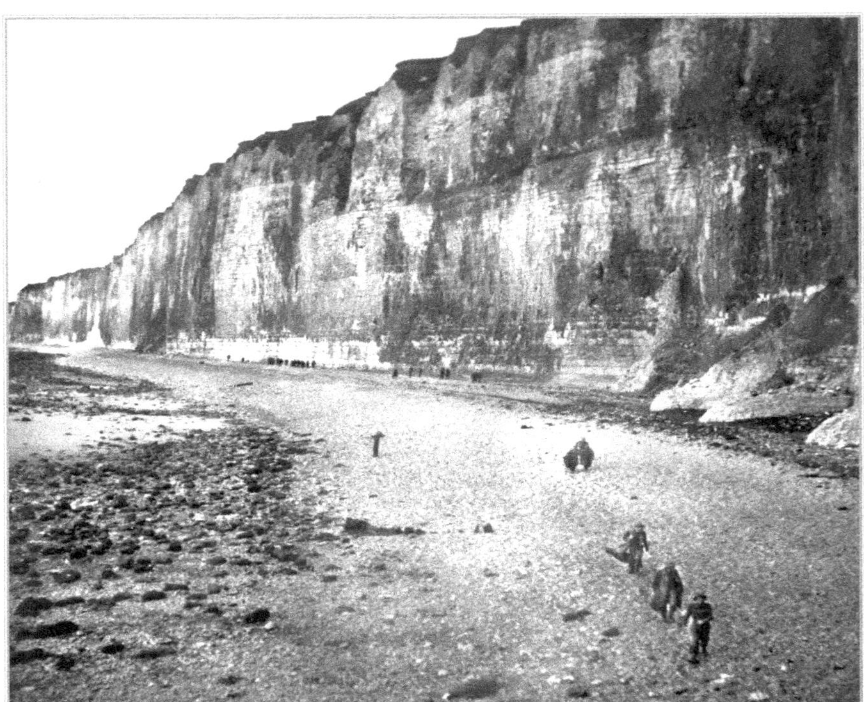

Groups of captive British soldiers walk near the coastline in France.

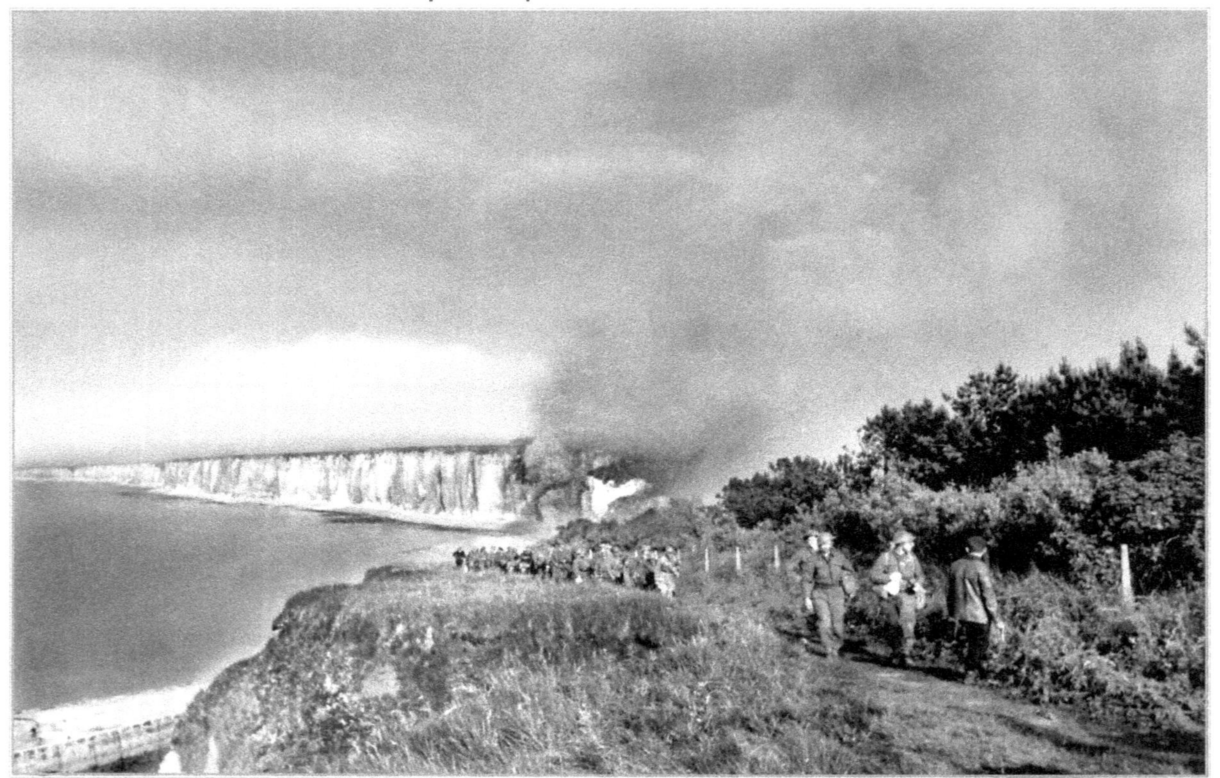

The captured soldiers have traveled a long distance from the beaches below up to this hillside.

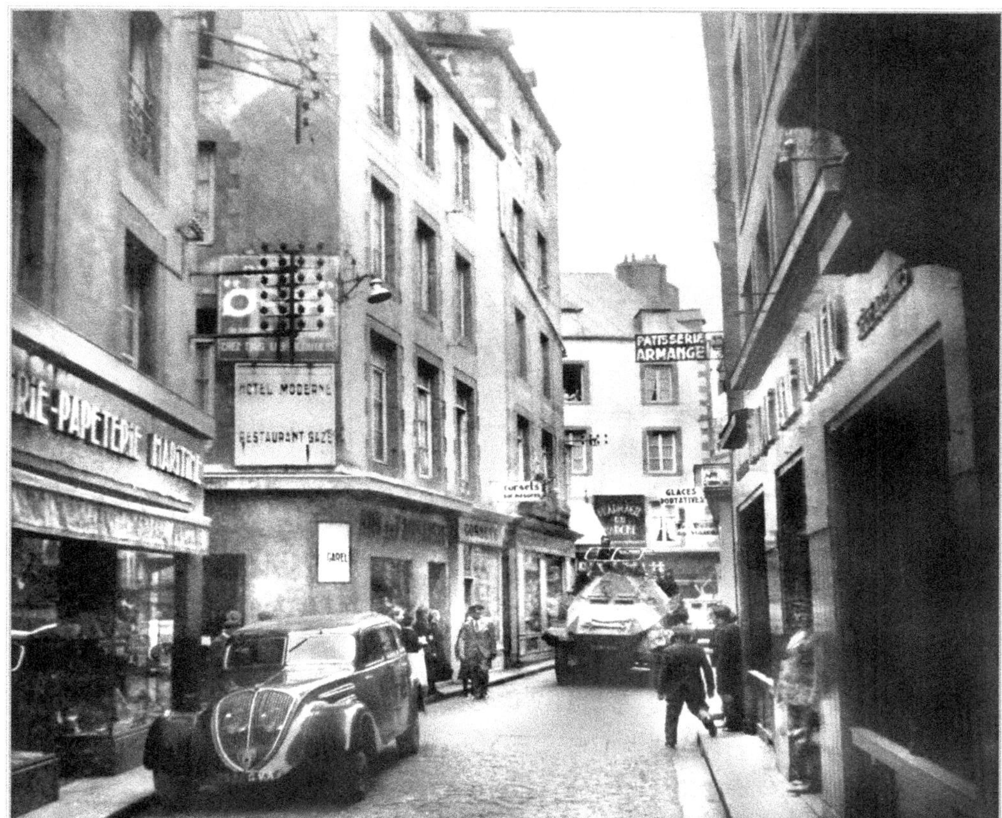

French civilians in urban areas step aside (above and below) as German soldiers pass besides them in tanks and armored vehicles in France.

The image below was taken in Landrecies, France on May 17, 1940. The Germans were crossing the Sambre river.

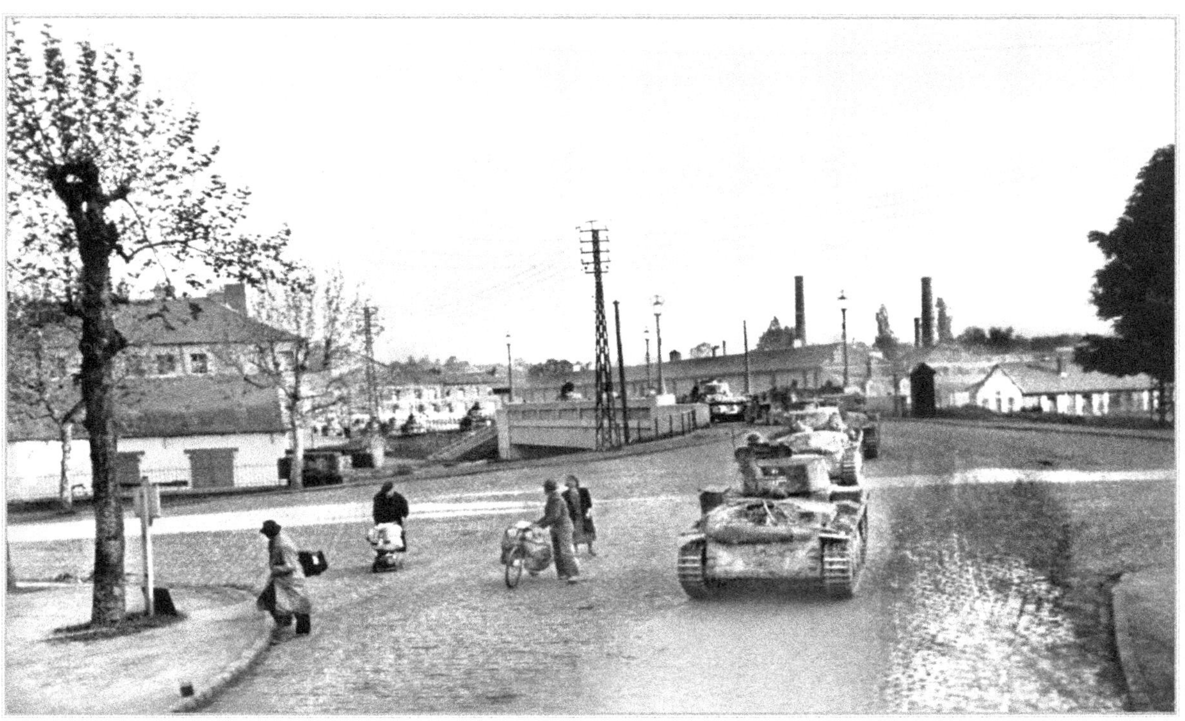

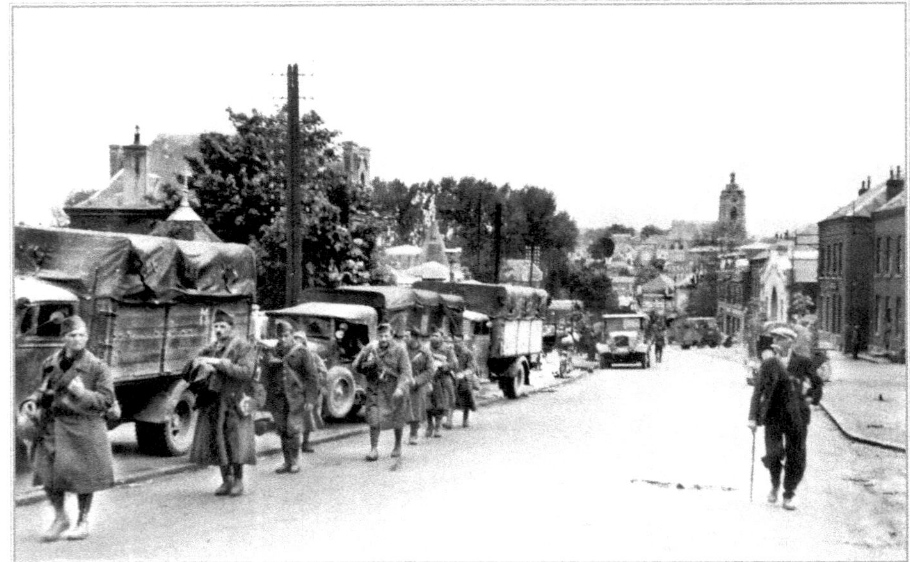

The old man with the cane looks towards the line of French troops, who carry their belongings as they march next to the vehicles parked on the street.

An elderly French civilian (right) stares at a band of French colonial troops walking on the opposite side of the street in Avesnes, France.

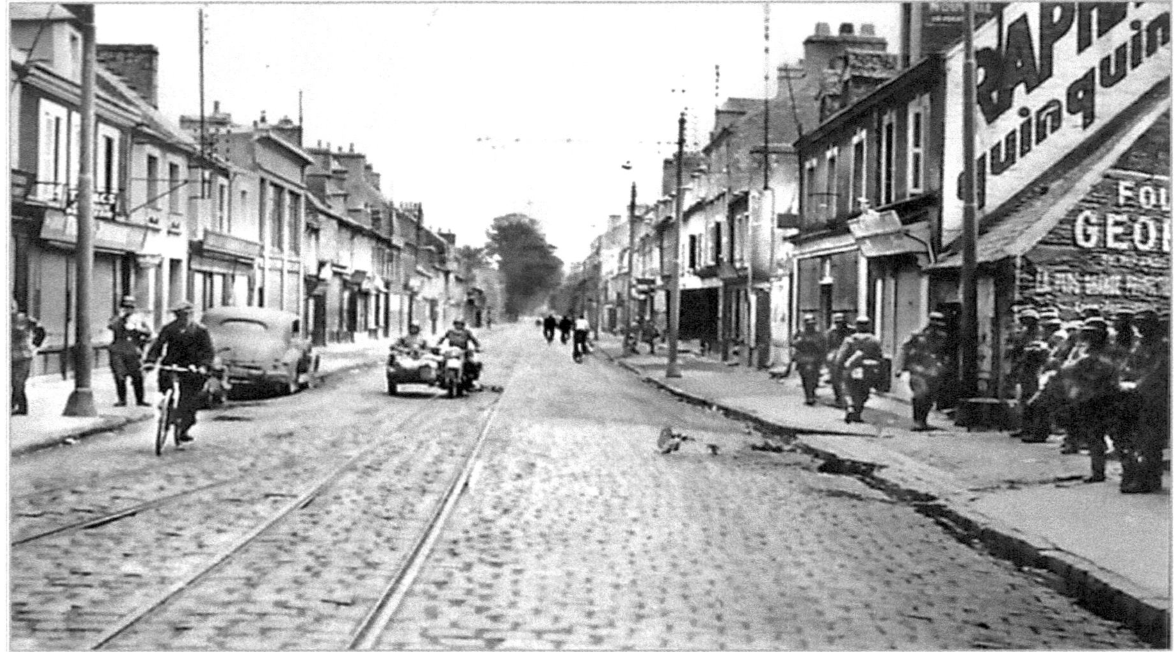

French civilians travel in both directions on a street among German officers and motorcyclists in Le Cateau, France.

The Frenchmen appear to pay no attention to the German soldiers. There are no women or children on the street.

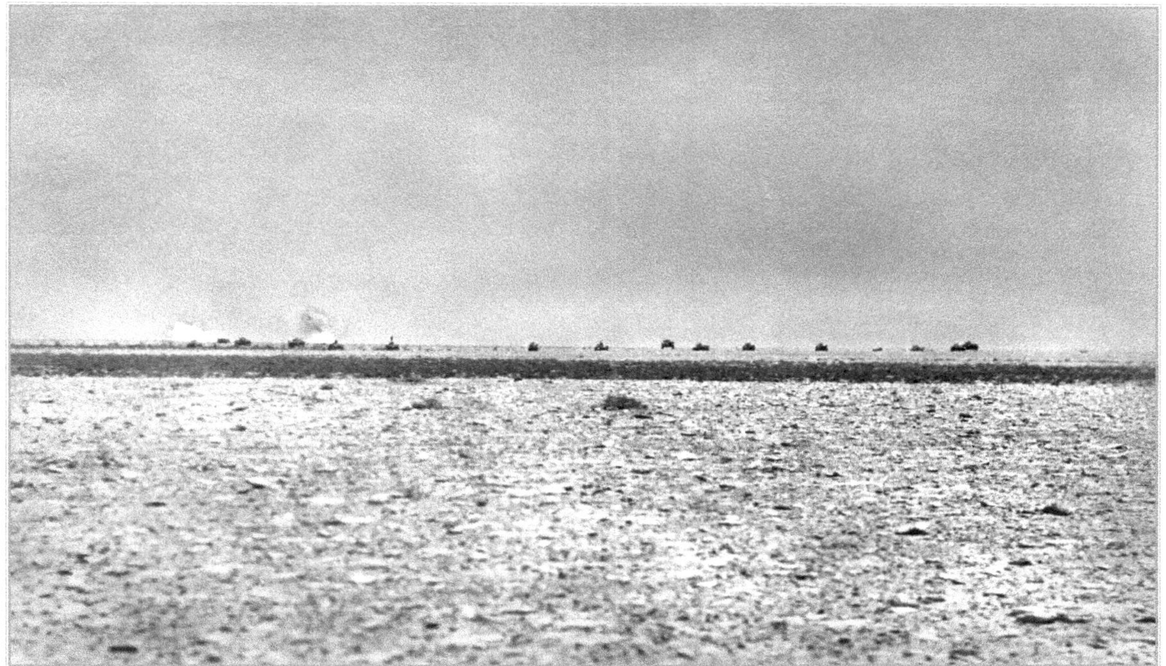

Two large blasts are visible beyond a line of German tanks in North Africa.

The tanks are aligned perfectly in the center of the frame, as if the vehicles are caught between the earth and sky.

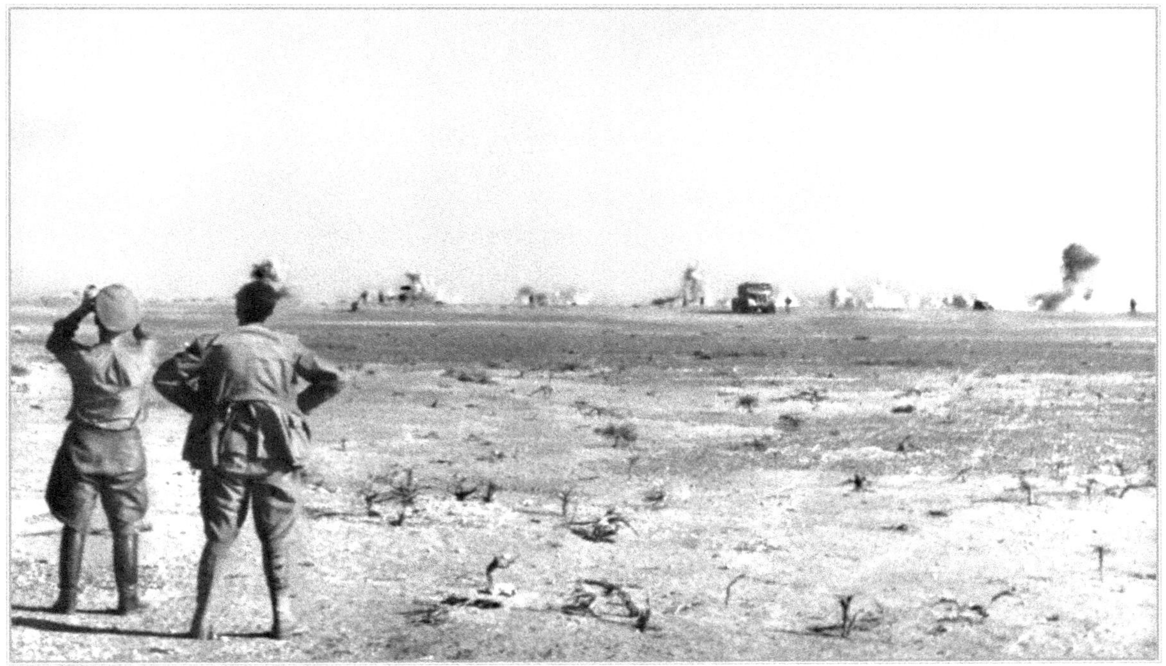

Rommel watches a battle unfold through binoculars in North Africa.

Columns of smoke, rising in the distance, divide the Germans from the Allies.

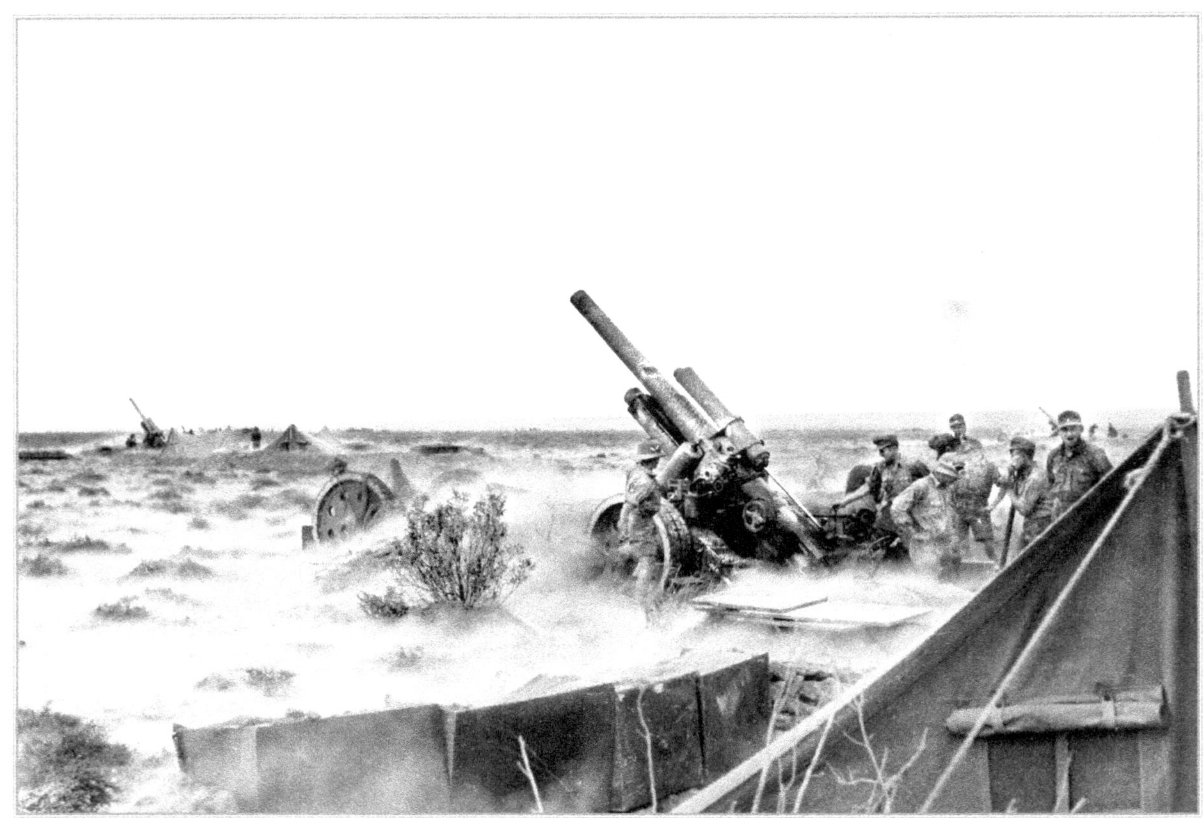

A dust storm sweeps through a German artillery crew in North Africa.

Strong gusts of wind lift sand up to the knee-level of the German soldiers, who gather around the artillery (right). One soldier in a pith helmet stands with his hands on his hips and looks downcast. A jagged bush, near the center of the image, rises from a mound. A gun behind it is nearly blocked from view by the blowing sand. The canvas on right side of this image belongs to a tent, which is similar to the tents located near the artillery posts on the left side of the frame.

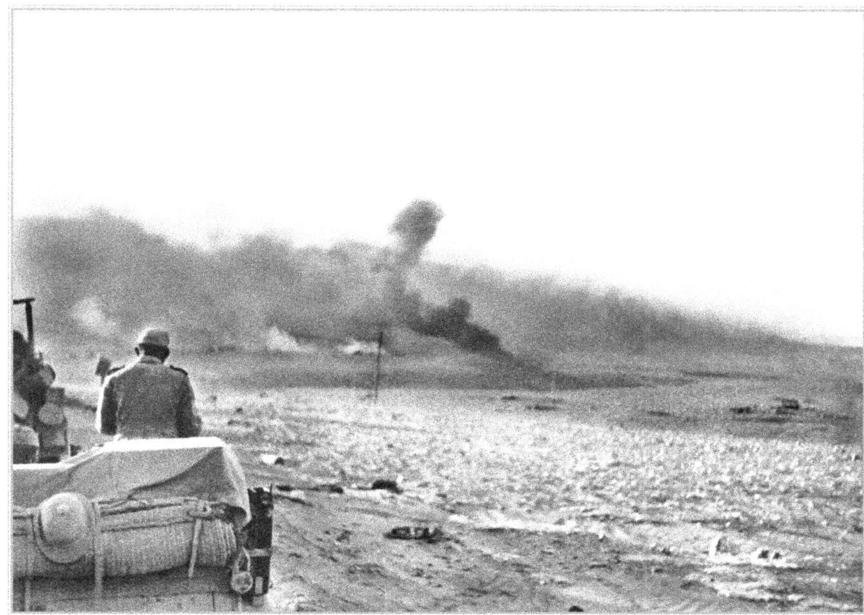

A battle rages in the desert.

The uniform of the officer in the car appears darkened by perspiration and dust. A pith helmet hangs from the back of the vehicle. The angle of this photo indicates that Rommel, like the officer in the car (left), also was monitoring the distant battle from a vehicle.

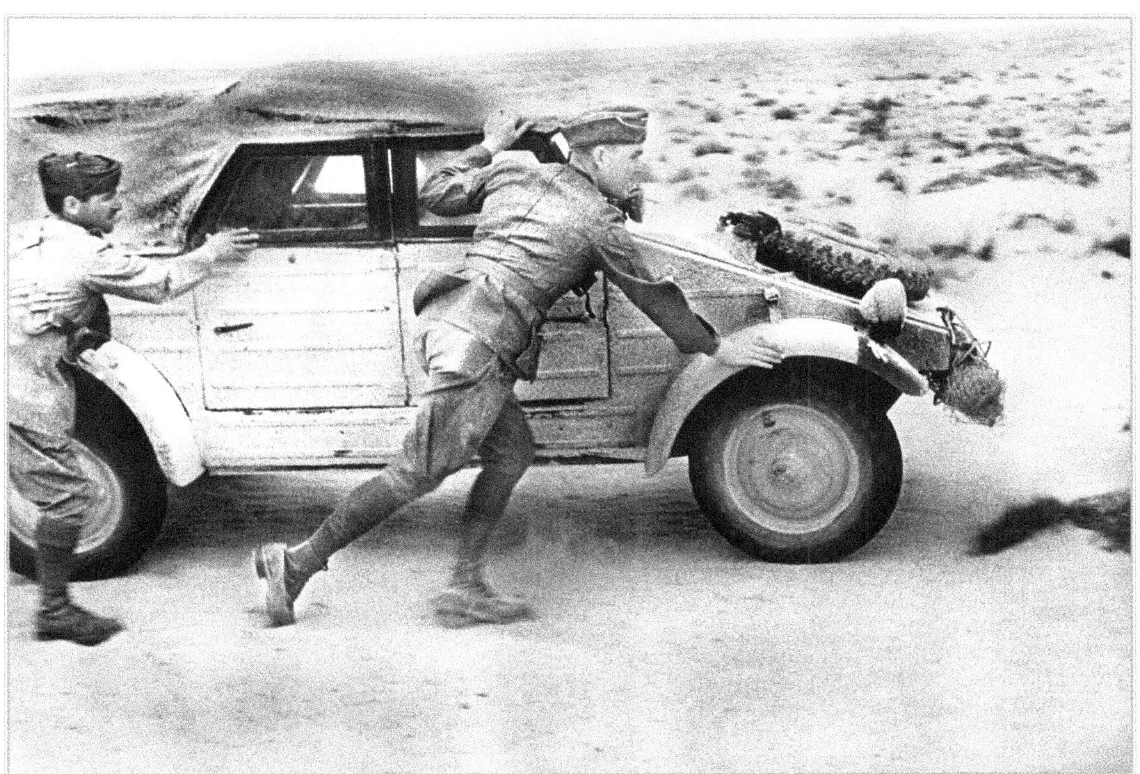

A German and Italian push a vehicle in the desert in North Africa.

The blur of the men's feet and ripple of the vehicle's canvas top show the men's fast motion to move the car. The driver behind the wheel is barely visible in the window.

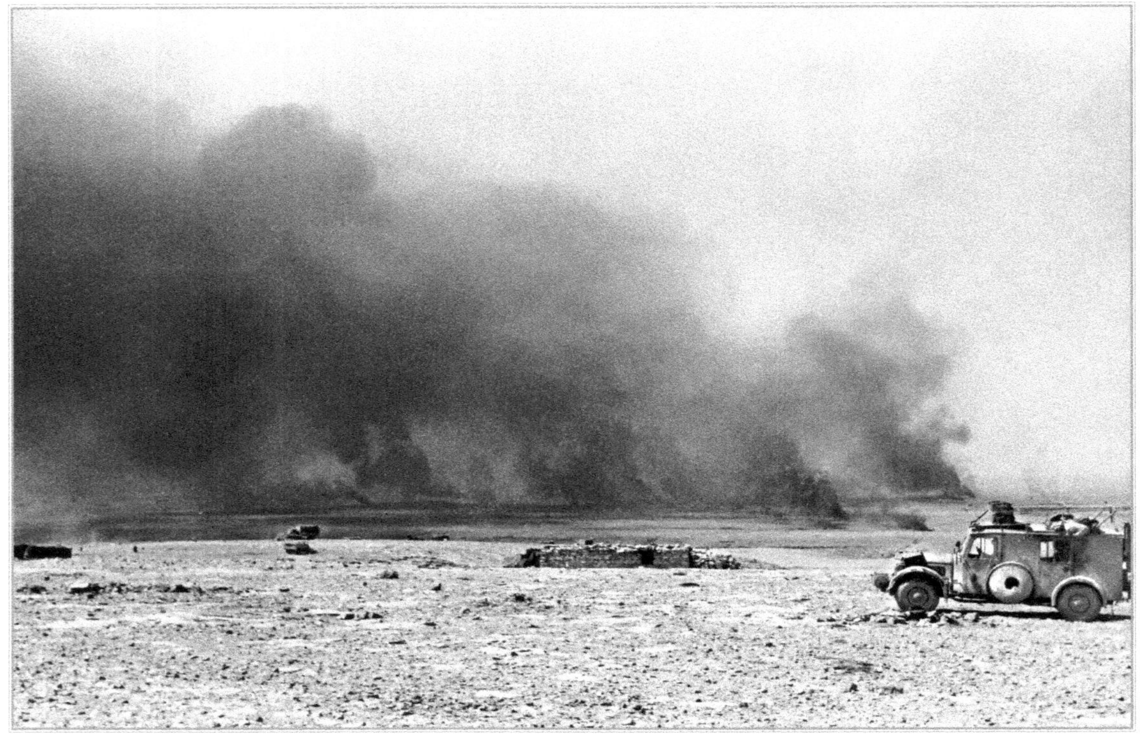

A dense wall of black smoke divides the sky above a scene of fighting in North Africa.

A driver waits in the vehicle (right). In the center of the frame, supplies and canvas coverings have been placed on top of a wall of sandbags.

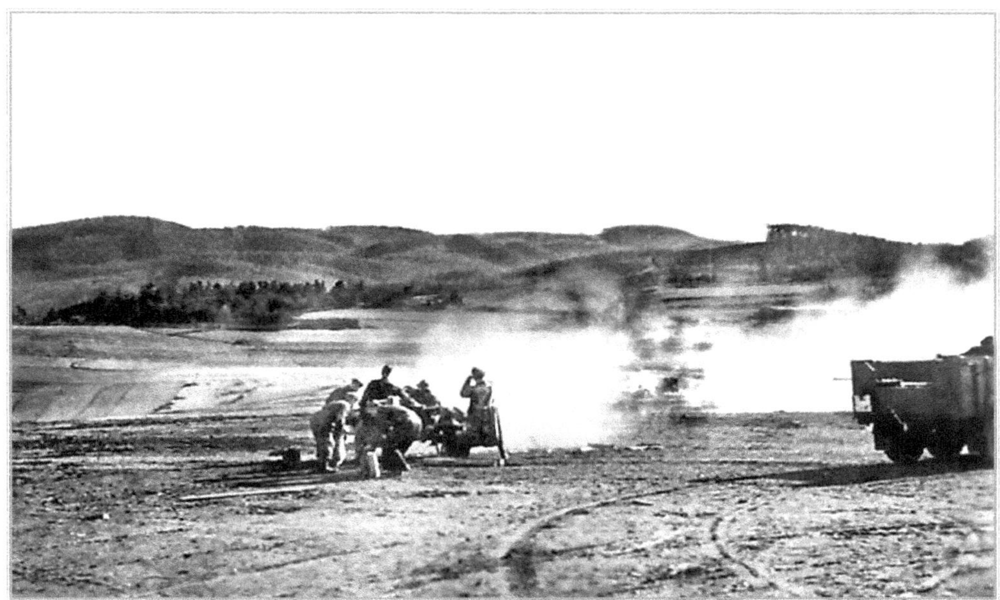

Rommel (right) directs artillery fire in France.

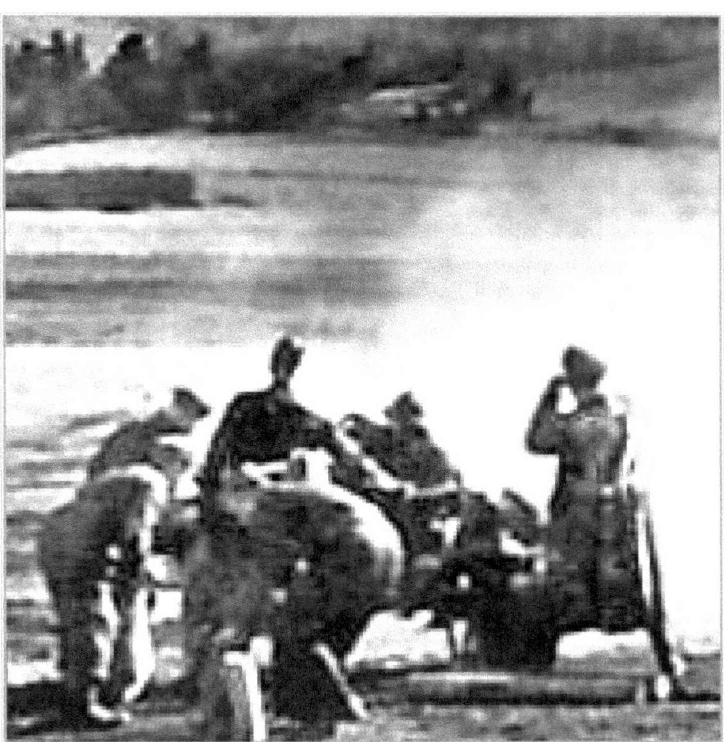

A close-up of Rommel, extracted from the image above, shows Rommel looking at the target through binoculars.

Rommel's distinctive camera and binocular straps, as well as his belt and pleated coat, are visible in this image. The photo was taken with Rommel's camera. He would have handed the camera to someone else to document his event, possibly for his military manual.

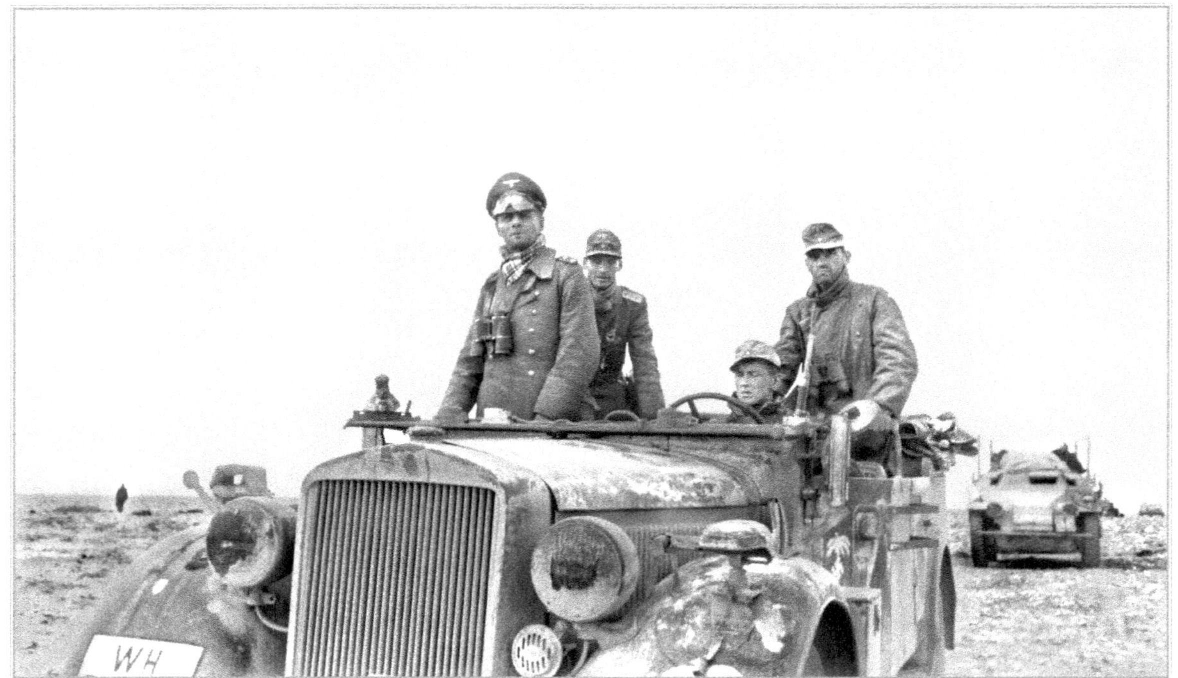

In this series, Rommel, covered in dust, stands in a vehicle with his staff near Sidi Omar.

Rommel appears to have been in the middle of commanding military operations when this photo was taken. He is wearing a scarf that his daughter Gertrud made for him. The vehicle, particularly the headlights, are caked with dust. The insignia of the Afrika Korps is visible on the front of the car near the driver's door.

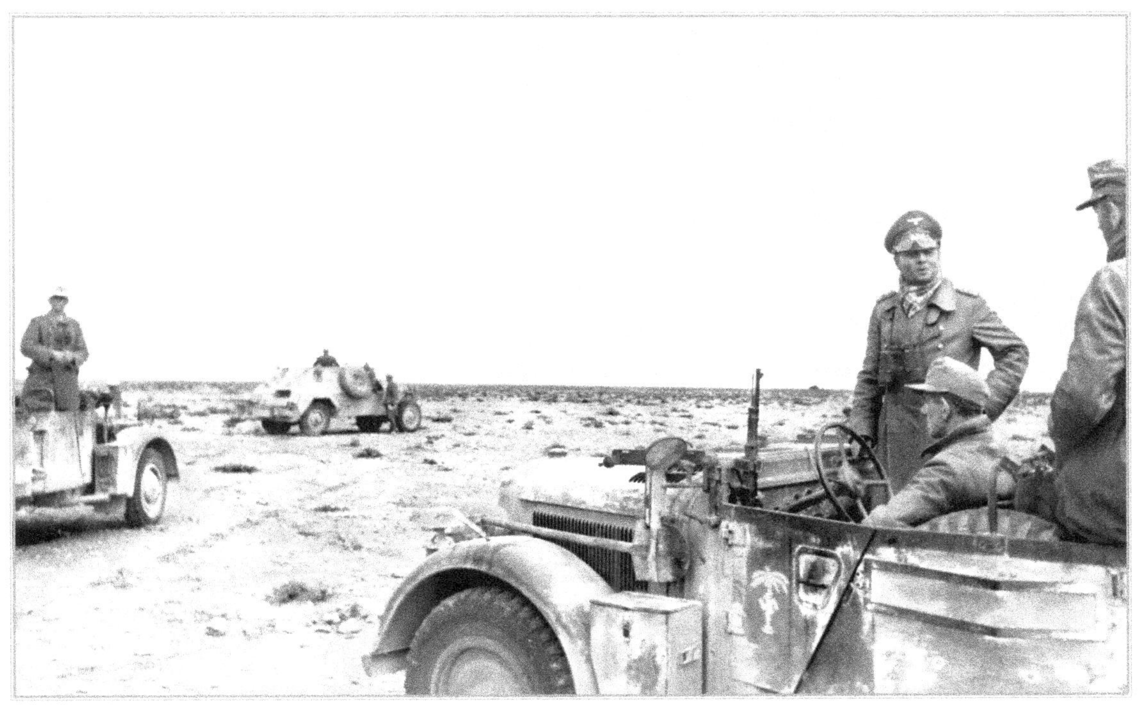

The Afrika Korps logo is more clearly visible. The vehicle has a rifle mounted in front of the steering wheel.

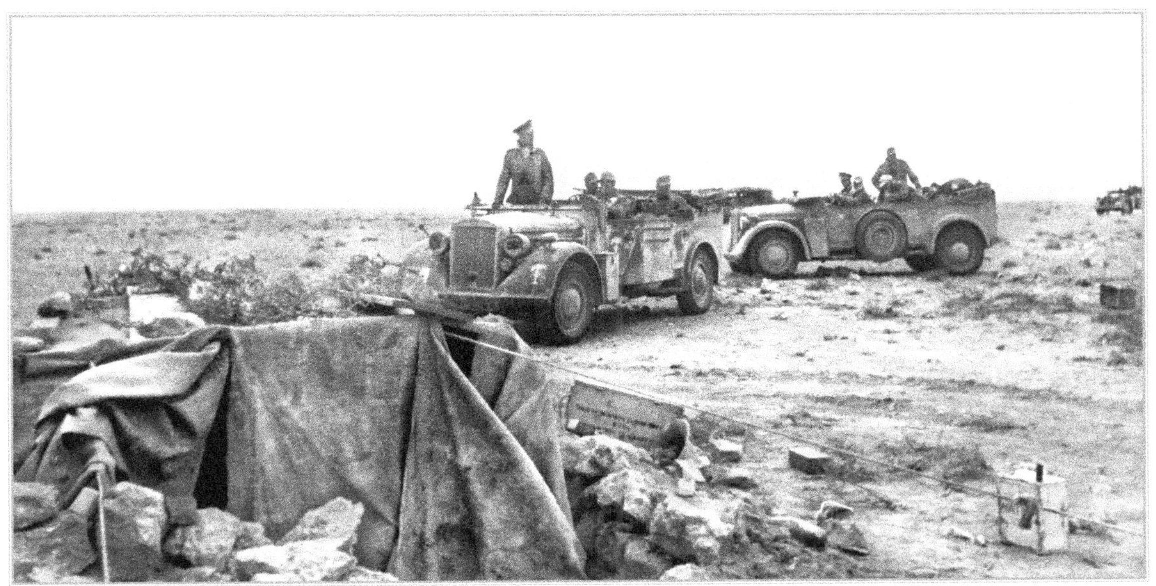

In the forefront is a dugout, covered with canvas, rocks, weeds, and boards.

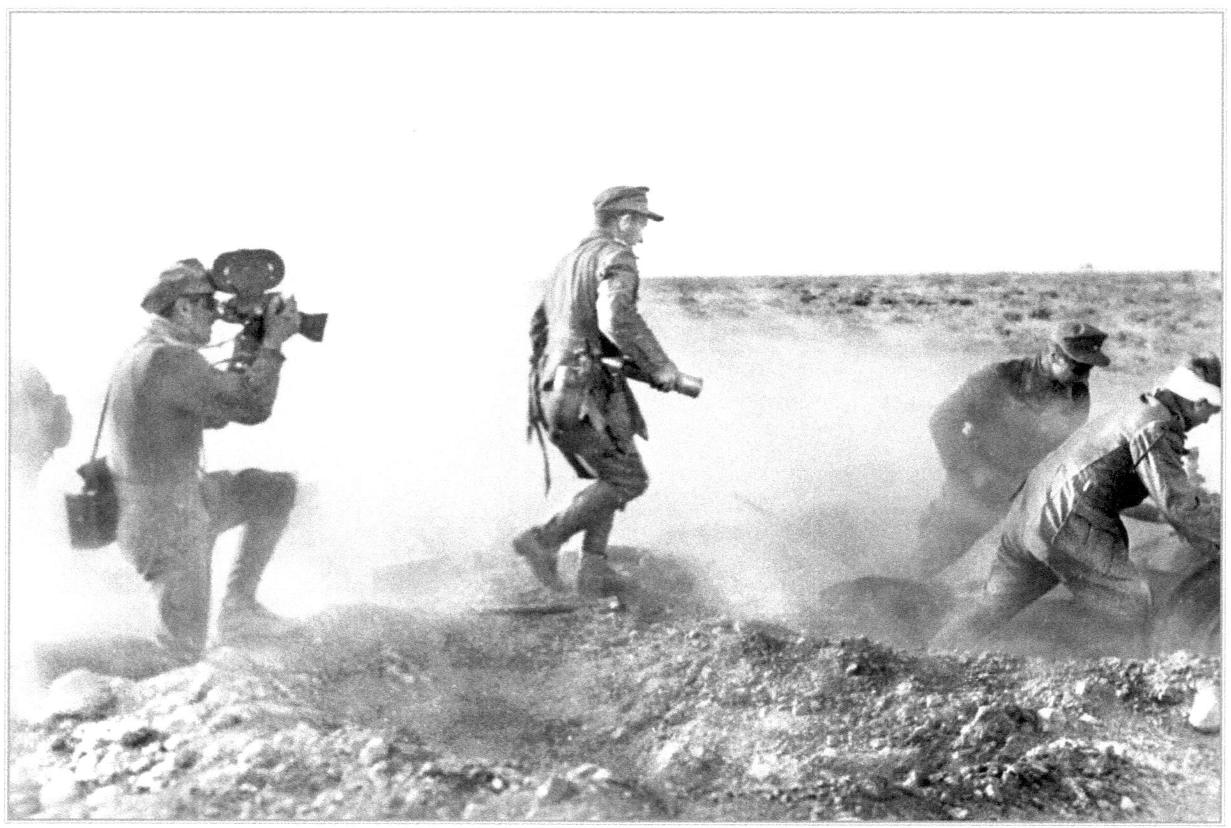

A propaganda cameraman hurriedly films German soldiers in combat in North Africa.

Two German soldiers (right), one with a bandage around his head, push a gun out of a deep rut in the soil. One of them wears goggles; his wedding ring is visible on his hand. Another soldier (center) runs behind with ammunition in his hand.

It is evident that Rommel paused during the hectic fray of battle to take this unusual photo. The subject matter is rather ironic—Rommel is documenting other men being documented.

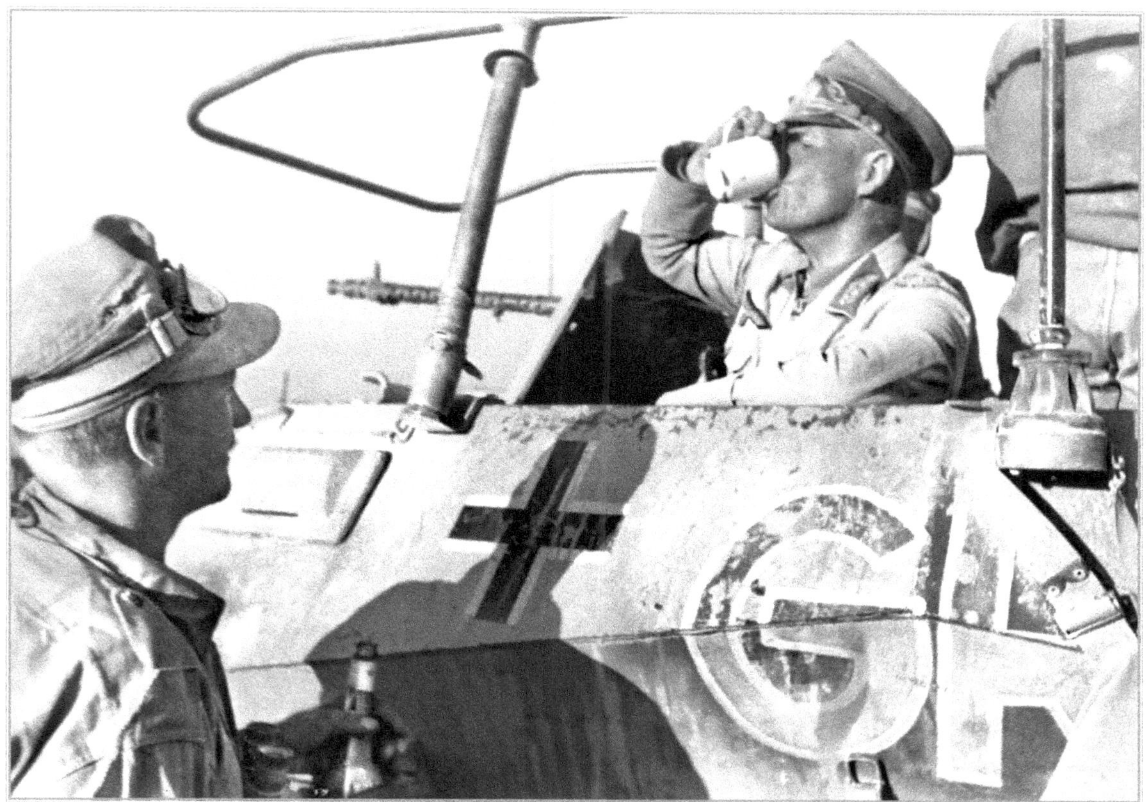

Rommel takes a drink while seated in his command vehicle in North Africa.

Covered in dust and with a flushed face, Rommel drinks from a chipped, enameled metal cup brought to him by a young German soldier, who stands waiting with a bottled drink in his hands. Behind Rommel (center, left) a gun barrel points out from the vehicle.

Although he had many available resources given his high rank, Rommel made it a point to eat the same rations as the enlisted men. Afrika Korps rations typically included black bread and canned beef. Most German and Italian soldiers viewed the canned beef as repulsive.

German soldiers considered themselves lucky to salvage British rations, particularly canned peaches. They sometimes hunted for gazelles and also bartered for chickens, eggs, and vegetables from Arab tribesmen. Rommel usually did not complain about the provisions—although he did comment on saltwater coffee and a leathery chicken, which he wrote, "must have been from the [chicken] coop of Ramses II."

Sanitation was also a major issue when it came to sustenance in North Africa. Water from the desert was usually dirty and contaminated with bacteria. Many German soldiers, including Rommel, became ill from unhealthy meals they consumed in North Africa.

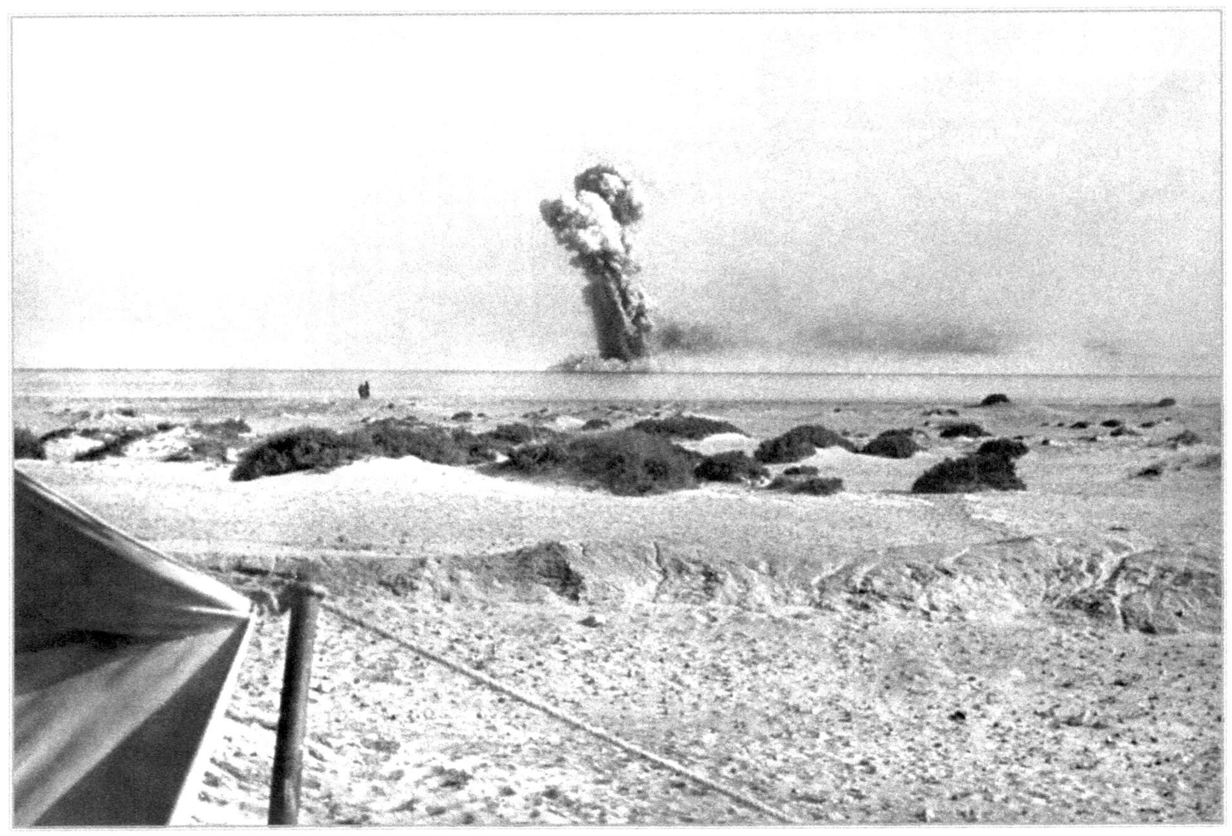

Beyond Rommel's tent, the silhouettes of two soldiers stand (center, left) in the distance as a giant cloud rises from a thunderous explosion on the ocean in North Africa.

This photo appears to have been taken from Rommel's headquarters on the beach outside of Tobruk in 1941. The blast rises from the ocean. It seems evident that a large ship has been destroyed.

In a letter to his wife, Rommel noted that a large British ship was sunk outside of Tobruk. As Rommel was eating breakfast outside his tent, the ship was spotted about a mile from the coast. German fighter planes attacked the ship, which after a few minutes exploded due to a gasoline fire. "I took pictures, of course," Rommel wrote.

The explosion in this image could possibly be the same one referred to in his letter.

As in many of his photos, Rommel framed the focal point—the explosion—in the exact center of the image.

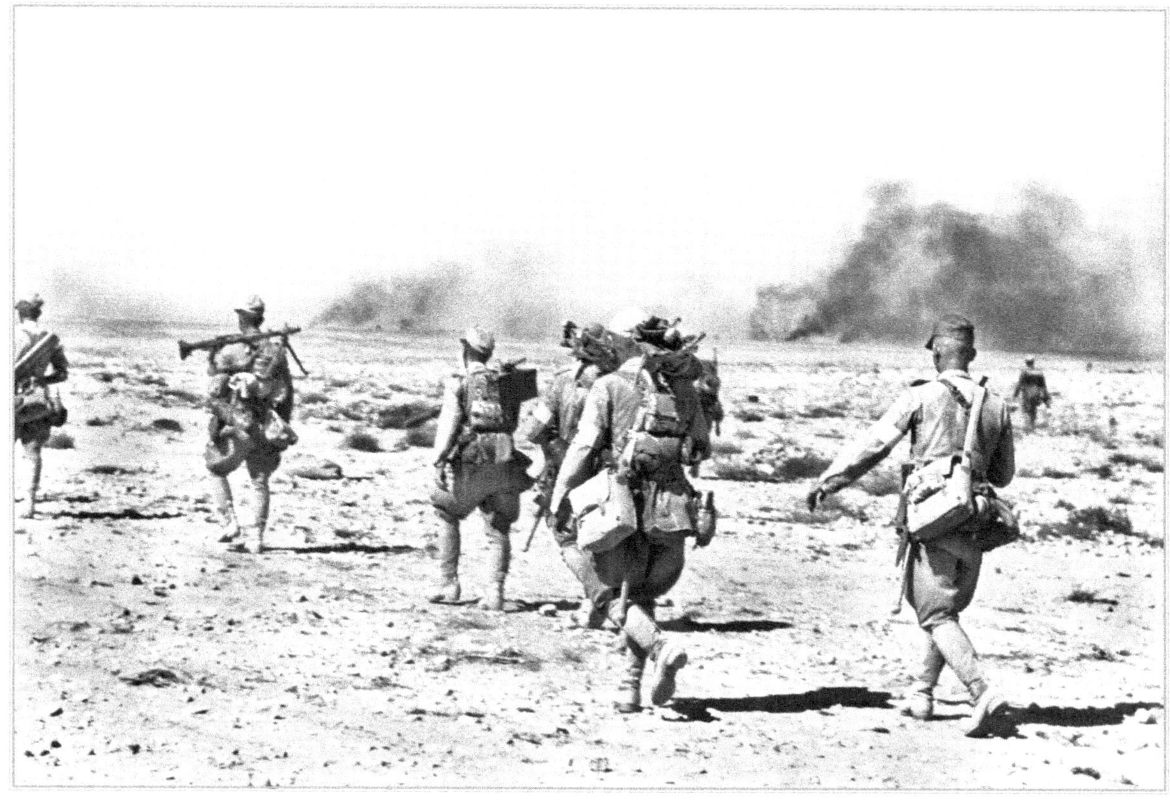

German medics trudge towards the scene of combat in North Africa.

Medics played an important role in the war in North Africa. Both on and off the battlefield it was difficult to maintain the health of soldiers in the desert. Many German soldiers caught dysentery and various other illnesses due to bacteria. Sand, which was everywhere, was also a contaminant. Wounds could become infected and gangrenous from dirty sand. Often the men were unable to wash or bathe for extended periods of time, and stood a greater risk of catching infections. Rommel at one time suffered from boils on his face and neck, as can be seen in various newsreels.

Additionally, the German troops were afflicted by insects. Swarms of flies, often numbering in the hundreds, would descend upon soldiers. These flies were known to bite and crawl on men's faces, looking for moisture. Many men also were plagued by fleas. Mosquitoes were a problem in some regions. In his personal letters, Rommel somewhat humorously recorded anecdotes of his "campaign" against numerous bugs which besieged him in his desert headquarters. In one instance, Rommel resorted to setting his iron bedstead on fire with gasoline in order to rid himself of persistent biting insects in the framework.

7

Devastation

Bombenangriffe

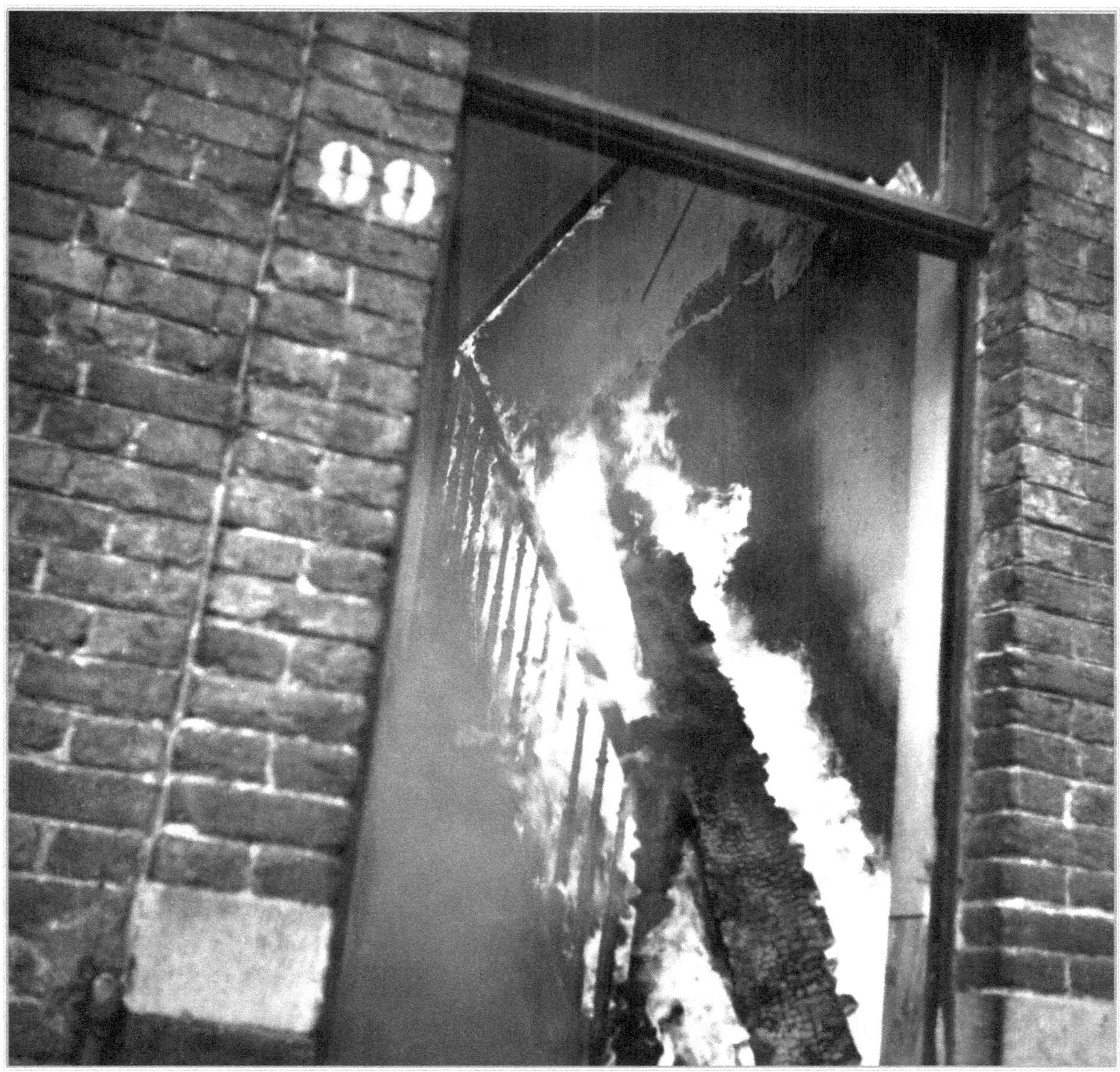

A staircase blazes inside a building in France.

A fire roars inside a brick building marked with the address Number 99. The angle of this photo is skewed. This sideways composition is unusual for Rommel, whose pictures tend to be symmetrical. The crooked angle draws attention to the ominous event taking place inside what appears to be a private home.

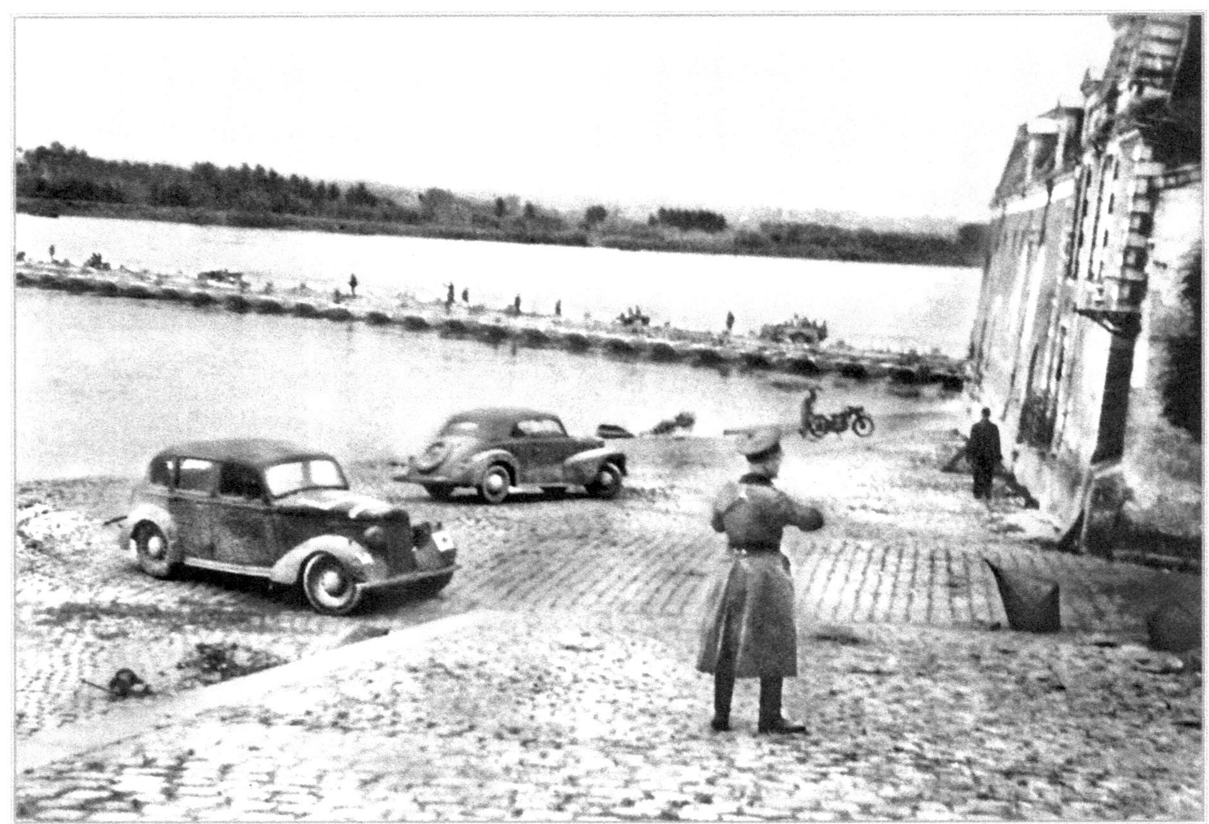

Rommel stops to explore and take photographs near a causeway in France.

Rommel stands beside a building looking to the right down a brick street. In the direction where he is looking, the side of the building has a gaping hole in it, and large pieces of debris are scattered on the street. Near Rommel are vehicles that apparently have been commandeered by German forces. Beyond on the causeway, there are many pedestrians and different types of vehicles. Like many photos of himself which Rommel saved in his collection, this picture appears to have been a spontaneous shot taken by an associate.

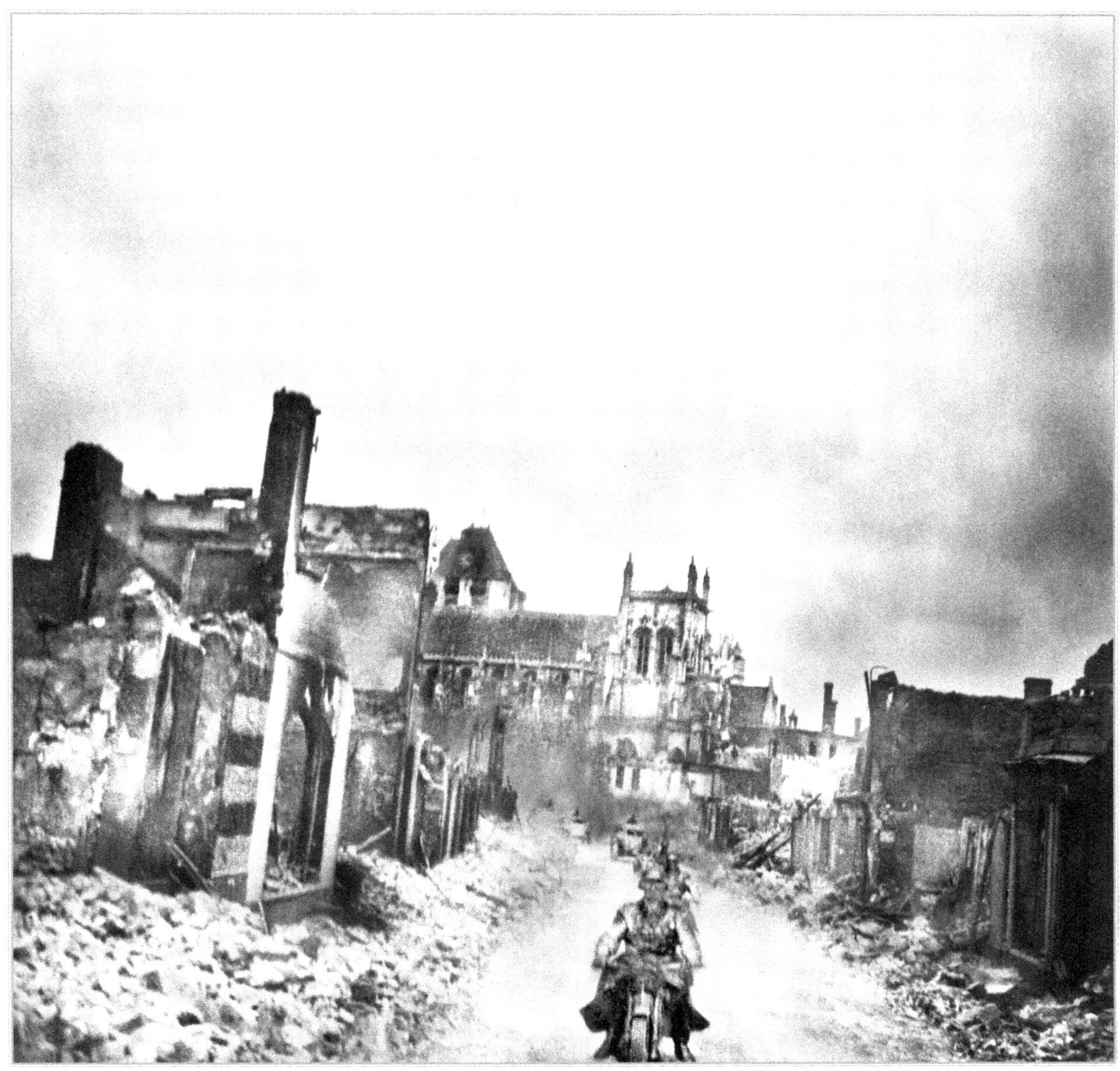

German motorcycle troopers precede Panzers as they speed through the ruins of a town in France.

Four motorcycle troopers drive ahead of three Panzers as they pass through a street where buildings have been reduced to rubble by heavy bombardments. The motorcyclist in front wears goggles. His uniform, like those of the other motorcyclists behind him, are covered in dust. In the background, a church and other buildings are blackened by smoke.

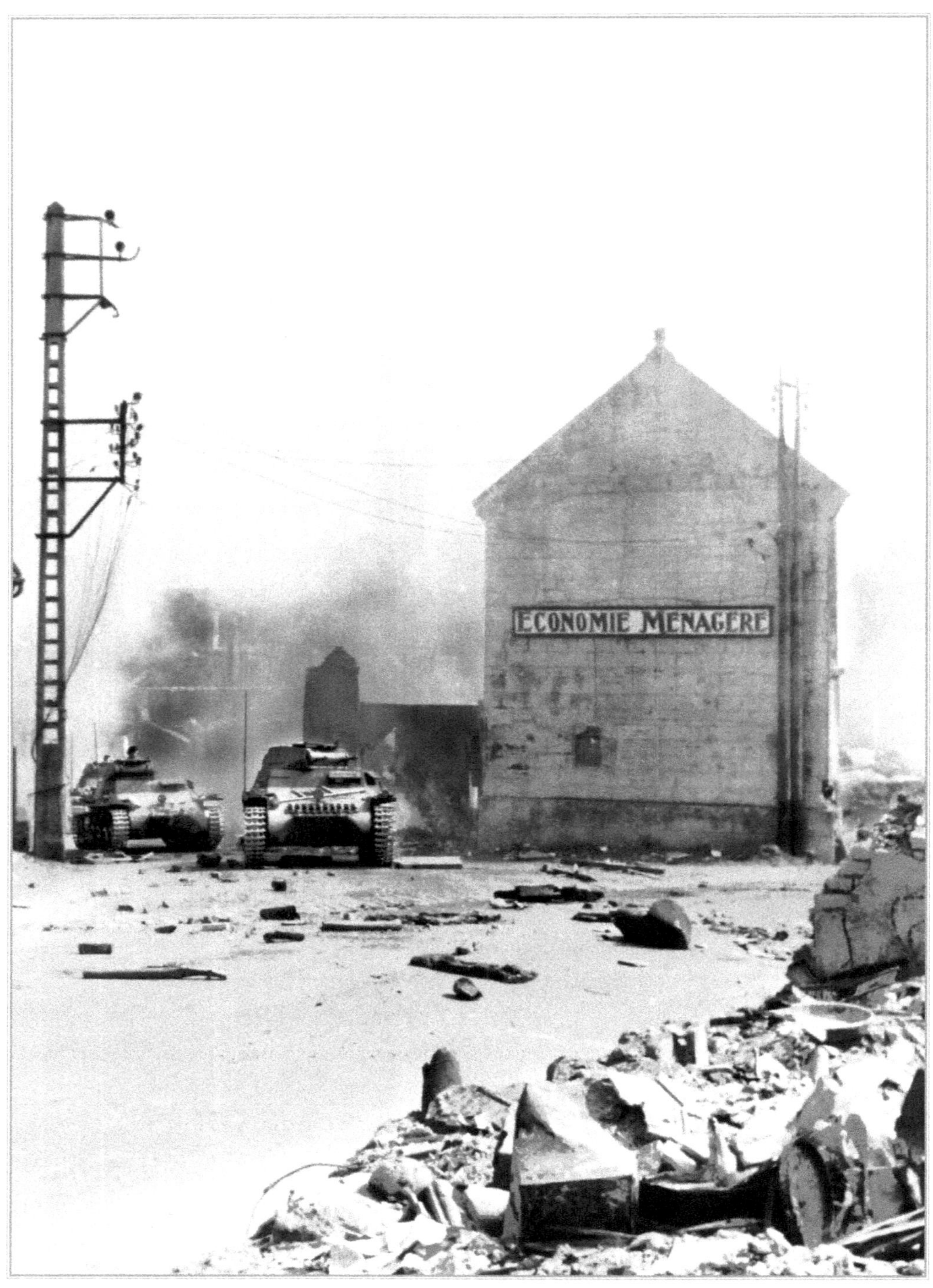

Rommel's Panzer column appears in a smoky, debris-strewn thoroughfare in France.

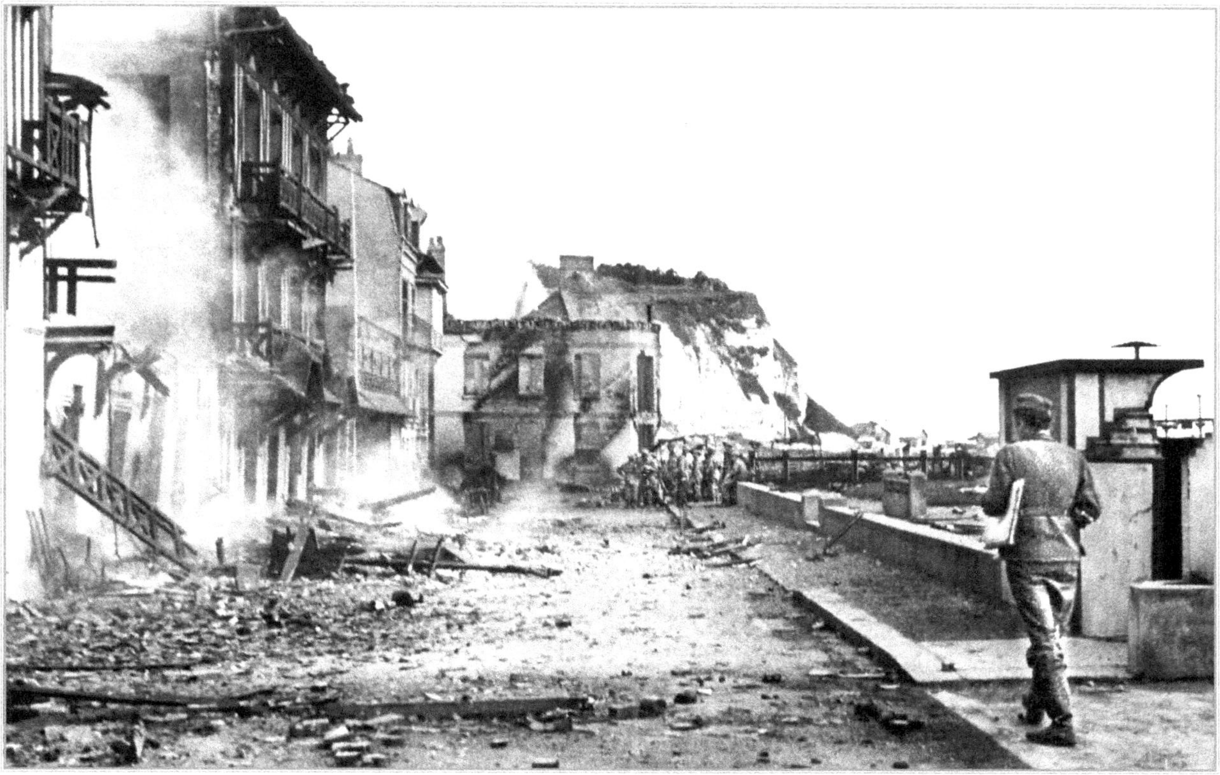

A soldier (right) strolls down the street in a devastated city on France's Normandy coast.

A group of soldiers (center) gather at an intersection near rows of smoldering houses.

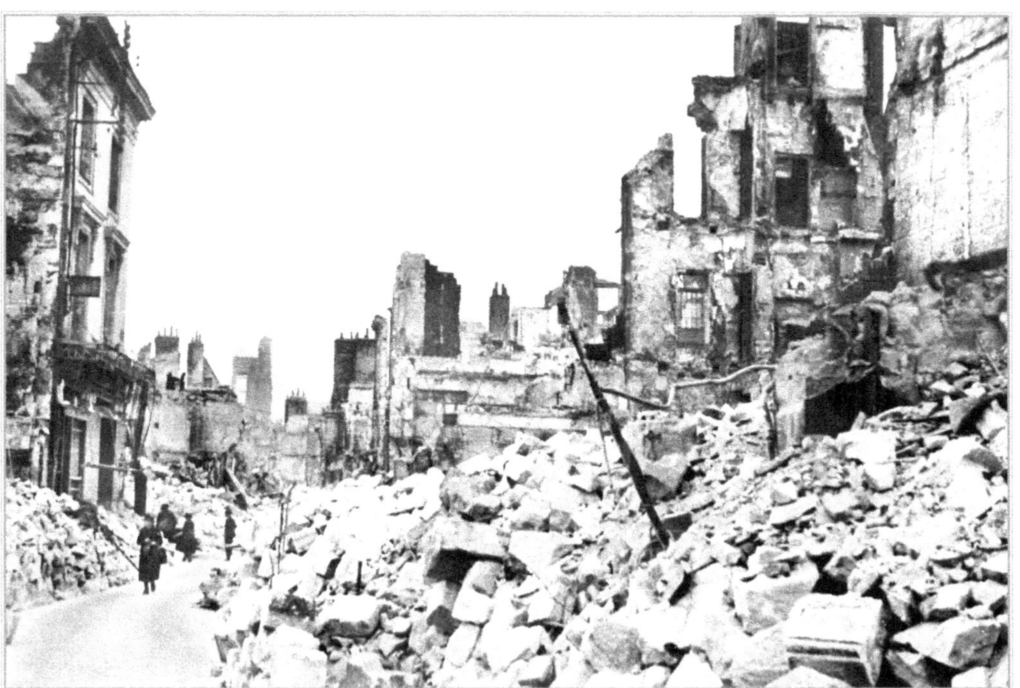

A group of civilians walk among rubble in France).

A woman clutching a purse looks at the destruction around her. Massive piles of rubble rise next to bombed buildings.

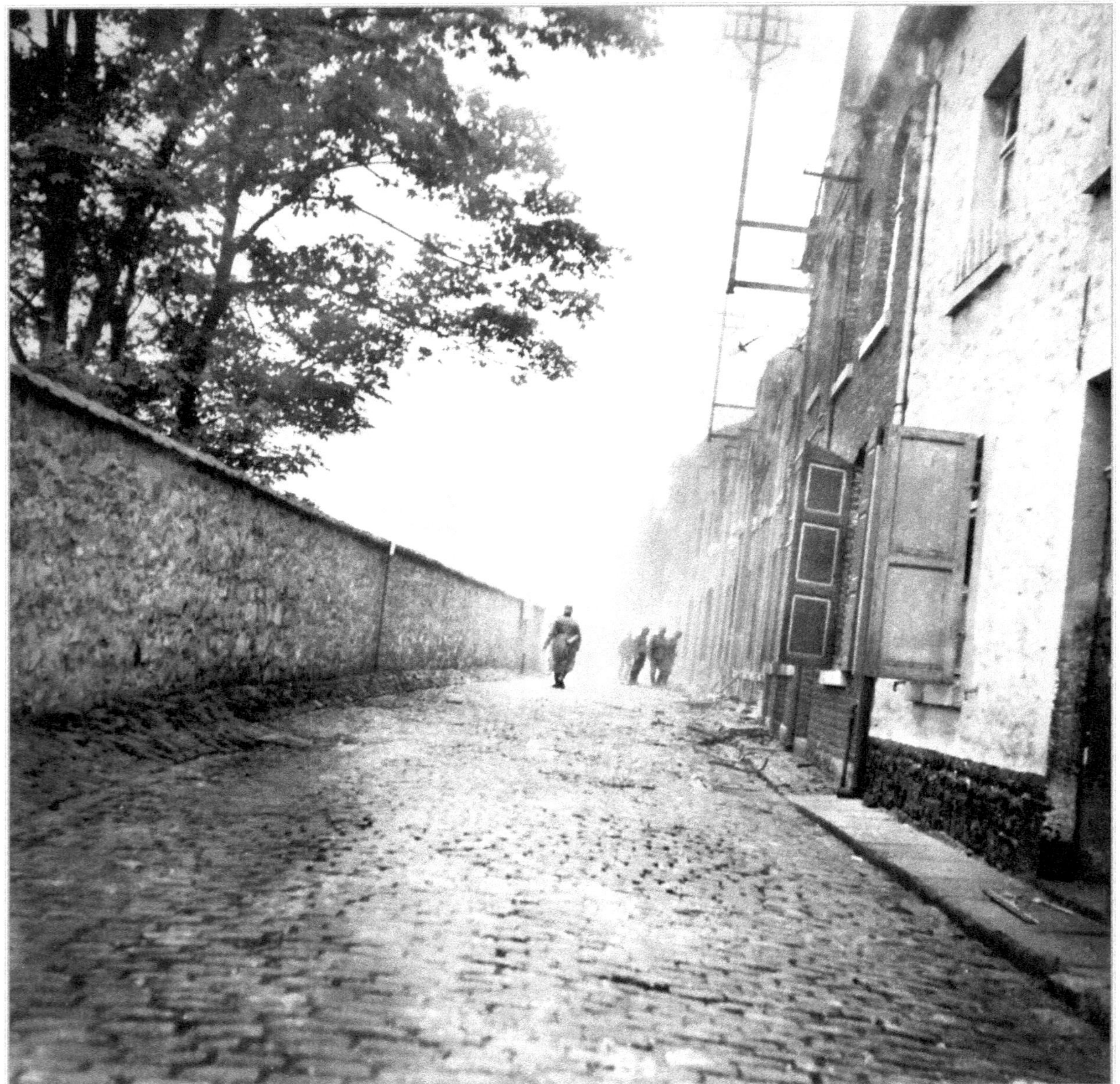

A solitary German soldier meanders down a street, approaching a group of four other soldiers who appear to be watching something on the right.

Rommel demonstrates his typical interest in a curving path surrounded by geometric shapes. The soldier in the foreground is perfectly centered in the frame. Rubble is strewn on the street just below the dark shutters (right).

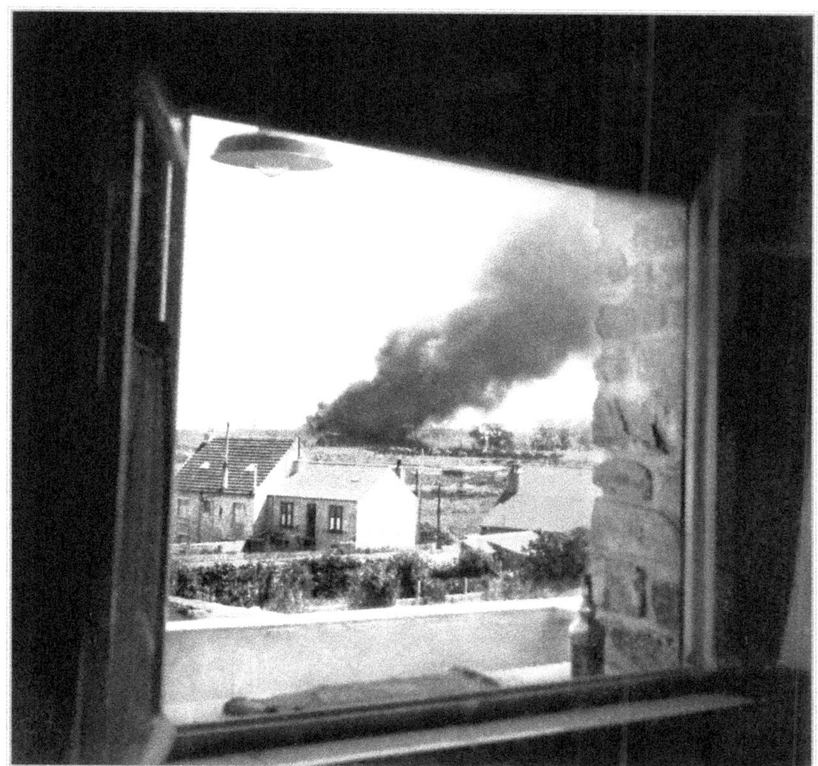

A military target burns in the distance behind a row of houses in France in two photos.

The first photo (upper left) shows a neighborhood view from a window inside a house.

Below, the same outdoor view of houses and gardens appear in the second photo. It seems Rommel was inside the house and stepped outside onto the balcony to take the second photo, which provides a less-constrained view of the smoke-filled sky.

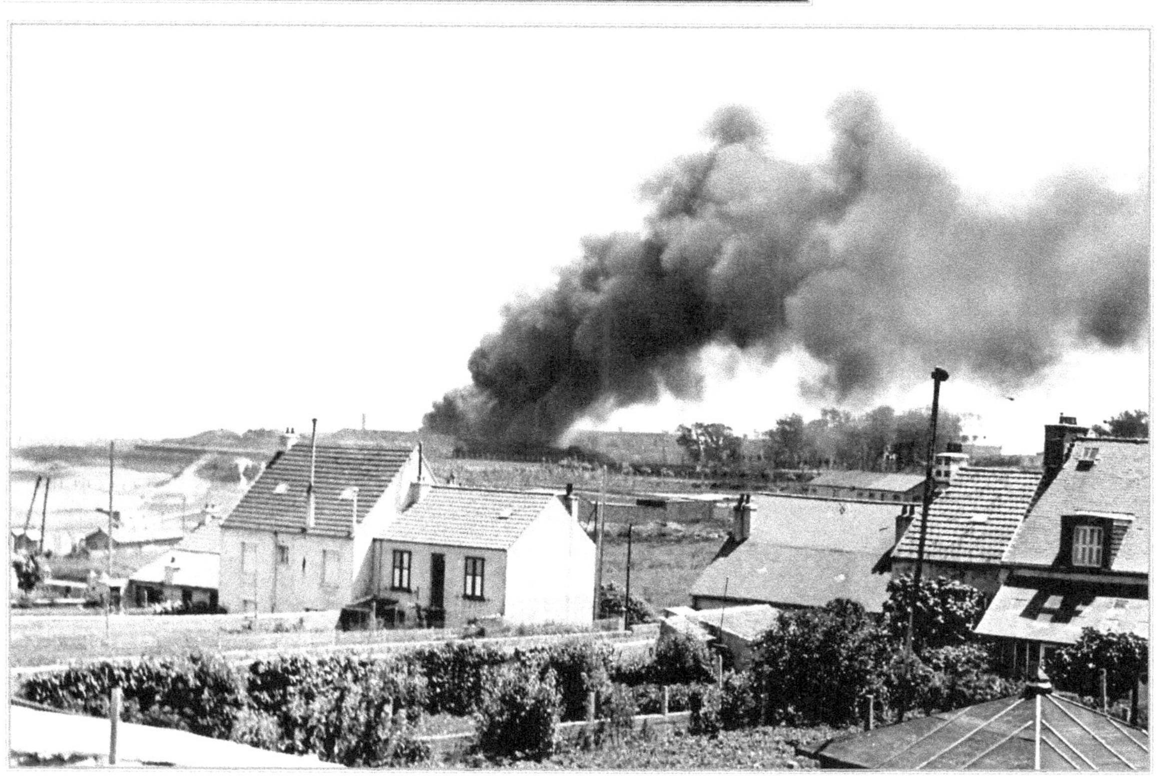

Wind pushes clouds of smoke into a neighborhood in France.

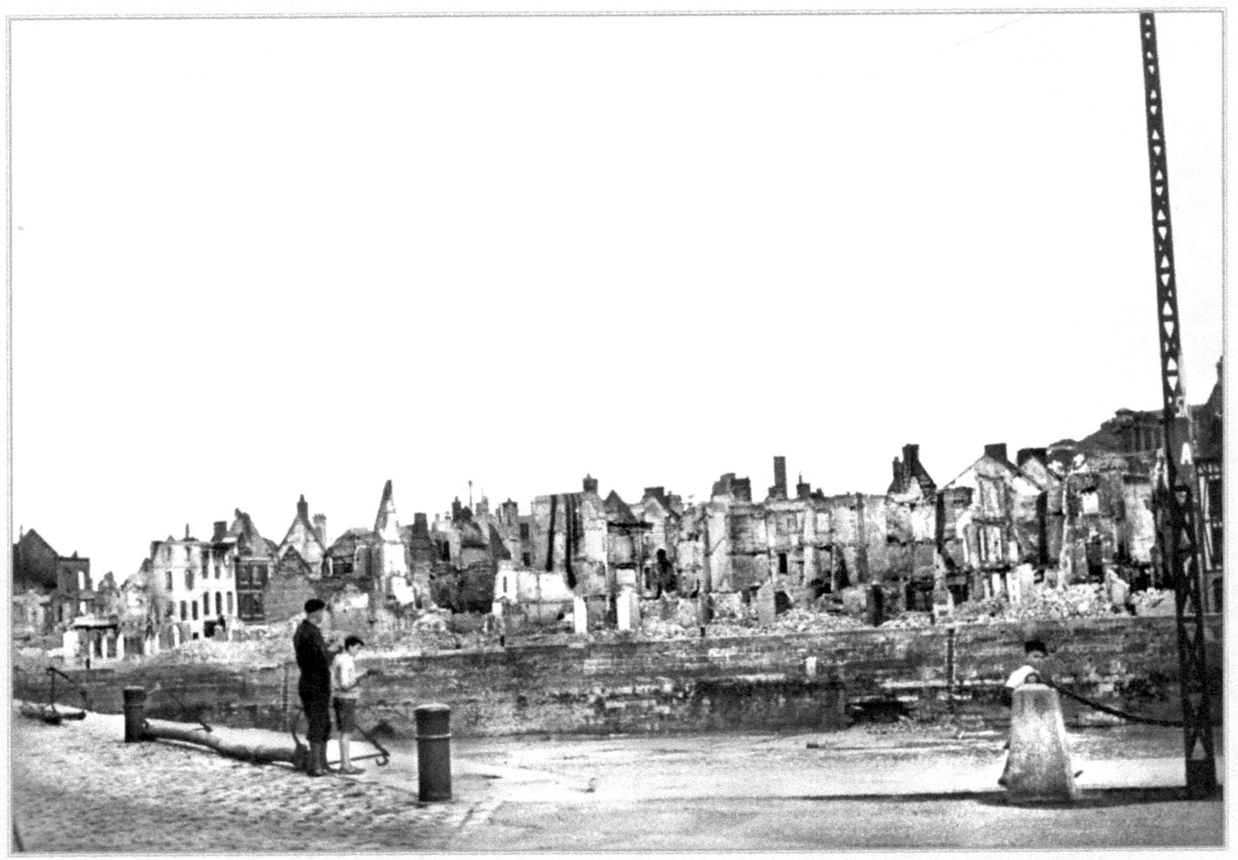

A man gazes at a shattered town in France.

This photo contains familiar themes. There are lone figures in the foreground set against the large backdrop of a city in ruins. A man and boy stand on the left. The man stares at the ruins while the boy looks at something he is holding in his hands. On the right, a smaller boy walks past in the foreground. He turns his head to look straight into the camera as Rommel snaps the photo. A utility pole marked "5k" looms high (right) next to the child.

Floors of a bombed building collapse in France.

This image shows an odd contrast. A perfectly intact building (far right) stands beside crumbling ones. The building seems undisturbed compared to the destruction next door. Rubble has spilled out onto the street.

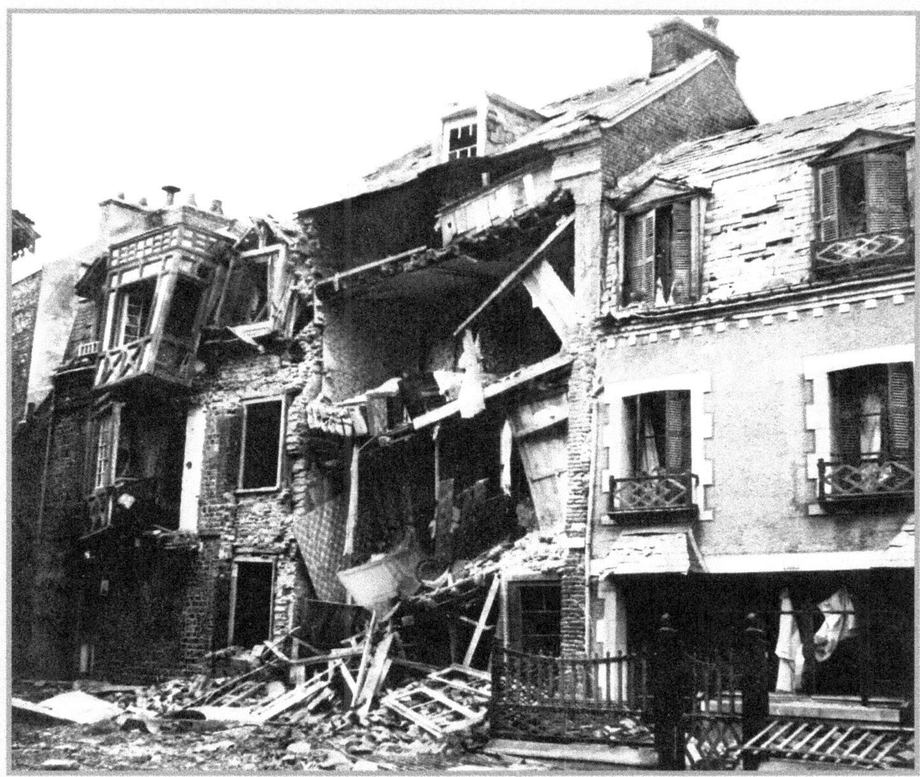

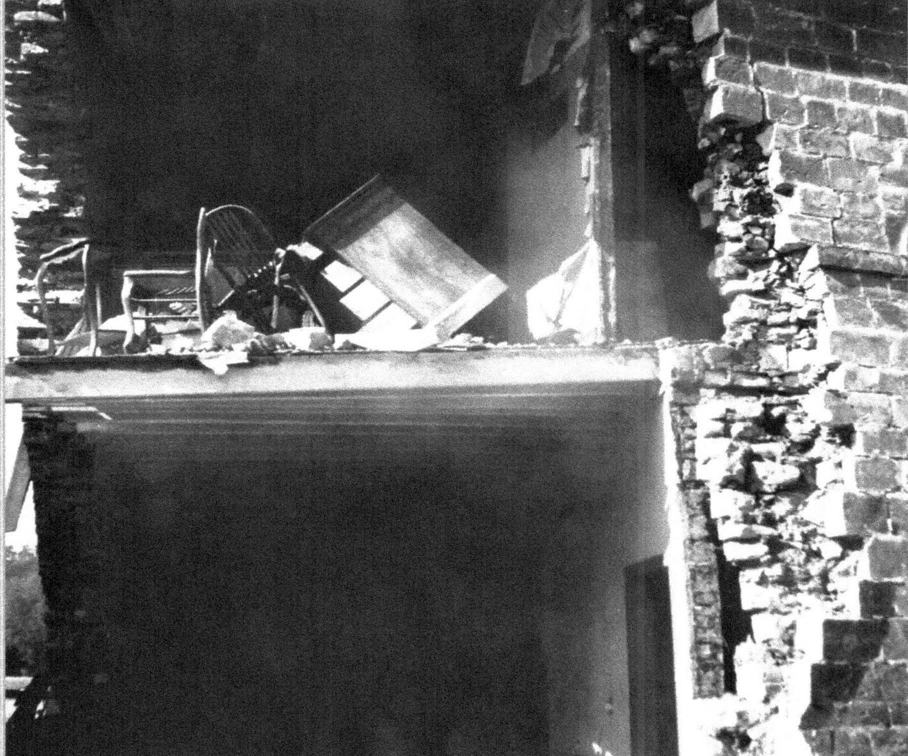

A sheared outer brick wall exposes disarrayed remnants of what was once the upper floor of a family home in France.

Two chairs and an end table still stand after a blast ripped the dwelling apart.

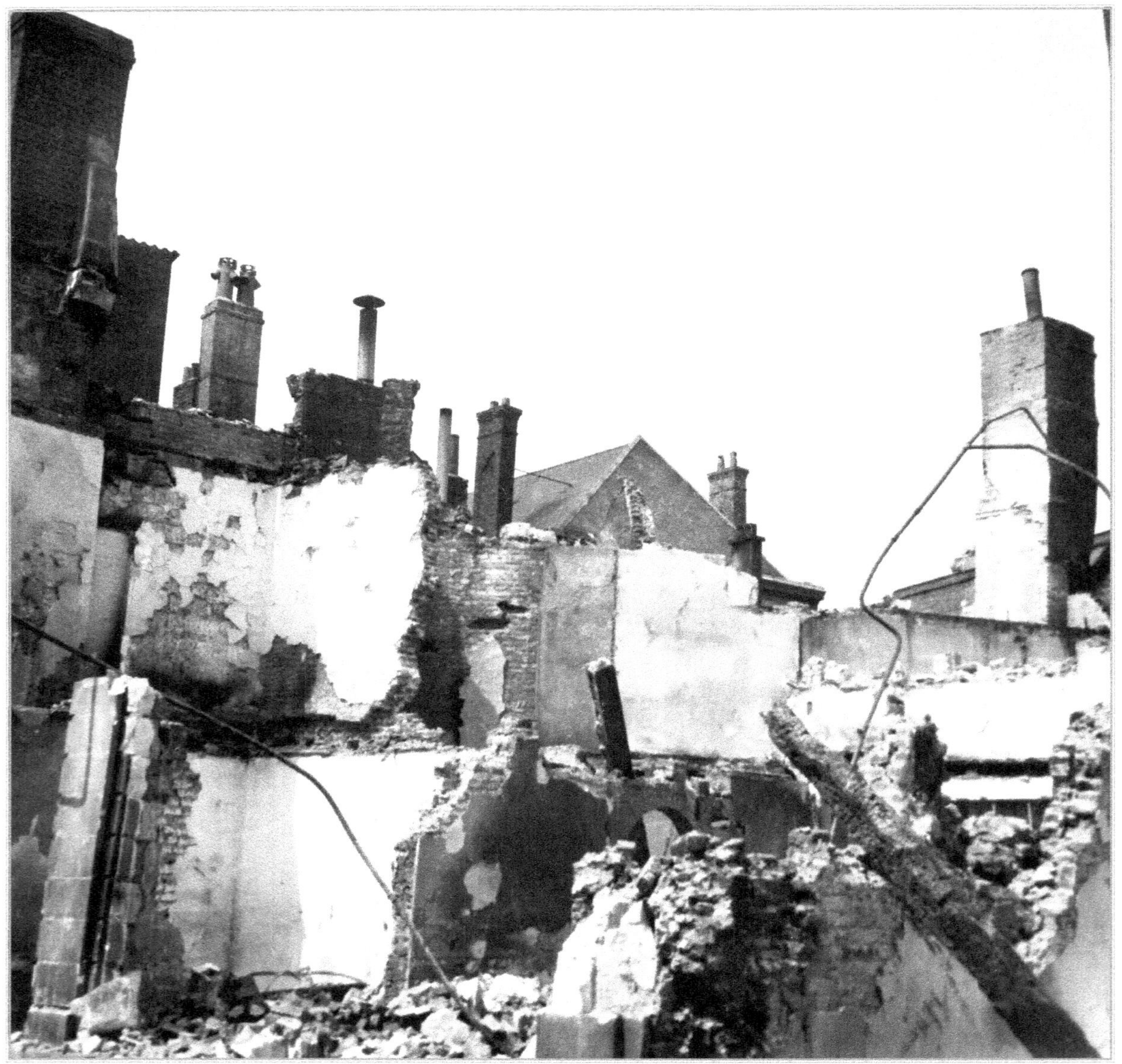

Only single walls remain of what were once rooms inside buildings in France.

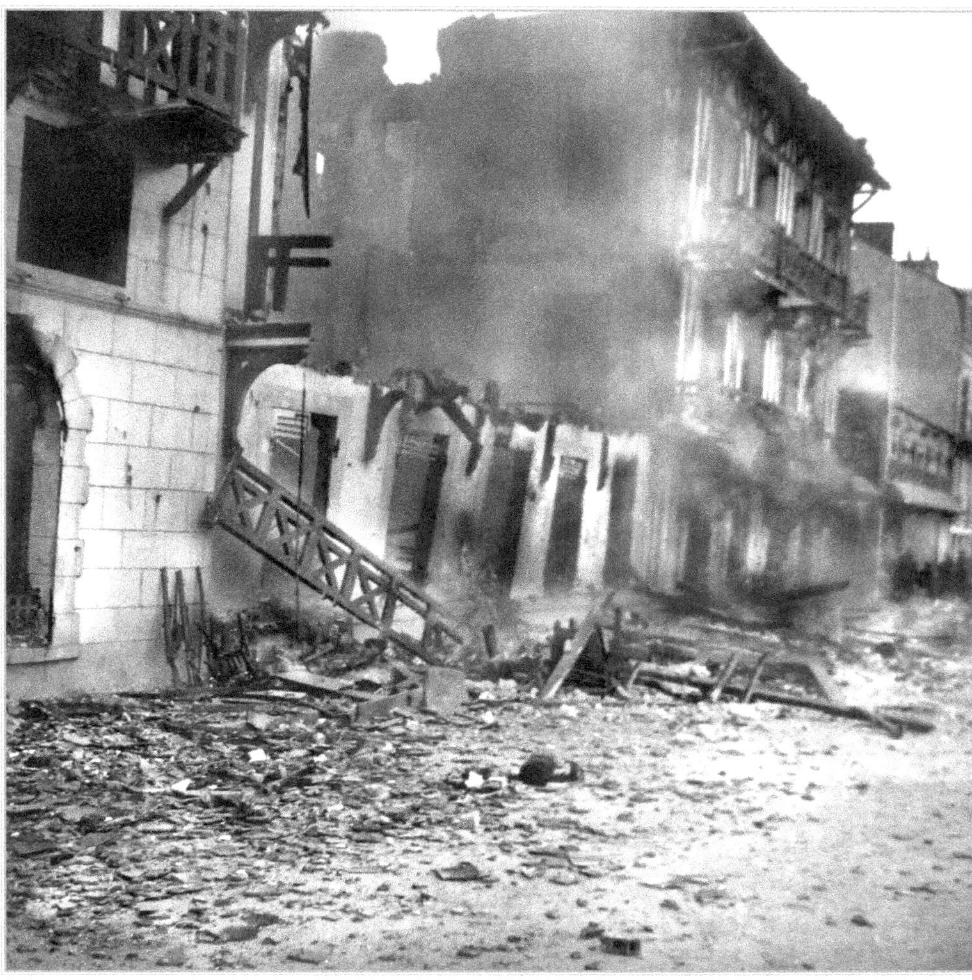

Three rifles are propped up on the ground (left) against a bombed out brick wall in France.

A demolished window reveals charred roof beams and the ruins of a building in France.

When composing this photo, Rommel used the "frame-within-a-frame" concept. The natural window frame in the foreground creates a border that gives way to inner frames within the rubble.

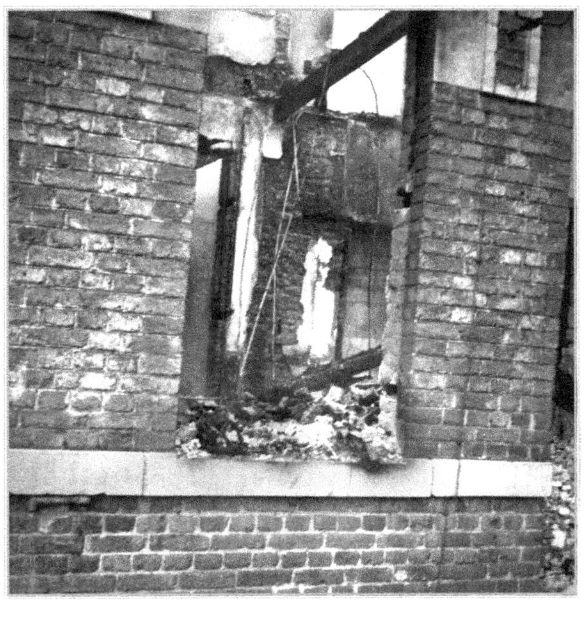

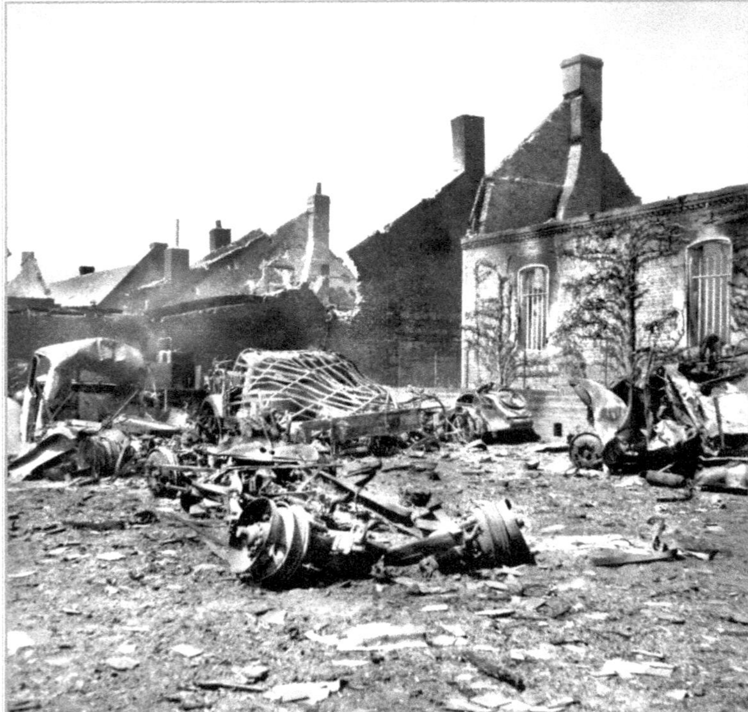

Wreckage covers a street in France.

Two views (right and opposite page) of destruction on one street in a town. A chunk has been torn out of a brick wall behind the vehicles (center).

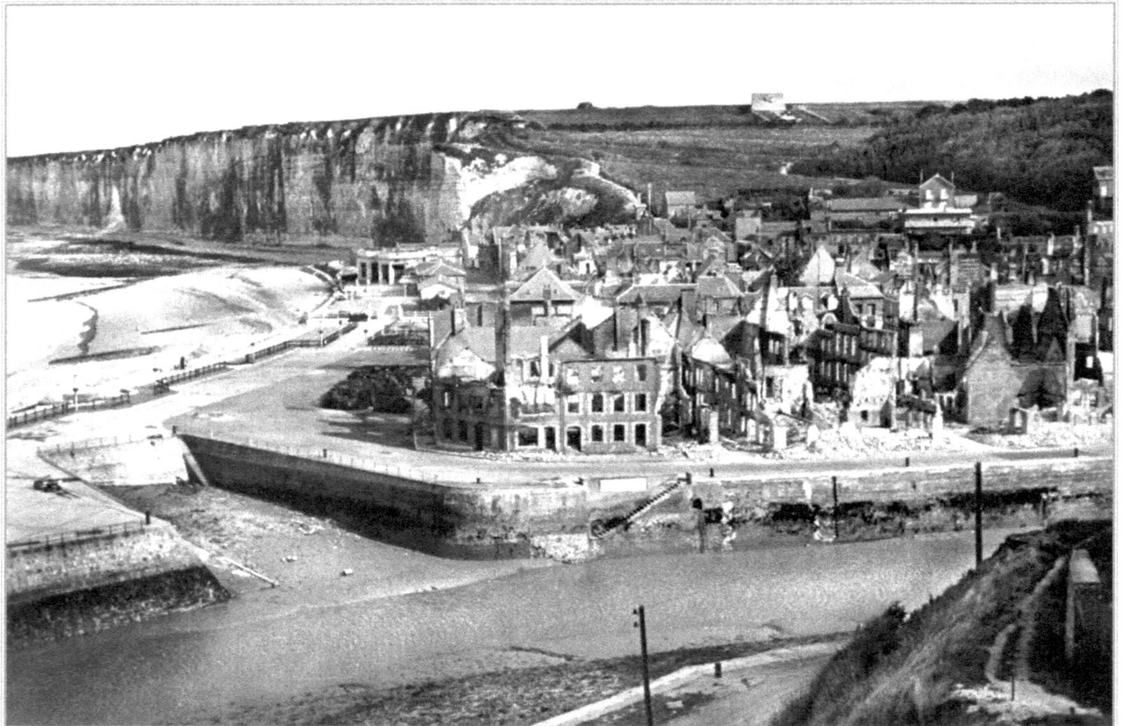

A view of the bombarded ruins of St. Valery-en-Caux, France after its surrender.

This view of the cliffs and hills show the route that POWs traveled in other photos. (See page 170.)

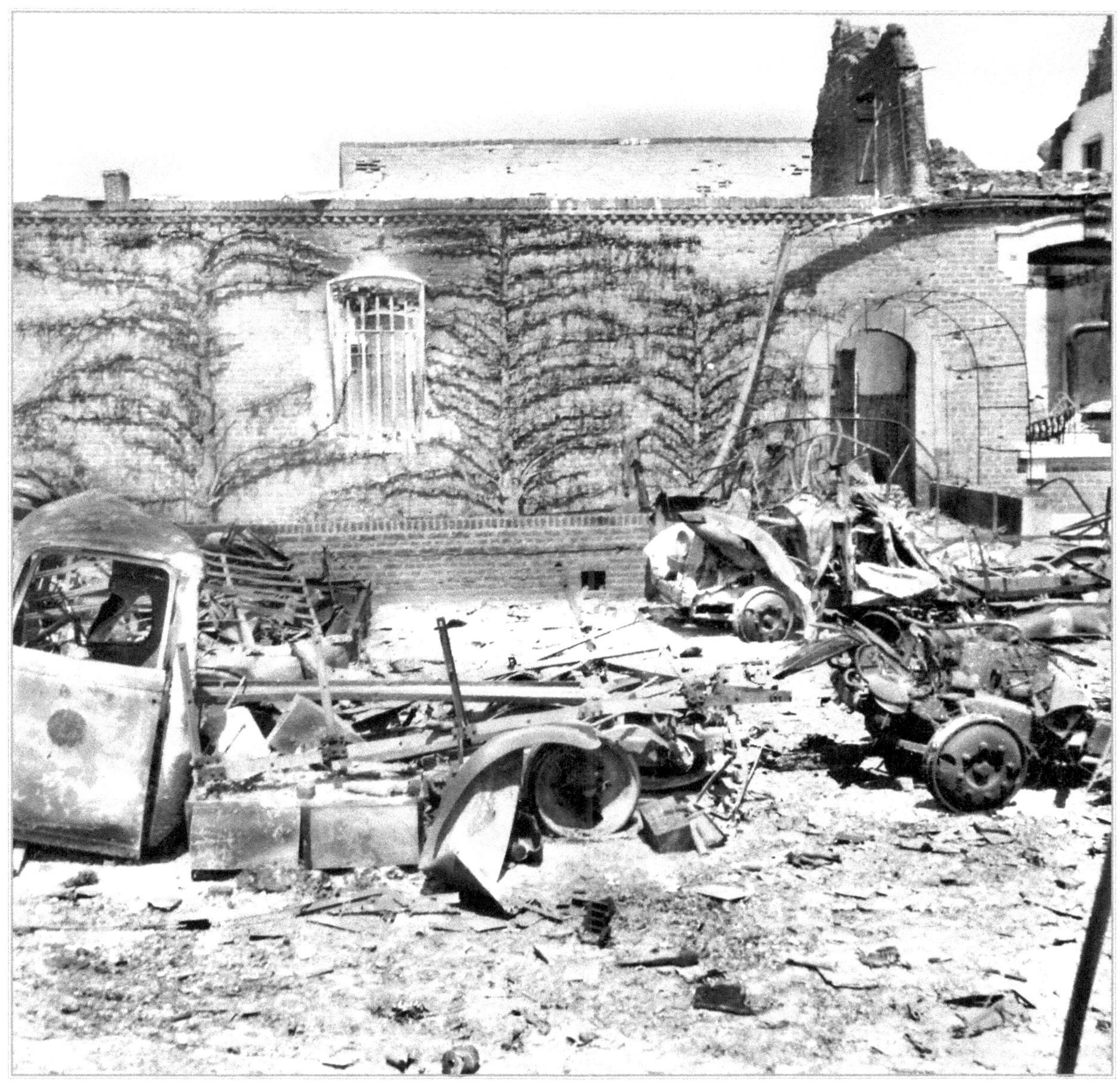

The skeleton of a truck (left) is surrounded by rubble and other demolished vehicles in France.

At first, the vine-covered brick building behind the vehicles appears intact. However, wreckage is visible on the roof. Also, to the far right of the frame, it appears that part of the building has been blown away.

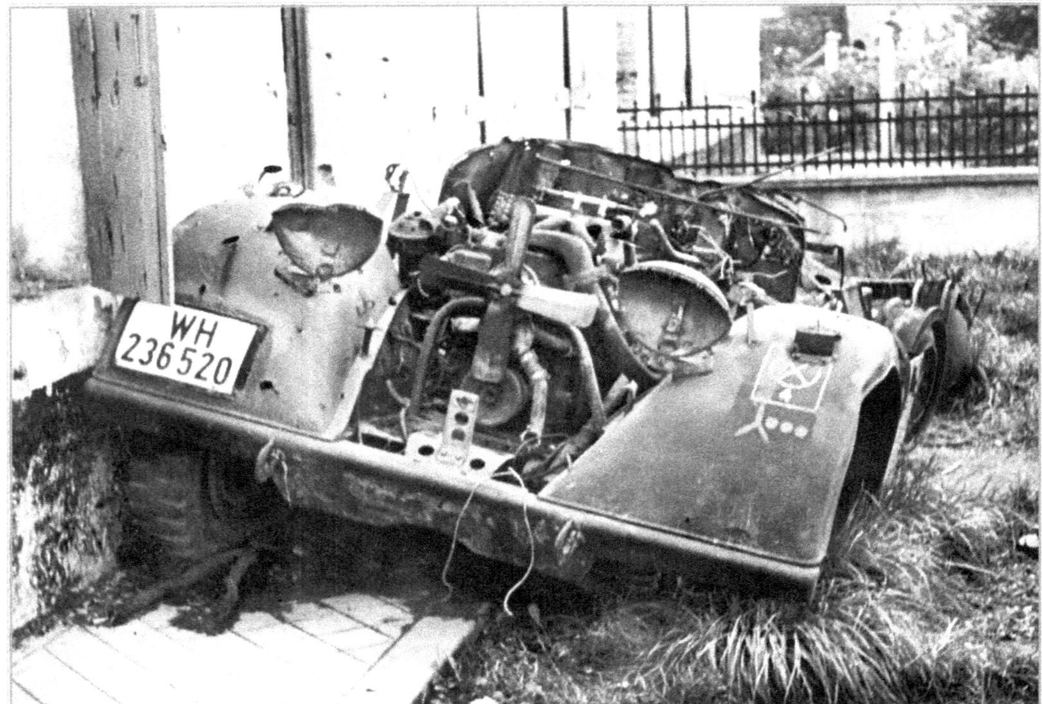

A shattered vehicle appears to have landed halfway in a garden after a blast in France.

Symbols on the fender suggest this was a German vehicle.

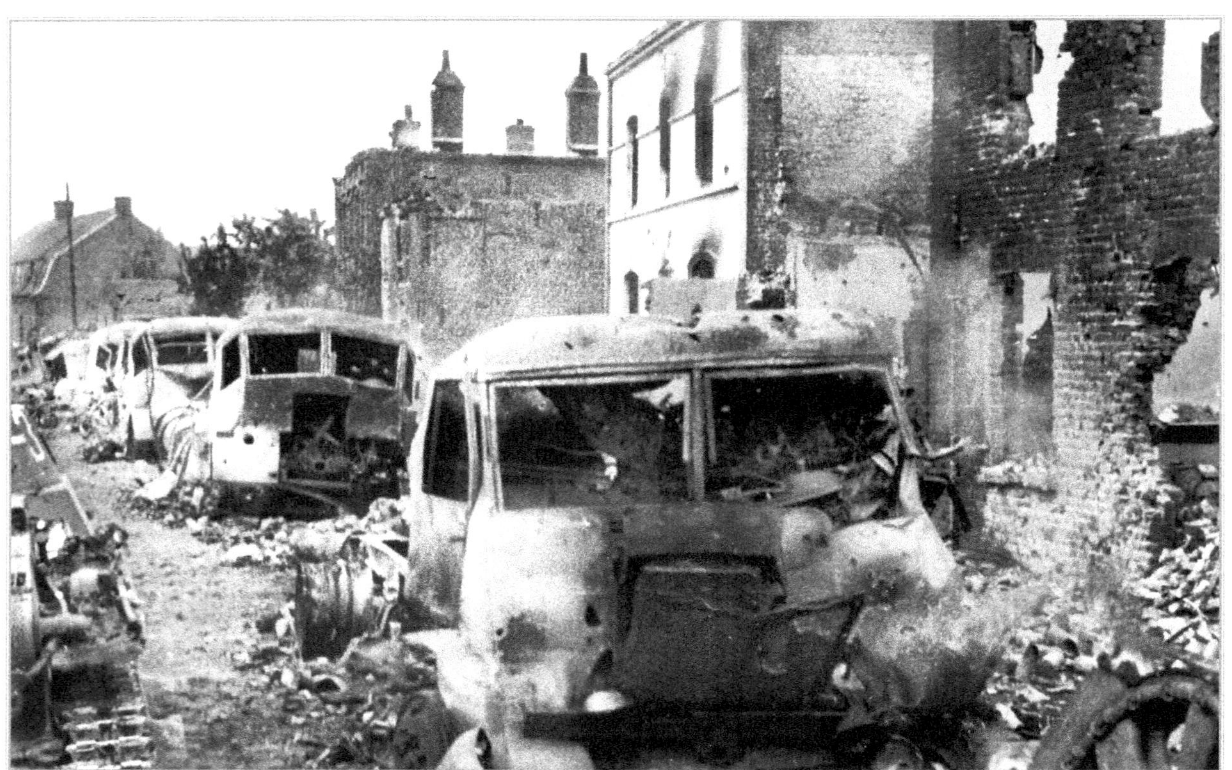

A Panzer on the left passes by a row of torched cars in France.

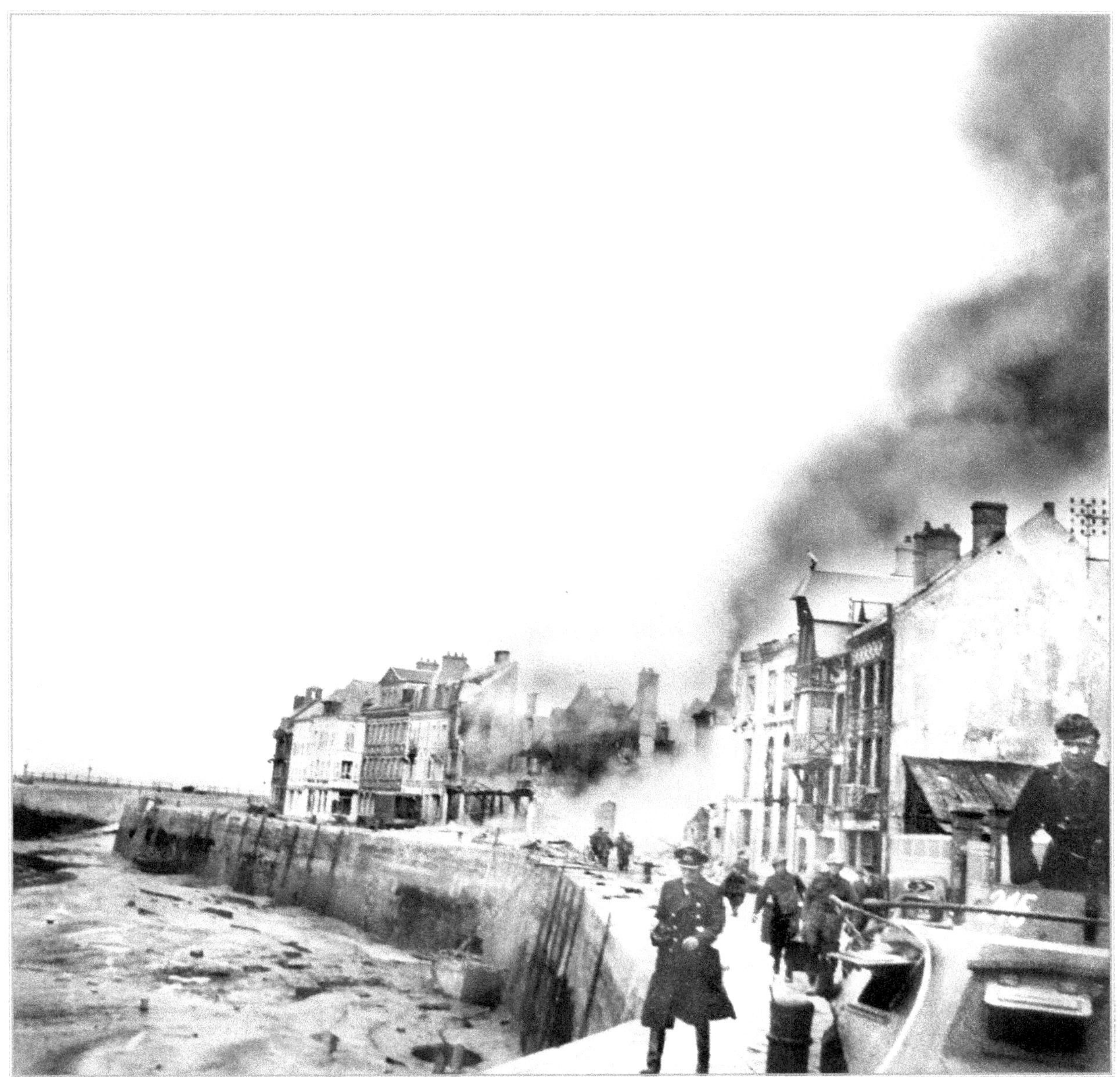

After the surrender of St. Valery-en-Caux, a German soldier in a tank (far right) precedes British soldiers of the 51st Highland Division on the road.

Rommel may have been riding in a Panzer or armored vehicle when he took this picture. The level of Rommel's camera is the same as that of the soldier in the Panzer traveling behind him.

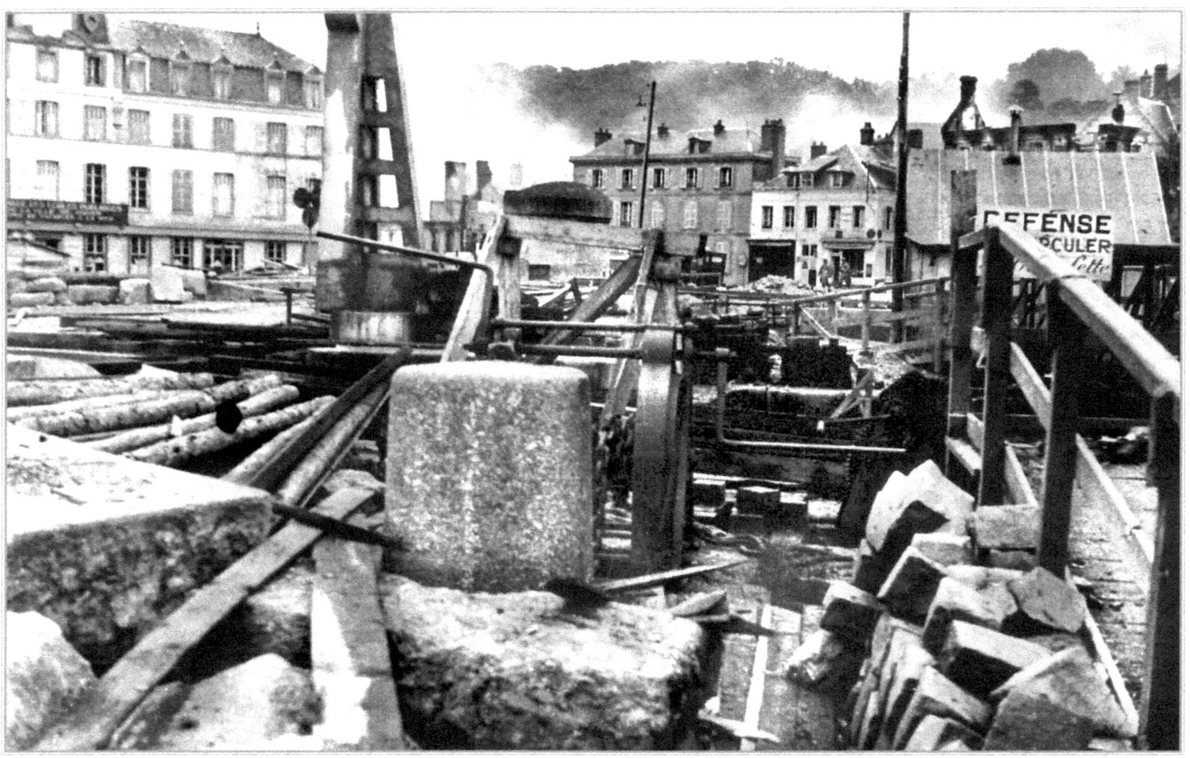

A handrail (right) is recognizable in the ruins of a fortified town center in France.

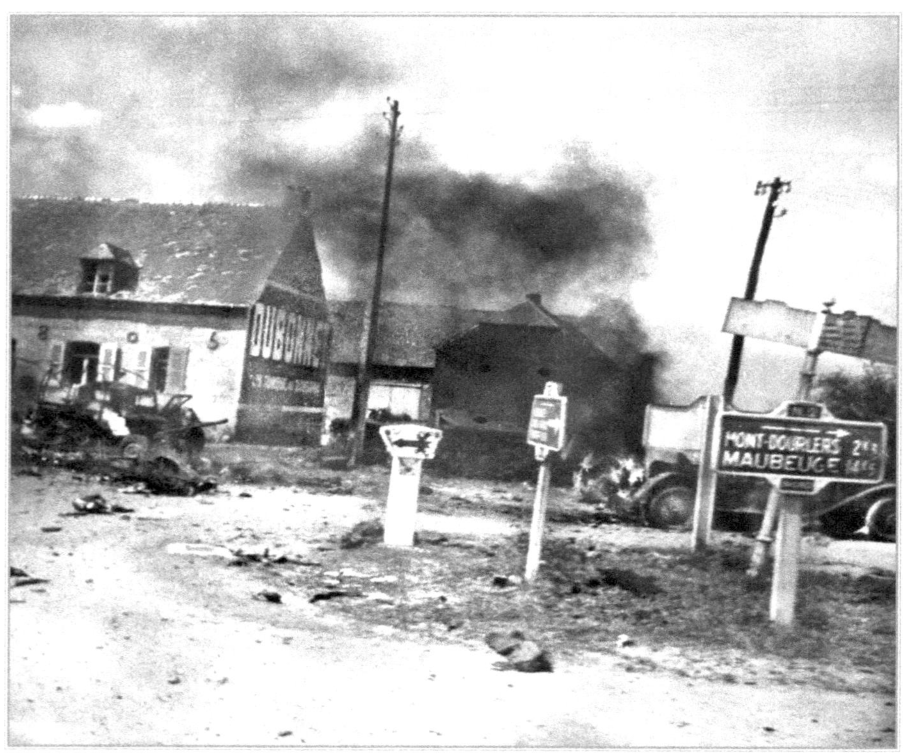

Wreckage covers a street in France.

An advertisement for an aperitif is painted on one side of a building, near an intersection surrounded by burning vehicles and rubble.

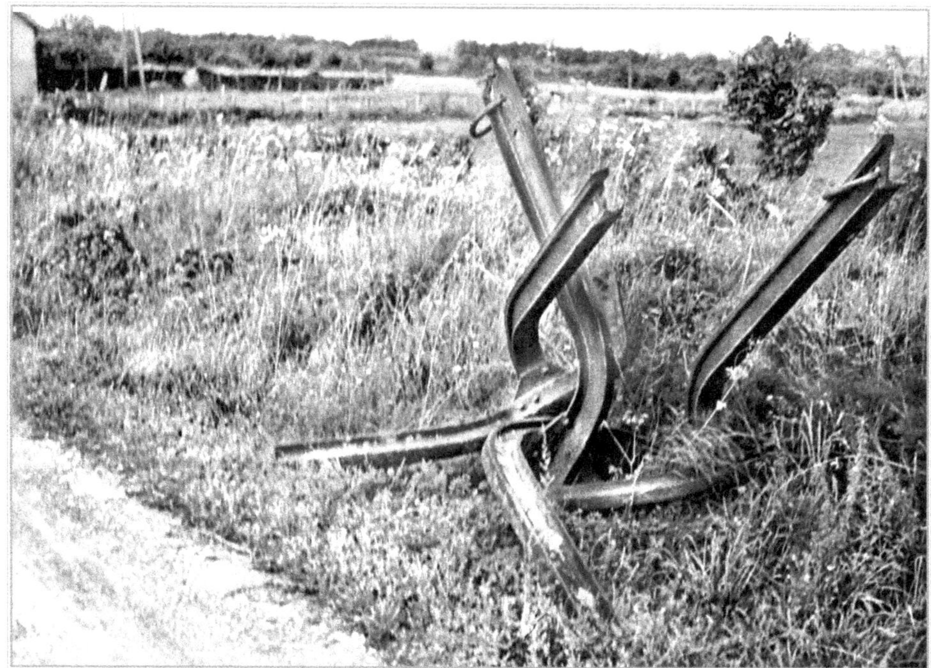

A large piece of a metal, twisted by battle, sits in isolation in a field alongside a dirt road in France.

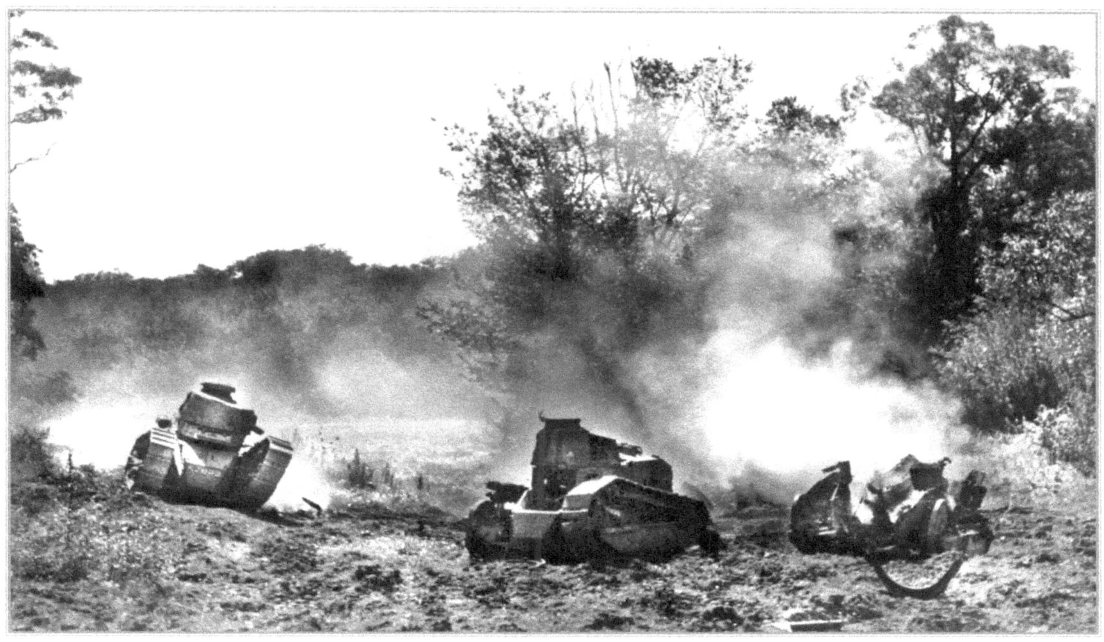

Three tanks smolder after a battle in France.

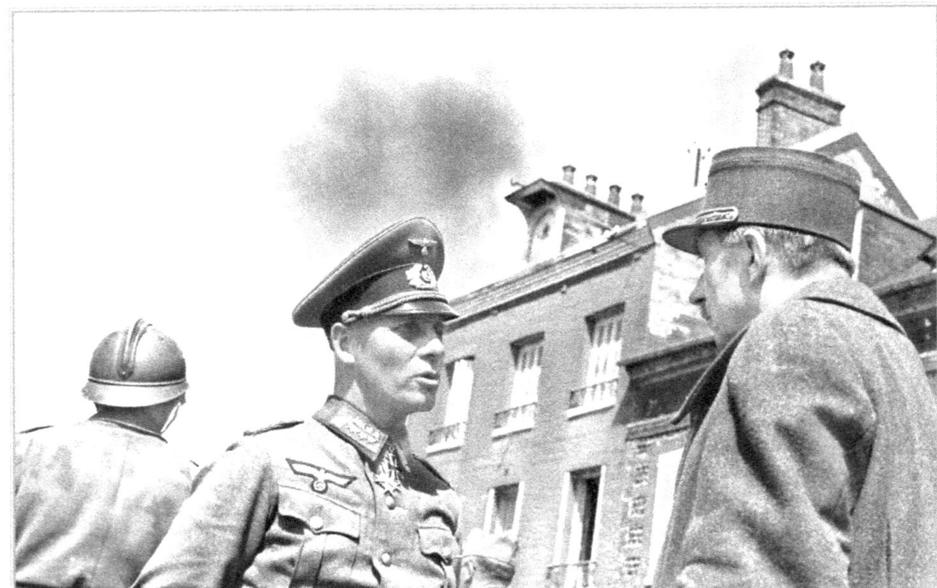

Rommel speaks with commanding General Marcel Ihler of the French 9th Army Corps in St. Valery-en-Caux (1940).

Ihler remained imprisoned in Germany until Hitler's defeat. In 1945, Ihler returned to France, where he died in 1975.

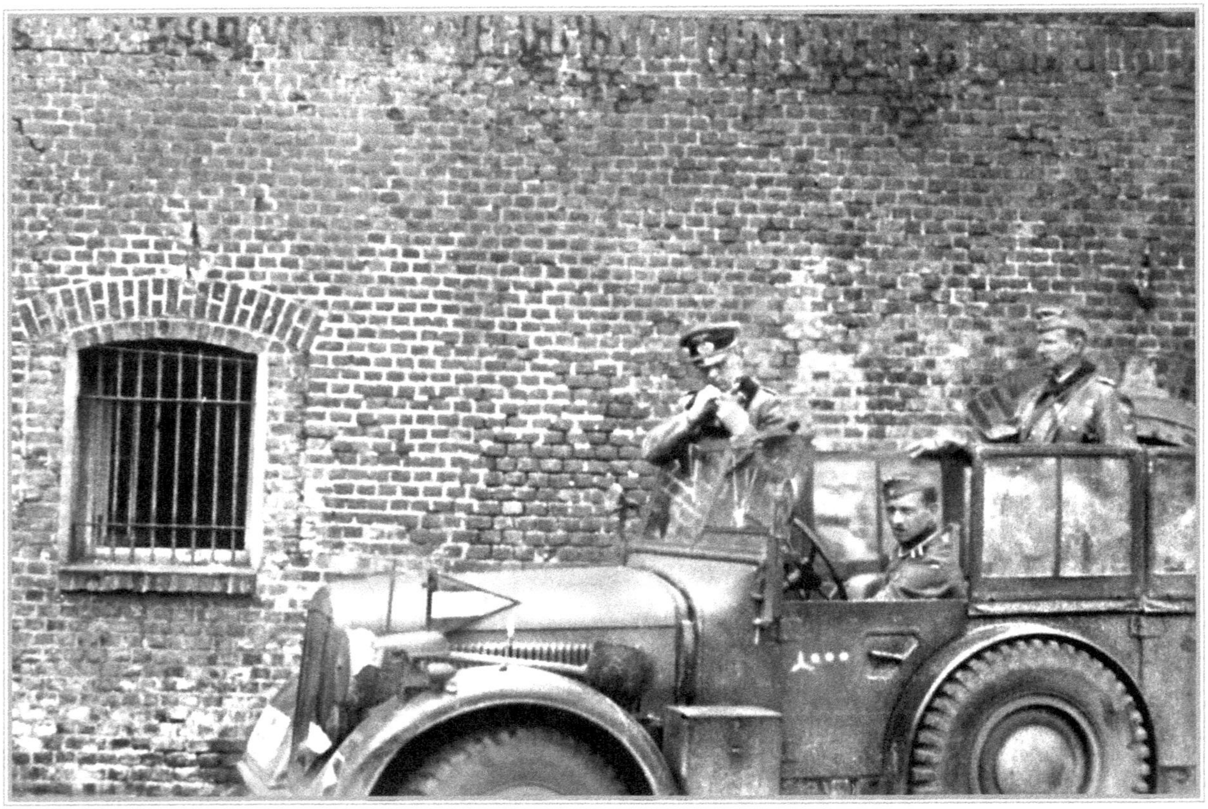

Rommel adjusts his binoculars in a parked car with two other German officers in France.

With a driver and assistant, Rommel lacked a large staff. He was not yet a Field Marshal at that time. He became a Field Marshal while serving in North Africa.

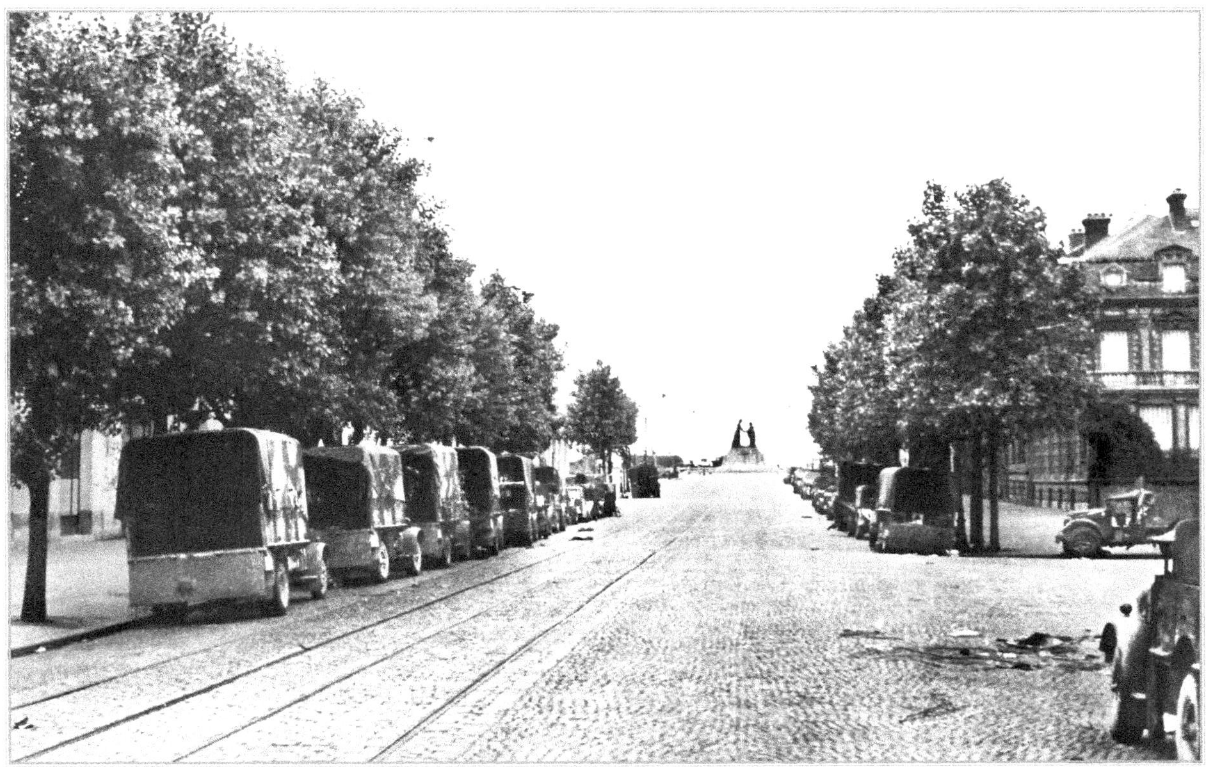

A classical monument stands at the end of a street bordered by military trucks in France.

The statue is the central focal point in this composition. Rommel stood slightly off-center in the street when he took this image. A pile of rubble is apparent (lower right) in the corner of the frame. The rows of trucks, trees, and streetcar tracks form diagonal lines that all point to the monument.

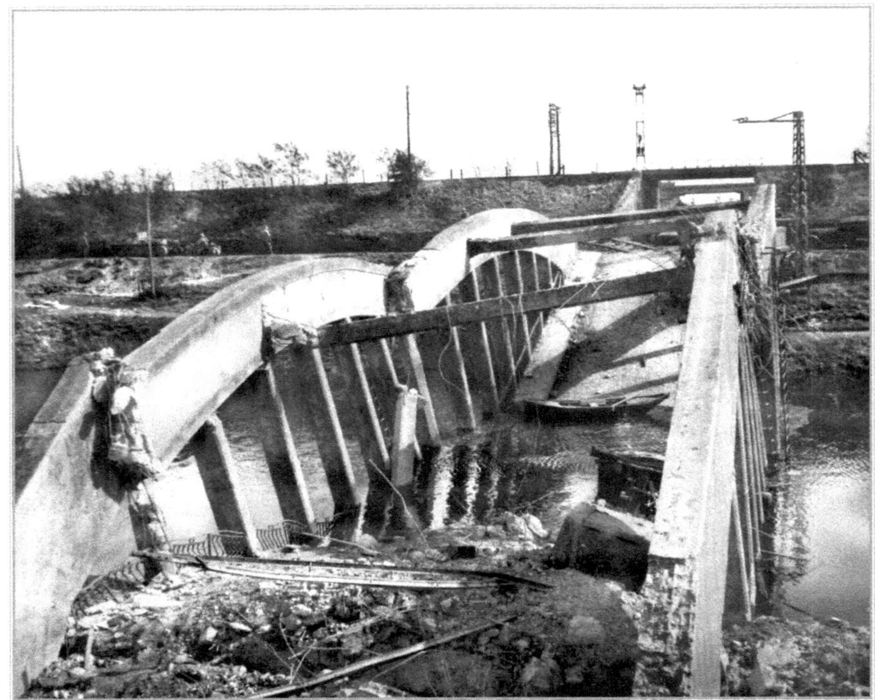

A damaged bridge sinks into the water in France.

Water flowing over the bridge separates a canoe from a destroyed vehicle. In the distance (left) German soldiers stand on a road next to a Panzer and motorcycle unit. Above the bridge (upper right) are the tiny figures of at least three men who are scaling a tower. The arches of the bridge form large diagonal lines.

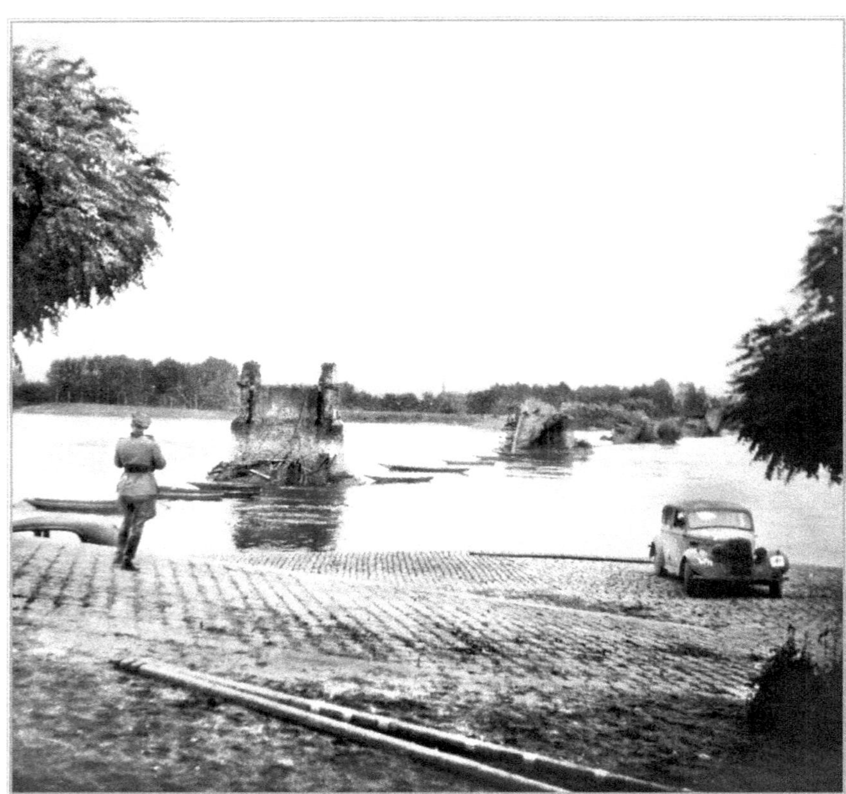

A German soldier stares at the fragments of a destroyed bridge in France.

The soldier stands near what appears to be a commandeered vehicle (right).

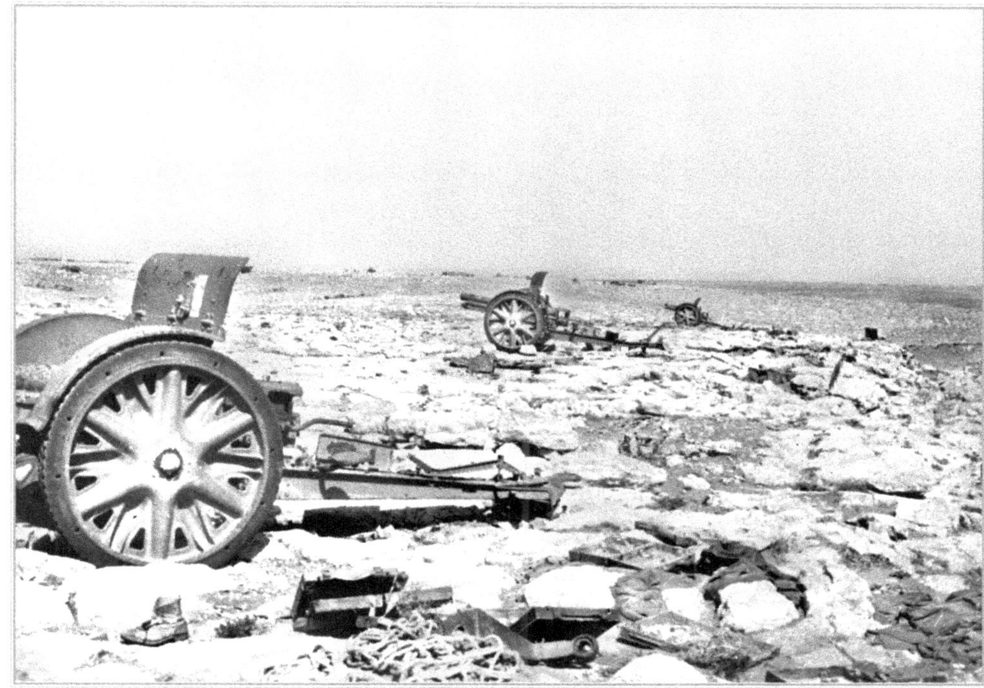

Remnants of a battle in North Africa.

In the foreground, a boot (left) and scattered equipment testify to the fact that a hard fight took place here. The guns decrease in size from left to right.

Two trees remain standing next a crumbled wall in North Africa.

Bricks have tumbled to the ground. The wall plaster is heavily pitted. The trees, however, appear untouched. Rommel composed this photo using the wall as a diagonal line through the center of the frame.

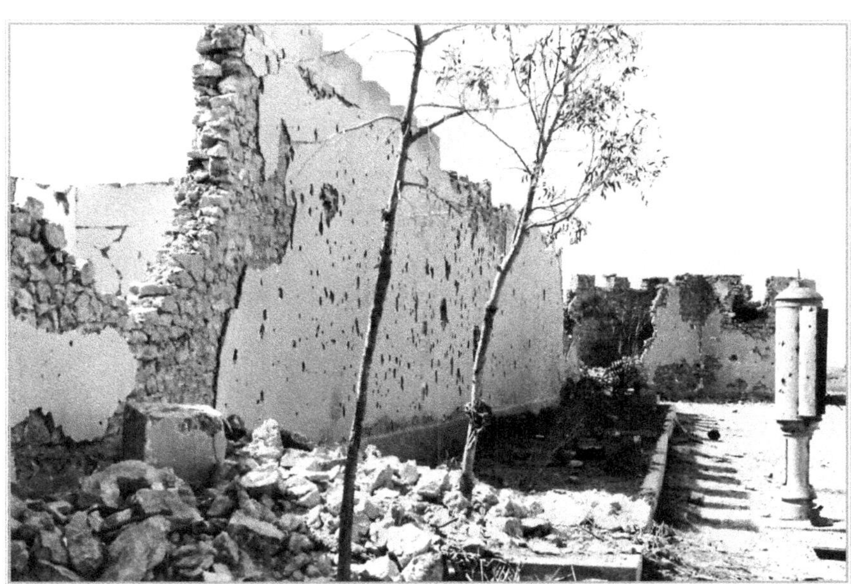

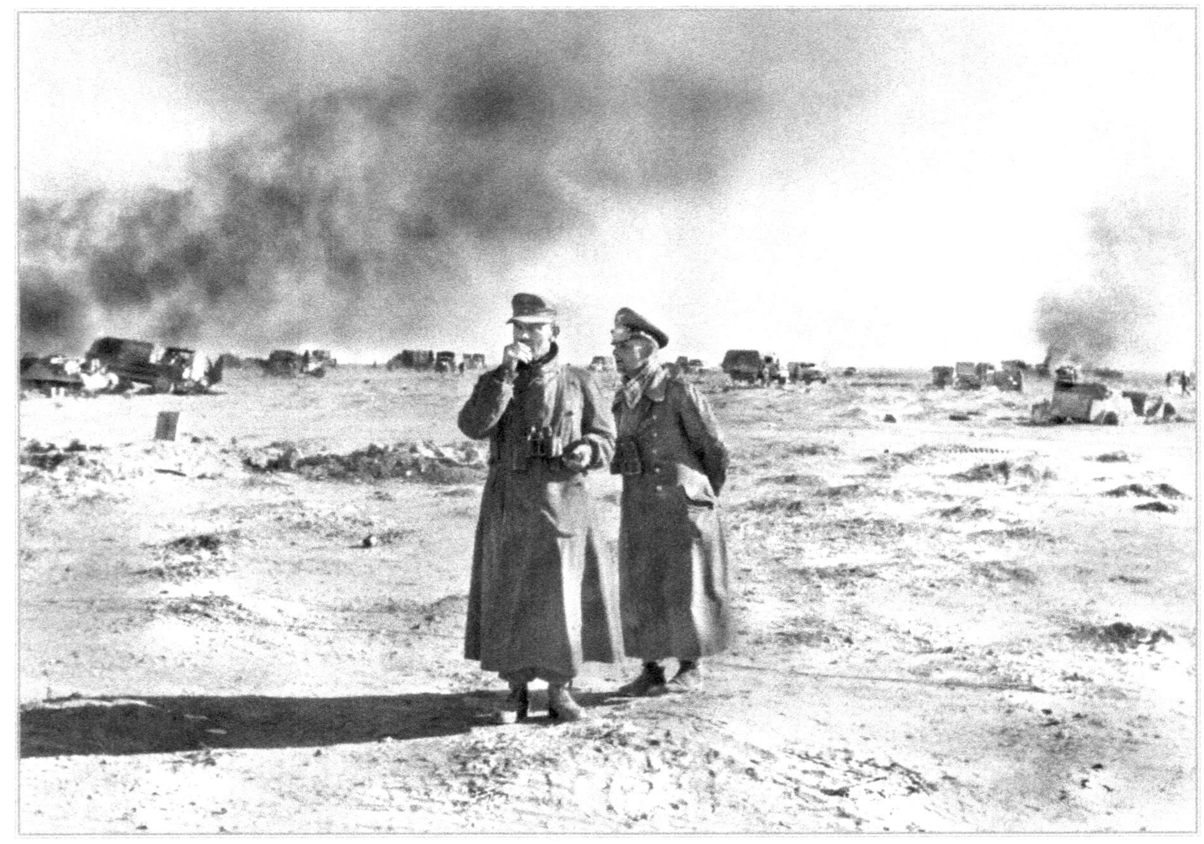

Rommel stands with Lieutenant General Fritz Bayerlein on the ground where a battle has just taken place in North Africa.

Rommel, wearing the scarf that his daughter made for him, has stubble on his face. This is unusual because normally he is pictured clean-shaven.

On Rommel's left, a disabled car without wheels is sunk into the sand. There is much activity in the background. Men are walking around the site, and clouds of dark smoke drift in the air.

Bayerlein was on good terms with Rommel and admired him as a commander. After Rommel's death, Bayerlein contributed to *"The Rommel Papers,"* in which he penned chapters about his time with Rommel in North Africa and Europe preceding the Allied Invasion. (See References.) Later Bayerlein surrendered his troops in Germany to American forces in 1945. He became a POW for two years and died in 1970.

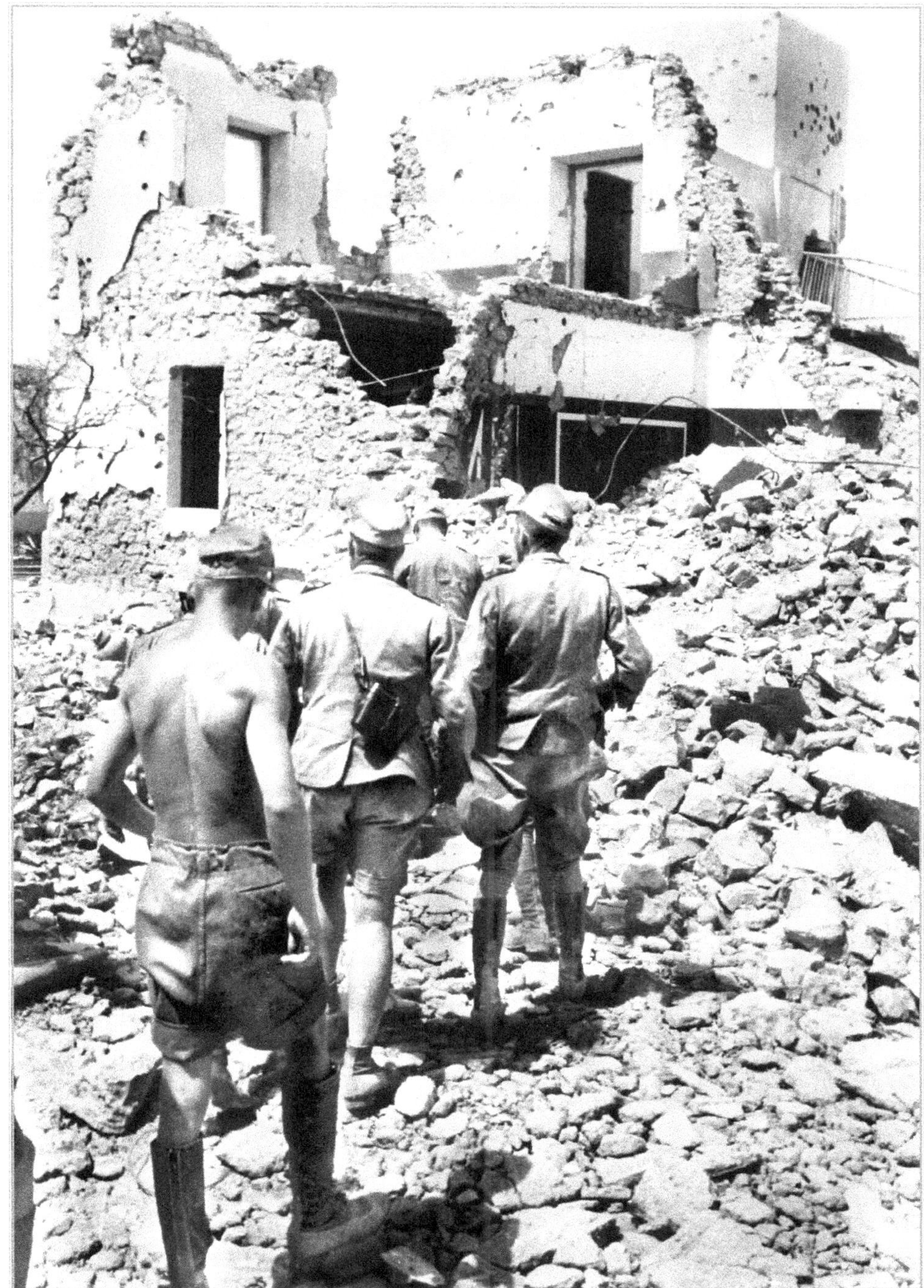

A group of German soldiers tread carefully through rubble in North Africa.

The soldiers form a diagonal line from the lower left to the center of the frame. The soldier in the middle has ankle boots, and the other men wear knee-high boots. Afrika Korps knee-high boots were made of high-quality suede and leather. They were well suited to the desert and coveted by British soldiers.

8

Soldiers

den deutschen Truppen

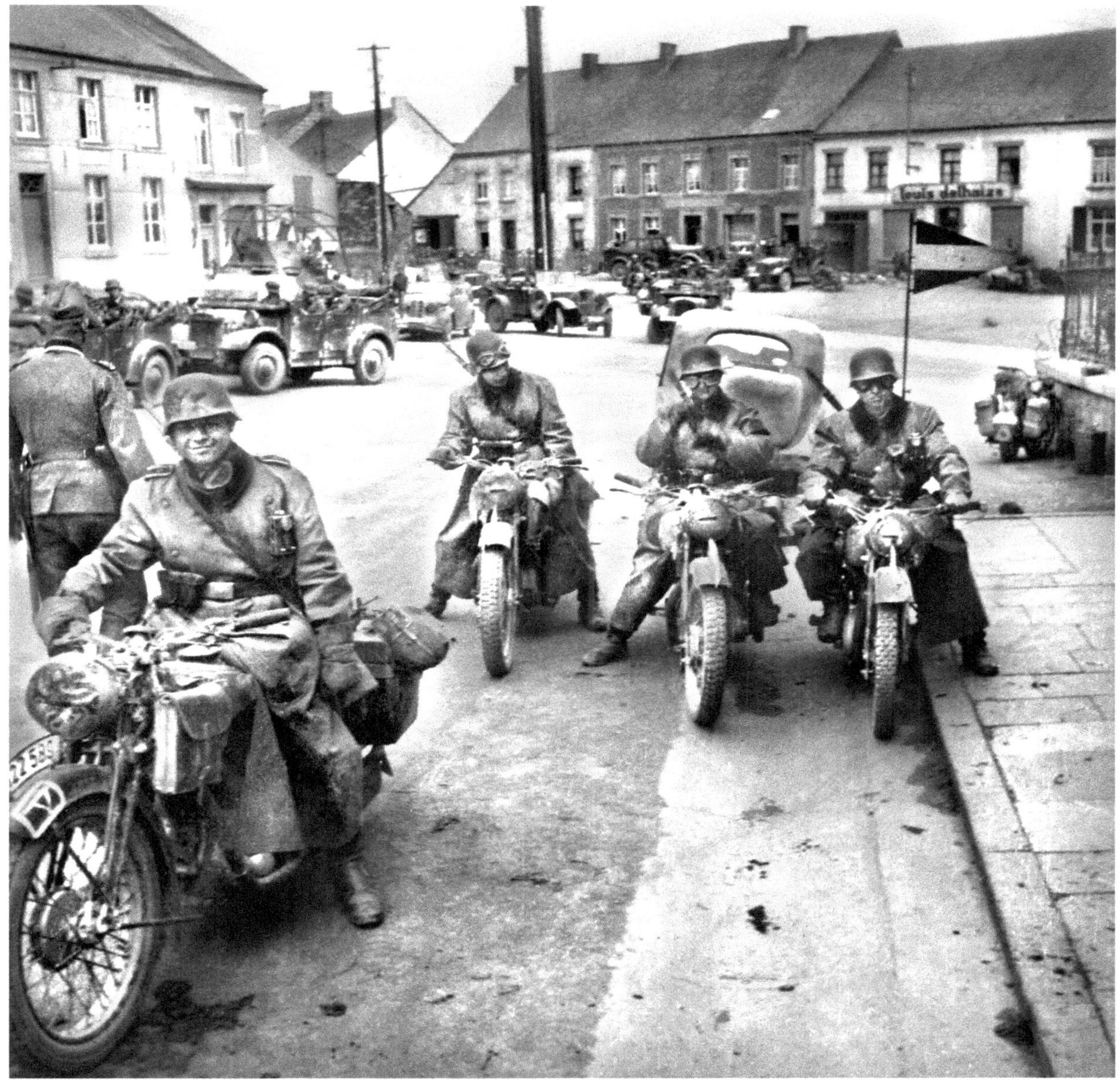

Four members of a German motorcycle unit pause to have their photo taken (in France or Belgium, 1940).

The motorcyclists, covered in dust, wear rifles strapped across their backs. The two motorcyclists on the left have pouches slung over their handlebars. Other German soldiers and vehicles converge in the streets behind them.

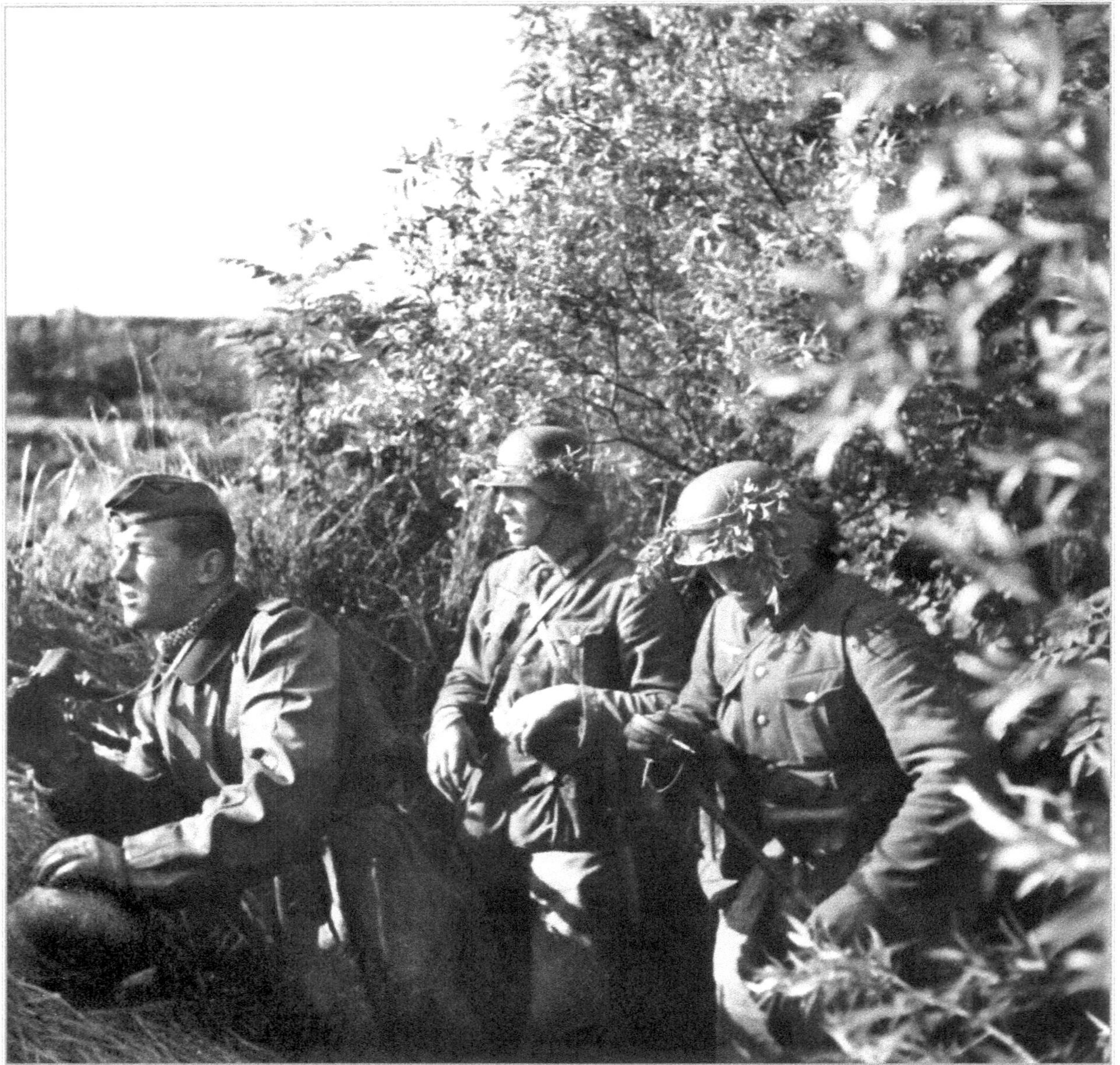

Camouflaged German soldiers blend into the foliage in France.

The soldier wearing the cap (left) rests his left hand on his steel helmet as he pauses with a pair of binoculars. His two companions have wrapped leafy branches around their helmets. The men appear to be tense and preparing for action. Rommel must have been standing in the same thicket with them when he took this picture.

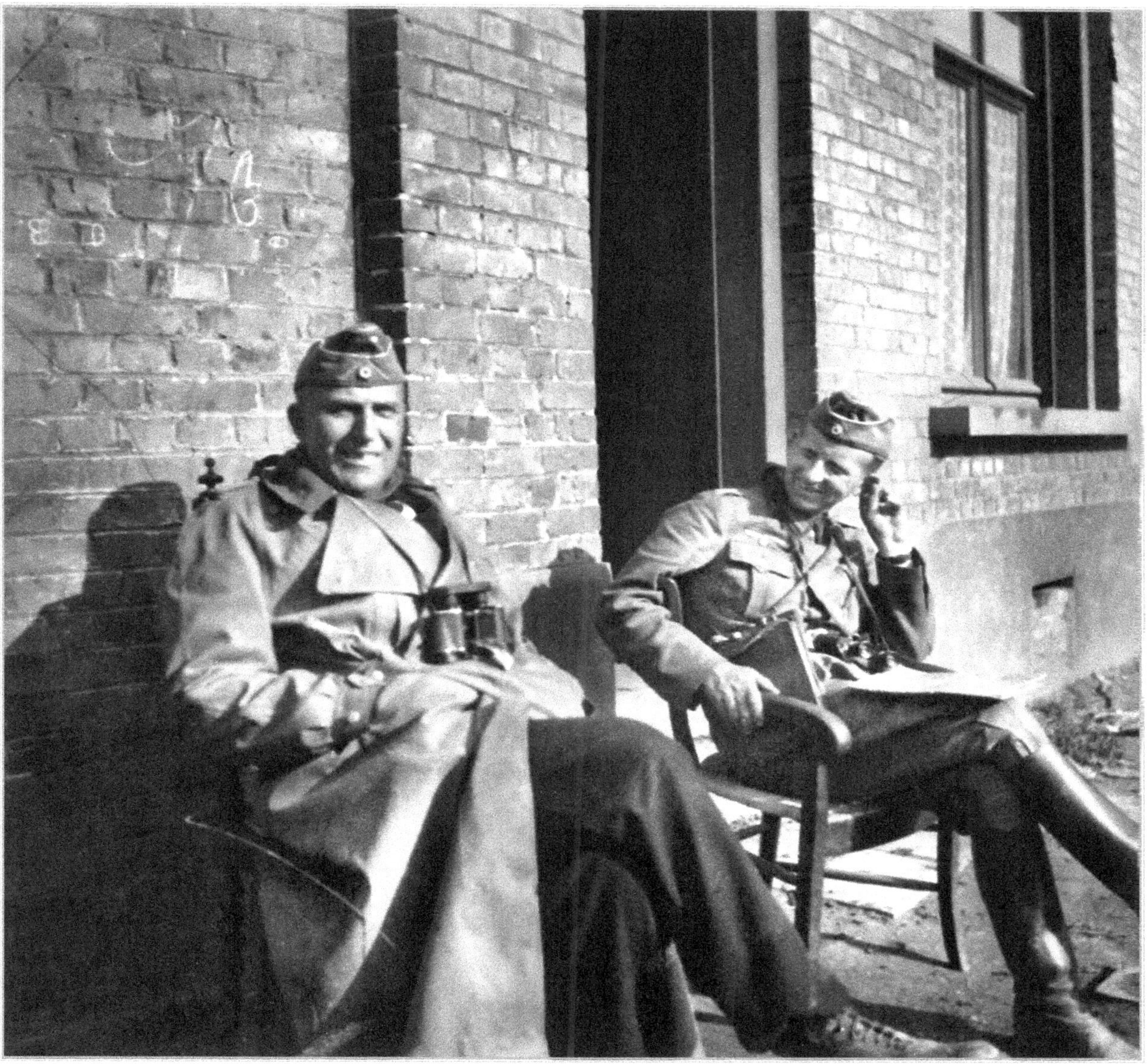

Two German officers recline in chairs outside a building (in France or Belgium, 1940).

Smiling for the camera, both men are wearing binoculars slung around their necks. The officer on the right is balancing documents on his lap and has a briefcase next to the armrest of his chair.

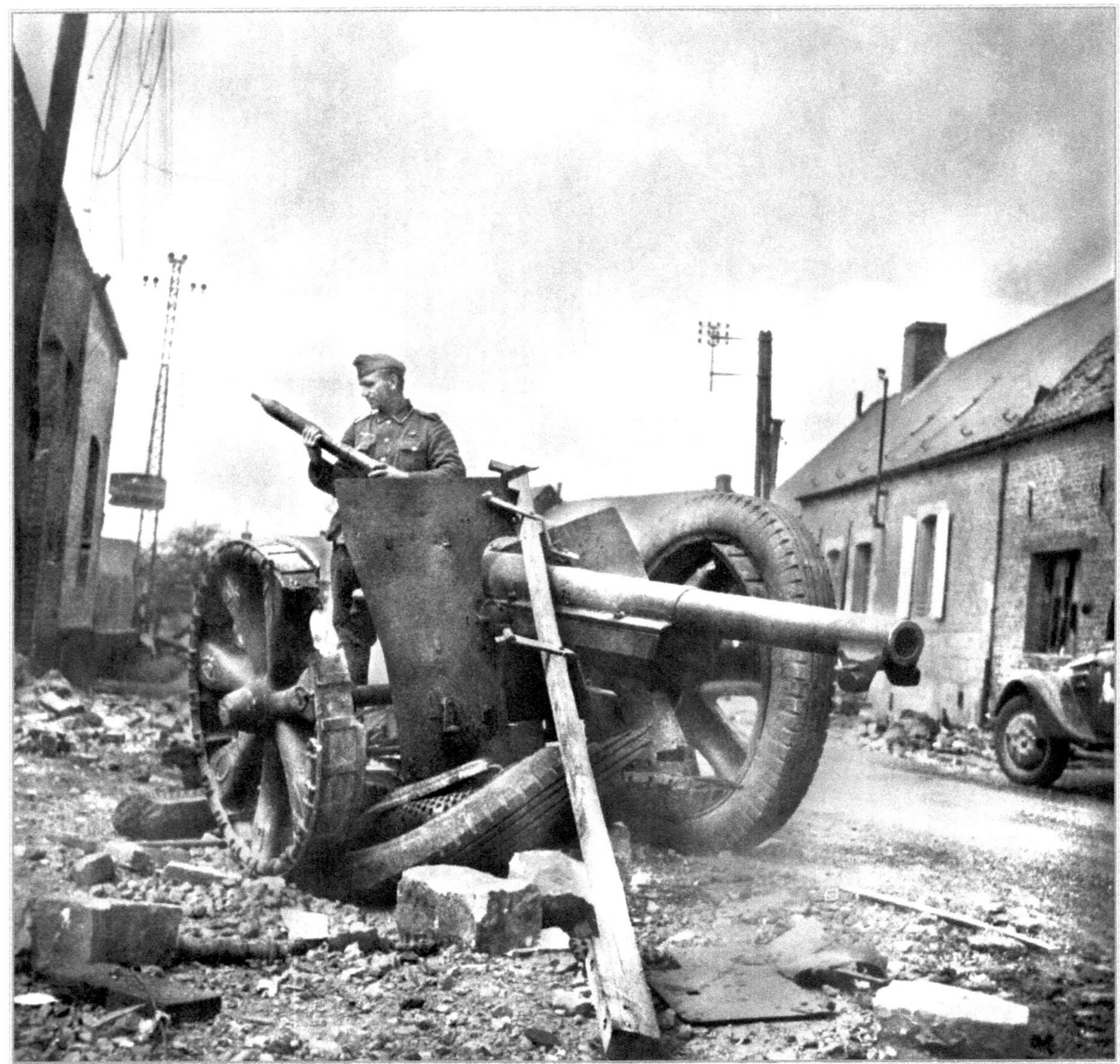

Surrounded by devastation, a lone German soldier holds a shell while standing on an antitank gun in France.

The fallen beam crossing the gun barrel is the central focal point. Large bricks and other rubble in the foreground may have rained down on the weapon from a nearby building. A chunk of the metal wheel rim is missing from this piece of artillery. The tire tread is ripped off and crumpled behind the wooden beam. The vantage point of this image indicates Rommel crouched down to take this photo.

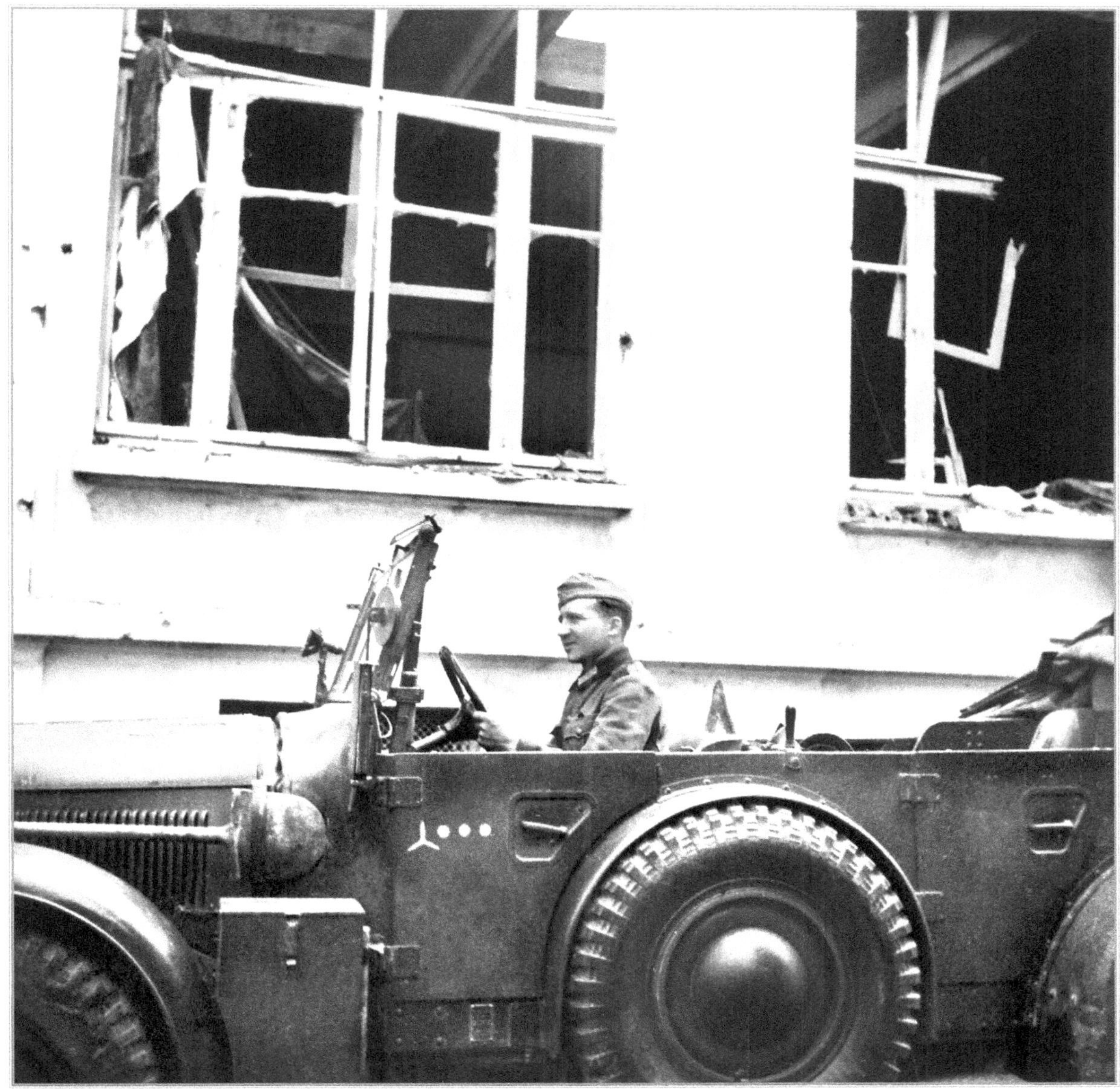

A German driver waits in a jeep outside a building with broken windows in France.

This is another contrasting image. Neither the immaculately attired driver nor the clean vehicle appear battle-worn. However, the building in the background tells a different story. There is no glass left in the broken windowpanes. Fabric from a torn curtain (left) has been blown across the frame. Possible bullet holes mark the exterior. In addition, part of the window ledge (right) is missing.

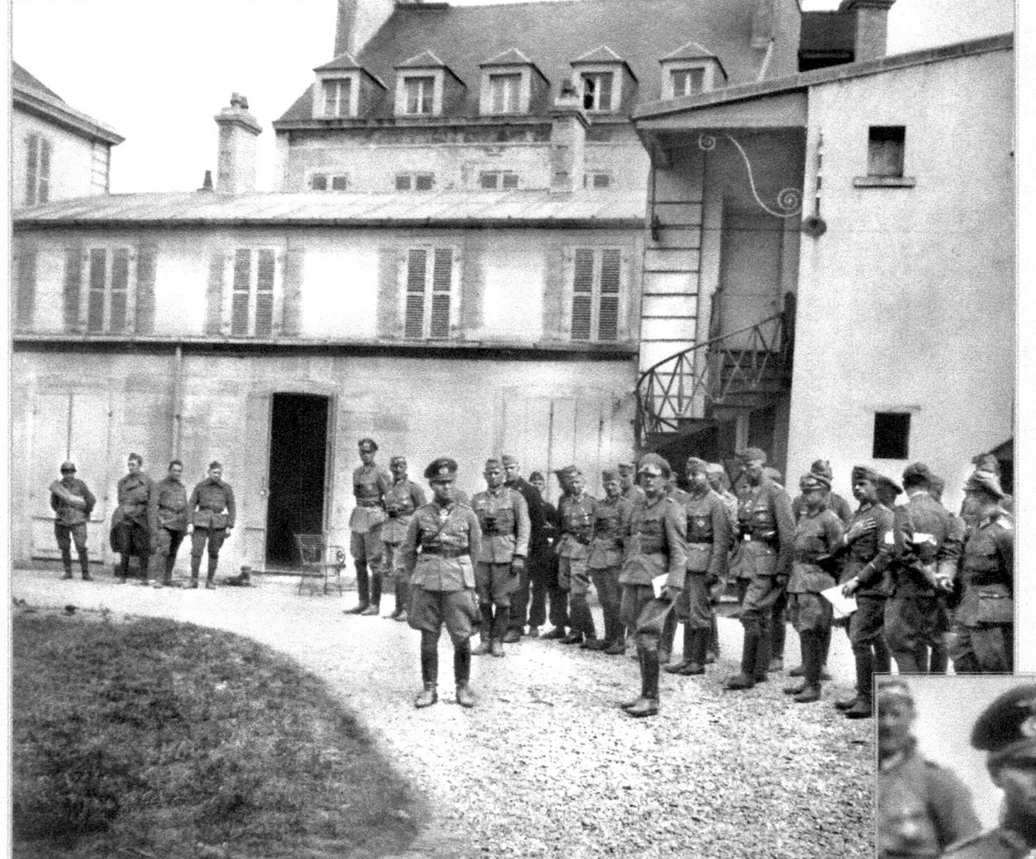

Rommel stands among an assembly of German officers outside a building in France on June 19, 1940.

The men appear to be assembled in front of the house as they await something. A few officers on the right clutch paperwork in their hands. A doorway is open (left) in the building. A dog sits nearby next to an empty chair.

A close-up of Rommel (right) has been extracted from the group photo. He stands with his arms folded behind him and his shoulders thrown back, assuming an air of confidence. Rommel often adopted this posture in photos.

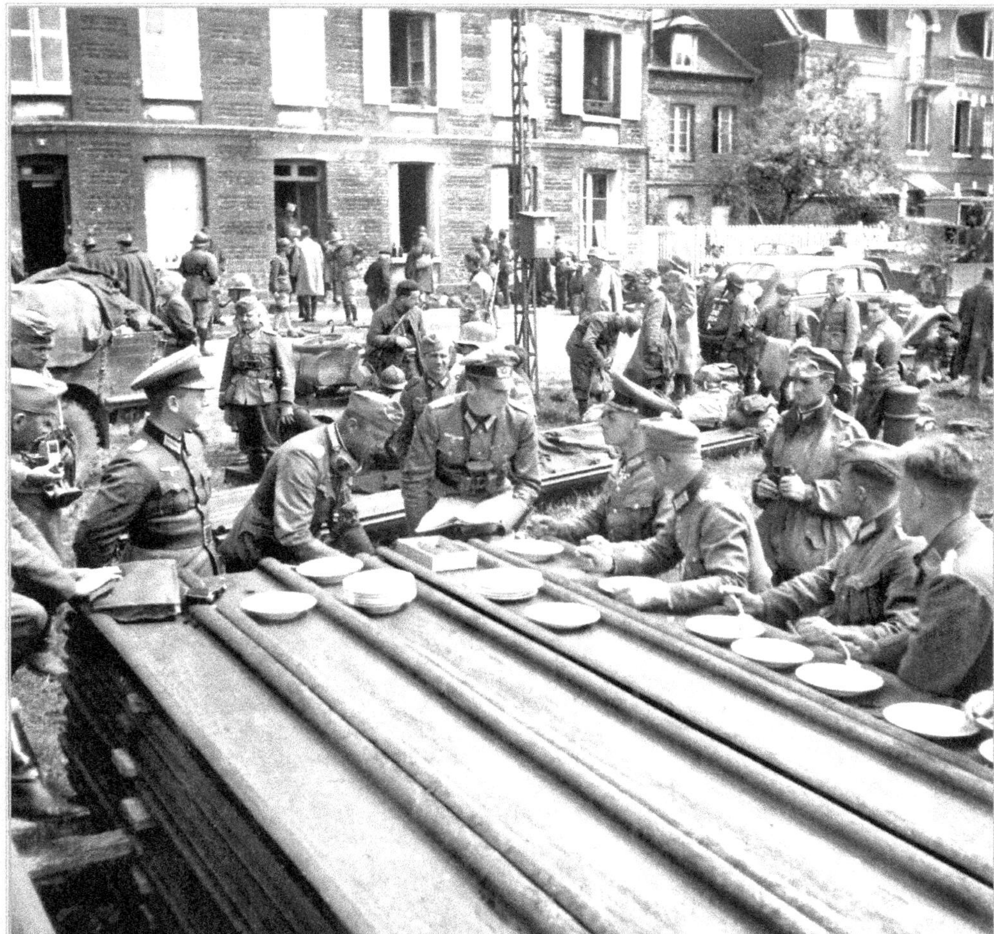

Rommel (center) shares a meal with fellow soldiers at an open-air field kitchen in France.

He appears to listen to the officer on his right, who leans over with papers. POWs walk and sit in the open area behind Rommel. Some POWs wear bérets.

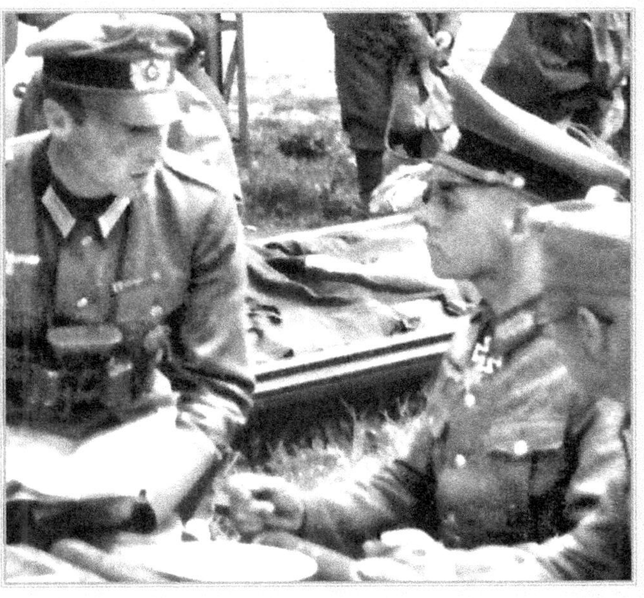

This image of Rommel (right) is blown up and cropped from the one above.

Rommel was admired by the average German soldier because of his down-to-earth demeanor and the camaraderie he showed towards the regular troops.

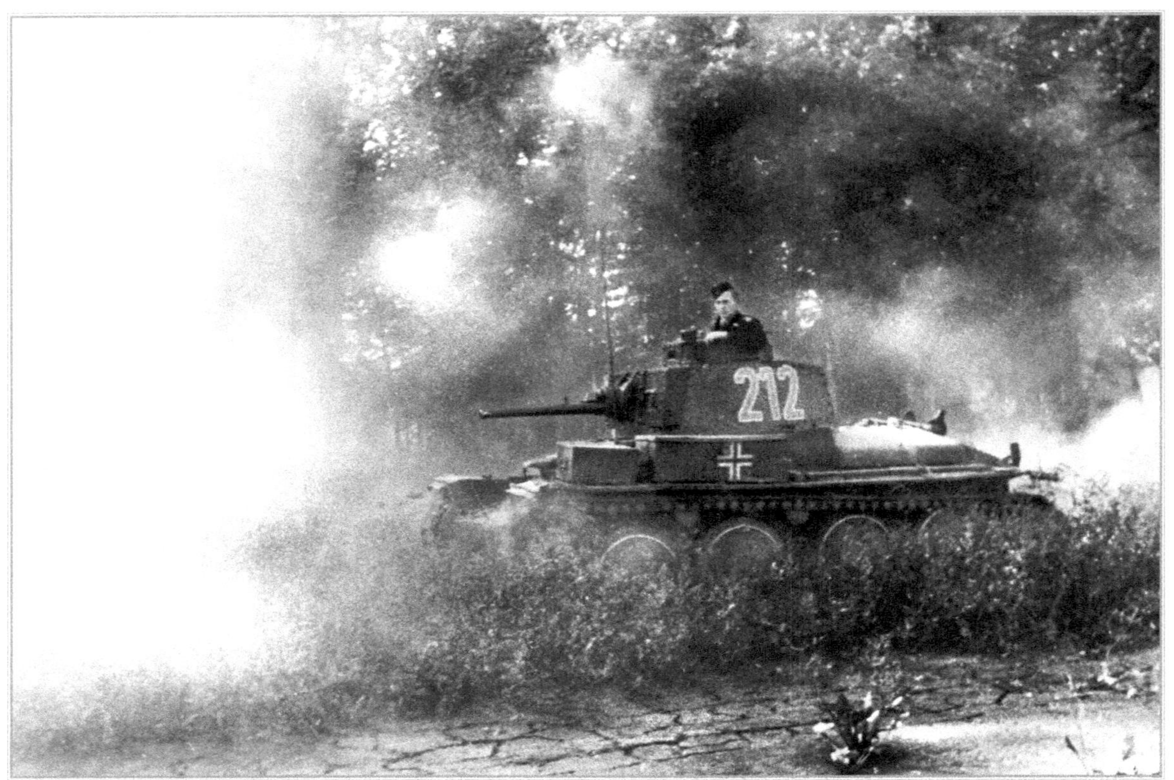

A German soldier sits in a Panzer surrounded by haze in France.

The soldier looks into the camera. The haze creates an eerie effect around the tank.

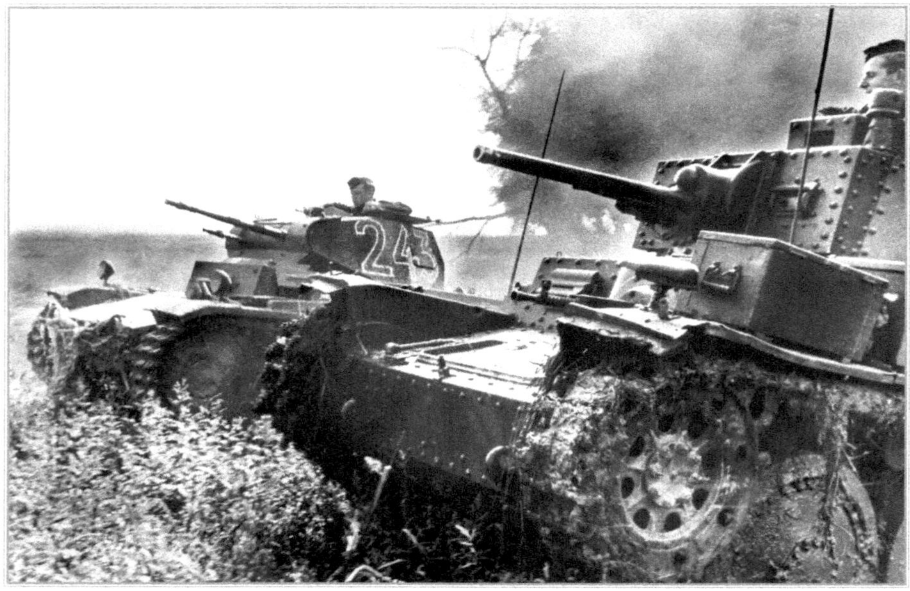

Two Panzers stand ready for action near a thicket of trees in France.

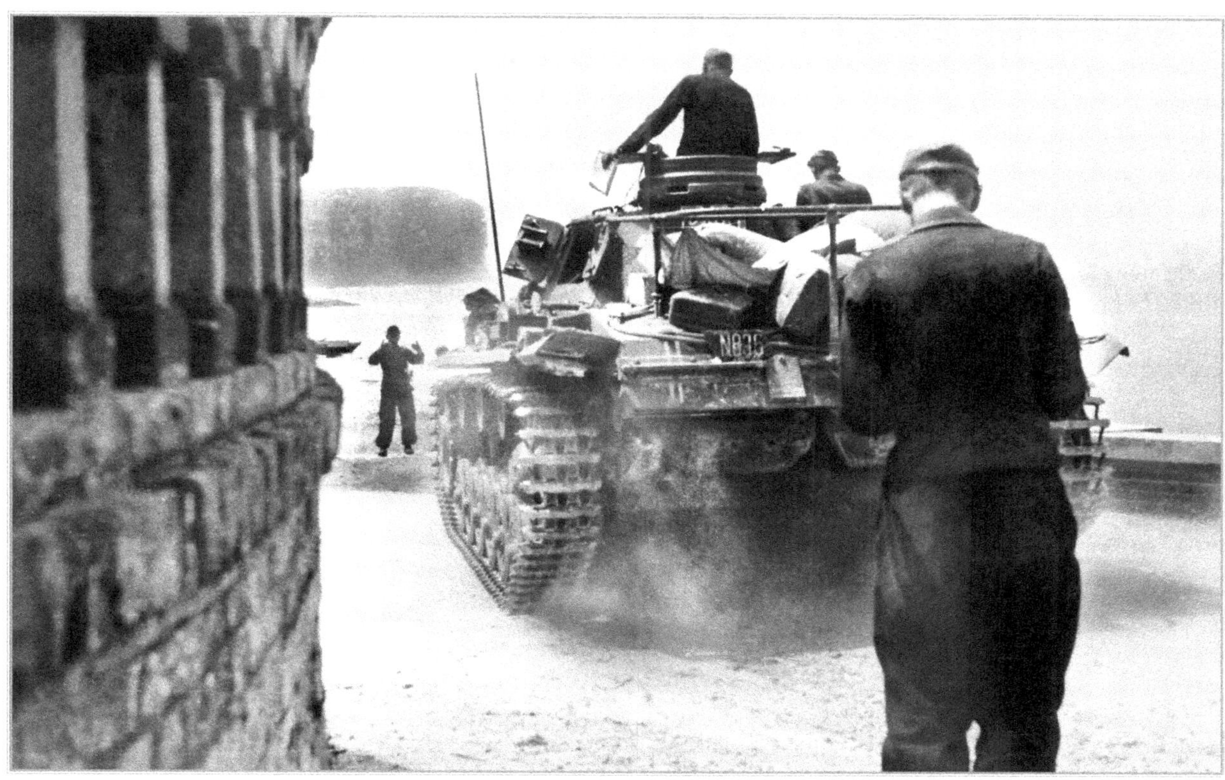

German tank crewmen guide Colonel Rothenburg's Panzer onto the beach of France's Normandy coast (June 10, 1940).

Rommel framed this picture using the wall (left), the action in the center, and the German soldier (right). Sand is kicked into the air as the Panzer rolls forward. A lone German soldier in the middle ground guides the tank into position. Col. Rothenburg, carrying papers, rides in the turret with a crewman beside him. A hatch is open on the tank's left side.

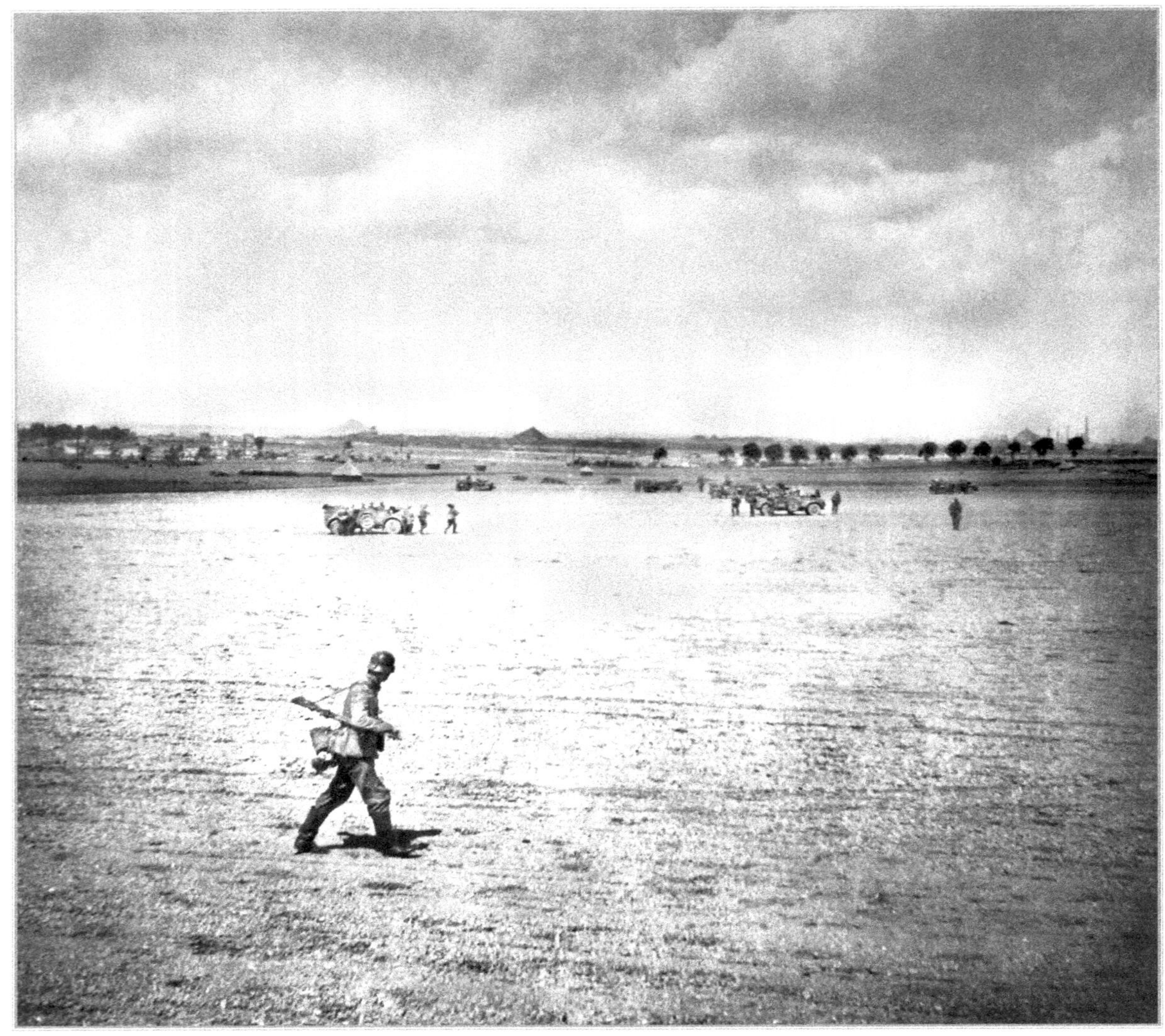

A solitary German soldier walks across a field under a moody sky (date and location unknown).

The soldier has a rifle slung over his shoulder and carries his gear as he gazes across a vast expanse. German troops gather at vehicles in the distance. Soldiers from one car in the middle ground assemble their gear and walk to meet others across the field. As in Rommel's other photos, this image features a lone person set against a large backdrop.

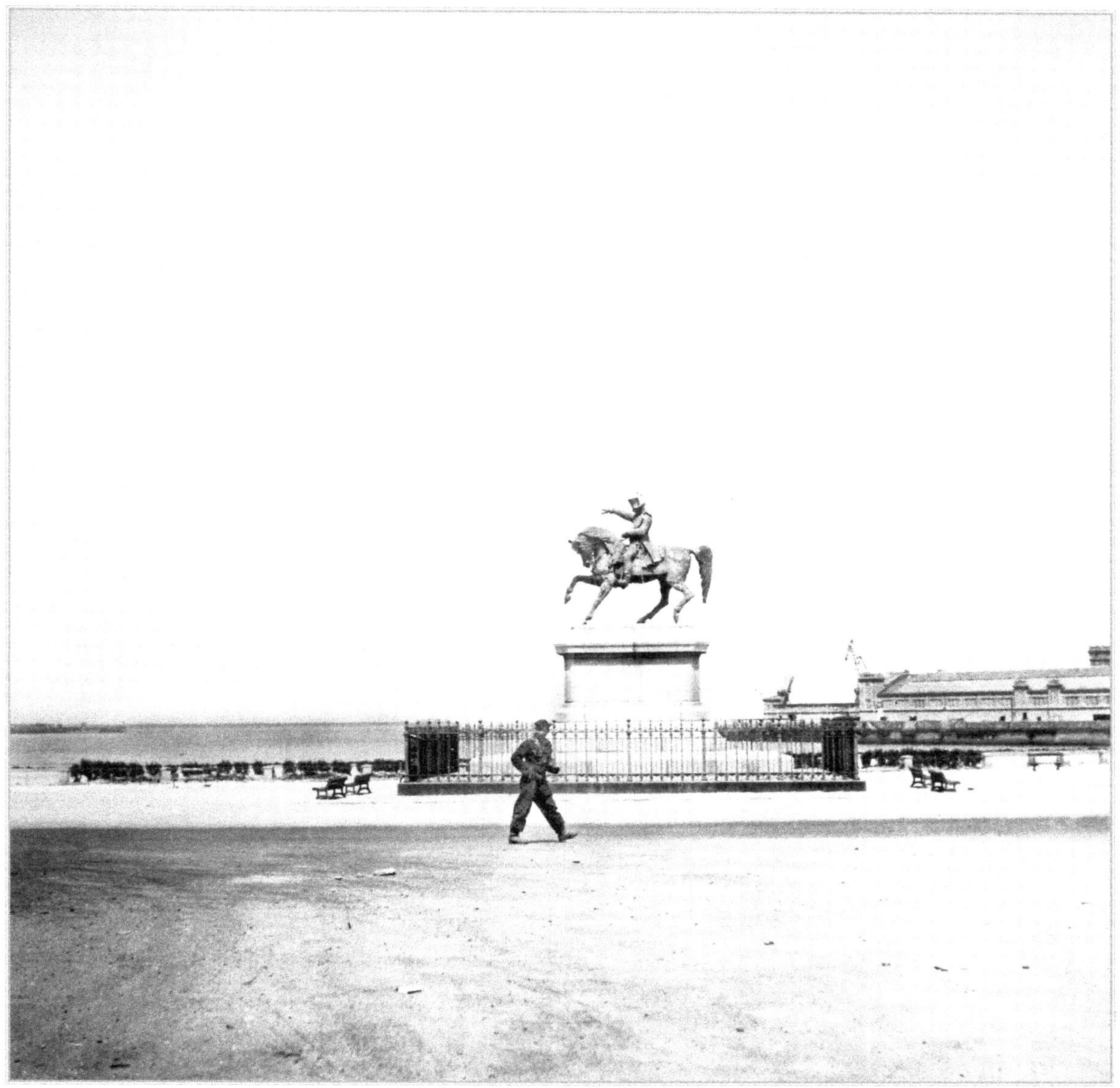

A French sailor walks in the opposite direction past a statue of Napoleon in Cherbourg, France.

Looking straight into the camera, the French seaman is the only figure on the harbor. The benches are empty. The upper and lower halves of the image contain negative space. Rommel may have been struck by the irony of the man and the statue facing opposite directions.

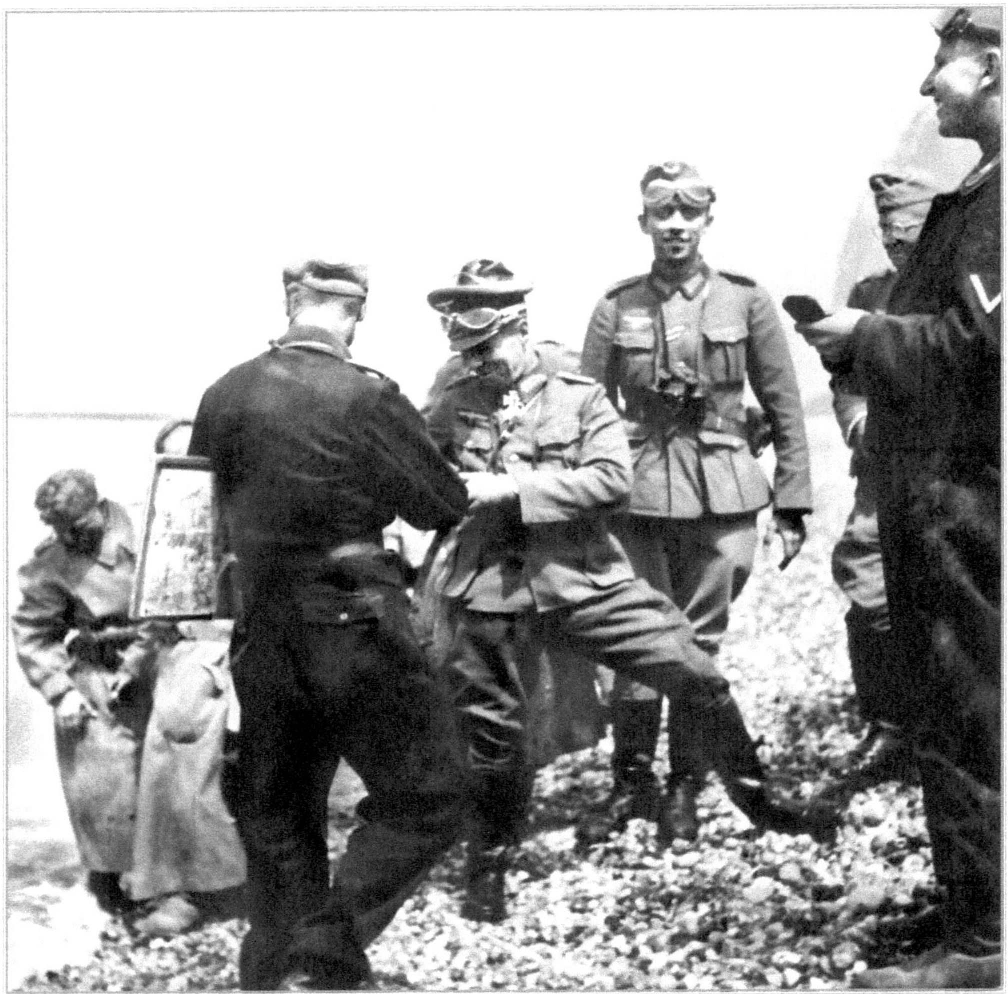

Rommel and his men relax on Les Petites-Dalles beach along the Normandy coast on June 10, 1940.

"The sight of the sea with the cliffs on either side thrilled and stirred every man of us; also the thought that we had reached the coast of France. We climbed out of our vehicles and walked down the shingle beach to the water's edge until the water lapped over our boots. Several dispatch riders in long waterproof coats walked straight out until the water was over their knees, and I had to call them back."

— *Rommel*

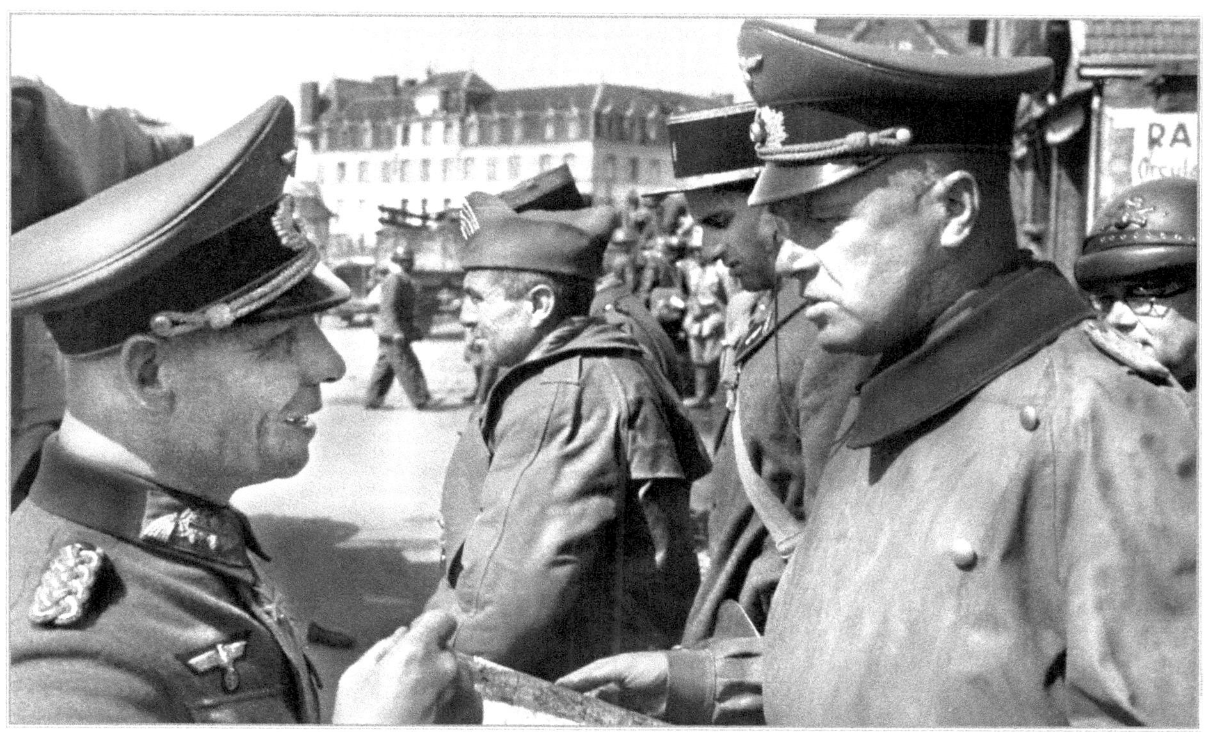

Rommel speaks with a German officer following the surrender at St. Valery-en-Caux, France (1940).

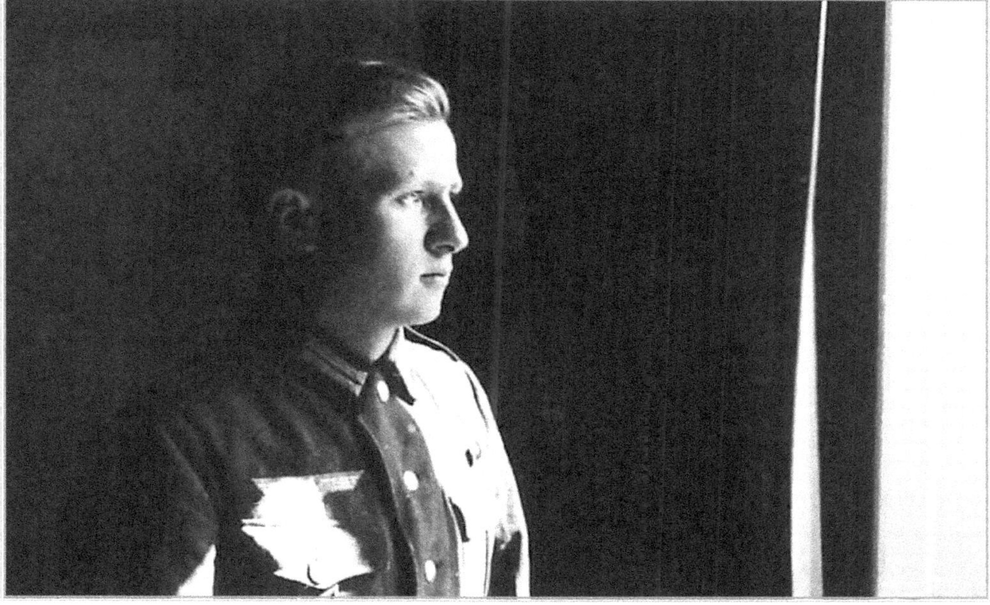

A close-up of an unknown German soldier (date unknown).

This man's image was included on a film strip among Rommel's pictures of his family and friends.

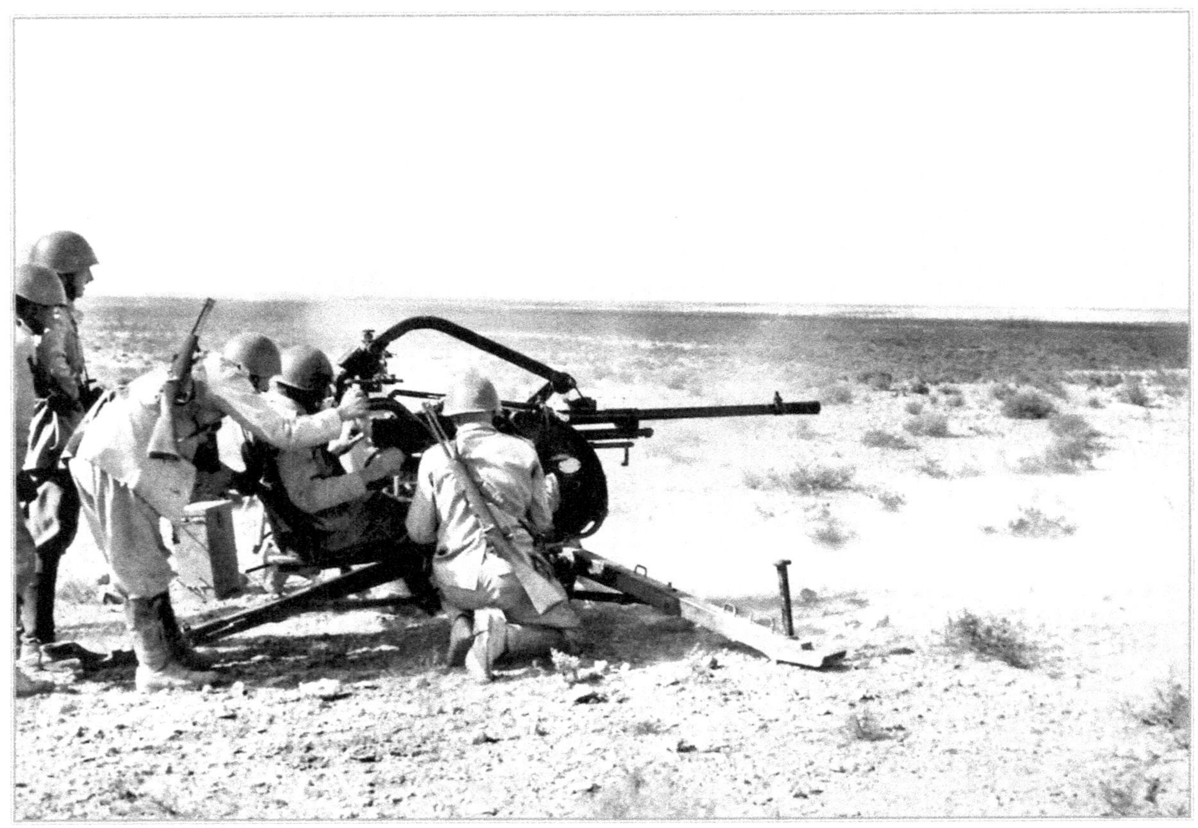

Italian soldiers practice using artillery during a training session in North Africa.

This photo series provides an interesting opportunity to see the different ways Rommel tried to capture the action with his camera. Rather than standing behind the group to include both the men and their target, he opts for a horizontal view. This angle shows the soldiers huddled around the gun. One bends down (left) behind the gunner to look at the target sight. The men pay no attention to Rommel as they focus their attention downrange.

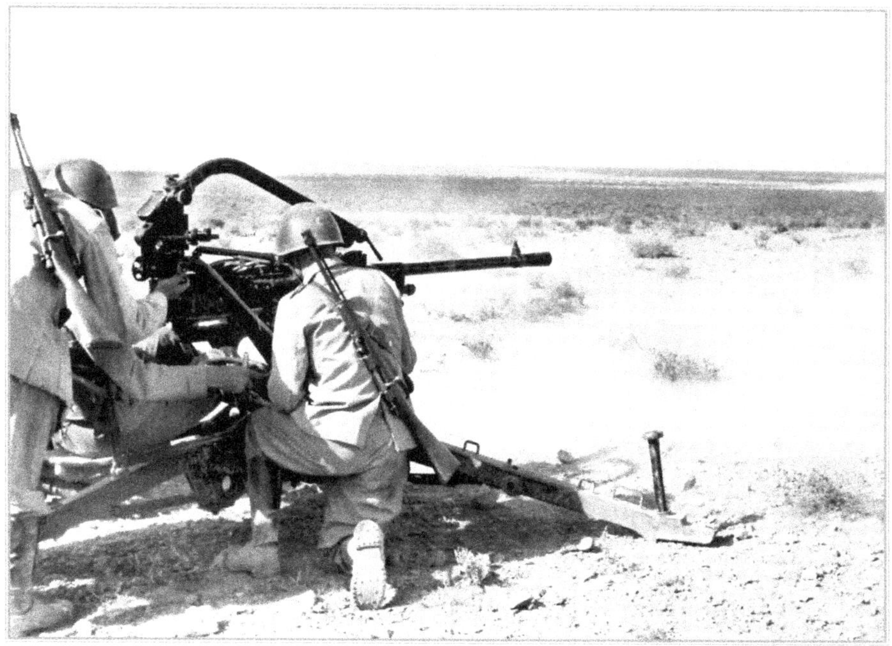

Stooping, Rommel steps closer to the men, who now fill half of the frame. The group around the gunner is out of view. The gun barrel is more prominent. The gunner's hands rest as the soldier behind him reaches over to adjust the sight.

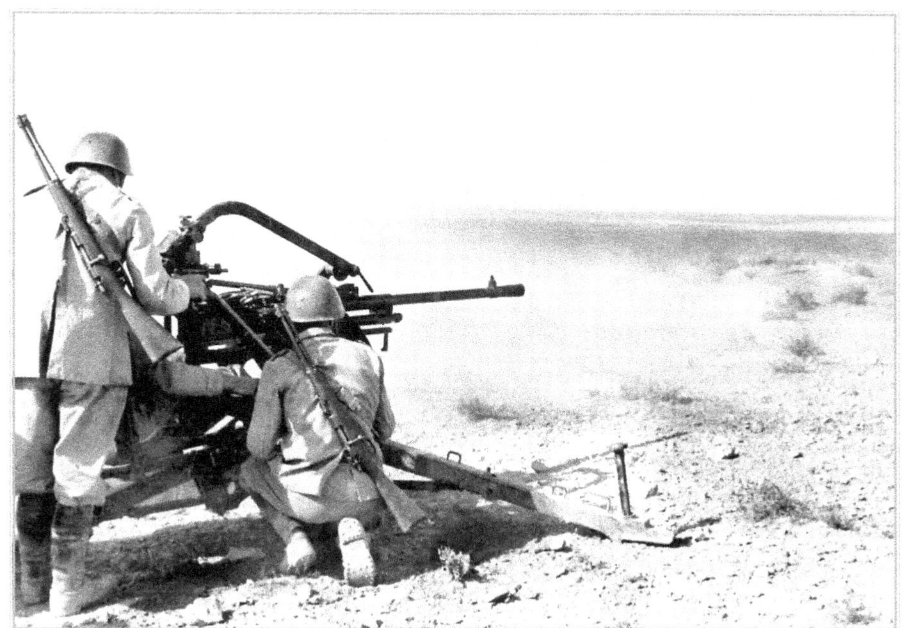

Rommel moves a few paces back. The barrel and surrounding dust become central focal points instead of the men. This image is more balanced than the others.

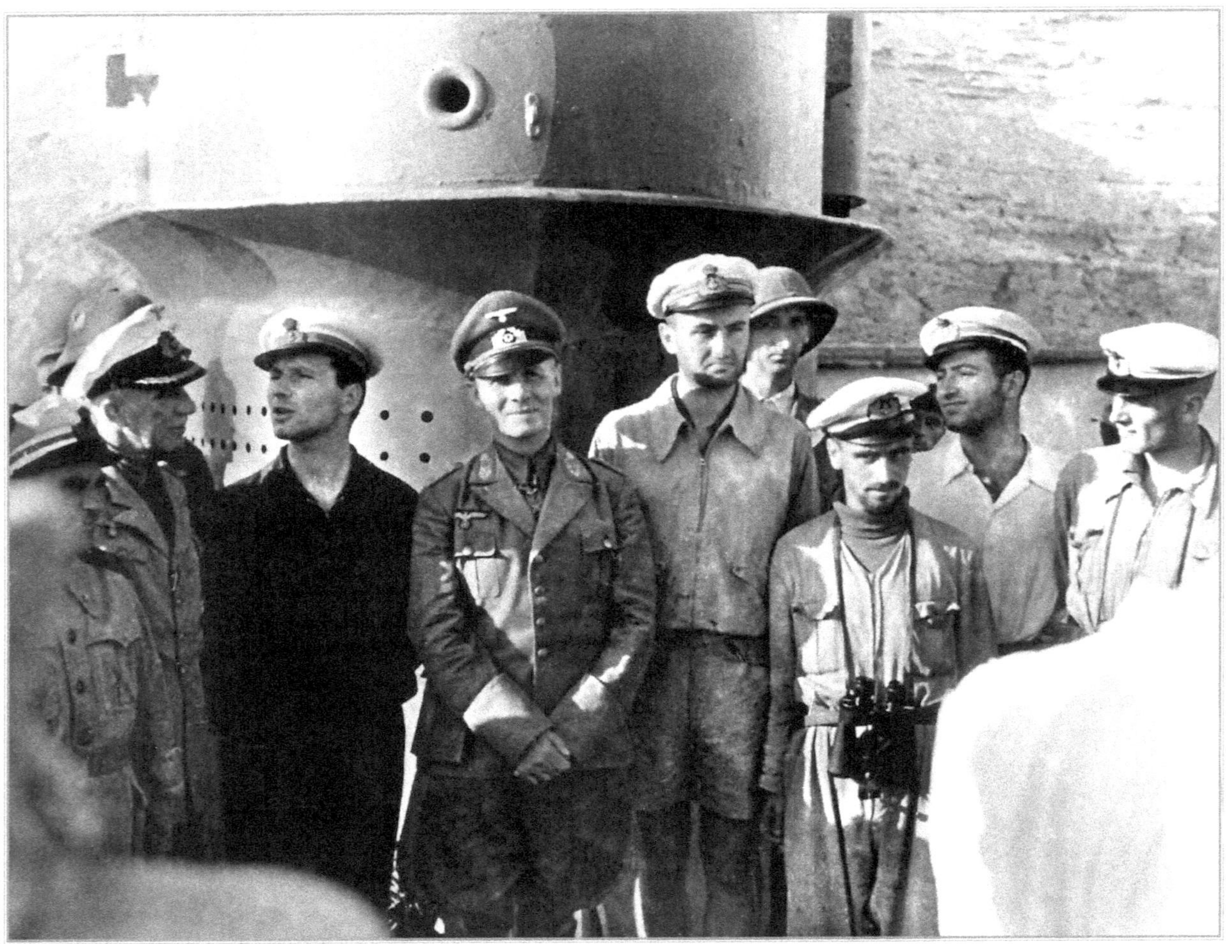

Rommel stands for a photo with several Italian sailors on the deck of an unidentified vessel in North Africa.

Rommel's uniform indicates that this picture was taken somewhere in North Africa. The men surrounding Rommel are Italian sailors. Italy's Navy, called the Regia Marina, was meant to support to Rommel's Army in North Africa, but most of the time their endeavors were ineffective.

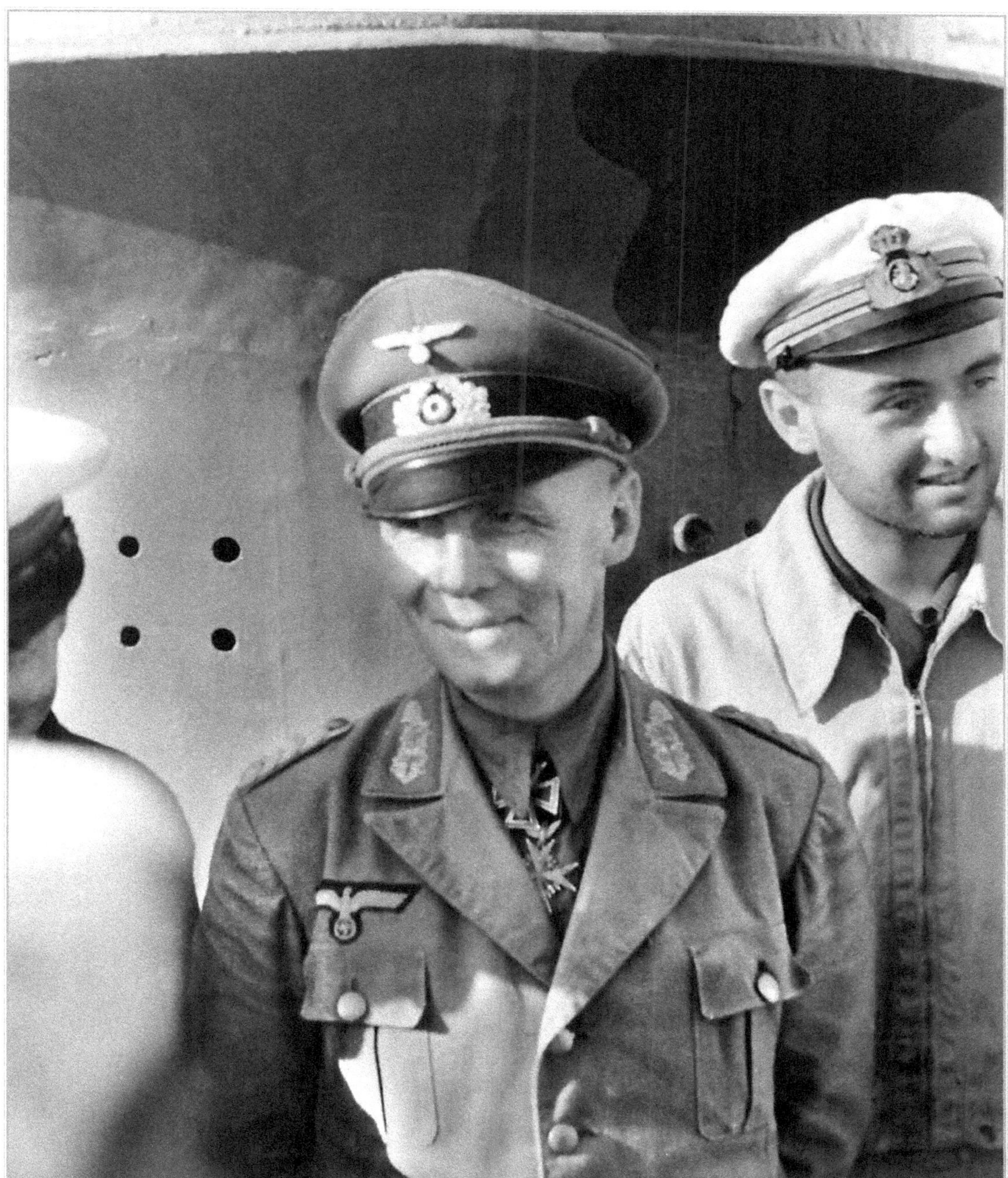

A close-up of Rommel with the sailors.

Rommel's World War I medal is visible under his collar. Called the Pour le Mérite, the medal was the Kaiser's highest decoration for military valor in World War I. Rommel wore it frequently.

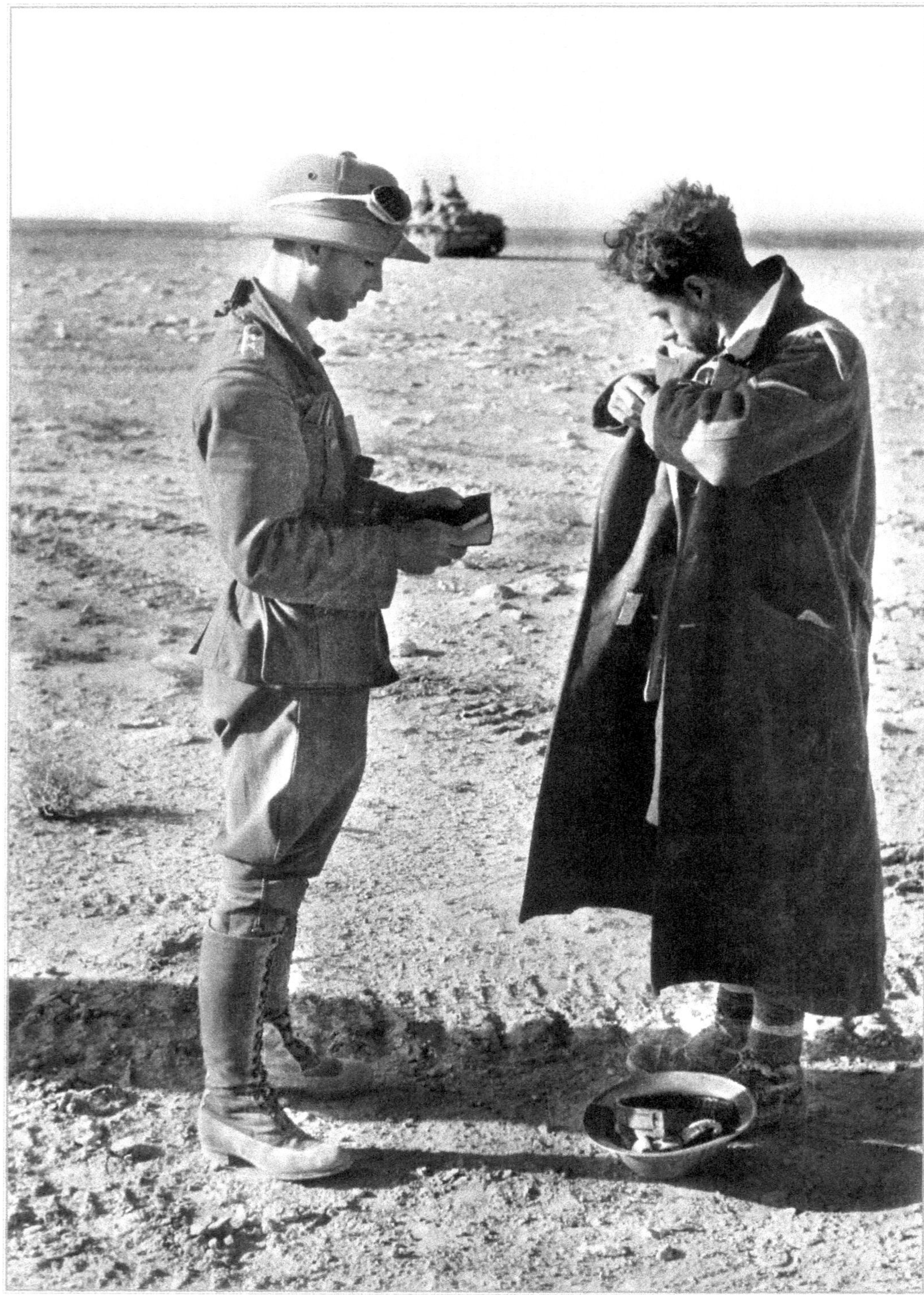

A British POW turns over his documents and empties his belongings into his helmet on the ground in North Africa, while a German soldier reads his identification papers.

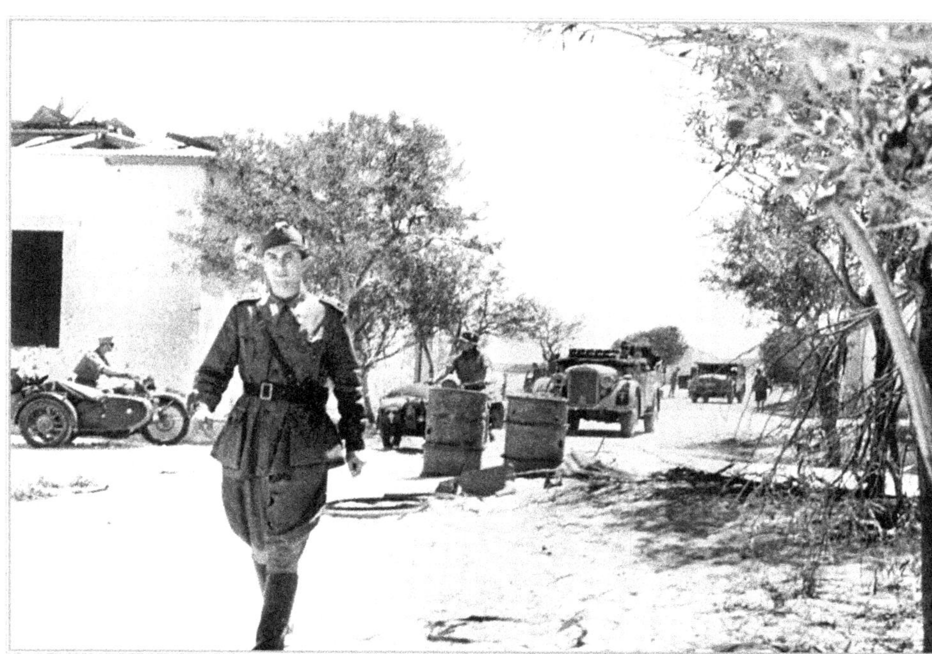

A soldier strides confidently through a small desert town in North Africa.

Two motorcycles with sidecars prepare to pass each other on the road. The soldier makes a half-smile and stares directly at Rommel's camera as the photo is taken.

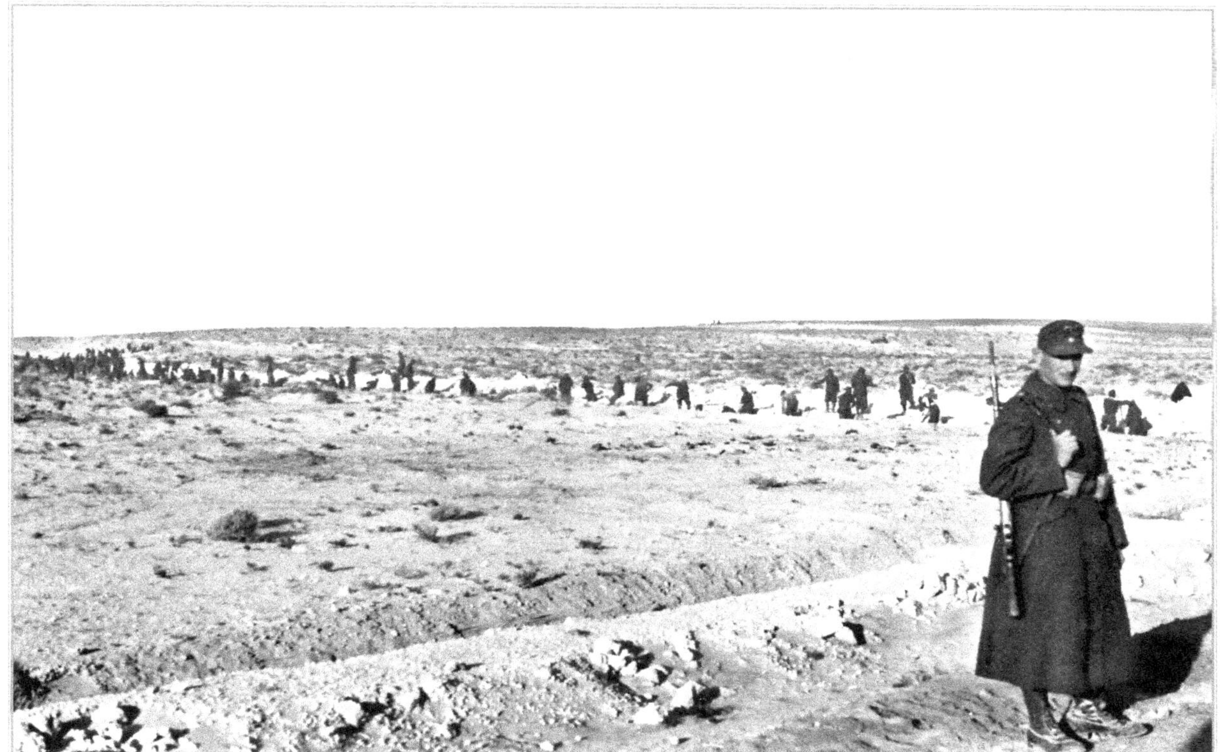

A German sentry in a greatcoat stands guard as men dig a trench in North Africa.

This image contains Rommel's familiar themes: a solitary figure against a large backdrop and converging diagonal lines.

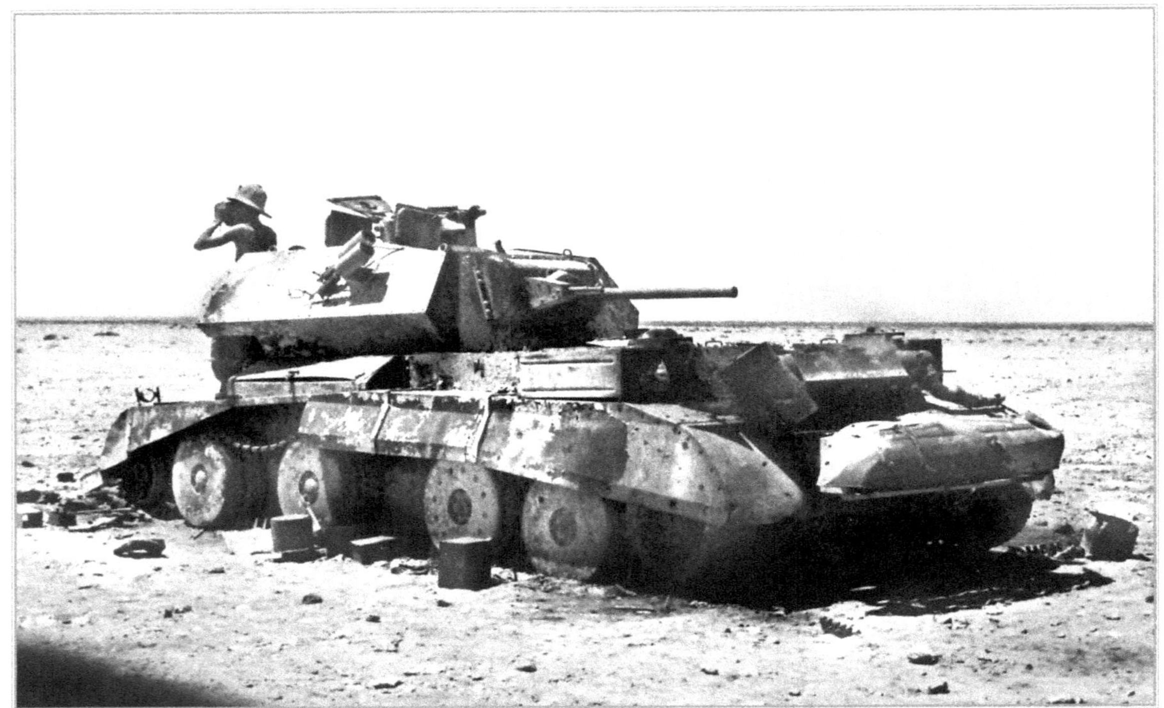

Under the scorching African sun, a shirtless German soldier on a tank scans the horizon through binoculars.

The rim of Rommel's car is visible in the lower left-hand corner. The barrel of the tank gun and the soldier face in opposite directions. The tank appears to be in bad condition.

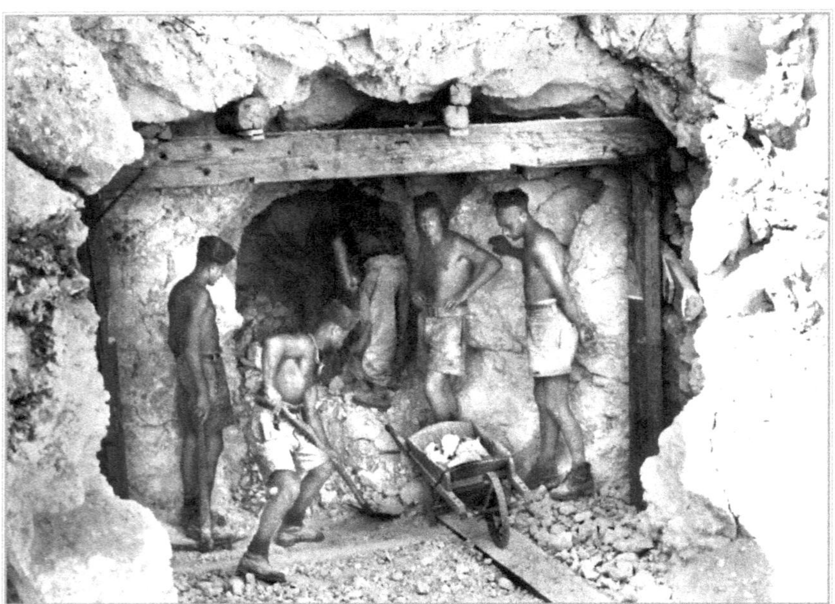

Half-dressed soldiers haul rocks from a strategic desert dugout.

One soldier holds a pickax (left). Another shovels rocks. The men probably would have had to make several trips to unload stones, given the small size of the wheelbarrow (center).

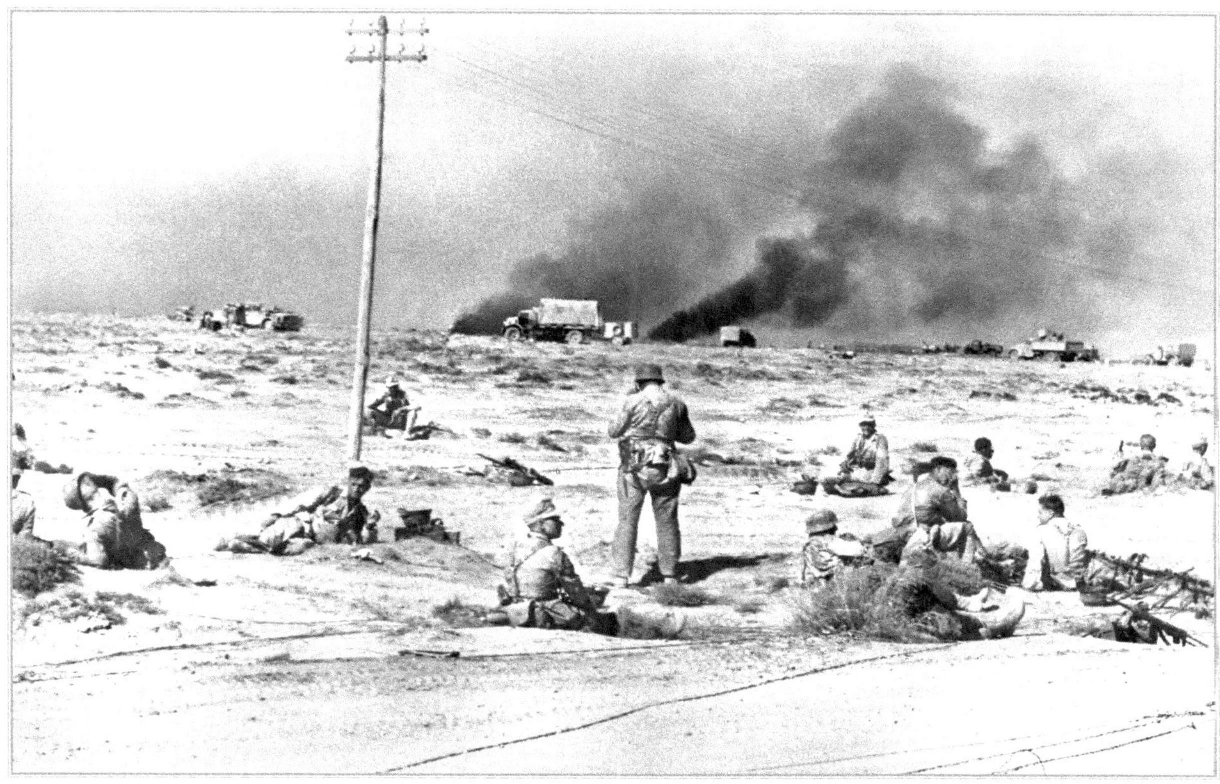

German troops rest after a battle in North Africa.

A soldier in a stained uniform stands in the center with his back to the camera. He is surrounded by others resting in the dirt. Black smoke spews beyond trucks in the distance.

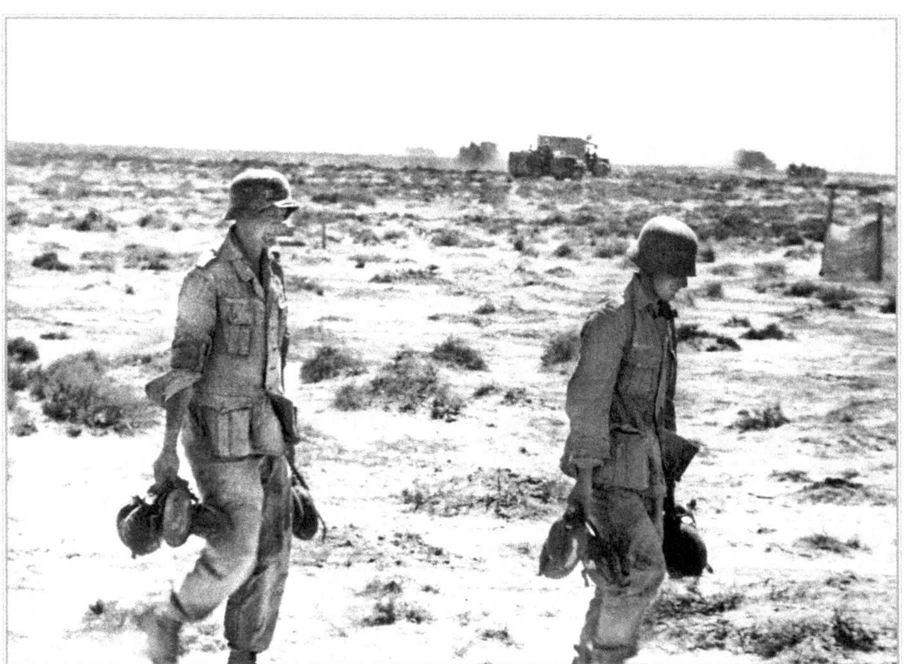

Two dusty German soldiers carry canteens of water across the hot desert in North Africa.

These young men, who look tired, trudge through the sand. Their expressions seem to show they were aware that Rommel was photographing them. In the background, vehicles on the road create dirt clouds.

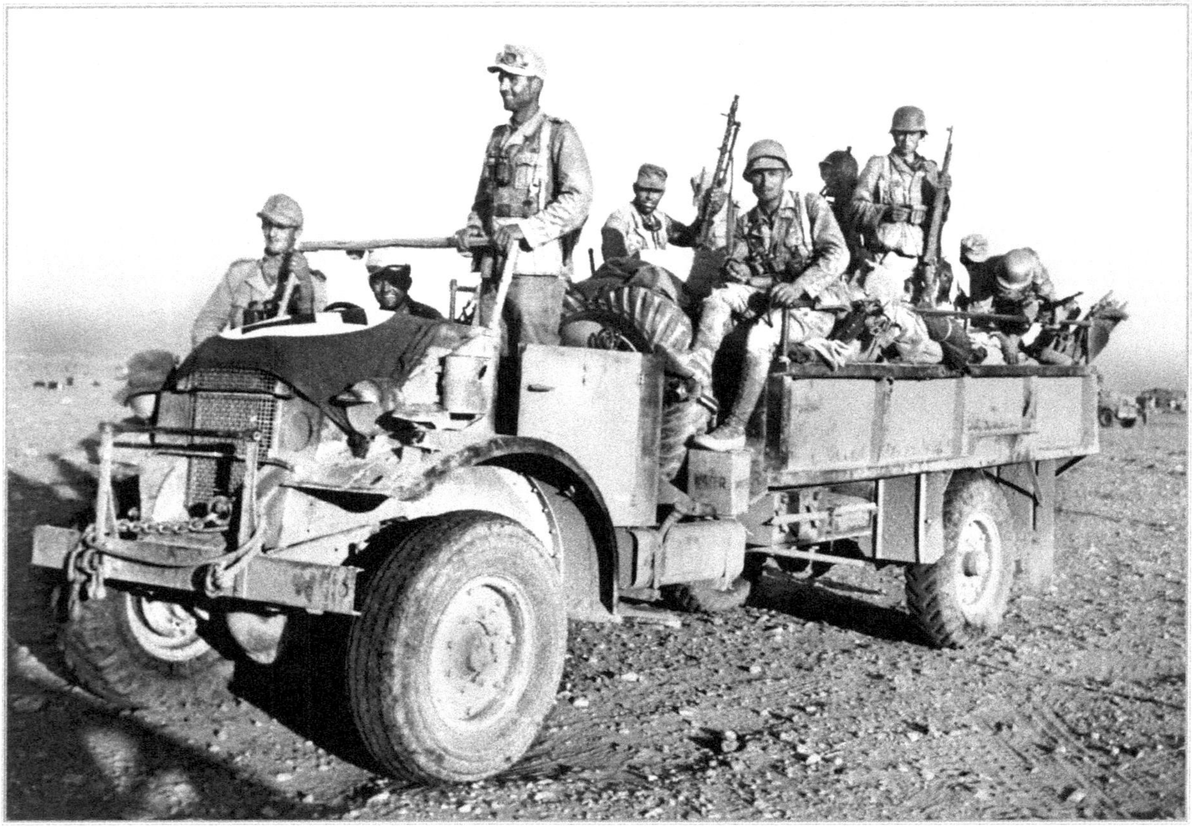

A truckload of German soldiers smile for the camera in North Africa.

They appear to be in good spirits as they set off for an unknown mission.

German soldiers push a piece of equipment in North Africa.

A disheveled man (right) looks away from the men. A soldier in the center of the group has a large hole in his pants and a torn pith helmet.

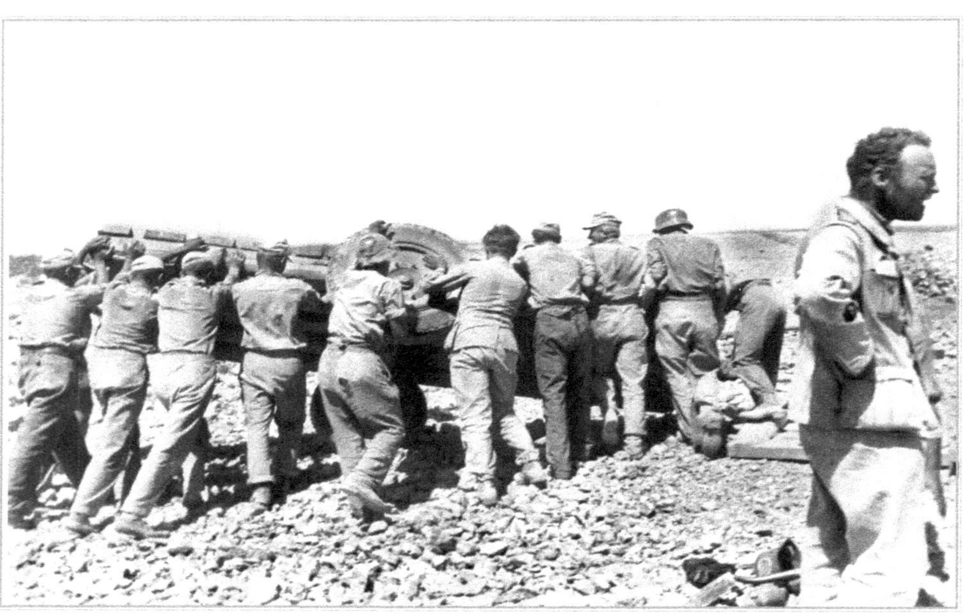

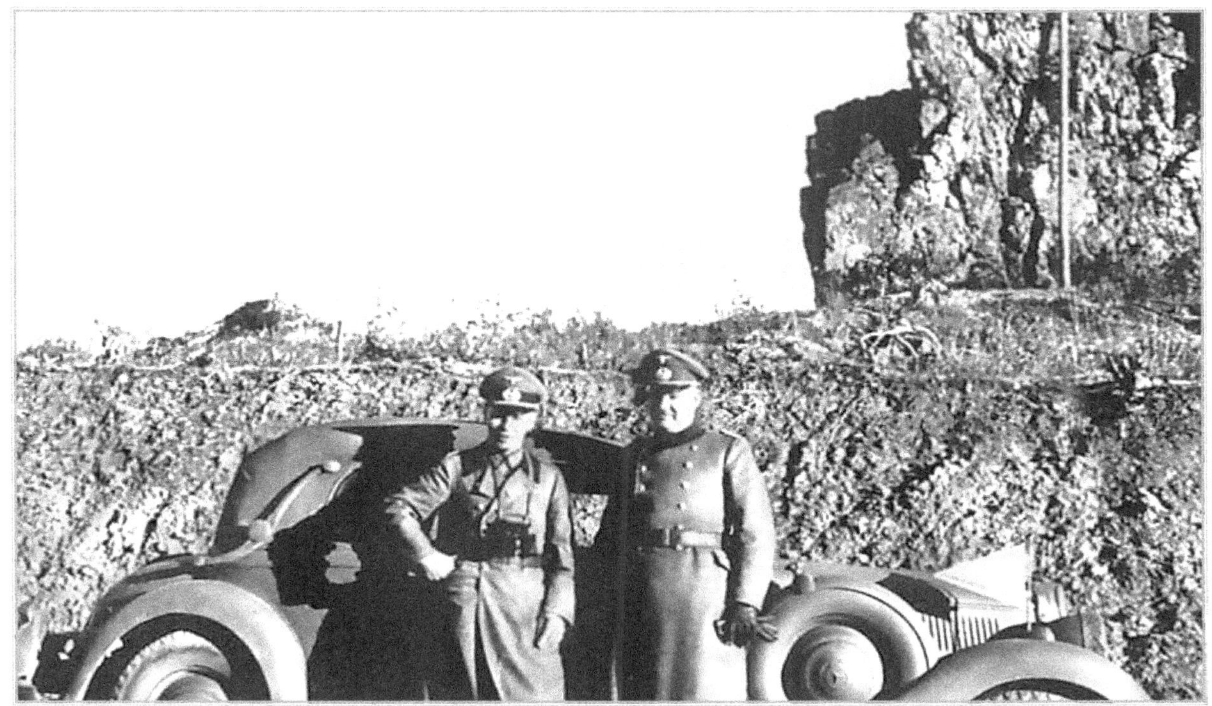

Rommel poses for a picture outside of a car with an unidentified German officer (date and location unknown).

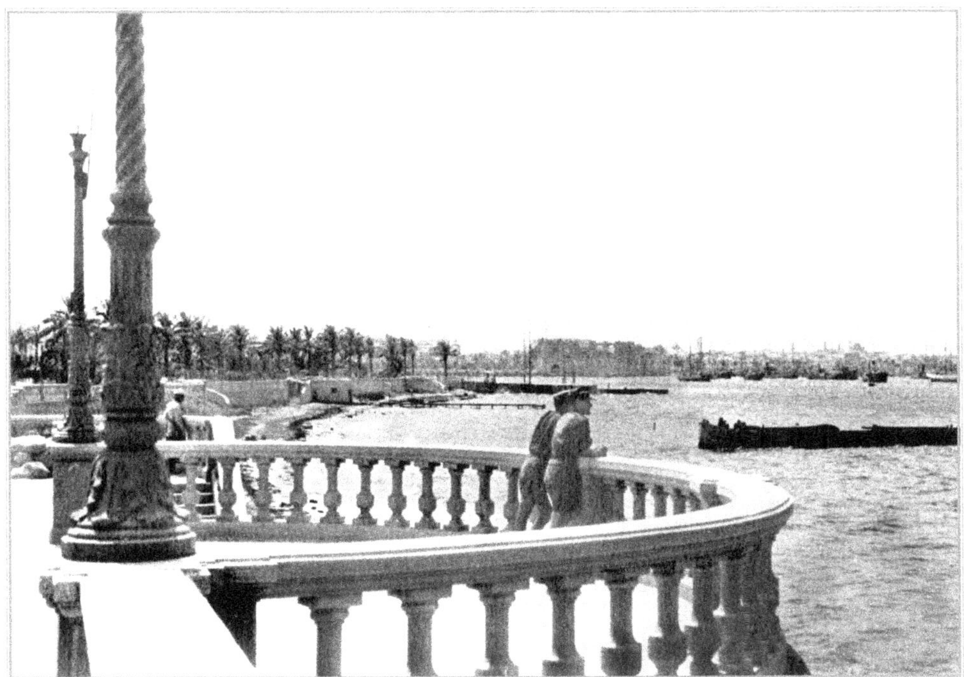

Two German soldiers lean over a balustrade and stare into a harbor in North Africa.

Rommel focused on the men instead of turning his lens out towards the harbor. The balustrade forms a strong curving element with the soldiers in the center.

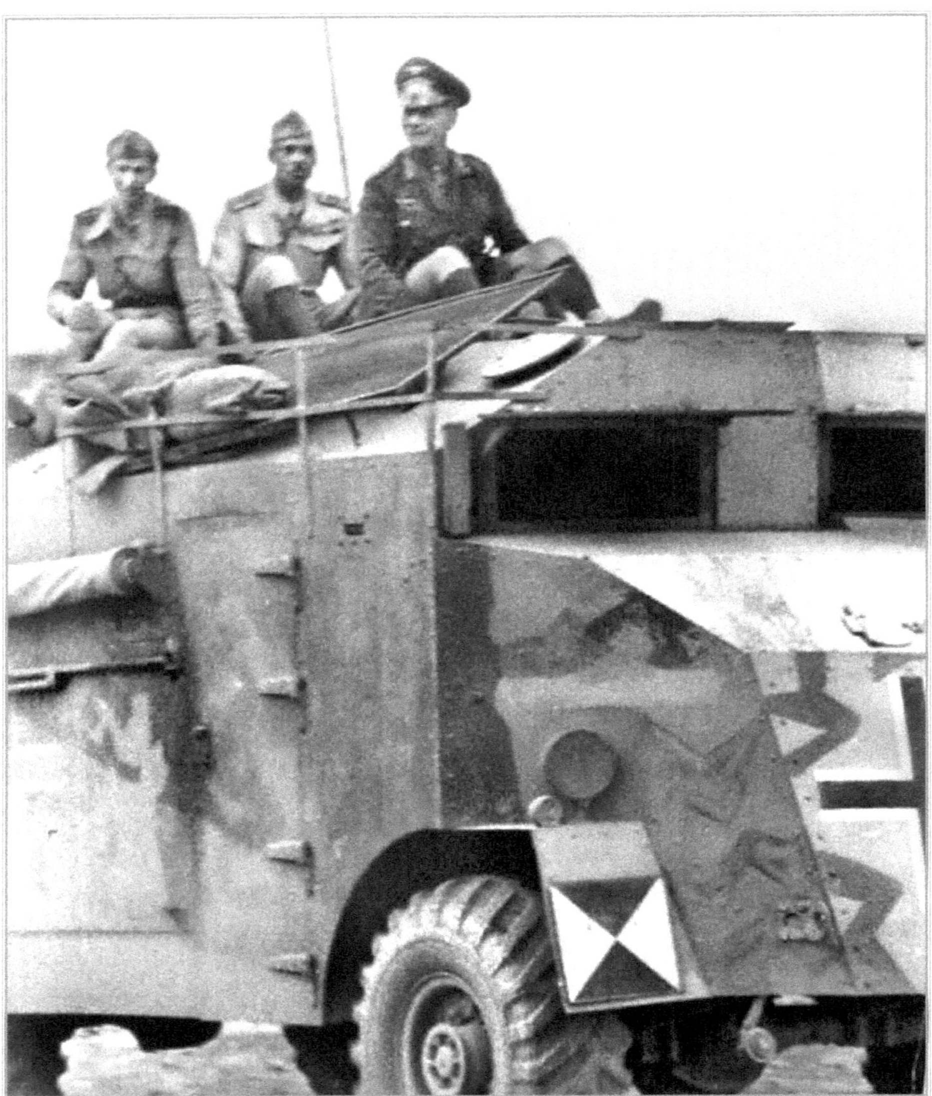

Rommel sits atop his favorite vehicle in North Africa.

Two Italian officers sit behind Rommel, who is smiling and wearing shorts. This AEC Armoured Command Vehicle (AEC 4x4 ACV), also known as the Mammoth, was made by the British and captured by German troops. The Mammoth was one of Rommel's preferred methods of transportation when commanding his army. Rommel was known to like different types of military vehicles, including the American jeep.

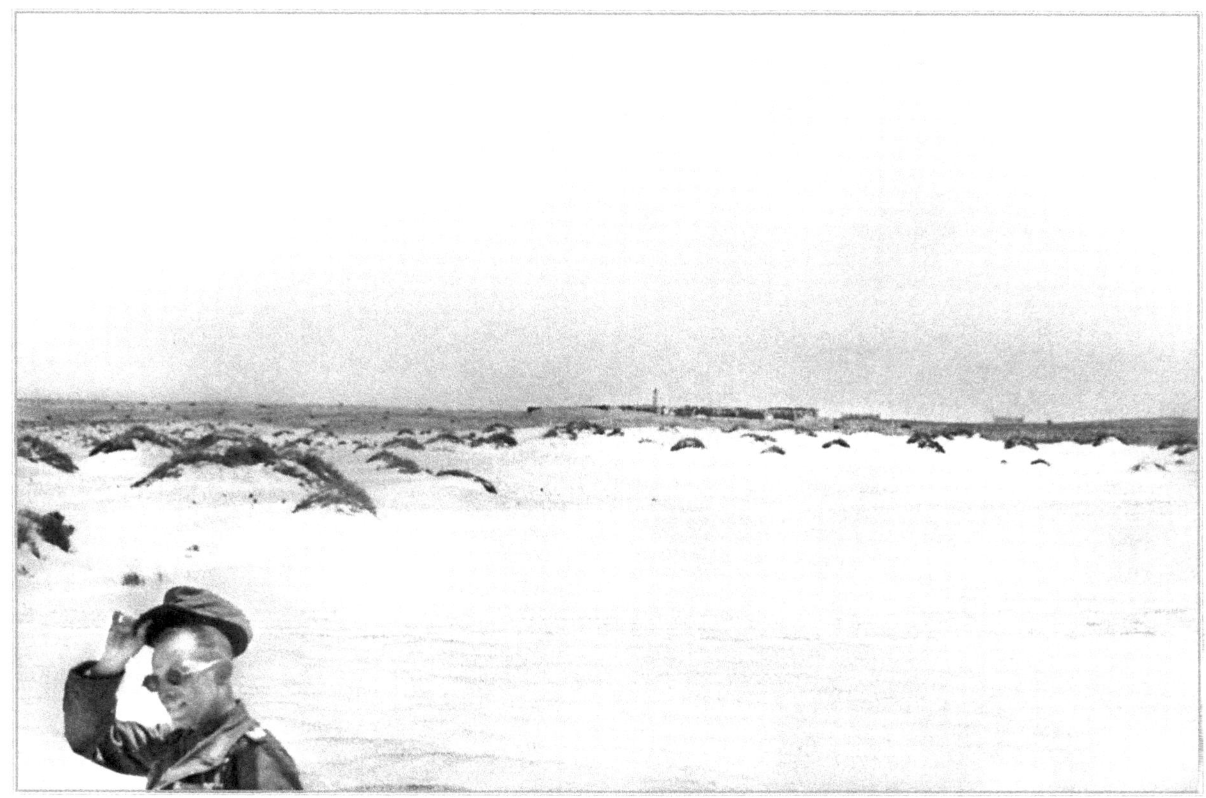

A German officer adjusts his hat in the harsh sunlight of the desert.

Rommel's focal point is atypically at a very low corner of the frame, with negative space above and below. The image was taken deliberately from a high angle. The officer is caught in motion as he adjusts his hat. His eyes are shielded from the sun, and his face looks tanned. What appears to be a minaret from a mosque is barely visible in the center of the frame. This picture gives a sense of isolation as a single human being is framed against the immensity of the formidable desert.

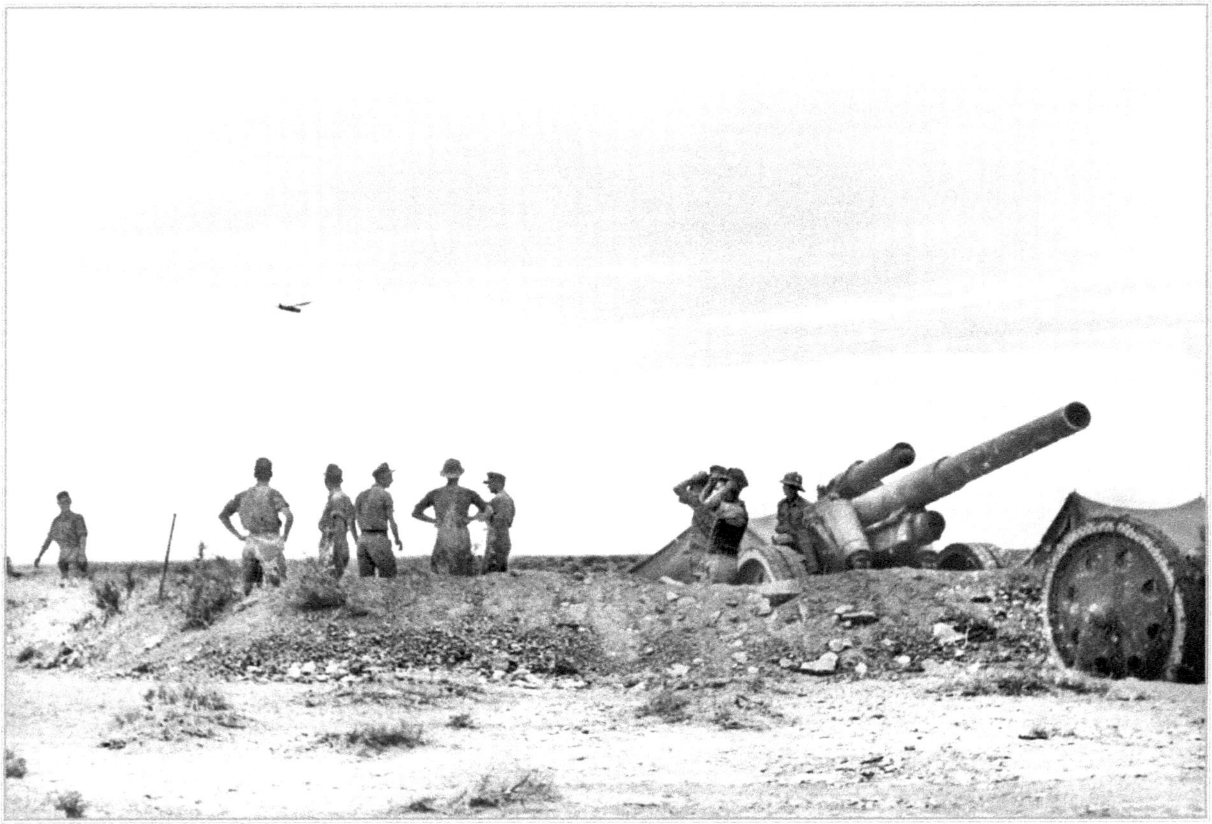

German soldiers watch an airplane fly overhead in North Africa.

German soldiers move supplies as wind and sand beat against them in North Africa.

The blowing sand obscures most of a vehicle (center). A soldier passes something into the vehicle's window.

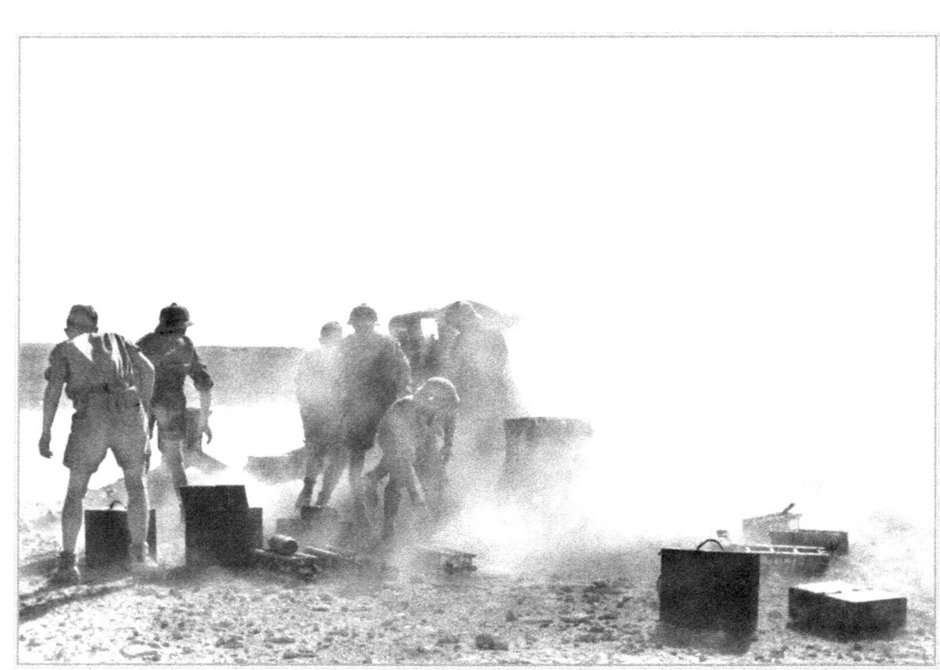

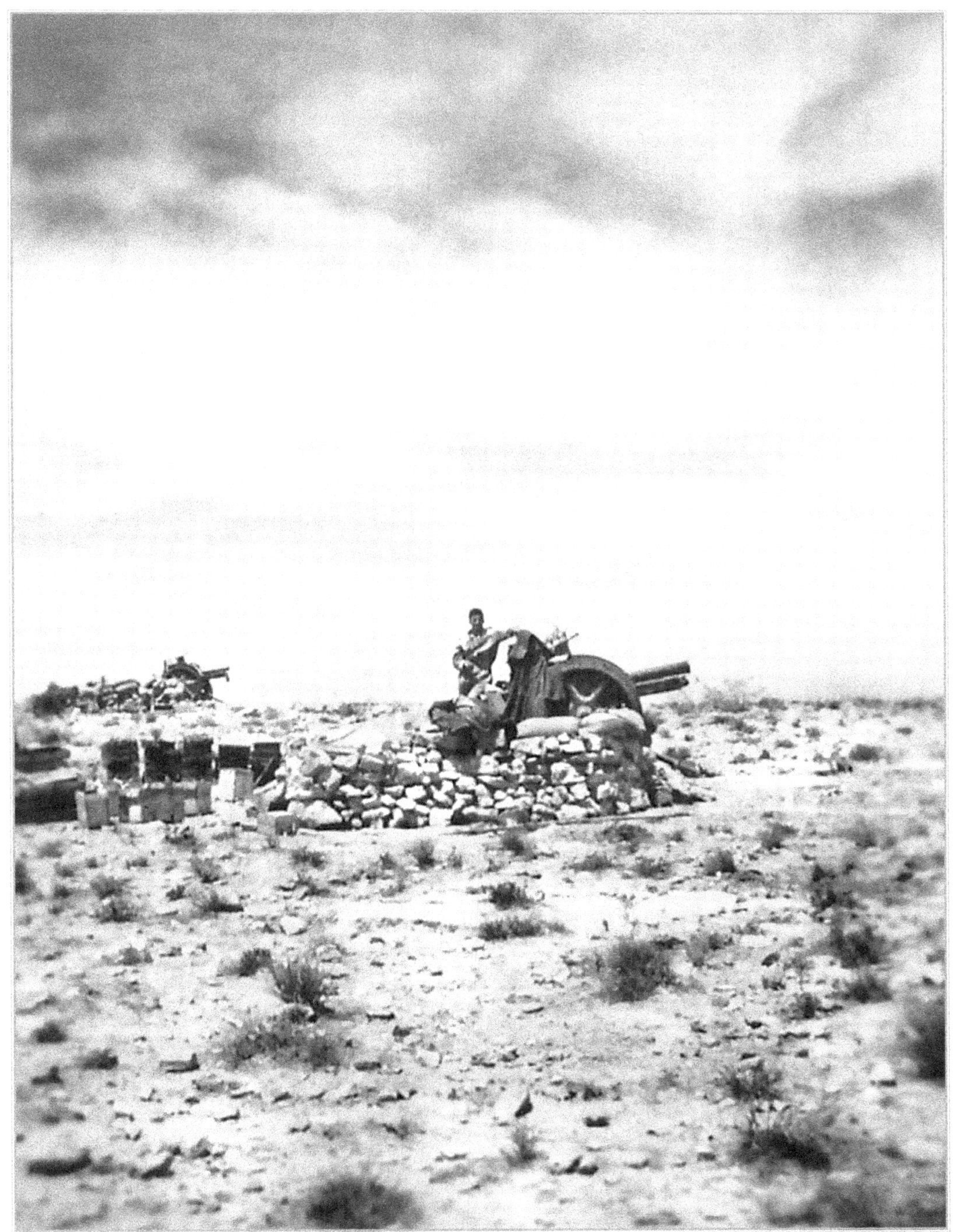

A gunner poses next to artillery in the North African desert.

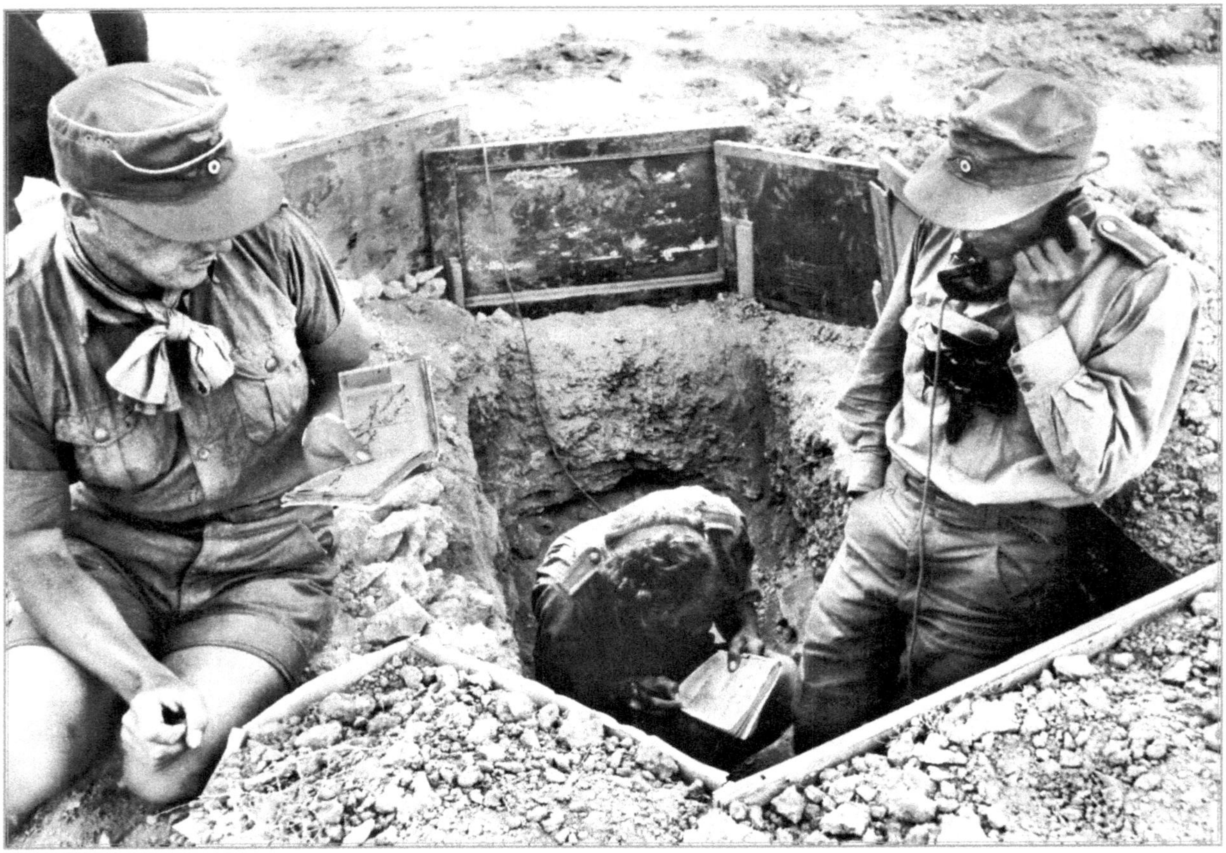

Men from Rommel's Afrika Korps conduct field communications from a hole in the ground.

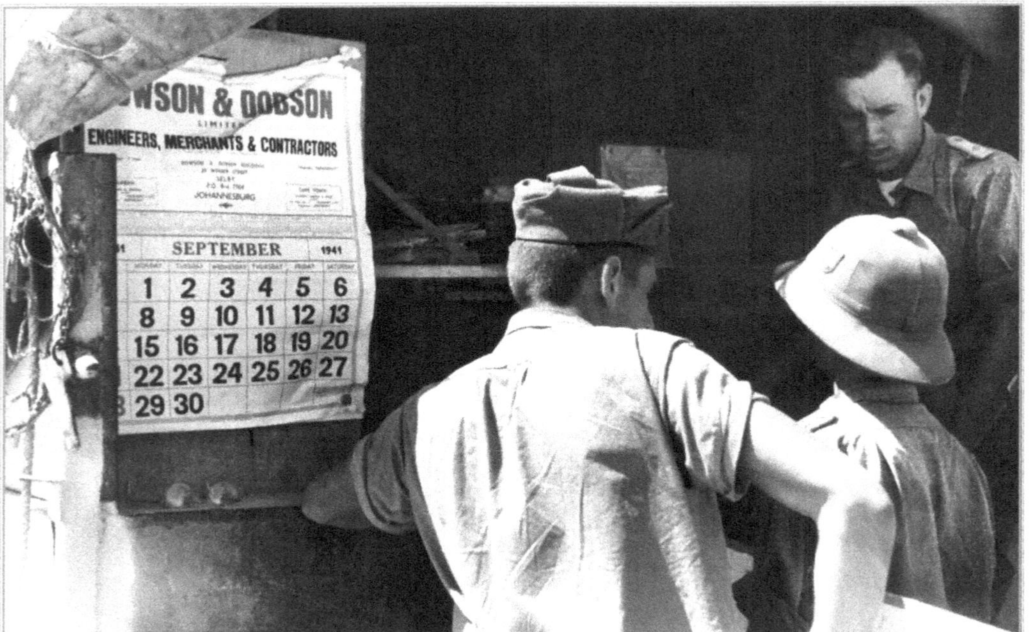

German soldiers hold a discussion in the back of a truck in North Africa.

Hanging beside them is an English calendar, from a firm in Johannesburg. The page is turned to September 1941.

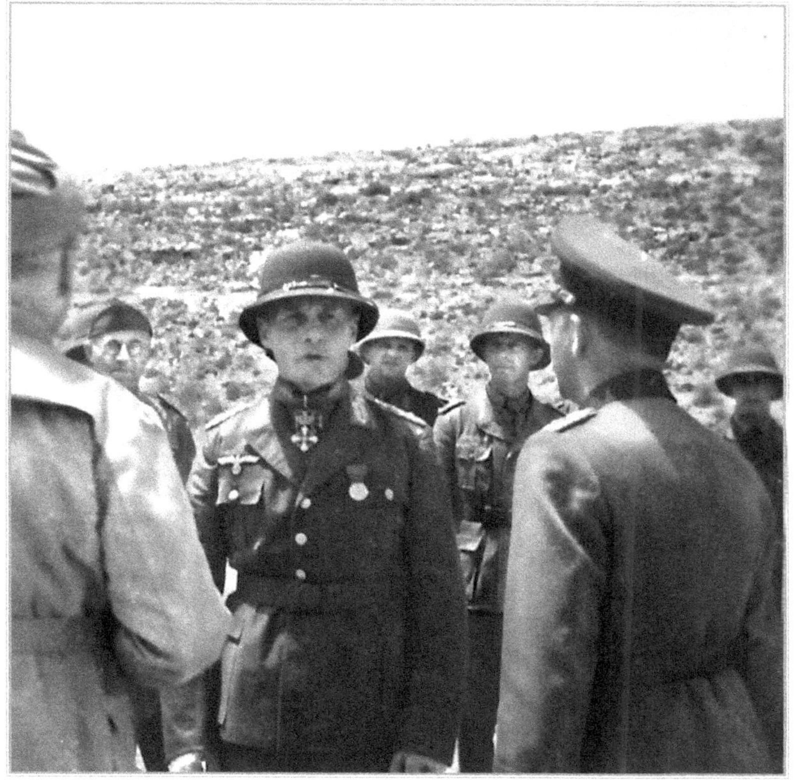

Rommel, wearing a pith helmet, receives a military decoration in North Africa (1941).

German soldiers, including Rommel, wore pith helmets when they first arrived in North Africa in 1941. However, the helmets soon proved to be ineffective in the harsh and hot desert. By 1942, German troops no longer wore them, instead favoring cooler and more convenient caps. Rommel himself was also quick to abandon the pith helmet. British soldiers were initially given pith helmets and had a similar experience. The inefficiency of this helmet was a source of ironic humor to desert veterans on both sides.

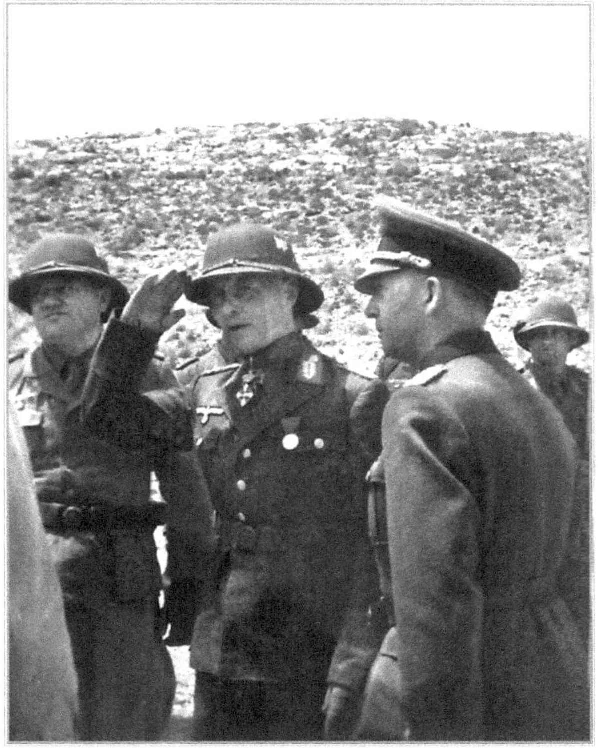

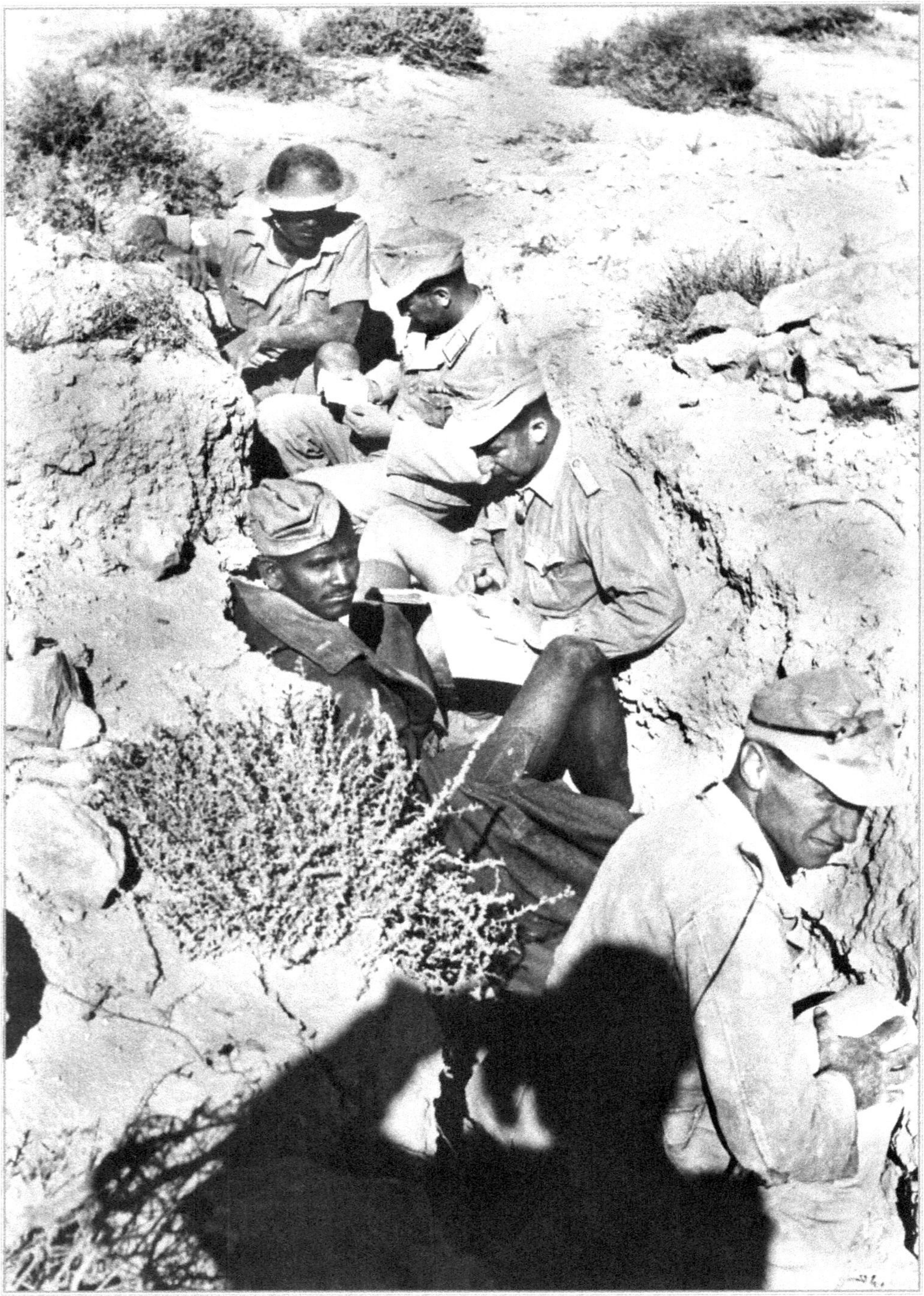

Rommel's shadow looms over British and German soldiers in a trench as he takes a photograph in North Africa.

The trench and the soldiers form a curving row that cuts through the center of the picture. Rommel's shadow can be seen below.

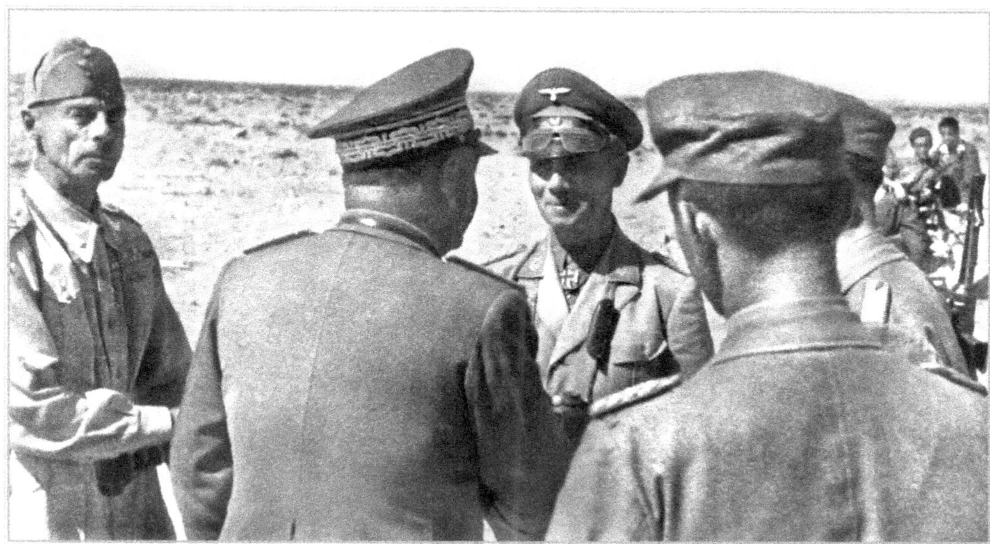

Two boys (right) look on as Rommel smiles during a conversation with German and Italian officers in North Africa.

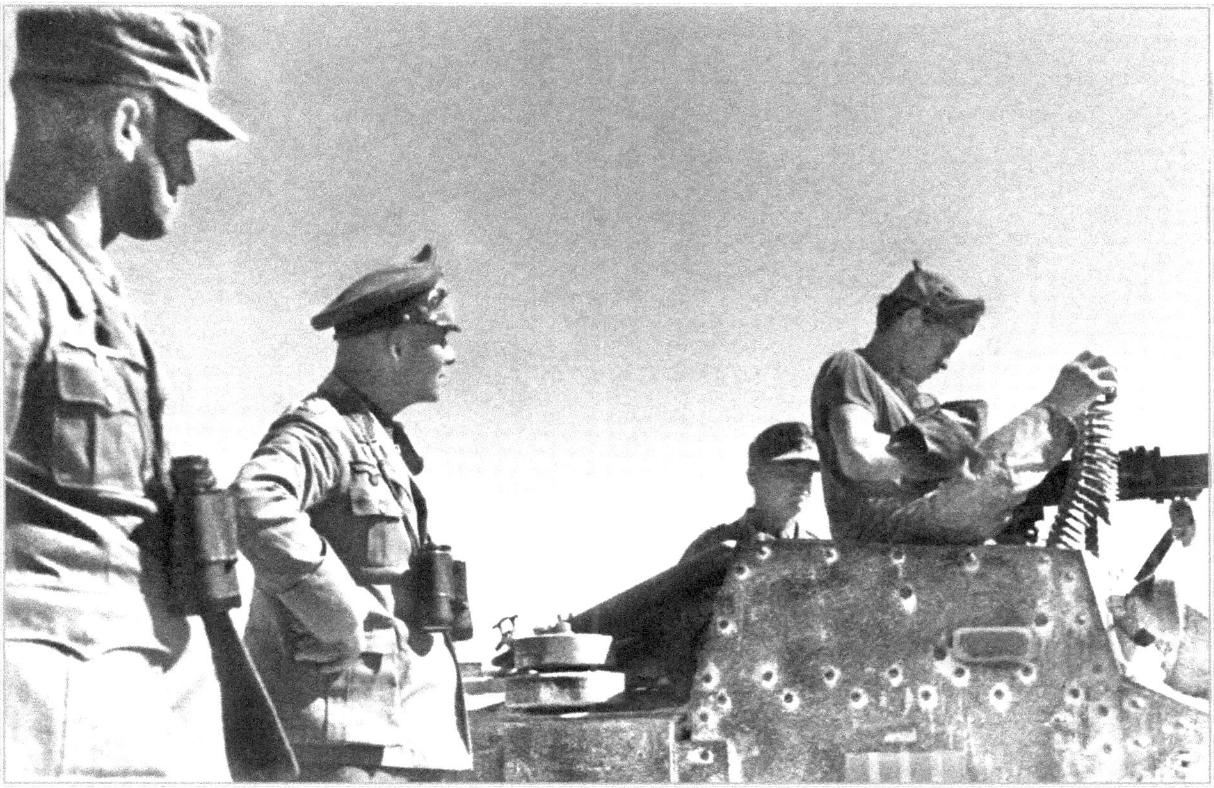

Rommel watches two Italian soldiers load a gun in a bullet-riddled Panzer in the desert.

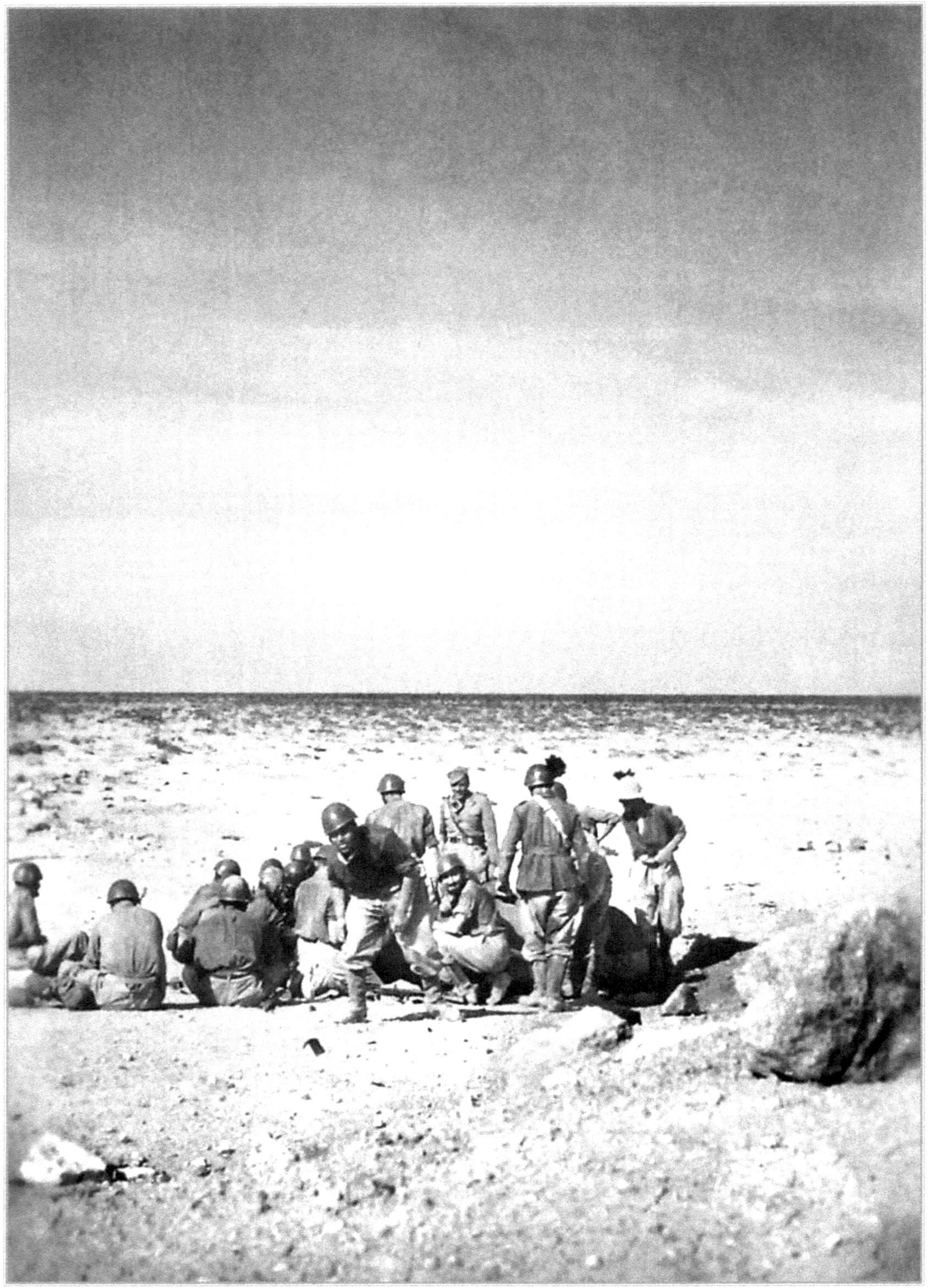

Italian soldiers band together in North Africa.

Oberst Montemurro
[illegible] EK I

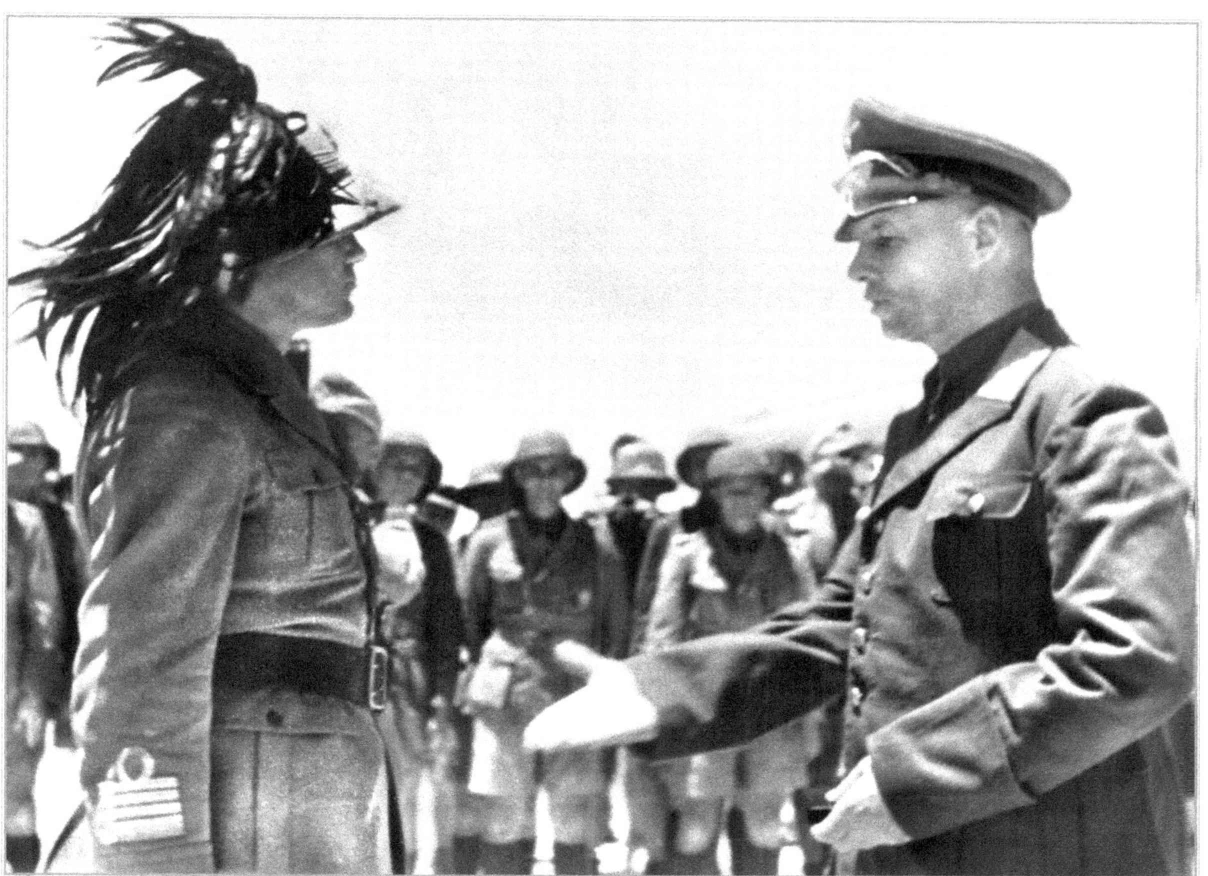

Rommel awards the Iron Cross military decoration to an Italian Bersaglieri officer in North Africa (1941).

Recognizable by the black wood grouse feathers on their headgear, the Bersaglieri are a famous Italian light infantry unit.

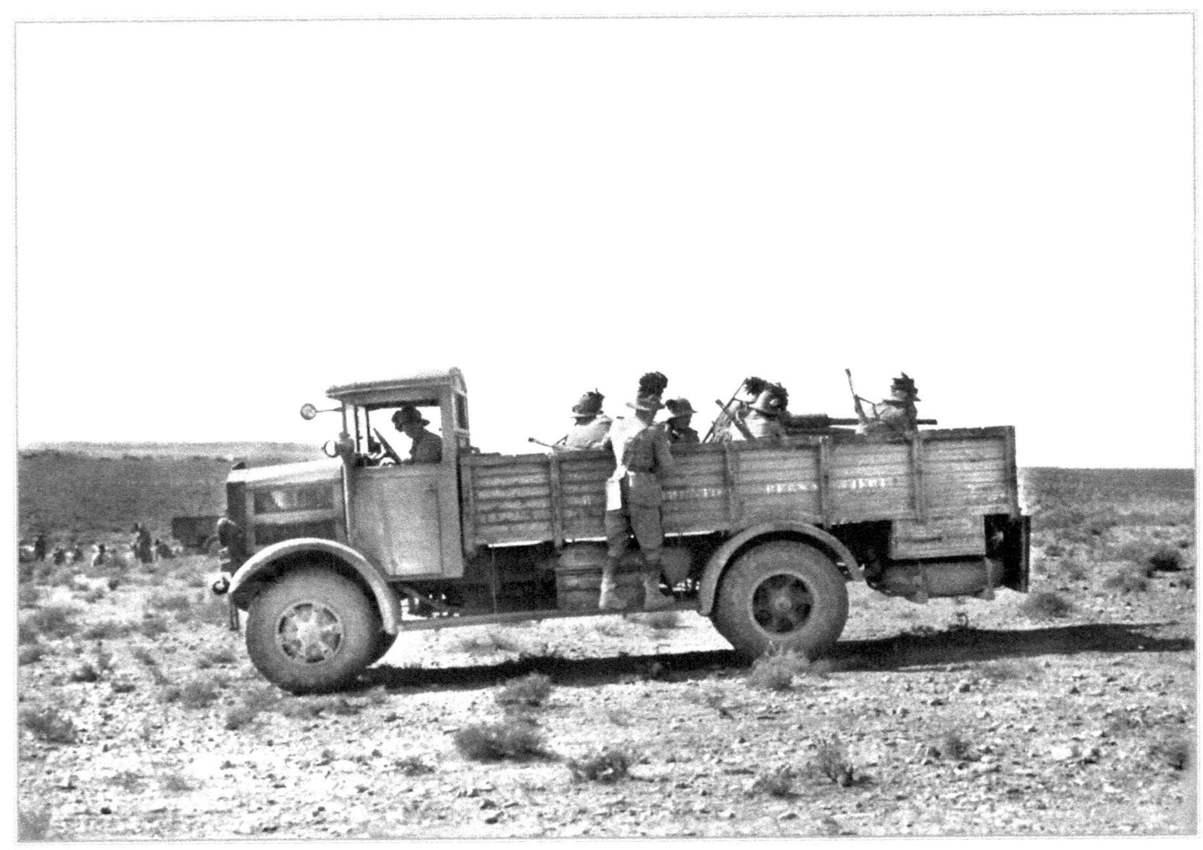

Italian troops transport artillery in North Africa.

The driver turns his head towards the camera as his six companions ride in the back of the truck. In the center of the truck, two Italian soldiers hold a gun steady. In the distance, a group of soldiers (left) climbs up a dirt hill towards the truck.

As usual, Rommel took this photo with mathematical precision. The man standing on the running board is centered exactly in the frame, and the truck appears evenly proportioned on both the left and right sides.

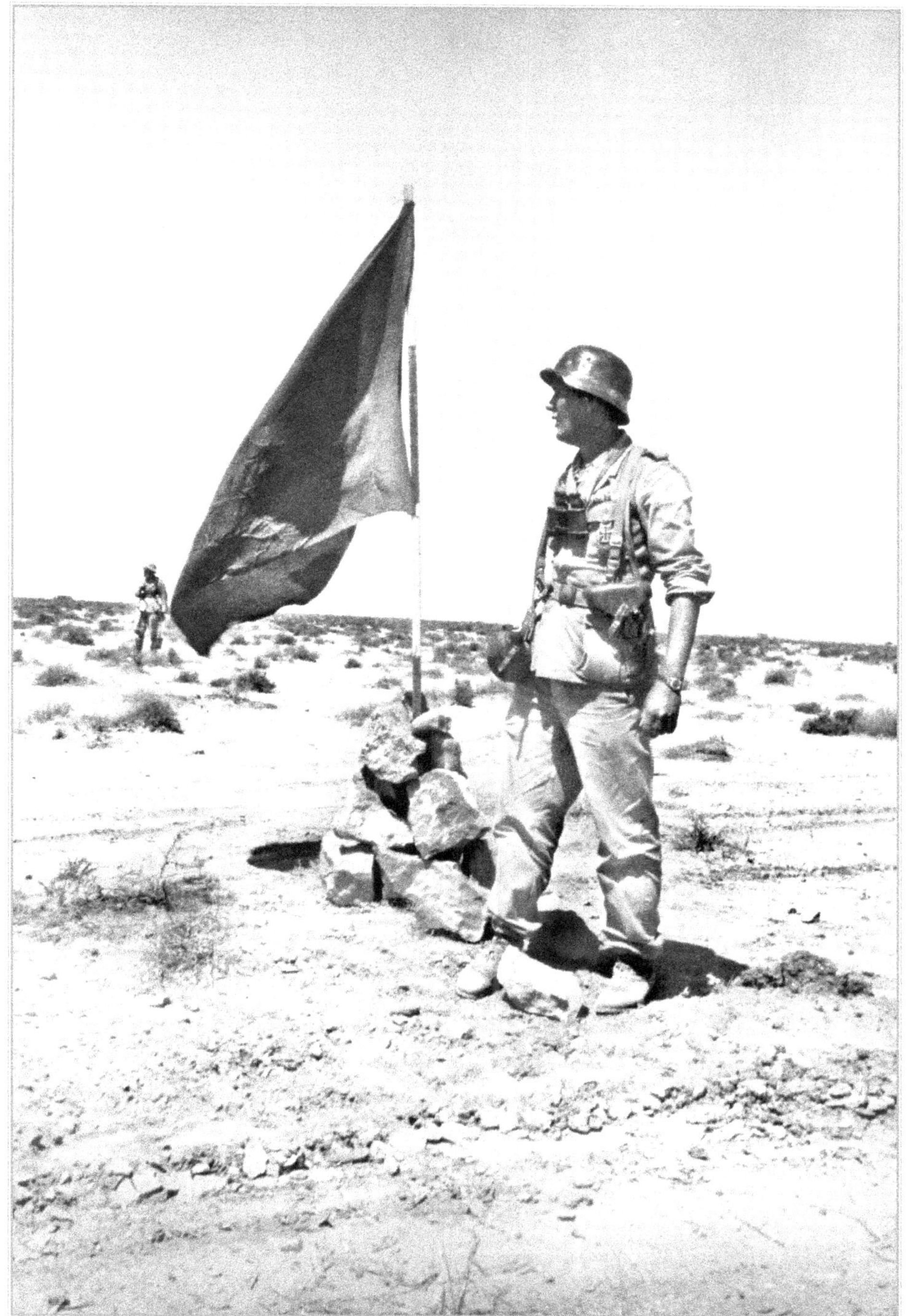

A flag flies beside a fatigued-looking German soldier in North Africa.

The soldier stands between parallel tracks running across the dirt. His uniform is dusty and crumpled. In the distance, another soldier stands among weeds.

9

The Fallen

2.6.40.

Grab des Ltn. Lauterbach 2/25.
gefallen beim Angriff auf Haute Bresnes.
am 21.5 1940.

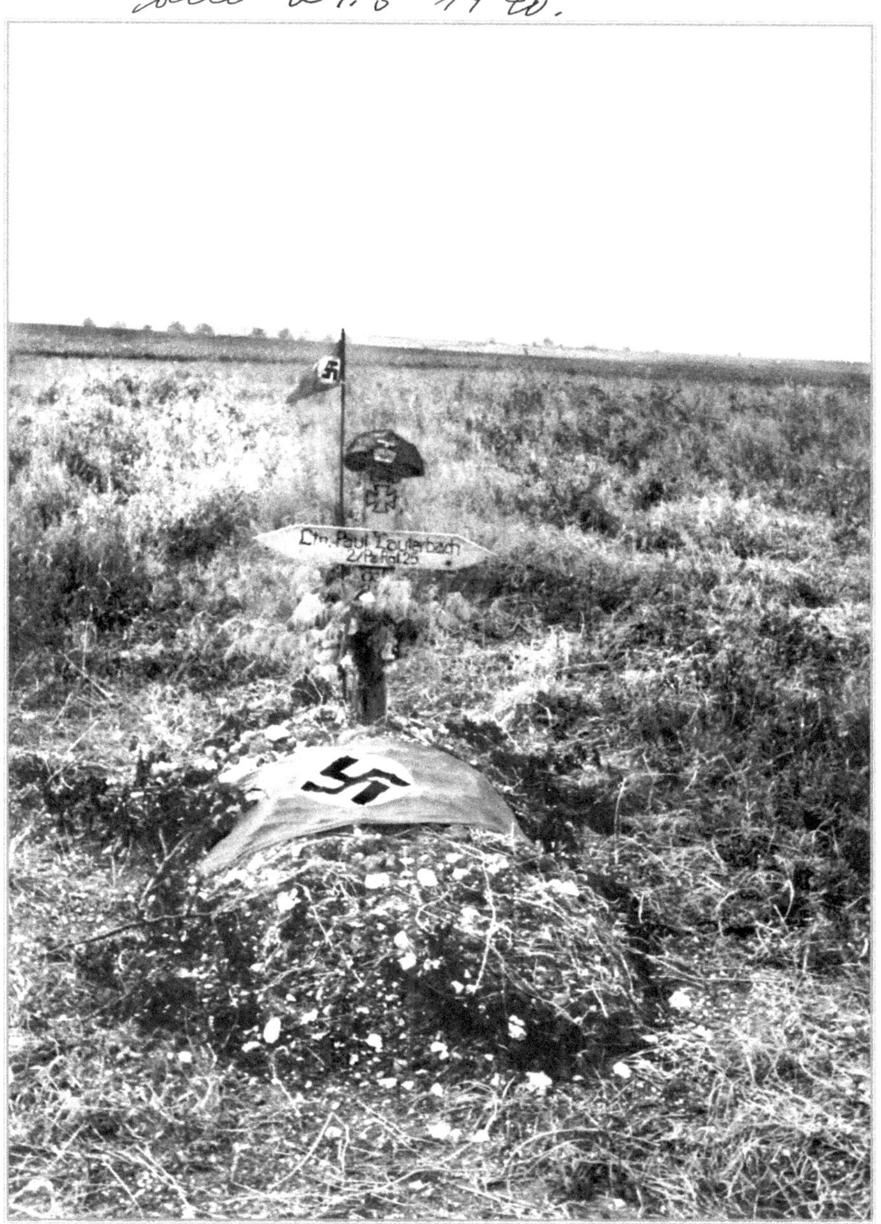

The grave of Lieutenant Paul Lauterbach lies in an open field in France.

Lauterbach saved German lives during a tank battle and was killed in action. (See pages 40 and 246.) His comrades honored his memory by adorning his grave.

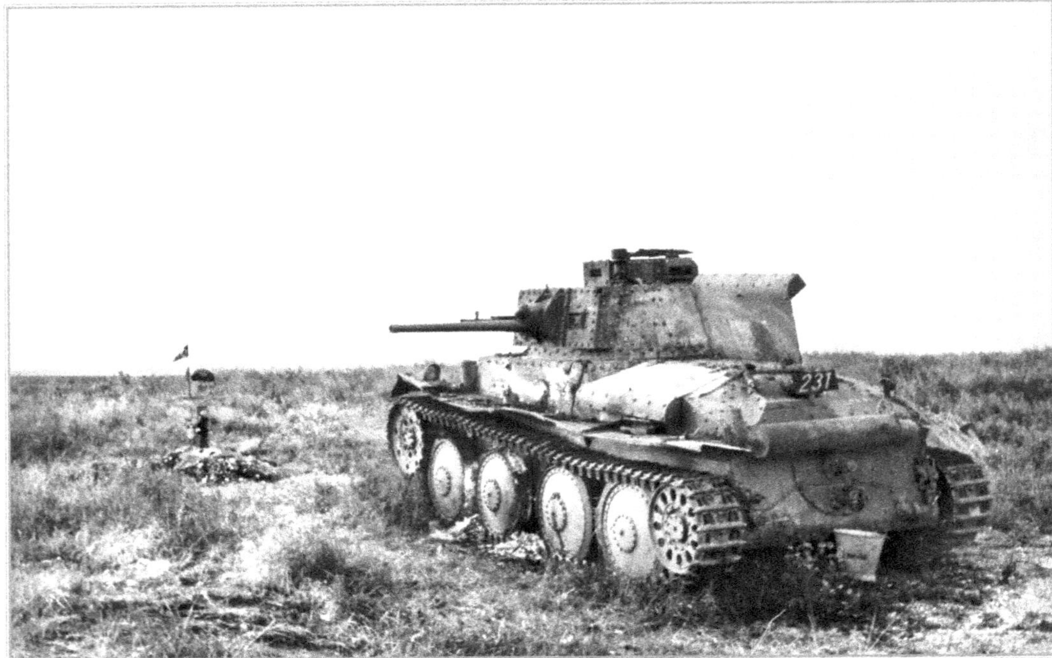

Another view of Lauterbach's grave.

A Panzer stands beside the grave in an apparent tribute to Lauterbach. He died in a Panzer III.

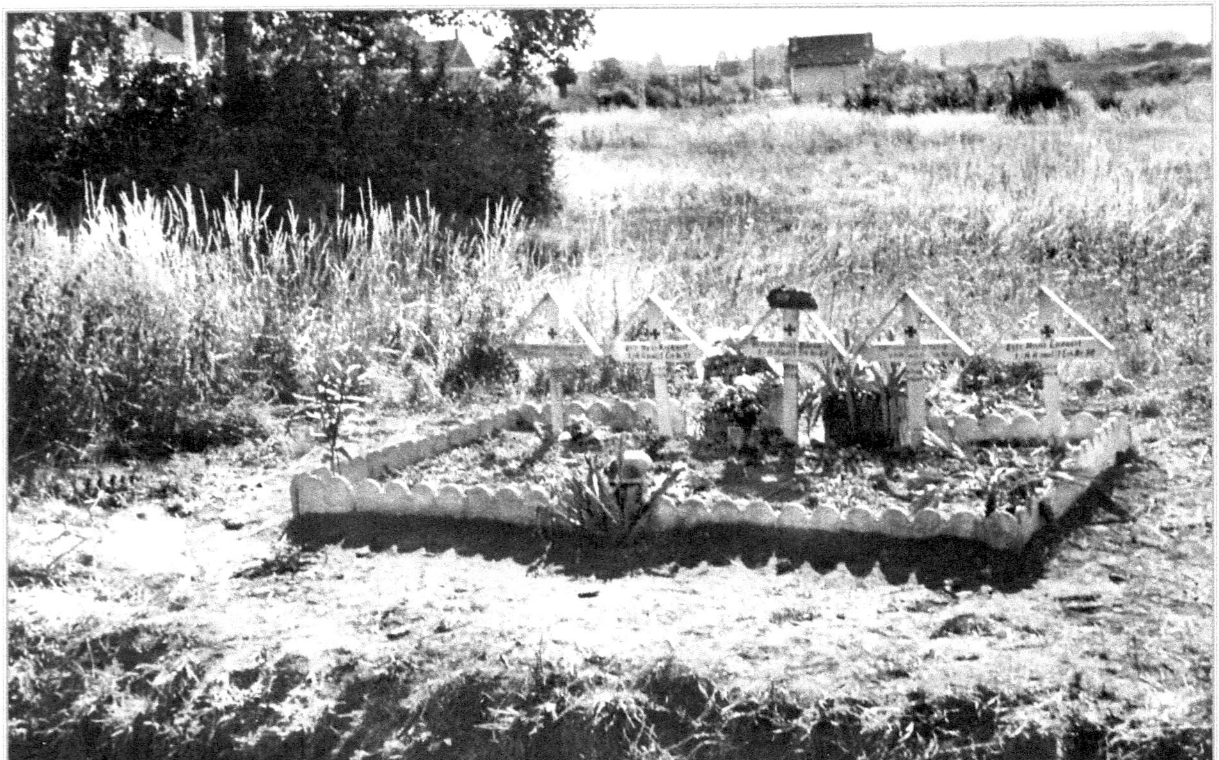

A helmet and a cap mark five German graves located near a farmhouse in France.

Bouquets of wildflowers and plants have been placed over this final resting place.

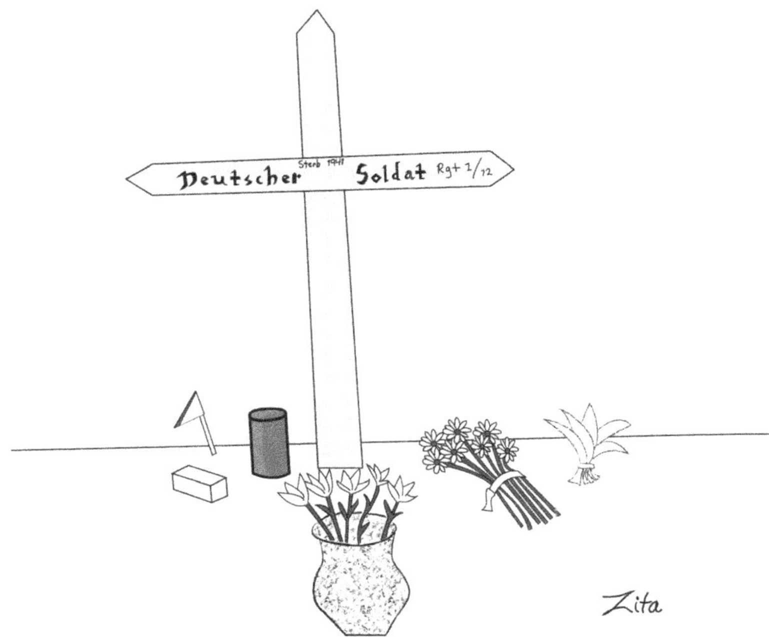

Germans attach a great importance to the burial of their war dead. They treat their fallen soldiers with affection and respect.

During WWII, the Germans made special efforts to give their men good burials. Most German graves were marked by wooden crosses, with hand-carved inscriptions detailing the men's names, ranks, and the dates of their deaths. The graves were decorated with bouquets of flowers or plants. Sometimes other forms of tribute and respect were added, such as flags, small stone borders, or other objects that were readily available. Generally speaking, the more time that German soldiers had in which to bury their fallen comrades, the more effort they put into decorating the graves.

Germans have a strong concept of homeland (sometimes called *Heimat*). Therefore, in addition to the sadness felt at a soldier's death, German families during wartime also experienced an added sense of loss and separation when the remains of their soldiers were buried in foreign countries, far away from their native land.

Even today, the German War Graves Commission (*Volksbund Deutsche Kriegsgräberfürsorge*), sponsored by the German government, attempts to provide personalized care for the graves of men who died in distant countries. The Volksbund also enables families and friends to send flowers to their loved ones' graves in foreign countries and provides photos of the graves to families in order to memorialize the fallen.

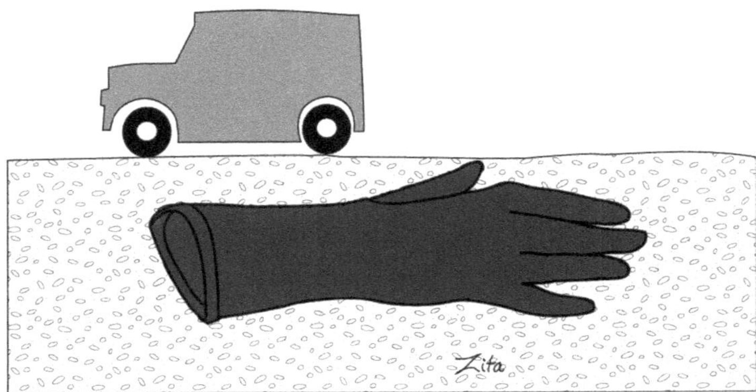

During WWII, Rommel experienced many brushes with death. Fellow soldiers were often killed beside or nearby him. Rommel recorded these losses in his memoirs. On one occasion in 1940, one of Rommel's corps commanders was killed before his eyes in France. German forces accidentally had begun to shell Rommel's command post in a dangerous case of friendly fire. As German shells rained down and bomb blasts rocked the house where Rommel and his men were standing inside, Rommel made a desperate attempt to reach the radio and order a ceasefire. The radio was located in a parked vehicle outside. Risking their lives, Rommel and one of his commanders ran out of the house into the thick of the bombing. Of the two of them, only Rommel survived. This event apparently left a deep impression on him, as can be seen in the unusually vivid account he recorded:

> "I was just making a dash for the signals vehicle, with Major Erdmann running a few yards in front, when a heavy shell landed close by the house door near which the vehicle was standing. When the smoke cleared, Major Erdmann, commander of the 37th Reconnaissance Battalion, lay face to the ground, dead, with his back shattered. He was bleeding from the head and from an enormous wound in his back. His left hand was still grasping his leather gloves. I had escaped unscathed, though the same shell had wounded several other officers and men."
>
> — *Rommel*

A similar incident occurred when Rommel and his staff were driving in North Africa. Their convoy of cars came under two attacks from low-flying British aircraft. Two of Rommel's staff officers were shot dead. One car took 25 hits. Wounding the driver, a large bullet pierced through the windscreen of Rommel's Mammoth vehicle. Rommel climbed into the driver's seat of the Mammoth, and drove himself and his staff officers away into the desert.

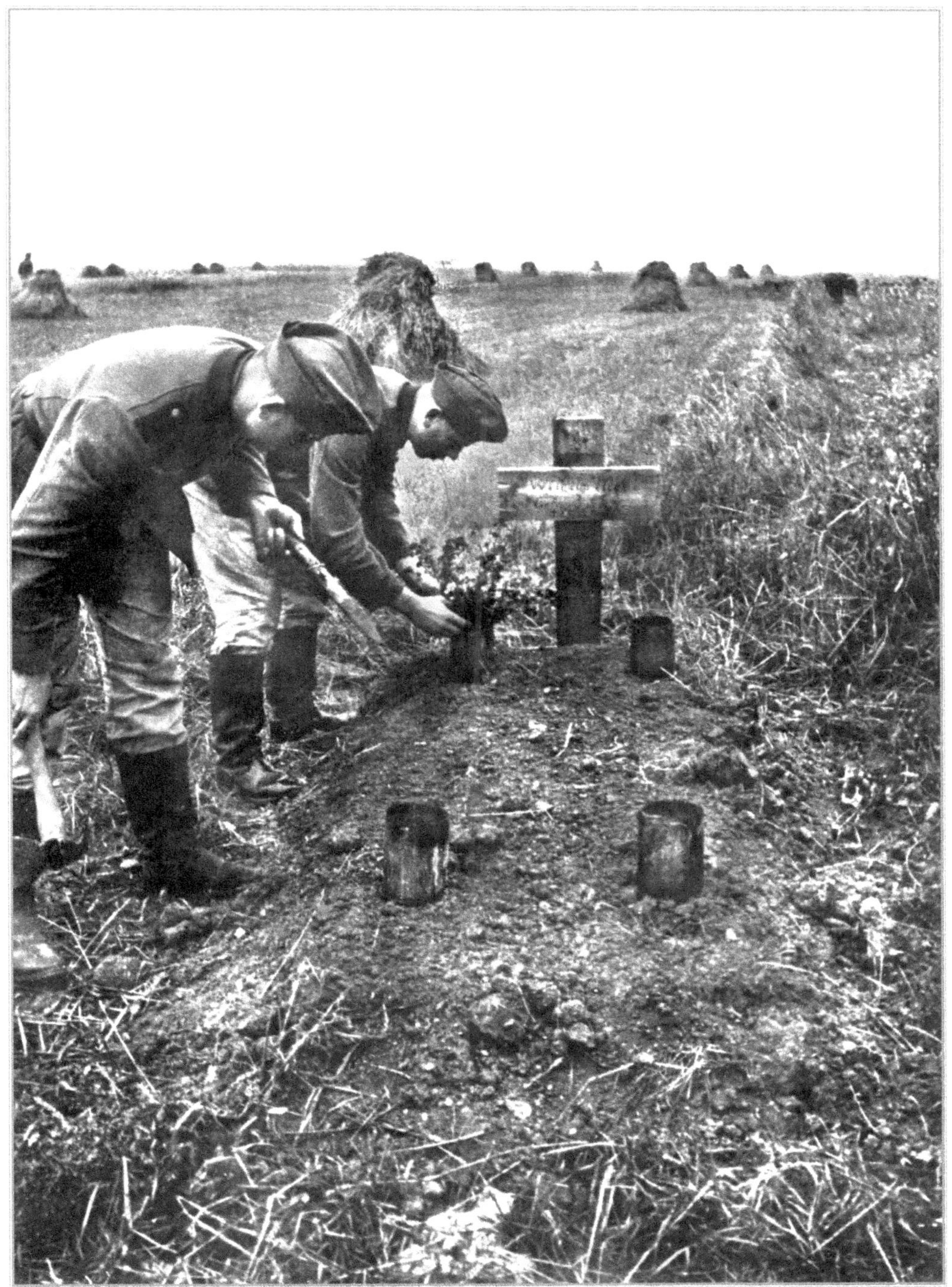

Two German soldiers conclude the burial of Private Wilhelm Mai in a hayfield in France.

Tank shells have been placed, almost like candles, to mark the outer corners of the grave. The soldier near the cross uses a shell as a makeshift vase in which to put a bouquet of flowers. The other soldier carries a hoe and a mud-covered knife. Haystacks dot the large field in the background.

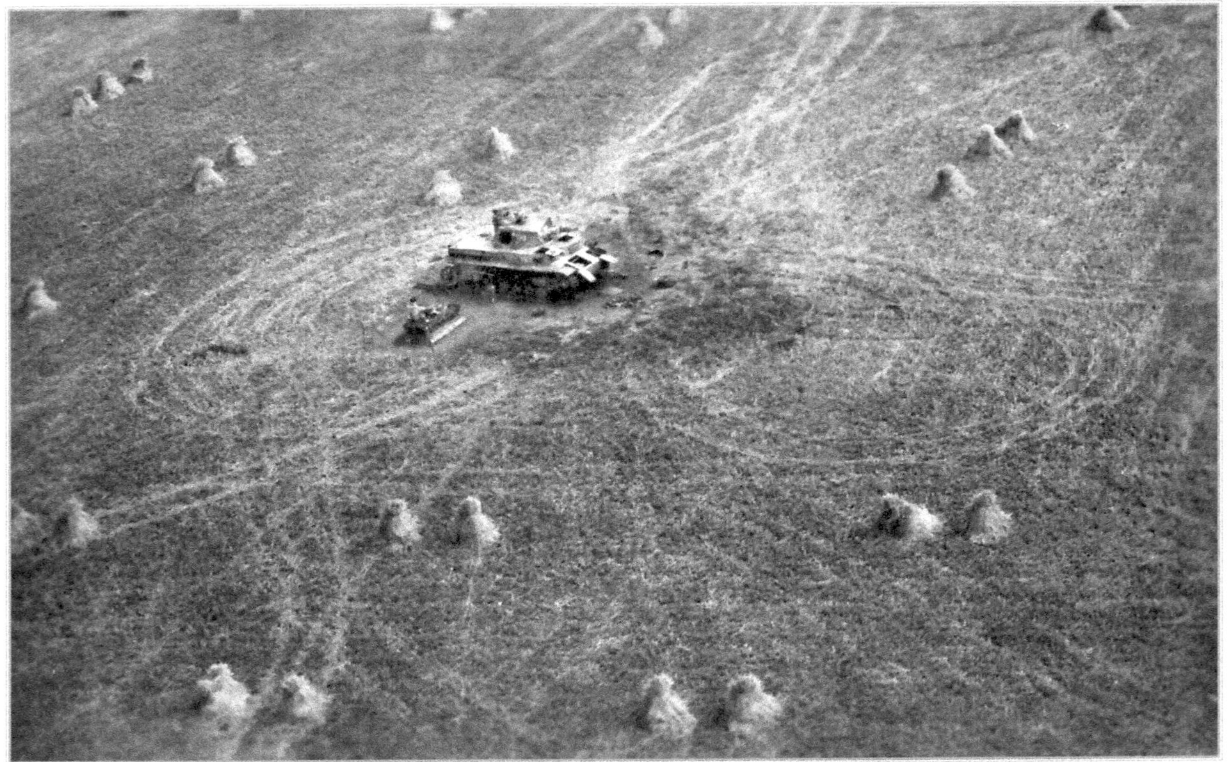

Aerial photos Rommel took to memorialize the death of a German soldier in a field of haystacks (date and location unknown).

These unusual images tell the story of the demise of a German soldier. The tank tracks indicate that the Panzer crossed a field and made wild circles before coming to a halt. Pieces of the demolished tank are littered on the ground near the grave of the soldier, who was obviously inside the vehicle when it was hit. The grave is marked with a white cross, upon which the soldier's cap is hanging.

Rommel evidently noticed this gravesite as he was passing by in an aircraft and took the photos.

In his memoirs, Rommel often noted the names of those around him who passed away.

> "One very sad loss was Major Kentel, one of the 25th Panzer regiment's Battalion commanders, who had been mortally wounded by a shell splinter."
>
> — *Rommel*

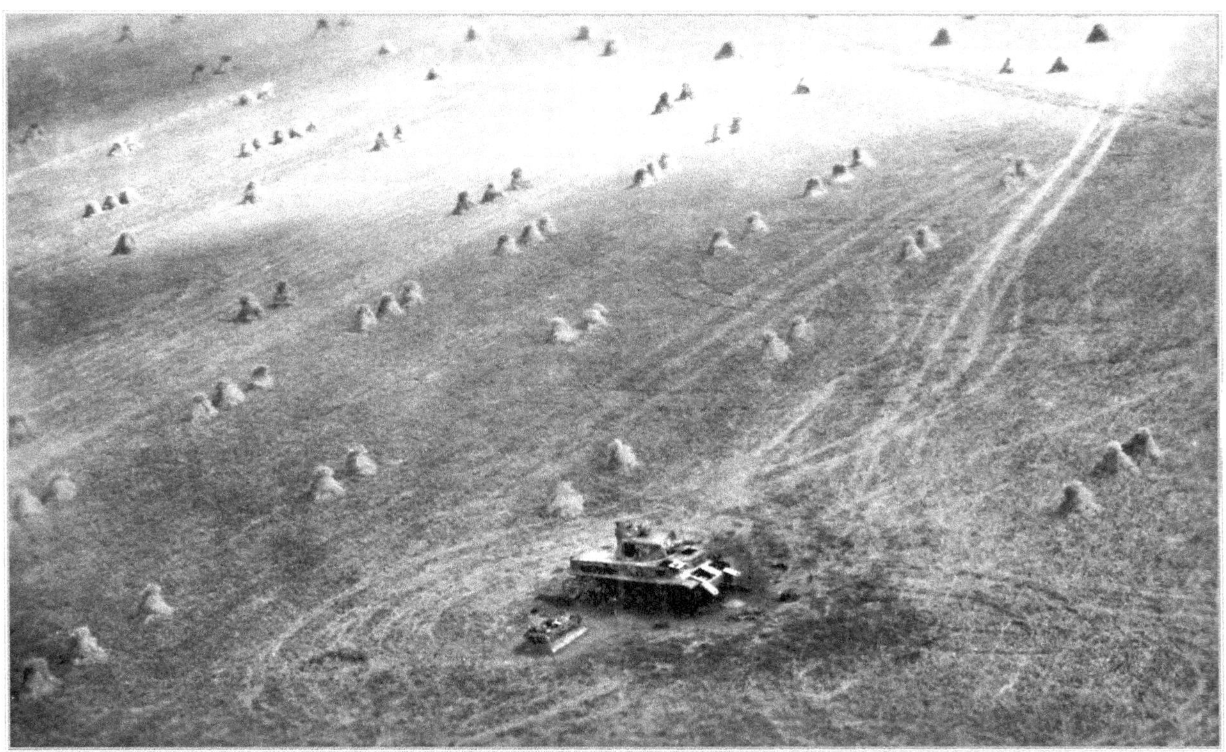

Another view of the tank in the field.

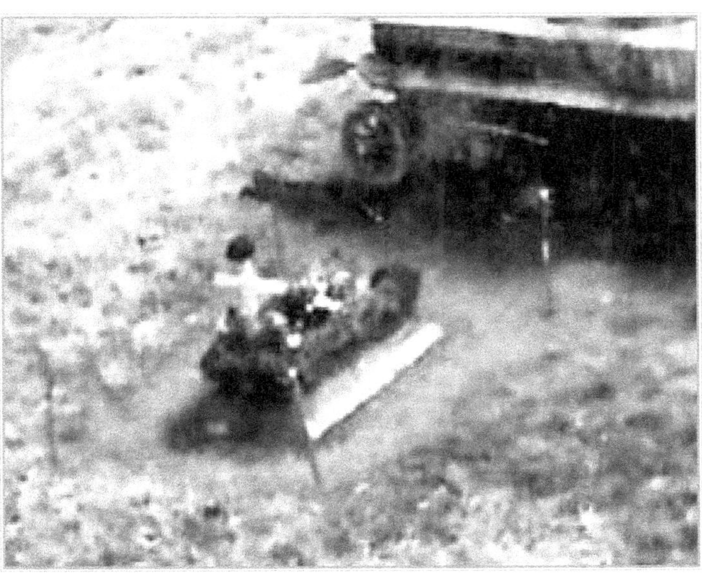

This photo is a close-up of the grave taken from Rommel's photo above, which provides greater detail of what Rommel saw as he flew past.

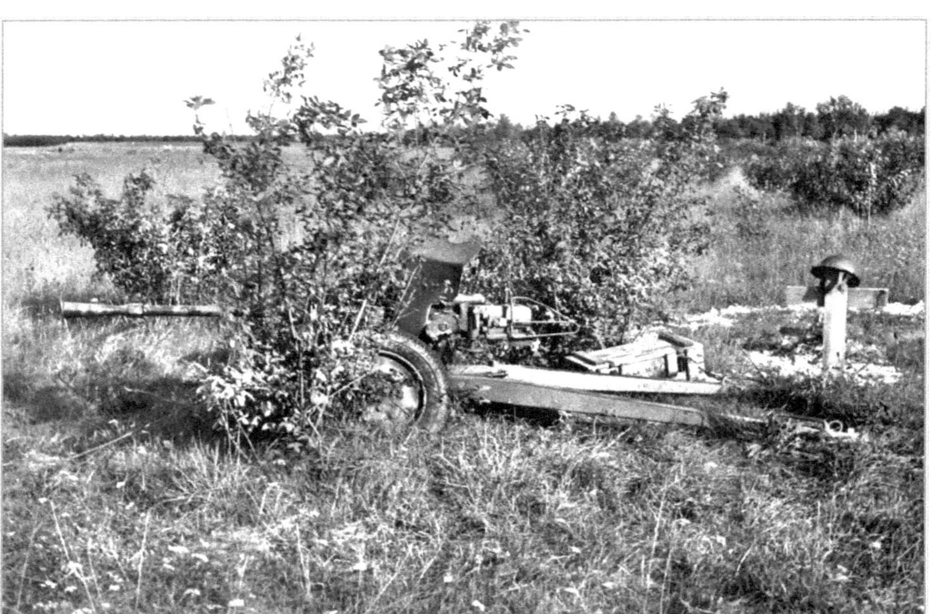

An unknown soldier's helmet marks his grave next to an antitank gun in a field in France.

The cross has no visible inscription. The helmet appears to be that of an Allied soldier, probably French.

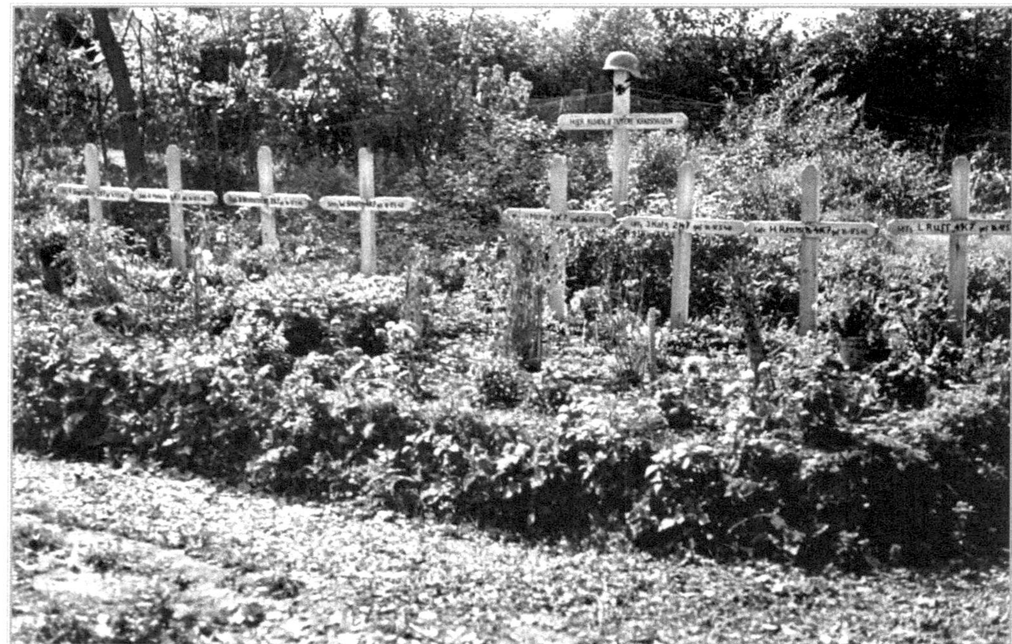

The graves of eight German motorcycle troopers in an unknown wooded area in France.

All of these men were killed between May 16–17, 1940. The central cross overlooking the graves, marked with a steel helmet, bears the inscription: "Here rest eight brave motorcycle troopers." Visible are the names of: Private O. Honack; H. Mohr; Sergeant J. Kalz; Private H. Rentsch; Sergeant L. Ruff; and W. Scharl, an enlisted rifleman. Their graves are covered with flowers. On some of the graves, bouquets have been placed in makeshift vases.

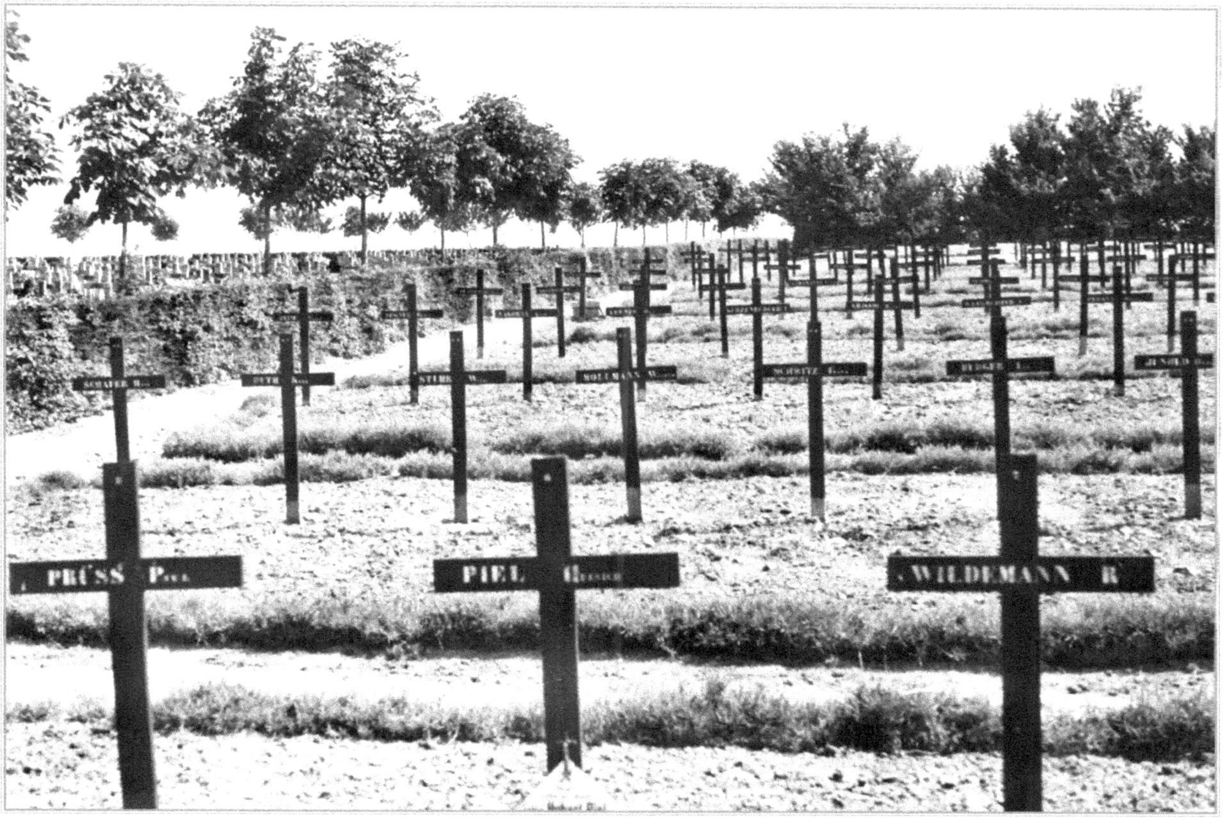

A German graveyard in a large cemetery in Europe.

This seems to be the German section of a World War I cemetery. Rommel, a veteran of WWI, likely visited here for personal reasons and took this photo as a memento.

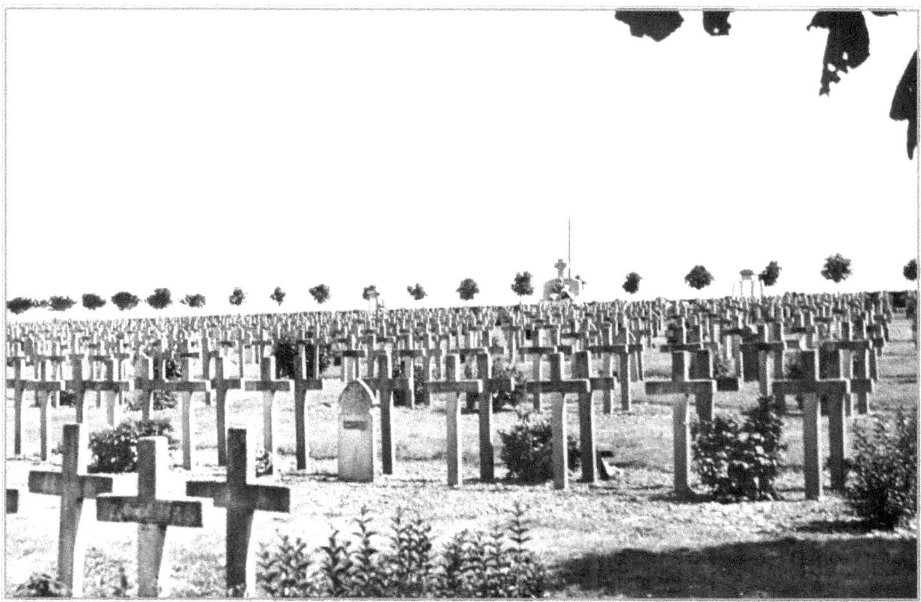

Stone crosses fill the same large cemetery in Europe.

Rommel seems to have walked all around the cemetery. These stone crosses appear in the photo above (left) beyond the line of trees in the distance. A monument (center) of the Pietà is visible.

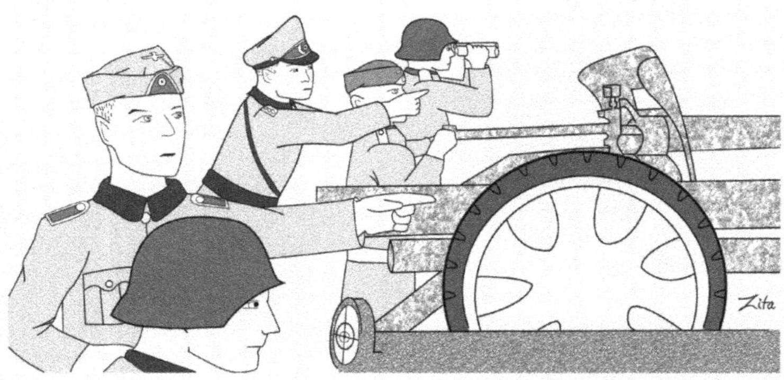

On May 21, 1940, a German-held town came under attack from a convergence of Allied tanks. As the tanks came speeding towards them from different directions, the German troops began to flee. Their vehicles became jammed in the roads of the small town. They were about to be overrun. Accompanied by Lieutenant Most, Rommel raced to a nearby hilltop where German artillery and anti-aircraft guns were in place. Watching enemy tanks speeding closer and closer below, Rommel and Most ran back and forth among the guns and spurred the crews to action. Under fire, Rommel sprinted to each gun and assigned it a target, with Most accompanying close at his side. Together he and Most managed to organize the German soldiers and beat off the assault. Many Allied tanks were destroyed or set on fire. Others retreated. A lull followed the violence. During this pause, Most met with an unexpected fate.

In the following passage, Rommel describes the moment that Most was killed. Rommel was usually very reserved and matter-of-fact in his war memoirs, which were intended to be published as military textbooks. This passage is a rare exception—it gives a uniquely sentimental account of a soldier's death. It seems evident Rommel was both very surprised and profoundly affected by Most's passing.

> "The worst seemed to be over and the attack beaten off, when suddenly Most sank to the ground beside a 20-mm anti-aircraft gun close beside me. He was mortally wounded and blood gushed from his mouth. I had had no idea that there was any firing in our vicinity at that moment, apart from that of the [German] 20-mm gun...Poor Most was beyond help and died before he could be carried into cover beside the gun position. The death of this brave man, a magnificent soldier, touched me deeply."
>
> — *Rommel*

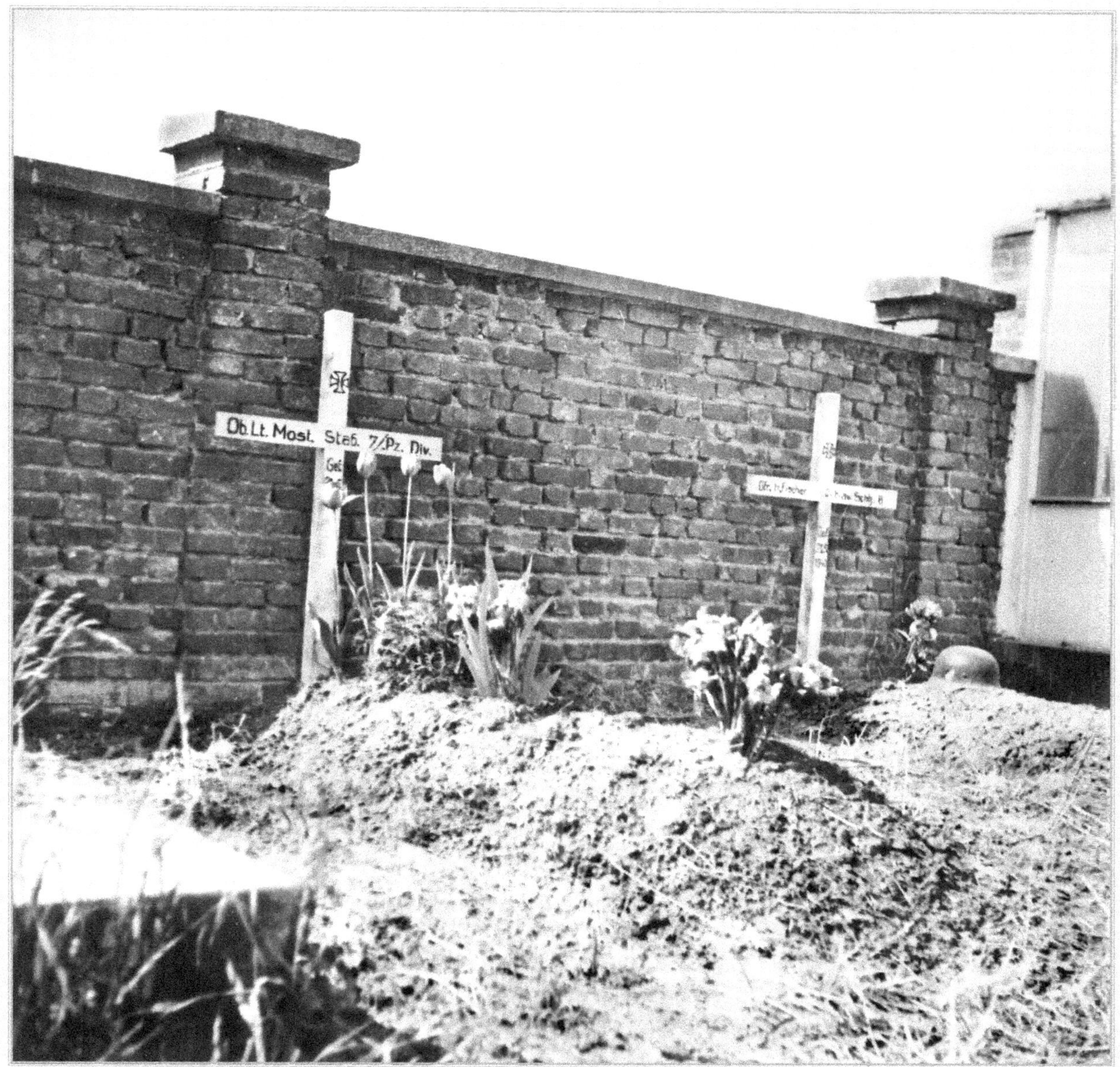

Rommel took this photo of the grave of Lieutenant Most, killed in action in France on May 21, 1940. Next to Most's final resting place is the grave of another German soldier, Private H. Fischer, whose helmet is near his cross.

Lieutenant Most was Rommel's aide in France. Together they braved many perilous situations during battles. (See page 141.) Most's grave is adorned with tulips and various bouquets of flowers. Rommel took this photo to memorialize Most, who was killed while standing a yard away from him.

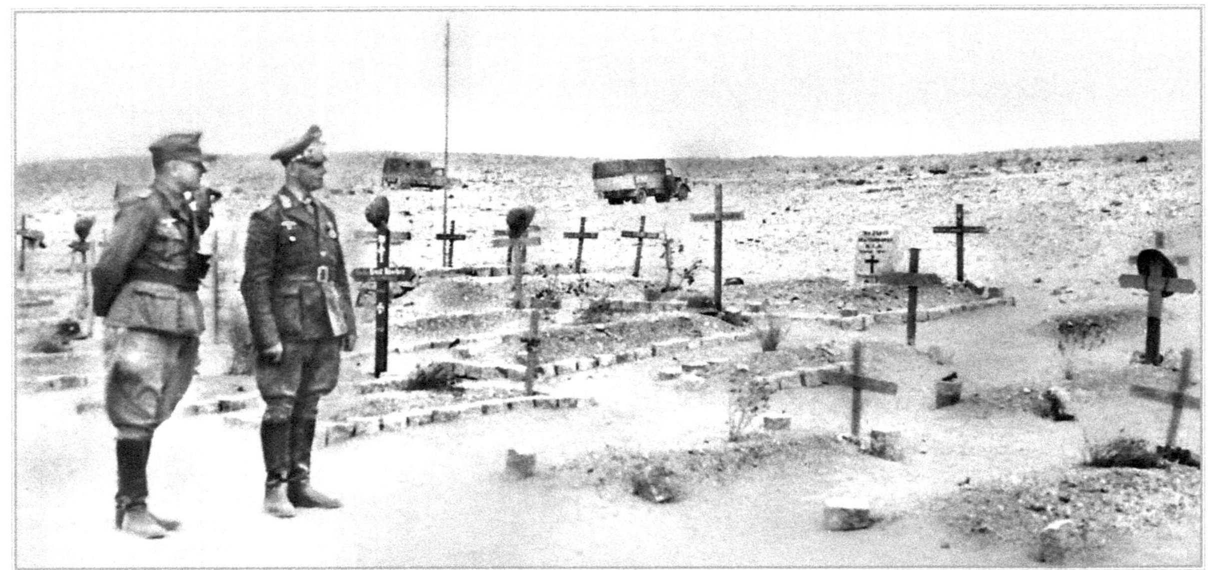

An officer accompanies Rommel on a visit to a cemetery in North Africa.

In the center of the image, a truck is driving away. It would seem that the truck was used to carried the fallen for burial. Crosses and helmets mark the graves of more than 20 men buried in the cemetery here.

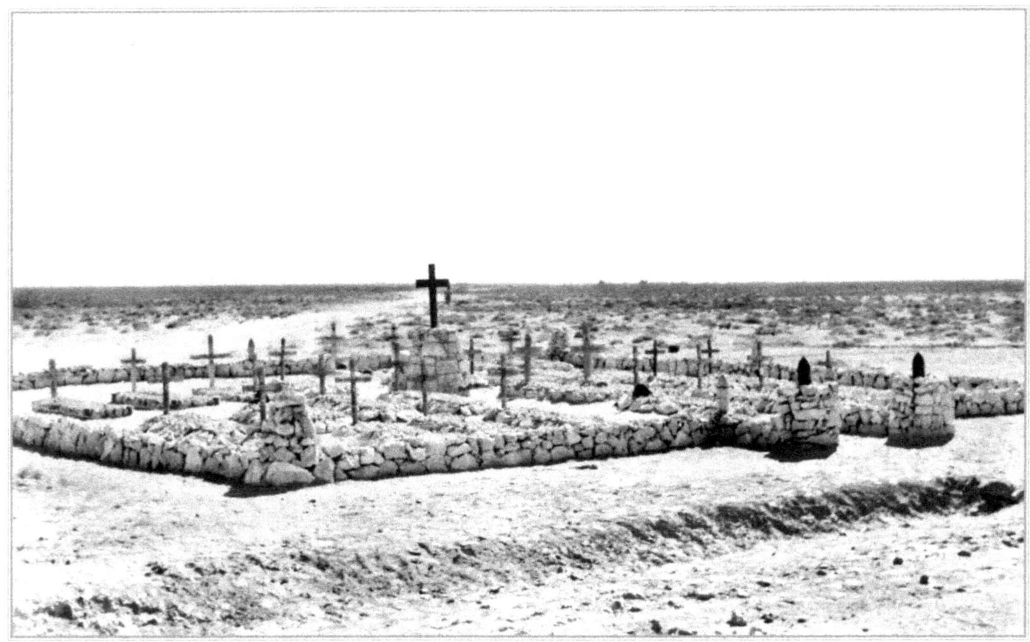

A more well-established graveyard with a cross monument as a centerpiece is bordered by a neat rock wall in North Africa.

This graveyard has been constructed with great care using rocks to form neat walls and burial plots. Rommel took this image while standing on a nearby hill.

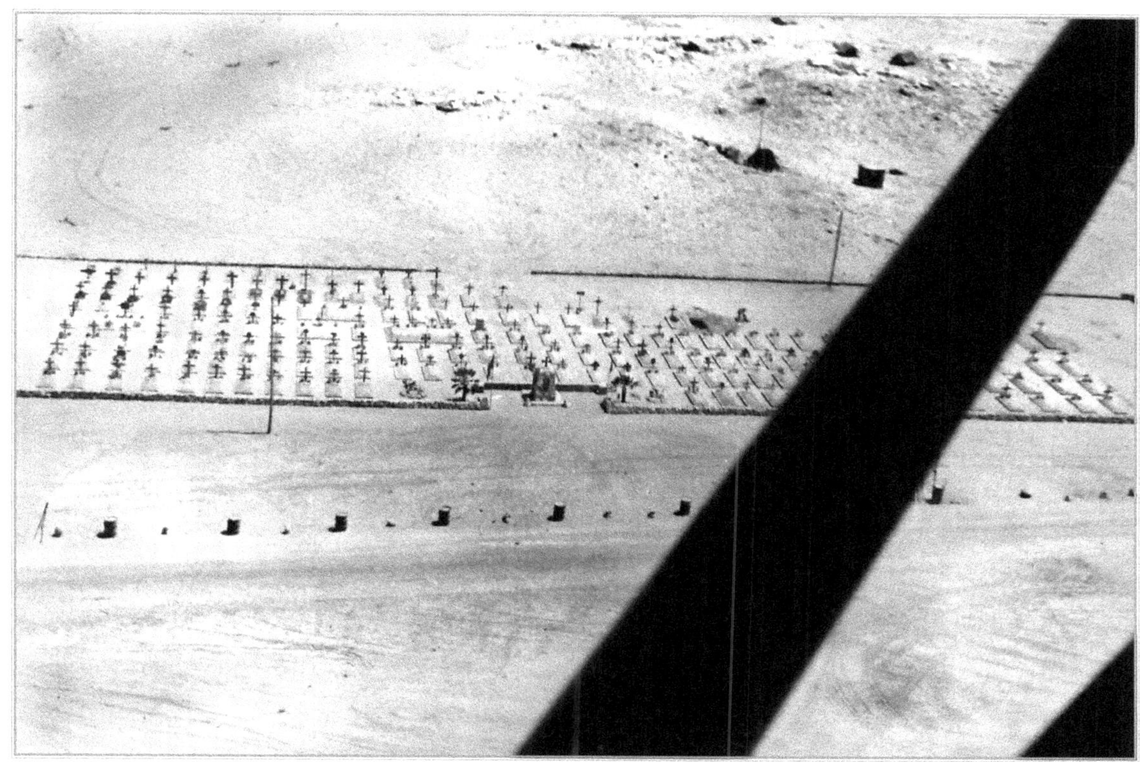

From his plane (upper right), Rommel took photos of a cemetery with over 170 graves in North Africa.

There are at least four oblong mass graves. One has four crosses on it. A man above (center, right) is bent over, apparently digging a new grave. Four tents are visible in the area near the cemetery.

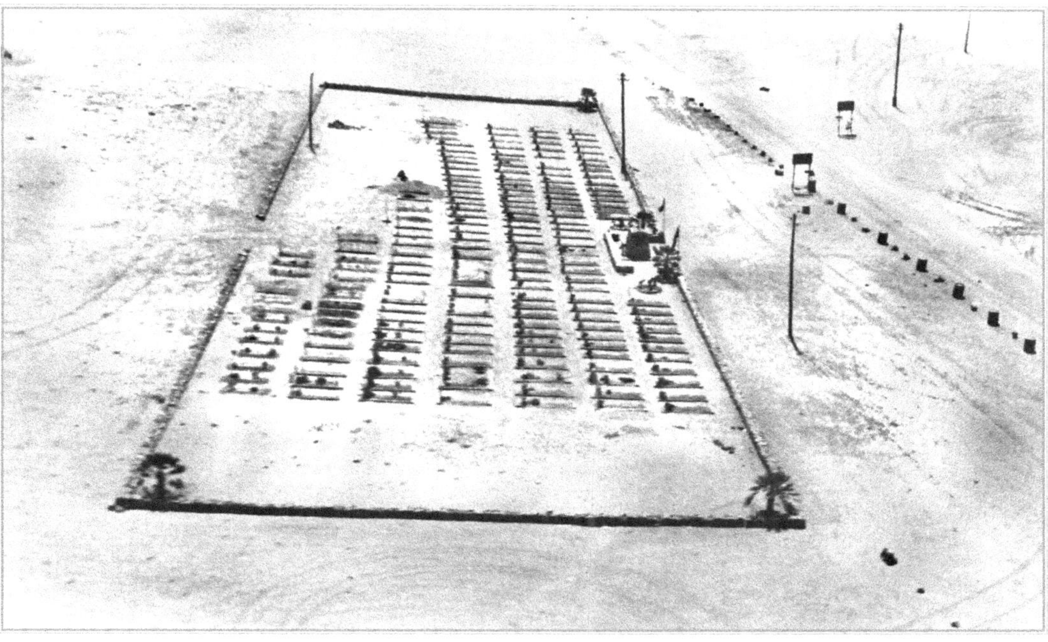

Dirt next to the open grave is apparent (left) from this view. Palm trees are planted at each side of the entrance and on three corners of the grounds.

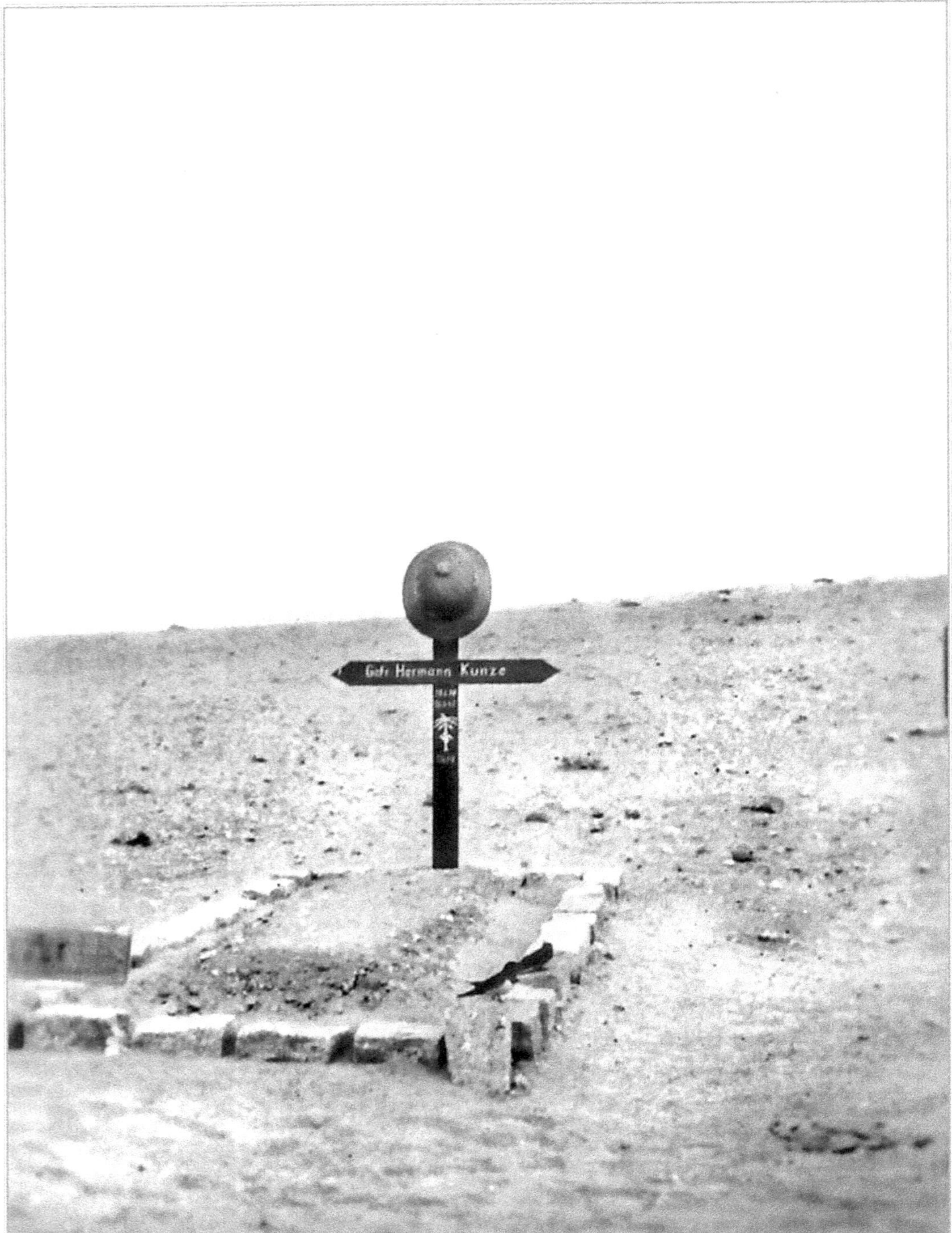

Rommel takes a close-up view of the grave of Private Hermann Kunze.

This sparsely decorated grave appears to stand isolated in a small, makeshift burial ground. The cross is marked with the seal of the Afrika Korps. Two birds (center) sit on bricks bordering the grave.

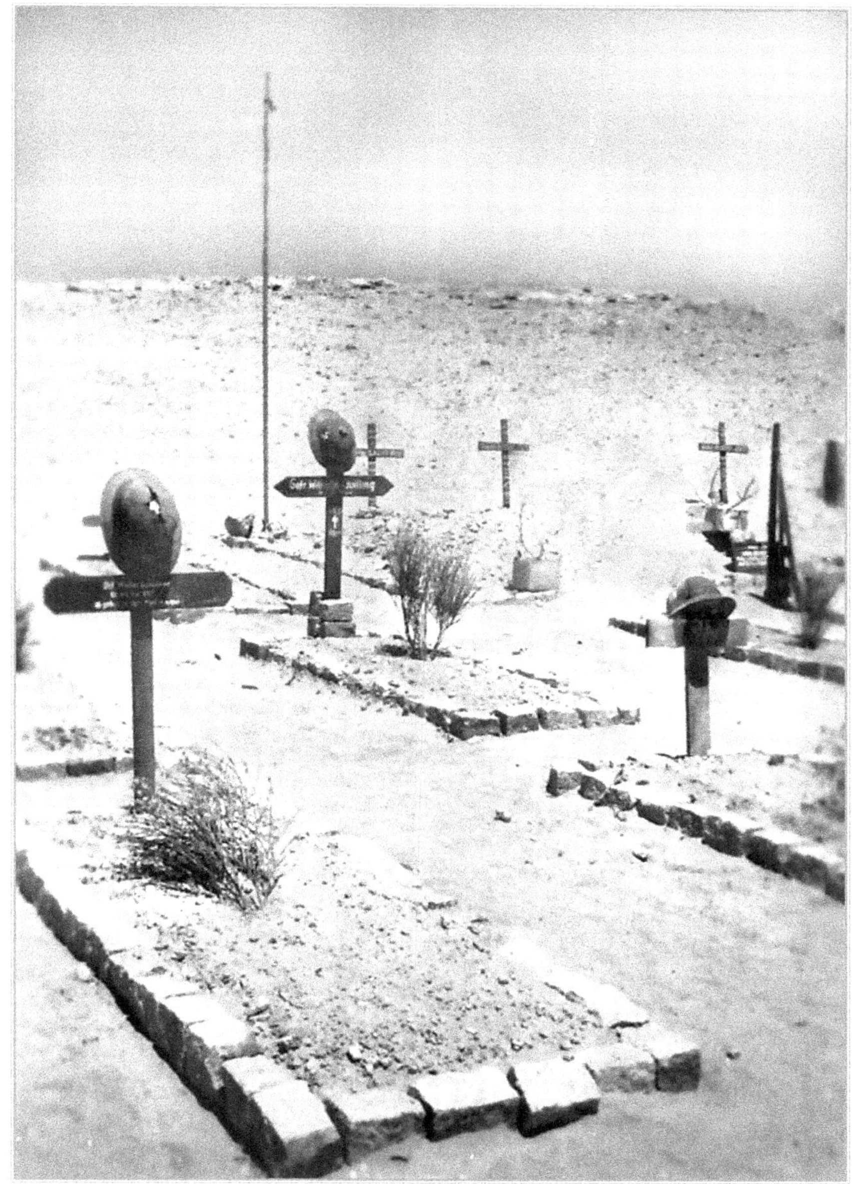

Helmets hang from German soldiers' graves in another lonely cemetery in North Africa.

Rommel took this photo of nine graves from a diagonal angle. A lack of resources didn't prevent soldiers from carefully marking and decorating the graves of the fallen. Desert brush and dry branches were used in place of flowers. On the grave of Private Wilhelm Zwilling (center), branches have been placed upright. On one grave there is a fuel canister on the mound. A pith helmet on the foremost grave (left) has a large hole in the center and is cracked.

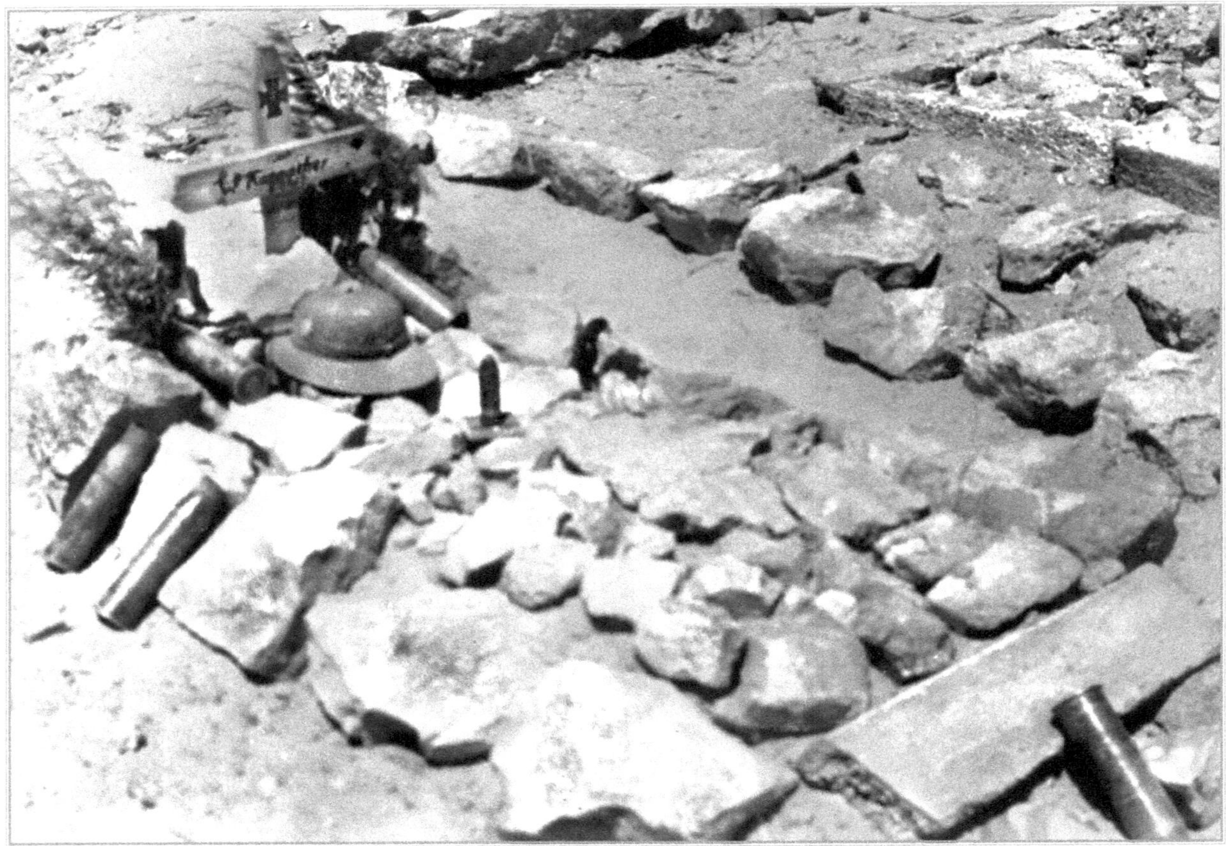

The hastily made grave of Lieutenant Kappacher is covered with stones.

Rommel took this image diagonally to show the ammunition casings around the grave. Two sprigs from shrubs adorn each side of the cross near the pith helmet. Although the image is somewhat blurry, Rommel still kept it among his personal collection of photos.

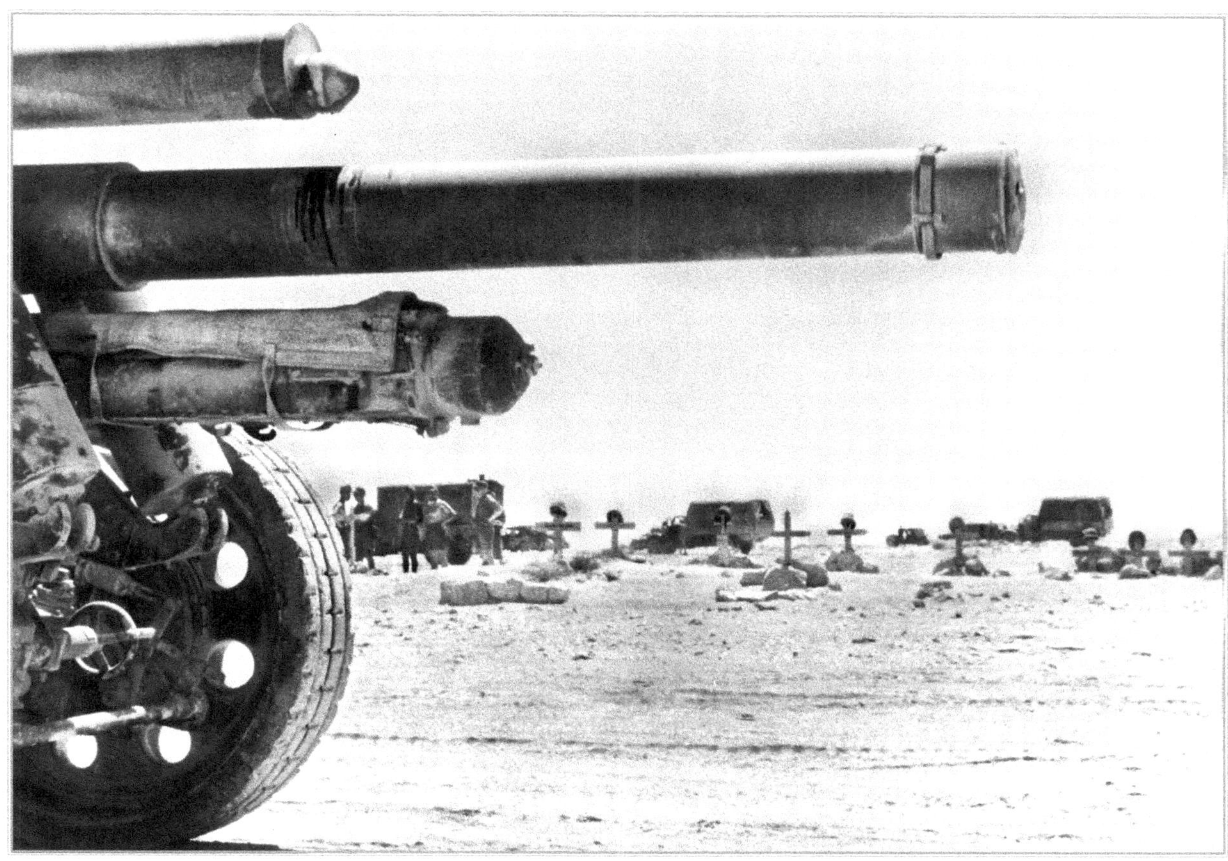

German soldiers bury the fallen in another makeshift cemetery in North Africa.

Rommel appears to have crouched low to the ground to capture the silhouette of the weapon barrels in front of the graveyard. Three trucks for transporting the dead are parked in the background. Soldiers stand near one of the trucks (left). In contrast to some of the other cemetery photos, this graveyard is smaller, with only 10 crosses visible. Also, the burial mounds are sparsely decorated with rocks and bushes.

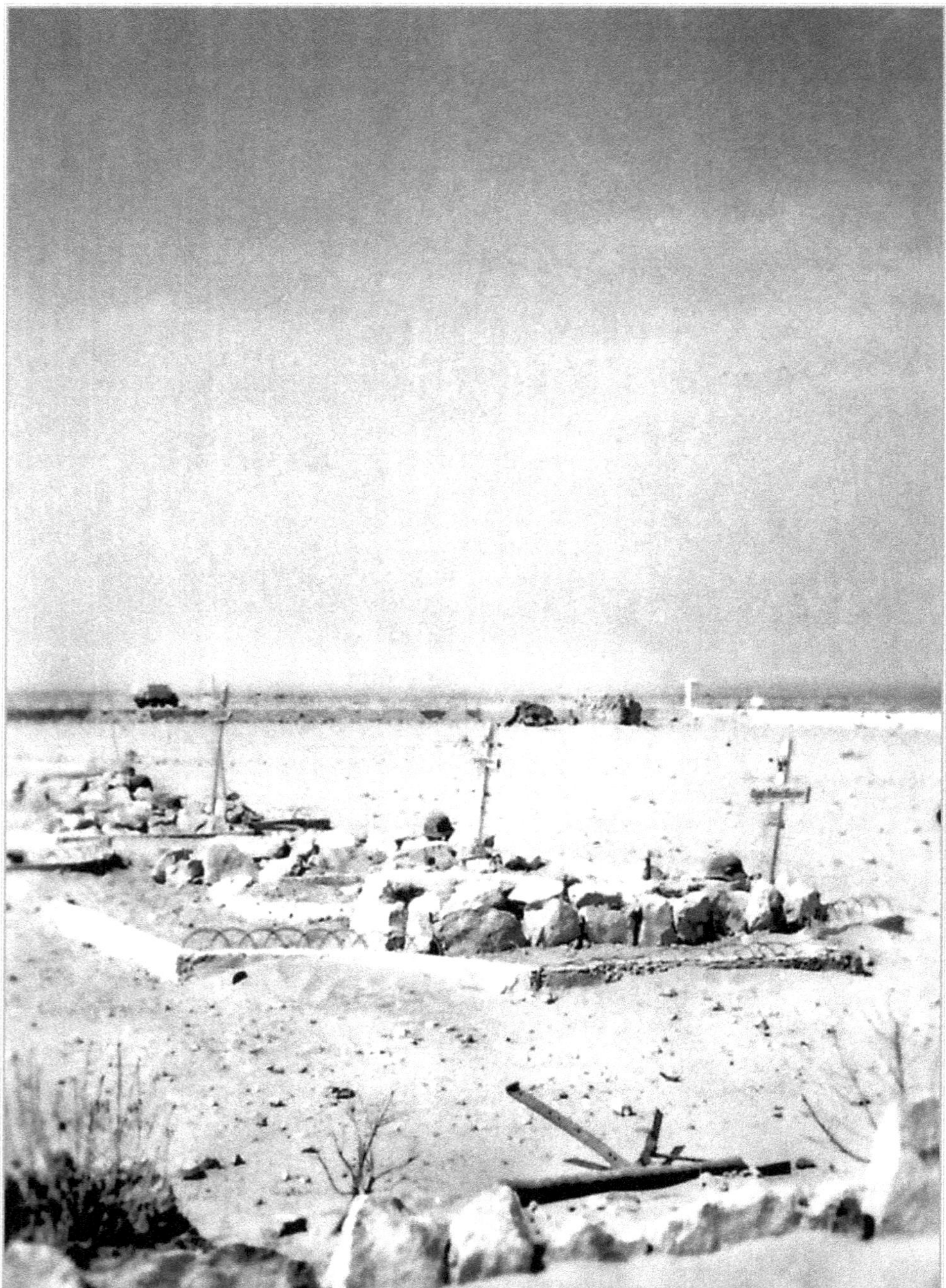

The mounds of four graves form the center of this barren cemetery.

Individual graves are topped with wooden crosses. Some are marked with the helmets of the fallen. In the distance, a transport truck drives away. The truck is similar to ones seen in Rommel's other photos at other cemeteries in North Africa.

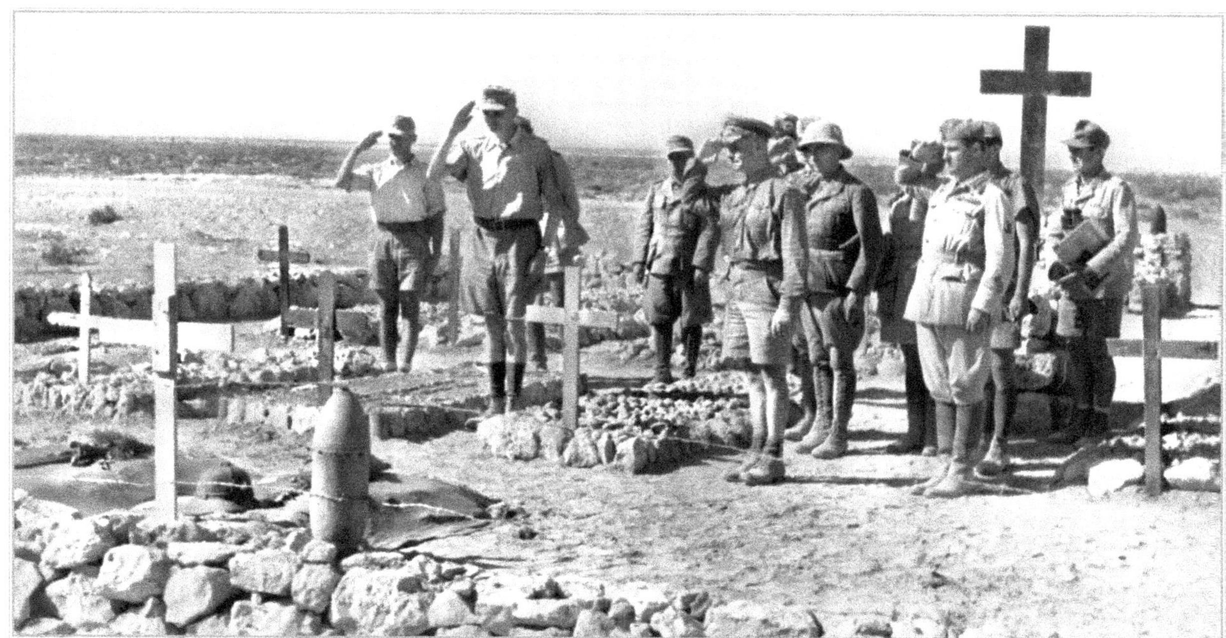

Rommel (above and below) salutes and pays his respects during a burial service for several fallen soldiers in two photos of the same event.

Two pith helmets rest on the dirt mounds. The bodies, covered with blankets, have not yet been buried. Both Italian and German officers attend the burial service.

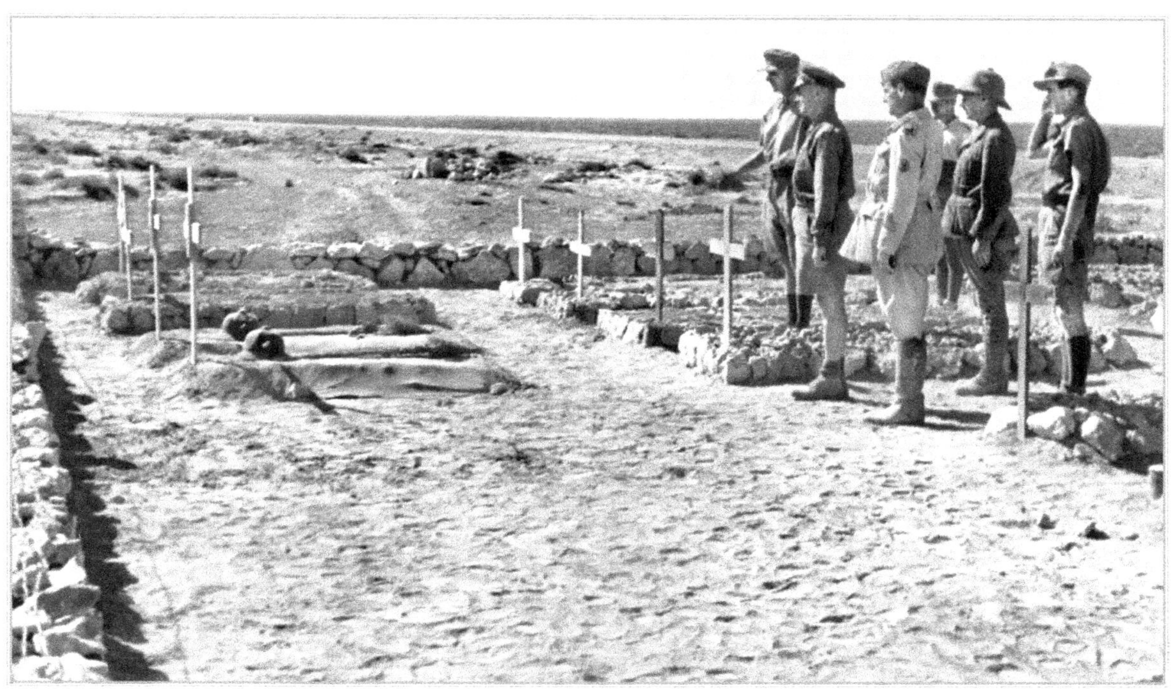

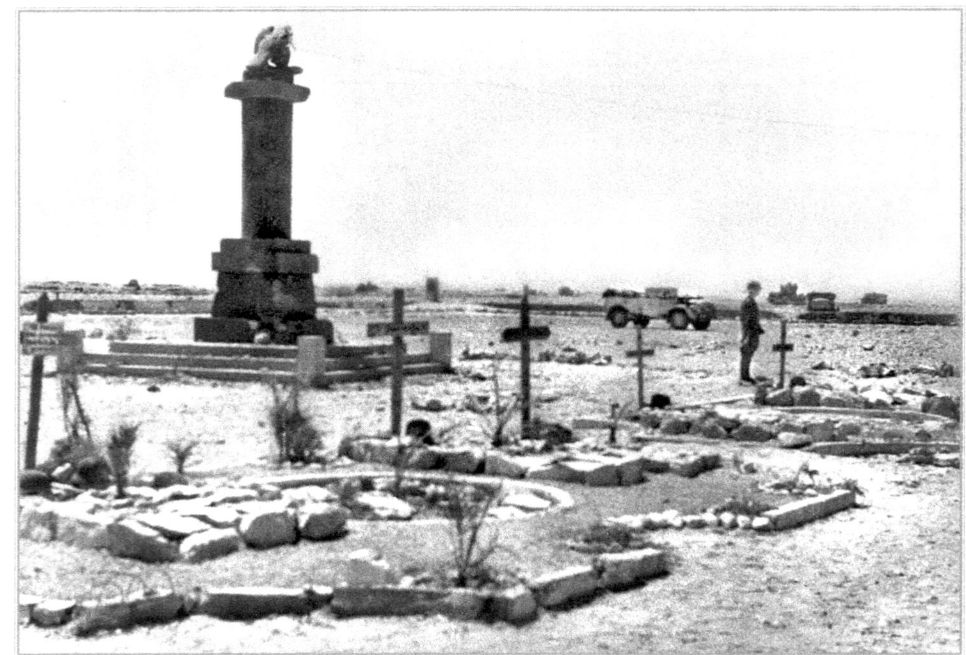

A German soldier pays his respects in a cemetery in North Africa.

This would appear to be a more permanent graveyard given the monument in the background.

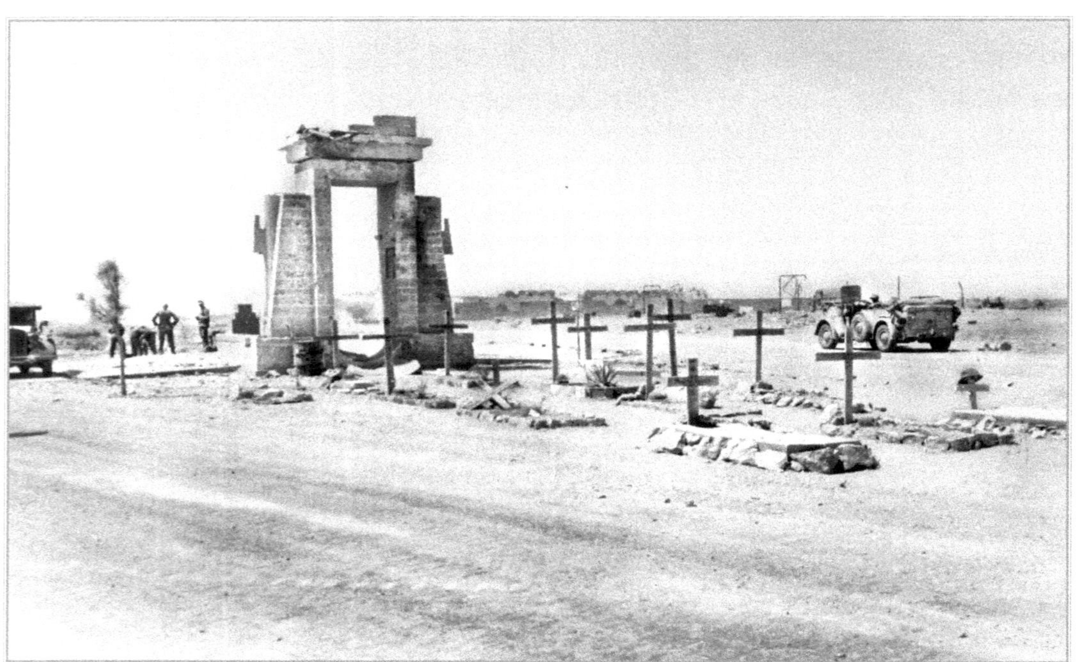

A dozen graves of German soldiers are located next to ancient ruins in North Africa.

What appears to be Rommel's vehicle and driver wait on the upper right of this photo, indicating that Rommel walked around the cemetery to take this picture. On the left side of the frame, part of a transport truck for the dead is shown, with soldiers beside it, who appear to be preparing a burial.

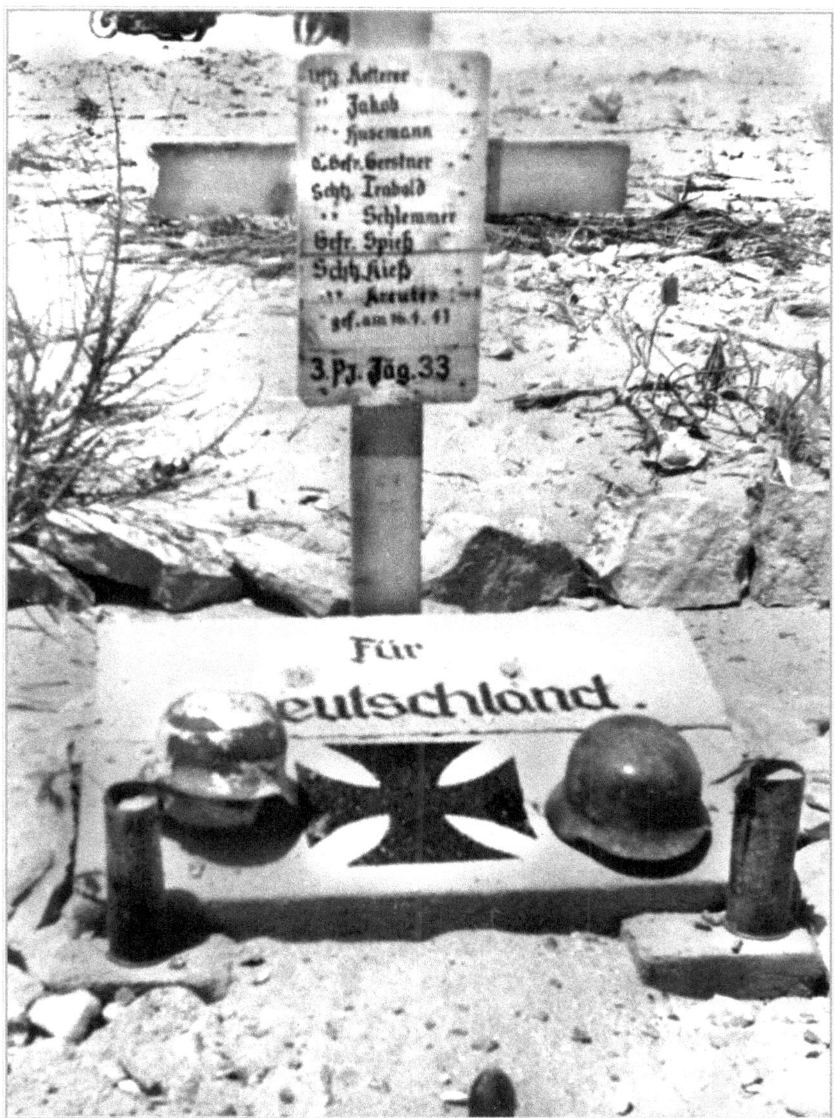

The names of nine men are clearly visible on this mass grave in the desert.

Motorcycles are partially visible at the top of the photo. The steel helmet on the left appears to have been burned. Names on the grave are:

Killed on April 16, 1941:

1. Ketterer (Sergeant, NCO)
2. Jakob
3. Husemann
4. Gerstner (Private 1st Class)
5. Irabold (Private, Enlisted Rifleman)
6. Schlemmer
7. Spietz (Private)
8. Kieß (Private, Enlisted Rifleman)
9. Kreuter

10

Family & Friends

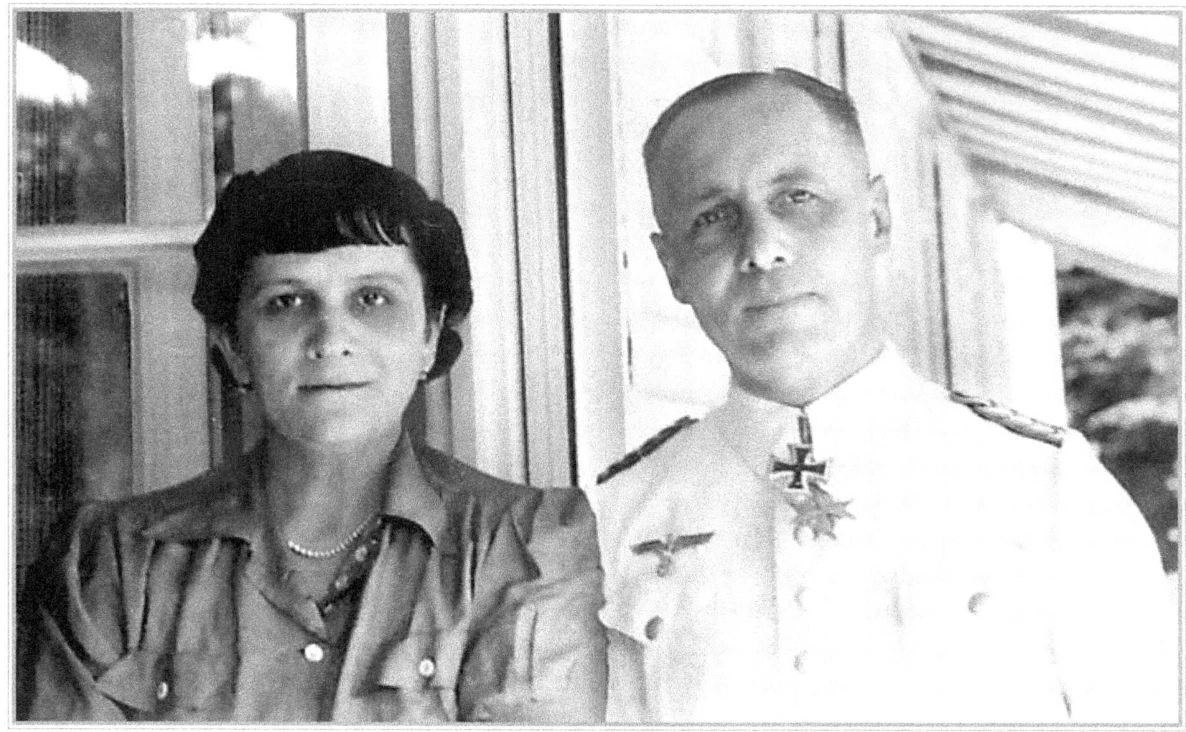

Rommel, in dress uniform, poses informally with his wife Lucie.

Rommel was 18 years old when he first met Lucia (Lucie) Maria Mollin in Danzig, a large city now known as Gdańsk in present-day Poland. Rommel had just joined the army and was attending a military academy.

At that time, Lucie, a student in boarding school, was studying to become a language teacher. Her family was of Italian origin. Years later, at age 25, Rommel married Lucie during the middle of World War I after he had been severely wounded.

In this photo, Rommel doesn't appear to have been made Field Marshal yet. He is wearing an Iron Cross medal and the Pour le Mérite medal.

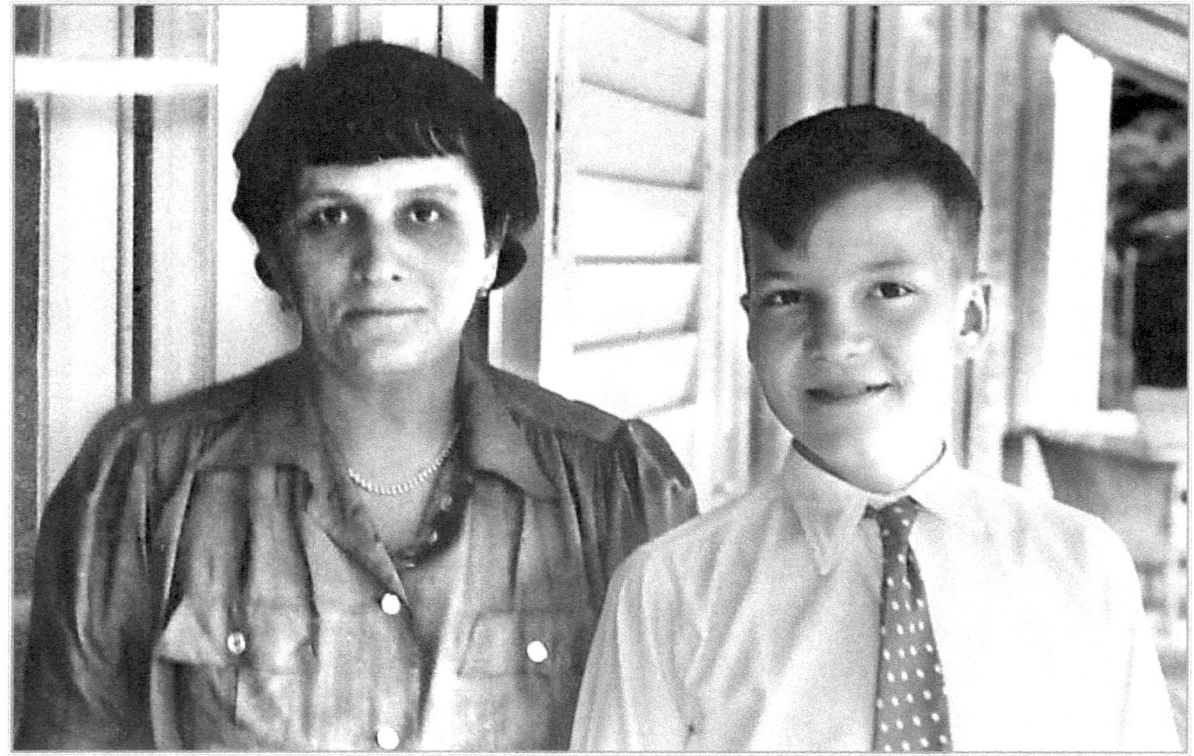

Rommel's wife and son pose for the camera.

Rommel seems to have taken this picture, given the precisely centered focal point and the even lines in the composition.

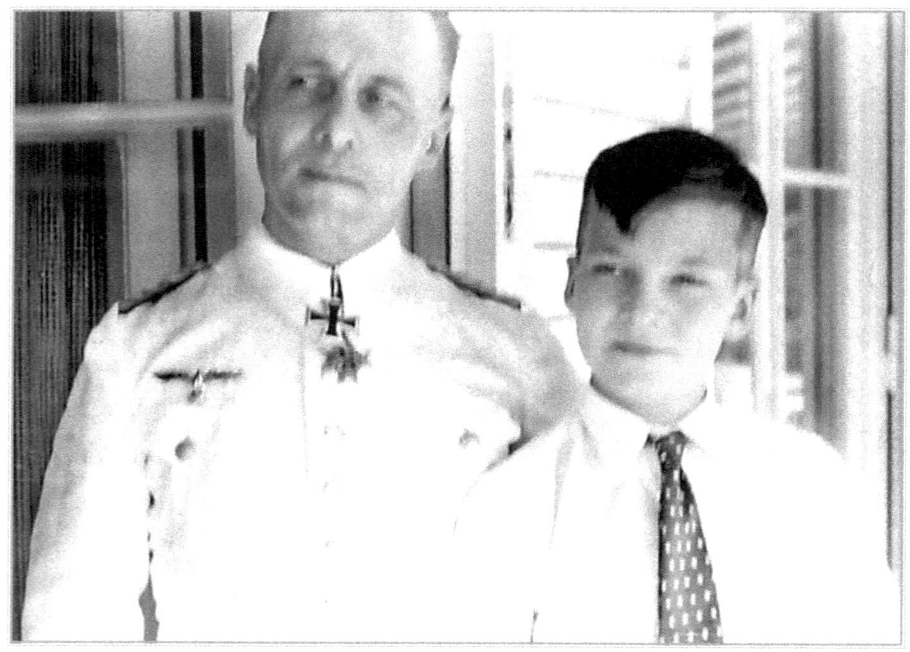

On the same day as the previous photos, Rommel poses with his son, Manfred.

This image (right) is slightly out of focus. It is possible that Rommel's wife took the photo.

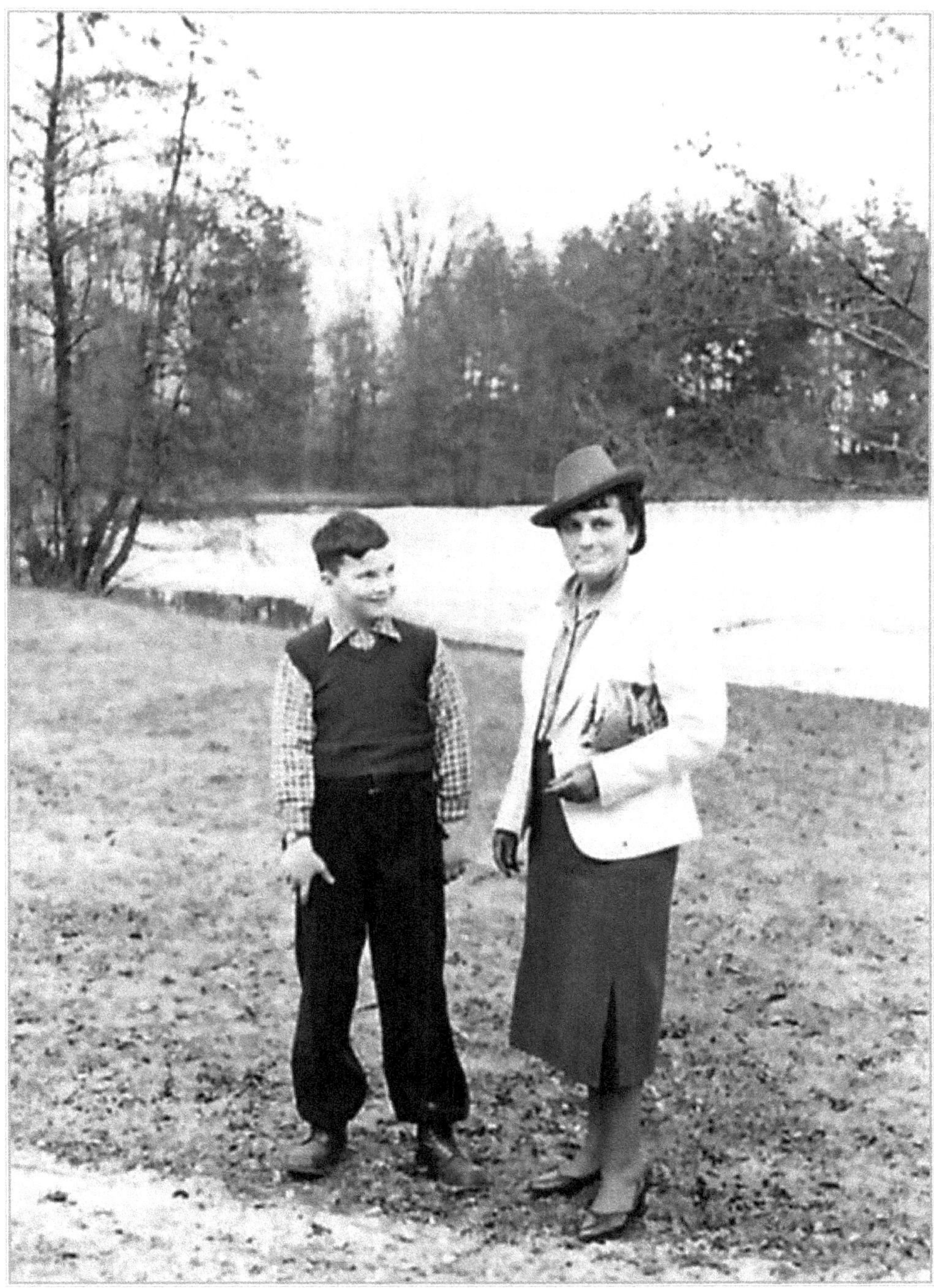

Rommel's only son, Manfred, looks slyly at his mother, Lucie, as they pose near a lake (date and location unknown).

It seems evident that Rommel took this picture. The water in the background forms a diagonal line cutting across the frame.

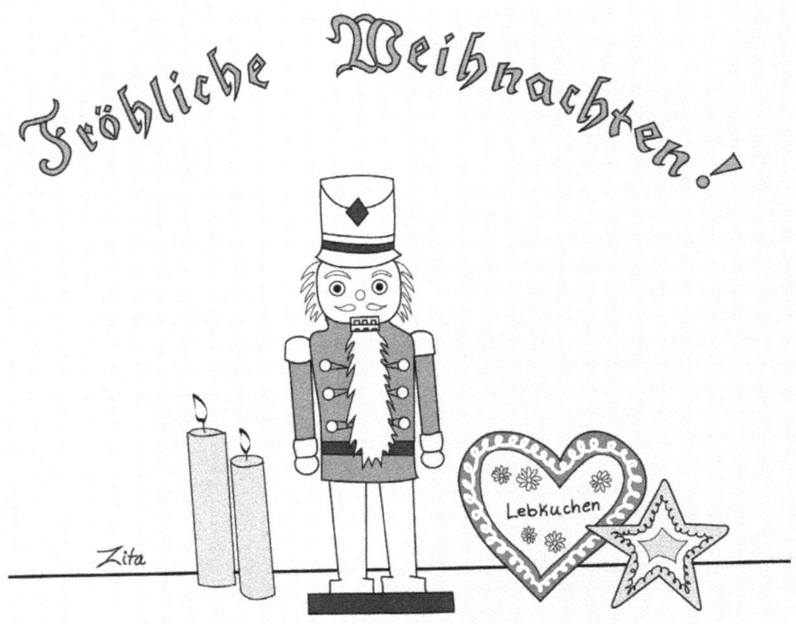

Rommel's only son Manfred was born Christmas Eve in 1928, when Rommel was 37 years old.

Christmas, called *Weihnachten*, is arguably the most important holiday in Germany. *Weihnachten* has a special place within the hearts of Germans. They have many traditions related to the Christmas season. The holiday is highly anticipated and preparations begin in Advent. The celebration of *Weihnachten* itself begins on Christmas Eve rather than on Christmas Day. The emphasis of *Weihnachten* isn't on materialism or decorations, but rather focuses on time spent with one's family and close friends.

For Erwin Rommel, *Weihnachten* had an even greater significance as Manfred's birthday. During the World War II, Rommel did not always remember dates or holidays. However, his memoirs and letters reveal that he never forgot Christmas and paid special attention to the occasion.

Rommel and Manfred had very different personalities. Although Manfred admired his father, he found Rommel to be a demanding parent. The two of them had dissimilar opinions and interests.

Despite their differences, both father and son still enjoyed a very close relationship.

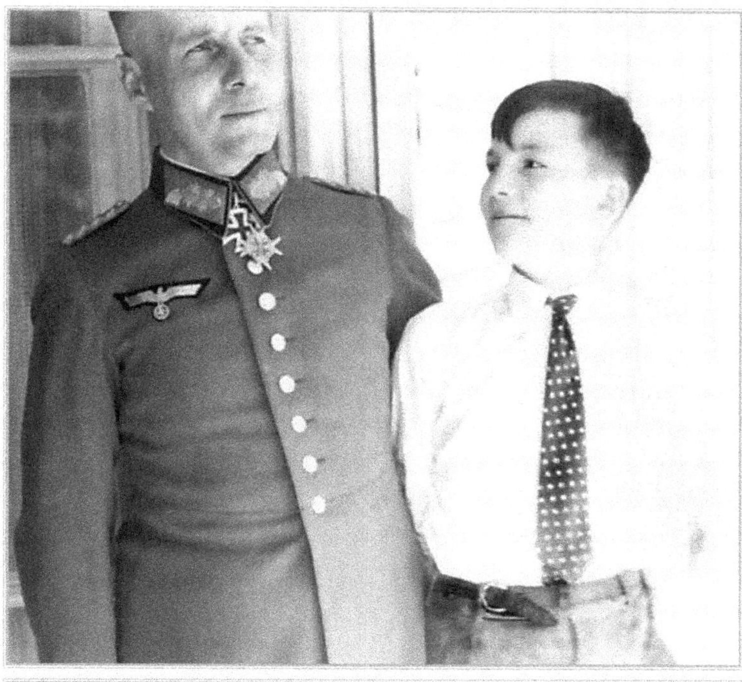

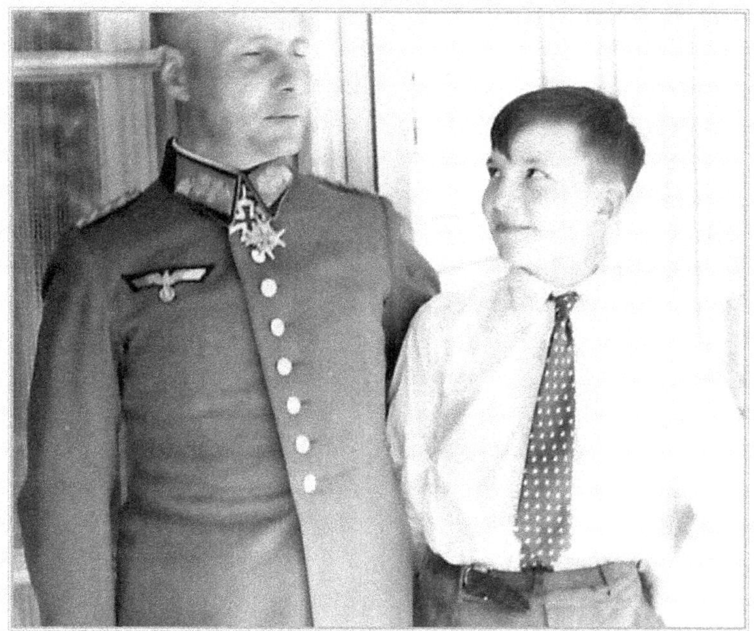

Rommel and Manfred stand together for another picture.

Manfred is wearing the same tie as in the previous photos. Rommel, however, has changed uniforms. Manfred appears to have been mischievous. His expressions in Rommel's photos are often playful. His belt buckle (above) is off-center, and his tie is a bit crooked.

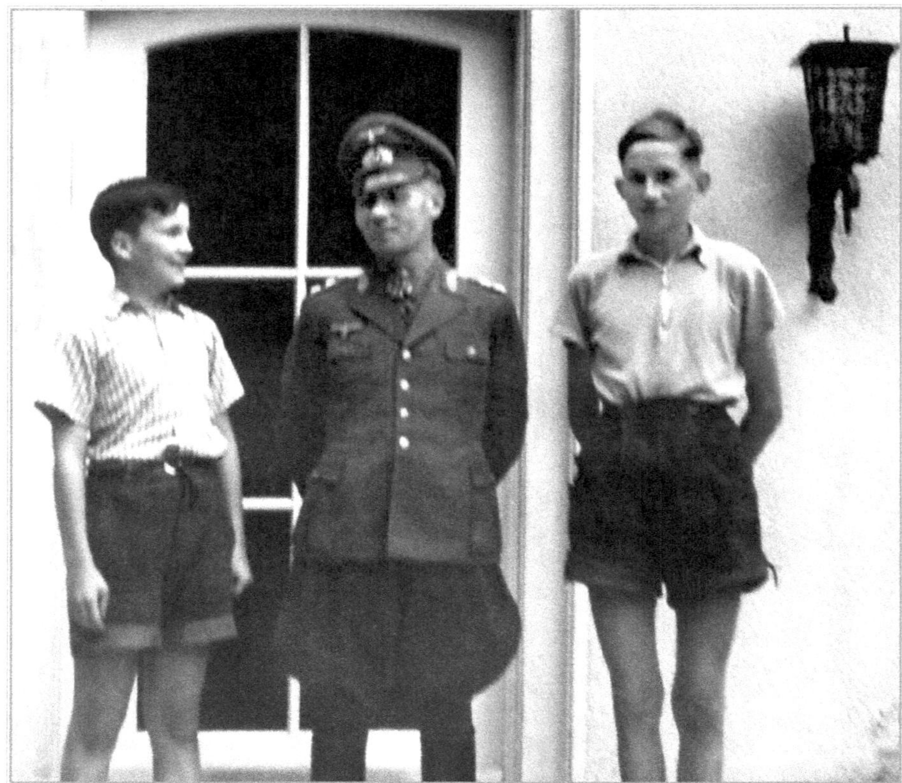

Rommel and Manfred smile at each other next to an unidentified boy.

The circumstances of Rommel's death in 1944 were difficult for Manfred, who was 15 years old at the time. Hitler decided to kill Rommel because of Rommel's opposition. On the morning of Rommel's death, father and son had breakfast together and took a walk. Then two emissaries from Hitler arrived hours later and threatened Rommel. The house and nearby area were surrounded by Gestapo and SS men. Rommel was told that if he committed suicide, his family and staff officers would be spared. Rommel accepted the offer. Manfred walked his father outside to the car, in which Rommel was driven further down the road from the house and forced to kill himself.

The Nazi regime kept Manfred and Lucie under surveillance and compelled them to keep the true nature of Rommel's death a secret, even from immediate family members. Like many other boys his age, Manfred was conscripted into a military unit in 1945 as Germany was being invaded. He was still being watched by Nazi agents. He fooled his commanding officers and escaped, deliberately becoming a prisoner of the French.

After WWII, Manfred went on to become a well-respected public official and longtime mayor of Stuttgart. He was honored with many awards and recognitions during his lifetime. He married Liselotte and they had a daughter, Catherine. Manfred made efforts to prevent misperceptions about his father. He died in 2013 at the age of 84.

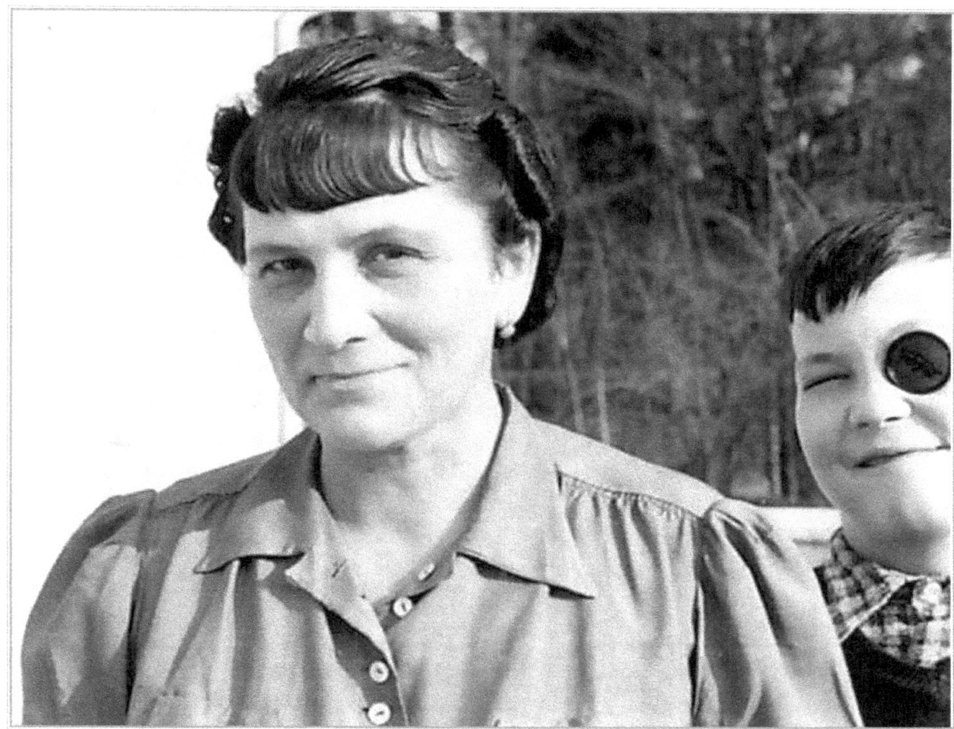

Manfred places a button in his eye and poses for the camera as his mother smiles (date and location unknown).

Given a lack of rations, Lucie often asked Rommel to bring back food items, such as sugar and wine, from countries he fought in. He indignantly refused due to his principles.

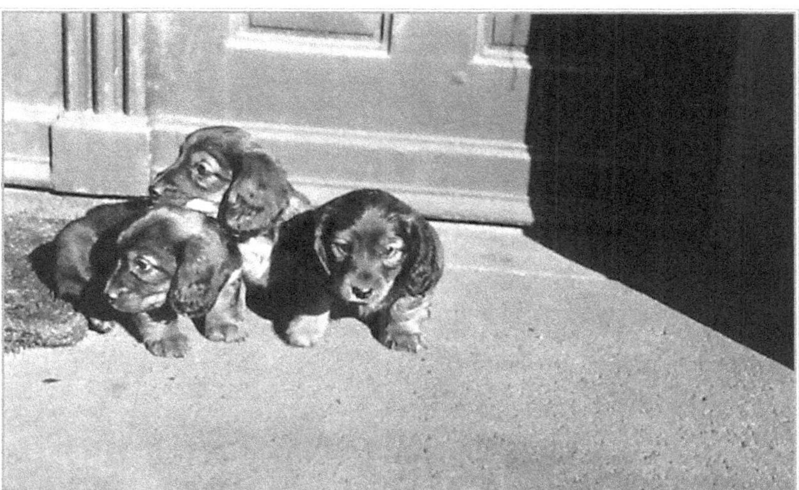

A group of dachshund puppies (date and location unknown).

Rommel had several dogs and enjoyed having animals as pets. One of his favorite dogs was a wire-haired dachshund named Elbo, who liked to eat sweets.

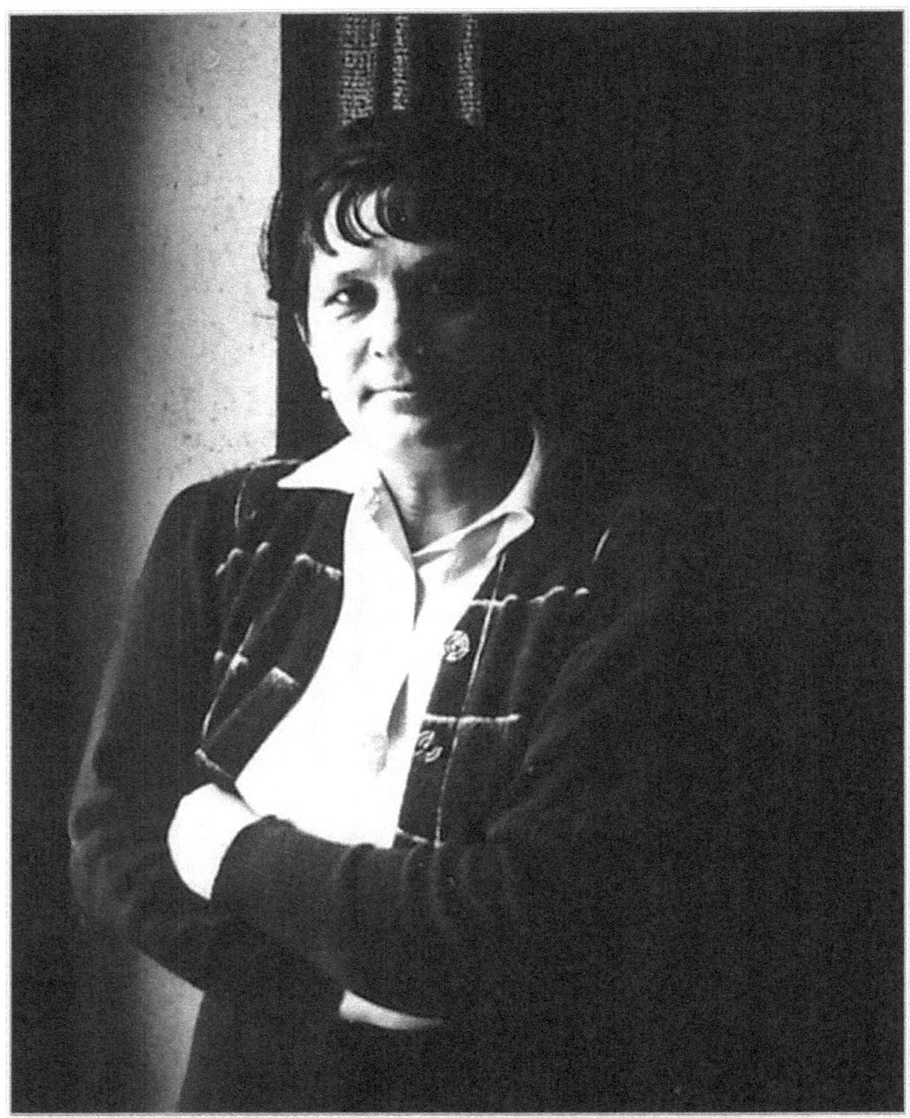

Rommel takes a portrait of his wife standing near a window.

Lucie was described as a vivacious, energetic, and strong-willed woman. She shared many common interests with Rommel, including a love of the outdoors, sports, and dancing. Unlike the wives of other German officers, Lucie discussed military matters with her husband and was well informed on military affairs. Rommel's death was devastating to Lucie. She also was outraged at the Nazi funeral given to her husband. She kept silent out of fear for Manfred's safety. Eventually, Lucie told American G.I.s the truth about what had happened. The G.I.s looted the Rommel home and stole many of Rommel and Lucie's belongings. Rommel's letters to Lucie also were stolen and reclaimed with great difficulty. In the years following WWII, Lucie lived a quiet life. She died in 1971 and is buried beside her husband.

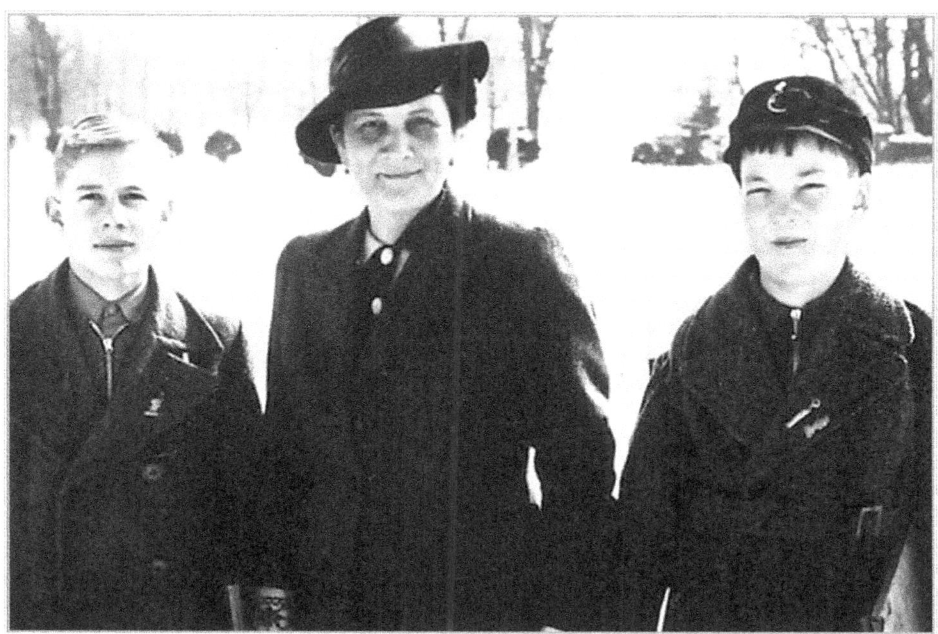

Lucie, Manfred, and an unidentified boy.

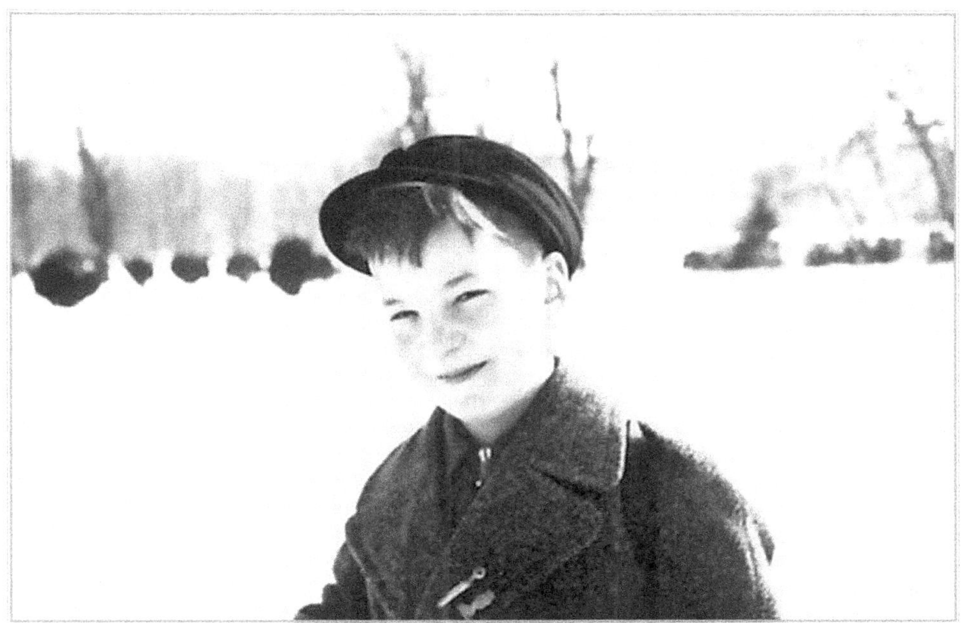

Manfred gives a playful expression on a winter's day.

During WWII, Manfred's time was divided between school and the Hitler Youth, which was mandatory for all German boys. Rommel reportedly was displeased with the Hitler Youth curriculum, and, in a personal letter, expressed annoyance that it took up so much of his son's time.

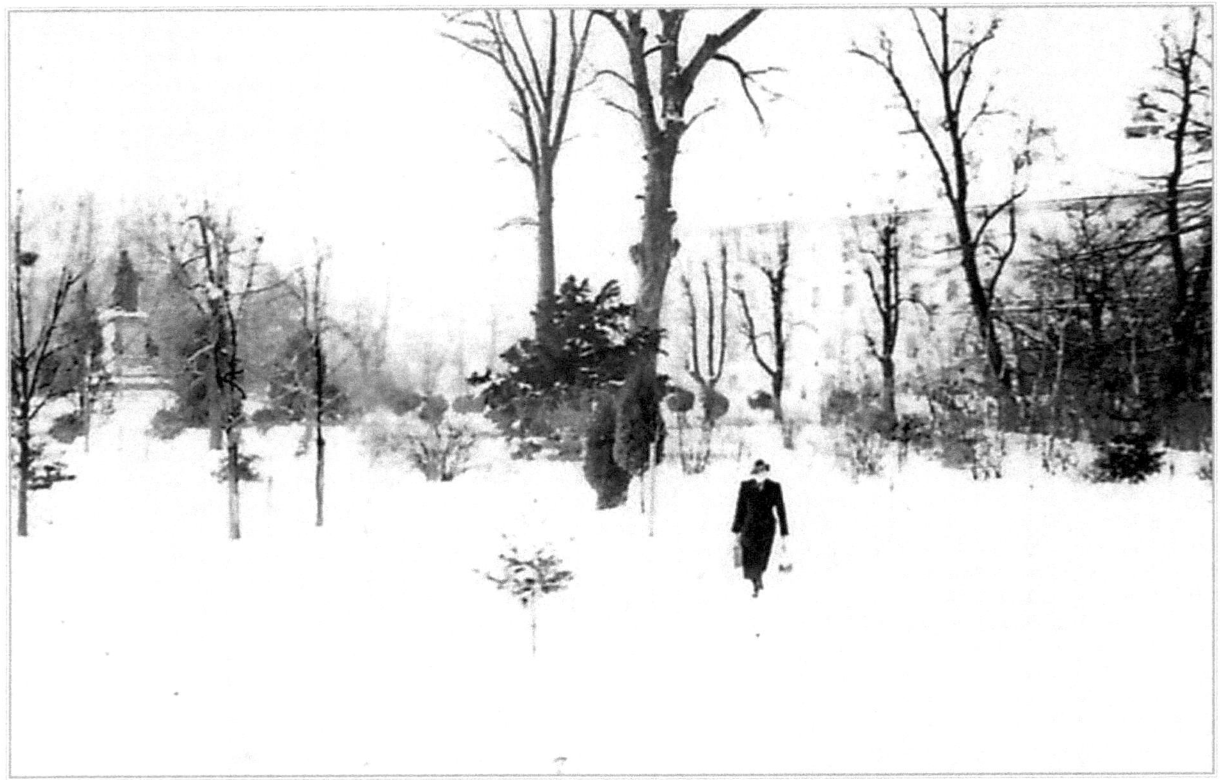

Rommel takes a picture of his wife walking through the snow in Austria (date unknown).

From 1938 until 1943, the Rommels lived in Wiener Neustadt, south of Vienna, until Rommel relocated his family to Germany due to intense Allied bombings.

In May 1945, months after Rommel's death, American soldiers arrived on Lucie's doorstep and ordered her to leave her home. They told her that American troops were to be billeted in the house and gave her one hour to get out. While Lucie was packing, American soldiers began searching the house and looting. Three American units were consecutively stationed in the house. They stole much of the Rommel family's property including clothing, bed sheets, interior decorations, kitchenware, and linens as well as many of Rommel's personal belongings and papers. American soldiers also broke into locked closets and trunks using force. During this time, Lucie found temporary shelter in a small room in the neighborhood. Eventually, she moved into a local school.

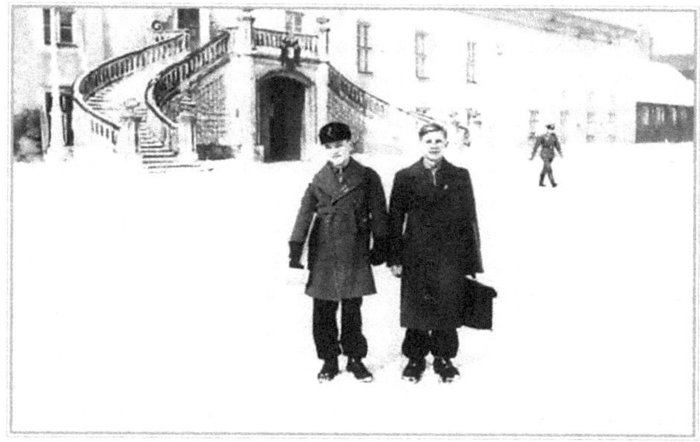

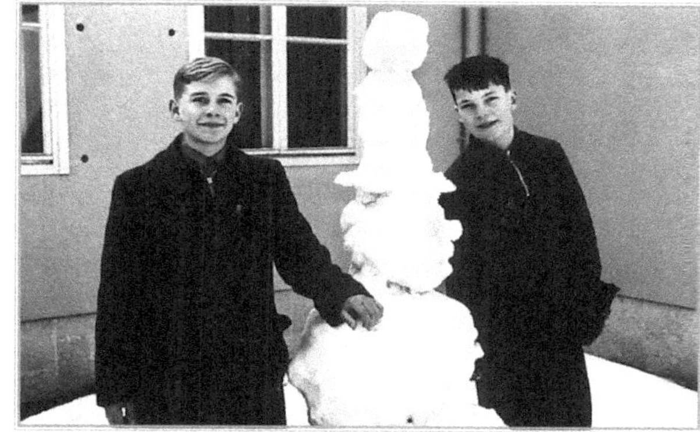

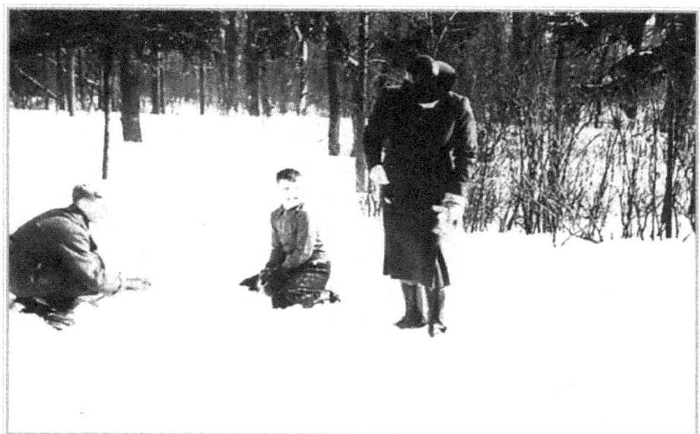

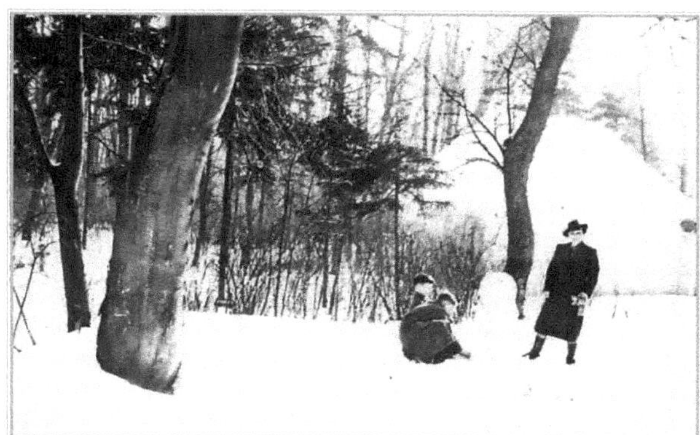

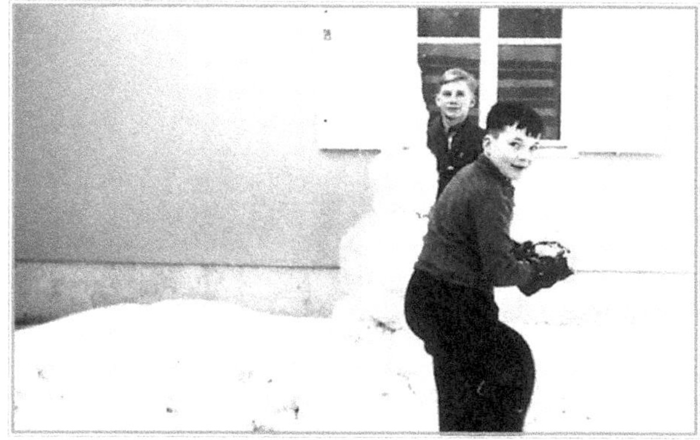

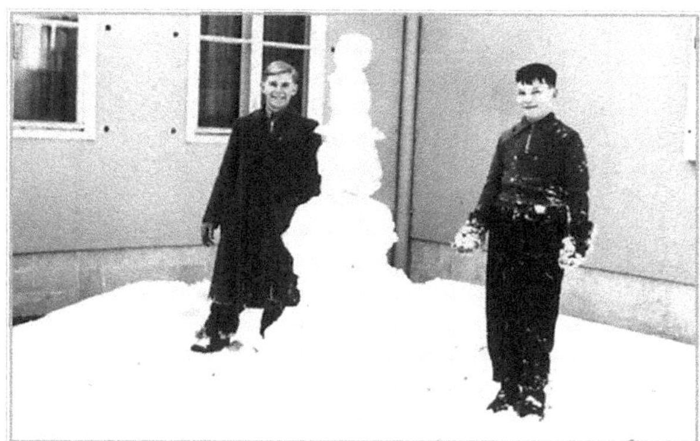

Manfred and his friend (upper left) pose together outside of the Theresian Military Academy in Wiener Neustadt, Austria. Manfred and a friend build snowmen and pose together in wintertime, while Rommel's wife stands nearby.

Rommel worked as a military instructor during the interwar years and became the commander of the Theresian Military Academy in 1938. Lucie shared Rommel's enthusiasm for outdoor trips. Once, when Rommel was on leave, he took his wife canoeing down the Rhine River to Lake Constance (called *Bodensee*), a large lake near the Alps.

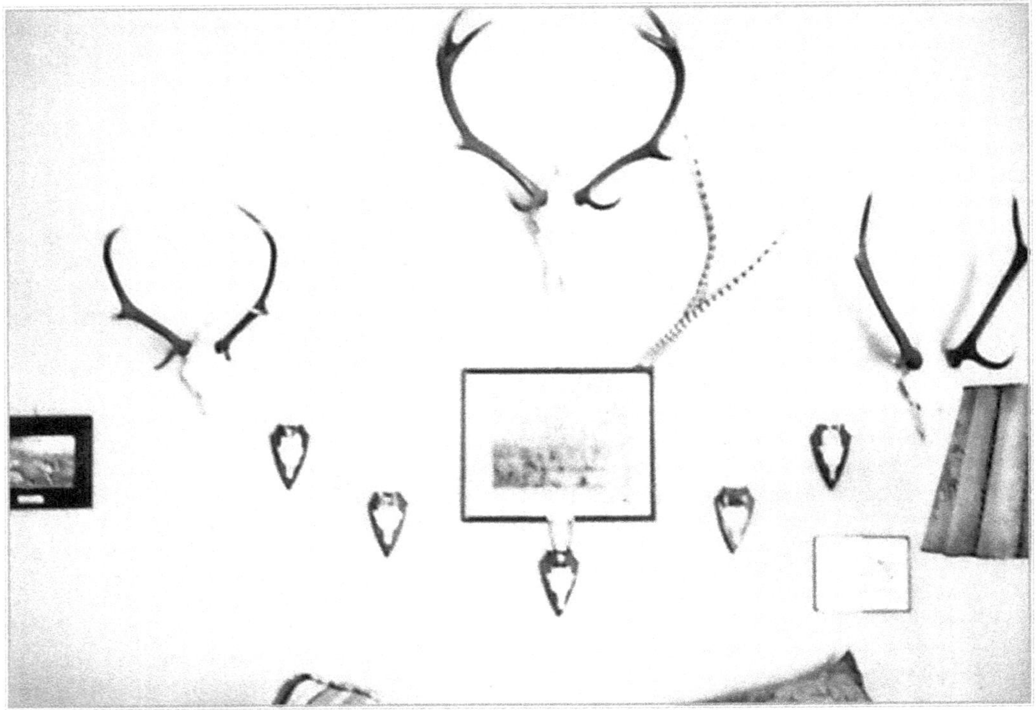

Rommel's hunting trophies hang on the wall of his home.

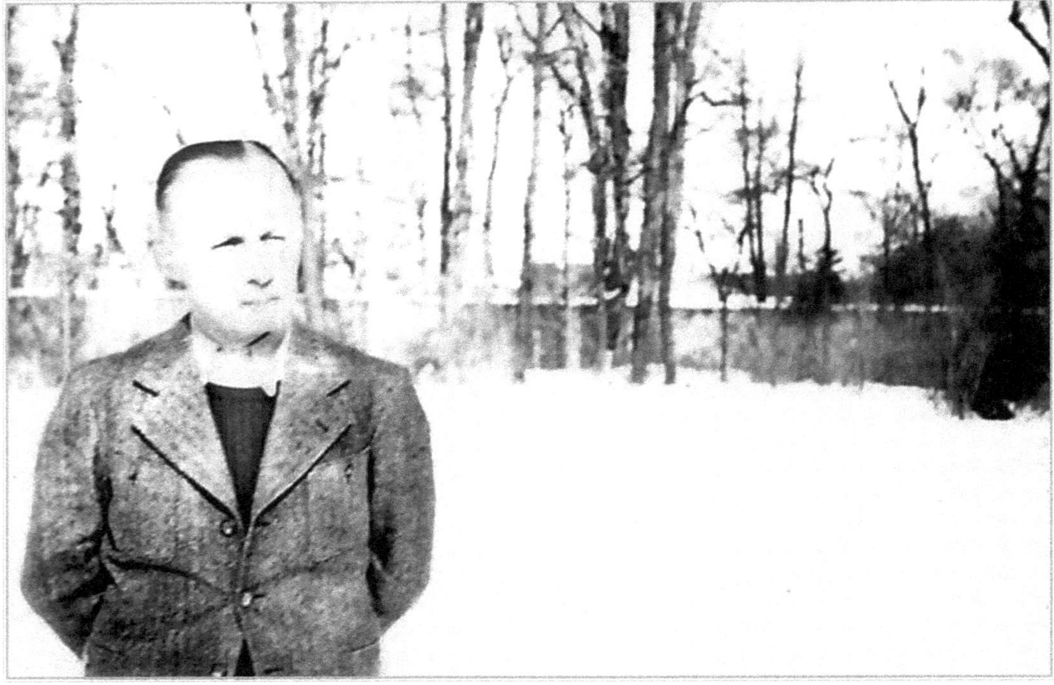

Rommel (above) poses outdoors in casual attire during the wintertime.

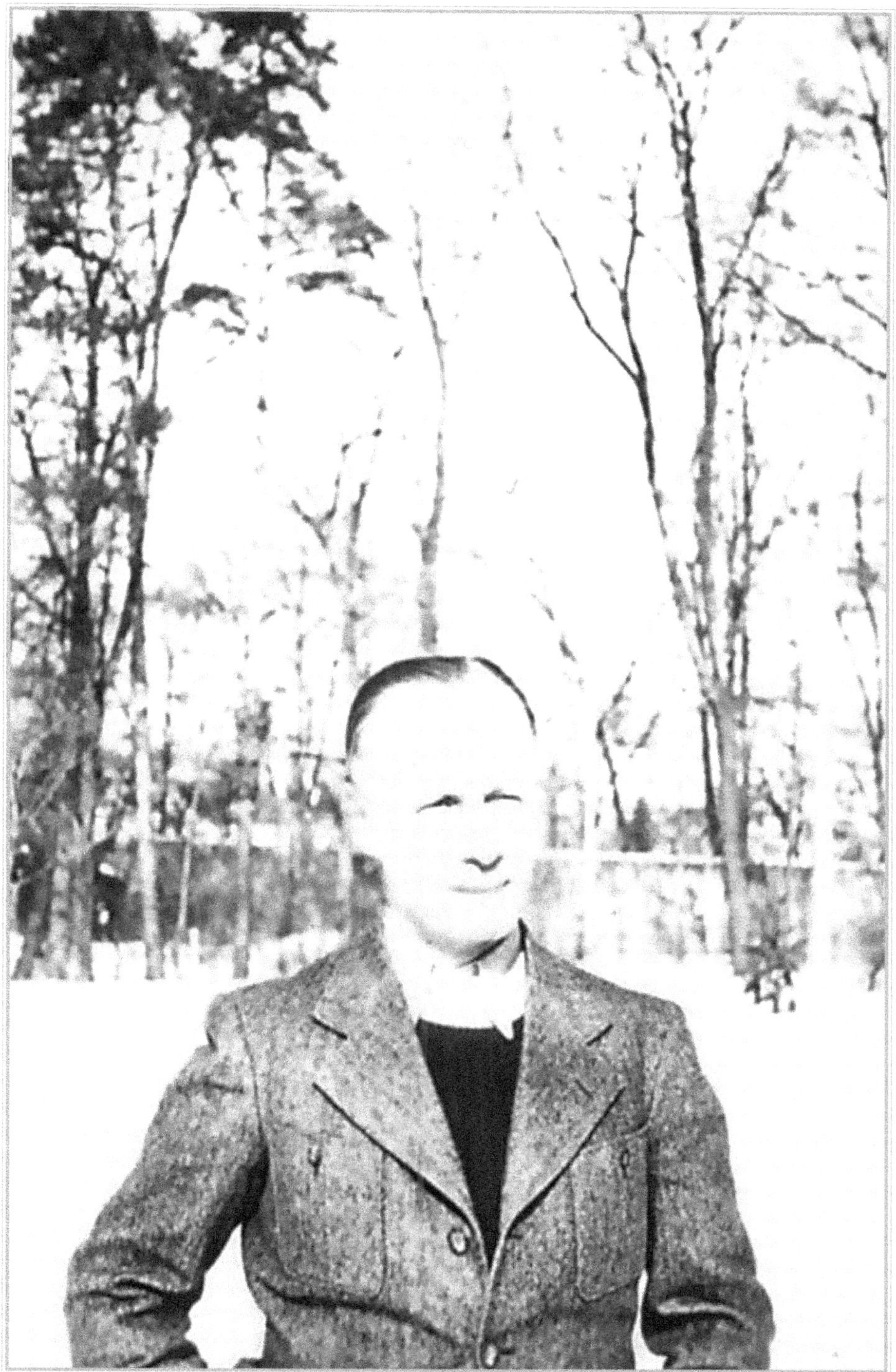

Rommel liked outdoor and athletic activities. He often went hiking, skiing, swimming, and horseback riding. He enjoyed trips to the countryside. Although Rommel was fond of animals, he was also an avid hunter and decorated his walls with many trophies.

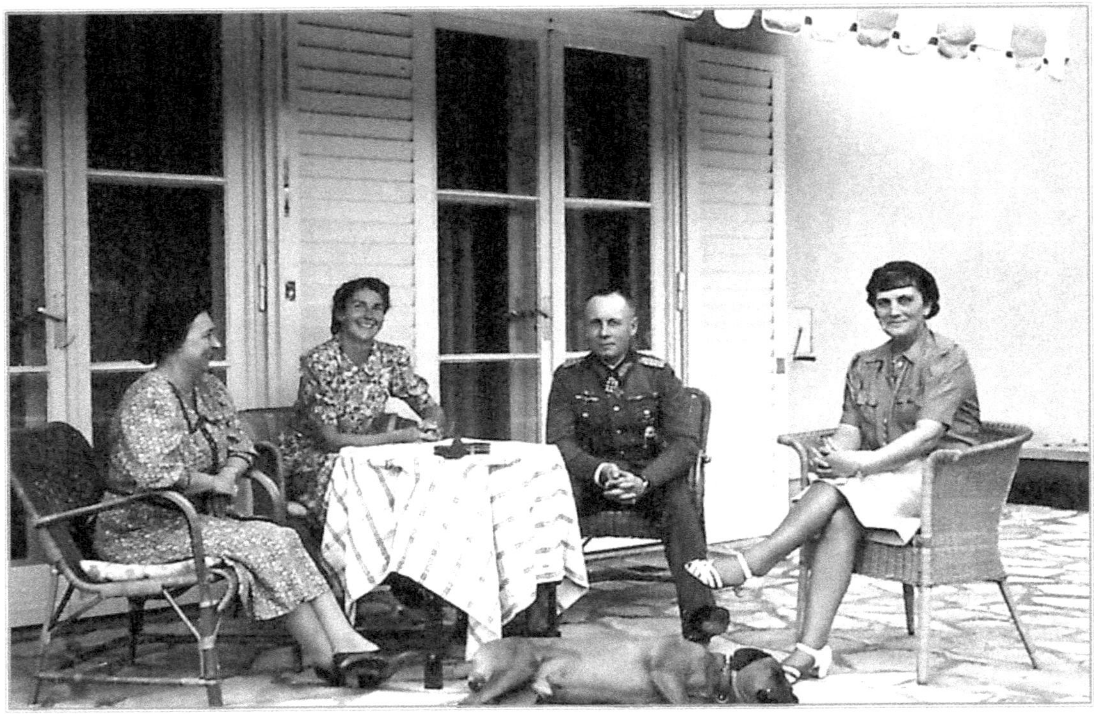

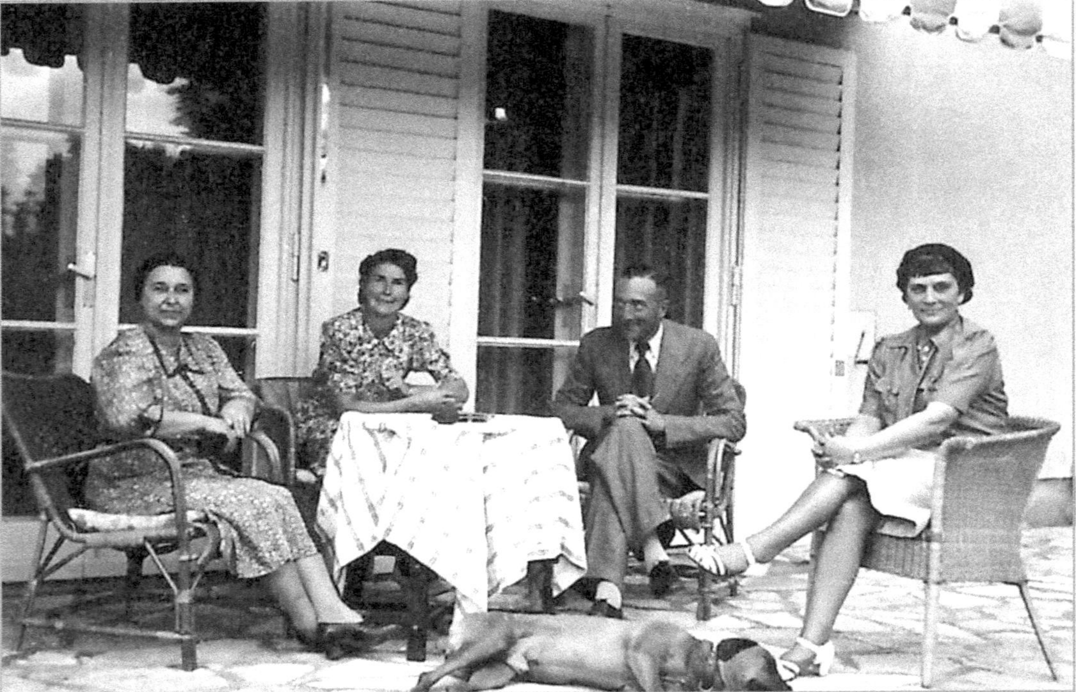

Rommel, his wife, and their acquaintances take turns behind the camera in this photo series of an informal gathering.

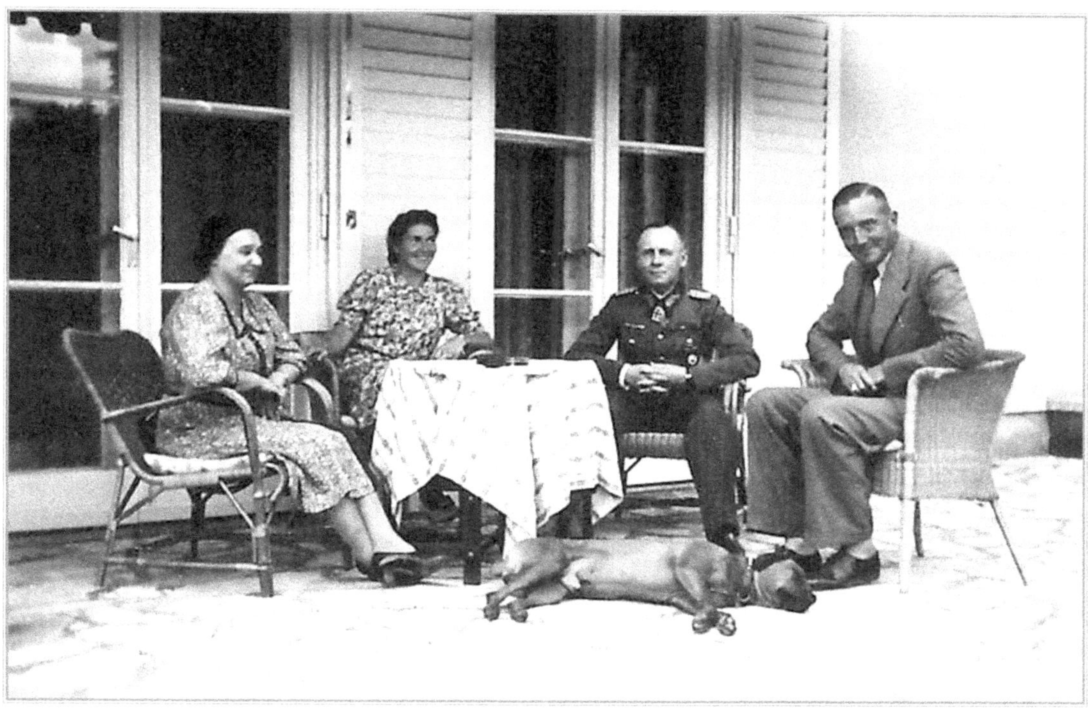

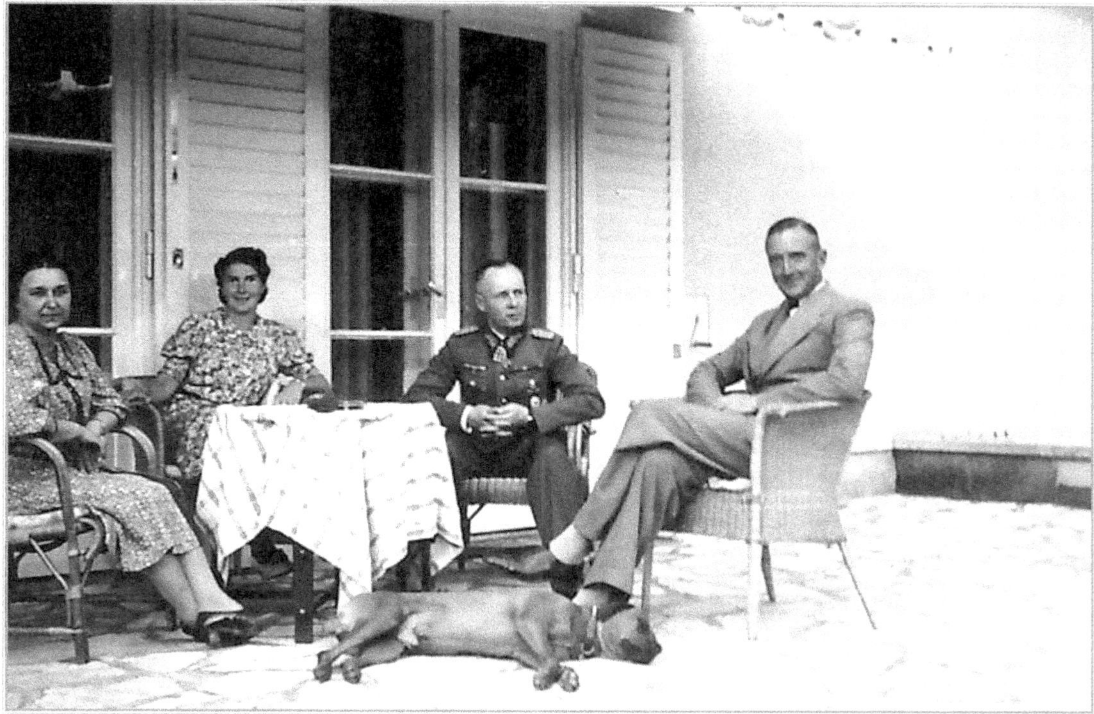

The Rommel family's circle of friends included other military officers and their wives.

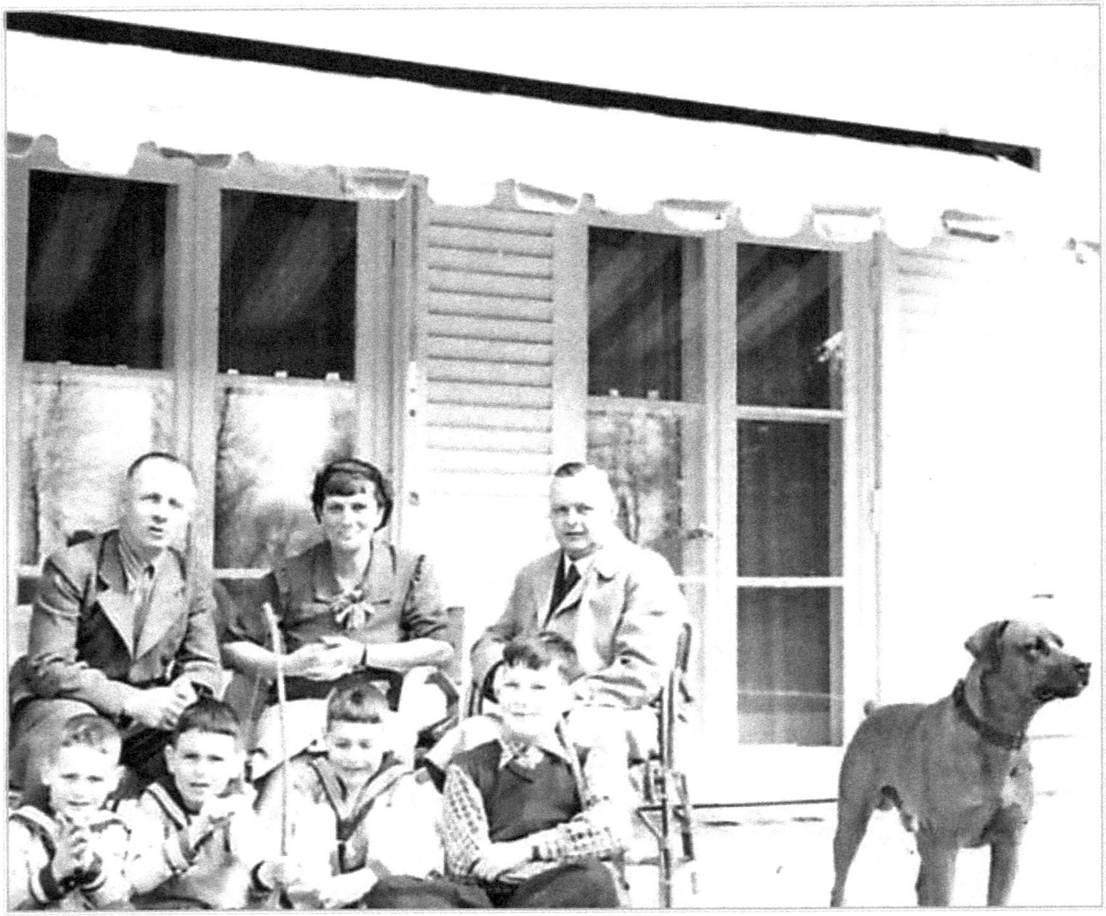

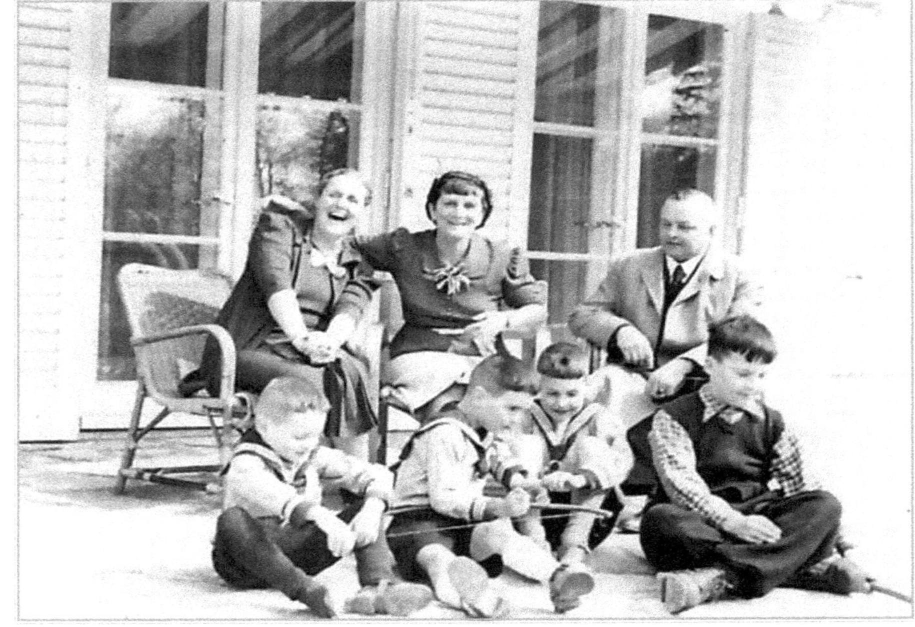

Rommel (top right and left) is shown enjoying himself with his wife and son in this photo series. The other people in the images are unidentified.

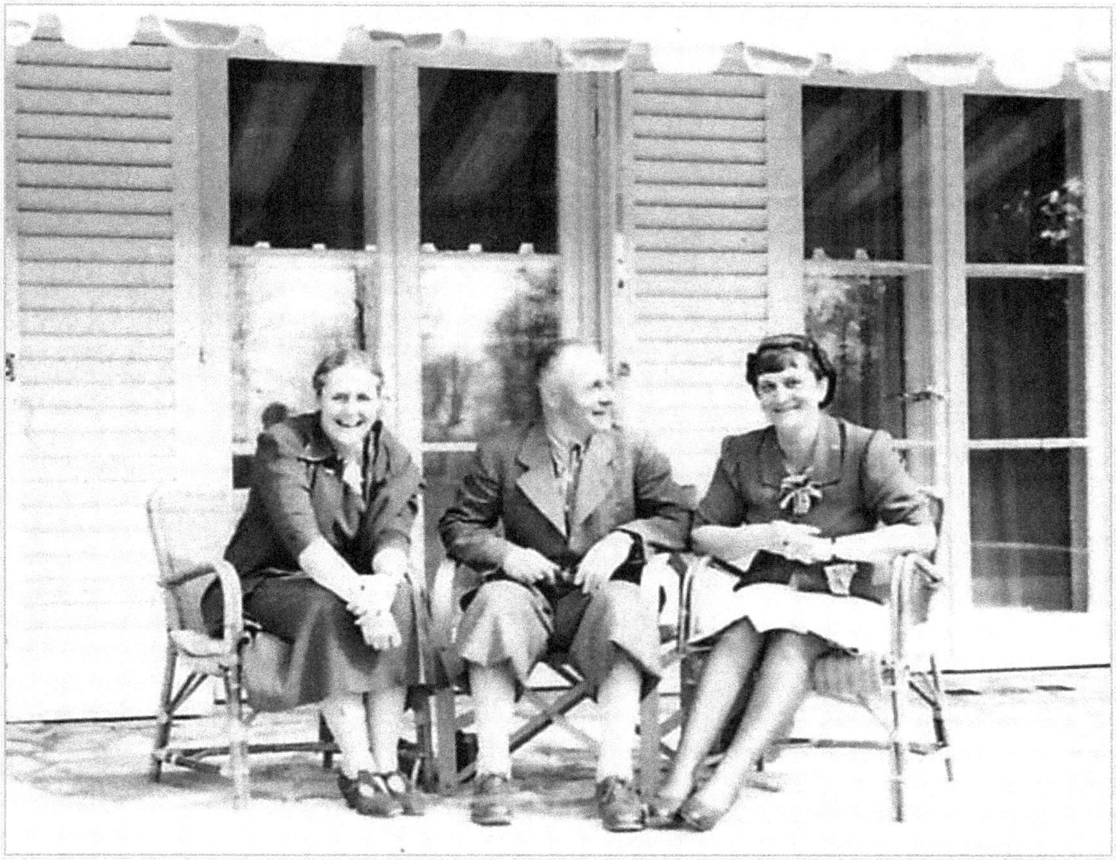

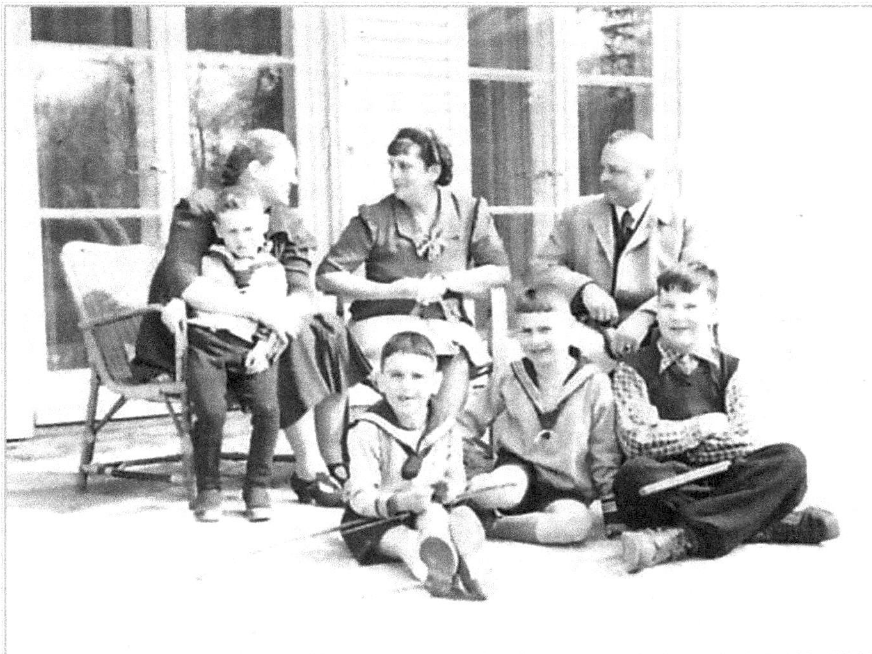

Along with his wife and son, Rommel's other close family members included his older sister, Helene, and his daughter Gertrud from a premarital relationship. He regularly wrote letters to Gertrud, who made a yellow scarf for Rommel. He constantly wore the scarf in North Africa, and it became part of his public image as Field Marshal.

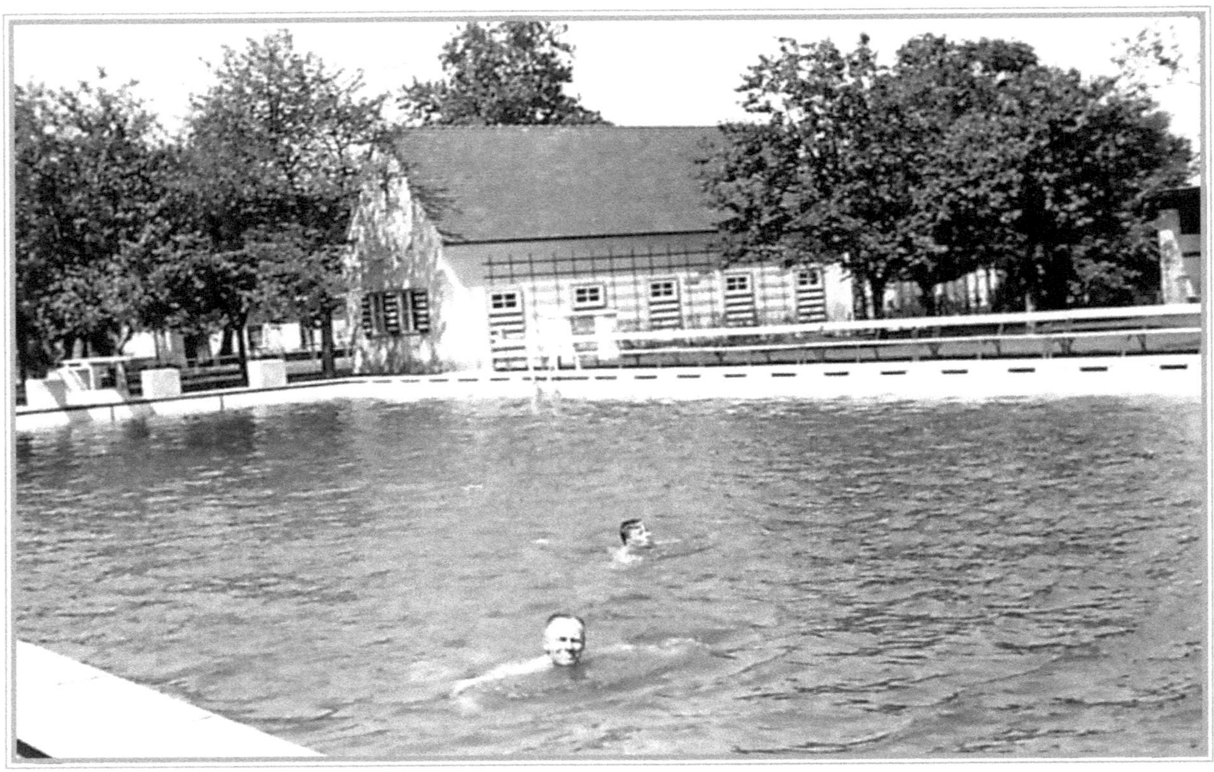

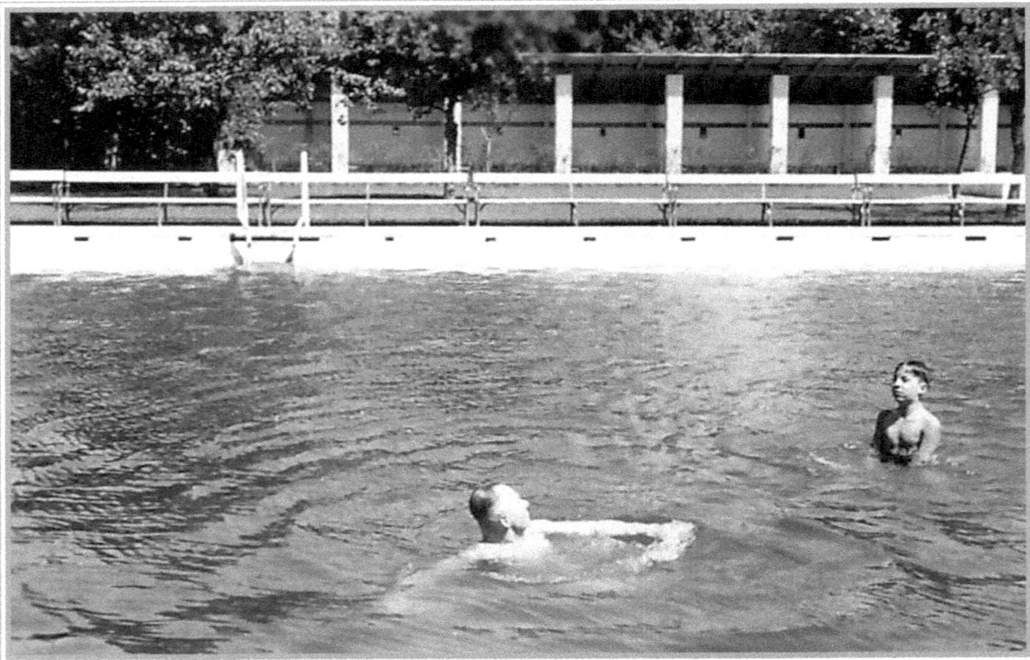

Rommel and Manfred enjoy family time swimming (date and location unknown).

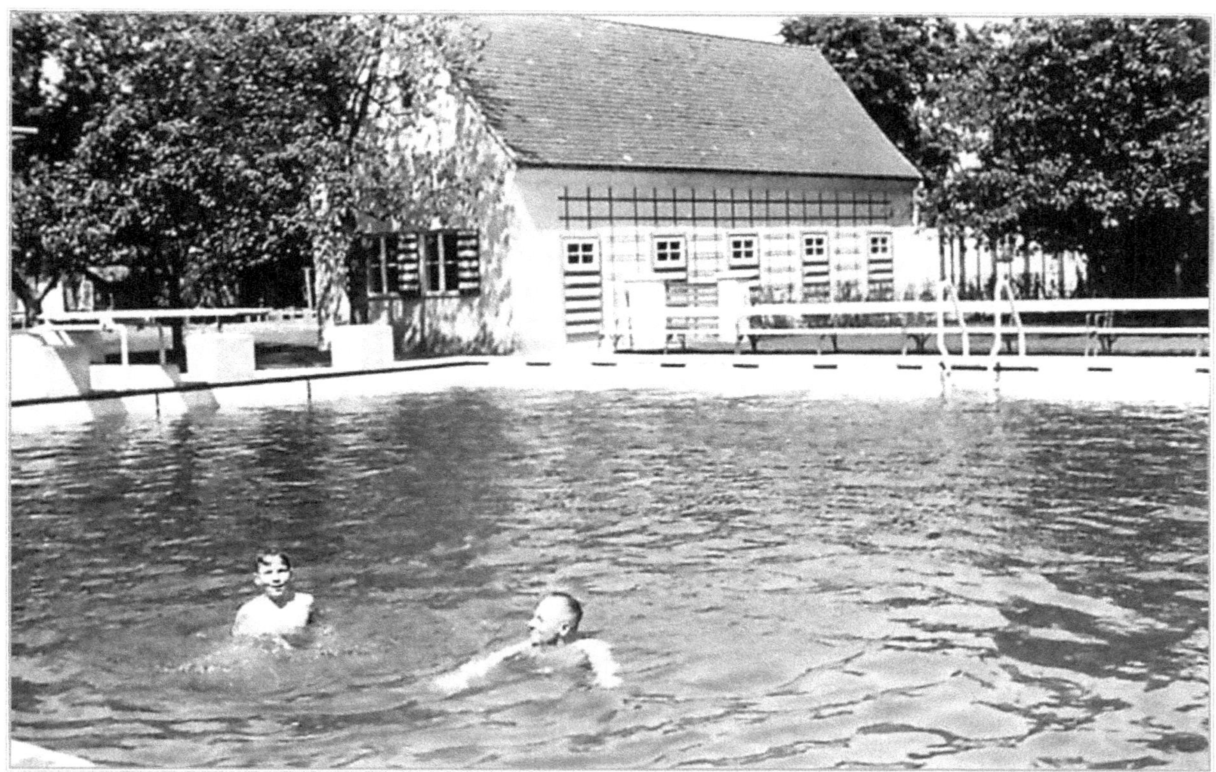

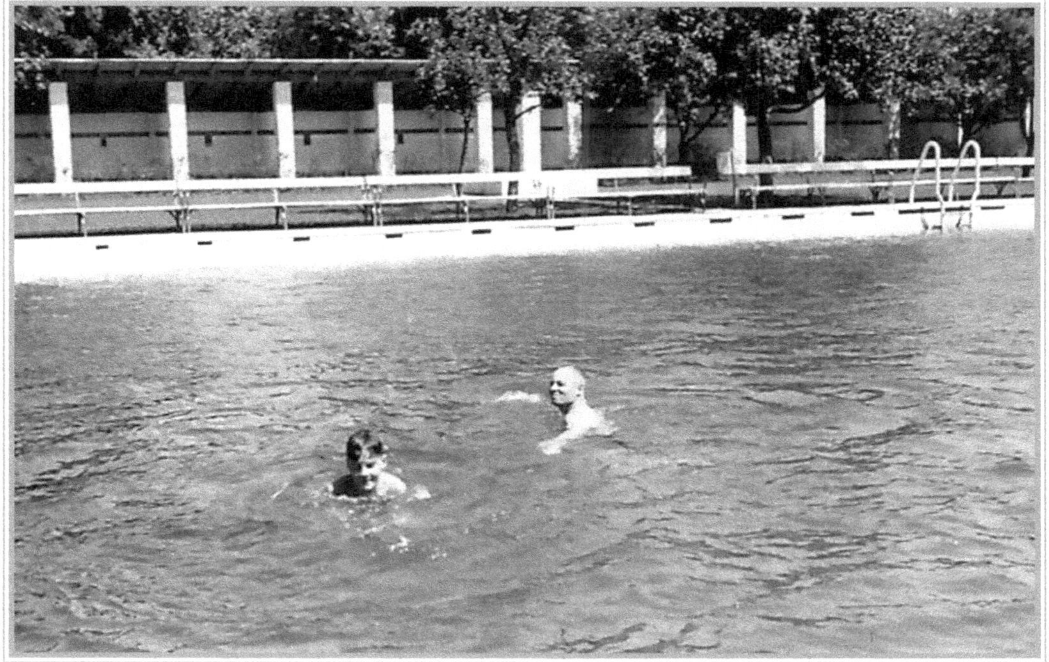

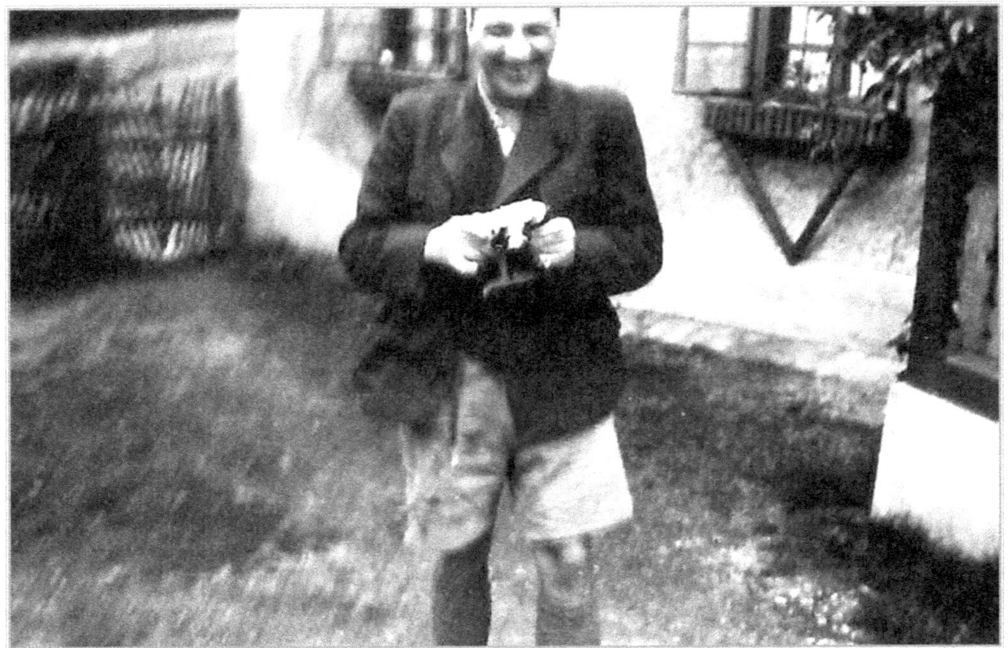

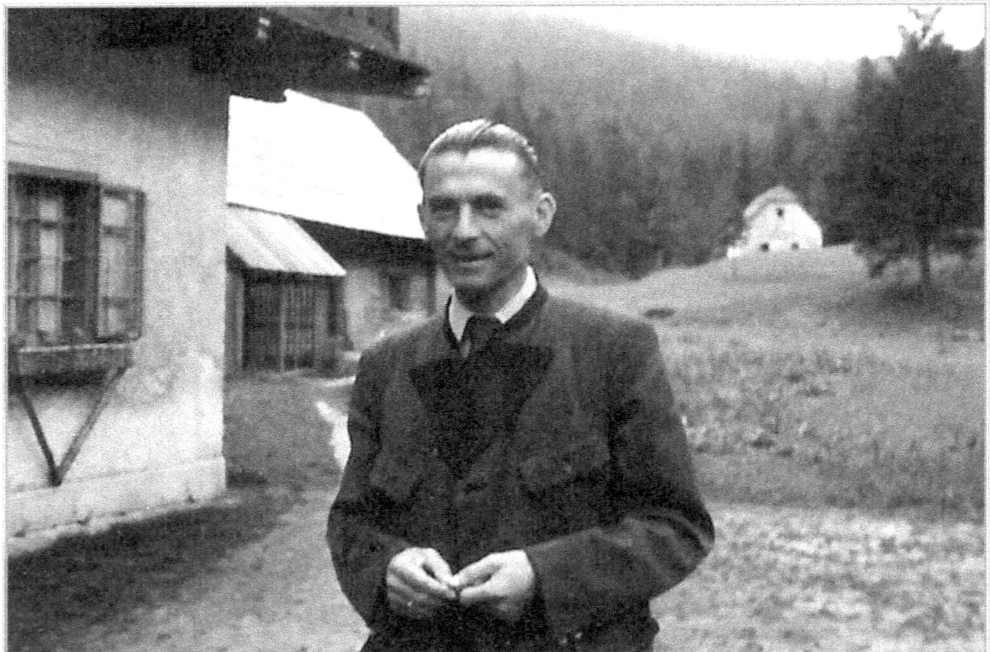

Photos of two unidentified men found in Rommel's personal photo collection.

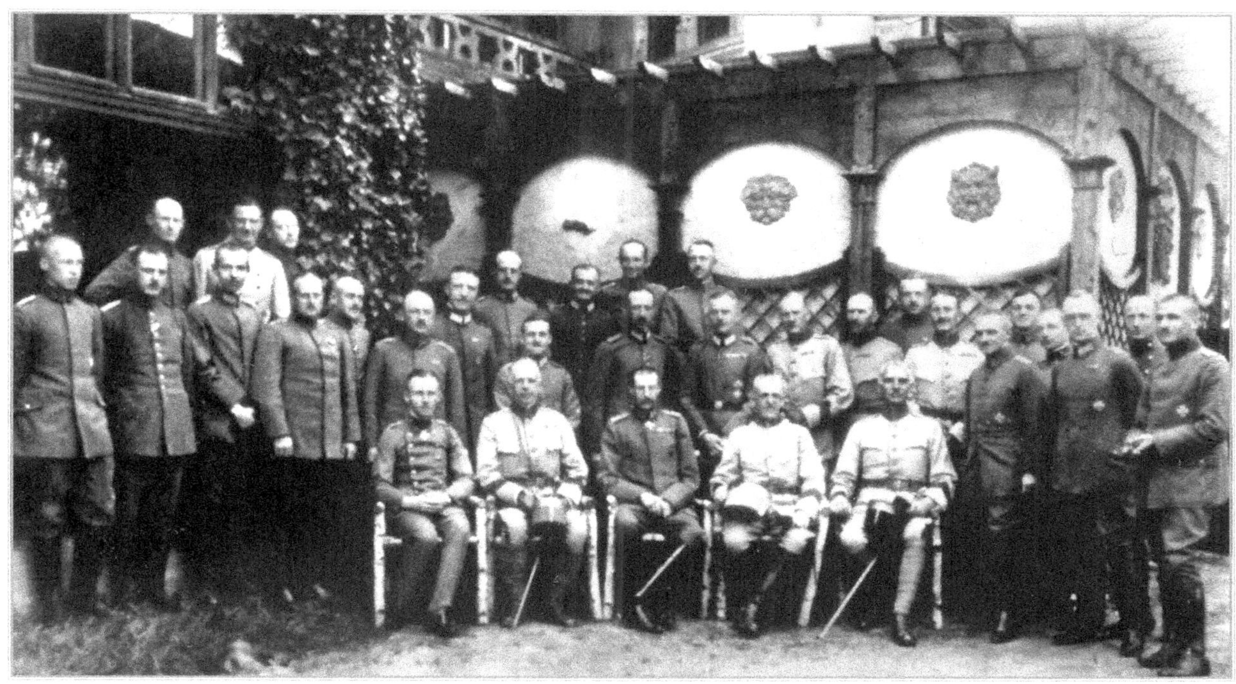

Rommel is pictured (1st row, left) with other members of the German military, either during WWI or sometime afterwards.

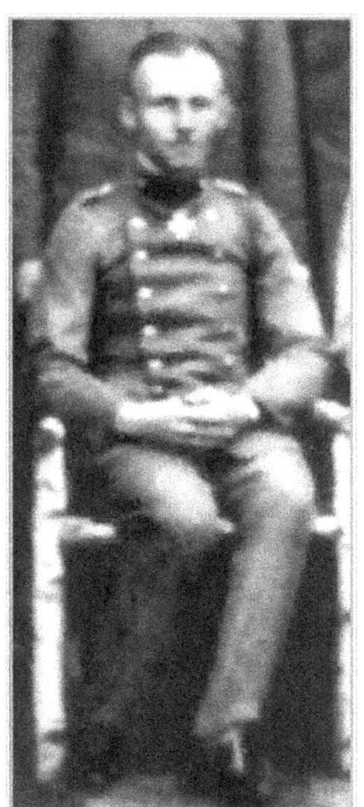

Close-up of Rommel taken from the group photo.

Rommel was in his late 20s when the war ended in 1918. He preserved friendships with his former comrades from World War I.

He founded a group called the "Old Comrades Association" in order to help other WWI veterans from his former battalion who had fallen on hard times. Rommel remained actively involved in this organization until his death in 1944.

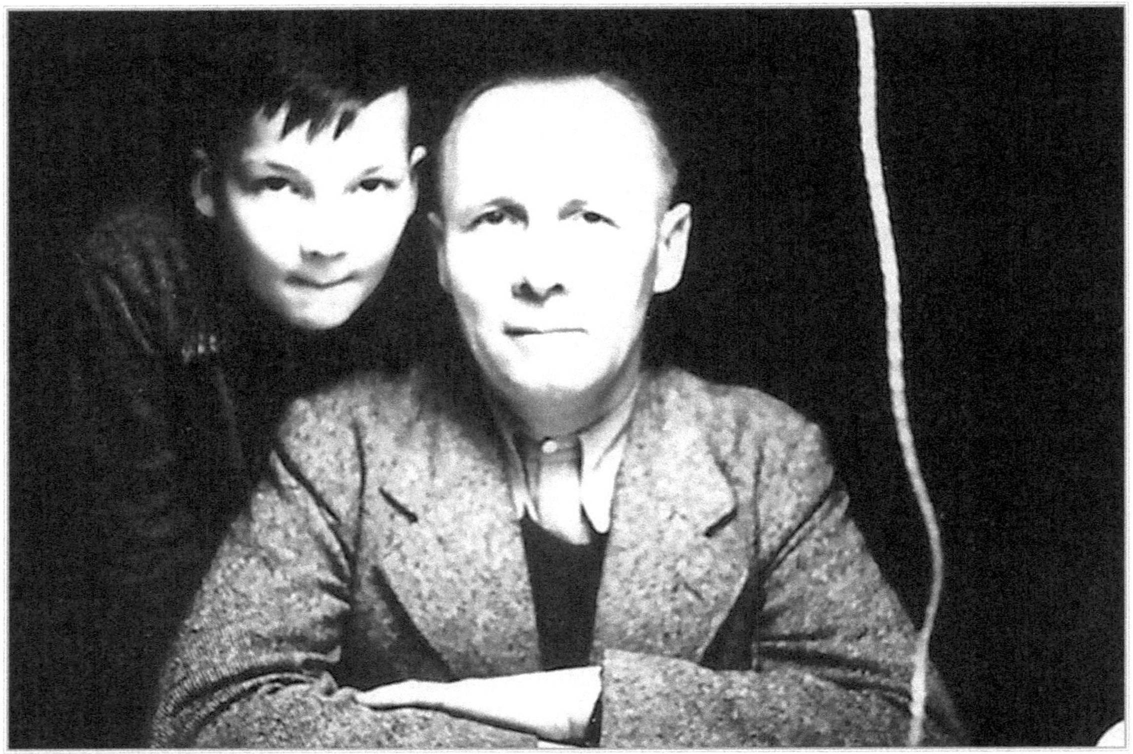

These photos of Rommel and Manfred were possibly taken in a darkroom with a tripod.

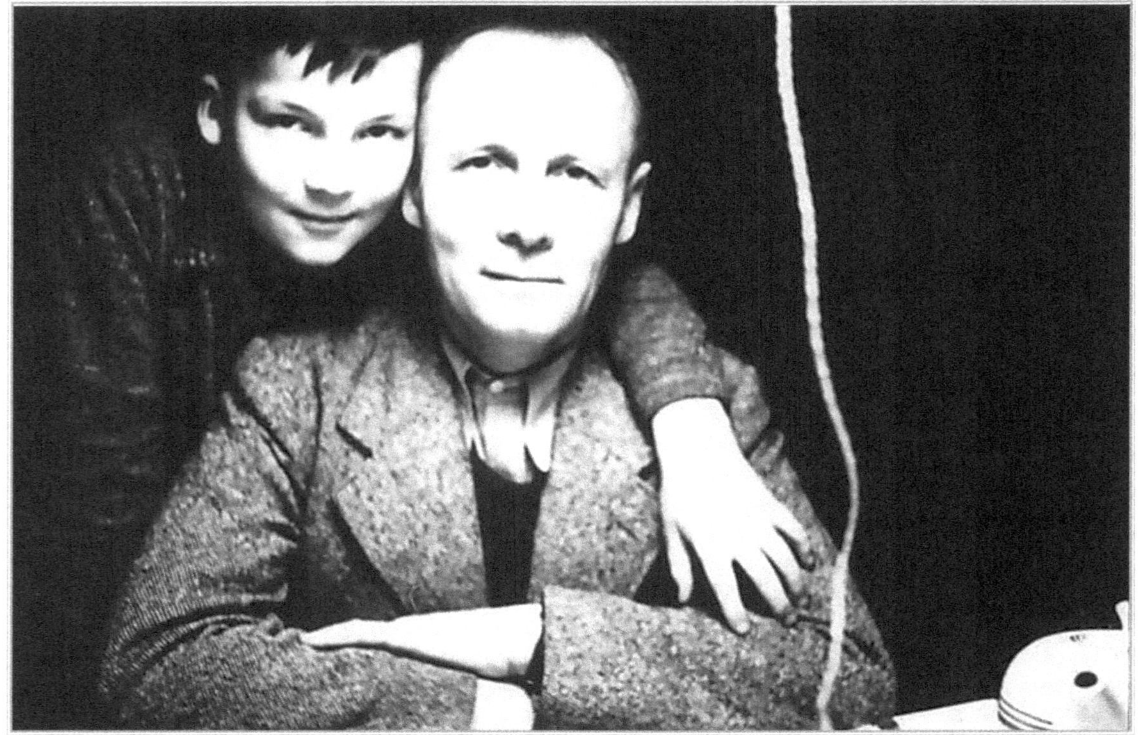

References

This book is not an academic work. It had its early origins as my undergraduate Honors Thesis, but evolved significantly over time. Therefore, I find it unnecessary to make a comprehensive list of all the materials that contributed to my knowledge about the topics in this book. I conducted years of in-depth research about Rommel and the war in North Africa. My writing and analyses on the subject matter are based on my own expertise. However, there are several important reference sources to which I owe credit. I cite them here as follows:

- *"The Rommel Papers,"* by Erwin Rommel (edited by B.H. Liddell-Hart and translated by Paul Findlay); with excerpts by Manfred Rommel and General Fritz Bayerlein (Da Capo Press: New York), 1953. Quoted on pp. 24, 30, 52, 62, 69, 93, 140, 169, 183, 220, 248, 250, 254, 272, and 276.

This collection of Erwin Rommel's writings and personal letters was published shortly after World War II. At the request of the Rommel family, it was edited by British military historian B.H. Liddell-Hart, whose work Rommel had admired during his lifetime. Various eyewitnesses contributed to the book, including Manfred Rommel, his mother Lucie, and General Fritz Bayerlein, who had fought alongside Rommel in North Africa.

- *"Rommel, the Desert Fox,"* by Desmond Young (Harper & Brothers: New York), 1950.

Desmond Young was a British officer in WWII who was captured as a POW by German troops in North Africa. He experienced the desert war firsthand and met Erwin Rommel in person. While gathering material for this book, he personally interviewed Rommel's family members, friends, fellow soldiers, and other eyewitnesses; gained access to original documents; and recorded firsthand testimony.

- *"The Rommel Murder,"* by Charles F. Marshall (Stackpole Books: Pennsylvania), 2002. [First published in 1994.] Quoted on pp. 181–182 and 276.

Charles F. Marshall, as an intelligence officer of the U.S. Army, entered Germany with American troops in 1945. He was in charge of a captured documents unit and interviewed captured German officers and other German military personnel. He was one of the first American soldiers to meet Rommel's widow. He also claimed to be the first American to break the true story behind Rommel's death to the press. During his investigation, Marshall interrogated Rommel's family members, personal acquaintances, and other military officers in 1945 and 1946.

Marshall appeared to have had ulterior motives during his military inquiry. While searching for military documents, he discovered a collection of Rommel's personal letters to his wife located at their home. Rommel's widow was still grieving for the recent loss of her husband.

Marshall took the letters after having promised her that he would return them after a few days.

However, in his book, Marshall revealed he had no intention of returning the letters. On the very same day he promised Lucie that he would give the letters back, Marshall stated that he intended to permanently confiscate them. The letters consisted of personal notes from Rommel to his wife and had little military relevance. Marshall said these notes were "a rich source of material for Rommel's biographers" and seemingly gathered excerpts from them for non-military purposes. He decided that "the original letters should wind up in the Library of Congress for future study by historians."

Having taken the letters from a grieving widow under false pretenses, Marshall apparently sent them to Washington, D.C. due to his belief that these would be useful to American citizens. Meanwhile, the Rommel family was told Marshall was "terribly sorry" that he was unable to keep his promise, and "the Army" had decided the documents needed to be sent to America.

Rommel's son, Manfred, later recalled Marshall's broken promise and the difficulty the Rommel family faced getting the letters returned from Washington. Many efforts failed. After the intervention of British military historian B.H. Liddell-Hart, the letters were eventually returned to the family. Some are still missing.

In 1994, decades after the WWII ended, Marshall published a book about Rommel using much of the information he had gathered in 1945 and 1946.

- *"Infantry Attacks,"* by Erwin Rommel, with an introduction by Manfred Rommel, (Greenhill Books: London), 2006. [First published in 1937.]

Based on his experiences in World War I, Erwin Rommel wrote this military textbook in the early 1930s. It gives detailed descriptions of Rommel's military tactics and approaches to battle. It contains sketches made by Rommel and his analyses of his own military strategies. It also includes Rommel's recollections of his first experiences as a soldier. This edition features an introduction by his son, Manfred, which provides firsthand personal details.

- *"Stuttgart's Mayor Rommel, Son of the Desert Fox, Says Tolerance Is the Way to Fight Terrorists,"* by Franz Spelman, in an interview with Manfred Rommel, *People Magazine,* Dec. 19, 1977. Quoted on p. 272.

In this interview, Manfred Rommel discusses his relationship with his father.

ENGLISH TRANSLATIONS OF ROMMEL'S WRITINGS

The excerpts quoted from Rommel's writings included in this book come from *"The Rommel Papers."* Because Findlay's English translations of Rommel's writings in German were made more than 50 years ago, I occasionally substituted some antiquated British words with modern English equivalents.

About the Author: Zita Steele

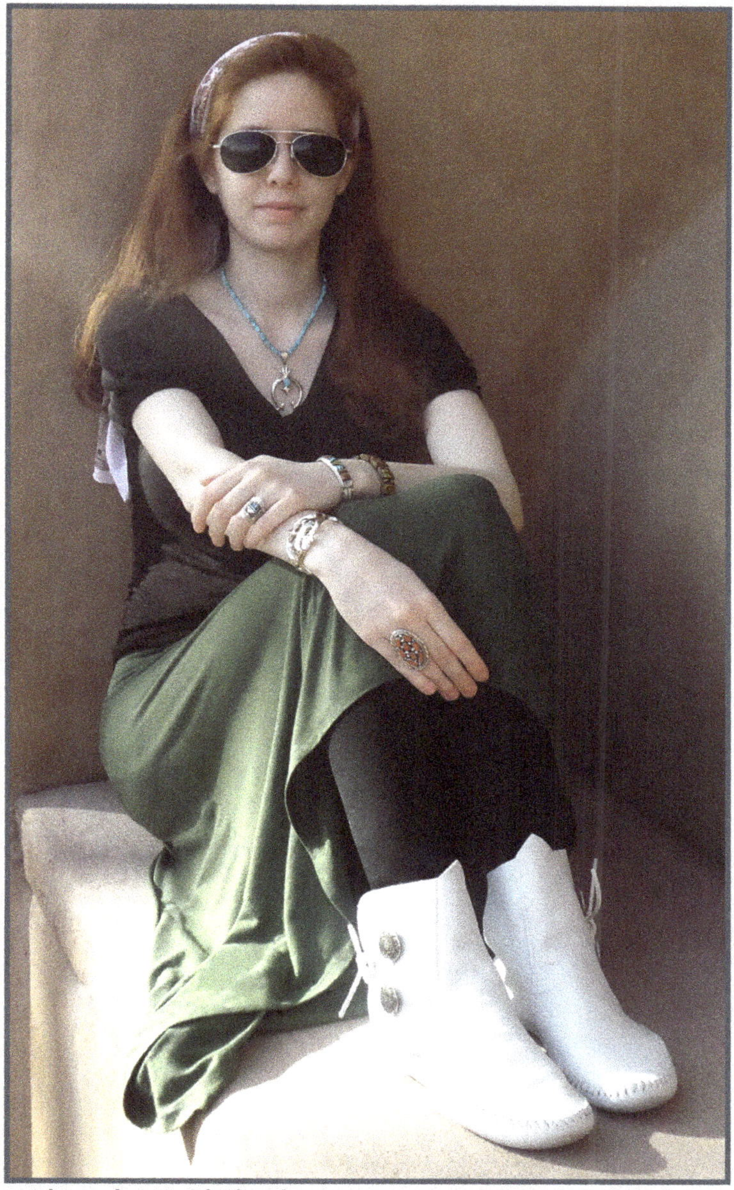
Photo by Noël Fletcher.

Zita Steele is a versatile author and artist. She grew up in the North Valley of Albuquerque, N.M., along the banks of the Rio Grande amid a vibrant Hispanic family of artists spanning three generations. Zita was raised by her mother, a writer and former foreign correspondent in China, in an environment filled with Asian art, a love of adventure, and the warmth of her extended family.

In her youth, it was common for those around her to be involved in various artistic endeavors, including painting, sculpture, and writing. Her great-uncle is an expert glass blower, painter, jeweler and illustrator. Her grandmother created fabric art, paintings, sculptures, and jewelry. Two great-aunts are painters. Her uncle, a former newspaper columnist, is a poet, author, and mixed-media artist. Her cousin is a photographer.

Typical family scenarios in Zita's formative life included having Mariachi music playing in the background, her great-uncle painting a religious mural, her grandmother designing jewelry for a museum exhibit, and her mother watching Polish historical movies with English subtitles.

This family atmosphere that valued aesthetic beauty and self-expression encouraged Zita to develop her intellectual interests and creative gifts.

From her earliest years, she demonstrated talent in drawing and writing.

In addition to writing novels and creating freehand illustrations, Zita expresses herself using advanced technology in graphic design, videos, and multimedia projects.

Zita loves foreign languages and has an impressive ability to learn them. Spanish and English were spoken in her family; her mother taught her some Mandarin Chinese while she was young. Zita studied Arabic and Latin in high school and expanded her capabilities while at university to include German, Russian, and Mandarin. In her spare time, she is learning Korean.

As a youth, she attended private schools. In high school, she had a unique home school curriculum designed to provide her with a classical education, an avenue to explore personal enrichment, and opportunities to travel. As a teen, she took adult-level community college courses of interest to her. She also traveled extensively to Washington, D.C., where she visited important historical sites and art museums. In addition, her travels took her to explore the Spanish missions in California and visit two presidential libraries there.

Zita completed her first fiction novel at age 15 and her second at 16. She attended the Honors College at the University of South Florida while completing her third fiction novel, *"Envoy: Rule of Silence,"* which was the first of her books to be published. Zita graduated with Magna Cum Laude honors at USF and earned a Bachelor of Arts degree in Social Sciences with emphases in criminology and international studies.

Like many from the Southwest, Zita enjoys the outdoors—hiking, skiing, horseback riding, and swimming. Her other interests include martial arts and fencing.

As an author, Zita is interested in combining her writing with strong visually artistic elements, such as photographs and illustrations. Her fiction and nonfiction frequently involve history and international themes. She sees her work as an opportunity to eliminate prejudice through stories that explore human motivations and issues. She creates characters who find themselves in situations in which they must cross cultural divides in order to understand each other.

At present, she is working on other books in the Rommel photography series as well as a modern fiction novel set in Asia.

More Books from Fletcher & Co. Publishers

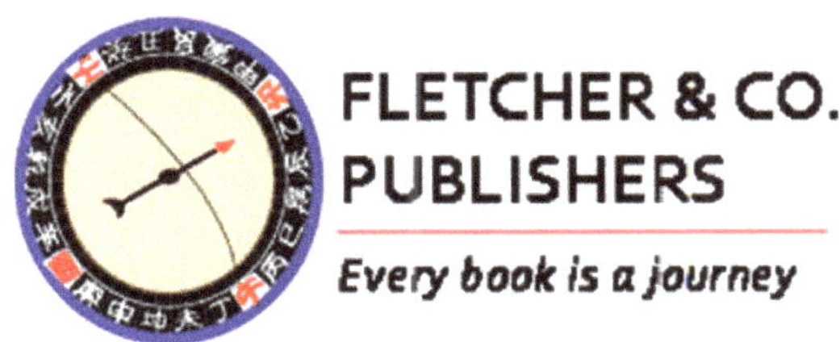

Every book is a journey. Fletcher & Co. Publishers is an independent, art-house publishing company. We use new media and graphic design techniques to transport you into the world of the novel.

Our books aren't just written words. They're experiences: international cultures, art, suspense, history, and adventure.

Watch our video trailers on Vimeo, Dailymotion, or YouTube to preview each book, see interesting images, and learn more about our newest releases. Visit our website to find out about our latest news.

Coming Soon!

Edge of Suspicion
by Zita Steele

Take a journey into danger and suspense. South Korean detective Moon chases an elusive cybercriminal and matches wits with a deadly blonde in Singapore.

Forts of the Old West:
A Journey across New Mexico
by Noël Fletcher

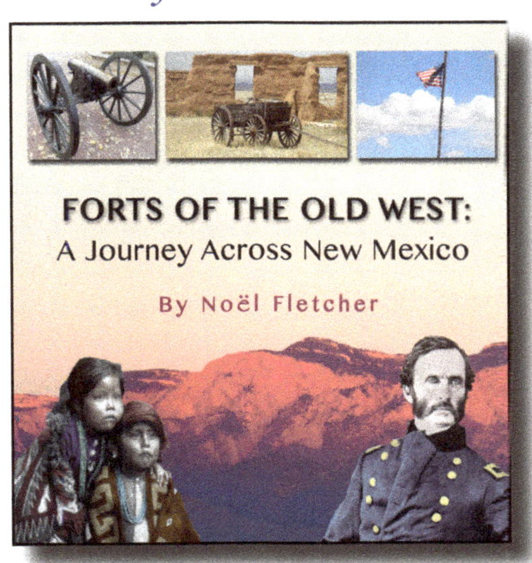

Take a journey into the forgotten forts of the Wild West and discover their dark secrets.

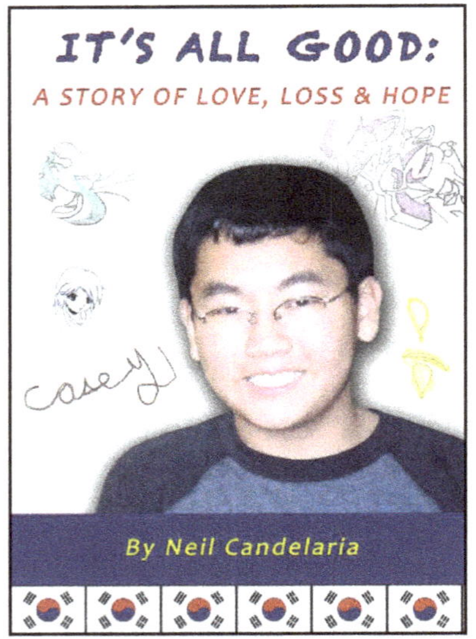

It's All Good: A Story of Love, Loss & Hope *by Neil Candelaria*

Take a journey of self-discovery and healing. Learn about the short but unforgettable life of Casey Jang-Joon Candelaria, a boy adopted from Busan, South Korea, who found a loving family and home in the American Southwest. His death at age 25 left his family shocked and devastated. Author Neil Candelaria, Casey's father, shares his experiences as a parent coping with the loss of a child. A former criminal court judge, Neil relates how he overcame his reliance on physical proof and came to believe in life after death.

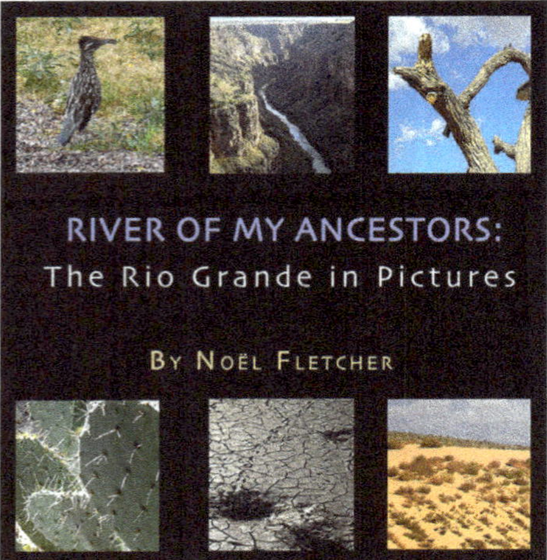

River of My Ancestors: The Rio Grande in Pictures *by Noël Fletcher*

Take a journey along the wild and rugged Rio Grande. Beautiful pictures capture the essence of the famous river and its importance in the arid Southwest. Native New Mexican author and photographer Noël Fletcher provides family stories and insights about frontier life. Follow the river through deserts, wetlands, and rocky cliffs. Experience natural wonders, including volcanic lands and river rapids. Encounter wildlife such as snakes, wolves, cranes, and bighorn sheep. With 180+ striking color photos, the book features interesting facts about local culture and life along the Rio Grande.

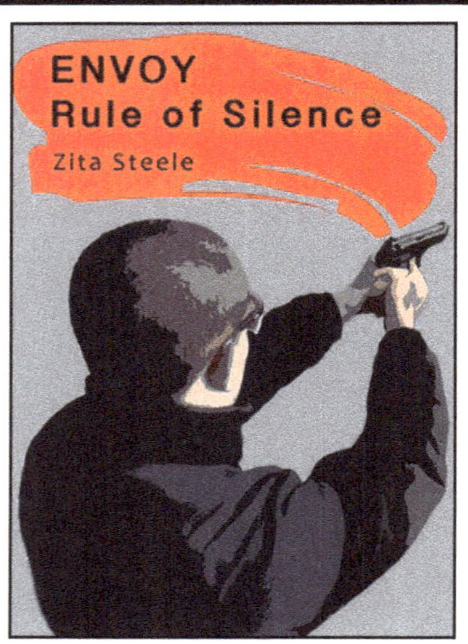

Envoy: Rule of Silence *by Zita Steele*

Take a journey into a thrilling world of secrets and lies in modern-day Europe. Polish ex-secret policeman Michal Krynski is tired of working as a double agent for France's security bureau. His last mission—to track down a runaway DJ. As he travels to the strange island of Malta, Krynski plots revenge against the system that ruined his life. Will he catch the DJ or kill him? Zita Steele is a novelist and artist. She writes with an expertise in criminology, cybercrime, and international relations. She creates her own illustrations.

NEW MEXICO GHOSTS &
HAUNTING IMAGES
by Ariela Desolina

New Mexico Ghosts and Haunting Images *by Ariela Desolina*

Let explorer-photographer Ariela Desolina spirit you away to New Mexico, where haunting ruins—some with ghostly inhabitants—will capture your imagination. With photos from the St. James Hotel, a notorious hangout of Western outlaws and gamblers. Mysterious shapes and ghostly forms (undetected when the pictures were taken) sometimes appear in her photos. This collection features photos of the haunted ruins of the Kelly Mine, once among the richest old gold and silver mines in the Southwest.

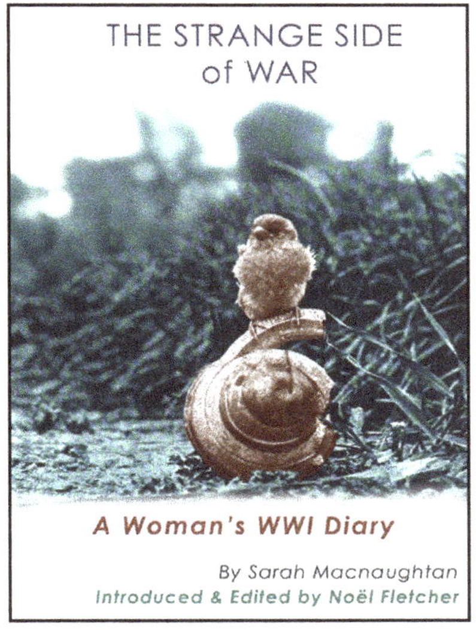

The Strange Side of War *by Sarah Macnaughtan & Noël Fletcher*

Take a journey across the dangerous battlefields of a world at war. Accompany Scottish novelist Sarah Macnaughtan as she volunteers alongside British humanitarian groups to alleviate the suffering in war-torn lands. Her many adventures tell unique stories of tragedy and triumph, taking readers on an unforgettable journey from the trenches of Belgium to the distant frontiers of Persia and tsarist Russia. Author/editor Noël Fletcher provides new historical context that brings Sarah's story to life and helps readers remember the bravery and sacrifice of those who died. Illustrated with 130+ rare photos from World War I, this important work features historical insights about the people and places involved in the conflict.

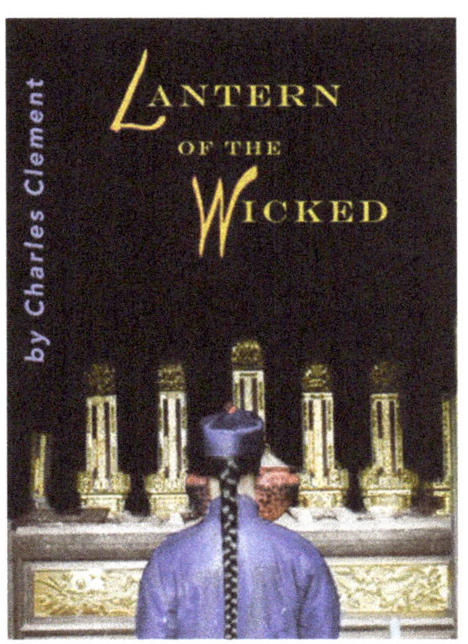

Lantern of the Wicked *by Charles Clement*

In the decadent and dangerous Shanghai of 1929, someone is spying for the Japanese, and the International Settlement's British police are on the hunt. Now, in the midst of the Mid-Autumn Moon Festival, American aviator Jack "Ace" Jordan becomes the prime suspect. A thrilling narrative blending fact, fiction, and rare photographs, *Lantern of the Wicked* creates an atmospheric window into the complexity and dark grandeur of the colonial Orient in this gripping historical mystery.

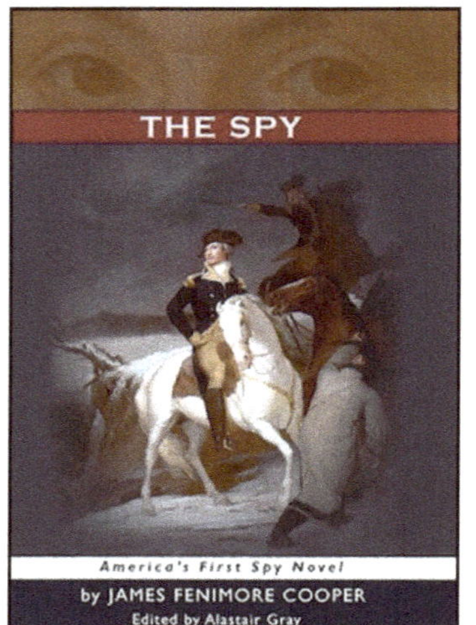

The Spy *by James Fenimore Cooper*

During the dark days of the Revolutionary War, America struggles for nationhood. Meanwhile, in the shadows, a spy is trading secrets of vital importance to the cause—but for whose side? Colonials and loyalists play a game of cloak and dagger in a classic historical tale of action and adventure. Our edition features 30+ color photographs and notations designed to give you a front-seat experience. This was the first major fiction novel on espionage ever written and published in America.

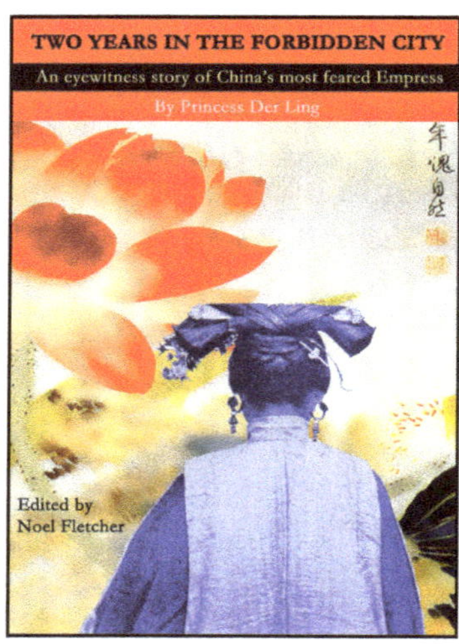

Two Years in the Forbidden City *by Princess Der Ling*

This true story was the first eyewitness account of the Imperial Court written by a Chinese aristocrat for Western readers. It provides an up-close view of the notorious Dowager Empress Tzu-hsi in her final years. Enhanced with rich imagery and additional historical notes, it includes interesting historical details and photos about China's infamous Dowager Empress, the Boxer Rebellion, and the Imperial Court. It is illustrated with 100+ historical photographs, illustrations, and paintings from the late 1800s to early 1900s. Author/editor Noël Fletcher provides context for this book in modern Chinese history.

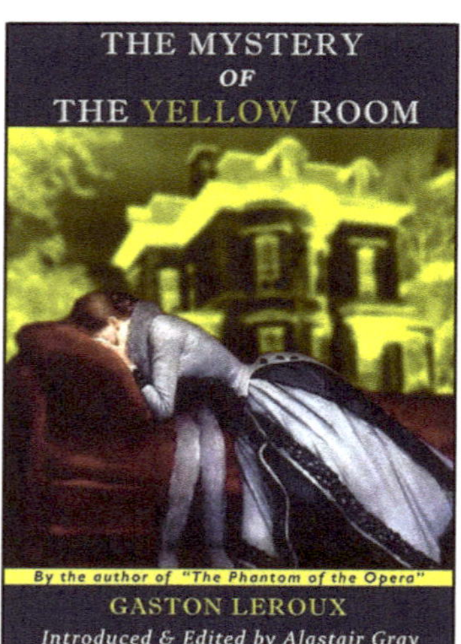

Mystery of the Yellow Room *by Gaston Leroux*

News of a strange crime spreads like wildfire in Paris. Someone has attempted to murder the daughter of a brilliant scientist. But nobody can explain how the murderer got in and out of a locked room in her isolated country home. Only Joseph Rouletabille, an impatient young journalist, has the genius to solve this crime. Written by the author of *"The Phantom of the Opera,"* this novel was published in 1907 as France's reply to Sherlock Holmes. Our edition has adapted text from archaic Victorian to standard English. It also features updated maps and is illustrated with 30+ historical paintings and illustrations from 19th-century France.

www.ingramcontent.com/pod-product-compliance
Lightning Source LLC
LaVergne TN
LVHW060629110826
845147LV00014B/878